Software
Agents

Software

Agents

Edited by
Jeffrey M. Bradshaw

AAAI Press / The MIT Press

Menlo Park, California • Cambridge, Massachusetts • London, England

Copublished and distributed by The MIT Press, Massachusetts Institute of Technology, Cambridge, Massachusetts and London, England.

Chapter 2 by Donald Norman, Chapter 8 by Patti Maes, Chapter 9 by David Smith, and Chapter 12 by Doug Riecken originally appeared in *Communications of the ACM,* July 1994 Volume 37 (7), Copyright, 1994, Association for Computing Machinerey. They are reprinted here with permission.

Portions of Chapter 3 originally appeared in *Being Digital* by N. Negroponte, copyright 1995, Alfred A. Knopf. It is reprinted here with permission.

Chapter 4 by Brenda Laurel is copyrighted by Apple Computer, Inc. It is reprinted here with permission.

Library of Congress Cataloging-in-Publication Data

Software agents / edited by Jeffrey M. Bradshaw.
     p. cm.
  ISBN 0-262-52234-9
  1. Intelligent agents (Computer software)   I Bradshaw, Jeffrey M.
  QA76.76.I58S64 1997
  006.3 =dc21
                                          97-1553
                                              CIP

Printed on acid-free paper in the United States of America.

To Kathleen

Contents

Preface

Recent trends have made it clear that software complexity will continue to increase dramatically in the coming decades. The dynamic and distributed nature of both data and applications require that software not merely respond to requests for information but intelligently anticipate, adapt, and actively seek ways to support users. Not only must these systems assist in coordinating tasks among humans, they must also help manage cooperation among distributed programs.

In response to these requirements, the efforts of researchers from several different fields have begun to coalesce around a common broad agenda: the development of software agents. On the one hand, researchers from the fields of human-computer interaction, intelligent and adaptive user interfaces, knowledge acquisition, end-user programming, and programming-by-demonstration have concerned themselves with the interaction between humans and software agents. On the other hand, researchers in the fields of distributed artificial intelligence, robotics, artificial life, and distributed object computing have advanced our understanding of how communities of agents can develop, reason, and cooperate.

These complementary lines of research are motivated by two main concerns: the limitations of direct manipulation interfaces, and the complexities of distributed computing. Following introductory pieces authored by well-known proponents (and a critic) of agent approaches, this book contains a set of chapters describing how agents have been used to enhance learning and provide intelligent assistance to users in situations where direct manipulation interfaces alone are insufficient. The final set of chapters details various approaches to agent-to-agent communication and agent mobility, as well as the use of agents to provide intelligent interoperability between loosely-coupled components of distributed systems. Woven within their accounts of technical issues and approaches are scores of examples of how agents are being applied to everyday problems in business, education, entertainment, and industry.

Although the limitations of time and space regretfully leave some important topics under discussed and the continuing evolution of agent technology will always preclude a definitive summary of the field, I hope that this book will provide greater accessibility to social and technical issues of enduring significance. Chapters by leading researchers from universities (the Massachusetts Institute of Technology, Stanford University, the University of Maryland, the University of Southern California, and the University of Toronto), computing companies (Apple, Microsoft, and General Magic), and industrial research centers (AT&T Bell Labs, Boeing, EURISCO, and Interval) not only aim to summarize the state of the art, but also to point the way in which standards and products incorporating agent technology are likely to evolve over the next few years. The variety of issues, approaches, and applications addressed enable this book's use as a classroom resource, as well as a reference for computing professionals. Because this book describes basic concepts and implementations without resorting to mathematical or undefined technical terms, I hope it will also be useful for many noncomputing professionals who are interested in a survey of this rapidly growing field.

In closing, I wish to express my thanks for the many months of painstaking efforts by the authors and the publisher to bring this book to press, as well as the patient support by colleagues at The Boeing Company, the Fred Hutchinson Cancer Research Center, and by my family.

Jeffrey Bradshaw
Seattle, Washington

Software Agents

CHAPTER I

An Introduction to Software Agents

Jeffrey M. Bradshaw

Since the beginning of recorded history, people have been fascinated with the idea of non-human agencies.[1] Popular notions about androids, humanoids, robots, cyborgs, and science fiction creatures permeate our culture, forming the unconscious backdrop against which software agents are perceived. The word "robot," derived from the Czech word for drudgery, became popular following Karel Capek's 1921 play *RUR: Rossum Universal Robots*. While Capek's robots were factory workers, the public has also at times embraced the romantic dream of robots as "digital butlers" who, like the mechanical maid in the animated feature "The Jetsons," would someday putter about the living room performing mundane household tasks. Despite such innocuous beginnings, the dominant public image of artificially intelligent embodied creatures often has been more a nightmare than a dream. Would the awesome power of robots reverse the master-slave relationship with humans? Everyday experiences of computer users with the mysteries of ordinary software, riddled with annoying bugs, incomprehensible features, and dangerous viruses reinforce the fear that the software powering autonomous creatures would pose even more problems. The more intelligent the robot, the more capable of pursuing its own self-interest rather than its master's. The more humanlike the robot, the more likely to exhibit human frailties and eccentricities. Such latent concerns cannot be ignored in the design of software agents—indeed, there is more than a grain of truth in each of them!

Though automata of various sorts have existed for centuries, it is only with the development of computers and control theory since World War II that anything resembling autonomous agents has begun to appear. Norman (1997) observes that perhaps "the most relevant predecessors to today's intelligent agents are servomechanisms and other control devices, including factory control and the automated takeoff, landing, and flight control of aircraft." However, the agents now being contemplated differ in important ways from earlier concepts.

Significantly, for the moment, the momentum seems to have shifted from hardware to software, from the atoms that comprise a mechanical robot to the bits that make up a digital agent (Negroponte 1997).[2]

Alan Kay, a longtime proponent of agent technology, provides a thumbnail sketch tracing the more recent roots of software agents:

> "The idea of an agent originated with John McCarthy in the mid-1950's, and the term was coined by Oliver G. Selfridge a few years later, when they were both at the Massachusetts Institute of Technology. They had in view a system that, when given a goal, could carry out the details of the appropriate computer operations and could ask for and receive advice, offered in human terms, when it was stuck. An agent would be a 'soft robot' living and doing its business within the computer's world." (Kay 1984).

Nwana (1996) splits agent research into two main strands: the first beginning about 1977, and the second around 1990. Strand 1, whose roots are mainly in distributed artificial intelligence (DAI), "has concentrated mainly on deliberative-type agents with symbolic internal models." Such work has contributed to an understanding of "*macro* issues such as the interaction and communication between agents, the decomposition and distribution of tasks, coordination and cooperation, conflict resolution via negotiation, etc." Strand 2, in contrast, is a recent, rapidly growing movement to study a much broader range of agent types, from the moronic to the moderately smart. The emphasis has subtly shifted from *deliberation* to *doing*; from *reasoning* to *remote action*. The very diversity of applications and approaches is a key sign that software agents are becoming mainstream.

The gauntlet thrown down by early researchers has been variously taken up by new ones in distributed artificial intelligence, robotics, artificial life, distributed object computing, human-computer interaction, intelligent and adaptive interfaces, intelligent search and filtering, information retrieval, knowledge acquisition, end-user programming, programming-by-demonstration, and a growing list of other fields. As "agents" of many varieties have proliferated, there has been an explosion in the use of the term without a corresponding consensus on what it means. Some programs are called agents simply because they can be scheduled in advance to perform tasks on a remote machine (not unlike batch jobs on a mainframe); some because they accomplish low-level computing tasks while being instructed in a higher level of programming language or script (Apple Computer 1993); some because they abstract out or encapsulate the details of differences between information sources or computing services (Knoblock and Ambite 1997); some because they implement a primitive or aggregate "cognitive function" (Minsky 1986, Minsky and Riecken 1994); some because they manifest characteristics of distributed intelligence (Moulin and Chaib-draa 1996); some because they serve a mediating role among people and programs (Coutaz 1990; Wiederhold 1989; Wiederhold 1992); some because they perform the role of an "intelligent assistant" (Boy 1991, Maes 1997) some because they can migrate in a self-directed way from computer to computer

(White 1996); some because they present themselves to users as believable characters (Ball et al. 1996, Bates 1994, Hayes-Roth, Brownston, and Gent 1995); some because they speak an agent communication language (Genesereth 1997, Finin et al. 1997) and some because they are viewed by users as manifesting intentionality and other aspects of "mental state" (Shoham 1997).

Out of this confusion, two distinct but related approaches to the definition of agent have been attempted: one based on the notion of agenthood as an *ascription* made by some person, the other based on a *description* of the attributes that software agents are designed to possess. These complementary perspectives are summarized in the section "What Is a Software Agent." The subsequent section discusses the "why" of software agents as they relate to two practical concerns: 1) simplifying the complexities of distributed computing and 2) overcoming the limitations of current user interface approaches. The final section provides a chapter by chapter overview of the remainder of the book.

What Is a Software Agent?

This section summarizes the two definitions of an agent that have been attempted: agent as an ascription, and agent as a description.

'Agent' as an Ascription

As previously noted, one of the most striking things about recent research and development in software agents is how little commonality there is between different approaches. Yet there is something that we intuitively recognize as a "family resemblance" among them. Since this resemblance cannot have to do with similarity in the details of implementation, architecture, or theory, it must be to a great degree a function of the eye of the beholder.[3] "Agent is that agent does"[4] is a slogan that captures, albeit simplistically, the essence of the insight that agency cannot ultimately be characterized by listing a collection of *attributes* but rather consists fundamentally as an *attribution* on the part of some person (Van de Velde 1995).[5]

This insight helps us understand why coming up with a once-and-for-all definition of agenthood is so difficult: one person's "intelligent agent" is another person's "smart object"; and today's "smart object" is tomorrow's "dumb program." The key distinction is in our expectations and our point of view. The claim of many agent proponents is that just as some algorithms can be more easily expressed and understood in an object-oriented representation than in a procedural one (Kaehler and Patterson 1986), so it sometimes may be easier for developers and users to interpret the behavior of their programs in terms of agents rather than as more run-of-the-mill sorts of objects (Dennett 1987).[6]

The *American Heritage Dictionary* defines an agent as "one that acts or has the power or authority to act... or represent another" or the "means by which something is done or caused; instrument." The term derives from the present participle of the Latin verb *agere:* to drive, lead, act, or do.

As in the everyday sense, we expect a software agent to act on behalf of someone to carry out a particular task which has been delegated to it.[7] But since it is tedious to have to spell out every detail, we would like our agents to be able to infer what we mean from what we tell it. Agents can only do this if they "know" something about the context of the request. The best agents, then, would not only need to exercise a particular form of expertise, but also take into account the peculiarities of the user and situation.[8] In this sense an agent fills the role of what Negroponte calls a "digital sister-in-law:"

"When I want to go out to the movies, rather than read reviews, I ask my sister-in-law. We all have an equivalent who is both an expert on movies and an expert on us. What we need to build is a digital sister-in-law.

In fact, the concept of "agent" embodied in humans helping humans is often one where expertise is indeed mixed with knowledge of you. A good travel agent blends knowledge about hotels and restaurants with knowledge about you... A real estate agent builds a model of you from a succession of houses that fit your taste with varying degrees of success. Now imagine a telephone-answering agent, a news agent, or an electronic-mail-managing agent. What they all have in common is the ability to model you." (Negroponte 1997).

While the above description would at least seem to rule out someone claiming that a typical payroll system could be regarded as an agent, there is still plenty of room for disagreement (Franklin and Graesser 1996). Recently, for example, a surprising number of developers have re-christened existing components of their software as agents, despite the fact that there is very little that seems "agent-like" about them. As Foner (1993) observes:

"... I find little justification for most of the commercial offerings that call themselves agents. Most of them tend to excessively anthropomorphize the software, and then conclude that it must be an agent because of that very anthropomorphization, while simultaneously failing to provide any sort of discourse or "social contract" between the user and the agent. Most are barely autonomous, unless a regularly-scheduled batch job counts. Many do not degrade gracefully, and therefore do not inspire enough trust to justify more than trivial delegation and its concomitant risks."[9]

Shoham provides a practical example illustrating the point that although anything *could* be described as an agent, it is not always advantageous to do so:

"It is perfectly coherent to treat a light switch as a (very cooperative) agent with the capability of transmitting current at will, who invariably transmits current when it believes that we want it transmitted and not otherwise; flicking the switch is simply our way of communicating our desires. However, while this is a coherent view, it does not buy us anything, since we essentially understand the mechanism sufficiently to have a simpler, mechanistic description of its behavior." (Shoham 1993).[10]

Physical Stance	Predict based on physical characteristics and laws
Design Stance	Predic t based on what it is designed to do
Intentional Stance	Precit based on assumption of rational agency

Table 1. Dennett's three predictive stances (from Sharp 1992, 1993).

Dennett (1987) describes three predictive stances that people can take toward systems (table 1). People will choose whatever gives the most simple, yet reliable explanation of behavior. For natural systems (e.g., collisions of billiard balls), it is practical for people to predict behavior according to physical characteristics and laws. If we understand enough about a *designed* system (e.g., an automobile), we can conveniently predict its behavior based on its functions, i.e., what it is designed to do. However as John McCarthy observed in his work on "advice-takers" in the mid-1950's, "at some point the complexity of the system becomes such that the best you can do is give advice" (Ryan 1991). For example, to predict the behavior of people, animals, robots, or agents, it may be more appropriate to take a stance based on the assumption of rational agency than one based on our limited understanding of their underlying blueprints.[11]

Singh (1994) lists several pragmatic and technical reasons for the appeal of viewing agents as intentional systems:

> "They (i) are natural to us, as designers and analyzers; (ii) provide succinct descriptions of, and help understand and explain, the behaviour of complex systems; (iii) make available certain regularities and patterns of action that are independent of the exact physical implementation of the agent in the system; and (iv) may be used by the agents themselves in reasoning about each other."

'Agent' As a Description

A more specific definition of "software agent" that many agent researchers might find acceptable is a software entity which functions continuously and autonomously in a particular environment, often inhabited by other agents and processes (Shoham 1997). The requirement for continuity and autonomy derives from our desire that an agent be able to carry out activities in a flexible and intelligent manner that is responsive to changes in the environment without requiring constant human guidance or intervention. Ideally, an agent that functions continuously in an environment over a long period of time would be able to learn from its experience. In addition, we expect an agent that inhabits an environment with other agents and processes to be able to communicate and cooperate with them, and perhaps move from place to place in doing so.

All this being said, most software agents today are fairly fragile and special-purpose beasts, no one of which can do very much of what is outlined above in a generic fashion. Hence the term "software agent" might best be viewed as an umbrella term that covers a range of other more specific and limited agent types (Nwana 1996). Though as individuals the capabilities of the agents may be rather restricted, in their aggregate they attempt to simulate the functions of a primitive "digital sister-in-law," as particular ones intimately familiar with the user and situation exchange knowledge with others who handle the details of how to obtain needed information and services. Consistent with the requirements of a particular problem, each agent might possess to a greater or lesser degree attributes like the ones enumerated in Etzioni and Weld (1995) and Franklin and Graesser (1996):

(handwritten margin note: Use to solidify)

- *Reactivity*: the ability to selectively sense and act
- *Autonomy*: goal-directedness, proactive and self-starting behavior
- *Collaborative behavior*: can work in concert with other agents to achieve a common goal
- *"Knowledge-level" (Newell 1982) communication ability:* the ability to communicate with persons and other agents with language more resembling human-like "speech acts" than typical symbol-level program-to-program protocols
- *Inferential capability*: can act on abstract task specification using prior knowledge of general goals and preferred methods to achieve flexibility; goes beyond the information given, and may have explicit models of self, user, situation, and/or other agents.
- *Temporal continuity:* persistence of identity and state over long periods of time[12]
- *Personality*: the capability of manifesting the attributes of a "believable" character such as emotion
- *Adaptivity*: being able to learn and improve with experience
- *Mobility*: being able to migrate in a self-directed way from one host platform to another.

(handwritten margin note: We better Description)

To provide a simpler way of characterizing the space of agent types than would result if one tried to describe every combination of possible attributes, several in the agent research community have proposed various classification schemes and taxonomies.

For instance, AI researchers often distinguish between *weak* and *strong* notions of agency: agents of the latter variety are designed to possess explicit mentalistic or emotional qualities (Shoham 1997; Wooldridge and Jennings 1995). From the DAI community, Moulin and Chaib-draa have characterized agents by degree of problem-solving capability:

> "A *reactive* agent reacts to changes in its environment or to messages from other agents.... An *intentional* agent is able to reason on its intentions and beliefs, to create plans of actions, and to execute those plans.... In addition to intentional agent

Use this

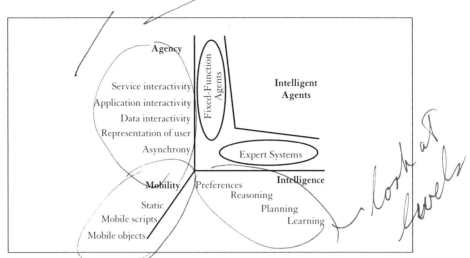

look at levels

Figure 1. Scope of intelligent agents (Adapted from Gilbert et al. 1995).

capabilities, a *social* agent possesses explicit models of other agents." (Moulin and Chaib-draa 1996, pp. 8-9).

An influential white paper from IBM (Gilbert et al. 1995) described intelligent agents in terms of a space defined by the three dimensions of *agency, intelligence,* and *mobility* (figure 1):

left view

left question

> "*Agency* is the degree of autonomy and authority vested in the agent, and can be measured at least qualitatively by the nature of the interaction between the agent and other entities in the system. At a minimum, an agent must run asynchronously. The degree of agency is enhanced if an agent represents a user in some way... A more advanced agent can interact with... data, applications,... services... [or] other agents.
>
> *Intelligence* is the degree of reasoning and learned behavior: the agent's ability to accept the user's statement of goals and carry out the task delegated to it. At a minimum, there can be some statement of preferences... Higher levels of intelligence include a user model... and reasoning.... Further out on the intelligence scale are systems that *learn* and *adapt* to their environment, both in terms of the user's objectives, and in terms of the resources available to the agent...
>
> *Mobility* is the degree to which agents themselves travel through the network... *Mobile scripts* may be composed on one machine and shipped to another for execution... [*Mobile objects* are] transported from machine to machine in the middle of execution, and carrying accumulated state data with them."

Nwana (1996) proposes a typology of agents that identifies other dimensions of classification. Agents may thus be classified according to:

- Mobility, as *static* or *mobile*
- Presence of a symbolic reasoning model, as *deliberative* or *reactive*

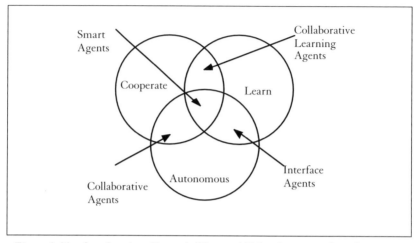

Figure 2. Typology based on Nwana's (Nwana 1996) primary attribute dimension.

- Exhibition of ideal and primary attributes, such as *autonomy, cooperation, learning.* From these characteristics, Nwana derives four agent types: *collaborative, collaborative learning, interface,* and *smart* (see figure 2).

- Roles, as *information* or *Internet*

- Hybrid philosophies, which combine two or more approaches in a single agent

- Secondary attributes, such as versatility, benevolence, veracity, trustworthiness, temporal continuity, ability to fail gracefully, and mentalistic and emotional qualities.

After developing this typology, Nwana goes on to describe ongoing research in seven categories: *collaborative agents, interface agents, mobile agents, information/Internet agents, reactive agents, hybrid agents,* and *smart agents.*

After listing several definitions given by others, Franklin and Graesser (1996) give their own: "an autonomous agent is a system situated within and part of an environment that senses that environment and acts on it, over time, in pursuit of its own agenda and so as to effect what it senses in the future." Observing that by this definition even a thermostat could qualify as an agent, they discuss various properties of agents and offer the taxonomy in figure 3 as one that covers most of the examples found in the literature. Below this initial classification, they suggest that agents can be categorized by control structures, environments (e.g., database, file system, network, Internet), language in which they are written, and applications.

Finally, Petrie (1996) discusses the various attempts of researchers to distinguish agents from other types of software. He first notes the difficulties in satisfactorily defining intelligence and autonomy. Then he shows how most of the

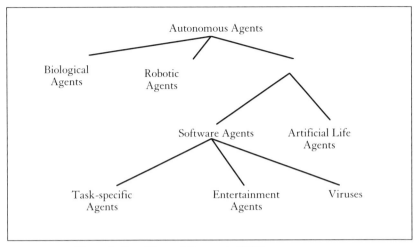

Figure 3. Franklin and Graesser's (1996) agent taxonomy.

current web-based searching and filtering "agents," though useful, "are essentially one-time query answering mechanisms" that are adequately described by the less glamorous computer science term "server." Similarly, "mobile process" would be a less confusing term than "mobile agent" for those Java applets whose only "agent-like" function is to allow processes to run securely on foreign machines. In contrast to these previous attempts to describe a set of unambiguous defining characteristics for agents in general, Petrie argues the case for one specific class: *typed-message agents.* Typed-message agents are distinguished from other types of software by virtue of their ability to communicate as a community using a shared message protocol such as KQML. In the shared message protocol, at least some of the message semantics "are typed and independent of the applications. And semantics of the message protocol necessitate that the transport protocol not be only client/server but rather a peer-to-peer protocol. An individual software module is not an agent at all if it can communicate with the other candidate agents only with a client/server protocol without degradation of the collective task performance."

Time and experience will ultimately determine both the meaning and the longevity of the term "agent." Like many other computing terms in common usage such as "desktop," "mouse," and "broker," it began with a metaphor but will end up denoting concrete software artifacts. As public exposure to useful and technically viable implementations of agent software increases, the term will either come to mean something that everyone understands because they have seen many examples of it, or it will fall into disuse because it describes a concept that is no longer appropriate. What is *unlikely* to disappear are the motivations that have incited the development of agent-based software. These are described in the following section.

Also Simpler. design

Why Software Agents?

While the original work on agents was instigated by researchers intent on studying computational models of distributed intelligence, a new wave of interest has
been fueled by two additional concerns of a practical nature: 1) simplifying the
complexities of distributed computing and 2) overcoming the limitations of current user interface approaches.[13] Both of these can essentially be seen as a contin-
uation of the trend toward greater abstraction of interfaces to computing services. On the one hand, there is a desire to further abstract the details of
hardware, software, and communication patterns by replacing today's program-
to-program interfaces with more powerful, general, and uniform agent-to-agent
interfaces; on the other hand there is a desire to further abstract the details of the
human-to-program interface by delegating to agents the details of specifying and
carrying out complex tasks. Grosof (Harrison, Chess, and Kershenbaum 1995)
argues that while it is true that point solutions not requiring agents could be devised to address many if not all of the issues raised by such problems, the aggregate advantage of agent technology is that it can address all of them at once.

In the following two subsections, I discuss how agents could be used to address the two main concerns I have mentioned. Following this, I sketch a vision
of how "agent-enabled" system architectures of the future could provide an unprecedented level of functionality to people.

Simplifying Distributed Computing

Barriers to Intelligent Interoperability. Over the past several years, Brodie
(1989) has frequently discussed the need for *intelligent interoperability* in
software systems. He defines the term to mean intelligent cooperation
among systems to optimally achieve specified goals. While there is little disagreement that future computing environments will consist of distributed
software systems running on multiple heterogeneous platforms, many of
today's most common configurations are, for all intents and purposes, disjoint: they do not really communicate or cooperate except in very basic ways
(e.g., file transfer, print servers, database queries) (figure 4). The current
ubiquity of the Web makes it easy to forget that until the last few years,
computer systems that *could* communicate typically relied on proprietary or
ad hoc interfaces for their particular connection. The current growth in popularity of object-oriented approaches and the development of a few important agreed-upon standards (e.g., TCP/IP, HTTP, IIOP, ODBC) has brought a
basic level of encapsulated connectivity to many systems and services. Increasingly, these connections are made asynchronously through message
passing, in situations where the advantages of loose coupling in complex cooperating systems can be realized (Mellor 1994; Perrow 1984; Shaw 1996).

We are now in the midst of a shift from the network operating system to In-

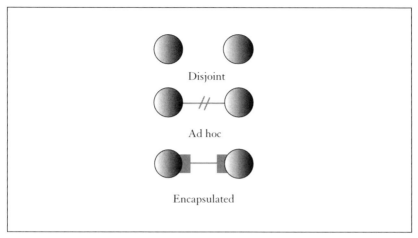

Figure 4. Evolution of system connectivity (Adapted from Brodie 1989).

ternet and intranet-based network computing (Lewis 1996). As this transition takes place, we are seeing the proliferation of operating system-independent interoperable network services such as naming, directory, and security. These, rather than the underlying operating systems, are defining the network, reducing the operating systems to commodities. Lewis (1996) asserts that Netscape is the best example of a vendor focused exclusively on such a goal. Federations of such vendors are defining standards-based operating system-independent services (directory, security, transactions, Web, and so forth), truly universal server-independent clients (Web browsers), and network-based application development support (Java, JavaScript, ActiveX). In such approaches, both the client and server operating systems become little more than a collection of device drivers.

Incorporating Agents as Resource Managers. A higher level of interoperability would require knowledge of the capabilities of each system, so that secure task planning, resource allocation, execution, monitoring, and, possibly, intervention between the systems could take place. To accomplish this, an intelligent agent could function as a global resource manager (figure 5).

Unfortunately, while a single agent might be workable for small networks of systems, such a scheme quickly becomes impractical as the number of cooperating systems grows. The activity of the single agent becomes a bottleneck for the (otherwise distributed) system. A further step toward intelligent interoperability is to embed one or more peer agents within each cooperating system (figure 6). Applications request services through these agents at a higher level corresponding more to user *intentions* than to specific *implementations*, thus providing a level of encapsulation at the planning level, analogous to the encapsulation provided at the lower level of basic communications protocols. As agents in-

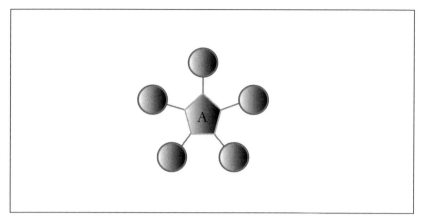

Figure 5. Cooperating systems with single agent as a global planner. Connections represent agent-to-application communication (Adapted from Brodie 1989).

creasingly evolve from stationary entities to mobile ones, we will see an even more radical redefinition of distributed object computing within corporate networks and on the World Wide Web (Chang and Lange 1996). These scenarios presume, of course, timely agreement on basic standards ensuring agent interoperability (Gardner 1996; Lange 1996; Virdhagriswaran, Osisek, and O'Connor 1995; White 1997).

Overcoming User Interface Problems

Limitations of Direct Manipulation Interface. A distinct but complementary motivation for software agents is in overcoming problems with the current generation of user interface approaches. In the past several years, *direct manipulation* interfaces (Hutchins, Hollan, and Norman 1986; Shneiderman 1983; Shneiderman 1984; Smith, et al. 1982) have become the standard. For many of the most common user tasks, they are a distinct improvement over command-line interfaces. Since direct manipulation requires software objects to be visible, users are constantly informed about the kinds of things they can act upon. If, in addition, the objects have a natural correspondence to real-world or metaphorical counterparts, users can apply previously acquired experience to more quickly learn what the objects can do and how to do it. Many advantages of direct manipulation begin to fade, however, as tasks grow in scale or complexity. For example, anyone who has had much experience with iconic desktop interfaces knows that there are times when sequences of actions would be better automated than directly performed by the user in simple, tedious steps.[14] Several researchers have analyzed the limitations of passive artifact metaphors for complex tasks (diSessa 1986; Erickson 1996; Kay 1990; Whittaker 1990). Among others, people are likely to encounter the following problems:

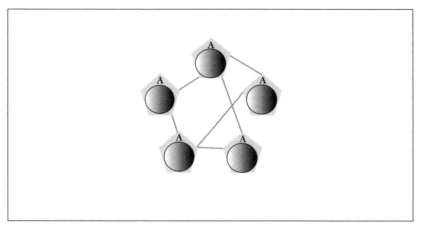

Figure 6. Cooperating systems with distributed agents. Connecting lines represent on-going agent-to-agent communication (Adapted from Brodie 1989).

- *Large search space:* In large distributed systems it is difficult to find what we need through browsing or the use of traditional indexing methods. What is practical and possible for a few hundred items becomes unwieldy and impossible for several thousand.
- *Actions in response to immediate user interaction only:* Sometimes instead of executing an action immediately, we want to schedule it for a specific time in the future. Or, we may want to have software automatically react to system-generated events when we are away from the machine.
- *No composition:* With most direct manipulation interfaces, we cannot easily compose basic actions and objects into higher-level ones.
- *Rigidity:* The consistency that makes passive artifact interfaces predictable and easy-to-learn for simple tasks makes them brittle and untrustworthy for complex ones.
- *Function orientation:* Software is typically organized according to generic software functions rather than the context of the person's task and situation.
- *No improvement of behavior:* Traditional software does not notice or learn from repetitive actions in order to respond with better default behavior.

Indirect Management Using Agents. Researchers and developers are attempting to address these problems by combining the expression of user intention through direct manipulation with the notion of an *indirect management* style of interaction (Kay 1990). In such an approach, users would no longer be obliged to spell out each action for the computer explicitly; instead, the flexibility and intelligence of software agents would allow them to give general guidelines and forget about the details.

Many of the actions now performed by users could be delegated to various software agents. Thus, in a glimpse of the future, Tesler (1991) imagines the following directives being given by a person to a software agent:

- On what date in February did I record a phone conversation with Sam?
- Make me an appointment at a tire shop that is on my way home and is open after 6 PM.
- Distribute this draft to the rest of the group and let me know when they've read it.
- Whenever a paper is published on fullerene molecules, order a copy for my library.

Later on in the day, Tesler imagines the agent catching up to the person with these follow-up messages:

- You asked me when you last recorded a phone conversation with Sam. It was on February 27. Shall I play the recording?
- You scribbled a note last week that your tires were low. I could get you an appointment for tonight.
- Laszlo has discarded the last four drafts you sent him without reading any of them.
- You have requested papers on fullerene research. Shall I order papers on other organic microclusters as well?

Direct manipulation and indirect management approaches are not mutually exclusive. Interface agent researchers are not out to completely do away with computing as we know it, but more modestly hope that complementing see-and-point interfaces with ask-and-delegate extensions will help reduce required knowledge and simplify necessary actions while maintaining a sufficient level of predictability. Specifically, the use of software agents will eventually help overcome the limitations of passive artifact interfaces in the following ways (table 2):

- *Scalability:* Agents can be equipped with search and filtering capabilities that run in the background to help people explore vast sources of information.
- *Scheduled or event-driven actions:* Agents can be instructed to execute tasks at specific times or automatically "wake up" and react in response to system-generated events.
- *Abstraction and delegation:* Agents can be made extensible and composable in ways that common iconic interface objects cannot. Because we can "communicate" with them, they can share our goals, rather than simply process our commands. They can show us how to do things and tell us what went wrong (Miller and Neches 1987).
- *Flexibility and opportunism:* Because they can be instructed at the level of goals and strategies, agents can find ways to "work around" unforeseen problems and exploit new opportunities as they help solve problems.

Typical Limitations of Direct Manipulation Interfaces	Advantages of Agent-Oriented Approach
Large search space	Scalability
Actions in response to immediate user interaction only	Scheduled or event-driven actions
No composition	Abstraction and delegation
Rigidity	Flexibility and opportunism
Function orientation	Task orientation
No improvement of behavior	Adaptivity

Table 2. Typical limitations of direct manipulation interfaces and advantages of agent-oriented approach.

- *Task orientation:* Agents can be designed to take the context of the person's tasks and situation into account as they present information and take action.
- *Adaptivity:* Agents can use learning algorithms to continually improve their behavior by noticing recurrent patterns of actions and events.

Toward Agent-Enabled System Architectures

In the future, assistant agents at the user interface and resource-managing agents behind the scenes will increasingly pair up to provide an unprecedented level of functionality to people. A key enabler is the packaging of data and software into components that can provide comprehensive information about themselves at a fine-grain level to the agents that act upon them.

Over time, large undifferentiated data sets will be restructured into smaller elements that are well-described by rich metadata, and complex monolithic applications will be transformed into a dynamic collection of simpler parts with self-describing programming interfaces. Ultimately, all data will reside in a "knowledge soup," where agents assemble and present small bits of information from a variety of data sources on the fly as appropriate to a given context (figure 7) (Neches et al. 1991; Sowa 1990). In such an environment, individuals and groups would no longer be forced to manage a passive collection of disparate documents to get something done. Instead, they would interact with active *knowledge media* (Barrett 1992; Bradshaw et al. 1993b; Brown and Duguid 1996; Glicksman, Weber, and Gruber 1992; Gruber, Tenenbaum, and Weber 1992) that integrate needed resources and actively collaborate with them on their tasks.

Figure 7 illustrates the various roles agents could play in an agent-enabled system architecture. Some could act in the role of intelligent user interface managers, drawing on the resources of other agents working behind the scenes (Arens et al. 1991; Browne, Totterdell, and Norman 1990; Kay 1990; Neal and Shapiro 1994;

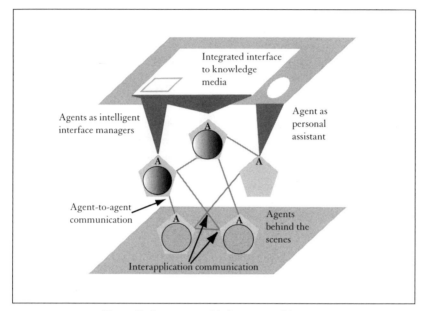

Figure 7 An agent-enabled system architecture.

Sullivan and Tyler 1991). Such agents would work in concert to help coordinate the selection of the appropriate display modes and representations for the relevant data (Bradshaw and Boose 1992; Johnson et al. 1994), incorporating semantic representations of the knowledge in the documents to enhance navigation and information retrieval (Boy 1992; Bradshaw and Boy 1993; Gruber, Tenenbaum, and Weber 1992; Lethbridge and Skuce 1992; Mathé and Chen 1994). Because the layout and content of the views would be driven by context and configuration models rather than by hand-crafted user-interface code, significant economies could be realized as the data and software components are reused and semi-automatically reconfigured for different settings and purposes. Some agents might be represented explicitly to the user as various types of personal assistants (Maes 1997). Ideally, each software component would be "agent-enabled," however for practical reasons components may at times still rely on traditional interapplication communication mechanisms rather than agent-to-agent protocols.

Overview of the Book

The first subsection summarizes the first set of chapters under the heading of "Agents and the User Experience," which contain introductory pieces authored by proponents (and a critic) of agent technology. The next set, "Agents for Learning and Intelligent Assistance," describes how agents have been used to enhance learning and provide intelligent assistance to users in situations where direct manipulation interfaces alone are insufficient. The final set, "Agent Communication, Collaboration, and Mobility," details various approaches to agent-oriented programming, agent-to-agent communication, and agent mobility, as well as the use of agents to provide intelligent interoperability between loosely-coupled components of distributed systems.

Agents and the User Experience

How Might People Interact with Agents? Norman's (1997) introductory chapter sets the stage for the first section of the book. "Agents occupy a strange place in the realm of technology," he opens, "leading to much fear, fiction, and extravagant claims." Because the new crop of intelligent agents differ so significantly in their computational power from their predecessors, we need to take into account the social issues no less than the technical ones if our designs are to be acceptable to people:

> "The technical aspect is to devise a computational structure that guarantees that from the technical standpoint, all is under control. This is not an easy task.
>
> The social part of acceptability is to provide reassurance that all is working according to plan... This is [also] a non-trivial task."

The reassurance that all is working according to plan is provided by an understandable and controllable level of feedback about the agent's intentions and actions. We must also think about how to accurately convey the agent's capabilities and limitations so that people are not misled in their expectations. Part of the problem is the natural overenthusiasm of agent researchers; part of the problem is people's tendency to falsely anthropomorphize.[15] Although designers can carefully describe agent capabilities and limitations within accompanying instructional manuals, it is even more important to find clever ways to weave this information naturally and effectively into the agent interface itself.

Safety and privacy are additional concerns. "How does one guard against error, maliciousness (as in the spread of computer viruses), and deliberate intent to pry and probe within one's personal records?" Legal policies to address these issues must be formulated immediately, at local, national, and global levels.

A final concern is how to design the appropriate form of interaction between agents and people. For example, how do ordinary people program the agent to do what they want? While programming-by-demonstration or simplified visual or scripting languages have been suggested, none of them seem adequate to specify the kinds of complex tasks envisioned for future intelligent agents.[16]

Since "agents are here to stay," we must learn how to cope with the dangers along with the positive contributions. "None of these negative aspects of agents are inevitable. All can be eliminated or minimized, but only if we consider these aspects in the design of our intelligent systems."

Agents: From Direct Manipulation to Delegation. In his chapter, Nicholas Negroponte (1997), a longtime champion of agent technology (Negroponte 1970, 1995), extols the virtues of delegation in intelligent interfaces:

We

> "The best metaphor I can conceive of for a human-computer interface is that of a well-trained English butler. The "agent" answers the phone, recognizes the callers, disturbs you when appropriate, and may even tell a white lie on your behalf. The same agent is well trained in timing… and respectful of idiosyncrasies. People who know the butler enjoy considerable advantage over a total stranger. That is just fine." (Negroponte 1997.)

What will such digital butlers do? They will filter, extract, and present the relevant information from bodies of information larger than we could ordinarily digest on their own. They will act as "digital sisters-in-law," combining their knowledge of information and computing services with intimate knowledge about the person on whose behalf they are acting.

To create agents that are intelligent enough to perform these tasks to our level of satisfaction, we will need to re-open profound and basic questions of intelligence and learning that past AI research has left largely untouched. An understanding of decentralized approaches to intelligence is key: coherence can emerge from the activity of independent agents who coordinate their actions indirectly through shared external influences in their common environment.[17]

User interface design will also be decentralized. Instead of being an effort by professionals to produce the best interface for the masses, it will become an individual affair, driven more by the personalized intelligence of one's local agents than the blanket application of general human-factors knowledge. The agent's long-time familiarity with a person, gained by numerous shared experiences, will be critical to the new beyond-the-desktop metaphor. Though direct manipulation has its place, Negroponte believes that most people would prefer to run their home and office life with a gaggle of well-trained butlers.

Interface Agents: Metaphors with Character. The thesis of Laurel's (1997) chapter is that unabashed anthropomorphism in the design of interface agents is both natural and appropriate:

> "First, this form of representation makes optimal use of our ability to make accurate inferences about how a character is likely to think, decide, and act on the basis of its external traits. This marvelous cognitive shorthand is what makes plays and movies work… Second, the agent as character (whether humanoid, canine, cartoonish, or cybernetic) invites conversational interaction… [without necessarily requiring] elaborate natural language processing… Third, the metaphor of *character* successfully draws our attention to just those qualities that form the essential nature of an agent: responsiveness, competence, accessibility, and the capacity to perform actions on our behalf."

Recognizing the considerable resistance many will have to this idea, she responds to some of the most common criticisms. First, is the objection to having to face "whining, chatting little irritants" each time you turn on the machine. Laurel notes that the problem is not "agents *per se*, but rather the traits they are assumed to possess." To address this problem, we must allow the traits of agents to be fully user-configurable. Another criticism is the indirection implied by the presence of an agent, "Why should I have to negotiate with some little dip in a bowtie when I know exactly what I want to do?" The answer is that if you know what you want to do and if you want to do it yourself, the agent should quickly get out of your way. Agent-based assistance should be reserved for tedious or complex tasks that you don't want to do yourself, and that you are comfortable entrusting to a software entity. Will people's acquired habit of bossing agents around lead them to treating real people the same way? Laurel argues that this is a real issue, but should not be handled by repression of the dramatic form—rather it should be addressed as an ethical problem for agent designers and the culture at large. Finally, there is the oft-heard criticism that "AI doesn't work." Laurel counters with examples of successful use of AI techniques in well-defined domains. Moreove, she asserts that most agents do not need a full-blown "artificial personality," but can be implemented much more simply.

Laurel concludes with a discussion of key characteristics of interface agents (agency, responsiveness, competence, and accessibility) and of an R&D agenda that includes an appreciation of the contribution of studies of story generation and dramatic character.[18]

Designing Agents as if People Mattered. Erickson (1997) explores the many difficulties surrounding adaptive functionality and the agent metaphor. With respect to adaptive functionality, he describes three design issues raised in a study of users of the DowQuest information retrieval system. In brief, people need to *understand* what happened and why when a system alters its response; they need to be able to *control* the actions of a system, even when it does not always wait for the user's input before it makes a move; and they need to *predict* what will happen, even though the system will change its responses over time. Several approaches to these problems have been suggested, including: providing users with a more accurate model of what is going on, managing overblown expectations of users at the beginning so they are willing to persist long enough to benefit from the system's incremental learning, and constructing a plausible 'fictional' model of what is going on.

Given the potential of the agent metaphor as a possible fiction for portraying system functionality, Erickson examines three strands of research that shed some light on how well this approach might work. Designed to encourage students to explore an interactive encyclopedia, the Guides project allowed researchers to observe the kinds of attributions and the level of emotional engagement people had with stereotypic characters that assisted in navigation. Erickson also reviews the extensive research that Nass and his colleagues have performed on the tendency of people to use their knowledge of people and social rules to make judgments about computers. Finally, he discusses recent research on the reaction of people to extremely realistic portrayals of agents.

In the final section of the chapter, Erickson contrasts the desktop object and agent conceptual models, and argues that they can be used together in the same interface so long as they are clearly distinguished from one another. Specific computing functionality can be portrayed either as an object or an agent, depending on what is most natural. The desktop metaphor takes advantage of users' previous knowledge that office artifacts are visible, are passive, have locations, and may contain things. "Objects stay where they are: nice, safe predictable things that just sit there and hold things." Ontological knowledge of a different sort comes into play when the agent metaphor is employed. Our common sense knowledge of what agents can do tells us that, unlike typical desktop objects, they can notice things, carry out actions, know and learn things, and go places.[19] "Agents become the repositories for adaptive functionality." The overall conclusion is that research "which focuses on the portrayal of adaptive functionality, rather than on the functionality itself, is a crucial need if we wish to design agents that interact gracefully with their users."

Direct Manipulation Versus Agents: Paths to Predictable, Controllable, and Comprehensible Interfaces. Breaking with the tone of cautious optimism expressed in the preceding chapters, Shneiderman, a longtime advocate of direct manipulation, is troubled by the concept of intelligent interfaces in general:

"First, such a classification limits the imagination. We should have much greater ambition than to make a computer behave like an intelligent butler or other human agent...

Second, the quality of predictability and control are desirable. If machines are intelligent or adaptive, they may have less of these qualities...

[Third,] I am concerned that if designers are successful in convincing the users that computers are intelligent, then the users will have a reduced sense of responsibility for failures...

Finally,... [m]achines are not people... [and if] you confuse the way you treat machines with the way you treat people... you may end up treating people like machines."[20]

Shneiderman backs up his general concerns with lessons from past disappointments in natural language systems, speech I/O, intelligent computer-assisted instruction, and intelligent talking robots.

Shneiderman observes that agent proponents have not come up with good definitions of what is and is not an agent. "Is a compiler an agent? How about an optimizing compiler? Is a database query an agent? Is the print monitor an agent? Is e-mail delivered by an agent? Is a VCR scheduler an agent?" His examination of the literature reveals six major elements of the agent approach: anthropomorphic presentation, adaptive behavior, acceptance of vague goal specification, gives you what you need, works while you don't, and works where you aren't. The first three, on closer examination, seem counterproductive, while the last three are good ideas that could be achieved by other means.

The alternative to a vision of computers as intelligent machines is that of predictable and controllable user interfaces, based on direct manipulation of representations of familiar objects. Shneiderman concludes with a description of two examples from his own lab (tree maps and dynamic queries) that show the power of visual, animated interfaces "built on promising strategies like informative and continuous feedback, meaningful control panels, appropriate preference boxes, user-selectable toolbars, rapid menu selection, easy-to-create macros, and comprehensible shortcuts." These, he argues, rather than vague visions of intelligent machines, will allow users to specify computer actions rapidly, accurately, and confidently.

Agents for Learning and Intelligent Assistance

Agents for Information Sharing and Coordination: A History and Some Reflections. The chapter by Malone, Grant, and Lai (1997) reviews more than ten years of seminal work on a series of programs which were intended to allow unsophisticated computer users to create their own cooperative work applications using a set of simple, but powerful, building blocks. The work is based on two key design principles, which each imply a particular kind of humility that should be required of agent designers:

> "1. Don't build computational agents that try to solve complex problems all by themselves. Instead, build systems where the boundary between what the agents do and what the humans do is a flexible one. We call this the principle of *semiformal systems*...
>
> 2. Don't build agents that try to figure out for themselves things that humans could easily tell them. Instead, try to build systems that make it as easy as possible for humans to see and modify the same information and reasoning processes their agents are using. We call this the principle of *radical tailorability*..."

Information Lens, the first program in the series, was a system for intelligent sorting and processing of electronic mail messages. *Object Lens* and *Oval* were successor programs providing much more general and tailorable environments that extended beyond the domain of electronic mail filtering.

The name "Oval" is an acronym for the four key components of the system: objects, views, agents, and links. "By defining and modifying templates for various semi-structured *objects*, users can represent information about people, tasks, products, messages, and many other kinds of information in a form that can be processed intelligently by both people and their computers. By collecting these objects in customizable folders, users can create their own *views* which summarize selected information from the objects. By creating semi-autonomous *agents*, users can specify rules for automatically processing this information in different ways at different times. Finally, *links*, are used for connecting and relating different objects" (Lai and Malone 1992).

The authors describe several different applications that were created to show the power and generality of the Oval approach.[21] All these demonstrate the surprising power that semiformal information processing can provide to people, and lend credence to the claim that people without formal programming skills can be enabled to create agent-based computing environments that suit their individual needs.

Agents that Reduce Work and Information Overload. While the developers of Oval have explored ways to simplify agent authoring, Pattie Maes and her colleagues at MIT have pursued an approach that allows personal assistants to *learn* appropriate behavior from user feedback (Maes 1997). The personal assistant starts out with very little knowledge and over time becomes more experienced, gradually building up a relationship of understanding and trust with the user:

> "[We] believe that the learning approach has several advantages over [end-user programming and knowledge-based approaches]... First, it requires less work from the end-user and application developer. Second, the agent can more easily adapt to the user over time and become customized to individual and organizational preferences and habits. Finally, the approach helps in transferring information, habits and know-how among the different users of a community."

A learning agent acquires its competence from four different sources. First, it can "look over the shoulder" of users as they perform actions. Second, it can learn through direct and indirect feedback from the user. Indirect feedback is provided when the user ignores the agent's suggested action. Third, the agent can learn from user-supplied examples. Finally, the agent can ask advice from other users' agents that have may have more experience with the same task.

Two assumptions determine whether the learning approach is appropriate for a given application:

1. *The application should involve a significant amount of repetitive behavior.* Otherwise, there would be no consistent situation-action patterns for the agent to learn.

2. *Repetitive behavior should be different for different users.* Otherwise, the behavior could be more efficiently hard-coded once and for all in a program, rather than implemented using learning agents.

Maes describes four agent-based applications built using the learning approach: electronic mail handling *(Maxims)*, meeting scheduling,[22] Usenet Netnews filtering *(Newt)*, and recommending books, music or other forms of entertainment *(Ringo)*[23] Through clever user feedback mechanisms and tailoring options, this approach provides a great deal of functionality from the combination of relatively simple mechanisms.

KidSim: Programming Agents without a Programming Language. Like Malone and his colleagues, Smith, Cypher, and Spohrer (1997) have focused their attention on the problem of agent authoring. What is unique to their application, however, is that they are trying to create a general and powerful tool for use by *children*. To make this possible, they have adopted a "languageless" approach:

> "We decided that the question is not: what language can we invent that will be easier for people to use? The question is: should we be using a language at all?...

We've come to the conclusion that since all previous languages have been unsuccessful…, *language itself is the problem.*.

… [The] graphical user interface eliminated command lines by introducing visual representations for concepts and allowing people to directly manipulate those representations… Today all successful editors on personal computers follow this approach. But most programming environments do not. This is the reason most people have an easier time *editing* than *programming.*"

KidSim[24] (now called "Cocoa") is a tool kit where children can build worlds populated by agents that they program themselves by demonstration and direct manipulation. Existing agents (simulation objects) can be modified, and new ones can be defined from scratch. Although agents cannot inherit from one another, they can share elements such as rules. In keeping with the design philosophy of direct manipulation, all elements of the simulation are visible in the interface.

"Languageless" programming is accomplished by combining two ideas: *graphical rewrite rules,* and *programming-by-demonstration.*[25] Graphical rewrite rules define transformations of a region of the game board from one state to another. Programming-by-demonstration is accomplished by letting the child put the system into "record mode" to capture all actions and replay them. A major strength of KidSim is that the results of recording user actions can be shown graphically, rather than as a difficult-to-understand script, as in most other such systems.

The authors describe a series of classroom studies in which children from ages eight to fourteen have used development versions of KidSim. The studies have led to a refinement of many of the concepts in KidSim, and have in turn provided convincing evidence that reasonably complex simulations of this sort can be constructed by very young children. No doubt there are many agent applications for adults that could take advantage of similar principles to make programming accessible.

Lifelike Computer Characters: The Persona Project at Microsoft. While many software agent researchers are content to make agents that are merely "useful," others seek the more ambitious goal of making "complete" agents that are highly visible in the user interface, project the illusion of being aware and intentioned, and are capable of emotions and significant social interaction. The *Persona* project (Ball et al. 1997) was formed to prototype possible interfaces to future computer-based assistants, in this case a "conversational, anthropomorphic computer character that will interact with the user to accept task assignments and report results." To be successful, such assistants will need to support interactive give and take including task negotiation and clarifying questions, understand how and when it is appropriate to interrupt the user with a report or request for input, and acknowledge the social and emotional impacts of interaction.

The creation of lifelike computer characters requires a wide variety of technologies and skills, including speech recognition, natural language understanding, animation, and speech synthesis. A sophisticated understanding of subtle dialogue mechanisms and social psychology is also essential. To add to this challenge, all the necessary computational machinery to support these technologies must ultimately be able to run with acceptable performance on garden variety computing platforms.

The application chosen for the project described in this chapter involves an animated character (Personal Digital Parrot One, PDP1, or Peedy for short) that acts as a knowledgeable compact disc changer: "The assistant can be queried as to what CDs are available by artist, title or genre, additional information can be obtained about the CDs, and a playlist can be generated." Peedy responds verbally and by doing things to spoken commands in a restricted subset of natural language.

The application relies on two major technology components: reactive animation and natural language. *ReActor* represents a visual scene and accompanying entities such as cameras and lights hierarchically. The most interesting aspect of the animation is its reactivity, i.e., the fact that complex behaviors, including "emotion," can be triggered by user input. The natural language capability relies on the *Whisper* speech recognition module and on a broad-coverage natural language parser.

The creation of such prototypes has allowed Ball and his colleagues to discover and explore many little-understood aspects of human-computer interaction and to point the way toward the creation of increasingly sophisticated lifelike conversational assistants in the future.

Software Agents for Cooperative Learning. Boy's chapter (1997) examines the role of agents in learning technology. He briefly reviews significant trends of the past, including computer-based training, intelligent tutoring systems, interactive learning systems, and cooperative learning systems. Computer-supported cooperative learning (CSCL) builds on the lessons learned from these past approaches to provide an environment where knowledge is exchanged via active electronic documents.

Four requirements guide the design of active documents: 1. providing the *appropriate illusion* that is useful and natural for the user to understand its content; 2. providing *appropriate indexing and linking mechanisms* to connect the document with other relevant documents; 3. providing *adaptivity* so that over time the document becomes increasingly tailored to the information requirements of particular users; and 4. including *dynamic simulations* to enable people to understand aspects of complex situations that cannot be adequately represented using a static medium such as paper.

Software agents for cooperative learning are designed to transform standard electronic documents into active ones. Drawing on extensive past research experience with the *Situation Recognition and Analytical Reasoning (SRAR)* model and the *knowledge block representation* (Boy 1992; Boy 1991; Boy and Mathé 1993; Mathé and Chen 1994), he defines an agent in the context of this chapter to be "a software entity that can be represented by a knowledge block with an interface metaphor (appearance)."

As an example of an agent-based CSCL system Boy describes ACTIDOC, a prototype environment for active documents that has been applied in the domain of physics instruction. ACTIDOC documents consist of an ordered set of pages containing content and software agents (to make the content active). Each agent contains a name, a context, a set of triggering conditions, a set of internal mechanisms, and a set of interface metaphors. From Schank and Jona's (1991) six learning architectures, Boy derives classes of agents useful in active document design: *case-based learning agent, incidental learning agent, problem-solving agent, video database agent, simulation agent, and suggestive-questions agent.* Additionally he defines the roles of *evaluation, instructor aid,* and *networking agents.* These are illustrated using a physics example that demonstrates one way that agents can be used to make document content come alive.

The M System. Based on Minsky's *Society of Mind* (SOM) theory (Minsky 1986), the M system (Riecken 1997) is designed to provide intelligent assistance in a broad range of tasks through the integration of different reasoning processes *(societies of agents).* The architecture has previously been applied in the domains of music composition and intelligent user interface agents; this paper describes how M assists users of a desktop multimedia conferencing environment to classify and manage metaphorical electronic objects such as documents, ink, images, markers, white boards, copy machines, and staplers.

In the Virtual Meeting Room (VMR) application, participants collaborate using pen-based computers and a telephone:

> "Each user is supported by a personalized assistant, which attempts to recognize and define relationships between domain objects, based on the actions performed by the users and the resulting new states of the world. For example, VMR participants may perform actions on a group of electronic documents such as joining them as a set or annotating them collectively. M attempts to identify all domain objects and classify relationships between various subsets based on their physical properties and relevant user actions."

Within M there are five major reasoning processes, each of which are viewed as individual agents: *spatial, structural, functional, temporal, and causal.* Other more simple agents function as *supporting agents.* Functioning as a set of SOM *memory machines,* these supporting agents represent conceptual knowledge about things like color, shape, and spatial relationships. As an architecture of integrated agents, M dynamically generates, ranks, and modifies simultaneous theories about what is going on in the VMR world. As a faithful implementation of SOM theory, M provides for an I/O system, a spreading activation semantic network (to implement Minsky's K-lines/polynemes), a rule-based system, a scripting system, a blackboard system (to implement Minsky's trans-frames and pronomes), and a history log file system.

To Riecken, an agent is fundamentally a simple, specialized "reasoning" process, whereas an assistant is composed of many "agencies of agents:" "To handle a common sense problem, one would not typically call on an agent—instead, one would want an assistant endowed with the talents of many integrated agents."

Agent Communication, Collaboration, and Mobility

An Overview of Agent-Oriented Programming. *Agent-oriented programming* (AOP) is a term that Shoham (1977) has proposed for the set of activities necessary to create software agents. What he means by 'agent' is "an entity whose state is viewed as consisting of mental components such as beliefs, capabilities, choices, and commitments." Agent-oriented programming can be thought of as a specialization of object-oriented programming approach, with constraints on what kinds of state-defining parameters, message types, and methods are appropriate. From this perspective, an agent is essentially "an object with an attitude."

An agent's "mental state" consists of components such as beliefs, decisions, capabilities, and obligations. Shoham formally describes the state in an extension of standard epistemic logics, and defines operators for obligation, decision, and capability. *Agent programs* control the behavior and mental state of agents. These programs are executed by an *agent interpreter.* In the spirit of speech act theory, interagent communication is implemented as speech act primitives of various types, such as inform, request, or refrain.

An agent interpreter assures that each agent will iterate through two steps at regular intervals: 1) read the current messages and update its mental state (including beliefs and commitments), and 2) execute the commitments for the current time, possibly resulting in further belief change. Shoham's original agent interpreter, AGENT-0, implements five language elements: *fact statements* ("Smith is an employee of Acme"), *communicative action statements* (inform, request, refrain), *conditional action statements* ("If, at time *t*, you believe that Smith is an employee of Acme, then inform agent A of the fact"), *variables*, and *commitment rules* ("If you receive message *x* while in the mental state *y*, perform action *z*").

The basic concepts described by Shoham have influenced the direction of many other agent researchers. He and his colleagues have continued their investigations an several fronts including mental states, algorithmic issues, the role of agents in digital libraries, and social laws among agents.

KQML as an Agent Communication Language. While Shoham's definition of an agent is built around a formal description of its mental state, other groups of researchers have taken agent communication as their point of departure.[26] In this chapter, Finin, Labrou and Mayfield (1997) justify such a rationale as follows:

> "The building block for intelligent interaction is knowledge sharing that includes both mutual understanding of knowledge and the communication of that knowledge. The importance of such communication is emphasized by Genesereth, who goes so far as to suggest that an entity is a software agent if and only if it communicates correctly

in an agent communication language (Genesereth and Ketchpel 1994). After all, it is hard to picture cyberspace with entities that exist only in isolation; it would go against our perception of a decentralized, interconnected electronic universe."

After an overview of the work of the Knowledge Sharing Effort (KSE) consortium (Neches et al. 1991) to tackle various issues relating to software agents and interoperability, the authors focus on one particular result of the effort: KQML (Knowledge Query Manipulation Language).

The authors suggest seven categories of requirements for an agent communication language:

- *Form.* It should be declarative, syntactically simple, and easily readable by people and programs.

- *Content.* A distinction should be made between the language that expresses communicative acts ("performatives") and the language that conveys the content of the message.

- *Semantics.* The semantics should exhibit those desirable properties expected of the semantics of any other language.

- *Implementation.* The implementation should be efficient, provide a good fit with existing software, hide the details of lower layers, and allow simple agents to implement subsets of the language.

- *Networking.* It should support all important aspects of modern networking technology, and should be independent of transport mechanism.

- *Environment.* It must cope with heterogeneity and dynamism.

- *Reliability.* It must support reliable and secure agent communication.

After a review of the features of KQML, the authors describe how the features of KQML support each of these requirements. The authors conclude by describing various applications of KQML and by giving a comparison with two related approaches: AOP and Telescript.

An Agent-Based Framework for Interoperability. Genesereth (1997) continues the theme of agent communication with his chapter on the role of agents in enabling interoperability, meaning that software created by different developers and at different times works together in seamless manner. He discusses two limitations of current software interoperability technologies: 1. they lack the ability to communicate definitions, theorems, and assumptions that may be needed for one system to communicate effectively with another, and 2. there is no general way of resolving inconsistencies in the use of syntax and vocabulary.

Like Finin and his colleagues, Genesereth has been a major contributor to the KSE. His *ACL* (agent communication language) draws on three cornerstones of the KSE approach: *vocabularies,* (ontologies) *KIF (Knowledge Interchange Format),* and *KQML.* The vocabulary of ACL is represented as a sophisticated open-ended dictionary of terms that can be referenced by the cooperating agents and applications.[27] KIF is a particular syntax for first order predicate calculus that provides for a common internal knowledge representation, an "inner" language for agents (Genesereth and Fikes 1992). It was originally developed by Genesereth's group and is currently being refined as part of an ISO standardization effort. In the ACL approach, KQML is viewed as a linguistic layer on top of KIF that allows information about the context (e.g., sender, receiver, time of message history) to be taken into account as part of agent messages. In short, "an ACL message is a KQML expression in which the 'arguments' are terms or sentences in KIF formed from words in the ACL vocabulary" (Genesereth and Ketchpel 1994).

The concept of a *facilitator* is central to ACL. Agents and facilitators are organized into a *federated system,* in which agents surrender their autonomy in exchange for the facilitator's services. Facilitators coordinate the activities of agents and provide other services such as locating other agents by name (white pages) or by capabilities (yellow pages), direct communication, content-based routing, message translation, problem decomposition, and monitoring. Upon startup, an agent initiates an ACL connection to the local facilitator and provides a description of its capabilities. It then sends the facilitator requests when it cannot supply its own needs, and is expected to act to the best of its ability to satisfy the facilitator's requests.

Genesereth describes several examples of applications and summarizes issues where further work is needed. ACL is an important step toward the ambitious long-range vision where "any system (software or hardware) can interoperate with any other system, without the intervention of human users or… programmers."

Agents for Information Gathering. The chapter by Knoblock and Ambite (1977) provides an in-depth example of the use of agents for an important class of problems: information gathering. The SIMS architecture for intelligent information agents is designed to provide:

1. *modularity* in terms of representing an information agent and information sources,

2. *extensibility* in terms of adding new information agents and information sources,

3. *flexibility* in terms of selecting the most appropriate information sources to answer a query,

4. *efficiency* in terms of minimizing the overall execution time for a given query, and

5. *adaptability* in terms of being able to track semantic discrepancies among models of different agents."

Each SIMS information agent provides expertise on a specific topic by drawing upon other information agents and data repositories. "An existing database or program can be turned into a simple information agent by building the appropriate interface code, called a *wrapper,* that will allow it to conform to the conventions of the [particular agent] organization… [Such an] approach greatly simplifies the individual agents since they need to handle only one underlying language. This arrangement makes it possible to scale the network into many agents with access to many different types of information sources." Agents that answer queries but do not originate them are referred to as *data repositories.*

"Each SIMS agent contains a detailed model of its domain of expertise [(an ontology)] and models of the information sources that are available to it. Given an information request, an agent selects an appropriate set of information sources, generates a plan to retrieve and process the data, uses knowledge about information sources to reformulate the plan for efficiency, and executes the plan." KQML is used as the communication language in which messages are transmitted among agents, while Loom (MacGregor 1990) is used as the content language in which queries and responses are formulated.

A learning capability helps agents improve their overall efficiency and accuracy. Three modes of learning are used: caching data that is frequently retrieved or which may be difficult to retrieve, learning about the contents of information sources so as to minimize the cost of retrieval, and analyzing the contents of information sources so as to refine its domain model.

To date, the authors have built information agents that plan and learn in the logistics planning domain. They are continuing to extend the planning and learning capabilities of these agents.

KAoS: Toward an Industrial-Strength Open Agent Architecture. It is ironic that as various sorts of agents are increasingly used to solve problems of software interoperability, we are now faced with the problem of incompatible competing agent frameworks:

> "The current lack of standards and supporting infrastructure has prevented the thing most users of agents in real-world applications most need: *agent interoperability* (Gardner 1996; Virdhagriswaran, Osisek, and O'Connor 1995). A key characteristic of agents is their ability to serve as universal mediators, tying together loosely-coupled, heterogeneous components—the last thing anyone wants is an agent architecture that can accommodate only a single native language and a limited set of proprietary services to which it alone can provide access."

The long-term objective of the KAoS (Knowledgeable Agent-oriented System) agent architecture (Bradshaw et al. 1997) is to address two major limitations of current agent technology: 1. failure to address infrastructure, scalability, and security issues; and 2. problems with the semantics and lack of principled extensibility of agent communication languages such as KQML. The first problem is addressed by taking advantage of the capabilities of commercial distributed object products (CORBA, DCOM, Java) as a foundation for agent functionality, and supporting collaborative research and standards-based efforts to resolve agent interoperability issues. The second problem is addressed by providing an open agent communication *meta*-architecture in which any number of agent communication languages with their accompanying semantics could be accommodated.

Each KAoS agent contains a *generic agent instance,* which implements as a minimum the basic infrastructure for agent communication. Specific extensions and capabilities can be added to the basic structure and protocols through ordinary object-oriented programming mechanisms. Unlike most agent communication architectures, KAoS explicitly takes into account not only the individual message, but also the various sequences of messages in which it may occur. Shared knowledge about message sequencing conventions *(conversation policies)* enables agents to coordinate frequently recurring interactions of a routine nature simply and predictably. *Suites* provide convenient groupings of conversation policies that support a set of related services (e.g., the *Matchmaker suite*). A starter set of suites is provided in the architecture but can be extended or replaced as required.

The authors experience with KAoS leads them to be "optimistic about the prospects for agent architectures built on open, extensible object frameworks and [they] look forward to the wider availability of interoperable agent implementations that will surely result from continued collaboration."

Communicative Actions for Artificial Agents. Cohen and Levesque's (1997) chapter identifies major issues in the design of languages for interagent communication, with specific application to KQML:

> "[The] authors of KQML have yet to provide a precise semantics for this language, as is customary with programming languages.[28] Without one, agent designers cannot be certain that the interpretation they are giving to a "performative" is in fact the same as the one some other designer intended it to have. Moreover, the lack of a semantics for communication acts leads to a number of confusions in the set of reserved "performatives" supplied. Lastly, designers are left unconstrained and unguided in any attempt to extend the set of communication actions."

In KQML, communicative actions are considered to belong to a specific class of speech acts called "performatives" which, in natural language, are utterances that succeed simply because speakers say or assert they are doing so (e.g., "I hereby bequeath my inheritance to my daughter"). The authors identify three general difficulties with KQML. First, the definitions of the performatives suffer from *ambiguity and vagueness.* Second, there are *misidentified performatives,* that should instead be classes as directives (e.g., requests) or assertives (e.g., informs). Third, there are missing *performatives* such as the commissives (e.g., promises).

The authors respond to these difficulties with an outline an analysis of rational action upon which their theory of speech acts rests. They then show how the speech acts of requesting and informing can be defined in terms of the primitives from this theory. The implications for future KQML design decisions are twofold. First, if developers are allowed to extend the set of KQML performatives, they must provide both correct implementations of the directive force of new actions as well as assure that the new actions enter into old and new conversation patterns correctly. Second, if the communication primitives are to be handled independently of the content of the message, developers must not allow any attitude operators in the content (e.g., not permit an agent who says that it requests an act to also say that it does not want the act done).

The authors provide a comparison with other agent communication languages including AOP, Telescript, and their own Open Agent Architecture (OAA) approach (Cohen and Cheyer 1994). Additional work in joint intention theory (Cohen 1994; Cohen and Levesque 1991; Smith and Cohen 1995) is required to clarify how communicative actions function in the initiation of team behavior, and how they may be able to predict the structure of finite-state models of interagent conversations as used in agent architectures such as KAoS.[29]

Mobile Agents. Telescript is an object-oriented remote programming language that is designed to address the problem of interoperability for network services (White 1997). What PostScript did for cross-platform, device-independent documents, Telescript aims to do for cross-platform, network-independent messaging:

> "In Telescript technology, mobile agents *go to places,* where they perform tasks on behalf of a user. Agents and places are completely programmable, but they are managed by security features such as *permits, authorities,* and *access controls.* Telescript technology is portable, allowing it to be deployed on any platform, over any transport mechanism, and through assorted media—wireline and wireless. Telescript technology can also handle different content types, including text, graphics, animations, live video, and sounds. Telescript technology turns a network into an open platform.[30] Simplified development, portability, and support for rich message content make the technology applicable to a range of communicating applications, from workflow automation to information services and from network management to electronic markets" (General Magic 1994).

Telescript technology allows developers to bundle data and procedures into an agent that will be sent over the network and executed remotely on the server.[31] The Telescript agent carries its own agenda and may travel to several places in succession in order to perform a task. Security for host systems is of paramount concern. The Telescript runtime engine can be set to prevent agents from examining or modifying the memory, file system, or other resources of the computers on which they execute. Moreover, each agent carries securely formatted and encrypted identification tickets that must be checked by the host before running code. The ticket may also carry information about what kinds of tasks the agent is permitted to perform, and the maximum resources it is allowed to expend.

White provides a motivation for mobile agent technology in terms of several example applications. A comprehensive overview of Telescript technologies and programming model and a brief discussion of related work round out the chapter.

Parting Thoughts

Readers may legitimately complain about the idiosyncratic selection of chapters for this book. Significant research topics and important bodies of work have certainly been neglected[32] although I hope that some of this may be rectified in a subsequent volume. What I have tried to provide is convenient access to an initial collection of exemplars illustrating the diversity of problems being addressed today by software agent technology. Despite the fact that the solutions described here will ultimately be replaced by better ones; regardless of whether the term "software agent" survives the next round of computing buzzword evolution, I believe that the kinds of issues raised and lessons learned from our exploration of software agent technology point the way toward the exciting developments of the next millennium.

Acknowledgments

Heartfelt thanks are due to Kathleen Bradshaw and to Ken Ford of AAAI Press, who nurtured this project from the beginning and patiently sustained it to a successful end. I am grateful to the authors of the individual chapters for allowing their contributions to appear in this volume, and for many stimulating discussions. Peter Clark, Jim Hoard, and Ian Angus provided helpful feedback on an earlier draft of this chapter. Significant support for this effort was provided by Boeing management including Cathy Kitto, Ken Neves, and Al Erisman; and by my colleagues in the agent research group: Bob Carpenter, Rob Cranfill, Renia Jeffers, Luis Poblete, Tom Robinson, and Amy Sun. The writing of this chapter was supported in part by grant R01 HS09407 from the Agency for Health Care Policy and Research to the Fred Hutchison Cancer Research Center.

Notes

1. Works by authors such as Schelde (1993), who have chronicled the development of popular notions about androids, humanoids, robots, and science fiction creatures, are a useful starting point for software agent designers wanting to plumb the cultural context of their creations. The chapter "Information beyond computers" in Lubar (1993) provides a useful grand tour of the subject. See Ford, Glymour, and Hayes (1995) for a delightful collection of essays on android epistemology.

2. This is perhaps an overstatement, since researchers with strong roots in artificial life (a-life) and robotics traditions have continued to make significant contributions to our understanding of autonomous agents (Maes 1993; Steels 1995). Although most researchers in robotics have concerned themselves with agents embodied in hardware, some have also made significant contributions in the area of software agents. See Etzioni (1993) for arguments that software presents a no-less-attractive platform than hardware for the investigation of complete agents in real-world environments. Williams and Nayak (1996) describe a software-hardware hybrid agent concept they call immobile robots (immobots).

3. For example, see the operational definition proposed by Shoham: "An agent is an entity whose state is *viewed as* consisting of mental components such as beliefs, capabilities, choices, and commitments."

4. With apologies to Oliver Goldsmith (Bartlett and Beck 1980, p. 369:9).

5. Alan Turing (Turing 1950) proposed what was perhaps the first attempt to operationalize a test for machine intelligence using the criterion of human ascription. Research on believable agents (Bates et al. 1994), lifelike computer characters (Ball 1996), and agent-based

computer games (Tackett and Benson 1985) carries on in the same tradition, aiming to produce the most realistic multimedia experience of computer-based agents possible. As discovered by organizers of the Loebner Prize Competitions (Epstein 1992) and the AAAI Robot Competitions (Hinkle, Kortenkamp, and Miller 1996; Simmons 1995), one significant challenge in objectively judging results of competitions based on pure ascription and performance measures is that unless the evaluation criteria are well-thought out, agents or robots relying on cheap programming tricks may consistently outperform those who may be demonstrating some more legitimate kind of machine intelligence.

6. Russell and Norvig (1995, p. 821) discuss the fact that while ascribing beliefs, desires, and intentions to agents (the concept of an *intentional stance*) might help us avoid the paradoxes and clashes of intuition, the fact that it is rooted in a relativistic folk psychology can create other sorts of problems. Resnick and Martin (Martin 1988; Resnick and Martin 1990) describe examples of how, in real life, people quite easily and naturally shift between the different kinds of descriptions of designed artifacts (see footnote 11). Erickson (1997), Laurel (1997), and Shneiderman (1997) offer additional perspectives on the consequences of encouraging users to think in terms of agents.

7. Milewski and Lewis (1994) review the organizational psychology and management science literature regarding delegation. They draw implications for agent design, including delegation cost-benefit tradeoffs, kinds of communication required, determinants of trust, performance controls, and differences in personality and culture.

8. "The difference between an automaton and an agent is a somewhat like the difference between a dog and a butler. If you send your dog to buy a copy of the *New York Times* every morning, it will come back with its mouth empty if the news stand happens to have run out one day. In contrast, the butler will probably take the initiative to buy you a copy of the *Washington Post,* since he knows that sometimes you read it instead" (Le Du 1994), my translation.

9. Newquist (1994) gives a similarly-flavored critique of the overhyping of "intelligence" in various products.

10. Shoham goes on to cite the following statement by John McCarthy, who distinguishes between the "legitimacy" of ascribing mental qualities to machines and its "usefulness" "To ascribe certain *beliefs, free will, intentions, consciousness, abilities* or *wants* to a machine or computer program is *legitimate* when such an ascription expresses the same information about the machine that it expresses about a person. It is *useful* when the ascription helps us understand the structure of the machine, its past or future behavior, or how to repair or improve it. It is perhaps never *logically required* even for humans, but expressing reasonably briefly what is actually known about the state of the machine in a particular situation may require mental qualities or qualities isomorphic to them. Theories of belief, knowledge and wanting can be constructed for machines in a simpler setting than for humans, and later applied to humans. Ascription of mental qualities is *most straightforward* for machines of known structure such as thermostats and computer operating systems, but is *most useful* when applied to entities whose structure is very incompletely known" (McCarthy 1979).

11. Of course, in real life, people quite easily and naturally shift between the different kinds of descriptions. For example, Resnick and Martin report the following about their research with children building LEGO robots: "As students play with artificial creatures, we are particularly interested in how the students think about the creatures. Do they think of the LEGO creatures as machines, or as animals? In fact, we have found that students (and adults) regard the creatures in many different ways. Sometimes students view their creatures on a *mechanistic* level, examining how one LEGO piece makes another

move. At other times, they might shift to the *information* level, exploring how information flows from one electronic brick to another. At still other times, students view the creatures on a *psychological* level, attributing intentionality or personality to the creatures. One creature 'wants' to get to the light. Another creature 'likes' the dark. A third is 'scared' of loud noises.

Sometimes, students will shift rapidly between levels of description. Consider, for example, the comments of Sara, a fifth-grader (Martin 1988). Sara was considering whether her creature would sound a signal when its touch sensor was pushed:

'It depends on whether the machine wants to tell... if we want the machine to tell us... if we tell the machine to tell us.'

Within a span of ten seconds, Sara described the situation in three different ways. First she viewed the machine on a psychological level, focusing on what the machine 'wants.' Then she shifted intentionality to the programmer, and viewed the programmer on a psychological level. Finally, she shifted to a mechanistic explanation, in which the programmer explicitly told the machine what to do.

Which is the correct level? That is a natural, but misleading question. Complex systems can be meaningfully described at many different levels. Which level is 'best' depends on the context: on what you already understand and on what you hope to learn. In certain situations, for certain questions, the mechanistic level is the best. In other situations, for other questions, the psychological level is best. By playing with artificial creatures, students can learn to shift between levels, learning which levels are best for which situations." (Resnick and Martin 1990).

12. Ideally, this would include some notion of episodic memory. Unfortunately, only two major examples of "agents" incorporating episodic memory in the literature easily come to mind: Winograd's (1973) SHRDLU and Vere and Bickmore's (1990) "basic agent." For a thought-provoking look into the consequences of a future where a personal "agent" might become the ultimate cradle-to-grave companion, experiencing and remembering every event of a lifetime, see "The Teddy" chapter in Norman (1992).

13. In his widely cited article "Eye on the Prize" (Nilsson 1995), Nilsson discusses the shift of emphasis in AI from inventing general problem-solving techniques to what he calls *performance programs,* and gives his reasons for believing that there will soon be a reinvigoration of efforts to build programs of "general, humanlike competence."

14. While macro and scripting languages are technically adequate to solve this problem, it seems unlikely that the majority of "end users" will ever want to endure what it takes to become proficient with them: "In the past two decades there have been numerous attempts to develop a language for end users: Basic, Logo, Smalltalk, Pascal, Playground, Hyper-Talk, Boxer, etc. All have made progress in expanding the number of people who can program. Yet as a percentage of computer users, this number is still abysmally small. Consider children trying to learn programming... We hypothesize that fewer than 10% of there children who are taught programming continue to program after the class ends... Eliot Soloway states, 'My guess is that the number... is less than 1%! Who in their right mind would use those languages—any of them—after a class?'" (Smith, Cypher, and Spohrer 1997). While the software agent perspective does not obviate the need for end-user programming, I believe it has potential as one means of simplifying some of the conceptual barriers that users and developers face in designing and understanding complex systems.

15. Fortunately, people have a lot of experience in judging the limitations of those with whom they communicate: "Sometimes people overstate what the computer can do, but what people are extremely good at is figuring out what they can get away with. Children can size up a substitute teacher in about five minutes" (Kahle 1993). For evidence that

developers of intelligent software are no less prone than other people to overestimate the capabilities of their programs, see McDermott (1976).

16. *Automatic programming* is an enterprise with a long history of insatiable requirements and moving expectations. For example, Rich and Waters (1988) remind us that "compared to programming in machine code, assemblers represented a spectacular level of automation. Moreover, FORTRAN was arguably a greater step forward than anything that has happened since. In particular, it dramatically increased the number of scientific end users who could operate computers without having to hire a programmer." Today, no one would call FORTRAN a form of automatic programming, though in 1958 the term was quite appropriate. The intractability of fully-automated, completely-general programming is analogous to the problem of automated knowledge acquisition (Bradshaw et al. 1993a; Ford et al. 1993). As Sowa observes: "Fully automated knowledge acquisition is as difficult as unrestricted natural language understanding. The two problems, in fact, are different aspects of exactly the same problem: the task of building a formal model for some real world system on the basis of informal descriptions in ordinary language. Alan Perlis once made a remark that characterizes that difficulty: *You can't translate informal specifications into formal specifications by any formal algorithm.*" (Sowa 1989).

17. Van de Velde (1995) provides a useful discussion of the three coupling mechanisms which can enable coordination between multiple agents: knowledge-level, symbol-level, and structural. Symbol-level coupling occurs when agents coordinate by exchange of symbol structures (e.g., "messages") and knowledge-level coupling occurs when an agent "rationalizes the behavior of multiple agents by ascribing goals and knowledge to them that, assuming their rational behavior, explains their behavior" (i.e., through taking an intentional stance). Structural coupling, as discussed extensively by Maturana and Varela (1992), occurs when two agents "coordinate without exchange of representation,... by being mutually adapted to the influences that they experience through their common environment... For example, a sidewalk... plays a coordinating role in the behavior of pedestrians and drivers... [and] the coordination of [soccer] players (within and across teams) is mediated primarily by... the ball." Similarly, as Clancey (1993) argues, the usefulness of the blackboard metaphor is that it provides an external representation that regulates the coordination between multiple agents.

18. These latter issues are discussed in more detail in a Laurel's (1991) book *Computers as Theatre*.

19. It is also easy for people to assume less tangible qualities about agents like that they are internally consistent, are rational, act in good faith, can introspect, can cooperate to achieve common goals, and have a persistent mental state.

20. A more blunt criticism of agents is voiced by Jaron Lanier (1996), who writes, "The idea of 'intelligent agents' is both wrong and evil. I also believe that this is an issues of real consequence to the near-term future of culture and society. As the infobahn rears its gargantuan head, the agent question looms as a deciding factor in whether this new beast will be much better than TV, or much worse." See also his extended online debate with Pattie Maes in Lanier and Maes (1996).

21. Several commercial products have subsequently incorporated Oval-like capability, though with less generality and sophistication. These include cooperative work tools and databases for semi-structured information such as Lotus Notes (Greif 1994) and Caere Pagekeeper, as well as mail readers with rule-based message sorting. Workflow management tools with some of these capabilities have also appeared.

22. For other approaches to defining agents for scheduling and calendar management tasks, see Kautz et al. (1993); Mitchell et al. (1994).

23. Maes has formed Firefly Network, Inc. in order to extend the technology developed in Ringo to the Web. Her *firefly* service uses knowledge about people with similar tastes and interests in music and movies as a means of personalizing its recommendations.

24. A sort of Java for kids.

25. For a similar approach that relies on graphical rewrite rules, see Repenning's (1995) Agentsheets.

26. This is of course a caricature of both approaches: Shoham does not ignore the importance of agent communication in AOP; neither would most agent communication researchers argue that some representation of "mental state" is unnecessary. Davies' (1994) Agent-K language is an attempt to build a hybrid that extends AGENT-0 to use KQML for communication.

27. One well-known tool that has been used to construct such vocabularies is *Ontolingua* (Gruber 1992a, 1992b).

28. Recent efforts to provide a semantic foundation for KQML are described in Labrou (1996) and Labrou and Finin (1994). Another more general approach to agent language semantics is currently under development by Smith and Cohen (1995).

29. Such a strategy parallels the approach of Rosenschein, who designed a compiler that generates finite state machines whose internal states can be proved to correspond to certain logical propositions about the environment (Kaelbling and Rosenschein 1990; Rosenschein 1995).

30. General Magic is working hard to assure that Telescript can take maximum advantage of developments in Internet technology. Its Tabriz AgentWare and Agent Tools products (General Magic 1996) integrate Telescript and Web technologies, and White has proposed a common agent platform intended to enable interoperability between Telescript and other mobile agent technology (White 1996).

31. With respect to the relationship between Telescript, Tabriz, and Java, General Magic writes: "It is important to note that Telescript and Java are complementary, interoperable languages. Telescript agents can set parameters for Java applets and Java applets can call Telescript operations on the server. This interoperability allows developers to create solutions that leverage the power of the two environments: Java can be used to create and manage compelling user experiences, while Tabriz can manage transactions, instructions, events, and processes" (General Magic 1996).

32. Much more, for example, could have been included about the veritable explosion of work on agents and the Internet (Bowman et al. 1994; Cheong 1996; Etzioni and Weld 1995; Weld, Marks, and Bobrow 1995). None of the many applications of agent technology in complex application areas ranging from digital libraries (Paepcke et al. 1996; Wiederhold 1995) to systems management (Benech, Desprats, and Moreau 1996; Rivière, Pell, and Sibilla 1996) to manufacturing (Balasubramanian and Norrie 1995) could be included. We have slighted the whole fields of artificial life (Langton 1995) situated automata (Brooks 1990; Kaelbling and Rosenschein 1991), learning and adaptation (Gaines 1996; Maes 1995; Sen et al. 1996), and large portions of the voluminous literature on DAI and other fields where important related work is taking place.

References

Apple. Computer 1993. *AppleScript Language Guide*. Reading, Mass.: Addison-Wesley.

Arens, Y.; Feiner, S.; Foley, J.; Hovy, E.; John, B.; Neches, R.; Pausch, R.; Schorr, H.; and Swartout, W. 1991. Intelligent User Interfaces, Report ISI/RR-91-288, USC/Information Sciences Institute, Marina del Rey, California.

Balasubramanian, S., and Norrie, D. H. 1995. A Multi-Agent Intelligent Design System Integrating Manufacturing and Shop-Floor Control. In *Proceedings of the First International Conference on Multi-Agent Systems (ICMAS-95),* ed. V. Lesser, 3–9. Menlo Park, Calif.: AAAI Press.

Ball, G. 1996. Lifelike Computer Characters (LCC-96) Schedule and Workshop Information. http://www.research.microsoft.com/lcc.htm.

Ball, G.; Ling, D.; Kurlander, D.; Miller, J.; Pugh, D.; Skelly, T.; Stankosky, A.; Thiel, D.; Dantzich, M. V; and Wax, T. 1996. Lifelike Computer Characters: The Persona Project at Microsoft Research. In *Software Agents,* ed J. M. Bradshaw. Menlo Park, Calif.: AAAI Press.

Barrett, E. 1992. Sociomedia: An Introduction. In *Sociomedia: Multimedia, Hypermedia, and the Social Construction of Knowledge,* ed. E. Barrett, 1–10. Cambridge, Mass.: MIT Press.

Bartlett, J., and Beck, E. M., eds. 1980. *Familiar Quotations.* Boston, Mass.: Little, Brown.

Bates, J. 1994. The Role of Emotion in Believable Agents. *Communications of the ACM* 37(7): 122–125.

Bates, J., Hayes-Roth, B., Laurel, B., & Nilsson, N. 1994. Papers presented at the AAAI Spring Symposium on Believable Agents, Stanford University, Stanford, Calif.

Benech, D.; Desprats, T.; and Moreau, J.-J. 1996. A Conceptual Approach to the Integration of Agent Technology in System Management. In *Distributed Systems: Operations and Management (DSOM-96).*

Bowman, C. M.; Danzig, P. B.; Manber, U.; and Schwartz, M. F. 1994. Scalable Internet Resource Discovery: Research Problems and Approaches. *Communications of the ACM* 37(8): 98–107, 114.

Boy, G. 1992. Computer-Integrated Documentation. In *Sociomedia: Multimedia, Hypermedia, and the Social Construction of Knowledge,* ed. E. Barrett, 507–531. Cambridge, Mass.: MIT Press.

Boy, G. A. 1991. *Intelligent Assistant Systems.* San Diego, Calif.: Academic Press.

Boy, G. A. 1997. Software Agents for Cooperative Learning. In *Software Agents,* ed J. M. Bradshaw. Menlo Park, Calif.: AAAI Press.

Boy, G. A., and Mathé, N. 1993. Operator Assistant Systems: An Experimental Approach Using a Telerobotics Application. In *Knowledge Acquisition as Modeling,* eds. K. M. Ford and J. M. Bradshaw, 271–286. New York: Wiley.

Bradshaw, J. M., and Boose, J. H 1992. Mediating Representations for Knowledge Acquisition, Boeing Computer Services, Seattle, Washington.

Bradshaw, J. M., and Boy, G. A. 1993. Adaptive Documents, Internal Technical Report, EURISCO.

Bradshaw, J. M., Dutfield, S., Benoit, P., & Woolley, J. D. 1997. KAoS: Toward an industrial-strength generic agent architecture. In *Software Agents,* ed J. M. Bradshaw. Menlo Park, Calif.: AAAI Press.

Bradshaw, J. M.; Ford, K. M.; Adams-Webber, J. R.; and Boose, J. H. 1993. Beyond the Repertory Grid: New Approaches to Constructivist Knowledge-Acquisition Tool Development. In *Knowledge Acquisition as Modeling,* eds. K. M. Ford and J. M. Bradshaw, 287–333. New York: Wiley.

Bradshaw, J. M.; Richards, T.; Fairweather, P.; Buchanan, C.; Guay, R.; Madigan, D.; and Boy, G. A. 1993. New Directions for Computer-Based Training and Performance Support in Aerospace. Paper presented at the Fourth International Conference on Human-Machine Interaction and Artificial Intelligence in Aerospace, 28–30 September, Toulouse, France.

Brodie, M. L. 1989. Future Intelligent Information Systems: AI and Database Technologies Working Together. In *Readings in Artificial Intelligence and Databases,* eds. J. Mylopoulos and M. L. Brodie, 623–642. San Francisco, Calif.: Morgan Kaufmann.

Brooks, R. A. 1990. Elephants Don't Play Chess. *Robotics and Autonomous Systems* 6.

Brown, J. S., and Duguid, P. 1996. The Social Life of Documents. *First Monday* (http://www.firstmonday.dk).

Browne, D.; Totterdell, P.; and Norman, M., eds. 1990. *Adaptive User Interfaces.* San Diego, Calif.: Academic.

Canto, C., and Faliu, O. (n.d.). *The History of the Future: Images of the 21st Century.* Paris: Flammarion.

Chang, D. T., and Lange, D. B. 1996. Mobile Agents: A New Paradigm for Distributed Object Computing on the WWW. In Proceedings of the OOPSLA 96 Workshop "Toward the Integration of WWW and Distributed Object Technology."

Cheong, F.-C. 1996. *Internet Agents: Spiders, Wanderers, Brokers, and Bots.* Indianapolis, Ind.: New Riders.

Clancey, W. J. 1993. The Knowledge Level Reinterpreted: Modeling Socio-Technical Systems. In *Knowledge Acquisition as Modeling,* eds. K. M. Ford and J. M. Bradshaw, 33–50. New York: Wiley.

Cohen, P. R. 1994. Models of Dialogue. In Cognitive Processing for Vision and Voice: Proceedings of the Fourth NEC Research Symposium, ed. T. Ishiguro, 181–203. Philadelphia, Pa.: Society for Industrial and Applied Mathematics.

Cohen, P. R., and Cheyer, A. 1994. An Open Agent Architecture. Paper presented at the AAAI Spring Symposium on Software Agents, 21–23 March, Stanford, California.

Cohen, P. R.; and Levesque, H. 1997. Communicative Actions for Artificial Agents. In *Software Agents,* ed J. M. Bradshaw. Menlo Park, Calif.: AAAI Press.

Cohen, P. R., and Levesque, H. J. 1991. Teamwork, Technote 504, SRI International, Menlo Park, California.

Coutaz, J. 1990. *Interfaces Homme Ordinateur: Conception et Réalisation.* Paris: Editions Bordas.

Davies, W. H. E. 1994. AGENT-K: An Integration of AOP and KQML. In Proceedings of the CIKM-94 Workshop on Intelligent Agents, eds. T. Finin and Y. Labrou. http://www.csd.abdn.ac.uk/~pedwards/publs/agentk.html.

Dennett, D. C. 1987. *The Intentional Stance.* Cambridge, Mass.: MIT Press.

diSessa, A. A. 1986. Notes on the Future of Programming: Breaking the Utility Barrier. In *User-Centered System Design,* eds. D. A. Norman and S. W. Draper. Hillsdale, N.J.: Lawrence Erlbaum.

Epstein, R. 1992. The Quest for the Thinking Computer. *AI Magazine* 13(2): 81–95.

Erickson, T. 1996. Designing Agents as If People Mattered. In *Software Agents,* ed J. M. Bradshaw. Menlo Park, Calif.: AAAI Press.

Etzioni, O. 1993. Intelligence without robotics. *AI Magazine*(Winter), 7-14.

Etzioni, O., & Weld, D. S. 1995. Intelligent agents on the Internet: Fact, fiction, and forecast. *IEEE Expert*, 10(4), 44-49.

Finin, T., Labrou, Y., & Mayfield, J. 1997. KQML as an agent communication language. In *Software Agents,* ed. J. M. Bradshaw. Menlo Park, Calif.: AAAI Press.

Etzioni, O. 1993. Intelligence without Robots: A Reply to Brooks. *AI Magazine* 14(4): 7–13.

Etzioni, O., and Weld, D. S. 1995. Intelligent Agents on the Internet: Fact, Fiction, and Forecast. *IEEE Expert* 10(4): 44–49.

Foner, L. 1993. *What's an Agent, Anyway? A Sociological Case Study*, Agents Memo, 93-01, Media Lab, Massachusetts Institute of Technology.

Ford, K. M.; Glymour, C.; and Hayes, P. J., eds. 1995. *Android Epistemology.* Menlo Park, Calif.: AAAI Press.

Ford, K. M.; Bradshaw, J. M.; Adams-Webber, J. R.; and Agnew, N. M. 1993. Knowledge Acquisition as a Constructive Modeling Activity. In *Knowledge Acquisition as Modeling,* eds. K. M. Ford and J. M. Bradshaw, 9–32. New York: Wiley.

Franklin, S., and Graesser, A. 1996. Is It an Agent or Just a Program? A Taxonomy for Autonomous Agents. In *Proceedings of the Third International Workshop on Agent Theories, Architectures, and Languages.* New York: Springer-Verlag.

Gaines, B. R. 1997. *The Emergence of Knowledge through Modeling and Management Processes in Societies of Adaptive Agents,* Knowledge Science Institute, University of Calgary. Forthcoming.

Gardner, E. 1996. Standards Hold Key to Unleashing Agents. *Web Week* 5, 29 April.

General Magic. 1996. Tabriz White Paper: Transforming Passive Networks into an Active, Persistent, and Secure Business Advantage, White Paper (http://www.genmagic.com/Tabriz/Whitepapers/tabrizwp.html), General Magic, Mountain View, California.

General Magic. 1994. Telescript Technologies at Heart of Next-Generation Electronic Services, News Release, 6 January, General Magic, Mountain View, California.

Genesereth, M. R. 1997. An Agent-based Framework for Interoperability. In *Software Agents,* ed. J. M. Bradshaw. Menlo Park, Calif.: AAAI Press.

Genesereth, M. R., and Fikes, R. 1992. Knowledge Interchange Format Version 3.0 Reference Manual, Logic Group Report, Logic-92-1, Department of Computer Science, Stanford University.

Genesereth, M. R., and Ketchpel, S. P. 1994. Software Agents. *Communications of the ACM* 37(7): 48–53, 147.

Gilbert, D.; Aparicio, M.; Atkinson, B.; Brady, S.; Ciccarino, J., Grosof, B., O'Connor, P.; Osisek, D.; Pritko, S., Spagna, R., and Wilson, L. 1995. IBM Intelligent Agent Strategy, IBM Corporation.

Glicksman, J.; Weber, J. C.; and Gruber, T. R. 1992. The NOTE MAIL Project for Computer-Supported Cooperative Mechanical Design. Paper presented at the AAAI-92 Workshop on Design Rationale Capture and Use, San Jose, California, July.

Greif, I. 1994. Desktop Agents in Group-Enabled Products. *Communications of the ACM* 37(7): 100–105.

Gruber, T. R. 1992a. ONTOLINGUA: *A Mechanism to Support Portable Ontologies, Version 3.0*, Technical Report, KSL 91-66, Knowledge Systems Laboratory, Department of Computer Science, Stanford University.

Gruber, T. R. 1992b. A Translation Approach to Portable Ontology Specifications. Paper presented at the Seventh Knowledge Acquisition for Knowledge-Based Systems Workshop, Banff, Alberta, Canada.

Gruber, T. R.; Tenenbaum, J. M.; and Weber, J. C. 1992. Toward a Knowledge Medium for Collaborative Product Development. In Proceedings of the Second International Conference on Artificial Intelligence in Design, ed. J. S. Gero.

Harrison, C. G.; Chess, D. M.; and Kershenbaum, A. 1995. Mobile Agents: Are They a Good Idea? IBM T. J. Watson Research Center.

Hayes-Roth, B.; Brownston, L.; and Gent, R. V. 1995. Multiagent Collaboration in Directed Improvisation. In *Proceedings of the First International Conference on Multi-Agent Systems (ICMAS-95),* ed. V. Lesser, 148–154. Menlo Park, Calif.: AAAI Press.

Hinkle, D.; Kortenkamp, D.; and Miller, D. 1996. The 1995 Robot Competition and Exhibition. *AI Magazine* 17(1): 31–45.

Hutchins, E. L.; Hollan, J. D.; and Norman, D. A. 1986. Direct Manipulation Interfaces. In *User-Centered System Design,* eds. D. A. Norman and S. W. Draper, 87–124. Hillsdale, N.J.: Lawrence Erlbaum.

Johnson, P.; Feiner, S.; Marks, J.; Maybury, M.; and Moore, J., eds. 1994. Paper presented at the AAAI Spring Symposium on Intelligent Multi-Media Multi-Modal Systems, Stanford, California.

Kaehler, T., and Patterson, D. 1986. A Small Taste of SMALLTALK. *BYTE,* August, 145–159.

Kaelbling, L. P., and Rosenschein, S. J. 1991. Action and Planning in Embedded Agents. In *Designing Autonomous Agents,* eds. P. Maes , 35–48. Cambridge, Mass.: MIT Press.

Kaelbling, L. P., and Rosenschein, S. J. 1990. Action and Planning in Embedded Agents. *Robotics and Autonomous Systems* 6(1–2): 35–48.

Kahle, B. 1993. Interview of Brewster Kahle. *Intertek* 4:15–17.

Kautz, H.; Selman, B.; Coen, M.; Ketchpel, S.; and Ramming, C. 1994. An Experiment in the Design of Software Agents. In Proceedings of the Twelfth National Conference on Artificial Intelligence (AAAI-94), 438–443. Menlo Park, Calif.: American Association for Artificial Intelligence.

Kay, A. 1990. User Interface: A Personal View. In *The Art of Human-Computer Interface Design,* ed. B. Laurel, 191–208. Reading, Mass.: Addison-Wesley.

Kay, A. 1984. Computer Software. *Scientific American* 251(3): 53–59.

Knoblock, C. A., & Ambite, J.-L. 1996. Agents for Information Gathering. In *Software Agents,* ed. J. M. Bradshaw. Menlo Park, Calif.: AAAI Press.

Labrou, Y. 1996. Semantics for an Agent Communication Language. Ph.D. diss., Dept of Computer Science, University of Maryland at Baltimore County.

Labrou, Y., and Finin, T. 1994. A Semantics Approach for KQML—A General-Purpose Communication Language for Software Agents. In Proceedings of the Third International Conference on Information and Knowledge Management, eds. N. R. Adam, B. K. Bhargava, and Y. Yesha, 447–455. New York: Association of Computing Machinery.

Lai, K.-Y., and Malone, T. W. 1992. Oval Version 1.1 User's Guide, Center for Coordination Science, Massachusetts Institute of Technology.

Lange, D. B. 1996. Agent Transfer Protocol ATP/0.1 Draft 4, Tokyo Research Laboratory, IBM Research.

Langton, C. G., ed. 1995. *Artificial Life: An Overview.* Cambridge, Mass.: MIT Press.

Lanier, J. 1996. Agents of Alienation. http://www.voyagerco.com/misc/jaron.html.

Lanier, J., and Maes, P. 1996. Intelligent Humans = Stupid Humans? *Hot Wired,* 15–24 July. http://www.hotwired.com/braintennis/96/29/index0a.html.

Laurel, B. 1991. *Computers as Theatre*. Reading, Mass.: Addison-Wesley.

Laurel, B. 1997. Interface agents: Metaphors with Character. In *Software Agents,* ed J. M. Bradshaw. Menlo Park, Calif.: AAAI Press.

Le Du, B. 1994. Issue 1309, 13 mai. Les Agents, des Assistants dotés d'Intelligence. 01 Informatique, p. 13.

Lethbridge, T. C., and Skuce, D. 1992. Beyond Hypertext: Knowledge Management for Technical Documentation. Submitted to SIGDOC '92. Ottawa, Ontario, Canada.

Lewis, J. 1996. NETSCAPE Gets Serious about Infrastructure. The Burton Group.

Lubar, S. 1993. *InfoCulture: The Smithsonian Book of Information and Inventions.* Boston, Mass.: Houghton Mifflin.

McCarthy, J. M. 1979. Ascribing Mental Qualities to Machines, Technical Report, Memo 326, AI Lab, Stanford University.

McDermott, D. 1976. Artificial Intelligence Meets Natural Stupidity. *SIGART Newsletter* 57:4–9.

MacGregor, R. 1990. The Evolving Technology of Classification-Based Knowledge Representation Systems. In *Principles of Semantic Networks: Explorations in the Representation of Knowledge,* ed. J. F. Sowa, 385–400. San Francisco, Calif.: Morgan Kaufmann.

Maes, P. 1997. Agents that Reduce Work and Information Overload. In *Software Agents,* ed. J. M. Bradshaw. Menlo Park, Calif.: AAAI Press.

Maes, P. 1995. Modeling Adaptive Autonomous Agents. In *Artificial Life: An Overview,* ed. C. G. Langton, 135–162. Cambridge, Mass.: MIT Press.

Maes, P., ed. 1993. *Designing Autonomous Agents.* Cambridge, Mass.: MIT Press.

Maes, P., and Kozierok, R. 1993. Learning Interface Agents. In Proceedings of the Eleventh National Conference on Artificial Intelligence (AAAI-93), 459–465. Menlo Park, Calif.: American Association for Artificial Intelligence.

Malone, T. W.; Grant, K. R.; and Lai, K.-Y. 1996. Agents for Information Sharing and Coordination: A History and Some Reflections. In *Software Agents,* ed. J. M. Bradshaw. Menlo Park, Calif.: AAAI Press.

Martin, F. 1988. *Children, Cybernetics, and Programmable Turtles*. Masters Thesis, Media Laboratory, Massachusetts Institute of Technology.

Mathé, N., and Chen, J. 1994. A User-Centered Approach to Adaptive Hypertext Based on an Information Relevance Model. Paper presented at the Fourth International Conference on User Modeling (UM '94), Hyannis, Massachusetts.

Maturana, H. R., and Varela, F. J. 1992. *The Tree of Knowledge: The Biological Roots of Human Understanding* (rev. ed.). Boston: Shambala.

Mellor, P. 1994. CAD: Computer-Aided Disaster, *SOFSEM 94.*

Milewski, A. E., and Lewis, S. M. 1994. Design of Intelligent Agent User Interfaces: Delegation Issues. Technical Report, Oct. 20. AT&T Information Technologies Services.

Miller, J. R., and Neches, R. 1987. Tutorial on Intelligent Interfaces Presented at the Sixth National Conference on Artificial Intelligence, 14–16 July, Seattle, Washington.

Minsky, M. 1986. *The Society of Mind*. New York: Simon & Schuster.

Minsky, M., and Riecken, D. 1994. A Conversation with Marvin Minsky about Agents. *Communications of the ACM* 37(7): 23–29.

Mitchell, T.; Caruana, R.; Freitag, D.; McDermott, J.; and Zabowski, D. 1994. Experience with a Learning Personal Assistant. *Communications of the ACM* 37(7): 81–91.

Moulin, B., and Chaib-draa, B. 1996. An Overview of Distributed Artificial Intelligence. In *Foundations of Distributed Artificial Intelligence*, eds. G. M. P. O'Hare and N. R. Jennings, 3–55. New York: Wiley.

Neal, J. G., and Shapiro, S. C. 1994. Knowledge-Based Multimedia Systems. In *Multimedia System*, ed. J. F. K. Buford, 403–438. Reading, Mass.: Addison-Wesley.

Neches, R.; Fikes, R.; Finin, T.; Gruber, T.; Patil, R.; Senator, T.; and Swartout, W. R. 1991. Enabling Technology for Knowledge Sharing. *AI Magazine* 12(3): 36–55.

Negroponte, N. 1997. Agents: From Direct Manipulation to Delegation. In *Software Agents*, ed. J. M. Bradshaw. Menlo Park, Calif.: AAAI Press.

Negroponte, N. 1995. *Being Digital*. New York: Alfred Knopf.

Negroponte, N. 1970. *The Architecture Machine: Towards a More Human Environment*. Cambridge, Mass.: MIT Press.

Newell, A. 1982. The Knowledge Level. *Artificial Intelligence* 18:87–127.

Newquist, H. P. 1994. Intelligence on Demand—Suckers. *AI Expert*, December, 42–43.

Nilsson, N. J. 1995. Eye on the Prize. *AI Magazine* 16(2): 9–17.

Norman, D. A. 1997. How Might People Interact with Agents? In *Software Agents*, ed J. M. Bradshaw. Menlo Park, Calif.: AAAI Press.

Norman, D. A. 1992. *Turn Signals Are the Facial Expressions of Automobiles*. Reading, Mass.: Addison-Wesley.

Nwana, H. S. 1996. Software Agents: An Overview. *Knowledge Engineering Review*, 11(3): 205-244.

Paepcke, A.; Cousins, S. B.; Garcia-Molina, H.; Hassan, S. W.; Ketchpel, S. P.; Röscheisen, M.; and Winograd, T. 1996. Using Distributed Objects for Digital Library Interoperability. *IEEE Computer*, May, 61–68.

Perrow, C. 1984. *Normal Accidents: Living with High-Risk Technologies*. New York: Basic.

Petrie, C. J. 1996. Agent-Based Engineering, the Web, and Intelligence. *IEEE Expert*, 11(6): 24-29.

Repenning, A. 1995. Bending the Rules: Steps toward Semantically Enriched Graphical Rewrite Rules. Paper presented at Visual Languages, Darmstadt, Germany.

Resnick, M., and Martin, F. 1990. Children and Artificial Life, E&L Memo, 10, Media Laboratory, Massachusetts Institute of Technology.

Rich, C., and Waters, R. C. 1988. Automatic Programming: Myths and Prospects. *IEEE Computer* 21(8): 40–51.

Riecken, D. 1997. The M System. In *Software Agents*, ed. J. M. Bradshaw. Menlo Park, Calif.: AAAI Press.

Rivière, A.-I.; Pell, A.; and Sibilla, M. 1996. Network Management Information: Integration Solution for Models Interoperability, Technical Report, Hewlett-Packard Laboratories.

Rosenschein, S. J. 1985. Formal Theories of Knowledge in AI and Robotics. *New Generation Computing* 3(4): 345–357.

Russell, S., and Norvig, P. 1995. *Artificial Intelligence: A Modern Approach*. New York: Prentice-Hall.

Ryan, B. 1991. DYNABOOK Revisited with Alan Kay. *BYTE*, February, 203–208.

Schank, R. C., and Jona, H. Y. 1991. Empowering the Student: New Perspectives on the Design of Teaching Systems. *The Journal of the Learning Sciences* 1(1).

Schelde, P. 1993. *Androids, Humanoids, and Other Science Fiction Monsters*. New York: New York University Press.

Sen, S.; Hogg, T.; Rosenschein, J.; Grefenstette, J.; Huhns, M.; and Subramanian, D., eds. 1996. Adaptation, Coevolution, and Learning in Multiagent Systems: Papers from the 1996 AAAI Symposium. Technical Report SS-96-01. Menlo Park, Calif.: AAAI Press.

Sharp, M. 1993. Reactive Agents, Technical Report, Apple Computer, Cupertino, Calif.

Sharp, M. 1992. Principles for Situated Actions in Designing Virtual Realities. Master's thesis, Department of Computer Science, University of Calgary.

Shaw, M. 1996. Some Patterns for Software Architectures. In *Pattern Languages of Program Design,* eds. J. O. Coplien and D. C. Schmidt, 453–462. Reading, Mass.: Addison-Wesley.

Shneiderman, B. 1997. Direct manipulation vs. agents: Paths to predictable, controllable, and comprehensible interfaces. In *Software Agents,* ed J. M. Bradshaw. Menlo Park, Calif.: AAAI Press.

Shneiderman, B. 1987. *Designing the User Interface: Strategies for Effective Human-Computer Interaction*. Reading, Mass.: Addison-Wesley.

Shneiderman, B. 1983. Direct Manipulation: A Step beyond Programming Languages. *IEEE Computer* 16(8): 57–69.

Shoham, Y. 1997. An Overview of Agent-oriented Programming. In *Software Agents,* ed J. M. Bradshaw. Menlo Park, Calif.: AAAI Press.

Shoham, Y. 1993. Agent-Oriented Programming. *Artificial Intelligence* 60(1): 51–92.

Simmons, R. 1995. The 1994 AAAI Robot Competition and Exhibition. *AI Magazine* 16(2): 19–30.

Singh, M. P. 1994. *Multiagent Systems: A Theoretical Framework for Intentions, Know-How, and Communication*. Berlin: Springer-Verlag.

Smith, D. C., Cypher, A., & Spohrer, J. 1997. KidSim: Programming Agents Without a Programming Language. In *Software Agents,* ed. J. M. Bradshaw. Menlo Park, Calif.: AAAI Press.

Smith, D. C.; Irby, C.; Kimball, R.; Verplank, W.; and Harslem, E. 1982. Designing the STAR User Interface. *BYTE* 4:242–282.

Smith, I. A., and Cohen, P. R. 1995. Toward a Semantics for a Speech Act–Based Agent Communications Language. In Proceedings of the CIKM Workshop on Intelligent Information Agents, eds. T. Finin and J. Mayfield. New York: Association of Computing Machinery.

Sowa, J. F. 1990. Crystallizing Theories out of Knowledge Soup. In *Intelligent Systems: State of the Art and Future Systems,* eds. Z. W. Ras and M. Zemankova. London: Ellis Horwood.

Sowa, J. F. 1989. Knowledge Acquisition by Teachable Systems. In *EPIA 89, Lecture Notes in Artificial Intelligence,* eds. J. P. Martins and E. M. Morgado, 381–396. Berlin: Springer-Verlag.

Steels, L. 1995. The Artificial Life Roots of Artificial Intelligence. In *Artificial Life: An Overview*, ed. C. G. Langton, 75–110. Cambridge, Mass.: MIT Press.

Sullivan, J. W., and Tyler, S. W., eds. 1991. *Intelligent User Interfaces*. New York: Association of Computing Machinery.

Tackett, W. A., and Benson, S. 1985. Real AI for Real Games: In *Technical Tutorial and Design Practice,* 467–486.

Tesler, L. G. 1991. Networked Computers in the 1990s. *Scientific American*, September, 86–93.

Turing, A. M. 1950. Computing Machinery and Intelligence. *Mind* 59(236): 433–460.

Van de Velde, W. 1995. Cognitive Architectures—From Knowledge Level to Structural Coupling. In *The Biology and Technology of Intelligent Autonomous Agents,* ed. L. Steels, 197–221. Berlin: Springer Verlag.

Vere, S., and Bickmore, T. 1990. A Basic Agent. *Computational Intelligence* 6:41–60.

Virdhagriswaran, S.; Osisek, D.; and O'Connor, P. 1995. Standardizing Agent Technology. *ACM Standards View*. In press.

Weld, D.; Marks, J.; and Bobrow, D. G. 1995. The Role of Intelligent Systems in the National Information Infrastructure. *AI Magazine* 16(3): 45–64.

White, J. 1997. A Common Agent Platform, http://www.genmagic.com/Internet/Cap/w3c-paper.htm, General Magic, Inc., Sunnyvale, California.

White, J. 1997. Mobile Agents. In *Software Agents,* ed. J. M. Bradshaw. Menlo Park, Calif.: AAAI Press.

Whittaker, S. 1990. Next-Generation Interfaces. Paper presented at the AAAI Spring Symposium on Knowledge-Based Human-Computer Interaction, Stanford, California, March.

Wiederhold, G. 1995. Digital Libraries, Value, and Productivity, Stanford University.

Wiederhold, G. 1992. Mediators in the Architecture of Future Information Systems. *IEEE Computer,* March, 38–49.

Wiederhold, G. 1989. The Architecture of Future Information Systems, Technical Report, Computer Science Department, Stanford University.

Williams, B. C., and Nayak, P. P. 1996. Immobile Robots: AI in the New Millennium. *AI Magazine* 17(3): 17–35.

Winograd, T. 1973. A Procedural Model of Language Understanding. In *Computer Models of Thought and Language,* eds. R. Schank and K. Colby, 249–266. New York: Freeman.

Wooldridge, M. J. and Jennings, N. R. 1995. Agent Theories, Architectures, and Languages: A Survey. In *Intelligent Agents: ECAI-94 Workshop on Agent Theories, Architectures, and Languages,* eds. M. J. Wooldridge and N. R. Jennings, 1–39. Berlin: Springer-Verlag.

Agents & the User Experience

Chapter 2

How Might People Interact with Agents

Donald A. Norman

A gents occupy a strange place in the realm of technology, leading to much fear, fiction, and extravagant claims. The reasons for this are not hard to find: the concept of an "agent," especially when modified by the term "intelligent," brings forth images of humanlike automatons, working without supervision on tasks thought to be for our benefit, but not necessarily to our liking. Probably all the major software manufacturers are exploring the use of intelligent agents. Myths, promises, and reality are all colliding. But the main difficulties I foresee are social, not technical: How will intelligent agents interact with people and perhaps more important, how might people think about agents?

Automata are not new concepts. Intelligent machines have existed in fact or fiction for centuries. Perhaps the most relevant predecessors to today's intelligent agents are servomechanisms and other control devices, including factory control and the automated takeoff, landing, and flight control of aircraft. The new crop of "intelligent agents" are different from the automated devices of earlier eras because of their computational power: they have Turing-machine powers, they take over human tasks, and they interact with people in humanlike ways, perhaps with a form of natural language, perhaps with animated graphics or video. Some agents have the potential to form their own goals and intentions, to initiate actions on their own without explicit instruction or guidance, and to offer suggestions to people. Thus, agents might set up schedules, reserve hotel and meeting rooms, arrange transportation, and even outline meeting topics, all without human intervention. Other, more complex interventions in human activities are contemplated. These humanlike activities and characteristics are what lead to the special concern over today's agents. Moreover, today's agents are simple in comparison to those that are being planned.

Two major themes are relevant for ensuring a smooth introduction of this technology. One theme deals with the way people feel about agents; the other, with comfort and acceptance of their automatic, autonomous actions.

- Ensuring that people feel in control of their computational systems;
- Hiding complexity while simultaneously revealing the underlying operations;
- Promoting accurate expectations (and minimizing false hopes);
- Providing built-in safeguards to prevent runaway computation;
- Addressing privacy concerns (a subset of the feeling of control problem);
- Developing appropriate forms of human-agent interaction.

The Feeling of Control

One of the first problems to face is that of the person's feeling of control. An important psychological aspect of people's comfort with their activities—all of their activities, from social relations, to jobs, to their interaction with technology—is the feeling of control they have over these activities and their personal lives. It's bad enough when people are intimidated by their home appliances: what will happen when automatic systems select the articles they should read, determine the importance and priority of their daily mail, and automatically answer mail, send messages, and schedule appointments? It is essential that people feel in control of their lives and surroundings, and that when automata do tasks for them, that they are comfortable with the actions, in part through a feeling of understanding, in part through confidence in the systems.

Confidence comes slowly, and the track record of existing automation does not lead to much optimism. Thus, the first introduction of automation into automobiles was met with resistance: the automatic spark advance, the automatic choke, the automatic transmission all took decades before they were accepted. The record of automation in the process control and transportation industries has not been good, with numerous failures. Although commercial airplanes can take off, navigate, and fly under automatic control, most passengers—including me—would not fly in a pilotless plane: indeed, we require two pilots partially because of workload, but partially because it is nice to have a spare: if one pilot becomes incapacitated, the other can take over. Pilots are not comfortable with all the automation; they feel "out of the loop" (Wiener 1988).

Mind you, the lack of confidence in automation is justified. We have a poor track record in developing large scale, complex systems. Systems do run amok (see, for example, Neumann 1995).

Agents pose especially complex technical questions because they are intended to be autonomous processes, sometimes capable of migrating across networks and processors in the most complex of asynchronous, autonomous, distributed processing environments. Moreover, each agent is apt to be created independently of the others, often in ignorance of the existence of others, so conflicts, contradictory actions, and synchronizing problems are bound to occur.

Providing Reassurance

Two things are necessary to make all this technology acceptable: one is technical, the other social. The technical aspect is to devise a computational structure that guarantees that from the technical standpoint, all is under control. This is not an easy task.

The social part of acceptability is to provide reassurance to the user that all is working according to plan. The best way to do this is through developing an appropriate conceptual model of the actions, one in which the actions of agents are understood in context so users feel comfortable in their ability to find out what actions have been taken in their behalf, that private matters remain private, that expensive or unwanted actions will not be taken without explicit permission, and that it is always possible to trace back the actual sequence of acts and undo any that are seen as unwarranted. Creating this conceptual model is a nontrivial task. We don't yet know how to do this, and to a large extent, the amount of information and explicit control that has to be provided is a function of the state of the individual's own comfort level: this will change over time, both for individuals and for society. Probably, in the early days, agents will have to make their presence and actions known through a conceptual model of the underlying operations and then, through graphics, sound, and appropriately chosen verbal messages, provide a continual updating of the conceptual state. As reliability increases, so too will people's comfort and acceptance. The user should therefore be able to change the amount and form of feedback, decreasing to some minimal level. I imagine that at first, people may want to know all the actions taken for them, but after they have come to trust the actions, they will be annoyed to have complete reporting. Nonetheless, I suspect there will always be the need to have the potential for such complete reports, even if they are seldom requested. Just as many people wish to be able to review their bank records each month, even though they seldom find an error, I suspect people will always want to be able to know about the actions of their agents.

Overblown Expectations

If the one aspect of people's attitudes about agents is fear over their capabilities and actions, the other is over-exaggerated expectations, triggered to a large extent because much more has been promised than can be delivered. Why? Part of this is the natural enthusiasm of the researcher who sees far into the future and imagines a world of perfect and complete actions. Part of this is in the nature of people's tendency to false anthropomorphizing, seeing human attributes in any action that appears in the least intelligent. Speech recognition has this problem: develop a system that recognizes words of speech and people assume that the system has full language understanding, which is not at all the same thing. Have a system act as if it has its own goals and intelligence, and there is an expectation of full knowledge and understanding of human goals.

The problem is amplified by the natural tendency of researchers and manufacturers to show their agents in human form. You can imagine the advertisements: "Want to schedule a trip, the new MacroAgent System offers you Helena, your friendly agent, ready to do your bidding." As soon as we put a human face into the model, perhaps with reasonably appropriate dynamic facial expressions, carefully tuned speech characteristics, and human-like language interactions, we build upon natural expectations for human-like intelligence, understanding, and actions.

There are some who believe that it is wrong—immoral even—to offer artificial systems in the guise of human appearance, for to do so makes false promises. Some believe that the more humanlike the appearance and interaction style of the agent, the more deceptive and misleading it becomes: personification suggests promises of performance that cannot be met. I believe that as long as there is no deception, there is no moral problem. Be warned that this is a controversial area. As a result, it would not be wise to present an agent in humanlike structures without also offering a choice to those who would rather not have them. People will be more accepting of intelligent agents if their expectations are consistent with reality. This is achieved by presenting an appropriate conceptual model—a "system image" (Norman 1986)—that accurately depicts the capabilities and actions.

Safety

Safety plays a part in the feeling of control: making sure that the agent does not do things that would jeopardize the physical, mental, or monetary well-being of the owner. But how can this be guaranteed when intelligent agents might enter one's system from outside? Sometimes one won't even know, as when they arrive in the mail, or are parts of some new set of capabilities being added to the computational system. How does one guard against error, maliciousness (as in the spread of computer viruses), and deliberate intent to pry and probe within one's personal records?

Privacy

Privacy could be considered a subset of the sense of control, but because the technical and social implications are considerably different, it deserves its own special consideration. Privacy is a complex topic, one deeply rooted in human cultural and legal systems. The concerns for privacy within the United States are not necessarily mirrored in the rest of the world, nor for that matter, even in the prior history of the United States.

Privacy often pits the interests of one group against another: the right of citizens to know what their government is doing; the right of one family to know what its neighbors are doing; the right or necessity of a government or person to keep its activities private and confidential.

Law enforcement has a need to be able to detect illegal actions: citizens have a right to be free from unwanted surveillance. Citizens do not trust their fellow citizens, industry, police, or government to use information about their activities in legitimate, beneficial ways. Business feels it can be more efficient and helpful the more information it has about the desires and behavior of its customers.

Not all the need for privacy is to avoid the detection of wrong-doing. White lies and other deceptions are an essential, positive aspect of social interaction, allowing for smoother, friendlier social discourse. Sometimes we want to protect a self-image. Sometimes we simply want to be removed from the hustle and bustle of modern communication — note the increasing prevalence of unlisted telephone numbers.

The issues are too complex to be given full treatment here. However, the idea that autonomous, intelligent agents could have access to personal records, correspondence, and financial activities is disturbing to many individuals, no matter how helpful the agents might be. Moreover, as the ability to imbed agents within electronic mail messages becomes more prevalent, who will be comfortable with the mail systems? Any mail message might release agents that search the recipient's records and return confidential information to the sender. I have already seen one such system demonstrated, and although it was shown with benign intent, where the agent "requested" permission before searching the recipient's address book and returning the information to the sender, it was easy to imagine other situations. Suppose the request was deceptive, with what was asked for differing from what was done.

Privacy and confidentiality of actions will be among the major issues confronting the use of intelligent agents in our future of a fully interconnected, fully communicating society. We must address those issues now, not just in the technical sense, but in the local, national, and global legal systems.

Human-Agent Interaction

What is the appropriate form of interaction between agent and person? The question has many different components, including the manner in which the person shall instruct and control the agent, the nature of the feedback from agent to person, the manner by which the person's conceptual model of the agent's method of operation and activities is presented, and the manner by which the agent offers advice and information to the person.

Take the problem of instruction: programming the agent. This is a complex issue. Various suggestions exist, from having the agent instruct itself by watching over people's activities and deciding how it can offer help, to instruction "by doing": "watch what I do," says the person," "and then do it for me." Other suggestions include the development of simple programming languages, some graphical, some declarative.

None of these seem satisfactory. The kinds of activities we assume will be performed by agents are quite complex. Scheduling events or ordering and making payments involve temporal relationships with other activities, distributed in space and time, not under control of the agent. Asynchronous coordination is not a simple task domain. The profound difficulty of programming complex tasks is well known by professional programmers.

Concluding Remarks

Agents are here to stay: once unleashed, technologies do not disappear. Agents may well have numerous positive contributions to our lives. They can simplify our use of computers, allowing us to move away from the complexity of command languages or the tedium of direct manipulation toward intelligent, agent-guided interaction. Agents offer the possibility of providing friendly assistance, so smoothly done that users need not even be aware, much as the modern automobile controls parts of the engine that used to require human intervention—e.g., the spark advance, choke, shifting—most of us are delighted to forget these things. Agents promise to hide complexity, to perform actions we could not or would rather not do ourselves. And agents could add to human intelligence, adding one more tool to the domain of cognitive artifacts that indeed do make people smarter (Norman 1993, 1991).

But along with the promise comes potential danger. Agents are unlike other artifacts of society in that they have some level of intelligence, some form of self-initiated, self-determined goals. Along with their benefits and capabilities come the potential for social mischief, for systems that run amok, for a loss of privacy, and for further alienation of society from technology through a diminishing sense of control. None of these negative aspects of agents are inevitable. All can be eliminated or minimized, but only if we consider these aspects in the design of our intelligent systems.

Acknowledgments

I thank Julie Norman, Tom Erickson, Harry Saddler and Pavel Curtis for critical readings and helpful suggestions.

References

Neumann, P. 1995. *Computer-Related Risk.* Reading, Mass.: Addison-Wesley.

Norman, D. A. 1993. *Things That Make Us Smart.* Reading, Mass.: Addison-Wesley.

Norman, D. A. 1991. Cognitive Artifacts. In *Designing Interaction: Psychology at the Human-Computer Interface*, ed. J. M. Carroll. New York: Cambridge University Press.

Norman, D. A. 1986. Cognitive Engineering. In *User Centered System Design*, eds. D. A. Norman and S. W. Draper. Hillsdale, N.J.: Lawrence Erlbaum.

Wiener, E. L. 1988. Cockpit Automation. In *Human Factors in Aviation*, eds. E. L. Wiener and D. C. Nagel. San Diego, Calif.: Academic.

Chapter 3

Agents: From Direct Manipulation to Delegation

Nicholas Negroponte

When I learned to make my bed, I was artfully taught and dutifully learned to make hospital corners. This simple fold had both functional and esthetic advantages and, with practice, added no time to the tedium of bedmaking. Today, notwithstanding this skill, I cherish the opportunity of delegating the task and have little interest in the direct manipulation of my bedsheets.

Likewise, I feel no imperative to manage my computer files, route my telecommunications, or filter the onslaught of mail, messages, news, and the like. I am fully prepared to delegate these tasks to agents I trust, as I tend to other matters (which could be as banal as getting dressed), while those other tasks are brought to a satisfactory conclusion. For the most part today, these agents are humans. Tomorrow they will be machines.

Intelligent Interfaces

My dream for the interface is that computers will be more like people. This idea is vulnerable to criticism for being too romantic, vague, or unrealizable. If anything, I would criticize it for shooting too low. There may be many exotic channels of communications of which we may not even be aware today. (As somebody married to an identical twin and with identical twin younger brothers, I am fully prepared to believe from observation that extrasensory communication is not out of the question.)

In the mid-1960s, I set my goals by trying to emulate face-to-face communication, with its languages of gesture and facial expressions and the motor involvement of our body and limbs. I used the admiral as my model.

In a landmark project called the Spatial Data Management System (circa 1976), the goal was to provide a human interface that would "bring computers directly to generals, presidents of companies, and six-year-old children." The system was designed to be learnable in thirty seconds. Familiarity with desktops and bookshelves was the tool used to browse and manipulate complex audio, video, and data.

That was radical for the late 1970s, but it still missed the more meaningful consequence of fashioning our communication after the conversation between the admiral and the seaman. Future human-computer interface will be rooted in delegation, not the vernacular of direct manipulation—pull down, pop up, click—and mouse interfaces. "Ease of use" has been such a compelling goal that we sometimes forget that many people don't want to use the machine at all. They want to get something done.

What we today call "agent-based interfaces" will emerge as the dominant means by which computers and people talk with one another. There will be specific points in space and time where bits get converted into atoms and the reverse. Whether that is the transmission of a liquid crystal or the reverberation of a speech generator, the interface will need size, shape, color, tone of voice, and all the other sensory paraphernalia.

Digital Butlers

In December 1980, Jerome Wiesner and I were the overnight and dinner guests of Nobutaka Shikanai at his lovely country house in the Hakone region of Japan, not far from Mount Fuji. We were so convinced that Mr. Shikanai's newspaper and TV media empire would benefit from being part of the inception of the Media Lab that we believed he would be willing to help pay for building it. We further believed that Mr. Shikanai's personal interest in contemporary art would play right into our dream of blending technology with expression, of combining the invention with the creative use of new media.

Before dinner, we walked around Mr. Shikanai's famous outdoor art collection, which during the daytime doubles as the Hakone Open Air Museum. At dinner with Mr. and Mrs. Shikanai we were joined by Mr. Shikanai's private male secretary who, quite significantly, spoke perfect English, as the Shikanais spoke none at all. The conversation was started by Wiesner, who expressed great interest in the work by Alexander Calder and told about both MIT's and his own personal experience with that great artist. The secretary listened to the story and then translated it from beginning to end, with Mr. Shikanai listening attentively. At the end, Mr. Shikanai reflected, paused, and then looked up at us and emitted a shogun-size "Ohhhh."

The male secretary then translated: "Mr. Shikanai says that he too is very impressed with the work of Calder and Mr. Shikanai's most recent acquisitions were under the circumstances of. . ." Wait a minute. Where did all that come from?

This continued for most of the meal. Wiesner would say something, it would be translated in full, and the reply would be more or less an "Ohhhh," which was then translated into a lengthy explanation. I said to myself that night, if I really want to build a personal computer, it has to be as good as Mr. Shikanai's secretary. It has to be able to expand and contract signals as a function of knowing me and my environment so intimately that I literally can be redundant on most occasions.

The best metaphor I can conceive of for a human-computer interface is that of a well-trained English butler. The "agent" answers the phone, recognizes the callers, disturbs you when appropriate, and may even tell a white lie on your behalf. The same agent is well trained in timing, versed in finding the opportune moments, and respectful of idiosyncrasies. People who know the butler enjoy considerable advantage over a total stranger. That is just fine.

Such human agents are available to very few people. A more widely played role of similar sorts is that of an office secretary. If you have somebody who knows you well and shares much of your information, that person can act on your behalf very effectively. If your secretary falls ill, it would make no difference if the temporary agency could send you Albert Einstein. This issue is not about IQ. It is shared knowledge and the practice of using it in your best interests.

The idea of building this kind of functionality into a computer until recently was a dream so far out of reach that the concept was not taken seriously. This is changing rapidly. Enough people now believe that such "interface agents" are buildable. For this reason, this backwater interest in intelligent agents has become the most fashionable topic of research in human-computer interface design. It has become obvious that people want to delegate more functions and prefer to directly manipulate computers less.

The idea is to build computer surrogates that possess a body of knowledge both about something (a process, a field of interest, a way of doing) and about you in relation to that something (your taste, your inclinations, your acquaintances). Namely, the computer should have dual expertise, like a cook, gardener, and chauffeur using their skills to fit your tastes and needs in cooking, planting, and driving. Delegating those tasks does not mean you do not like to prepare food, grow plants, or drive cars. It means you have the option to do those things when you wish, because you want to, not because you have to.

Likewise with a computer. I really have no interest whatsoever in logging into a system, going through protocols, and figuring out your Internet address. I just want to get my message through to you. Similarly, I do not want to be required to read thousands of bulletin boards to be sure I am not missing something. I want my interface agent to do those things.

Digital butlers will be numerous, living both in the network and by your side, both in the center and at the periphery of your own organization (large or small).

I tell people about the intelligent pager that I have and love: how it delivers in full sentences of perfect English only timely and relevant information, how it behaves so intelligently. The way it works is that only one human being has its number, and all messages go through that person, who knows where I am, what is important, and whom I know (and their agent). The intelligence is in the head end of the system, not at the periphery, not in the pager itself.

But you should have intelligence at the receiving end as well. I was recently visited by the CEO of a large corporation and his assistant, who wore the CEO's pager and fed him its prompts at the most opportune moments. The assistant's functions of tact, timing, and discretion will eventually be built into the pager.

Personal Filters

Al Gore need not be right or wrong in his conception of details. It almost doesn't matter whether he calls it an information superhighway, an infobahn, or a national information infrastructure. What matters is his personal and sincere interest in computers and communications and the fact that his enthusiasm has raised our popular consciousness of telecommunications. The media cacophony over phenomena like the Internet fosters an open architecture and emphasizes access by all Americans.

The clamor, however, has perpetuated a tacit assumption that more bandwidth is an innate, a priori, and (almost) constitutional good. The right to 1,000 channels of TV! Continental Cable, the local cable company in Cambridge, Massachusetts, now offers Internet access at 500,000 bits per second. With that service, *The Wall Street Journal* takes sixteen seconds to transmit its entirety (as structured data mostly, not fax, please!). When fiber reaches the home, by some estimates, we will have access to as much as 100 billion bits per second. Hmmm. Most people generally make a false assumption that more bits are better. More is more.

In truth, we want fewer bits, not more. What I really need is intelligence in the network and in my receiver to filter and extract relevant information from a body of information that is orders of magnitude larger than anything I can digest. I am willing to project an enormous new industry based on a service that helps navigate through massive amounts of data.

Imagine an electronic newspaper delivered to your home as bits. Assume it is sent to a magical, paper-thin, flexible, waterproof, wireless, lightweight, bright display. The interface solution is likely to call upon mankind's years of experience with headlining and layout, typographic landmarks, images, and a host of techniques to assist browsing. Done well, this is likely to be a magnificent news medium. Done badly, it will be hell.

There is another way to look at a newspaper, and that is as an interface to news. Instead of reading what other people think is news and what other people justify as worthy of the space it takes, being digital means that you can change the economic model of news selections, make your interests play a bigger role, and, in fact, use pieces from the cutting-room floor that did not make the cut on popular demand.

Imagine a future in which your interface agent can read every newswire and newspaper and catch every TV and radio broadcast on the planet, and then construct a personalized summary. This kind of newspaper is printed in an edition of one.

A newspaper is read very differently on Monday morning than it is on Sunday afternoon. At 7 a.m. on a workday, you browse a newspaper as a means of filtering the information and personalizing a common set of bits that were sent to hundreds of thousands of people. Most people tend to trash whole sections of newspapers without a glance, browse some of the rest, and read very little in detail.

What if a newspaper company were willing to put its entire staff at your beck and call for one edition? It would mix headline news with "less important" stories relating to acquaintances, people you will see tomorrow, and places you are about to go to or have just come from. It would report on companies you know. In fact, under these conditions, you might be willing to pay the Boston *Globe* a lot more for ten pages than for a hundred pages, if you could be confident that it was delivering you the right subset of information. You would consume every bit (so to speak). Call it *The Daily Me*.

On Sunday afternoon, however, we may wish to experience the news with much more serendipity, learning about things we never knew we were interested in, being challenged by a crossword puzzle, having a good laugh with Art Buchwald, and finding bargains in the ads. This is *The Daily Us*. The last thing you want on a rainy Sunday afternoon is a high-strung interface agent trying to remove the seemingly irrelevant material.

These are not two distinct states of being, black and white. We tend to move between them, and, depending on time available, time of day, and our mood, we will want lesser or greater degrees of personalization. Imagine a computer display of news stories with a knob that, like a volume control, allows you to crank personalization up or down. You could have many of these controls, including a slider that moves both literally and politically from left to right to modify stories about public affairs.

These controls change your window onto the news, both in terms of its size and its editorial tone. In the distant future, interface agents will read, listen to, and look at each story in its entirety. In the near future, the filtering process will happen by using headers, those bits about the bits.

Digital Sisters-In-Law

The fact that *TV Guide* has been known to make larger profits than all four networks combined suggests that the value of information about information can be greater than the value of the information itself. When we think of new information delivery, we tend to cramp our thoughts with concepts like "info grazing" and "channel surfing." These concepts just do not scale. With a thousand channels, if you surf from station to station, dwelling only three seconds per channel, it will take almost an hour to scan them all. A program would be over long before you could decide whether it is the most interesting.

When I want to go out to the movies, rather than read reviews, I ask my sister-in-law. We all have an equivalent who is both an expert on movies and an expert on us. What we need to build is a digital sister-in-law.

In fact, the concept of "agent" embodied in humans helping humans is often one where expertise is indeed mixed with knowledge of you. A good travel agent blends knowledge about hotels and restaurants with knowledge about you (which often is culled from what you thought about other hotels and restaurants). A real estate agent builds a model of you from a succession of houses that fit your taste with varying degrees of success. Now imagine a telephone-answering agent, a news agent, or an electronic-mail-managing agent. What they all have in common is the ability to model you.

All of us are quite comfortable with the idea that an all-knowing agent might live in our television set, pocket, or automobile. We are rightly less sanguine about the possibility of such agents living in the greater network. All we need is a bunch of tattletale or culpable computer agents. Enough butlers and maids have testified against former employers for us to realize that our most trusted agents, by definition, know the most about us.

I believe there is a whole new business in confiding our profiles to a third party, which will behave like a Swiss bank. I fear this will not be one of my credit card companies, which have sold my name for all sorts of purposes, and have thus shot themselves in the foot. It must be a credible third party, perhaps a local telephone company, perhaps a long distance company like AT&T, perhaps a new venture altogether. What we should be looking for is an entity which is able and willing to keep our identities confidential while at the same time passing along newsworthy advertising and information.

Such services will work only with a high degree of machine learning. It is not a matter of a questionnaire or a fixed profile. Agents must learn and develop over time, like human friends and assistants. It is not only the acquisition of a model of you; it is using it in context. Timing alone is an example of how human agents distinguish themselves. But it is all too easy to wave your hand and say "learning." What constitutes learning?

The only clue I have found goes back two decades to the work of the English cybernetician Gordon Pask, who taught me to look at the second- and third-order models. In human-to-computer interaction, your model of the computer is less telling than its model of your model of it. By extension, your model of its model of your model of it is even more critical. When this third-order model matches the first (your model of it), we can say that you know each other.

Artificial Intelligence

When I talk about interface agents, I am constantly asked, "Do you mean artificial intelligence?" The answer is clearly "yes." But the question carries implicit doubts raised by the false hopes and hyped promises of AI in the past. In addition, many people are still not comfortable with the idea that machines will be intelligent.

Alan Turing is generally considered the first person to seriously propose machine intelligence in his 1950 paper, "Computer Machinery and Intelligence." Later pioneers, such as Marvin Minsky, continued Turing's deep interest in pure AI. They ask themselves questions about recognizing context, understanding emotion, appreciating humor, and shifting from one set of metaphors to another. For example, what are the subsequent letters in a sequence that starts *O. T. T. F. F?*

I think AI may have suffered a turn for the worse around 1975 when computing resources started to achieve the kind of power that might be needed to solve intuitive problems and to exhibit intelligent behavior. What happened is that scientists suddenly opted for the very doable and marketable applications, like robotics and expert systems (i.e., stock trading and airline reservations), thereby leaving untouched the more profound and basic questions of intelligence and learning.

Minsky is quick to point out that even while today's computers can exhibit an uncanny grasp of airline reservations (a subject almost beyond logic), they absolutely cannot display the common sense exhibited by a three- or four-year-old child. They cannot tell the difference between a dog and a cat. Subjects like common sense are now moving off the back burner onto the center stage of scientific research, which is very important because an interface agent without common sense would be a pain in the neck.

By the way, the answer to the question raised above is *S. S.* The sequence is determined by the first letter of each word as you count: *one, two, three, four, five.*

Decentralization

A future interface agent is often seen as some centralized and omniscient machine of Orwellian character. A much more likely outcome is a collection of computer programs and personal appliances, each of which is pretty good at one thing and very good at communicating with the others. This image is fashioned after Minsky's (1986) *The Society of Mind* , in which he proposes that intelligence is not found in some central processor but in the collective behavior of a large group of more special-purpose, highly interconnected machines.

This view runs against a set of prejudices that Mitchel Resnick (1994), in his book, *Turtles, Termites, and Traffic Jams,* calls the "centralized mind-set." We are all strongly conditioned to attribute complex phenomena to some kind of controlling agency. We commonly assume, for example, that the frontmost bird in a V-shaped flock is the one in charge and the others are playing follow-the-leader. Not so. The orderly formation is the result of a highly responsive collection of processors behaving individually and following simple harmonious rules without a conductor. Resnick makes the point by creating situations in which people are surprised to find themselves part of such a process.

I recently experienced such a demonstration by Resnick in the Kresge Auditorium at MIT. The audience of roughly 1,200 people was asked to start clapping and try to clap in unison. Without the slightest lead from Resnick, within less than two seconds, the room was clapping a single beat. Try it yourself; even with much smaller groups the result can be startling. The surprise shown by participants brings home how little we understand or even recognize the emergence of coherence from the activity of independent agents.

This is not to say that your calendar agent will start planning meetings without consulting your travel agent. But every communication and decision need not go back to a central authority for permission, which might be a crummy way to manage an airline reservation system, but this method is viewed more and more as a viable way to manage organizations and governments. A highly intercommunicating decentralized structure shows far more resilience and likelihood of survival. It is certainly more sustainable and likely to evolve over time.

For a long time, decentralism was plausible as a concept but not possible as an implementation. The effect of fax machines on Tiananmen Square is an ironic example, because newly popular and decentralized tools were invoked precisely when the government was trying to reassert its elite and centralized control. The Internet provides a worldwide channel of communication that flies in the face of any censorship and thrives especially in places like Singapore, where freedom of the press is marginal and networking ubiquitous.

Interface agentry will become decentralized in the same way as information and organizations. Like an army commander sending a scout ahead or a sheriff sending out a posse, you will dispatch agents to collect information on your behalf. Agents will dispatch agents. The process multiplies. But remember the way this started: it started at the interface where you delegated your desires, versus diving into the World Wide Web itself.

This model of the future is distinctly different from a human-factors approach to interface design. The look and feel of the interface certainly count, but they play a minor role in comparison to intelligence. In fact, one of the most widely used interfaces will be the little tiny hole (or two) in plastic or metal, through which your voice accesses a small microphone.

It is also important to see the interface agent approach as very different from the current rage about the Internet and browsing it with Netscape. The Internet hackers can surf that medium, explore enormous bodies of knowledge, and indulge in all kinds of new forms of socialization. This strikingly widespread phenomenon is not going to abate or go away, but it is only one kind of behavior, one more like direct manipulation than delegation.

Our interfaces will vary. Yours will be different from mine, based on our respective information predilections, entertainment habits, and social behavior—all drawn from the very large palette of digital life.

Why Winking Works

At a recent dinner party I winked at my wife,[1] and she knew all the paragraphs of information it would have taken me (otherwise) to explain the same to some stranger. The reason is quite obvious. A vast amount of shared experiences and robust models of each other make the epitome of communication be the lack of it.

In a agent-model of computers, similar familiarity is required in order to preclude relentless explicitness that would destroy the value of agencies. In daily life it can often be the case that it is easier to do something oneself than to explain it to somebody "new." No, the computer must be an old friend with as many shared experiences (facts, at least) as the future computer presence will allow. This is absolutely critical to a new metaphor, beyond the desktop.

The Theatrical Metaphor

If you are prepared to accept the promise of delegation and the viability of speech, the desktop metaphor is subject to serious change, soon.[2]

My view of the future of desktop computing is one where the bezel becomes a proscenium and agents are embodied to any degree of literalness you may desire. In the longer term, as holography prevails, little people will walk across your desk (if you have one) dispatched to do what they know how.

The picture is simple. The stage is set with characters of your own choice or creation whose scripts are drawn from the ploy of your life. Their expressiveness, character, and propensity to speak out are driven by an event (external) and a style (yours). If you want your agents to wear bow ties, they will. If you prefer talking to parallelepipeds, fine.

This highly literal model of agents can be dismissed as a foolish scheme to replace serious icons with Snow White and the Seven Dwarfs.[3] But this begs the question about delegation and speech. In some form we can expect surrogates who can execute complex functions, filter information, and intercommunicate in our interest(s).

Conclusion: Direct Manipulation and Digital Butlers

Direct manipulation has its place and in many regards is part of the joys of life: sports, food, and for some, driving. But wouldn't you really prefer to run your home and office life with a gaggle of well trained butlers (to answer the telephone), maids (to make the hospital corners), secretaries (to filter the world), accountants or brokers (to manage your money),[4] and on some occasions, cooks, gardeners, and chauffeurs when there were too many guests, weeds, or cars on the road?

Acknowledgments

The material in this chapter has been adapted from: Negroponte, N. (1989). A Personal Perspective: An Iconoclastic View Beyond the Desktop Metaphor. *International Journal of Human-Computer Interaction,* 1(1), 109-113; Negroponte, N. (1994). Less is More: Interface Agents as Digital Butlers. *Wired,* June 1994, 142; and Negroponte, N. (1995). *Being Digital.* New York: Alfred A. Knopf, pp. 101-102, 149-158.

Notes

1. In some perverted measure of information theory, this could be construed as one bit.

2. I have not addressed animation because I think it goes without saying that there will be a dramatic change in three-dimensional engines and low-cost, real-time, high-resolution animation will be as commonplace as pull-down menus.

3. In 1977 I recall almost being laughed out of an auditorium when I suggested that a calculator icon would invoke that object on the screen and ease of use would naturally stem from familiarity.

4. This one might make you nervous.

References

Minsky, M. 1986. *The Society of Mind.* New York: Simon & Schuster.

Resnick, M. 1994. *Turtles, Termites, and Traffic Jams: Explorations in Massively Parallel Microworlds.* Cambridge, Mass.: The MIT Press.

CHAPTER 4

Interface Agents:
Metaphors with Character

Brenda Laurel

O n the bridge of the USS *Enterprise*, a decidedly clipped female voice announces that the computer is "working." On board the Nostromo, Rip-
ley hunches over her console seeking advice from "Mother." On the
moon, Adam Selene foments a revolution. HAL refuses to open the pod bay
doors, and his sibling SAL wonders whether she'll dream when her creator
powers her down.

Since the beginning of this century, people have dreamed about the new
companions they might create with high technology. Some of those dreams are
nightmares about malevolent computers enslaving mankind as techno-evolu-
tion catapults them far beyond our puny carbon-based brains. Most are wistful
longings for new helpers, advisors, teachers, playmates, pets, or friends. But all
of the computer-based personae that weave through popular culture have one
thing in common: they mediate a relationship between the labyrinthine preci-
sion of computers and the fuzzy complexity of people.

Why is this tendency to personify interfaces so natural as to be virtually universal in our collective vision of the future?

Computers behave. Computational tools and applications can be said to have
predispositions to behave in certain ways on both fuctional and stylistic levels. Interfaces are designed to communicate those predispositions to users, thereby enabling them to understand, predict the results of, and successfully deploy the associated behaviors.

When we think and communicate about behavioral predispositions, we naturally use metaphors based on living organisms. Even the most technologically
savvy user will feel quite comfortable comparing the Macintosh and the IBM-
PC in terms of their "personalities" and may characterize software with adjectives based on a living-organism metaphor: WORD is fussy, my spelling checker

is illiterate, EMACS is obtuse. Where agentlike activities already exist, they are often perceived as having character—one interface designer has described error messages as "wrist-slapping grannies."

An interface agent can be defined as a character, enacted by the computer, who acts on behalf of the user in a virtual (computer-based) environment. Interface agents draw their strength from the naturalness of the living-organism metaphor in terms of both cognitive accessibility and communication style. Their usefulness can range from managing mundane tasks like scheduling, to performing customized information searches which combine both filtering and the production (or retrieval) of alternative representations, to providing companionship, advice, and help throughout the spectrum of known and yet-to-be-invented interactive contexts.

Objections to Agents

Although the notion of interface agents seems natural and desirable to many, considerable resistance exists. One negative view can be described as the "agent as virus" problem. One of this book's authors characterized agents as "whining, chatting little irritants." She dreaded waking up one day to find "a whining little secretary stuck in my machine." Here the problem is not agents *per se*, but rather the traits that they are assumed to possess. One solution is to offer the user a number of agents from which to choose (rather like a job interview or theatrical audition); another is to provide an "identa-kit" whereby agents could be configured by their users.

Closely related to "agent as virus" is the notion that agents are just plain silly. "I would feel incredibly stupid pretending that there was a person in my computer," one programmer told me (however, this same person has often been observed shouting obscenities at his screen). In a lively conversation on the subject on the WELL (Whole Earth 'Lectronic Link), one user confided that he had been saving digitized images of his dog to immortalize him as an agent after his death. This idea was greeted with a mixture of derision and horror. Yet the idea of a canine agent (perhaps not one's own departed pet) readily suggests a class of activities (fetching the morning paper and announcing intruders, for instance), a level of competence (the agent will deliver the paper but will not provide commentary), and a kind of communication (a small repertoire of simple commands and an equally small repertoire of behavioral responses) that may be entirely appropriate.

For some users, the idea of agents smacks of indirection. "Why should I have to negotiate with some little dip in a bowtie when I know exactly what I want to do?" The answer, of course, is equivocal. Few of us would hire an agent to push the buttons on our calculator; most of us would hire an agent to scan 5,000 pieces of junk mail. If I were looking for a specific book for a research project, I'd probably use a reference librarian; if I were browsing with an opportunistic eye, I'd want to go into the stacks. When I have to negotiate with UNIX, I call my husband. It doesn't feel like indirection when an agent does something for me that I can't or don't want to do myself. I have often railed against interfaces that force me to plead with a system (in exotic language) to do a very simple thing (Laurel 1986a). But that is quite different from having a competent agent at my beck and call. Agents, like anything else, can be well or poorly designed. A good one will do what I want, tell me all I want to know about what it's doing, and give me back the reins when I desire. Good interfaces usually allow for more than one way of doing things, too. Only users who want to use agents should have them; others should have other choices.

Perhaps a more thought-provoking objection to agents rests on an ethical argument that goes something like this: if an agent looks and acts a lot like a real person, and if I can get away with treating it badly and bossing it around without paying a price for my bad behavior, then I will be ecouraged to treat other, "real" agents (like secretaries and realtors, for instance) just as badly. This argument seems to hinge on the fear that humans will mistake a representation for the real thing, possibly first expressed by Plato when he banned the dramatic arts from his Republic on the same grounds. Yet few would trade the plays of Shakespeare and Molière for the apparent unambiguity of Plato's world. Today, many parents are concerned that their children will confuse the violence in the news with that in the latest commando movie (or video game). These are real issues which must be addressed by artists and citizens. The solution lies, I believe, not in repression of the form (which is a strategy that is bound to fail, if history is any indicator), but rather in the ethics of the artist, the entrepreneur, the parent, and the culture at large.

Another objection is that implementing agents would necessarily involve Artificial Intelligence, a discipline whose star is currently in eclipse. "AI doesn't work," the litany goes, "and even if it did, an agent would gobble up more cycles than it's worth." Two responses apply. First, although the grand platform of AI may not have been satisfactorily realized, there are numerous examples of the successful use of AI techniques. For example, Object Lens, an "intelligent groupware" system under development at the Sloane School of Management at MIT, enables users to create agents that can sort mail, issue reminders, and find things in object-oriented databases (Crowston and Malone 1988). Second, there are already examples of agents that employ no AI at all (Oren et al. 1990). The problem here may be that an anthropomorphic agent is being confused with a full-blown "artificial personality," the implementation of which is, of course, a daunting prospect. But an agent can — indeed, must — be much simpler than that, as we shall see.

In Defense of Anthropomorphism

Anthropomorphizing interface agents is appropriate for both psychological and functional reasons. Psychologically, we are quite adept at relating to and communicating with other people. We utilize this ability in dealing with nonsentient beings and inanimate objects through the process of anthropomorphism. This mode of operating in the world is so natural that we often engage in anthropomorphizing objects in our daily lives — ships, countries, cars, and vacuum cleaners. Where an anthropomorphic persona is not readily apparent, one is often created for us by advertisers: Reddy Kilowatt, the Pillsbury Doughboy, and the California Raisins come to mind (indeed, the anthropomorphic Raisins are so attractive that they have generated more revenue than their fruity friends).

Anthropomorphism is not the same thing as relating to other people but is rather the application of a metaphor with all its concomitant selectivity. Metaphors draw incomplete parallels between unlike things, emphasizing some qualities and suppressing others (Lakoff and Johnson 1980). When we anthropomorphize a machine or an animal, we do not impute human personality in all its subtle complexity; we paint with bold strokes, thinking only of those traits which are useful to us in the particular context.

The kinds of tasks that computers perform for (and with) us require that they express two distinctly anthropomorphic qualities: *responsiveness* and the *capacity to perform actions*. These qualities alone make up the metaphor of agency. To flesh out a particular agent, the computer can be made to represent its unique skills, expertise, and predispositions in terms of character traits. As in drama, traits can be represented directly through appearance, sound, and communication style (external traits), which in turn cause us to infer traits on the level of knowledge and thought (internal traits). Evaluating action taken by an agent provides a feedback loop through which we refine and embellish our understanding of its character. The point here is that, as the ultimate device for making dynamic, mimetic representations, the computer is ideally suited to the task of manifesting agents as dramatic characters (Laurel 1986b).

By capturing and representing the capabilities of agents in the form of character, we realize several benefits. First, this form of representation makes optimal use of our ability to make accurate inferences about how a character is likely to think, decide, and act on the basis of its external traits. This marvelous cognitive shorthand is what makes plays and movies work; its universality is what makes the same play or story work for a variety of cultures and individuals. With interface agents, users can employ the same shorthand—with the same likelihood of success—to predict, and therfore control, the actions of their agents. Second, the agent as character (whether humanoid, canine, cartoonish, or cybernetic) invites conversational interaction. This invokes another kind of shorthand — the ability to infer, co-create, and employ simple communication conventions. As Susan Brennan (1990) and Bill Buxton (1990) demonstrate, the essence of conversationality can be captured without elaborate natural language processing. Third, the metaphor of *character* successfully draws our attention to just those qualities that form the essential nature of an agent: responsiveness, competence, accessibility, and the capacity to perform actions on our behalf.

Key Characteristics of Interface Agents

There are four key characteristics of interface agents: agency, responsiveness, competence, and accessibility. Each characteristic will be discussed in the following subsections.

Agency

In a purely Aristotelean sense, an agent is one who takes action. In social and legal terms, an agent is one who is empowered to act on behalf of another. Researcher Susan Brennan observes that most people whom we refer to as "our agents"—real estate agents, insurance agents, and the like—are not working for us at all, but rather for the companies who pay their salaries (Brennan 1984). An interface agent would exercise its agency entirely on behalf of the user. Alan Kay traces the development of the concept:

> The idea of an agent originated with John McCarthy in the mid-1950's, and the term was coined by Oliver G. Selfridge a few years later, when they were both at the Massachusetts Institute of Technology. They had in view a system that, when given a goal, could carry out the details of the appropriate computer operations and could ask for and receive advice, offered in human terms, when it was stuck. An agent would be a "soft robot" living and doing its business within the computer's world. (Kay 1984)

Agents provide expertise, skill, and labor. They must of necessity be capable of understanding our needs and goals in relation to them (either explicitly or implicitly), translating those goals into an appropriate set of actions, performing those actions, and delivering the results in a form that we can use. They must also know when further information is needed from us and how to get it. In life, any person or institution who is empowered by us to take action on our behalf is an agent. Examples include secretaries, gardeners, craftspeople and laborers, teachers, librarians, and accountants.

What kinds of tasks do we perform with computers for which agents are appropriate? They are tasks with the same requirements as those for which we employ agents in real life: tasks which require expertise, skill, resources, or labor that we need to accomplish some goal, and which we are unwilling or unable to perform ourselves. Figure 1 provides examples of computer-related tasks where agents would be appropriate.

Information	Work
Navigation and Browsing	Reminding
Information Retrieval	Programming
Sorting and Organizing	Scheduling
Filtering	Advising
Learning	**Entertainment**
Coaching	Playing against
Tutoring	Playing with
Providing Help	Performing

Figure 1. Kinds of tasks an agent might perform.

Some of these tasks are appropriate for an agent because they are too complex for either straightforward algorithmic solutions or for complete parametric specification by the human user. An obvious example is a search for information in a large database, which may involve linguistic, numeric, formal, and a variety of heuristic and stylistic concerns. The nature of the complexity of such problems makes them excellent candidates for an expert-systems approach (Hayes-Roth, Waterman, and Lenat 1983). Like the human experts who give expert systems their not-so-metaphorical name, agents based on such systems probably require considerable detailing and subtlety in their character traits. Other kinds of tasks (such as sorting mail or preparing monthly invoices) require much less "intelligence"; the associated agents are valuable because they are diligent, quick, accurate, and impervious to boredom. Representing such agents would require relatively fewer, more simplistic traits. Both functional implementation and external representation (i.e., character) will vary widely according to the nature of the agent's tasks.

Responsiveness

Because of its social contract with the user, an interface agent is a prime example of user-centered interface design. An agent succeeds or fails on the basis of its ability to be responsive to the user. What are the dimensions of responsiveness?

Most other forms of human-computer interface exhibit *explicit responsiveness*; that is, user and system communicate through a series of highly constrained, explicit transactions. Typically, a system accomodates users' expressions of goals and intentions only in ways that are formally compatible with its operating requirements. Even when commands are camouflaged in comfortable metaphors like "cut," "paste," or "paint," users must parse their actions and intentions in terms dictated by the system (and therefore the interface) and must express them explicitly.

Because it is the function of an agent to take action on behalf of a user, it follows that the value of the agent derives, at least in part, from its ability to formulate and execute a set of actions solely on the basis of a user's goals. Whether those goals are explicitly stated by the user or inferred by the system, the way an agent interprets and attempts to meet them constitutes *implicit responsiveness*. This is the principal means whereby an agent amplifies the user's personal power.

One aspect of implicit responsiveness is the ability of an agent to tune its actions to the user's traits and preferences. If my French tutor notices that I'm a theatre buff, she'll enhance my learning process by assigning readings in Molière. Noting my intransigence regarding the three-comma rule, my writing coach should probably beat on me mercilessly until I either succumb to the new grammar or exchange him for Edgar Allan Poe. Knowledge about the user can be both explicitly obtained (by questioning) and inferred (by noticing).

Users also change over time. Even when the user's goals are explicitly the same from day to day, the way they should be interpreted changes. If I ask my news agent to tell me what's going on in the Middle East, for instance, he should not present me with the same article I read yesterday. And if he's smart, he'll notice that I seem to have become especially interested in the Persian Gulf and will gather materials accordingly. Responsiveness therefore requires that the agent have access to a dynamic model of the user, or at the very least, a log of his experience in a particular application or environment with rules for interpreting that experience when formulating actions.

Depending upon how it is implemented, an interface agent may be associated primarily with a single user or with an application or environment that has multiple users. In the latter case, the agent must be able to distinguish among users, at least on the basis of experience and preferences, in order to be genuinely responsive.

Interface designers often have a strong aversion to implicit responsiveness because it requires inference, and inference is fuzzy. The belief is that an incorrect inference is more disturbing to the user than no inference at all (i.e., insistence on explicit transactions). But a failed inference need not be painful if it results only in a request for more information. If a system knows enough to generate an error message, then it also knows enough to ask a question. The risk of incorrect inference can be mitigated by a variety of strategies for disambiguation, including dialogue, user modeling, and the creation of redundancy through the use of multiple input channels (Chen and Leahy 1990; Mountford and Gaver 1990).

Competence

Suggestions about building and employing the first area of competence, knowledge about the user, are included in the discussion of responsiveness above. Clearly, an interface agent must also be competent in the domain of the application or environment in which it operates. An agent can be said to have access to all of the information and possible operations in its domain by virtue of its being part of the same system. But in order to serve the user well, an agent must possess (or be able to generate) both meta-knowledge and multiple representations.

By meta-knowledge I mean knowledge about problem-solving in a domain. If the domain is a database, then knowledge is required about both the information content and the process of retrieving and representing that information to the user. If the domain is a table of airline schedules and fares, the meta-knowledge consists in knowing how to formulate a travel plan based on both domain information and the preferences of the traveler, and then how to present it in a clear and actionable way.

The ability to provide multiple representations of information is a key aspect of responsiveness. Brennan observes:

> [M]ultiple respresentations increase the odds that the user and the system will be able to communicate effectively and that ambiguities in one representation will be disambiguated by another; multiple representations also provide a basis for a learning environment. Good teachers and good students are skilled at providing feedback by trading multiple representations back and forth... (Brennan 1984)

At the very least, competence consists of knowing how to select from among multiple representations already extant in a single database. Ultimately, however, such limited competence will prove to be inadequate. Users will eventually want agents to assemble information from multiple sources containing huge volumes of information in a wide variety of forms. It seems impractical to create a new information-linking industry where humans attempt to stitch all the information in the world together so that we can build interfaces which simply follow the threads. It also seems impractical to include multiple representations for every item in even a small database. Competence will ultimately include the ability to both retrieve and generate alternate representations of information according to the needs and personal styles of users. Agents will be selected or configured by users partially on the basis of their distinctive searching heuristics and representation-making abilities.

Accessibility

An agent's traits and predispositions must be made accessible to the user. Perceptually, users must be given cues by the external representation of an agent which allow them to infer its internal traits. Selection of the modes of representation (e.g., visual, verbal, auditory, etc.) should be driven by a consideration of the whole character, the environment, and the traits in question. For some agents and environments, text is just enough (ELIZA's disembodied phrases may be its greatest strength), while for others completely different modalities are required (imagine capturing Marilyn Monroe without a picture or Donald Duck without a voice). For example, in the Guides project (Oren et al. 1990), graphical icons that minimize facial detail and emphasize emblematic props are adequate for distinguishing among points of view in the task of navigating through the textual database, but for providing alternate representations of information in storytelling style, motion video and character voice are required.

On the conceptual level, an agent is accessible if a user can predict what it is likely to do in a given situation on the basis of its character. Equally important is the criterion that an agent must be conceived by users as a coherent entity. It is in the area of accessibility that the idea of structuring agents as dramatic characters has the greatest value.

Design and Dramatic Character

The case for modeling interface agents after dramatic characters is based on both the familiarity of dramatic characters as a way of structuring thought and behavior and the body of theory and methodology already in place for creating them. Most cultures have a notion of dramatic form, and people are quite familiar with both the differences and similarities between characters and real people. Character traits function as stereotypic "shorthand" for understanding and predicting character behavior (Schank and Lebowitz 1979).

Somewhat ironically, dramatic characters are better suited to the roles of agents than full-blown simulated personalities. The art of creating dramatic characters is the art of selecting and representing only those traits which are appropriate to a particular set of actions and situations (Schwamberger 1980). For most uses, an interface agent, like a dramatic character, must pass a kind of anti-Turing test in order to be effectively understood and employed by the user. We want to know that the choices and actions of our agents, whether computational or human, will not be clouded by complex and contradictory psychological variables. In most cases, we want to be able to predict their actions with greater certainty than those of "real" people.

Although designers and scholars like Alan Kay worry that oversimplification of character will destroy the illusion of lifelikeness (Kay 1984), the fact is that, thanks to well-internalized dramatic convention, we can enjoy (and believe in) even one-dimensional dramatic characters. In fact, when a minor dramatic character possesses only one or two functional traits, audience members will impute elaborate histories and motivations as needed to make it believable (Schwamberger 1980). Whether the character is as simple as Wiley Coyote or as complex as Hamlet, we take pleasure when — and *only* when — even the surprises in a character's behavior are causally related to its traits.

Happily, the selectivity and causality inherent in the structure of dramatic characters simplifies the task of representing them computationally (Laurel 1986b). In the area of story generation, James Meehan, Michael Lebowitz, and others have created functional and entertaining characters from a small cluster of well-conceived traits that are realized as goal-formulating and problem-solving styles (Lebowitz 1984; Meehan 1976). Increasingly in the world of adventure and role-playing computer games, designers are implementing characters with traits that are *dynamic* (modified by learning and experience) and *relational* (modified in relation to objects and situations).

The artistic side of the design problem is to represent the character (in this case, an interface agent) to the user in such a way that the appropriate traits are apparent and the associated styles and behaviors can be successfully predicted. External traits like diction and appearance must be shaped to suggest those internal traits (values, heuristics, etc.) which determine a how a character will make choices and perform actions. A character is coherent—whole—when its traits are well-integrated through careful selection and planned interaction. The designer can look to the considerable body of work on playwriting, as well as to the area of modeling and representing character traits computationally (see, for instance, Carbonell 1980) for guidance.

An R & D Agenda

As we are discovering with all types of interfaces, good design is no longer the exclusive province of the applications programmer, the graphic designer, the AI researcher, or even the multimedia hacker. In the effort to make interface agents a reality, several areas of technology and design must be explored simultaneously.

In the theoretical arena, work must proceed on the analysis of user needs and preferences vis-à-vis applications and environments. What are the qualities of a task that make it a good candidate for an agent-like interface? What kinds of users will want them, and what are the differences among potential user populations? How might interface agents affect the working styles, expectations, productivity, knowledge, and personal power of those who use them?

In terms of design, the meatiest problem is developing criteria that will allow us to select the appropriate set of traits for a given agent—traits which can form coherent characters, provide useful cues to users, and give rise to all of the necessary and appropriate actions in a given context. Contributions will be needed from the disciplines of dramatic theory and practice, literary criticism and storytelling, and aspects of psychology and communication arts and sciences.

In the area of implementation, much ongoing work can be appropriated. We must explore and refine existing AI techniques for understanding, inference, and computational representation of character. Techniques for constructing and enacting characters can also be imported from the field of computer game design. Expert-systems techniques can be applied to such "soft" problems as learning and assimilating the user's style and preferences, developing navigational strategies, and creating alternate representations. Work on such technologies as language and speech processing, paralinguistics, story generation, image recognition, and intelligent animation can be refocused and revitalized by the agents platform.

Finally, rapid prototyping techniques must be developed to facilitate user testing and evaluation. If we can continue to gather feedback from individual users and inspiration from popular culture as a whole, then the notion of agents will evolve—as it should—in collaboration with the people from whose fantasies it arose.

References

Brennan, S. 1990. Conversation as Direct Manipulation: An Iconoclastic View. In *The Art of Human-Computer Interface Design,* ed. B. Laurel, 393–404. Reading, Mass.: Addison-Wesley.

Brennan, S. 1984. Interface Agents, Technical Report, Atari Systems Research Laboratory, Sunnyvale, California.

Buxton, W. 1990. The Natural Language of Interaction: A Perspective on Nonverbal Dialogues. In *The Art of Human-Computer Interface Design,* ed. B. Laurel, 405–416. Reading, Mass.: Addison-Wesley.

Carbonell, J. G. 1980. Towards a Process Model of Human Personality Traits. *Artificial Intelligence* 15:49–50.

Chen, M., and Leahy, F. 1990. A Design for Supporting New Input Devices. In *The Art of Human-Computer Interface Design,* ed. B. Laurel, 299–308. Reading, Mass.: Addison-Wesley.

Crowston, K., and Malone, T. W. 1988. Intelligent Software Agents. *Byte* 13(13): 267–274.

Hayes-Roth, F.; Waterman, D. A; and Lenat, D. B., eds. 1983. *Building Expert Systems.* Teknowledge Series in Knowledge Engineering 1. Reading, Mass.: Addison-Wesley.

Kay, A. 1984. Computer Software. *Scientific American* 251(3): 52–59.

Lakoff, G., and Johnson, M. 1980. *Metaphors We Live By.* Chicago: University of Chicago Press.

Laurel, B. 1986a. Interface as Mimesis. In *User-Centered System Design: New Perspectives on Human-Computer Interaction*, eds. D. A. Norman and S. Draper. Hillsdale, N.J.: Lawrence Erlbaum..

Laurel, B. 1986b. Toward the Design of a Computer-Based Interactive Fantasy System. Ph.D. diss., Computer Science Department, The Ohio State University.

Lebowitz, M. 1984. Creating Characters in a Story-Telling Universe. *Poetics* 13:171–194.

Meehan, J. R. 1976. The Metanovel: Writing Stories by Computer. Ph.D. diss., Computer Science Department, Yale University.

Mountford, J., and Gaver, W. W. 1990. Talking and Listening to Computers. In *The Art of Human-Computer Interface Design,* ed. B. Laurel, 319–334. Reading, Mass.: Addison-Wesley.

Oren, T.; Salomon, G.; Kreitman, K.; and Don, A. 1990. Guides: Characterizing the Interface. In *The Art of Human-Computer Interface Design,* ed B. Laurel, 367–382. Reading, Mass.: Addison-Wesley.

Schank, R. C., and Lebowitz, M. 1979. The Use of Stereotype Information in the Comprehension of Noun Phrases. Alexandria, Va.: Defense Technical Information Center.

Schwamberger, J. 1980. The Nature of Dramatic Character. Ph.D. diss., Department of Theatre, The Ohio State University.

Chapter 5

Designing Agents as if People Mattered

Thomas Erickson

One of Apple Computer's buildings used to have an advanced energy management system. Among its many features was the ability to make sure lights were not left on when no one was around. It did so by automatically turning the lights off after a certain interval, during times when people weren't expected to be around. I overheard the following dialogue between a father and his six year old daughter, one Saturday evening at Apple. The energy management system had just noticed that the lights were on during 'off hours,' and so it turned them off.

Daughter: "Who turned out the lights?"

Father: "The computer turned off the lights."

Daughter (pause): "Did you turn off the lights?"

Father: "No, I told you, the computer turned off the lights."

(someone else manually turns the lights back on)

Daughter: "Make the computer turn off the lights again!"

Father (with irony in his voice): "It will in a few minutes."

I like this vignette. It illustrates a number of the themes we're going to be exploring in this chapter. It is evident that the child is struggling to understand what is going on. She clearly had a model of how the world worked: people initiate actions; computers don't. But the world didn't behave as expected. Even after double checking to make sure Dad really didn't turn off the lights, she still assumed that ultimately he was in control: surely he could make the computer turn off the lights again. In this, too, she was mistaken. One wonders how the little girl revised her model of the world to account for the apparently capricious, uncontrollable, but semi-predictable behavior of the computer. The computer as weather? The computer as demigod?

Just like the little girl, we all strive to make sense of our world. We move through life with sets of beliefs and expectations about how things work. We try to understand what is happening. We make up stories about how things work. We try to change things. We make predictions about what will happen next. The degree to which we succeed in doing these things is the degree to which we feel comfortable and in control of our world.

As the opening vignette illustrates, we have no guarantees that technology will behave in accordance with our expectations and wishes. We may suddenly find ourselves in the dark, wondering what on earth happened. The goal of this chapter is to explore ways of preventing this. The central theme is that we need to focus not just on inventing new technologies, not just on making them smarter, but on designing technologies so that they fit gracefully into our lives.

Agents are a case in point. As this volume illustrates, a lot of work is being directed at the development of agents. Researchers are exploring ways to make agents smarter, to allow them to learn by observing us, to make them appear more lifelike. However, relatively little work is being focused on how people might actually experience agents and on how agents might be designed so that we feel comfortable with them.

What Does "Agent" Mean?

To begin, let's take a look at the concept of agent. "Agent" is the locus of considerable confusion. Much of this confusion is due to the fact that "agent" has two different meanings that are often conflated.

One way in which the word is used is to designate an autonomous or semi-autonomous computer program. An agent is a program that is, to some degree, capable of initiating actions, forming its own goals, constructing plans of action, communicating with other agents, and responding appropriately to events—all without being directly controlled by a human. This sense of "agent" implies the existence of particular functional capacities often referred to as intelligence, adaptivity, or responsiveness. To discuss agents in this sense of the term, I will use the phrase *adaptive functionality*.

The second meaning of agent is connected with what is portrayed to the user. Here, "agent" is used to describe programs which *appear* to have the characteristics of an animate being, often a human. This is what I will call the *agent metaphor*. The agent metaphor suggests a particular model of what the program is, how it relates to the user, and what its capabilities and functions are. Examples of the agent metaphor include the bow-tied human figure depicted in Apple's Knowledge Navigator video (Apple 1987), the digital butler envisioned by Negroponte (see chapter 3 in this volume), and the Personal Digital Parrot described by Ball and his colleagues (see chapter 10 in this volume).

Now, of course, these two meanings of agent often go together. A common scenario is that of a program which intercepts incoming communications and schedules meetings based on a set of rules derived from its understanding of its user's schedule, tasks, and responsibilities. Such a program might be portrayed using the metaphor of an electronic secretary and would, of course, require adaptive functionality to learn and appropriately apply the rules. But it is important to recognize that the metaphor and functionality can be decoupled. The adaptive functionality that allows the 'agent' to perform its task need not be portrayed as a talking head or animated character: it could, for example, be presented as a smart, publicly accessible calendar. Thus, someone wanting to schedule a meeting could log on to it and directly schedule a meeting in an available slot. The rules would still be present, but rather than being portrayed through an agent which handled the scheduling, they would be reflected in which (if any) calendar slots were made available to the person seeking the meeting.

It is important to distinguish between these two meanings of agent because each gives rise to different problems. Adaptive functionality raises a number of design issues—as we saw in the opening vignette—that are independent of how it is portrayed to users. Programs that take initiative, attempt to act intelligently (sometimes failing), and change their behavior over time fall outside our range of experience with computer programs. Likewise, the agent metaphor has its own set of problems that are distinct from those caused by adaptive functionality. Portraying a program as a human or animal raises a variety of expectations that designers have not had to deal with in the past.

In this chapter I will explore the difficulties surrounding adaptive functionality and the agent metaphor, respectively. In the first case, I describe the three basic problems that computer researchers and developers will have to address, regardless of whether or not they use an agent metaphor. In the second case, I discuss how people react to the agent metaphor and consider the implications of these reactions for designing agents. Finally, I look beyond the surface of the agent metaphor and note that it suggests a very different conceptual model for human-computer interfaces. This model, in turn, has implications for when and how the agent metaphor should be used. Throughout the chapter, the ultimate concern is with how to design agents that interact gracefully with people. What good are agents? When should functionality—adaptive or not—be portrayed through the agent metaphor? What benefits does depicting something as an agent bring, and what sorts of drawbacks? While there are no absolute answers, an understanding of some of the tradeoffs, as well as issues that require further research, can only aid us as we move into the future.

Adaptive Functionality: Three Design Issues

Whether our future is filled with agents or not, there is no question that there will be lots of adaptive functionality. Consider just a few of the things brewing in university and industry laboratories:

- After observing its user performing the same set of actions over and over again, a computer system offers to produce a system-generated program to complete the task (Cypher 1991).

- An adaptive phone book keeps track of which numbers are retrieved; it then uses that information to increase the accessibility of frequently retrieved numbers (Greenberg and Witten 1985).

- A "learning personal assistant" fits new appointments into the busy calendar of its user, according to rules inferred by observing previous scheduling behavior (Mitchell et al. 1995).

- A multi-user database notices that over time certain seemingly unrelated bibliographic records—call them X and Y—are frequently retrieved in the same search session. It uses that information to increase the probability that Y is retrieved whenever X is specified, and vice versa (Belew 1989).

- A full text database allows its users to type in questions in plain English. It interprets the input, and returns a list of results ordered in terms of their relevance. Users can select an item, and tell it to 'find more like that one' (Dow Jones 1989).

- A variety of recognition systems transform handwriting, speech, gestures, drawings, or other forms of human communication from fuzzy, analog representations into structured, digital representations.

In general, systems with adaptive functionality are doing three things:

- Noticing: trying to detect potentially relevant events

- Interpreting: trying to recognize the events (generally, this means mapping the external event into an element in the system's 'vocabulary') by applying a set of recognition rules

- Responding: acting on the interpreted events by using a set of action rules, either by taking some action that affects the user, or by altering their own rules (i.e. learning)

Thus, a speech recognition system tries to *notice* sounds that may correspond to words, tries to *interpret* each sound by matching it to a word in its vocabulary (using rules about phonetics and what the user is likely to be saying at the moment), and then *responds* by doing an action that corresponds to the word it recognized, reporting an error if it couldn't interpret the word, or adjusting its recognition rules if it is being trained.

Such adaptive functionality holds great promise for making computer systems more responsive, personal, and proactive. However, while such functionality is necessary for enhancing our systems, it is not sufficient. Adaptive functionality does no good if it is not, or can not be used; it may do harm if it confuses its users, interferes with their work practices, or has unanticipated effects.

Notice that there are many chances for adaptive functionality to fail. The system may fail to notice a relevant event (or may mistakenly notice an irrelevant event). It may misinterpret an event that has been noticed. Or it may respond incorrectly to an event that it has correctly noticed and interpreted (that is, the system does everything right, but the rules that it has for responding to the event don't match what the user expects). These failures are important to consider because they have a big impact on the user's experience. Let's take a closer look at some of the design issues which are raised by adaptive functionality.

Understanding: What Happened and Why?

Consider an intelligent tutoring system that is teaching introductory physics to a teenager. Suppose the system notices that the student learns best when information is presented as diagrams and adapts its presentation appropriately. But even as the system is watching for events, interpreting them, and adjusting its actions, so is the student watching the system, and trying to interpret what the system is doing. Suppose that after a while the student notices that the presentation consists of diagrams rather than equations: it is likely that the student will wonder why: 'Does the system think I'm stupid? If I start to do better, will it present me with equations again?' There is no guarantee that the student's interpretations will correspond with the system's. How can such potentially negative misunderstandings on the user's part be minimized?

Control: How Can I Change It?

If the system makes an error—either because it has failed in notification or interpretation, or because its actions are not in line with the users wishes or expectations—what should the design response be? In most circumstances the user ought to be given a way to take control of the system and to undo what the adaptive functionality has wrought. But how is this to be done?

The problem is not simply one of providing an undo capability. That works well for today's graphic user interfaces where users initiate all actions and the "undo" command can be invoked when a mistake is made. However, with adaptive functionality, the difficulty is that the user did not initiate the action. This leads to several problems.

First, since the user didn't initiate the change, it may not be clear how to undo it. Thus, the student who wants the teaching system to continue presenting equations will have no idea what to do, or even where to look, to make the system return to its earlier behavior. This is complicated by the fact that it may take the user a while to notice that the system has changed in an undesirable way, and so clues about what actually happened have vanished.

Second, there may be a mismatch between the user's description of what has happened and the system's description of its action. What the user notices may be only a side effect of the system's action. Users may need assistance in discovering what the relevant action was in the first place, and it is an open question of whether the system will be able to provide it. If the tutoring system shifted to *content* which just happened to consist of diagrams, a student searching for a way to modify the *style* of presentation may be baffled. If the energy management system describes its action as shutting off a particular power subsystem, a user searching for a way to control the lights on the fourth floor may have difficulty.

All of this presupposes that the users understand that the system can be controlled in the first place. What kind of model of the system is necessary to make this clear? It would be important for the model not only to indicate what aspects of the system can be controlled, but to provide an obvious representation and set of methods for exercising control.

Prediction: Will it Do What I Expect?

Prediction goes hand in hand with understanding and trying to control what is happening. Let's take a close look at an actual example of adaptive functionality, found in a program called DowQuest (Dow Jones 1989). DowQuest is a commercially available system with a basic command line interface, but very sophisticated functionality. It provides access to the full text of the last 6 to 12 months of over 350 news sources and permits users to retrieve information via relevance feedback (Stanfill and Kahle 1986).

Rather than using a sophisticated query language, DowQuest allows users to type in a sentence (e.g. 'Tell me about the eruption of the Alaskan volcano'), get a list of articles, and then say—in essence—'find more like that one.' Figures 1 and 2 show two phases of the process of constructing a query. In figure 1 the user has entered a question and pressed return. DowQuest does not try to interpret the meaning of the question; in the example shown, the system will drop out the words "tell," "me," "about," "the," and "of," and use the lower frequency words to search the database. Next the system returns the titles of the 16 most 'relevant' articles, where relevance is defined by a sophisticated statistical algorithm based on a variety of features over which the user has no control (and often no knowledge). While this list frequently contains articles relevant to the user's question, it also usually contains items which appear—to the user—to be irrelevant. At this point, the user has the option of reading the articles retrieved or continuing to the second phase of the query process.

In phase 2 of the process (figure 2), the user tells the system which articles are good examples of what is wanted. The user may specify an entire article or may open an article and specify particular paragraphs within it. The system takes the full text of the selections, drops out the high frequency noise words, and uses a limited number of the most informative words for use in the new query. It then returns a new list of the 16 'most relevant' items. This second, relevance feedback phase may be repeated as many times as desired.

New users generally had high expectations of DowQuest: it seemed quite intelligent. However, their understanding of what the system was doing was quite different from what the system was actually doing. The system appeared to un-

```
tell me about the eruption of the alaskan volcano
DOWQUEST          STARTER LIST      HEADLINE PAGE 1 OF 4
    1 OCS: BILL SEEKS TO IMPOSE BROAD LIMITS ON INTERIOR . . .
        INSIDE ENERGY, 11/27/90  (935 words)
    2 Alaska Volcano Spews Ash, Causes Tremors
        DOW JONES NEWS SERVICE , 01/09/90  (241)
    3 Air Transport: Volcanic Ash Cloud Shuts Down All Four . . .
        AVIATION WEEK and SPACE TECHNOLOGY, 01/01/90  (742)
    4 Volcanic Explosions Stall Air Traffic in Anchorage
        WASHINGTON POST: A SECTION, 01/04/90  (679)
                    * * * * *
```

Figure 1. The first phase of DowQuest interaction: the user types in a 'natural language' query and the system searches the database using the non-'noise words' in the query and returns a list of titles of the 'most relevant' articles.

```
search 2 4 3
DOWQUEST          SECOND SEARCH   HEADLINE PAGE 1 OF 4
    1 Air Transport: Volcanic Ash Cloud Shuts Down All Four . . .
        AVIATION WEEK and SPACE TECHNOLOGY, 01/01/90  (742 words)
    2 Alaska Volcano Spews Ash, Causes Tremors
        DOW JONES NEWS SERVICE , 01/09/90  (241)
    3 Volcanic Explosions Stall Air Traffic in Anchorage
        WASHINGTON POST: A SECTION, 01/04/90  (679)
    4 Alaska's Redoubt Volcano Gushes Ash, Possibly Lava
        DOW JONES NEWS SERVICE , 01/03/90  (364)
                    * * * * *
```

Figure 2. The second phase of DowQuest interaction: the user instructs the database to find more articles like 2, 3 and 4, (of figure 1) and the system returns a new set of relevant articles. (Note that the first three, 'most relevant' articles are those that were fed back (an article is most 'like' itself); the fourth article is new.

derstand plain English; but in reality it made more effort to understand the question that was typed in—it just used a statistical algorithm. Similarly, the system appeared to be able to 'find more items like this one'; but again, it had no understanding of what an item was like—it just used statistics. These differences were important because they led to expectations that could not be met.

Users' expectations were usually dashed when, in response to the first phase of the first query, DowQuest returned a list of articles containing many obviously irrelevant items. When this happened some users concluded that the system was 'no good,' and never tried it again. While reactions like this may seem hasty and extreme, they are not uncharacteristic of busy people who do not love technology for its own sake. Furthermore, such a reaction is perfectly appropriate in the case of conventional application: a spreadsheet that adds incorrectly should be rejected. Users who had expected DowQuest to be intelligent could plainly see that it was not. They did not see it as a semi-intelligent system that they had control over and that would do better as they worked with it. This was quite ironic, as the second stage of the process, relevance feedback, was the most powerful and helpful aspect of the system.

Only a few users gave up after the first phase. However, efforts to understand what was going on and to predict what would happen continued to influence their behavior. In the second phase of a DowQuest query, when users requested that the system retrieve more articles 'like that one,' the resulting list of articles was ordered by 'relevance.' While no computer scientist would be surprised to find that an article is most relevant to itself, some ordinary users lacked this insight: when they looked at the new list of articles and discovered that the first, most relevant article was the one they had used as an example, they assumed that there was nothing else relevant available and did not inspect the rest of the list. Obviously, a system with any intelligence at all would not show them articles that they had already seen if it had anything new.

DowQuest is a very compelling system. It holds out the promise of freeing users from having to grapple with arcane query languages. But, as is usually the case with adaptive functionality, it doesn't work perfectly. Here we've seen how users have tried to understand how the system works (it's smart!) and how their expectations have shaped their use of the system.

How can designers address these problems? One approach is to provide users with a more accurate model of what is going on. Malone, Grant, and Lai (see chapter 7 in this volume), advocate this sort of approach, with their dictum of 'glass boxes, not black boxes,' suggesting that agents' rules be made visible to and modifiable by users. This is certainly a valid approach, but it is not likely to always work. After all, the statistical algorithm which computes the 'relevance' of stories is sufficiently complex that describing it would probably be futile, if not counterproductive, and allowing users to tinker with its parameters would probably lead to disaster. In the case of DowQuest, perhaps the aim should not be to give users an accurate picture of what is going on. One approach might be to encourage users to accept results that seem to be of low quality, so that they will use the system long enough to benefit from its sophistication. Another approach might be to construct a 'fictional' model of what the system is doing, something that will set up the right expectations, but without exposing them to the full complexity of the system's behavior. See Erickson and Salomon (1991) and Erickson (1995) for a discussion of other issues in this task domain, and a glimpse of one type of design solution.

Understanding how to portray a system which exhibits partially intelligent behavior is a general problem. Few will dispute that, for the foreseeable future, intelligent systems will fall short of the breadth and flexibility which characterize human-level intelligence. But how can the semi-intelligence of computer systems be portrayed? People have little if any experience with systems which are extremely (or even just somewhat) intelligent in one narrow domain, and utterly stupid in another, so appropriate metaphors or analogies are not easy to find. Excellent performance in one domain or instance is likely to lead to expectations of similar performance everywhere. How can these expectations be controlled?

The Agent Metaphor: Reactions and Expectations

In this section I turn to the agent metaphor and the expectations it raises. Why should adaptive functionality be portrayed as an agent? What is gained by having a character appear on the screen, whether it be a bow-tied human visage, an animated animal character, or just a provocatively named dialog box? Is it somehow easier or more natural to have a back-and-forth dialog with an agent than to fill in a form that elicits the same information? Most discussions that advance the cause of agents focus on the adaptive functionality that they promise—however, as I've already argued, adaptive functionality need not be embodied in the agent metaphor. So let's turn to the question of what good are agents as ways of *portraying* functionality? When designers decide to invoke the agent metaphor, what benefits and costs does it bring with it?

First it must be acknowledged that in spite of the popularity of the agent metaphor, there is remarkably little research on how people react to agents. The majority of work has been focused either on the development of adaptive functionality itself or on issues having to do with making agents appear more lifelike: how to animate them, how to make them better conversants, and so on. In this section, we'll look at three strands of research that shed some light on the experience of interacting with agents.

Guides

The Guides project involved the design of an interface to a CD ROM–based encyclopedia (Oren et al. 1990; Salomon, Oren, and Kreitman 1989). The intent of the design was to encourage students to explore the contents of the encyclopedia. The designers wanted to create a halfway point between directed searching and random browsing by providing a set of travel guides, each of which was biased towards a particular type of information.

The interface used stereotypic characters such as a settler woman, an Indian, and an inventor (the CD-ROM subset of the encyclopedia covered early American history). The guides were represented by icons that depicted the guide's role—no attempt was made to reify the guide, either by giving it a realistic-looking picture or by providing information such as a name or personal history.

As users browsed though stories in the encyclopedia, each guide would create a list of articles that were related to the article being looked at and were in line with its interests. When clicked on, the guide would display its 'suggestions.' Thus, if the user were reading an article about the gold rush, the Indian guide might suggest articles about treaty violations, whereas the inventor guide might suggest an article about machines for extracting gold.

The system was implemented and was then tested on high school students. The students had a variety of reactions. They tended to assume that the guides, which were presented as stock characters, embodied particular characters. For example, since many of the articles in the encyclopedia were biographies, users would assume that the first biography suggested by a guide was its own. If the inventor guide first suggested an article on Samuel Morse, users often assumed that Morse was now their guide. Students also wondered if they were seeing the article from the guide's point of view (they weren't). And they sometimes assumed that guides had specific reasons for suggesting each story and wanted to know what they were (in line with users' general wish to understand what adaptive functionality is actually doing).

In some cases, the students also became emotionally engaged with the guides. Oren et al. (1990) report some interesting examples of this: "…the preacher guide brought one student to the Illinois history article and she could not figure out why. The student actually got angry and did not want to continue with the guide. She felt the guide had betrayed her." While anecdotes of users getting angry with their machines are common, stories about users getting angry with one interface component are much less so. In another case, a bug in the software caused the guide to disappear. Oren, et al., write: "One student interpreted this as '…the guide got mad, he disappeared.' He wanted to know '…if I go back and take his next choice, will he come back and stay with me?'" Here the tables are turned. The user infers that the guide is angry. While no controlled experiment is available, it is hard to believe that the user would have made such an inference if the suggested articles been presented in a floating window that had vanished.

While this evidence is anecdotal, it is nevertheless interesting and relevant. Here we again see users engaged in the effort to understand, control, and predict the consequences of adaptive functionality. What is particularly interesting is how these efforts are shaped by the agent metaphor, The students are trying to understand the guides by particularizing them and thinking about their points of view. One student wants to control his guide (the one that 'got mad and disappeared') by being more agreeable, suspecting that the guide will come back if his recommendations are followed. All of this happens in spite of the rudimentary level of the guides' portrayals.

Computers as Social Actors

Nass, and his colleagues at Stanford, have carried out an extensive research program on the tendency of people to use their knowledge of people and social rules to make judgments about computers. Two aspects of their results are interesting in relation to the agent metaphor. First, they show that very small cues can trigger people's readiness to apply social rules to computers. For example, simply having a computer use a human voice is sufficient to cause people to apply social rules to the computer (Nass and Steuer 1993). This suggests that the agent metaphor may be invoked very easily—human visages with animated facial expressions, and so forth, are not necessary. This is in accord with the finding from the Guides study, in which stereotypic pictures and role labels triggered attributions of individual points of views and emotional behavior. The second aspect of interest is the finding that people do, indeed, apply social rules when making judgments about machines.

Let's look at an example. One social rule is that if person B praises person A, a third person will perceive the praise as more meaningful and valid than if person A praises himself. Nass, Steuer, and Tauber (1994) designed an experiment to show that this social rule holds when A and B are replaced with computers. The experiment went something like this (it has been considerably simplified for expository purposes):

- In part 1, a person went through a computer-based tutorial on a topic.
- In part 2, the person was given a computer-based test on the material covered.
- In part 3, the computer critiqued the effectiveness of the tutorial in part 1.

The experimental manipulation was that in one condition, parts 1, 2, and 3 were all done on computer A (i.e. computer A praised itself), whereas in the second condition, computer A was used for giving the tutorial and computer B was used to give the test and critique the tutorial (i.e., B praised A). Afterwards, the human participants in the study were asked to critique the tutorial themselves. The result was that their ratings were much more favorable when computer B had praised A's tutorial than when computer A had praised itself. That is, they were more influenced by B's praise of A than by A's praise of itself.

The finding that people are willing apply their social heuristics to computers is surprising, particularly since the cues that trigger the application of the social rules are so minimal. In the above experiment, the only cue was voice. There was no attempt to portray the tutorial as an agent or personal learning assistant—no animation, no picture, no verbal invocation of a teacher role, just a voice that read out a fact each time the user clicked a button. This finding appears to be quite general. Nass and colleagues are engaged in showing that users apply a wide variety of social rules to computers, given the presence of certain cues: to date, these range from rules about politeness, to gender biases, to attributions about expertise (Nass, Steuer, and Tauber 1994; Nass and Steuer 1993).

While this research is important and interesting, there is a tendency to take it a bit too far. The finding that people apply social rules to interpret the behavior of computers is sometimes generalized to the claim that individuals' interactions with computers are fundamentally social (e.g., Nass, Steuer, and Tauber 1994; see also chapter by Ball et al., also in this volume). I think that this is incorrect. It is one thing for people to apply social heuristics to machines; it is quite another to assume that this amounts to social interaction, or to suggest that the ability to support social interaction between humans and machines is now within reach. Interaction is a two-way street: just as people act on and respond to computers, so computers act on and respond to people. Interaction is a partnership. But social interaction relies on deep knowledge, complex chains of inferences and subtle patterns of actions and responses on the part of all participants (see, for example, Goffman [1967]). Computers lack the knowledge, the inferential ability, and the subtlety of perception and response necessary to be even marginally competent social partners. Does this mean that this research should be disregarded? Certainly not. If anything, the willingness of people to apply social rules to entities that can't hold up their end of an anticipated social interaction raises more problems for designers.

Faces

Thus far we have looked at cases where rather minimal portrayals of agents have evoked surprising reactions. For an interesting contrast, let's move to the other end of the spectrum and examine work on extremely realistic portrayals of agents.

One of the more famous examples of a highly realistic agent is "Phil," an agent played by a human actor in the Knowledge Navigator video tape (Apple 1987). During the video, Phil interacts via natural language, and uses vocal inflection, direction of gaze, and facial expressions to support the interaction. While, as noted in the previous section, the intelligence and subtlety necessary to support such interaction is far beyond the capacities of today's software and hardware, it is possible to create portrayals of agents which synchronize lip movements with their speech and make limited use of gaze and facial expression (e.g. Takeuchi and Taketo 1995, and Walker, Sproull, and Subramani 1994).

Walker, Sproull, and Subramani (1994) report on a controlled study of human responses to two versions of a synthesized talking face that was used to administer a questionnaire. One group simply filled in a textual questionnaire presented on the computer. Two other groups listened while synthesized talking faces (a different one for each group) read a question, and then typed their answer on the computer. Compared to people who simply filled out the questionnaire, those who answered the questions delivered by the synthesized faces spent more time, wrote more comments, and made fewer errors. People who interacted with the faces seemed more engaged by the experience.

Of particular interest was the difference between people's responses to the two synthesized faces. The faces differed only in their expression: one face was stern, the other was more neutral. Although the difference in expression was extremely subtle—the only difference was that the inner portion of the eyebrows were pulled inward and downward—it did make a difference. People who answered questions delivered by the stern face spent more time, wrote more comments, and made fewer errors. Interestingly enough, they also liked the experience and the face less.

Is the Agent Metaphor Worth the Trouble?

So far it looks like the agent metaphor is more trouble than it's worth. Designers who use the agent metaphor have to worry about new issues like emotion and point of view and politeness and other social rules and—if they put a realistic face on the screen—whether people *like* the face's expression! Perhaps the agent metaphor should be avoided.

I think there are several reasons not to give up on agents. First, it is too soon to give up on the agent metaphor. The difficulties noted above are problems for designers—not necessarily for users. They may very well be solvable. We simply don't know enough about how people react to agents. Far more research is needed on how people experience agents. Second, the research by Nass and his colleagues suggests that we may not have much of a choice. Very simple cues like voice may be sufficient to invoke the agent metaphor. Perhaps our only choice is to try to control expectations, to modulate the degree to which the agent metaphor is manifested. It's not clear. The third reason is that I believe the agent metaphor brings some clear advantages with it.

The Agent Conceptual Model

We've discussed the two meanings of agent—adaptive functionality and the agent metaphor—and some of the new problems they raise. In this section I want to look below the surface of the agent metaphor at its most fundamental characteristics. The agent metaphor brings with it a new conceptual model, one that is quite different from that which underlies today's graphic user interfaces. It is at this level that the agent metaphor has the most to offer. To begin with, let's look at the conceptual model that underlies today's interfaces, and then we'll consider the agent conceptual model in relation to it.

The Object-Action Conceptual Model

Today's graphic interfaces use a variety of different metaphors. The canonical example is the desktop metaphor, in which common interface components such as folders, documents, and the trash can, can be laid out on the computer screen in a manner analogous to laying items out on a desktop. However, I don't think the details of the metaphors—folders, trash cans, etc.—are what is most important. Rather, it is the conceptual model that underlies them.

The underlying conceptual model of today's graphical user interfaces has to do with objects and actions. That is, graphic user interface elements are portrayed as objects on which particular actions may be done. The power of this object-action conceptual model is rooted in the fact that users know many things about objects. Some of the general knowledge that is most relevant to the objects found in graphic user interfaces includes the following:

- Objects are visible.
- Objects are passive.
- Objects have locations.
- Objects may contain things.

This knowledge translates into general expectations. An object has a particular appearance. Objects may be moved from one location to another. Because objects are passive, if users wish to move them, they must do so themselves. Objects that contain things may be opened, their contents inspected or changed, and then closed again.

Graphic user interfaces succeed in being easy to use because these expectations are usually met by any component of the interface. When users encounter an object—even if they have absolutely no idea what it is—they know that it is likely that they can move it, open it, and close it. Furthermore, they know that clicking and dragging will move or stretch the object, and that double clicking will open it. They know that if they open it up and find text or graphics inside it, they will be able to edit the contents in familiar ways, and close it in the usual way. Because this general knowledge is applicable to anything users see in the interface, they will always be able to experiment with any new object they encounter, regardless of whether they recognize it.

The Agent Conceptual Model

The agent metaphor is based on a conceptual model that is different from the object-action conceptual model. Rather than passive objects that are acted upon, the agent metaphor's basic components (agents, of course) have a degree of animacy and thus can respond to events. We'll call this the responsive agent conceptual model.

Consider some of the general knowledge people have about agents:

- Agents can notice things.
- Agents can carry out actions.
- Agents can know things.
- Agents can go places.

This knowledge translates into expectations for agents that differ from those for objects. Since agents can notice things and carry out actions, in contrast to inanimate objects where these attributes don't apply, the responsive agent conceptual model is well suited to representing aspects of a system which respond to events. The sorts of things an agent might notice, and the ways in which it might respond, are a function of its particular portrayal.

Another basic difference is that while objects can contain things, agents know things, and, as a corollary, can learn things. Thus, the agent conceptual model is suitable for representing systems which acquire, contain, and manage knowledge. What sort of things are agents expected to learn or know? That depends on the way in which the agent is portrayed. To paraphrase Laurel (1990), one might expect an agent portrayed as a dog to fetch the electronic newspaper, but one would not expect it to have a point of view on its contents. A 'stupid' agent might know only a few simple things that it is taught and might be unable to offer explanations for its actions beyond citing its rules; a more intelligent agent might be able to learn by example and construct rationales for its actions. Note that more intelligence or knowledge is not necessarily better: what is important is the match between the agent's abilities and the user's expectations. Ironically, the agent metaphor may be particularly useful not because agents can represent intelligence, but because agents can represent very low levels of intelligence.

Another difference between object-action and agent conceptual model is that agents can go places. Users expect objects to stay where they're put; agents, on the other hand, are capable of moving about. Where can agents go? That depends both on the particular portrayal of the agent, as well as on the spatial metaphor of the interface. At the very least, an agent is well suited for representing a process that can log onto a remote computer, retrieve information, and download it to its user's machine. Another consequence of an agent's ability to go places is that it need not be visible to be useful or active. The agent may be present 'off stage,' able to be summoned by the user when interaction is required, but able to carry out its instructions in the background.

Objects and Agents

These arguments about the differences between the object and agent conceptual models could be ignored. After all, interface components ignore many properties of the real things on which they are based. For example, 'Folder objects' in graphic user interfaces can be deeply nested, one inside another inside another inside another, unlike their real world counterparts. Yet in spite of this departure from our knowledge of the real world objects, it works well. Perhaps we could simply integrate adaptive functionality into what were formerly passive, unintelligent objects. It's easy to conceive of an interface folder that is 'smart,' or that can 'notice' particular kinds of documents and 'grab' them, or that can 'migrate' from a desktop machine to a portable when it is time to go home. However, the drawback of such a design tack is that it undermines the object-action conceptual model. If that tack were pursued, users wouldn't know as much about what they see on the screen. If they encounter a new object, what will it do? Perhaps it will just sit there, or perhaps it will wake up and do something. Perhaps double clicking will open it, or perhaps double clicking will start it running around, doing things.

I believe that there is much to be said for maintaining the separation between the object and agent conceptual models. It becomes a nice way of dividing up the computational world. That is, objects and agents can be used in the same interface, but they are clearly distinguished from one another. Objects stay what they are: nice, safe, predictable things that just sit there and hold things. Agents become the repositories for adaptive functionality. They can notice things, use rules to interpret them, and take actions based on their interpretations. Ideally, a few consistent methods can be defined to provide the users with the knowledge and control they need. That is, just as there are consistent ways of moving, opening, and closing objects, so can there be consistent ways of finding out what an agent will notice, what actions it will carry out, what it knows, and where it is. Such methods get us a good deal of the way to providing users with the understanding, control, and prediction they need when interacting with adaptive systems.

There is a risk of over emphasizing the importance of metaphors and conceptual models. Normally, people are not aware of the conceptual model, the metaphor, or even individual components of the interface. Rather, they are absorbed in their work, accomplishing their actions with the kind of unreflective flow that characterizes expert performance. It is only when there are problems—the lights go out, the search agent brings back worthless material, the encyclopedia guide vanishes—that we begin to reflect and analyze and diagnose.

But this is why metaphors and conceptual models are particularly important for adaptive functionality. For the foreseeable future, it will fall short of perfection. After all, even humans make errors doing these sorts of tasks, and adaptive functionality is immeasurably distant from human competence. As a consequence, systems will adapt imperfectly, initiate actions when they ought not, and act in ways that seem far from intelligent.

Concluding Remarks

In this chapter we've explored a number of problems that are important to consider when designing agents. First I noted that there are two distinct senses of agent: the metaphor that is presented to the user and the adaptive functionality that underlies it. Each gives rise to particular problems. The agent metaphor brings a number of expectations that are new to user interface design. And adaptive functionality raises a number of other issues that are independent of how the functionality is portrayed.

The chief challenge in designing agents, or any other portrayal of adaptive systems, is to minimize the impact of errors and to enable people to step in and set things right as easily and naturally as possible. We've discussed two approaches to this. One is to make sure that adaptive systems are designed to enable users to understand what they're doing and predict and control what they may do in the future. Here I've suggested that the agent conceptual model may provide a good starting point, providing general mechanisms for accessing and controlling agents. Second, since the agent metaphor can create a wide variety of expectations, we need to learn more about how portrayals of agents shape users' expectations and then use that knowledge to adjust (which usually means lower) people's expectations. Research which focuses on the portrayal of adaptive functionality, rather than on the functionality itself, is a crucial need if we wish to design agents that interact gracefully with their users.

Acknowledgments

Gitta Salomon contributed to the analysis of the DowQuest system. A number of the findings about the use of DowQuest are from an unpublished manuscript by E. Meier and his colleagues (1990), carried out as project for a Cognitive Engineering class under the supervision of Don Norman, with Salomon and myself as outside advisors. The paper benefited from the comments of Stephanie Houde, Gitta Salomon, and three anonymous reviewers.

References

Apple. 1987. *The Knowledge Navigator.* Cupertino, Calif.: Apple Computer. Videotape.

Belew, R. K. 1989. Adaptive Information Retrieval: Using a Connectionist Representation to Retrieve and Learn about Documents. In Proceedings of the Twelfth Annual International ACMSIGIR Conference on Research and Development in Information Retrieval, 11–20. New York: ACM Press.

Cypher, A. 1991. EAGER: Programming Repetitive Tasks by Example. In Human Factors in Computing Systems: The Proceedings of CHI '91, 33–39. New York: ACM Press.

Dow Jones. 1989. Dow Jones News/Retrieval User's Guide. Princeton, N.J.: Dow Jones and Company.

Erickson, T. 1995. Feedback and Portrayal in Human Computer Interface Design. In *Dialogue and Instruction: Modeling Interaction in Intelligent Tutoring Systems*, eds. R. J. Beun, M. Baker, and M. Reiner, 302–320. Berlin: Springer-Verlag.

Erickson, T., and Salomon, G. 1991. Designing a Desktop Information System: Observations and Issues. In Human Factors in Computing Systems: The Proceedings of CHI '91, 49–54. New York: ACM Press.

Goffman, E. 1967. *Interaction Ritual.* New York: Anchor.

Greenberg, S., and Witten, I. 1985. Adaptive Personalized Interfaces—A Question of Viability. *Behavior and Information Technology* 4(1): 31–45.

Laurel, B. 1990. Interface Agents: Metaphors with Character. In *The Art of Human-Computer Interface Design*, ed. B. Laurel, 355–365. Reading, Mass.: Addison Wesley.

Mitchell, T.; Caruana, R.; Freitag, D.; McDermott, J.; and Zabowski, D. 1995. Experience with a Learning Personal Assistant. *Communications of the ACM* 37(7): 1–91.

Nass, C., and Steuer, J. 1993. Anthropomorphism, Agency, and Ethopoeia: Computers as Social Actors. *Human Communication Research* 19(4): 504–527.

Nass, C.; Steuer, J; and Tauber, E. R. 1994. Computers Are Social Actors. In Human Factors in Computing Systems: CHI '94 Conference Proceedings, 72–78. New York: ACM Press.

Oren T.; Salomon, G.; Kreitman K.; and Don, A. 1990. Guides: Characterizing the Interface. In *The Art of Human-Computer Interface Design*, ed. B. Laurel, 367–381. Reading, Mass.: Addison Wesley.

Salomon, G.; Oren, T.; and Kreitman, K. 1989. Using Guides to Explore Multimedia Databases. In Proceedings of the Twenty-Second Annual Hawaii International Conference on System Science, 3–11. Washington, D.C.: IEEE Computer Society.

Stanfill, C., and Kahle, B. 1986. Parallel Free-Text Search on the Connection Machine System. *Communications of the ACM* 29(12): 1229–1239.

Takeuchi, A., and Taketo, N. 1995. Situated Facial Displays: Towards Social Interaction. In Human Factors in Computing Systems: CHI '95 Conference Proceedings, 450–455. New York: ACM Press.

Walker, J.; Sproull, L.; and Subramani, R. 1994. Computers Are Social Actors. In Human Factors in Computing Systems: CHI '94 Conference Proceedings, 85–91. New York: ACM Press.

Chapter 6

Direct Manipulation Versus Agents: Paths to Predictable, Controllable, and Comprehensible Interfaces

Ben Shneiderman

U ser interface agents offer exciting new opportunities, but progress might be greater if goals and terms were clarified. Promoters of agent-oriented interfaces, as I understand them, wish to allow users to carry out complex actions at later times on multiple and, possibly, remote machines. As with most user interface designs, the challenge is to create a mechanism that is powerful, yet comprehensible, predictable, and controllable. A well-designed agent interface would enable users to specify tasks rapidly, be confident that they will get what they want, and have a sense of accomplishment when the job is done

If users are unsure about what the agent will do, if they cannot repeat previously successful actions, or if they cannot understand the instructions, dialog boxes, and error messages, they will not tolerate the interface. There is a growing danger that agents will be a deception and an empty promise. I fear that many promoters of "intelligent agents" have inadequately considered their designs, have not learned the lessons of history, and will omit adequate user testing to refine their vague notions (Shneiderman 1997).

General Concerns About Intelligent Interfaces

A generally troubling issue is the choice of "intelligent" as a label for much of agent technology. The obvious comparison is to humans. But is such a comparison necessarily a good thing? The metaphors and terminology we choose can shape the thoughts of everyone from researchers and designers to members of

Congress and the press. We have a responsibility to choose the best metaphor possible for the technology we create.

I am opposed to labeling computers as "intelligent" for several reasons. First, such a classification limits the imagination. We should have much greater ambition than to make a computer behave like an intelligent butler or other human agent. Computer-supported cooperative work, hypertext/hypermedia, multimedia, information visualization, and virtual reality are powerful technologies that enable human users to accomplish tasks that no human has ever done. If we describe computers in human terms, we run the risk of limiting our ambition and creativity in the design of future computer capabilities. In the same way that most of us have learned to use terminology not specific to any gender, we should now learn not to limit designers of computers with the tag "intelligent" or "smart."

Second, the quality of predictability and control are desirable. If machines are intelligent or adaptive, they may have less of these qualities. Usability studies at the University of Maryland show that users want the feelings of mastery, competence, and understanding that come from a predictable and controllable interface. Most users seek a sense of accomplishment at the end of the day, not the sense that some intelligent machine magically did their job for them.

Another reason I'm concerned about this label is that it limits or even eliminates human responsibility. I am concerned that if designers are successful in convincing the users that computers are intelligent, then the users will have a reduced sense of responsibility for failures. The tendency to blame the machine is already widespread and I think we will be on dangerous ground if we encourage this trend. As part of my work, I collect newspaper articles about computers, some of which bear the headlines "Victims of Computer Error Go Hungry," "IRS Computers Err on Refund Reports," and "Computers That 'Hear' Taking Jobs," all of which seem to absolve human operators by implicating the machine.

Finally, I have a basic philosophical objection to the "intelligent" label. Machines are not people, nor can they ever become so. For me, computers have no more intelligence than a wooden pencil. If you confuse the way you treat machines with the way you treat people, you may end up treating people like machines, which devalues human emotional experiences, creativity, individuality, and relationships of trust. I know that many of my colleagues are quite happy to call machines intelligent and knowledgeable, but I prefer to treat and think about machines in very different ways from the way I treat and think about people.

Learning From History

While some productive work has been done under the banner of "intelligent," often those who use this term reveal how little they know about what users want or need. The user's goal is not to interact with an intelligent machine, but to create, communicate, explore, plan, draw, compose, design, or learn. Ample evidence exists of the misguided directions brought by intelligent machines.

- Natural-language interaction seems clumsy and slow compared to direct manipulation and information-visualization methods that use rapid, high-resolution, color displays with pointing devices. Lotus HAL is gone, Artificial Intelligence Corporation's Intellect hangs on but is not catching on. Although there are some interesting directions for tools that support human work through natural-language processing (aiding human translators, parsing texts, and generating reports from structured databases), these functions are different from natural-language interaction.

- Speech I/O in talking cars and vending machines has not flourished. Voice recognition is fine for handicapped users and special situations, but it doesn't seem to be viable for widespread use in office, home, or school settings. Our recent studies suggest that speech I/O has a greater interference with short-term and working memory than hand-eye coordination for menu selection by mouse. Voice store and forward, phone-based information retrieval, and voice annotation have great potential, but these are not intelligent applications.

- Intelligent computer-assisted instruction, as compared to traditional CAI, served only to prolong the point at which users felt they were victims of the machine. Newer variations such as intelligent tutoring systems are giving way to interactive learning environments. in which students are in control and actively cresting or exploring.

- Intelligent talking robots with five-fingered hands and human facial features (a quaint fantasy that did well in Hollywood but not in Detroit) are mostly gone in favor of flexible manufacturing systems that enable supervisors to specify behavior with predictable results.

It seems that some designers continue to ignore this historical pattern and still dream of creating intelligent machines. It is an ancient and primitive fantasy, and it seems most new technologies must pass though this child-like animistic phase. Lewis Mumford identified this pattern (*Technics and Civilization*, Harcourt Brace, 1934) when he wrote "the most ineffective kind of machine is the realistic mechanical imitation of a man or another animal... for thousands of years animism has stood in the way of development."

What Is an Agent?

The first question I would ask a proponent of agents is—what is an agent (and what is not an agent)? Is a compiler an agent? How about an optimizing compiler? Is a database query an agent? Is the print monitor an agent? Is e-mail delivered by an agent? Is a VCR scheduler an agent? Most agent promoters that I ask say no to these questions because they have some vague dream that an agent is more "intelligent," probably anthropomorphic (human form), and somehow more adaptive than these applications.

Further questioning reveals a disturbingly vague set of responses. The usual example of having the computer monitor previous database queries so that it can automatically find relevant items in the future is often offered under the term "know-bots." However, the detailed mechanisms for such an agent are not well enough specified to allow an implementer to go to work. While many scenarios, including Apple Computer's famous 1987 videotape on the Knowledge Navigator, include an anthropomorphic representation of an agent, there are some designers who recognize the unwanted and unnecessary deception.

An appealing example emerged in recent stories on General Magic's Magic Cap. Your purchase of an airline ticket generates a planned action that checks the airline schedule two hours before departure and sends you e-mail if there is a delay. This is comprehensible, predictable, and specific and can be invoked or modified with a simple template or dialog box. Maybe the designers and marketeers like calling this an agent, but I'll bet that the public won't.

Looking at the Components

My autopsy on agents reveals these components:

- Anthropomorphic presentation
- Adaptive behavior
- Accepts vague goal specification
- Gives you just what you need
- Works while you don't
- Works where you aren't

The first three seem appealing at first but have proven to be counterproductive. The latter three are good ideas but can be achieved more effectively with other interface mechanisms. Our results with dynamic queries, user-controlled information visualization, query templates, direct manipulation, triggers, control panels, scheduled procedures, planned actions, and other concepts have been demonstrated to be effective, whereas the agent scenarios have a quarter century history of failure. Many of the same people who have made exaggerated promises for artificial intelligence, natural language processing, voice and handwriting recognition, and robots are now pushing agents.

Some designers continue to be seduced by anthropomorphic scenarios, even though these have repeatedly been rejected by consumers. The effective paradigm for now and the future is comprehensible, predictable, and controllable interfaces that give users the sense of power, mastery, control, and accomplishment.

The control panel on your computer, like the cruise control on your car (have you noticed that it is not called the intelligent driving assistant nor the auto agent?), emphasizes the ways you, the users, are in control. The users have goals and make choices, and the computer responds promptly to carry out the users' instructions. Users want to be in control.

Similarly, bank terminals have matured through the early phase in which anthropomorphic designs (Tillie the Teller, Harvey Wallbanker, BOB the Bank of Baltimore) dominated. The anthropomorphic styles are cute the first time, silly the second time, and an annoying distraction the third time. The designs have also passed through the second phase, focusing on technology, in which terms like "electro," "auto," and "compu" dominate. The third, and more durable, phase emphasizes names that convey the service provided to the user: CashFlow, MoneyMover, Money Exchange, 24-hour Bank, etc. Even the generic term Automated Teller Machines (ATMs) has become Advanced Transaction Machines.

Anthropomorphic terms and concepts have continually been rejected by consumers, yet some designers fail to learn the lesson. Talking cash registers and cars, SmartPhone. SmartHome, Postal Buddy, Intelligent Dishwasher, and variations have all come and gone. Even the recent variation of Personal Digital Assistant had to give way to the more service-oriented name now used in the Apple Newton ads: MessagePad. We'll leave it to the psychoanalysts to fathom why some designers persist in applying human attributes to their creations.

Adaptivity under the hood of your car is positive (the computer adjusts the carburetor based on air and engine temperature, etc.), but it is more tricky if it interferes with your choices. If your car decided that since your windshield wipers were on, you should be driving 20% slower, you would be quite unhappy. Similarly, you probably would not like cars to monitor your driving habits and if you had too many abrupt stops, it would slow you down or suggest that you take a rest. On the other hand simple, predictable linkages such as turning on the interior lights when you open the door are an acceptable automation. The lesson is to be cautious in choosing how automatic or adaptive systems should be. A few mistaken choices and the users are angry — high accuracy is necessary. There is a Gresham's Law of Interaction: Bad experiences drive out good users.

Vague goal specification is dangerous, just ask the Sorcerer's Apprentice. On the other hand, high-level goals that translate into many smaller predictable actions are great, for example, dragging a directory to the trash can conveniently delete all the contents with a single action (reversible where possible). Who would use a system that allowed a vague command like "Delete all old files" or even vaguer "Delete all useless files"? I believe that specific predictable actions are desired. Allow users to display files in order by age or by frequency of use and then allow them to invoke specific predictable actions.

Realizing a New Vision

The vision of computers as intelligent machines is giving way to one based on the use of predictable and controllable user interfaces. The computer appears to vanish, and users directly manipulate screen representations of familiar objects and actions to accomplish their goals. Predictable and controllable interfaces have certain desirable qualities that let users

- Have a clear mental model of what is possible and what will happen in response to each action
- Repeat desired sequences of action to achieve their goals
- Recover from errors easily
- Alter the interface to suit their needs

None of these qualities are found to the same degree in intelligent machines. Indeed, users often don't know what the machine is going to do next.

I see a future filled with powerful but predictable and controllable computers that will genuinely serve human needs. Visual, animated, colorful, high-resolution interfaces will be built on promising strategies like informative and continuous feedback, meaningful control panels, appropriate preference boxes, user-selectable toolbars, rapid menu selection, easy-to-create macros, and comprehensible shortcuts. Users will be able to specify rapidly, accurately, and confidently how they want their e-mail filtered, what documents they want retrieved and in what order, and how their documents will be formatted.

Our Human-Computer Interaction Laboratory has applied these principles to information-visualization methods that give users X-ray vision to see through their mountains of data. Techniques include tree maps and dynamic queries.

Tree Maps

Tree maps let users see (and hear) two to three thousand nodes of hierarchically structured information by using every pixel on the display. Each node is represented by a rectangle whose location preserves the logical tree structure and whose area is proportional to one of its attributes. Color represents a second attribute and sound a third.

Brian Johnson (Johnson and Shneiderman 1991) applied tree maps to Macintosh directory browsing. Figure 1 shows a screen from TreeViz, an interface that uses this technique. Users can set area to file size, color to application type. and sound to file age.

When users first try TreeViz they usually discover duplicate or misplaced files, redundant and chaotic directories, and many useless files or applications be cause they can now see all their files at once. They can then apply their human perceptual skills to detect patterns and exceptions with remarkable speed.

Treemaps have also been applied by David Turo (Asahi, Turo, and Shneiderman 1995; Turo and Johnson 1992) to the management of stock-market portfolios, sales data, voting patterns. and even sports (in basketball alone, there are 48 statistics on 459 NBA players, in 27 teams, in four divisions).

Marko Teittinen has built a more advanced viewer for the Windows environment which also does all the tasks of the File Manager, such as delete, rename,

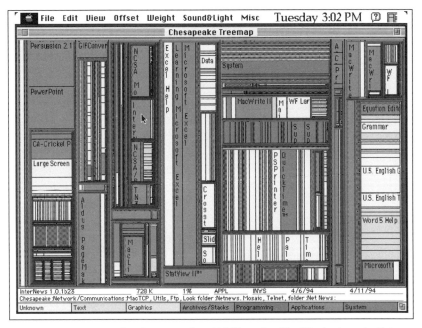

Figure 1. A treemap showing more than 600 files using TreeViz (written by Brian Johnson of UM). Alphabetical order and directory structure are preserved, color (shades of gray) shows file type, and area is proportional to file size.

copy, etc. WinSurfer™ lets network data managers and individual users gracefully and rapidly examine directories and invoke file actions.

Initially each tile's area matches the file size, and the color shows the file type, but you can also show file age or use a constant size. The overview shows you how you are using your disk space, and then zooming in on directories lets you get down deep into the details.

Dynamic Queries

These animations let you rapidly adjust query parameters and immediately display updated result sets, which makes them very effective when a visual environment like a map, calendar, or schematic diagram is available. The immediate display of results lets users more easily develop intuitions, discover patterns, spot trends, find exceptions, and see anomalies (Shneiderman 1994).

Figure 2 shows a screen from Dynamic HomeFinder, a prototype interface for real-estate agents that uses dynamic queries, written by Christopher Williamson (Williamson and Shneiderman 1992). Users can adjust the cost, number of bedrooms. and location of the A and B markers, among other characteristics, and points of light appear on a map to indicate a home that matches

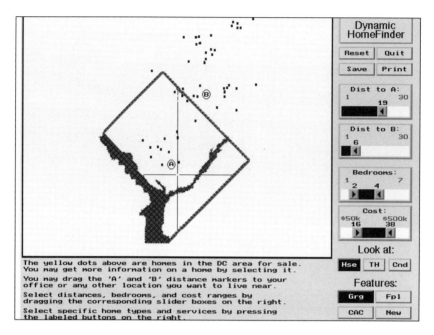

Figure 2. Dynamic HomeFinder lets users adjust sliders to express queries and see points of light, which represent homes for sale, come and go dynamically (written by Christopher Williamson of UM).

their specifications. Clicking on a point of light brings up a home description or image.

Users of Dynamic HomeFinder can execute up to 100 queries per second (rather than one query per 100 seconds as is typical in a database query language), producing a revealing animated view of where high- or low-price homes are found_and there are no syntax errors. Our empirical study of 18 users showed Dynamic HomeFinder to be more effective than a natural-language interface using Q&A from Symantec (Ahlberg, Williamson, and Shneiderman 1992, Williamson and Shneiderman 1992).

Dynamic queries can also be easily applied with standard text-file output, as figure 3 shows. Dynamic queries exemplify the future of interaction: you don't need to describe your goals, negotiate with an intelligent agent, and wait for a response, you *just do it!* Furthermore, dynamically seeing the results enables you to explore and rapidly reformulate your goals in an engaging videogame-like manner (Ahlberg and Shneiderman 1994, 1992).

Open problems in information visualization include screen organization, widget design, algorithms for rapid search and display, use of color and sound, and strategies to accommodate human perceptual skills. We also see promise in

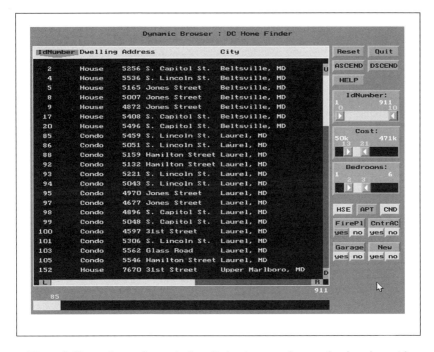

Figure 3. Dynamic queries method applied to home-real-estate database but with textual output that is rewritten after each slider is adjusted (written by Vinit Jain of UM).

expanding macro makers into the graphical environment with visual triggers based on the controlled replay of desired actions.

I especially want to encourage the exploration of new metaphors and visions of how computers can empower people by presenting information, allowing rapid selection, supporting personally specified automation, and providing relevant feedback. Metaphors related to controlling tools or machines such as driving, steering, flying, directing, conducting, piloting, or operating seem more generative of effective and acceptable interfaces than intelligent machine.

Back to a Scientific Approach

I close by invoking the basic principle of user interface research: move past first intuitions to scientific evaluations. If you think you have an idea for a successful agent, build one and test it against viable alternatives, such as direct manipulation on action templates. Measure learning time, speed of performance, error rates, retention over time, and subjective satisfaction. Then we can talk some more. But possibly, just possibly, all this heated debate is excessive, and agents will merely become the Pet Rock of the 1990s—everyone knows they're just for fun.

Acknowledgments

This article was based on two earlier pieces with the kind help of Jeffrey Bradshaw and the permission of ACM and IEEE: "Beyond Intelligent Machines," *(IEEE Software)* and "Looking for the Bright Side of Agents" *(ACM Interactions)*. (Full citations appear in the references.)

References

Ahlberg, C., and Shneiderman, B. 1994a. ALPHASLIDER: A Compact and Rapid Selector. In Proceedings of the ACM CHI94 Conference, 365–371. New York: ACM Press.

Ahlberg, C., and Shneiderman, B. 1994b. Visual Information Seeking: Tight Coupling of Dynamic Query Filters with Starfield Displays. In Proceedings of the ACM CHI94 Conference, 313–317. New York: ACM Press. Reprinted in Baecker, R. M.; Grudin, J.; Buxton, W. A. S.; and Greenberg, S., ed. 1995. *Readings in Human-Computer Interaction: Toward the Year 2000,* 2d ed., 450–456. San Francisco, Calif.: Morgan Kaufmann.

Ahlberg, C.; Williamson, C.; and Shneiderman, B. 1992. Dynamic Queries for Information Exploration: An Implementation and Evaluation. In Proceedings of the ACM CHI'92: Human Factors in Computing Systems, 619–626. New York: ACM Press.

Asahi, T.; Turo, D.; and Shneiderman, B. 1995. Using Treemaps to Visualize the Analytic Hierarchy Process. *Information Systems Research* 6(4): 357–375..

Johnson, B., and Shneiderman, B. 1991. Tree-Maps: A Space-Filling Approach to the Visualizaton of Hierarchical Information Structures. In Proceedings of the IEEE Visualization '91, 284–291. Washington, D.C.: IEEE Computer Society.

Plaisant, C.; Carr, D.; and Shneiderman, B. 1995. Image-Browser Taxonomy and Guidelines for Designers. *IEEE Software* 12(2): 21–32.

Shneiderman, B. 1997. *Designing the User Interface: Strategies for Effective Human-Computer Interaction,* 3d ed. Reading, Mass.: Addison-Wesley.

Shneiderman, B. 1995. Looking for the Bright Side of Agents. *ACM Interactions* 2(1): 13–15.

Shneiderman, B. 1994. Dynamic Queries for Visual Information Seeking. *IEEE Software* 11(6): 70–77.

Shneiderman, B. 1993. Beyond Intelligent Machines: Just Do It! *IEEE Software* 10(1): 100–103.

Turo, D., and Johnson, B. 1992. Improving the Visualization of Hierarchies with Treemaps: Design Issues and Experimentation. In Proceedings of IEEE Visualization '92, 124–130. Washington, D.C.: IEEE Computer Society.

Williamson, C., and Shneiderman, B. 1992. The Dynamic HOMEFINDER: Evaluating Dynamic Queries in a Real-Estate Information Exploration System. In Proceedings of the ACM SIGIRU92 Conference, 338–346. New York: ACM Press. Reprinted in Shneiderman, B., ed. 1993. *Sparks of Innovation in Human-Computer Interaction,* 295-307. Norwood, N.J.: Ablex.

Agents for Learning and Intelligent Assistance

CHAPTER 7

Agents for Information Sharing and Coordination: A History and Some Reflections

Thomas W. Malone, Kum-Yew Lai, and Kenneth R. Grant

I t is now more than ten years since we began work on the first of our "intelligent agent" systems: a system called the Information Lens, which was designed to help users intelligently find, filter, sort, and prioritize electronic messages. During these ten years, much has changed in the world: Computers are far cheaper, more powerful, and more common. Information networks are no longer the province of esoteric technical specialists, but have become the focus of significant public policy debate. And "intelligent agents" have moved from being a somewhat obscure research topic to being an important element in the product strategies of some of the world's largest technology companies.

As participants in one of the earliest projects developing "intelligent agents" (in the current sense of this term), we have taken the writing of this chapter as an opportunity to recount the history of our work and to reflect upon the lessons that can be drawn from it. This reflection has highlighted for us two key design principles whose importance has struck us repeatedly through the years and whose importance we believe is still not widely appreciated. We call these two principles the principles of *semiformal systems* and *radical tailorability*, and we will describe them further below.

Both these design principles are based upon the premise that computers are not likely, in the foreseeable future, to have the cognitive capabilities that humans do. It is, of course, true that computers can already do many things that humans cannot, and it is certainly possible that someday computers may be able to do so many human-like things that this premise will no longer be a useful basis for design. For the foreseeable future, however, it seems safe to assume significant limitations on the cognitive capabilities of computers.

The question this raises, therefore, is what role "intelligent" computational agents can play in the world of human activities. It is, of course, tempting to think of "intelligent agents" as being much like intelligent humans. We would like them to be able to perform important tasks by themselves, communicating with humans using natural human languages when necessary, and inferring as many things as possible without ever being told (e.g., Maes, also in this volume). But to the extent computers are unable to do these things in the ways that humans do, we may be led astray by models of computational agents that are based too closely on how humans behave. For instance, computational agents that try to communicate using natural language but have severely limited capabilities for doing so may be much less useful than agents that simply use a restricted artificial language which is easily understandable by humans. Similarly, agents that attempt to infer things without ever being told may cause more trouble than they save if they take actions based on seriously incorrect inferences.

Our experience has convinced us that a certain amount of humility is desirable in proceeding toward the goal of building truly useful computational agents. In particular, we have found the following two design principles to embody useful forms of humility:

1. Don't build computational agents that try to solve complex problems all by themselves. Instead, build systems where the boundary between what the agents do and what the humans do is a flexible one. We call this the principle of *semiformal systems* because it involves blurring the boundary between formally represented information acted upon by agents and informally represented information acted upon by humans.

2. Don't build agents that try to figure out for themselves things that humans could easily tell them. Instead, try to build systems that make it as easy as possible for humans to see and modify the same information and reasoning processes their agents are using. We call this the principle of *radical tailorability* because one way of applying this principle is to create "tailoring languages" with which people who are not skilled programmers can easily "tailor" new applications for themselves.

In recounting the history of our work, we will attempt to illustrate the implications of these two design principles. We proceed as follows: First, we will describe the Information Lens system, an early intelligent tool for helping people find, filter, sort, and prioritize electronic messages. In addition to describing the design of the system, we will briefly report on empirical studies of the use of this system. Next, using this early work as a basis, we will describe in more detail the two design principles of semiformal systems and radical tailorability. Then, we will describe the Oval system, a much more general tool for supporting information sharing and collaboration. The Oval system can be thought of as a radically tailorable, semiformal environment in which communities of intelligent agents and humans can interact. Finally, we will describe a number of examples of agent-oriented applications we have developed in the Oval environment.

Information Lens: An Intelligent Tool for Managing Electronic Messages

In late 1984, we began work on the original version of the Information Lens (see Malone, Grant, Turbak, et al. [1987] and Malone, Grant, Lai, et al. [1988] for complete descriptions).

The system was motivated by a desire to help people cope intelligently with the increasingly common problem of having large amounts of electronic mail: it helped people filter, sort, and prioritize messages that were already addressed to them, and it also helped them find useful messages they would not otherwise have received. In some cases, the system responded automatically to certain messages, and in other cases it suggested likely actions for human users to take.

Key Ideas

The Information Lens system was based on four key ideas:

1. A rich set of semistructured message types (or frames) can form the basis for an intelligent information sharing system. For example, meeting announcements can be structured as templates that include fields for "date," "time," "place," "organizer," and "topic," as well as any additional unstructured information. These templates can help people compose messages in the first place (e.g., by reminding them of what information to include). More importantly from our present point of view, by putting much of the essential information in special fields, these templates also enable computational agents to automatically process a much wider range of information than would be possible with simple keyword methods or automatic parsing.

2. Sets of "if-then" rules can be used to conveniently specify automatic processing for these messages. These rules may include multiple levels of reasoning, not just Boolean selection criteria.

3. The use of semistructured message types and automatic rules for processing them can be greatly simplified by a consistent set of display-oriented editors for composing messages, constructing rules, and defining new message templates.

4. The initial introduction and later evolution of a group communication system can be much easier if there is an incremental adoption path, that is, a series of small changes, each of which has the following properties: (a) individual users can continue to use their existing system with no change if they so desire, (b) individual users who make small changes receive some

immediate benefit, and (c) groups of users who adopt the changes receive additional benefits beyond the individual benefits.

System Overview

In order to provide a natural integration of this system with the capabilities that people already used, the system was built on top of an existing electronic mail system. Users could continue to send and receive their mail as usual, including using centrally maintained distribution lists and manually classifying messages into folders. In addition, the Information Lens provided four important optional capabilities: (1) people could use structured message templates to help them compose their messages; (2) receivers could specify rules to automatically filter and classify messages arriving in their mailbox; (3) senders could include as an addressee of a message in addition to specific individuals or distribution lists, a special mailbox (named "Anyone") to indicate that the sender was willing to have this message automatically redistributed to anyone else who might be interested; and (4) receivers could specify rules to find and show messages addressed to "Anyone" that the receiver would not otherwise have seen (see figure 1). Our primary implementations of this system were in the Xerox Interlisp environment.

Messages

Figure 2 shows a sample of the highly graphical interaction through which users could construct messages using semistructured message templates. After selecting a field of a message by pointing with a mouse, the user could point with the mouse again to see the field's default value, an explanation of the field's purpose, or a list of likely alternatives for filling in the field. If the user selected one of these alternatives, that value was automatically inserted in the message text. The user could also edit any fields directly at any time using the built-in display-oriented text editor. Users who did not want to take advantage of these message construction aids could simply select the most general message type ("Message") and use the text editor to fill in the standard fields ("To," "From," and "Subject") just as they would have done in the underlying mail system.

The templates for different types of messages were arranged in an "inheritance hierarchy" with some message types being specializations of others (e.g., see Fikes and Kehler [1985]). For example, the "Seminar Announcement" template was a specialization of the "Meeting Announcement" template, and it included an additional field for speaker that was not present in "Meeting Announcements."

Rules

Just as the structure of messages simplified the process of composing messages, it also simplified the process of constructing rules for processing messages. For instance, figure 3 shows an example of the display-oriented editor used to con-

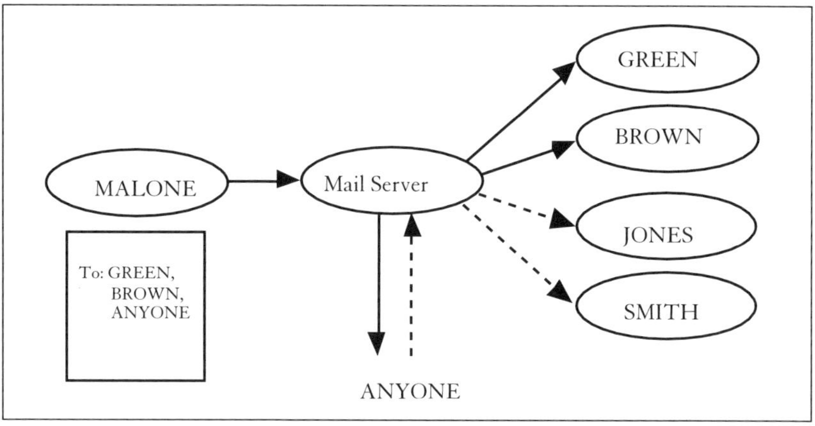

Figure 1. The Information Lens system includes components in the users' worksta-tions and in a central server (called "Anyone"). Messages that include "Anyone" as an addressee are automatically distributed (via the dotted lines) to all receivers whose in-terest profiles select the messages as well as to the other explicit addressees.

struct rules in the Information Lens system. This editor used rule templates based on the same message types as those used for message construction, and it used a similar interaction style with menus available for defaults, alternatives, and explanations.

Figure 4 shows some sample rules for performing actions such as moving messages to specific folders (figure 4a), deleting messages (figure 4b), and auto-matically "resending" messages to someone else (figure 4c). "Resending" a mes-sage is similar to "forwarding" it, except that instead of copying the entire origi-nal message into the body of a new message, the new message preserves the type and all but the "To" and "cc" fields of the original message. Rules could also "set characteristics" of a message that could then be tested by later rules (figure 4d). When the local rules finished processing all incoming messages, the numbers of new messages that had been automatically moved into different folders since the last time the folder was viewed were shown on a hierarchical display of the folder names. In order to help users understand and modify their rules, a simple explanation capability allowed users to see a history of the rules that fired on a given message.

In addition to the local rules applied when messages were retrieved to a user's workstation, an individual user could also specify central rules to select mes-sages addressed to "Anyone" that the user wanted to see (see figure 4e).

Group Use of Message Types

Users of systems like the Information Lens can take advantage of simple sorting rules, even if they do not use any of the specialized message templates the sys-

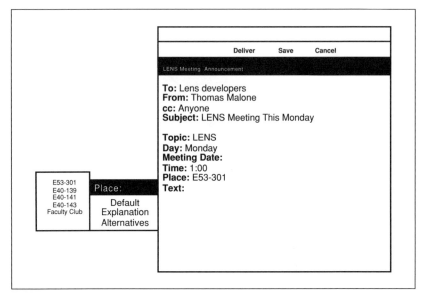

Figure 2. Messages are composed with a display-oriented editor and templates that have pop-up menus associated with the template fields. (Note: The format of screen displays in this figure and others throughout the chapter differ in minor ways because different figures are taken from different generations of the systems described.)

tem provides. But, to the extent that a group of people all use the same message templates, they can benefit even more from rules based on the shared message structures.

One of the important questions, therefore, is how groups of people can develop and evolve a shared language of common message types. One simple solution is to require everyone to use the same message types, perhaps determined by some central administrator or standards committee. Another, more complicated, solution is to let anyone create new message types as long as they also write "translation rules" that translate these types into and out of the common language.

Lee and Malone (1990) describe one way of categorizing all possible solutions to this translation problem and propose a hybrid solution called "Partially Shared Views" that combines many of the best features of the different schemes. Essentially this solution lets different (and possibly overlapping) groups of people develop and use shared sets of message type definitions (called "views"). When someone adopts a view, they can receive messages directly from other users of the view. When someone receives a message created in a view they have not adopted, the message is translated automatically into one of the message types they have adopted.

The most interesting case of this automatic translation occurs when the "for-

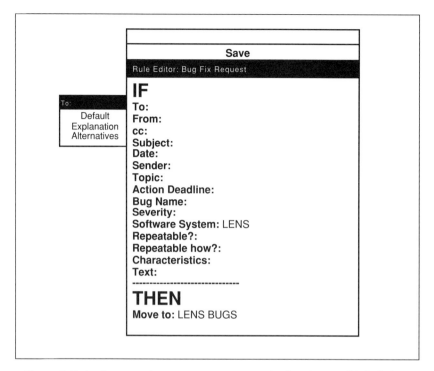

Figure 3. Rules for processing messages are composed using the same kind of editor and the same templates as those used for composing messages in the first place.

eign" message type is a specialization of one already known to the receiver. In this case, the foreign message type is automatically translated into the "nearest common ancestor" type known to both groups. For instance, if you received a "Seminar Announcement" message, and you had not adopted a definition for this type of message, then the message would be automatically translated into the nearest "parent" type, say "Meeting Announcement," which you had adopted. Information from any fields not present in "Meeting Announcements" (e.g., "Speaker") would simply be added into the "Text" field of the "Meeting Announcement" message. Then all the rules you had defined for "Meeting Announcements" would be applied to the incoming message.

Users' Experiences with Information Lens

In order to see how people outside our own group would actually use a system like the Information Lens, we worked for several years (approximately 1985-1988) with a corporate test site to implement a version of the system in their environment and observe their usage experience. These studies are described in

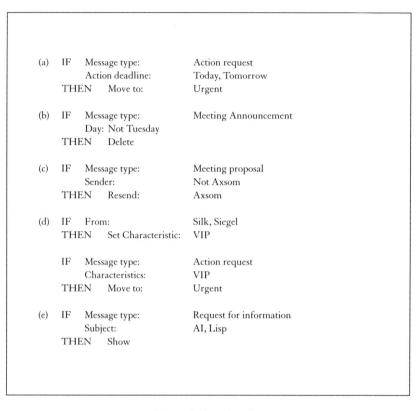

Figure 4. Sample rules.

detail by MacKay (1988) and MacKay et al. (1989). In this section we summarize some of the key results.

Can Nonprogrammers Use Rules? One of the most important questions we had was whether nonprogrammers would be able to use rules effectively. The test site we studied was very advanced in its use of computer technology, and a number of our test users were skilled computer programmers. However, our test sample also included secretaries, managers, and other non-computer scientists. We were happy to find that no one at the test site had trouble understanding how to create and use rules. Even users who had never had any computer programming experience at all told us they found the template-based method of constructing rules to be quite easy to use. For instance, one user, with no computer training, described his first experience with the rule editor as follows: "It's obvious. You just go into the [fields] and type whatever you want."

When Do Users Run Rules? When we designed the Information Lens system, we expected that people would use rules to sort and process their messages before reading the messages. However, it was also possible for users to read all their messages first and then apply the rules to sort the messages into folders. To our surprise, we found that a number of users preferred to use rules in this way. These users said they liked to feel "in control" by seeing all their messages before any rules moved them, and then they could use the rules to file the messages in folders for later retrieval. We called the first kind of users "prioritizers" and the second kind of users "archivers" (MacKay 1988).

What Kinds of Rules Do Users Write? In the sample of people we studied most carefully, users created an average of 15 rules each (with a range from 2 to 35 rules per person). The most common kind of rules sorted messages based on the distribution lists to which the messages were addressed. For instance, users often used rules to move messages addressed to a particular distribution list into a folder with the same name, thus creating a kind of computer conferencing system based on electronic mail.

Another important observation was that some of the users who reported the most satisfaction with the system had only a few rules. For instance, one user who was on the verge of being overwhelmed (with more than 30 messages per day), created only two rules: One rule moved messages into a special folder if their "Subject" field contained the name of a conference this person was organizing. The other rule moved messages into a different folder if they were addressed to this person by name (rather than simply to a distribution list of which this person was a member). This person said that these two rules "changed her life!"

Semiformal Systems and Radical Tailorability

In reflecting upon our experience with Information Lens, we had the feeling that there were some underlying—but largely inarticulate—design principles that contributed to its apparent success and that could be useful in designing many other kinds of systems. Eventually we were able to articulate two of these principles using the terms *semiformal systems* and *radical tailorability*.

Semiformal Systems

One of the things that struck us most strongly about our experience with Information Lens was the usefulness of letting people structure their messages to a certain degree (e.g., by putting some information in special fields), but still letting them include other unstructured information. For instance, there may well be times when people want to put "I don't know yet" in the "Place" field of a "Meeting Announcment" message. In this case, the system can still be useful, even though perhaps not as useful as it would be if the field contained the expected kind of information.

More generally, the agents in the Information Lens system operate in a very complex human-centered environment of interpersonal messaging. In this complicated environment, the agents "understand" very little of what is actually going on, but they can still be useful. This usefulness is possible, we believe, because the agents do simple things with the bits of structure they do "understand" and then "degrade gradually" (e.g., by doing nothing) when there is not enough recognizable structure for them to take any sensible action. These observations led us to become more reflective about the benefits of systems that formalize certain things for automatic processing by computers, while leaving other things informal for processing by humans.

Definition of Semiformal Systems. We eventually came to call such systems *semiformal systems*, and we defined a semiformal system as a computer system that has the following three properties:

1. it represents and automatically processes certain information in formally specified ways;

2. it represents and makes it easy for humans to process the same or other information in ways that are not formally specified; and

3. it allows the boundary between formal processing by computers and informal processing by people to be easily changed.

In the past, computer systems have almost always been at one extreme or the other. At one extreme are very highly structured systems like conventional databases and knowledge bases with strict requirements about the contents of different kinds of fields and with structured procedures for processing the information represented in the system. At the other extreme are very unstructured systems like conventional electronic mail and word processing where the computer's role is primarily to record, store, and transmit information that is to be understood only by people, not to "understand" or otherwise process the information it stores. The concept of semiformal systems opens up a vast middle ground between these two extremes and suggests how computers can be useful in a much wider range of ways than we have previously come to expect.

Semistructured information. One important consequence of this definition is that information in a semiformal system is "semistructured" with some structured elements such as named fields and some unstructured elements such as free text, voice, or images. It is also often useful for a semiformal system to be "tolerant" of unstructured or unexpected information, even in places where some kind of structured information might usually be expected.

Visible reasoning. Another important attribute of semiformal systems that is implied by this definition is that the reasoning processes used by the system are often accessible to their human users. In other words, rather than creating intelligent agents whose operations are "black boxes", designers should try to create "glass boxes" where the essential elements of the agents' reasoning can be seen and modified by users.

A serious risk, for example, of "learning agents" like those described by Maes (1997) is that agents will infer incorrect rules (or fail to infer correct ones) when users could have easily described the rules they actually wanted to use. A semi-formal approach to designing such systems would suggest that any attempts to have agents automatically "learn" from observing users' behavior should occur only *after* the system already provides a way for users to directly specify what they want.

Of course, this does not mean that unsophisticated computer users should be exposed to details of low-level programming languages. It does mean, however, that designers should try to create user interfaces where the essence of what is going on in a system is exposed to users in a form that is meaningful and understandable to them. One approach to part of this problem is suggested by the "explanation" facilities in traditional knowledge-based systems. Another approach is suggested by the principle of radical tailorability to be described below.

When Are Semiformal Systems Useful? Semiformal systems are most useful when we understand enough to formalize in a computer system some, but not all, of the knowledge relevant to acting in a given situation. We believe that this includes almost all of the real-world situations in which agents might be used. A number of commentators, for example, have pointed out that there is, in some sense, an essentially infinite amount of potential complexity in any real situation (e.g., Suchman 1983). On the other hand, there are also clearly many situations where patterns and structural knowledge can be useful.

The trick, we believe, is to design flexible systems that allow us to exploit the patterns and knowledge we understand when they are useful without getting in the way when they are not. And this is precisely the goal of the design principle we have called semiformal systems.

Radical Tailorability

Another aspect of the Information Lens system that struck us as being particularly important was the ability of users to change the formal structures that the system supported for them.

The most important example of this was the ability of users to create and modify their own mail-processing rules. It would, of course, have been possible to build a system with a few "pre-canned" and generally useful rules. It would also be possible (though not usually economically feasible) to have skilled programmers modify the rules used by people whenever the people's mail-processing needs changed. Neither of these alternatives, however, is as desirable as having a system that is easy enough to use that most people can understand their own mail processing rules and can change them whenever the need arises.

A second example of how people could change the formal structure of the Information Lens system was by modifying the message types. By adding new message types to their own system, individual users could simplify the creation of messages they frequently send. And by agreeing upon new message types to be shared in a group, users could make possible more powerful filtering rules for these new types of messages.

Both of these ways of modifying Information Lens are examples of how people can shape the formal structure in their systems to fit the situations in which the systems are used. This process of letting end users modify their own systems is often called "end user programming," and Information Lens embodied—in rudimentary form—a kind of end user programming we have since come to call *radical tailorability*.

Definition of Radical Tailorability. Loosely speaking, we call a system radically tailorable if it allows end users to create a wide range of different applications by progressively modifying a working system. Radically tailorable systems are not new; perhaps the best known examples of existing radically tailorable systems are spreadsheets. However, we believe it is useful to articulate two desirable properties of such systems in order to help create more systems with these properties.

First, we use the term "tailorable" to mean that these systems can be changed without ever "really programming." More specifically, by "tailorable," we mean that *end users* (not skilled programmers) can progressively modify a working system (such as a spreadsheet) without ever having to leave the application domain and work in a separate underlying "programming" domain. With conventional programming languages, it is, of course, possible to change a working application. Doing so, however, requires that someone (usually a trained programmer) modify instructions that are related in potentially very complex ways to what the end user of the application sees on the screen. In radically tailorable systems, on the other hand, changes are made directly in the context of a working application, usually on the same screens. In this way, radically tailorable systems can help reduce the "cognitive distance" between using an application and designing it (Hutchins, Hollan, and Norman 1986).

Second, we use the term "radically" to suggest that very large changes can be made by tailoring. Radically tailorable systems, therefore, differ from "ordinary" tailorable systems (such as word processing programs with "Preferences" parameters) in the degree to which users can create a wide range of substantially different applications. For instance, starting with the same blank spreadsheet, users can create applications ranging from personal budgeting to sales forecasting to corporate finance.

When Are Radically Tailorable Systems Useful? As the continuing needs for "maintenance" and "systems integration" of nearly all computer systems demonstrates, the need for adapting computer systems to the situations in which they are used is very pervasive.

One of the critical questions in determining whether a "radically tailorable" approach to system modification is feasible, however, is whether a designer can create a set of building blocks at the "right" level of abstraction. That is, the building blocks should not be so low-level that they require significant effort to do anything useful, nor so high-level that they require significant modification whenever the users' needs change (diSessa 1985).

Fortunately, our experiences with Information Lens led us toward a set of building blocks that turned out to be widely useful. To begin with, we were genuinely surprised at how useful the semistructured messages turned out to be. For instance, in one of our papers (Malone, Grant, Lai, et al. 1987), we described how adding a few specialized action types to certain kinds of messages greatly simplified the process of designing a variety of different applications such as computer conferencing, task tracking, and calendar management.

Even though simple versions of these new applications were relatively easy to program using the basic architecture in Information Lens, there were some obvious limitations to them. For instance, it was possible to automatically sort "Action Request" messages into a "To do" folder, but like any other folder, the table of contents format for messages in the folder would show only the "From," "Date," and "Subject" fields of the messages. To see other information (such as the "Due Date" or "Requestor"), we would have to display each message individually. Clearly this application called for a more general display format for the contents of objects in folders.

As we continued along this line of thinking, we felt ourselves inexorably drawn toward generalizing the Information Lens to include more types of objects (besides just messages), more types of display formats for collections of objects (besides the tables of contents for messages), and more types of agents (besides those used to sort and route messages). As described in the next section, the result of these generalizations became the system we called Oval.

Oval: A Radically Tailorable Tool for Information Management and Cooperative Work

In 1987, we began work on the first version of the Oval system[1] (Lai, Malone, and Yu 1988). The name "Oval" is an acronym for the four key components of the system: Objects, Views, Agents, and Links. Unlike the Information Lens system, which was focused exclusively on electronic messaging, we wanted Oval to be a much more general tool for supporting many kinds of cooperative work and information management applications. In particular, we had two primary goals in designing this system that differed from the goals of many previous systems to support similar tasks:

1 *Integration*. The system should combine many different kinds of formal and informal information and many different applications into a single integrated environment where people use a simple and consistent interface

for everything from reading mail to querying databases and where these applications can interact with each other.

2 *Tailorability.* The system should let ordinary people create and modify these applications for themselves without requiring the help of professional programmers.

In order to achieve these goals, the system helps people keep track of and share knowledge about various "objects" such as people, tasks, projects, companies and many other things with which they work. For example, people can use hypertext links to represent relationships between a message and its replies, between people and their supervisors, and between different parts of a complex product.

The system also lets people create various kinds of "intelligent agents" to help them organize and respond to this knowledge. For instance, people can use intelligent agents to find electronic messages in which they are interested, to notice overdue tasks, and to notify others of upcoming deadlines.

A key aspect of the system, for our purposes here, is that both the people and their agents use and modify the same knowledge base of linked objects. Among other things, this means that information people maintain in the system for their own purposes can also be used by their agents to be more helpful. For instance, information people store in the system about hierarchical reporting relationships and task assignments might also be used by their agents to select problem reports about projects for which people in a particular group are responsible.

In order to make it feasible for people to maintain many different kinds of information in the system, it must be both easy and useful for them to do so. By designing Oval as a radically tailorable system, we have tried to accomplish both of these goals.

Overview of Oval

Oval is based upon four key building blocks: *objects, views, agents,* and *links*. In the next four subsections, we provide an overview of how these four components allow us to expose semiformal knowledge to users in a way that is both visible and changeable. Much more detailed descriptions of the system features can be found in Lai, Malone, and Yu (1988) and Malone, Yu, and Lee (1989).

Objects. Semistructured *objects* represent things in the world such as people, tasks, messages, and meetings. Each object includes a collection of fields and field values and a set of actions that can be performed upon it. For example, Figure 5 shows a template for an object of type "Task." These objects are semistructured in the sense that users can fill in as much or as little information in different fields as they desire and the information in a field is not necessarily of any specific type (e.g., it may be free text, a link to another object, or a combination of text and links). Users see and manipulate these objects

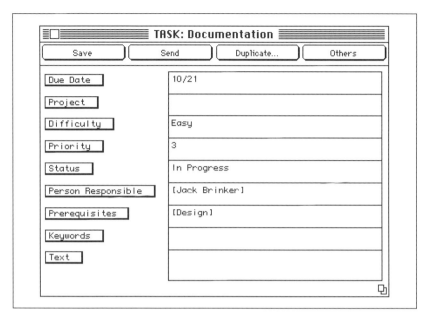

Figure 5. Objects can be edited with a simple template editor.
Fields can include text, graphics, or links to other objects.

via a particularly natural form of template-based interfaces.

These object types are arranged in a hierarchy of increasingly specialized types with each object type inheriting fields, actions, and other properties from its parents in the hierarchy. For example, objects include fields for "Name," "Keywords," and "Text" and standard actions (like "Save," "Send," and "Add Link") which can be performed on them. In addition, some object types have other specialized actions that are appropriate only for that kind of object. For instance, messages have actions like "Reply" and "Forward," and agents (see below) have a "Trigger" action that triggers them to start running.

Views. User customizable *views* summarize collections of objects and allow users to edit individual objects. For instance, figure 6(a) shows a "table" view that includes the values of selected fields from the tasks in the folder pertaining to a specific project. Users can easily tailor the format of these displays by selecting from a menu the fields they want to have included in the table.

In cases (like this one) where the objects in a folder are related to each other, Oval can also display these relationships in a "network" format. For instance, figure 6(b) shows the same folder, but with the display format changed to show the relationships represented by links in the "Prerequisites" field. In this case, the display resembles a simple PERT chart. Figure 6(c) shows the same folder

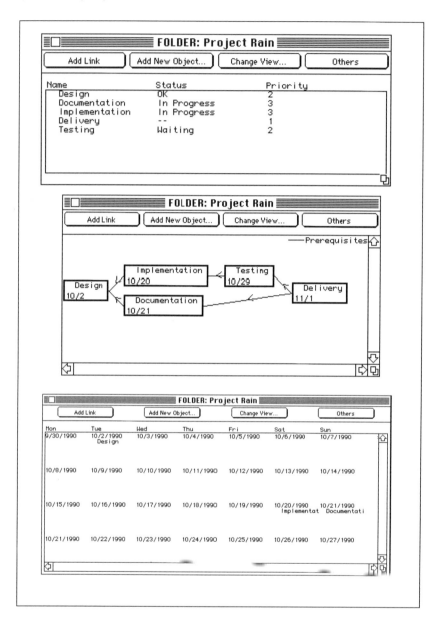

Figure 6. In (a), users can select which fields to display in tables that summarize a collection of objects. In (b), users can choose which fields to be used as edges in a network that summarizes the relationships among objects. Finally, in (c), users can choose a field containing dates that will be used to display the objects in a calendar.

of task objects with a third view, the "calendar" format which places objects in a calendar according to the dates shown in their "Due Date" fields.

Users can select any view format (e.g., table, network, or calendar) for any collection of objects. In keeping with the semiformal philosophy, the system will do its best to apply the view, even if it doesn't make sense for all the objects. For instance, if a calendar view contains objects for which there is no recognizable date in the appropriate field, those objects will be shown in a calendar cell called "No date."

Agents. Rule-based *agents* perform active tasks for people without requiring the direct attention of their users. Agents can be triggered by events such as the arrival of new mail, the appearance of a new object in a folder, or the arrival of a prespecified time. For instance, figure 7 shows an example of a simple agent designed to help a user keep track of tasks to be done. This agent is triggered whenever a task is added to the "New Tasks" folder or when a task already in the folder is changed.

When an agent is triggered, it applies a set of rules to a collection of objects. Rules contain descriptions of the objects to which they apply and actions to be performed on those objects. For instance, the agent shown in figure 7 includes several rules, one of which is shown. This rule finds any tasks with a "Due Date" less than today and copies them to the "Late Tasks" folder. Some other possible actions include moving and deleting objects from folders and mailing them to other users.

Embedded Descriptions. With the capabilities we have described so far, all rules must depend only on information contained in the objects to which they are being applied. For instance, a rule about a message can depend only on information contained in the message itself. It is often desirable, however, to be able to specify rules that also depend on other information contained elsewhere in the knowledge base. For instance, in the Information Lens system, if a user wanted to specify a rule that applied to all messages from vice presidents, the rule would have to include the names of all the vice presidents in the "From" field.

In Oval, it is possible to draw upon other information by having descriptions embedded within other descriptions. For instance, the rule shown in figure 8 is satisfied if the message is from any person with a job title that includes "vice president." To apply this rule, the system checks to see whether the string in the "From" field of the message is the same as the "Name" of any "Person" object in the knowledge base that satisfies the description.

Other agent actions. For users who can (and want to) write programs more complex than the sequences of rules described so far, it is a simple matter conceptually for systems like Oval to include "escapes" to more powerful scripting or programming languages. The current prototype of Oval illustrates this possiblity by allowing users to invoke any arbitrary program (written in Lisp, the language in which Oval is implemented) as the action of a rule. It would also be

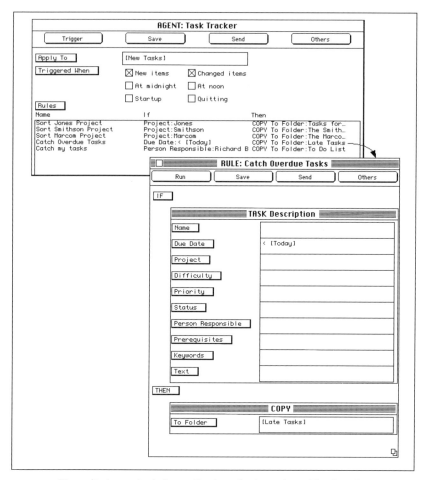

Figure 7. Agents include a collection of rules and specifications for when and where to apply them. Rules describe the objects that satisfy them and specify what action to perform on those objects.

possible (though not implemented in our current prototype) for an agent itself to be any arbitrary program that is triggered by some specified condition.

Links. Users of Oval can easily see and change the relationships among objects by inserting and deleting *links* between the objects. For example, by inserting in the fields of some objects links (or "pointers") to other objects, users can represent relationships between messages and their replies, between people and their supervisors, or between different parts of a complex product. Users can then follow these hypertext links by clicking on them. In addition to this "manual" navigation using links, the knowledge represented by the links can also be test-

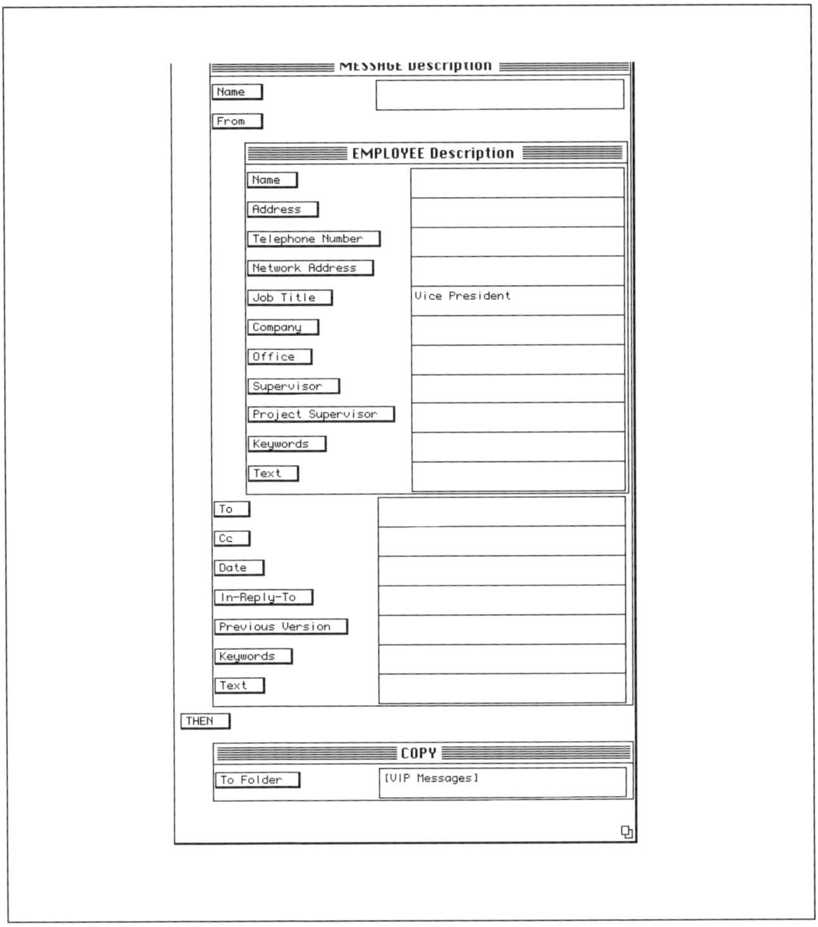

Figure 8. Rules can use embedded descriptions to create complex queries.

ed by agents and used for creating displays that summarize relationships.

For instance, figure 5 contains a link to two objects; (1) a "Person" object called "Jack Hunker" that represents the person responsible for the task and (2) a "Task" object called "Design" that is a prerequisite to documentation.

User Tailoring

The primary user level modifications to the system include (1) defining new object types, (2) adding fields to existing object types, (3) selecting views for objects and collections of objects (from a prespecified set of display formats), (4) specifying parameters for a given view (such as which fields to show), (5) creating new agents and rules, and (6) inserting new links.

Implementation Environment

The primary implementations of Oval were as a proof-of-concept prototype in Macintosh Common Lisp on networked Apple Macintoshes. This implementation of Oval was not robust enough for daily use in most environments, and therefore, we have not done formal empirical tests of the usability of the system in "real world" situations. The implementation was, however, sufficiently robust for rapid prototyping and demonstration of many applications. For instance, over 100 copies of the software were distributed to other researchers and developers for demonstration purposes.[2]

Sharing Information

Even though the "low level" systems issues involved in data sharing were not the primary focus of this project, we implemented three primary ways for people to save and share information in Oval:

1. *Mailing objects.* Users can mail any collection of objects back and forth to each other in messages. For instance, all the objects linked (directly or indirectly) to a given object can be automatically collected and mailed. This is done by inserting a link to the object in a message and then choosing the option of mailing "all levels" of other objects linked to the first object.

   When users receive a message containing objects, the identity of the objects is preserved (i.e., pre-existing links will point to the newest versions of the objects, and the previous versions will be stored as "previous versions"). Users are notified of these changes and, if they desire, can undo them in specific cases.

   This method of explicitly mailing objects is sometimes more awkward than having a shared database. However, many applications can be supported quite satisfactorily in this way for groups of people who are connected only by email gateways, without the necessity of shared databases.

2. *Sharing databases.* We also implemented a rudimentary version of "live" sharing of objects stored on remote databases. To do this, we used a remote relational database and mapping functions to translate between Oval objects and records in the relational database. Even though we did not do so, it would also be quite consistent with the overall Oval framework to use an object-oriented database for data storage and sharing.

3. *Sharing files.* Finally, users can save any collection of Oval objects in a file which they (or other people) can load later. These files can, of course, be shared in all the ways other files can be shared: on a file server, on floppy disks, etc. This is, in many ways, the least interesting way of sharing objects, but it is, in practice, the way we have used most often so far.

A key issue that arises when people share information in Oval is how to share definitions of new object types. As mentioned above, Lee and Malone (1990) discuss this issue in detail and propose a general solution called "partially shared views" which involves grouping type definitions into "views," explicitly sharing these views, and automatically translating unknown types into the nearest "ancestor" type in a view shared by both the sender and the receiver. In the current version of the system, we implemented the following special case of this general solution: When users save or mail objects not defined in the basic system, the type definitions are saved or mailed along with the objects themselves.

What's New Here?

Because the novel contribution of Oval is a subtle one, it is useful to be explicit about what we believe the contribution to be. The individual components of Oval (objects, views, agents, and links) are not new; each of them has been used before in at least some (and sometimes many) previous systems.

What we believe is novel about the Oval system is the choice of this set of building blocks and the particular way of combining them that is both simple and surprisingly powerful. That is, we believe the primary innovation in Oval is a user interface that has two important properties: (1) it is simple and intuitive for users to understand, and (2) it provides users a surprisingly large amount of functionality for creating and modifying a wide range of applications.

It would, of course, be no surprise to say that we could implement many applications in a general purpose programming language or that primitives like objects, views, agents, and links were helpful in doing so. The surprising thing, we believe, is that so many applications can be implemented using only the extremely restricted and simplified tailoring language provided by Oval.

Examples of Applications and Agents in Oval

To test our hypothesis that Oval is radically tailorable, we used the system to try to implement the functionality of a variety of cooperative work applications. The applications we used for these tests included well-known systems such as gIBIS (Conklin and Begeman 1988), Coordinator (Winograd 1987), Notes (Lotus 1989), and Information Lens (Malone, Grant, Turbak, et al. 1987). With a few exceptions described in detail by Malone, Lai, and Fry (1995), we found that it was possible to emulate the basic functionality of each of these systems using only the user-level tailoring facilities of Oval described above. We also implemented a number of more generic applications for tasks such as project management, software maintenance, and workflow management.

In this section, we will briefly describe several of these examples, emphasizing the use of agents in these applications. Since an important focus of our work was on making a system that would be easy for users to tailor, we will describe the construction of the first application in somewhat more detail than the others. Based on this description, readers can get some sense of the ease of tailoring new applications.

It is important to note, by the way, that we were concerned primarily with whether the overall user interface paradigm and user-level capabilities provided by Oval could accommodate in a "natural" way the primary functionality of the applications we tried to emulate. Since our system is only a research prototype, we did not attempt to replicate the level of attention to robustness, speed, live sharing of data, access controls, and so forth present in the commercial products we analyzed. These attributes are clearly essential in creating widely usable software systems, but they were not the primary focus of our work. It is also important to realize that these applications provide a kind of "stress test" for the tailorability of the system. We would not expect beginning users of a system like Oval to be immediately able do all the tailoring needed for these applications. For instance, some of the applications require the use of tailoring features (such as defining new object types) that we would expect only experienced users to have. In general we had, as a rough goal, the notion that the kinds of people who could use spreadsheets should be able to use Oval.

Also, just as spreadsheets are used by people at many different levels of sophistication, we expect that radically tailorable systems like Oval will be used in very different ways by end users, by power users, and by programmers (MacKay 1990; Nardi and Miller 1990). Since the system provides a wide spectrum of tailoring options, we believe that many users would make only minimal changes to applications developed by others, while some power users would develop applications for other people, and programmers would use the system to dramatically reduce the time and effort required to develop completely new applications.

gIBIS : Argumentation Support

gIBIS (Conklin and Begeman 1988) is a tool for helping a group explore and capture the qualitative factors that go into making decisions. Elements of a policy analysis in gIBIS are represented as a network containing three types of nodes: Issues, Positions, and Arguments. Each Issue may have several Positions that "Respond to" it, and each Position, in turn, may have various Arguments that "Support" or "Object to" it. Users can create new nodes of any type, and they can browse through a network by following the hypertext links between nodes or by looking at summary views that graphically display the different kinds of nodes and their relationships.

Defining New Object Types and Creating Examples of Them. To emulate gIBIS in Oval, we first defined the three types of objects used by gIBIS: Issues, Positions, and Arguments. For instance, to define the new type of object called "Argument," we performed the actions illustrated in figure 9. First, we selected the basic object type called "Thing" and then chose the "Create Subtype" action

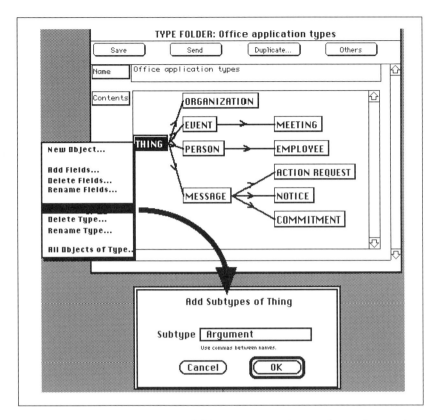

Figure 9(a). To define a new type of object, users create it as a subtype of some existing object type. (Note: In this and subsequent figures, the heavy curved arrow is added for clarity. It is not part of the actual screen display.)

(figure 9(a)). To create individual examples of this type, we selected the new type and chose the "New object" action. The new Arguments have the fields "Name," "Keywords," and "Text" by default, since these fields are present in all Things. To add the fields (like "Supports," "Objects to," and "Futured by") that are present in Argument objects but not in all Things, we used the "Add Field" action on one of the new Argument objects (figure 9(b)). Finally, we filled in the fields of this (and other objects) by typing and by adding links (figure 9(c)).

As an example of the kind of "shortcuts" that Oval includes to enhance the convenience of users, consider how new fields were added in figure 9(b). In designing a way for users to add fields to an object type, programmers who have worked with object-oriented systems would commonly have an operation that is performed on a "type definition" somewhere in the system. In some early versions of the Oval system, this is exactly what we did. However, in working with

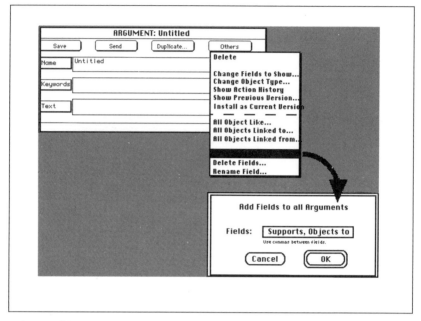

Figure 9(b). Users can add fields to an object type with the "Add Fields" action on any instance of that type. The fields then appear in all objects of that type.

Oval, we realized that nearly every time a user wants to perform a "type operation" (such as adding fields, setting default values for a field, and so forth) the user is already in the context of a specific instance of the type. Therefore, we made all these type operations accessible from the instances themselves. This approach seems to enhance the "immediacy" of using the system significantly; instead of making changes indirectly to an abstract type definition, users are directly changing a specific object that is of interest to them.

Linking Objects. The square brackets in figure 9(c) indicate "live" links to other objects that can be traversed by clicking on them. To add these links in the first place the user selects the "Add link" action in a field and then points to the object to which the link goes. It is also possible to use the "Add New Object" action on a field as a shortcut to both create a new object and insert a link to that object into the field.

Viewing Collections of Objects. When a field in an Oval object contains links to other objects, users can tailor views to specify how they wish to have these objects displayed. For instance, in figure 10, the objects in the "Contents" field of the Folder are initially displayed in a "Table" view, with the "Name" and "Entered by" fields shown in the table.

In the original gIBIS system, users can also view the relationships between

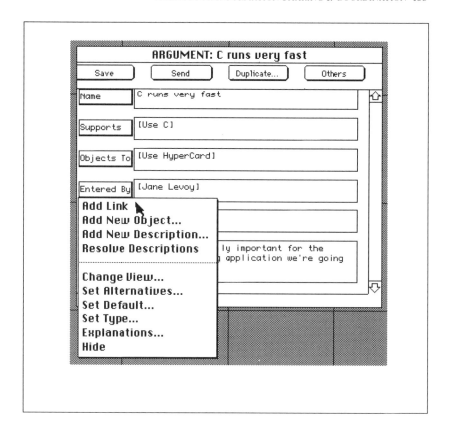

*Figure 9(c). Users can fill in the fields of an object by typing
or by inserting links to other objects.*

the nodes in an argument network graphically. To do this with Oval, we selected the "Change View" action for a field containing the nodes and then chose the
"Network" display format (see figures 10 and 11). This format allows us to
choose the fields from which links will be shown in the network. For example,
in figure 10, we chose to show links from three fields "Supports," "Objects to,"
and "Responds to." We also chose to display in each node the "Name" and "Object Type" fields. The result is shown in figure 11.

   In one sense, of course, there is nothing new about this notion of using general display formats for many kinds of objects. We have been genuinely suprised,
however, at how widely useful and powerful this feature is when users can
apply it themselves to create new applications. For instance, it makes it possible
for end users to create in seconds specialized displays like organization charts,
PERT charts, and part explosion graphs that might otherwise require days or
weeks of programming.

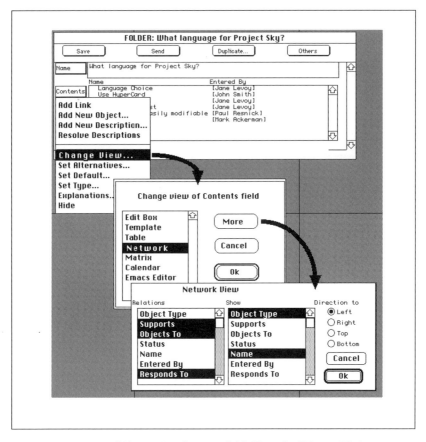

Figure 10. Users can "Change View" on any field. Here, the "Network" view was se-lected. Then, two other choices were made: (1) the fields from which links will be used to construct the network and (2) the fields to be shown in the nodes of the network.

Coordinator: Conversation Structuring and Task Tracking

The Coordinator is an electronic mail-based system that helps people structure conversations and track tasks (Action Technologies 1988; Winograd and Flores 1986). For instance, a typical "Conversation for Action" begins with a "Request" message from person A to person B, explicitly requesting person B to do something by a certain date. Person B is then prompted to respond with a "Promise" message (promising to perform the action), with a "Decline" message (declining to perform the action), or with a "Counteroffer" message (offering to perform the action by a different date or to perform a different action). If B promises to do the action, then a typical conversation might continue with B eventually

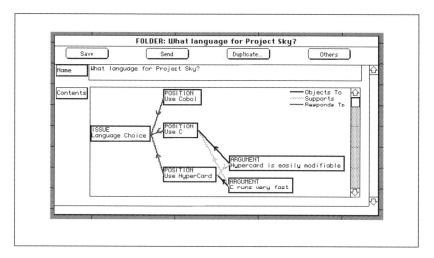

Figure 11. This network view, the result of the choices made in figure 10, shows the relationships between Issues, Positions, and Arguments as in the gIBIS system.

sending a "Report completion" message (indicating that the action has been performed) and A replying with a "Close" message (indicating that the action was performed satisfactorily).

In addition to this prototypical conversational sequence, a variety of other message sequences are possible when, for instance, A is not satisfied with B's performance or when the conversation begins with B "offering" to do something rather than with A "requesting" something. In all these cases, the system automatically groups all messages for a single conversational "thread" together, and allows users to easily see the status of various conversations. For example, users can easily see all the outstanding requests they have made to other people or all the things they have promised to do for others (along with their due dates).

This system was originally implemented without any components called "agents." However, to emulate this system, we found it useful to create a number of agents to sort the messages into appropriate folders based on their contents. As described in more detail by (Malone, Lai, and Fry 1995), we created 23 folders (such as "Open Matters" and "My promises") and 14 agents with 47 rules that move messages into and out of these folders. For instance, figure 12 shows an agent that moves conversations with promises from the user into two folders: "My Promises" and "All Open Promises and Offers."

Notes: Semistructured Information Sharing

Of the other systems analyzed here, Lotus Notes (Lotus 1989) is the most simi-

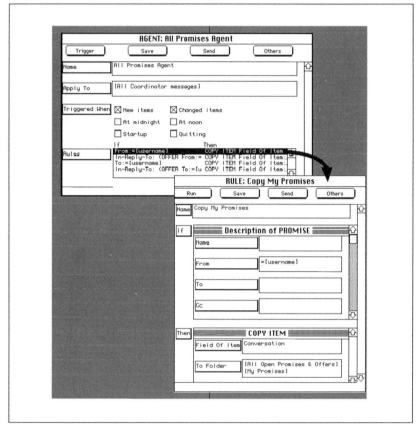

Figure 12. An agent that tracks conversations involving promises. The rule shown puts conversations that include Promise messages from the user into the appropriate folders.

lar to Oval. It was developed independently and announced soon after the basic ideas of Oval were first published (Lai, Malone, and Yu 1988). Notes is also similar to earlier computer conferencing systems with the important additions that (1) the documents in a database are semistructured templates (with optional "hot links" to other documents) and (2) the documents in a database can be filtered and summarized according to various user-definable views.

For example, a typical Notes application might help a company keep track of information gleaned from various sources about its competitors. Such an application might include a template that includes fields for which competitor the information is about, which customer(s) are involved (if any), and how important the creator of the item feels the information is. The template could also include a field for unstructured text describing the information in detail. The application might also include customized views of the data that, for example, show only high priority reports or sort reports by what competitors and customers are involved.

As this example illustrates, Notes—like Oval—can be used to create many different applications. Thus, we did not literally tailor Oval to emulate Notes itself, but rather we can tailor Oval in different ways to emulate different Notes applications. For instance, figure 13 shows a simple application for competitive information tracking like the one just described. It requires the definition of a new object type ("Competitive Information Report") and a table view for a folder containing objects of this type.

In general, the primitives that Notes provides for creating applications have equivalents in Oval, and thus the kinds of applications that can be created in Notes can also be emulated in Oval. For instance, the templates in Notes are equivalent to object types in Oval; the databases in Notes are equivalent to folders in Oval; and the views in Notes are equivalent to views of collections of objects in Oval. Notes views are all variations of a kind of "outline" display format that does not currently exist in Oval but is similar to the table format display that does exist (see figure 13).

In certain ways, however, Notes is significantly more limited than Oval. For instance, Notes does not include any of the other folder display formats in Oval such as networks and calendars. More importantly from our point of view in this chapter, Notes does not have active agents like those in Oval. If agents were integrated into Notes, they could help users do all of the kinds of things described in the other examples in this chapter.

One useful way of thinking about the relationship between Oval and Notes, therefore, is to view Oval as illustrating an integrated user interface paradigm and a number of additional features that Notes could, in principle, be extended to include.

Information Lens: Intelligent Mail Sorting

Implementing Information Lens in Oval is quite straightforward. For instance, users can define new message types as subtypes of Message in the object type hierarchy and create rules to filter and sort messages (see figure 14).

Other Applications

In addition to the applications described in detail above, we have developed a number of other applications using the Oval system. The range of these applications provides a further demonstration of the tailorability of Oval, and this section briefly summarizes a sample of these other applications. (All of these applications, except (1), are included with the demonstration version of Oval that is available to other researchers. They are described further in documentation that accompanies that system (Lee 1992):

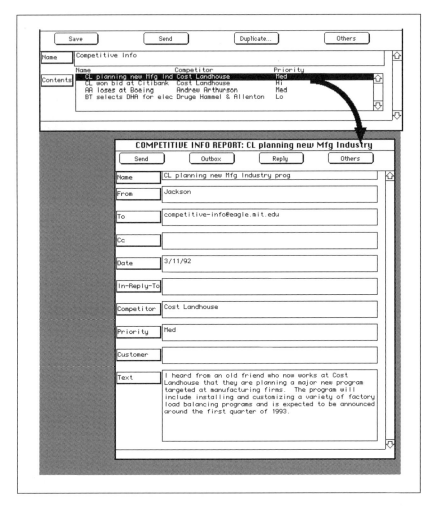

Figure 13. A table format display summarizing documents like those in a Notes database.

1. a project management system that tracks the tasks to be done, people responsible, prerequisites, overdue tasks, etc. A user can create this system by defining a new type of object called "Task" and viewing collections of these tasks using different views. For instance, a network view is used to summarize the links in the "prerequisite" fields (thus creating a PERT chart), and a calendar view is used to display objects according to the date in their "Due date" field. An agent finds overdue tasks (using a rule that looks for tasks whose "Due date" is less than today) and moves them to a

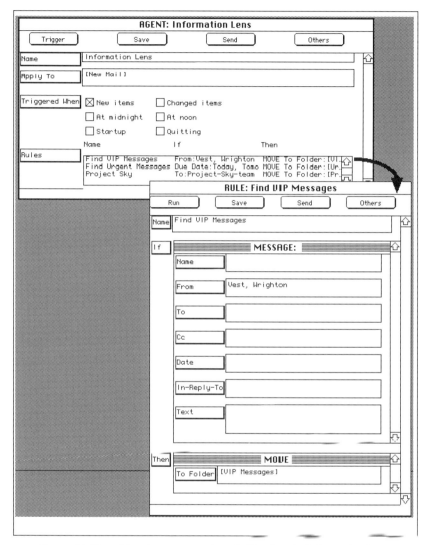

Figure 14. Examples of an agent and a rule like those in Information Lens.

special folder. It is also possible for people to mail tasks back and forth to each other. For example, a project manager can mail new tasks to people responsible for performing them, and those individuals can then mail back new versions of the tasks as the status of the tasks changes.

2. a system for tracking software bug reports and automatically routing them to appropriate people. For instance, the demonstration includes agents that

route bug reports to the programmers responsible for modules in which the bugs occur. Other agents route bug reports to programmers responsible for modules that call the ones containing bugs (on the theory that programmers may be interested in knowing about bugs in modules they use, even if they are not responsible for fixing them). This system is based, in part, on field studies of support "hot lines" in software companies (Pentland 1992, 1991) and of engineering change processes in manufacturing organizations (Crowston 1991).

3. a workflow system for order approval. This application is not a complete workflow system, but it demonstrates how rule-based agents can be used to route forms to appropriate people. For instance, the demonstration includes an agent with rules that route purchase requests to different managers for approval depending on the dollar amount of the purchase request.

Conclusions

Our experience with all the systems described above has strengthened our belief in the importance of using semiformal systems—where computational agents can gradually support more and more of the knowledge and processing involved when humans work together, without ever having to "understand" it all.

Our experience has also strengthened our belief in the importance of trying to design radically tailorable systems which end users (not skilled programmers) can modify to suit the needs of the changing situations in which they find themselves. Such systems, we believe, will make it feasible for many more people to maintain in computer systems information that is useful for themselves, for other people, and for their computational agents. These systems will also make it feasible for many people to directly tell their agents what to do, rather than having to depend on the limited abilities of their agents to figure out what needs to be done or having to depend on skilled programmers to program the agents.

We were also struck by the the usefulness of the particular "tailoring language" (composed of objects, views, agents, and links) that we used. We suspect that these building blocks may provide a surprisingly powerful basis for creating a wide variety of information management and cooperative work applications.

As we look to the future, we can imagine a world in which people share massively interconnected databases containing the kinds of semistructured objects we have seen here. The people in this world will be assisted by armies of computational agents that work constantly on their owners' behalf: searching for relevant information, notifying their owners when important things change, and responding automatically to certain conditions in the database.

A variety of technical challenges remains before such a world can come to pass. Among the most important of these technical challenges are issues of scaling: How can we manage globally distributed databases with millions of interconnected objects shared by hundreds of thousands of users and agents? How can we help numerous, partially overlapping communities of users collectively evolve shared definitions for different types of objects and shared understandings about what these objects mean?

Perhaps even more important than these technical challenges, however, are social and organizational questions: What kinds of information do people want to share in the first place? What kinds of incentives would lead people to contribute to and maintain these knowledge bases? Can systems like these help reduce the tiresome details of successful collaboration without leading people to feel overwhelmed by computerized "red tape"? And, for that matter, what makes work satisfying for people in the first place, and how can systems like these increase those satisfactions?

An Addendum: The Relationship between Oval and Object Lens

As noted above, we have used the name "Oval" in this chapter to include versions of the system that we originally called "Object Lens" (Lai, Malone, and Yu 1988). We eventually changed the system name from "Object Lens" to "Oval" to avoid confusion with the Information Lens system.

The primary differences between later versions of Oval and the system that was originally called Object Lens are the following: (1) Later versions of Oval were implemented in Macintosh Common Lisp on Macintoshes; Object Lens was implemented in Interlisp-D on Xerox 1100 workstations. (2) Later versions of Oval included two new kind of views that were not implemented in Object Lens: calendars and matrices. (3) Later versions of Oval included the capabilities described above for mailing objects around in a way that preserved instance identity. These capabilities were not present in Object Lens. (4) Later versions of Oval included several "user convenience" features which were not present in Object Lens. For instance, in later versions of Oval, type operations could be performed on instances (see more detailed description above).

Acknowledgements

Portions of this chapter appeared previously in Malone, Lai, and Fry (1995); Malone and Lai (1992); MacKay et al. (1989); Malone, Yu, and Lee (1989); Lai, Malone, and Yu (1988); Malone, Grant, Lai, et al. (1987); and Malone, Grant, Turbak, et al. 1987.

The work described here was performed by many people over a number of years. Here is a partial list of the people who contributed to these projects: Steven Brobst, Stu Card, Michael Cohen, Kevin Crowston, Christopher Fry,

Jintae Lee, Wendy MacKay, Ramana Rao, David Rosenblitt, Franklyn Turbak, and Keh-Chiang Yu. Financial support for this work was provided by Digital Equipment Corporation, the National Science Foundation, Apple Computer, Xerox Corporation, Wang Laboratories, General Motors/Electronic Data Systems, Bankers Trust Company, and by the corporate sponsors of the Center for Coordination Science, the Management in the 1990s Research Program and the International Financial Services Research Center at the Sloan School of Management, MIT.

Notes

1. The early versions of Oval were called "Object Lens" (Lai, Malone, and Yu 1988; Malone, Yu, and Lee 1989). However, we eventually changed the name to "Oval" to reduce the widespread confusion between Information Lens and Object Lens. In this paper, therefore, we will use the name "Oval" to refer to all versions of the system, including those that were originally called "Object Lens." A detailed description of the differences between the system originally called "Object Lens" and the later versions of Oval is included as an appendix to this chapter.

2. For information on how to obtain a copy of the software for research purposes at no charge, contact Heather Mapstone, MIT Technology Licensing Office, E32-300, 28 Carleton Street, Cambridge, MA 02139 (Telephone: (617) 253-6966. Fax: (617) 258-6790. E-mail: mapstone@mit.edu.)

References

Action Technologies. 1988. The Coordinator, Version 2, User's Guide, Action Technologies, Inc., Emeryville, California.

Conklin, J., and Begeman, M. 1988. GIBIS: A Tool for Exploratory Policy Discussion. *ACM Transactions on Office Information Systems* 6(4).

Crowston, K. 1991. Towards a Coordination Cookbook: Recipes for Multi-Agent Action. Ph.D. thesis, Sloan School of Management, Massachusetts Institute of Technology.

diSessa, A. A. 1985. A Principled Design for an Integrated Computational Environment. *Human Computer Interaction* 1:1–47.

Fikes, R., and Kehler, T. 1985. The Role of Frame-Based Representation in Reasoning. *Communications of the ACM* 28(9): 904–920.

Hutchins, E. L.; Hollan, J. D.; and Norman, D. A. 1986. Direct Manipulation Interfaces. In *User-Centered System Design,* eds. D. Norman and S. Draper, 87–124. Hillsdale, N.J.: Lawrence Erlbaum.

Lai, K.-Y.; Malone, T. W.; and Yu, K.-C. 1988. OBJECT LENS: A Spreadsheet for Cooperative Work. *ACM Transactions on Office Information Systems* 6(4): 332–353.

Lee, G. 1992. Oval Applications Catalog, September. Cambridge, Mass.: MIT Center for Coordination Science.

Lee, J., and Malone, T. W. 1990. Partially Shared Views: A Scheme for Communicating among Groups That Use Different Type Hierarchies. *ACM Transactions on Information Systems* 8(1): 1–26.

Lotus. 1989. Lotus Notes Users' Guide. Cambridge, Mass.: Lotus Development Corp.

MacKay, W. E. 1990. Patterns of Sharing Customizable Software. In Proceedings of the

CSCW 1990 Conference on Computer-Supported Cooperative Work, 209–222. New York: ACM Press.

MacKay, W. E. 1988. More Than Just a Communication System: Diversity in the Use of Electronic Mail. In Proceedings of the ACM Conference on Computer-Supported Cooperative Work, 26–28. New York: ACM Press.

MacKay, W. E.; Malone, T. W.; Crowston, K.; Rao, R.; Rosenblitt, D.; and Card, S. K. 1989. How Do Experienced Information Lens Users Use Rules? In ACM Conference on Human Factors in Computing Systems, eds. K. Bice and C. Lewis, 211–216. New York: ACM Press.

Maes, Pattie. 1997. Agents that Reduce Work and Information Overload. In *Software Agents* ed. J. Bradshaw, 145-164. Menlo Park, Calif.: AAAI Press

Malone, T. W., and Lai, K. Y. 1992. Toward Intelligent Tools for Information Sharing and Collaboration. In *Computer-Augmented Teamwork: A Guided Tour*, eds. R. P. Bostrom, R. T. Watson, and S. T. Kinney, 86–107. New York: Van Nostrand Reinhold.

Malone, T. W.; Lai, K.-Y.; and Fry, C. 1995. Experiments with OVAL: A Radically Tailorable Tool for Cooperative Work. *ACM Transactions on Information Systems* 13(2): 177–205.

Malone, T. W.; Yu, K.-C.; and Lee, J. 1989. What Good Are Semistructured Objects? Adding Semiformal Structure to Hypertext, Working Paper, 102, Center for Coordination Science, Massachusetts Institute of Technology.

Malone, T. W.; Grant, K. R.; Lai, K.-Y.; Rao, R.; and Rosenblitt, D. 1987. Semi-Structured Messages Are Surprisingly Useful for Computer-Supported Coordination. *ACM Transactions on Office Information Systems* 5:115–131.

Malone, T. W.; Grant, K. R.; Turbak, F. A.; Brobst, S. A.; and Cohen, M. D. 1987. Intelligent Information-Sharing Systems. *Communications of the ACM* 30(5): 390–402.

Nardi, B. A., and Miller, J. R. 1990. An Ethnographic Study of Distributed Problem Solving in Spreadsheet Development. In Proceedings of the CSCW 1990 Conference on Computer-Supported Cooperative Work, 197–208. New York: ACM Press.

Pentland, B. 1992. Organizing Moves in Software Support Hotlines. *Administrative Science Quarterly* 37(4): 527–548.

Pentland, B. 1991. Making the Right Moves: Toward a Social Grammar of Software Support Hot Lines. Ph.D. thesis, Sloan School of Management, Massachusetts Institute of Technology.

Suchman, L. A. 1983. Office Procedure as Practical Action: Models of Work and System Design. *ACM Transactions on Office Information Systems* 1(4): 320–328.

Winograd, T. 1987. A Language-Action Perspective on the Design of Cooperative Work. In *Human-Computer Interaction* 3:3–30

Winograd, T., and Flores, F. 1986. *Understanding Computers and Cognition: A New Foundation for Design*. Norwood, N.J.: Ablex.

Chapter 8

Agents that Reduce Work and Information Overload

Pattie Maes

C omputers are becoming the vehicle for an increasing range of everyday activities. Acquisition of news and information, mail and even social interactions and entertainment become more and more computer-based. At the same time, an increasing number of untrained users are interacting with computers, and this number will continue to rise as technologies such as handheld computers and interactive television become popular.

Unfortunately, these technological developments are not going hand in hand with a change in the way people interact with computers. The currently dominant interaction metaphor of *direct manipulation* (Shneiderman 1983) requires the user to initiate all tasks explicitly and to monitor all events. This metaphor will have to change if untrained users are to make effective use of the computers and networks of tomorrow.

Techniques from the field of artificial intelligence, in particular so-called "autonomous agents," can be used to implement a complementary style of interaction, which has been referred to as *indirect management* (Kay 1990). Instead of user-initiated interaction via commands and/or direct manipulation, the user is engaged in a cooperative process in which human and computer agents both initiate communication, monitor events, and perform tasks. The metaphor used is that of a *personal assistant* who is *collaborating with the user* in the same work environment. The assistant becomes gradually more effective as it learns the user's interests, habits, and preferences (as well as those of his or her community). Notice that the agent is not necessarily an interface between the computer and the user. In fact, the most successful interface agents are those that do not prohibit the user from taking actions and fulfilling tasks personally (see figure 1).

Agents assist users in a range of different ways:

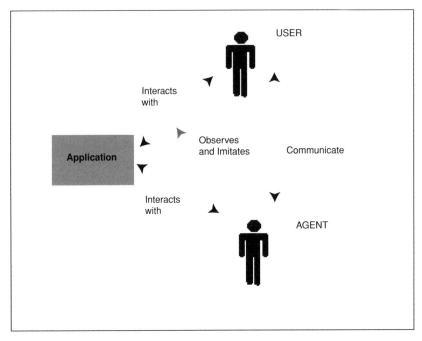

Figure 1. The interface agent does not act as an interface or layer between the user and the application. It rather behaves as a personal assistant which cooperates with the user on the task. The user is able to bypass the agent.

- They hide the complexity of difficult tasks.
- They perform tasks on the user's behalf.
- They can train or teach the user.
- They help different users collaborate.
- They monitor events and procedures.

The set of tasks or applications with which an agent can assist the user is virtually unlimited: information filtering, information retrieval, mail management, meeting scheduling, selection of books, movies, music, etc.

Approaches to Building Agents

The idea of employing agents in the interface to delegate certain computer-based tasks was introduced by visionaries such as Nicholas Negroponte (1990), Alan Kay (1984), and Tom Malone (Crowston and Malone 1988). More recently, several computer manufacturers have adopted this idea to illustrate their vision of the interface of the future (cf. videos produced in 1990-1991 by Apple, Hewlett Packard, Digital and the Japanese FRIEND21 project). Even though a great amount of work has gone into the modeling and construction of agents, currently available techniques are still far from being able to produce the high-level, human-like interactions depicted in these videos. Two main problems have to be solved when software agents are built. The first problem is that of *competence*: how does an agent acquire the knowledge it needs to decide when to help the user, what to help the user with, and how to help the user? The second problem is that of *trust*: how can we guarantee that the user feels comfortable delegating tasks to an agent? Two previous approaches for building interface agents can be distinguished. Neither one provides a satisfactory solution to these problems.

The first approach consists in making the end-user program the interface agent. Malone and Lai's *Oval* (formerly *Object-Lens*) system (Lai, Malone, and Yu 1988), for example, has "semi-autonomous agents" which consist of a collection of user-programmed rules for processing information related to a particular task. For example, the Oval user can create an electronic mail sorting agent by creating a number of rules that process incoming mail messages and sort them into different folders. Once created, these rules perform tasks for the user without having to be explicitly invoked by the user. Similarly, one can buy "agents" that can be programmed by the user to provide information filtering services (e.g. select any new article that mentions MIT Media-Lab, etc.).

The main problem of this approach is that it does not deal with the competence criterion in a satisfactory way. The approach requires too much insight, understanding, and effort from the end-user, since the user has to

- Recognize the opportunity for employing an agent
- Take the initiative to create an agent
- Endow the agent with explicit knowledge (specifying this knowledge in an abstract language)
- Item maintain the agent's rules over time (as work habits or interests change, etc.).

Trusting the agent is less of a problem in this approach, provided that the user trusts his or her own programming skills. However, the programs we write typically behave differently than expected, even when we trust our programming skills.

The second approach, called the "knowledge-based approach," consists of endowing an interface agent with extensive domain-specific background knowledge about the application and the user (called a domain model and user model respectively). This approach is adopted by the majority of people working in Artificial Intelligence on intelligent user interfaces (Sullivan and Tyler 1991). At run-time, the interface agent uses its knowledge to recognize the user's plans and to find opportunities for contributing to them. For example, UCEgo (Chin

1991) is an interface agent designed to help a user solve problems in using the UNIX operating system. The UCEgo agent has a large knowledge base about how to use UNIX, incorporates goals and meta-goals, and does planning (e.g. UCEgo can volunteer information or correct the user's misconceptions).

Both competence and trust constitute problems in the knowledge-based approach. The first problem related to competence is that the approach requires a huge amount of work from the knowledge engineer. A large amount of application-specific and domain-specific knowledge has to be entered into the agent's knowledge base. Little of this knowledge or the agent's control architecture can be used when building agents for other applications. The second problem is that the knowledge of the agent is fixed once and for all. It cannot be customized to individual user habits and preferences. The possibility of providing an agent with all the knowledge it needs to always comprehend the user's sometimes unpredictable actions is questionable.

In addition to the competence problem, there is also a problem with trust. It is probably not a good idea to give a user an interface agent that is very sophisticated, qualified, and autonomous from the start. Shneiderman has argued convincingly that such an agent would leave the user with a feeling of loss of control and understanding (Don 1992). Since the agent has been programmed by someone else, the user may not have a good model of the agent's limitations, the way it works, etc.

Training a Personal Digital Assistant

In my work, I explore an alternative approach to building interface agents that relies on Machine Learning techniques. A similar approach has been reported by Dent et al. (1992) as well as Cypher (1991). The hypothesis that is tested is that, under certain conditions, an interface agent can "program itself," in other words it can acquire the knowledge it needs to assist its user. The agent is given a minimum of background knowledge, and it learns appropriate "behavior" from the user and from other agents. Particular conditions have to be fulfilled: (1) the use of the application has to involve a substantial amount of repetitive behavior (within the actions of one user or among users), and (2) this repetitive behavior is potentially different for different users. If the latter condition is not met, i.e. the repetitive behavior demonstrated by different users is the same, a knowledge-based approach might prove to yield results faster than a learning approach. If the former condition is not met, a learning agent will not be able to learn anything (because there are no regularities to learn in the user's actions).

The machine learning approach is inspired by the metaphor of a personal assistant. Initially, a personal assistant is not very familiar with the habits and preferences of his or her employer and may not even be very helpful. The assistant needs some time to become familiar with the particular work methods of the employer and organization at hand. However, with every experience, the assistant learns, either by watching how the employer performs tasks, by receiving instructions from the employer, or by learning from other more experienced assistants within the organization. Gradually, more tasks that were initially performed directly by the employer can be taken care of by the assistant.

The goal of my research is to demonstrate that a learning interface agent can, in a similar way, become gradually more helpful and competent. In addition, I attempt to demonstrate that the learning approach also presents a satisfactory solution to the trust problem. If the agent gradually develops its abilities—as is the case in my approach—the user is also given time to gradually build up a model of how the agent makes decisions, a development which is one of the prerequisites for a trust relationship. Furthermore, the particular learning approach adopted allows the agent to give "explanations" for its reasoning and behavior in a language with which the user is familiar, namely in terms of past examples that are similar to the current situation. For example, "I thought you might want to take this action because this situation is similar to this other situation we have experienced before, in which you also took this action" or "because assistant Y to person Z also performs tasks that way, and you and Z seem to share work habits."

Finally, I believe that the learning approach has several advantages over the previous two approaches. First, it requires less work from the end-user and application developer. Second, the agent can more easily adapt to the user over time and become customized to individual and organizational preferences and habits. Finally, the approach helps in transferring information, habits and know-how among the different users of a community. The results described in a later section support all of the above hypotheses and predictions.

A learning agent acquires its competence from four different sources (see figure 2). First of all, the interface agent learns by continuously "looking over the shoulder" of the user as the user is performing actions. The interface agent can monitor the activities of the user, keep track of all of his or her actions over long periods of time (weeks or months), find regularities and recurrent patterns, and offer to automate these. For example, if an electronic mail agent notices that a user almost always stores messages sent to the mailing list "intelligent-interfaces" in the folder pattie-mailint int rot, dwn It can oller to automate this action the next time a message sent to that mailing list is read. Similarly, if a news filtering agent detects some patterns in the articles the user reads, then it can offer similar articles to the user when it discovers them.

A second source for learning is direct and indirect user feedback. Indirect feedback happens when the user neglects the suggestion of the agent and takes a different action instead. This occurence can be as subtle as the user changing the order in which he or she reads incoming messages, not reading some articles suggested by the agent, or reading articles not suggested by the agent. The user can also give explicit negative feedback for actions automated by the agent

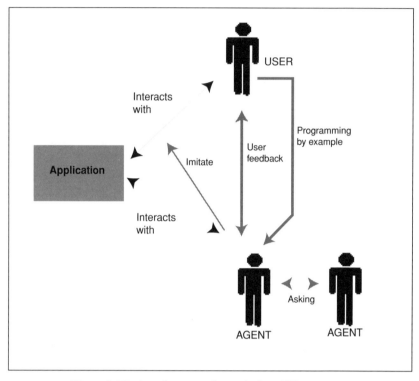

Figure 2. The interface agent learns in four different ways:
(1) it observes and imitates the user's behavior, (2) it adapts based on user feedback,
(3) it can be trained by the user on the basis of examples, and
(4) it can ask for advice from other agents assisting other users.

("don't do this again" or "I dislike this article").

Third, the agent can learn from examples given explicitly by the user. The user can train the agent by giving it hypothetical examples of events and situations and telling the agent what to do in those cases (Lieberman 1993, Myers 1988). The interface agent records the actions, tracks relationships among objects, and changes its example base to incorporate the example that it is shown. For instance, the user can teach a mail clerk agent to save all messages sent by a particular person in a particular folder by creating a hypothetical example of an e-mail message (which has all aspects unspecified except for the sender field) and dragging this message to the chosen folder. Similarly, the user can instruct a news filtering agent by giving it examples of (partially specified) articles (e.g. "select any article in which the word MIT appears").

Finally, a fourth method used by the interface agent to acquire competence is to ask for advice from agents that assist other users with the same task (and that may have built up more experience). If an agent does not know itself what action is appropriate in a certain situation, it can present the situation to other agents and ask "what action they recommend for that situation". For example, if an e-mail message arrives which has been sent by Nicholas Negroponte (the director of the Media Lab), then the e-mail agent can ask other agents what to do with that message. If a majority of the other agents recommends that the message has high priority and should be presented to the user for reading right away, then the agent can offer this recommendation to its user, even though the agent never previously observed the user deal with messages from Nicholas Negroponte. Rather than averaging the recommendations of all other agents in the community, a user might also inform his or her agent to accept suggestions from one or more specific agents which assist specific users. For example, if one person in the lab is an expert in the use of a particular piece of software, then other users can instruct their agents to accept advice about that software from the agent of that expert user. Additionally, the agent can learn from experience which agents are good sources for suggestions. It can learn to trust agents that in the past have proven to recommend actions that the user appreciated. The entertainment selection agent discussed below uses this technique to learn which other users have entertainment tastes similar to its user's tastes and thus are good sources of suggestions.

Some Examples of Existing Agents

Four agents have been built using the learning approach discussed above:
- An agent for electronic mail handling
- An agent for meeting scheduling
- An agent for electronic news filtering (Usenet Netnews)
- An agent that recommends books, music or other forms of entertainment

The choice of these domains was motivated by my dissatisfaction with the ways these tasks are currently handled. Many valuable hours are wasted dealing with junk mail; scheduling and rescheduling meetings; searching for relevant information among heaps of irrelevant information, and browsing through lists of books, music, and television programs in search of something interesting.

Electronic Mail Agent

Maxims (Lashkari, Metral, and Maes 1994) is an agent which assists the user with electronic mail. Maxims learns to prioritize, delete, forward, sort, and archive mail messages on behalf of the user (figures 3 and 4). Maxims is implemented in Macintosh Common Lisp. It communicates with the commercial elec-

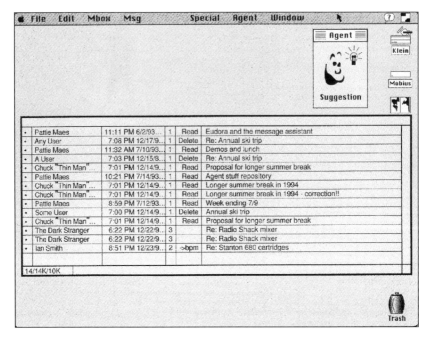

Figure 3. The e-mail agent makes recommendations to the user (middle column). It predicts what actions the user will perform on messages, such as which messages will be read and in which order (one can ask the agent to sort them), which messages will be deleted, forwarded, archived, etc.

tronic mail package Eudora (Dorner 1992) using Apple Events. The main learning technique used by Maxims is Memory-Based Reasoning (Stanfill and Waltz 1986, Maes and Kozierok 1993). The agent continuously "looks over the shoulder" of the user as the user deals with electronic mail. As the user performs actions, the agent memorizes all of the situation-action pairs generated. For example, if the user saves a particular electronic mail message after having read it, the mail agent adds a description of this situation and the action taken by the user to its memory of examples. Situations are described in terms of a set of features which are currently handcoded. In this domain, the agent keeps track of the sender and receiver of a message, the Cc: list, the keywords in the Subject: line, whether the message has been read or not, whether it is a reply to a previous message, and so on.

When a new situation occurs, which can be due to the user's taking an action or due to some external event such as a message arriving, the agent will try to predict the action(s) of the user, based on the examples stored in its memory. The agent compares the new situation with the memorized situations and tries

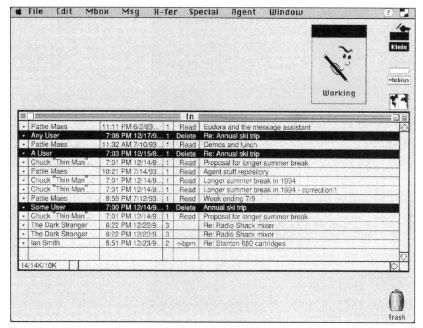

Figure 4. The user can select some of the suggestions made by the agent and ask the agent to execute them. Suggestions that have a confidence level above the "do-it" threshold are automated by the agent without asking for prior approval.

to find a set of nearest neighbors (or close matches). The most similar of these memorized situations contribute to the decision of which action to take or suggest in the current situation. The distance metric used is a weighted sum of the differences for the features that make up a situation. Some features carry more weight than others. The weight of a feature is determined by the agent. Occasionally (e.g. at night), the agent analyzes its memory and determines the correlations between features and actions taken. For example, the agent may detect that the "from" field of an e-mail message is highly correlated to whether its user reads the message, while the "date" field is not correlated. The detected correlations are employed as weights in the distance metric.

The agent not only predicts which action is appropriate for the current situation. It also measures its confidence in each prediction. The confidence level is determined by:

- Whether or not all the nearest neighbors recommended the same action
- How close/distant the nearest neighbors are
- How many examples the agent has memorized (a measure of the accuracy of the correlation weights)

Two thresholds determine how the agent uses its prediction. When the confidence level is above the "do-it" threshold, then the agent autonomously takes the action on behalf of the user. In that case, it writes a report for the user about the action it automated. The user can ask the agent for its report of automated actions at any time. If the confidence level is above the "tell-me" threshold, then the agent will offer its suggestion to the user but will wait for the user's confirmation to automate the action. The user is responsible for setting the "tell-me" and "do-it" thresholds for actions at levels the user feels comfortable with. For example, if the user feels paranoid about the agent autonomously deleting messages, then the user can set the "do-it" threshold for that action at a maximum.

The agent communicates its internal state to the user via facial expressions (see figure 5). These appear in a small window on the user's screen. The faces have a functional purpose: they make it possible for the user to get an update on what the agent is doing "in the blink of an eye." There are faces for "thinking" (the agent is comparing the current situation to memorized situations), "working" (the agent is automating an action), "suggestion" (the agent has a suggestion), "unsure" (the agent does not have enough confidence in its suggestion), etc. The "pleased" and "confused" faces help the user gain information about the competence of the agent (if the agent never offers its suggestion but always shows a pleased face after the user takes an action, then clearly the "tell-me" threshold should be lowered. The agents have deliberately all been drawn as simple cartoon faces, in order not to encourage unwarranted attribution of human-level intelligence.

The Maxims agent gradually gains competence by observing the user and acquiring more examples. In order to deal with this slow start problem, two additional competence acquisition schemes exist. First of all, it is possible for the user to instruct the agent explictly. If the user does not want to wait for the agent to pick up a certain pattern, then the user can create a hypothetical situation and show the agent what should be done. This functionality is implemented by adding the example to the agent's memory, including "wildcards" for the features which were not specified in the hypothetical situation. For instance, the user can create a hypothetical message from Negroponte and show the agent that that message has high priority. The new situation-action pair will match all situations in which an e-mail message has been received from Negroponte. By varying the way in which such hypothetical examples are treated when selecting an action and when compiling statistics, both *default* and *hard-and-fast rules* can be implemented within the memory-based learning framework (Kozierok 1993).

A second method which allows the agent to start from more than scratch is multi-agent collaboration (Lashkari 1994). When the agent does not have enough confidence in its prediction (confidence lower than "tell-me" threshold), it asks for help from other agents that are assisting other users with electronic mail. The agent sends part of the description of the situation to other agents via

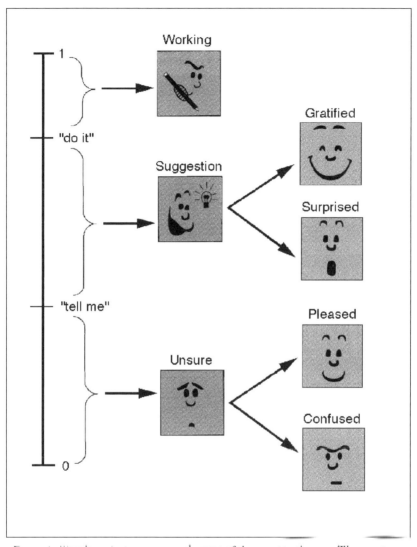

Figure 5 Simple caricatures convey the state of the agent to the user. The agent can be "alert" (tracking the user's actions), "thinking" (computing a suggestion), "offering a suggestion" (confidence in suggestion is above "tell-me" threshold), "surprised" if the suggestion is not accepted, "gratified" if the suggestion is accepted, "unsure" about what to do in the current situation (confidence below "tell-me" threshold, and thus suggestion is not offered), "confused" about what the user ends up doing, "pleased" that the suggestion it was not sure about turned out to be the right one after all, and "working" or performing an automated task (confidence in prediction above "do-it" threshold).

e-mail and awaits their response. For example, if a new Media Lab user/agent pair receives a message from Negroponte, then that agent will ask other agents what it should do with that message. Some other agents will recommend that the message is important and should be immediately presented to the user for reading. The agent will make a prediction based on the different suggestions that are returned. The agent gradually learns which other agents are trustworthy sources of information for certain classes of problems. Every agent models how much it trusts other agents' advice. The trust level is increased or decreased when the action eventually taken by the user is compared with the recommendations (and confidence levels) of peer agents. The multi-agent communication is an excellent method for transfer of information and competence among different users in a workgroup.

Meeting Scheduling Agent

The learning agent described above is generic. It can be attached to any application, provided the application is scriptable and recordable. The same agent was attached to a meeting scheduling software package (Kozierok 1993; Kozierok and Maes 1993).

The resulting agent assists a user with the scheduling of meetings (accept/reject, schedule, reschedule, negotiate meeting times, etc.). The meeting scheduling agent is again implemented in MCL (see figure 6 for a screen shot). Meeting scheduling is another example of a task which fulfills the criteria for learning interface agents: the behavior of users is repetitive, but nevertheless very different for individual users. Some people prefer meetings in the morning; others, in the afternoon. Some like to group meetings; others spread them out. Different people have different criteria for which meetings are important, which meeting initiators are important (and should be accomodated), etc. The learning interface agent approach is ideally suited for assisting the user in a very personalized way by automating the scheduling task according to the unique habits of the user.

Both the Maxims agent and the meeting scheduling agent have been tested by real users. The results of these user tests are very encouraging. Users are eager to try out interface agents. They welcome whatever help they can get with their work overload. Users reported that they felt comfortable delegating tasks to the agents. The tests revealed that it is important to provide the agent with an extensive set of features to describe situations. The more features the agent has, the better the agent performs. The useless features eventually become disregarded by the agent (the weights become 0 because they do not correlate with certain actions). The tests also revealed that several areas need further improvement. First, the agents have to be made to run faster, and second, users requested that they be able to instruct the agent to forget or disregard some of their behavior. Figure 7 shows some of the results obtained with the meeting scheduling agent. The agent's confidence in correct predictions increases with

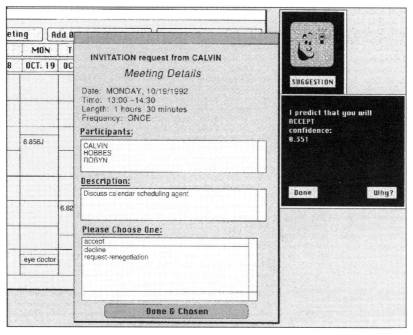

Figure 6. The calendar agent offers its suggestion to the user. The user can accept, take a different action, or ask for an explanation.

time, while its confidence in wrong predictions tends to decrease.

News Filtering Agent

Probably one of the more widely useful agents is an agent that helps the user select articles from a continuous stream of news (Sheth 1994; Sheth and Maes 1993). As more and more information becomes available on the network (see World Wide Web, on-line news feeds, etc.), users become more and more desperate for tools that will help them filter this stream of information and find articles of interest to them. NewT is a system which helps the user filter Usenet Netnews. It is implemented in C++ on a Unix platform. A user can create one or many "news agents" and train them by means of examples of articles that should or should not be selected. For example, figure 8 shows four agents (and icons) created by a user: one for business news, one for political news, one for computer news and one for sports news. An agent is initialized by giving it some positive and negative examples of articles to be retrieved. The agent performs a full text analysis (using the vector-space model (Salton and McGill 1983) for documents) to retrieve the words in the text that may be relevant. It also remembers the structured information about the article, such as the author,

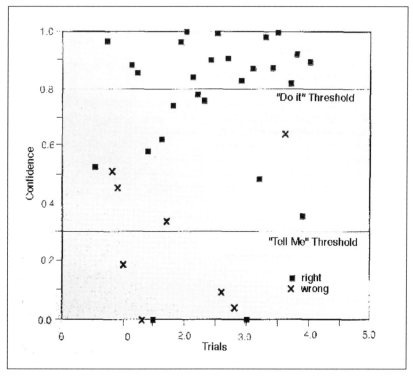

Figure 7. Typical results from a learning meeting scheduling agent. The confidence level in correct predictions increases with time, while the confidence level in wrong predictions tends to decrease.

source, assigned indices, etc. The user can also program the agent explictly and fill out a set of templates of articles that should be selected (e.g. select all articles by Michael Schrage in the Los Angeles *Times*).

Once an agent has been bootstrapped, it will start recommending articles to the user. The user can give it positive or negative feedback for articles or portions of articles recommended. For example, the user can highlight a word or paragraph and give selective positive or negative feedback. The user can also select the author or source and give positive and negative feedback. Giving the agent such an example will increase or decrease the probability that the agent will recommend similar articles in the future. The current implementation only performs content filtering, in the sense that the agent tries to correlate the positive and negative feedback with the contents of the article. It does not perform "collaborative filtering," which would mean that agents of different users would exchange recommendations with one another. However, a weaker form

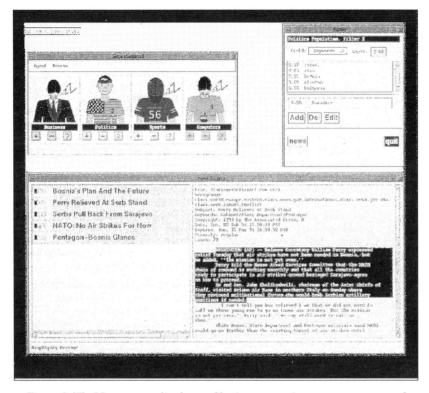

Figure 8. The Newt personalized news filtering system. A user can create a set of agents (four in this case) which assist the user with the filtering of an on-line news source. The agents are trained by means of positive and negative examples of articles to be selected or not selected respectively. Feedback is given, either for the complete article, or for a partial selection of an article, e.g. a paragraph, a proper name, the author, the source, etc.

of collaborative filtering is implemented in the NewT system: a user can train an agent for a while and then create a duplicate of that agent and give it to an other user.

The NewT agents were tested by a group of twelve users. A larger group is using the system on a daily basis. As is the case with the other agent systems described above, the NewT agents are not meant to automate all of the user's news interests. The agents are able to recommend articles to the user which concern topics (or authors or sources) in which the user has shown a continued interest. The user is still responsible for browsing the news sources to find less predictably interesting articles. Once such articles have been discovered, the user can train the agent to select those kinds of articles in the future. Again, the results obtained with the news agents were very promising. Users liked using the system and found it very useful. The main limitation of the system is that it is restricted to keywords only. However, if a method for deeper semantic analysis of texts becomes available (e.g. as a result of natural language understanding research), this deeper representation can be learned with the same statistical learning techniques as are currently used for relevant keywords.

Entertainment Selection Agent

A fourth and final application area is entertainment selection. Of all four applications discussed, this one might have the best potential to become the next "killer application." Currently, critics publish reviews and recommendations which are meant for a large, general audience, but no individualized mechanisms exist to help people select movies, books, or television and radio shows based on their personal tastes. However, as soon as entertainment becomes more interactive, agents can offer personalized, "readership of one" recommendations and critiques. *Ringo* is a personalized music recommendation system implemented on the Unix platform in Perl (Shardanand and Maes 1995). A similar system was built for recommending science fiction books (Feynman 1993). The firefly website lists a directory of sites that employ this technology. The agents in these systems use "collaborative filtering." They do not attempt to correlate the user's interests with the contents of the items recommended. Instead, they rely solely on correlations between different users.

In these systems, every user has an agent which memorizes which books or music albums its user has evaluated and how much the user liked them. Then, agents compare themselves with other agents. An agent finds other agents that are correlated, that is, agents that have values for similar items and whose values are positively correlated to the values of this agent. Agents accept recommendations from other correlated agents. Basically, if user A and user B have related musical tastes, and A has evaluated an album positively which B has not yet evaluated, then that album is recommended to user B. The actual algorithm is slightly more complex in the sense that agents combine the recommendations from a collection of related agents rather than from a single related agent. Figure 9 illustrates some of the results obtained.

One problem with this approach is how to bootstrap the whole system, so that enough data is avaliable for the agents to start noticing correlations and make recommendations. A second problem is that users can end up relying too much on the recommendation system and may not enter into the system any new items that they discovered themselves.

In order to deal with both of these problems, "virtual users" are created which represent a particular taste, e.g. a virtual "Madonna fan" user, who has high ratings for all Madonna albums and no other ratings, or a virtual "cyberspace fan" user, who rates all books on cyberspace highly and has no other

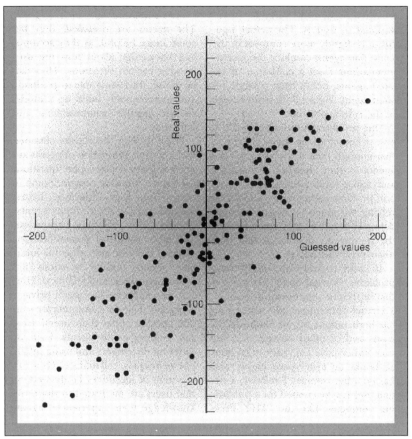

Figure 9. Results obtained with the entertainment selection agents. The Y-axis repre-sents actual values assigned by users to items. The X-axis represents values guessed by the agents based on correlations among users.

ratings. Similarly, a virtual user can be created for a publishing company, like the "MIT Press fan" who rates all MIT Press books highly. By entering such virtual user data into the system, the agent system can bootstrap itself, and agents for actual users can correlate themselves with virtual users.

Discussion

As computers are used for more tasks and become integrated with more ser-vices, users will need help dealing with the information and work overload. In-terface agents radically change the style of human-computer interaction. The user delegates a range of tasks to personalized agents that can act on the user's behalf. We have modeled an interface agent after the metaphor of a personal assistant. The agent gradually learns how to better assist the user by

- Observing and imitating the user
- Receiving positive and negative feedback from the user
- Receiving explicit instructions from the user
- Asking other agents for advice

These agents have been shown to tackle two of the hardest problems involved in building interface agents. The agents are *competent*: they become more helpful, as they accumulate knowledge about how the user handles certain situations. They can be *trusted*: the user is able to gradually and incrementally build up a model of the agent's competencies and limitations.

Even though the results obtained with this first generation of agents are encouraging, many open questions for future research remain. Some of these are user interface issues: Should there be one or many agents? Should agents use facial expressions and other means of personification (Don 1992, Laurel 1990)? What is the best metaphor for interface agents? Other questions are more algorithmic and technical: How can we guarantee the user's privacy, especially if agents communicate with one another about their users? How can heterogeneous agents, built by different developers and using different techniques, collaborate? How can a system of incentives be devised, so that users are motivated to share the knowledge their experienced agents have learned? Most importantly, from a legal standpoint, should a user be held responsible for his or her agents' actions and transactions?

Acknowledgments

Beerud Sheth, Robyn Kozierok, Yezdi Lashkari, Max Metral, Carl Feynman, Upendra Shardanand, Cecile Pham, and Henry Lieberman were responsible for many of the concepts and for the implementation of the four prototype agents. Christie Davidson, Yezdi Lashkari, and Henry Lieberman helped in the preparation of this article. This research is sponsored by Apple Computer, by the NSF under grant number IRI-92056688, and by the News in the Future Consortium of the MIT Media Laboratory.

References

Chin, D. 1991. Intelligent Interfaces as Agents. In *Intelligent User Interfaces*, eds. J. Sullivan and S. Tyler, 177-206. New York: ACM Press.

Crowston, K., and Malone, T. 1988. Intelligent Software Agents. *BYTE* 13(13): 267-271.

Cypher, A. 1991. EAGER: Programming Repetitive Tasks by Example. In Proceedings of the CHI'91 Conference, 33-39. New York: Association of Computing Machinery.

Dent, L.; Boticario, J.; McDermott, J.; Mitchell, T.; and Zabowski, D. 1992. A Personal

Learning Apprentice. In Proceedings of the Tenth National Conference on Artificial Intelligence, 96–103. Menlo Park, Calif.: American Association for Artificial Intelligence.

Don, A. 1992. Anthropomorphism: From ELIZA to TERMINATOR 2, Panel Description. In Proceedings of the CHI'92 Conference, PP–PP. New York: Association of Computing Machinery.

Dorner, S. 1992. EUDORA Reference Manual. Qualcomm Inc., San Diego, Calif.

Feynman, C. 1993. Nearest-Neighbor and Maximum-Likelihood Methods for Social Information Filtering, Internal Report, Media Laboratory, Massachusetts Institute of Technology.

Kay, A. 1990. User Interface: A Personal View. In *The Art of Human-Computer Interface Design*, ed. B. Laurel, 191-207. Reading, Mass.: Addison-Wesley.

Kay, A. 1984. Computer Software. *Scientific American* 251(3): 53-59.

Kozierok, R. A. 1993. Learning Approach to Knowledge Acquisition for Intelligent Interface Agents, Master's thesis, Department of Electrical Engineering and Computer Science, Massachusetts Institute of Technology.

Kozierok, R., and Maes, P. 1993. A Learning Interface Agent for Scheduling Meetings. Paper presented at the *ACM SIGCHI International Workshop on Intelligent User Interfaces*, 4-7 January, Orlando, Florida.

Lai, K.; Malone, T.; and Yu, K. 1988. OBJECT LENS: A "Spreadsheet" for Cooperative Work. *ACM Transactions on Office Information Systems* 6(4): 332-353.

Lashkari, Y.; Metral, M.; and Maes, P. 1994. Collaborative Interface Agents. In Proceedings of the Twelfth National Conference on Artificial Intelligence, 444–450. Menlo Park, Calif.: American Association for Artificial Intelligence.

Laurel, B. 1990. Interface Agents: Metaphors with Character. In *The Art of Human-Computer Interface Design*, ed. B. Laurel, 355-365. Reading, Mass.: Addison-Wesley.

Lieberman, H. 1993. MONDRIAN: A Teachable Graphical Editor. In *Watch What I Do: Programming by Demonstration*, ed. A. Cypher, 341-358. Cambridge, Mass.: MIT Press.

Maes, P., and Kozierok, R. 1993. Learning Interface Agents. In Proceedings of the Eleventh National Conference on Artificial Intelligence, 459–464 Menlo Park, Calif.: American Association for Artificial Intelligence.

Myers, B., ed. 1991. Demonstrational Interfaces: Coming Soon? In Proceedings of CHI'91, 393-396. New York: Association of Computing Machinery.

Myers, B. 1988. *Creating User Interfaces by Demonstration*. San Diego, Calif.: Academic.

Negroponte, N. 1970. The Architecture Machine: Toward a More Human Environment. Cambridge, Mass.: MIT Press.

Salton, G., and McGill, M. 1983. *Introduction to Modern Information Retrieval*. New York: McGraw-Hill.

Shneiderman, B. 1983. Direct Manipulation: A Step beyond Programming Languages. *IEEE Computer* 16(8): 57–69.

Shardanand, U., and Maes P. 1994. RINGO: A Social Information-Filtering System for Recommending Music, Internal Report, Media Laboratory, Massachusetts Institute of Technology.

Sheth, B. 1994. A Learning Approach to Personalized Information Filtering, Master's thesis, Department of Electrical Engineering and Computer Science, Massachusetts Institute of Technology.

Sheth, B., and Maes, P. 1993. Evolving Agents for Personalized Information Filtering. In Proceedings of the Ninth Conference on Artificial Intelligence for Applications, 345-352. Washington, D.C.: Institute of Electrical and Electronics Engineers.

Stanfill, C., and Waltz, D. 1986. Toward Memory-Based Reasoning. *Communications of the ACM* 29(12): 1213–1228.

Sullivan, J. W., and Tyler, S. W., eds. 1991. *Intelligent User Interfaces*. New York: ACM Press.

CHAPTER 9

KidSim:
Programming Agents
without a Programming Language

David Canfield Smith, Allen Cypher, & Jim Spohrer

Software agents are our best hope during the 1990s for obtaining more power and utility from personal computers. Agents have the potential to *actively participate* in accomplishing tasks, rather than serving as passive tools as do today's applications. However, people do not want generic agents—they want help with *their* jobs, *their* tasks, *their* goals. Agents must be flexible enough to be tailored to each individual. The most flexible way to tailor a software entity is to program it. The problem is that programming is too difficult for most people today. Consider the following:

- How can ordinary people program agents? Most people today would say they cannot.
- How can ordinary people understand what agents are doing? Will they turn dozens or hundreds of agents loose in their computers if they cannot? Or even one?

The End-User Programming Problem

Although most people can perform tasks of similar difficulty, few people are able to program. We examine the reasons why this is the case, and also explore some previous approaches to end-user programming, in the following subsections.

Why Are So Few People Able to Program?

How can people tell agents what to do? More generally, how can ordinary people who are not professional programmers program computers? This problem—the "end-user programming problem"—is an unsolved one in computer science. In spite of many previous attempts to develop languages for end users, today only a small percentage of people are able to program. Why are most people unable to program, in spite of all the attempts to empower them? Is programming inherently too difficult? Or does the fault lie with computer scientists? Have we developed languages and approaches best suited to the skilled practitioner, languages that take months or years to master? We take the latter view: computer scientists have not made programming easy enough. Consider the following evidence:

First, observe that most people can follow a recipe, give directions, make up stories, imagine situations, plan trips—mental activities similar to those involved in programming. It seems well within the capacity of humans to construct and understand concepts like sequences (first add rice, then add salt), conditionals (if the water boils too fast, turn down the heat), and variables (double each quantity to serve eight).

Can we make programming as easy as giving directions?

Second, notice that most people can use personal computers. Today, over 100 million people use them to write letters and reports, draw pictures, keep budgets, maintain address lists, access data bases, experiment with financial models, play games, and so forth. Children as young as two years old can use a mouse and paint with programs like KidPix (a child's painting program, at one time the world's best selling application) or explore worlds like The PlayRoom (a child's adventure game). So computers are not inherently unusable. The key observation is that most of these applications are *editors:* with them, users produce an artifact by invoking a sequence of actions and examining their effects. When the artifact is the way they want it, they stop.

Can we make programming as easy as editing?

Let us define the term "end users" to mean people who use computers but who are not professional programmers. Such people are typically skilled in some job function, but most have never taken a computer course. They use programs ("applications") written by other people. They can't modify these programs unless the designer explicitly built in such modification, and then the modification is typically limited to setting preferences. Perhaps 99% of the hundred million computer users can be classified as "end users." If we could empower these people to program computers, the impact would be enormous.

Previous Approaches to End-User Programming

In the past two decades, there have been numerous attempts to develop a language for end users (Soloway and Spohrer 1989): Basic, Logo, Smalltalk, Pascal, HyperTalk, Boxer (diSessa and Abelson 1989), Playground (Fenton and Beck 1989), etc. All have made progress in expanding the number of people who can program. Yet as a percentage of computer users, this number is still abysmally small. Consider children trying to learn programming. When they are in class, most children will learn anything. But do they continue to program after the class ends? Today programming classes are characterized by the "Whew, I'm glad that's over!" syndrome. As soon as children do not have to program anymore, they go on to something that is actually fun.

We hypothesize that fewer than 10% of the children who are taught programming continue to program after the class ends. This percentage is based on personal experience and observation. Surprisingly there are no published studies on this issue, to our best knowledge. Nevertheless, we expect that most readers will agree with this hypothesis. Elliot Soloway states "My guess is that the number… is less than 1%!!! Who in their right mind would use those languages—any of them—after a class??"[1] Single digit percentiles indicate that the end-user programming problem has not yet been solved.

As a step towards solving this problem, we will describe a prototype system designed to allow children to program agents in the context of simulated microworlds. Our approach is to apply the good user interface (UI) principles developed during the 1980s for personal computer applications to the *process of programming*. The key idea is to combine two powerful techniques—graphical rewrite rules and programming by demonstration. The combination appears to provide a major improvement in end users' ability to program agents.

Good User Interface Principles for Programming Environments

In this section we examine the problem with programming languages and describe principles for solving the end-use programming problem.

The Problem with Programming Languages

Why have previous attempts to develop a usable end user programming language not been more successful? We have, ourselves, developed languages for end users, none of which were successful either. When people are not making progress on a problem, it is often because they are asking the wrong question. We decided that the question is not "What language can we invent that will be easier for people to use?" The question is "Should we be using a language at all?" This question was the starting point for the work described here. We have come to the conclusion that since all previous languages have been unsuccessful by the criterion described here, *language itself is the problem*. It does not matter what the syntax is. Learning another language is difficult for most people. The solution is to get rid of the programming language.

But if we do, what do we use instead? The answer is all around us in the form of personal computers. Today, all successful personal computer applications and many workstation applications follow certain human-computer interface principles that were developed in the late 1970s (Smith et al. 1982) and codified during the 1980s (Apple 1992). The most common embodiment of these principles is the so-called graphical user interface (GUI) consisting of windows, menus, icons, the mouse, and so forth. The principles that make this interface work can and should guide computer scientists in attacking the end-user programming problem. We will briefly describe a few of these principles. However, we want to emphasize that we did not invent these principles in the work reported here. We are merely applying them to programming. Furthermore, the description here is by no means complete; many books have been written on these principles. See, for example, Laurel (1990), Baecker and Buxton (1987), and Heckel (1982).

Principles for Solving the End-User Programming Problem

The following are the most important principles for solving the end-user programming problem.

- *Visibility.* Make everything relevant to people's operation of a computer system visible on the display screen. This is the single most important UI principle. People have an easier time understanding what is going on and what to do next if things are visible than if things are kept internal to the program and hidden from users. Without visibility it is almost impossible to achieve an easy-to-use interface. Visibility has a couple of related principles: The first principle is *interactive vs. batch:* Establish a cause-effect relationship between user actions and system semantics. When users do something, show the effects immediately. Systems that do not show results are confusing. The second principle is *modeless vs. modal:* A "mode" is a state of a system in which user actions are interpreted differently than they would be ordinarily. Systems get in trouble when either (a) they have many modes or (b) their modes are invisible. Both confuse people, leading to (usually unpleasant) surprises at the results of actions.

- *Copying and modifying versus creating from scratch:* Allow people to copy and modify existing items in a system as a way to create new ones. It is often easier to start with something that works and figure out how to modify it than to create the same thing from scratch. Revealingly, this is the way most professional programmers work.

- *Seeing and pointing versus remembering and typing:* Allow users to point to entities on the display screen with a pointing device, instead of making them describe the entities by typing text. It is the foundation for the popular concept of "direct manipulation."

- *Concrete versus abstract:* Make the entities presented to users concrete. People have an easier time with the concrete than with abstractions.

- *Familiar user's conceptual model:* Cast the concepts in a system into terms the user can understand. When faced with a new situation, people try to apply their existing knowledge to understand it. This is the inspiration for the use of metaphor in computer interfaces, especially the so-called desktop metaphor invented for the Xerox Star by the first author (Smith et al. 1982).

- *Minimum translation distance:* One principle of utmost importance for programming environments but not so much for other applications was proposed by Sloman (1971): minimize the conceptual distance between people's mental representations of concepts and the representations that the computer will accept. In our opinion, the failure to do so is the single biggest reason that languages designed for children such as Logo and Smalltalk have not attained wider use. Time and again we have watched children try to accomplish simple programming tasks such as making a fish swim away from a shark, only to be frustrated by the difficulty in having to deal with coordinate systems and vectors. The most articulate representations are the ones that minimize this translation distance. Of course this is also a principle of good program design: create data structures and operations that are close to those in the problem domain.

In summary, the GUI eliminated command lines by introducing visual representations for concepts and allowing people to act on those representations by direct manipulation. It has empowered millions of people to use computers. Today, all successful editors on personal computers follow this approach. But most programming environments do not. This is the reason most people have an easier time editing than programming.

Actually, some programming systems *have* adopted an editing interface, and these systems are beginning to broaden the community of programmers. Spreadsheets, the most widely used programming technology, have done this for years. The popularity of some user interface management systems with their "drag-and-drop" interface builders is a result of their allowing direct manipulation of interface elements. Similarly, most people can construct buttons and fields in HyperCard, which has an editing feel, but few of those same people can program in HyperTalk.

There are a few brilliant examples of programming systems that have applied all of these principles. Our favorite is Bill Budge's video game for personal computers called "The Pinball Construction Set." It allows people to program pinball games by directly editing the layouts, i.e. by dragging and dropping pinball elements such as flippers and bumpers. The elements begin functioning as soon as they are dropped into place. Everyone can create pinball games this way. We call this "programming by direct manipulation," and when done well, it is wonderfully successful. The problem with The Pinball Construction Set is that you can program only pinball games with it. The challenge is to increase the generality without losing the ease of use.

Simulations

The end-user programming problem in its full generality is a tough one. It has resisted solution for over two decades. So we decided to attack it in a domain that is more general than The Pinball Construction Set but more restricted than general programming, the domain of symbolic simulations. A symbolic (as opposed to numeric) simulation is a computer-controlled microworld made up of individual objects (agents) which move around a game board interacting with one another. We chose as our target audience children from the ages of 5 to 18.

Why simulations? They are a powerful tool for education. Simulations encourage unstructured exploratory learning. They allow children to *construct* things, supporting the constructivist approach to education. Alan Kay (private communication) contends "We build things not just to have them, but to learn about them." He quotes the philosopher Cesare Pavese: "To know the world, one must construct it." Scardamalia (Scardamalia and Bereiter 1991) argues that children learn best when constructing things. They enter Vygotsky's "zone of proximal development." Simulations such as SimCity and SimEarth allow children (of all ages) to construct unique microworlds, giving them a sense of ownership in their creations. Able to observe and modify and experiment with these microworlds, children are the "gods" of their worlds. This pride of ownership and feeling of power are compelling qualities that motivate even professional programmers.

However, most simulations today do not permit users to modify their fundamental behaviors and assumptions. For example, one cannot alter the fact that if one puts in a railroad in SimCity, the pollution problems go away—not exactly a realistic consequence. This inflexibility is the reason that most school teachers do not use SimCity as a teaching tool, even if the class is studying city building. It does not model what they want to communicate. Simulations that do allow fundamental modifiability, such as numeric simulations built with Stella, require extensive programming skills. Few children or teachers can or want to do it.

What is needed is a way for children without programming knowledge to have more control over the behavior of simulations. What is also needed is a way for teachers to tailor simulations to support their curriculum goals. Kid-Sim™ provides a way to do both.

KidSim

KidSim ("Kids' Simulations") is a tool kit that allows children to build symbolic simulations. Kids can modify the programming of existing simulation objects and define new ones from scratch. KidSim simulations consist of the following:

- A *game board* divided into discrete spaces, like a checkerboard

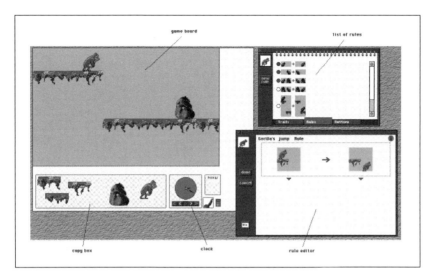

Figure 1. A KidSim jungle simulation.

- A *clock* whose time is divided into discrete ticks
- One or more *simulation objects* (agents)
- A *copy box* which is the source of new simulation objects
- A *rule editor* where rules are defined and modified
- Various other elements.

In this chapter we will focus on simulation agents and the way kids program them.

The game board represents the simulation microworld. It is the environment in which simulation objects interact with one another. Dividing the board into discrete squares makes it easier for kids to communicate their intentions to the computer. The game board shown in figure 1 displays a monkey in a simple jungle scene. We will use this simulation throughout this article.

The clock starts and stops a simulation running. Dividing time into discrete ticks makes it easy for kids to control their simulations. The clock provides both fine grain control over time (single stepping) and the ability to run time backward. Running the clock backward undoes everything that happened during the previous tick, encouraging kids to experiment and take chances. If something goes wrong, they can just back up the clock to before that point.

The copy box is a container for simulation objects that automatically makes copies of things inside it. Whenever a child drags an object out of the copy box, the system clones the object and puts the original back. This provides an infinite source of new objects. Kids can place their own objects in the copy box, allowing them to duplicate infinitely their own objects as well.

Figure 2. Examples of agents.

Agents in KidSim

Let us define an *agent* as a persistent software entity dedicated to a specific purpose. "Persistent" distinguishes agents from subroutines; agents have their own ideas about how to accomplish tasks, their own agendas. "Specific purpose" distinguishes them from entire multifunction applications; agents are typically much smaller. (This is by no means a universally accepted definition, but it is the one we will use here.)

In KidSim, the active objects in simulations are agents. During each clock tick, agents move around on the game board interacting with one another. Metaphorically, agents are characters in a microworld, and we will use the terms "character" and "agent" interchangeably. KidSim agents have three attributes:

- *Appearance:* Kids can draw their own appearances for agents, encouraging metaphorical thinking.

- *Properties:* Kids can define their own data and characteristics for agents. Typical ones for a monkey character might be "name," "age," "height," "weight," "sex," "hunger," "fear" and "climbing ability." Properties are name-value pairs. They serve the same function in KidSim that variables do in traditional programming languages. Properties have no inherent meaning to KidSim. They have meaning only if kids use them in rules.

- *Rules:* Kids can define rules of behavior for agents. The set of rules for an agent constitutes its program.

Thus KidSim agents are full objects in the object-oriented programming sense. They have state (properties), behavior (rules), and an appearance. There is no inheritance between agents, but there is a way to give every agent the same rule.

KidSim agents are similar to those in Logo Microworlds. The difference is in how they are programmed. In Logo Microworlds, kids program objects with Logo. In KidSim, kids construct "graphical rewrite rules."

In KidSim, kids usually start with several predefined characters in various microworlds. The kids can play with these microworlds immediately, as with ordinary video games. This gets them involved. After a while, the kids typically want something to work differently. At this point, KidSim differs from video games. Kids can modify the way the characters work by changing their programming. Pedagogically this is an important difference, because the act of changing things forces kids to think. They have to decide what to change, how to change it, and how to fix it when their changes do not work. At every step their brains are engaged. In fact, we believe that any video game can be turned into a learning experience by allowing kids to modify it.

We also give kids a "lump of clay" from which they can create new characters, indeed entire worlds. The lump of clay is sufficient to build everything. Typically kids begin by modifying the predefined characters, but they quickly move on to defining totally new ones.

Languageless Programming, the Key Idea

The main innovation in KidSim is the way in which children specify the behavior of agents: KidSim does it without a programming language. Instead KidSim combines two powerful ideas:

1. Graphical rewrite rules
2. Programming by demonstration

Each has been tried before in isolation by various researchers, including the present authors, and each has been found insufficient by itself to enable people to program computers. This is the first time they have been combined in a general programming environment. We call the result "languageless programming."

Graphical Rewrite Rules

A graphical rewrite rule is a transformation of a region of the game board from one state to another. It consists of two parts: a "before" part and an "after" part. Each part is a small scene that might occur during the running of the simulation:

A rule is said to *match* if its "before" part is the same as some area of the game board at some moment in time. When a rule matches, KidSim transforms the region of the game board that matched to the scene in the "after" part of the rule. (Actually a recorded program is executed, as described later.)

Rewrite rules or "if-then rules" or "production systems" are well known in artificial intelligence (Rychener 1976; Davis and King 1975; Newell and Simon 1972). They form the control structure for expert systems, of which OPS5 from Carnegie Mellon is an example (Maher, Sriram, and Fenves 1984). Rule-based systems have some marvelous characteristics. Since rules are independent of one another, it is possible to add a rule to an existing system without affecting the rules that are already there. This assumes that the added rule is specific enough so that it does not override other rules and that the system is smart enough to factor the rule into the correct order. The Lisp70 production system automati-

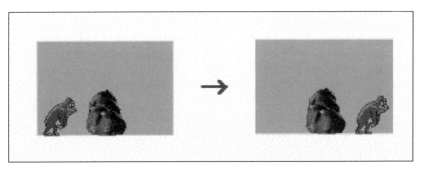

Figure 3. A typical graphical rewrite rule.

cally factored rules using an algorithm called "specificity" in which the more specific rules were tried before the more general ones, which worked well in most cases (Tesler, Enea, and Smith 1973). Furthermore, in rule-based systems it is easy to understand and debug each rule by itself, without having to be concerned with the other rules. Of course a good rule tracer and stepper are essential, as in any programming language.

Graphical rewrite rules are two dimensional versions of rewrite rules. They too have been applied to the end-user programming problem by several researchers (Repenning 1993; Furnas 1991). While they work well for simple tasks, graphical rewrite rules have encountered two problems that have limited their utility for complex tasks: (a) The "rule-generality" problem—pictures, being inherently literal, are hard to generalize to apply to multiple situations. (b) The "rule-semantics" problem—it is difficult to specify how the computer is to perform the transformation from the left to the right side of a rule. Some systems have applied AI techniques to try to infer the transformation, but to date no one has developed a general method for doing so. Additionally, graphical rewrite rules suffer from a problem that all rule-based systems have, graphical or not: (c) The "rule-sequencing" problem—it is difficult to specify a series of transformations, i.e. do rule A then rule B then rule C, since rules by definition are independent of each other. KidSim's graphical rewrite rules solve the first problem by abstraction and the second by programming by demonstration. We have not yet addressed the third problem, sequencing.

Children may generalize KidSim's graphical rewrite rules in two ways:

- *Picture abstraction:* Kids may select an object in the "before" part of a rule, and a pop-up menu will appear listing possible generalizations of that object: In this example, a child has clicked on a rock in the "before" (left) part of a rule. Its list of possible generalizations appears: "this particular rock (gray rock 7), any gray rock, any rock, or any object." The child may specify that the rule is to apply to any of these types of objects.
- *Property abstraction:* Kids can specify tests on the properties of the objects

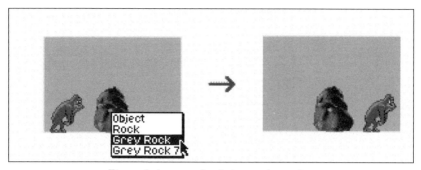

Figure 4. An example of picture abstraction.

in the "before" part of a rule. These constitute additional tests (conjuncts) that must be satisfied for the rule to match. For example, suppose a child wants to restrict a rule in which a monkey jumps over any rock to apply only to rocks that are less than the monkey's height. Adding the property test in figure 5 to the rule does this. If a child buttons down on the < symbol, a pop-up menu of operators appears showing the allowable tests on numeric properties ($< \le = \ne \ge >$). Text properties have other operators. A child may choose any operator.

Now we can fully define a graphical rewrite rule in KidSim:

A *graphical rewrite rule* consists of a (possibly generalized) visual image and zero or more property tests. In order for a rule to match, its visual image must conform to a situation on the game board, and all of its property tests must evaluate to true.

Programming by Demonstration

Programming by demonstration is a technique in which the user puts a system in "record mode," then continues to operate the system in the ordinary way, and the system records the user's actions in an executable program (Cypher 1993a; Smith 1977). The key characteristic is that *the user interacts with the system just as if recording were not happening.* Users do not have to do anything differently or learn anything additional. Halbert (1984) calls this "programming a software system in its own user interface," a phrase that accurately expresses the user's experience.

There have been a number of programming by demonstration (PBD) systems prior to KidSim. The major ones are described in Cypher (1993b). These systems have proved to be exceptionally easy for people. However, most PBD systems to date have suffered from two deficiencies:

- PBD systems have been experimental, used by small numbers of people for simple tasks but not by large numbers of people for complex tasks. The exceptions are macro recorders, which are in wide use, but they have such a

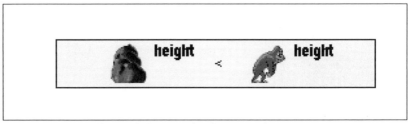

Figure 5. An example of property abstraction.

limited ability to generalize that they are not general purpose programming systems. KidSim will attempt to solve this problem by delivering a commercially available, general purpose programming product. It is designed to be powerful enough to enable children to construct simulations as complicated as the game "PacMan." In fact, our test for generality is not Turing equivalence, which is easy; it is "PacMan equivalence."

- PBD systems do not represent recorded programs in a way that users can understand. We might call this the "PBD representation problem." Often they show programs as scripts. But it does not work to let people record programs in a way they can handle—by demonstration—and then turn around and force them to learn a programming language! KidSim solves this problem by using graphical rewrite rules as visual reminders for recorded actions.

An Example of Programming in KidSim

Suppose a child wants to teach a monkey how to jump over rocks. Here are the steps involved:

1. The child sets up the simulation situation which he or she wants to affect. In this example, the child places the monkey next to a rock. KidSim allows children to define rules only when the actual simulation situation exists. This makes defining rules a concrete process, reducing the need to visualize simulation states abstractly. The child can be sure that the rule will work at least for this one example, and the child can generalize it to a wider class of situations later.

2. The child specifies the region of the game board with which the rule is to deal (figure 6). This is the region that will be pattern matched against the game board when the simulation runs. The child specifies this region by direct manipulation, by dragging the border of a "spotlight" which appears during recording. The "before" and "after" pictures in the rule copy the "spotlight's" area.

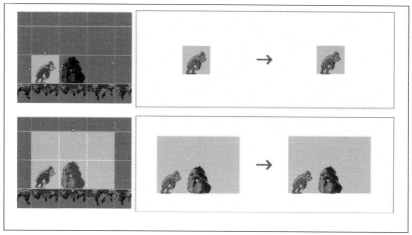

Figure 6. Defining the context for a rule.

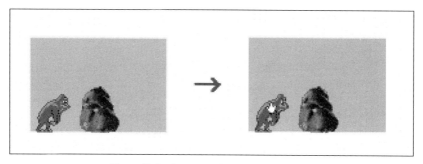

Figure 7. Defining a rule by demonstration.

3. Initially the "before" and "after" parts of a rule are identical, i.e. each rule begins as an identity transformation. The child defines the rule semantics by *editing the "after" picture* to produce a new simulation state:

   First the child places the cursor (a small hand) over the monkey and drags it to the square above the rock (figure 8). Then the child drags it to the square to the right of the rock (figure 9). Done. That is all there is to it. Nowhere did the child have to type "begin...end", "if...then...else," semicolons, or other language syntax. Yet the effect when executed is that the monkey jumps over the rock. The child has programmed the monkey. This is the essence of programming in KidSim: *programming by direct manipulation editing.*

Suppose now that the child wants to restrict the monkey to climbing over rocks that are up to twice its height (monkeys being good climbers) but no higher. Suppose the monkey's height is 60, and the height of the current rock is 70.

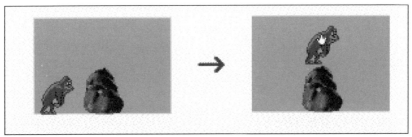

Figure 8. Dragging the monkey above the rock.

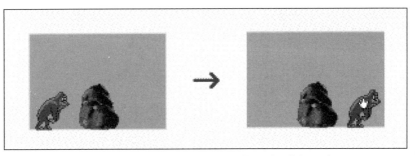

Figure 9. Dragging the monkey to the right of the rock.

Here is how to do it.

4. The child clicks on the triangle below the left side of the rule (figure 10). This displays a box in which property tests may be defined. KidSim always provides an empty test.

5. The child drags the height property from the rock's viewer into the left side of the test.

6. Since the right side of the test is to contain a calculation, the child displays the KidSim calculator:

   The child drags the monkey's height property into the calculator display, pushes the multiplication button and the 2 button, then pushes the = button. 120 appears in the display. The child drags this value into the right side of the property test. The resulting rule is shown in figure 12. Since 70 (the height of the rock) is less than 120 (twice the monkey's height), this rock passes the test. However, other rocks the monkey encounters in its travels may be higher than 120, so this rule would not match, and the monkey could not climb over those rocks.

7. Finally the child closes the rule editor window. A miniature image of the rule is placed in the monkey's viewer at the top of its list of rules (figure 13). This image visually suggests its behavior. KidSim can display (upon

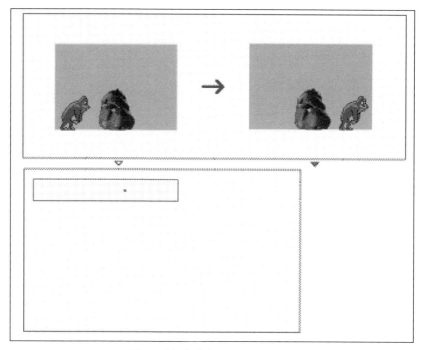

Figure 10. Defining a property test.

Figure 11. KidSim calculator.

request) the program that was built as the child edited the right side of the rule (figure 14).

These are the actions that were recorded "by demonstration." Now we can define what it means to execute a graphical rewrite rule:

> When a graphical rewrite rule matches, KidSim executes the program that was recorded by demonstration for it.

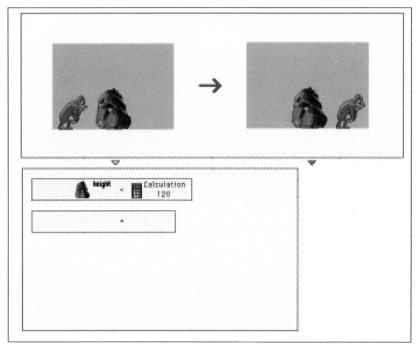

Figure 12. Checking if a rock is less than twice the monkey's height.

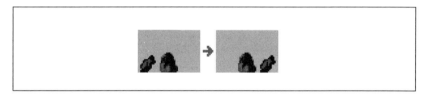

Figure 13. A miniature image.

The iconic-symbolic representation for the program is an attempt to be close to what children are thinking when they edit—the "minimum translation dis- tance" principle. However, we feel children will rarely want to see this repre- sentation, and we make no particular claims for it. It will usually be enough for kids to look at the miniature images of rules to understand what they do. We have found that children can look at dozens of graphical rewrite rules and (a) tell them apart, and (b) explain what they do, even rules written by other chil- dren (figure 15).

Here is where combining graphical rewrite rules and programming by demonstration results in a system that is stronger than either. Graphical rewrite

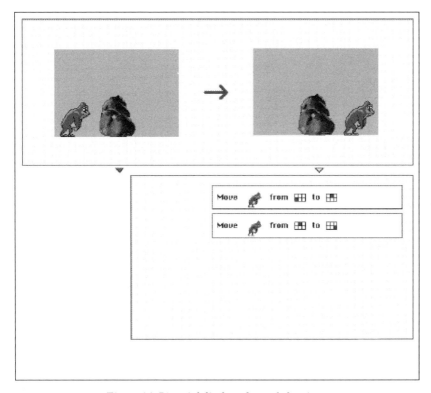

Figure 14. Pictorial display of recorded actions.

rules solve the PBD representation problem, and programming by demonstration solves the rule-semantics problem.

A problem with rule-based systems is that rule order is crucial and often hard to get right. The problem grows with the number of rules. This problem is somewhat mitigated in KidSim because its rules are quite high level. We have found that we can accomplish interesting tasks in relatively few rules. For example, an optimized strategy for playing the game "MasterMind" requires only about 15 rules in KidSim. Rules can be grouped into subroutines, thereby forming larger conceptual chunks. Nevertheless, this problem could become serious when the number of rules gets large. We may adopt a strategy like Lisp70's in which rules are automatically factored into a discrimination tree by specificity, removing the need for children to manually order the rules.

Of course, graphical rewrite rules really do constitute a programming language. The language has a syntax: left side –> right side, and it has an ordering of "statements": top to bottom. Nevertheless, we feel justified in calling KidSim "languageless programming" because of the complete absence of a traditional linguistic syntax such as if-then-else, and because the left and right sides of rules

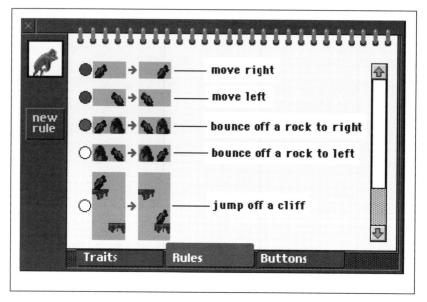

Figure 15. The rules for a monkey.
(The annotations are not part of the actual display.)

are images of the game board, not abstract representations of it. Furthermore, KidSim follows all of the UI principles listed above, making it feel more like direct manipulation editing than programming.

Kid Tests of KidSim

KidSim has been tested with fifth grade students in two US elementary schools, and also at an informal user study at the University of Nottingham. In this section, we'll explore the results of those early tests.

Early Tests with Fifth Graders

Over the past two years we have formed a close association with fifth-grade classrooms in two elementary schools. As part of other projects, Apple Computer had endowed both schools with numerous Macintosh computers. Each of the classrooms has about fifteen computers, one for every two children. While this ratio is not representative of schools in general, it did provide a good laboratory for experimenting with ways to improve education through technology.

This association with the schools has been essential in the development of KidSim. If you want to design a program for children, then children must participate in the design. Feedback from the kids has caused us to change the design of KidSim several times. After each revision, we went back to the children for their reaction to the new design, often causing us to revise it further. An example was our approach to specifying arithmetic expressions on property values, such as computing twice the monkey's height. We invented several clever (we thought) notations, most having a data-flow flavor. The kids repeatedly said they could not understand them, much less write them. Finally we went back to the principle of direct manipulation. We introduced a calculator to allow interactive creation of expressions, rather than forcing kids to type them statically. Kids drag property values to the calculator and push buttons to operate on them, much as they would with a physical calculator. The calculator metaphor obeys almost all of the good UI principles mentioned earlier—concrete, interactive, direct manipulation, seeing and pointing, familiar conceptual model, and modeless. We found that all the children could use it. (A calculator "tape" is available for displaying the steps should a child want to see them.)

Having a working prototype is also essential in getting feedback from children. They are able to respond more easily when they can try out a design rather than having to imagine how it might work. But even before we got a prototype working, we tested the ability of children to write graphical rewrite rules via "Post-It Notes programming," in which they wrote rules on note pads and then acted out their "programs." Among the thirty fifth graders (ten-year olds) we tested, both boys and girls, none had any trouble writing rules. Furthermore, they enthusiastically responded to the concept. When we gave them new problems, they raced back to their desks, scribbled out a new rule or two, then raced back to us and demanded "Test us now!" There was no writer's block as is often observed with programming languages, in which kids do not know how to proceed.

Several refinements were made as a result of these early user tests. We found that a trash can was inappropriate for disposing characters, that allowing users to erase individual items in a conditional expression was excessive and unnecessary, and that adding the text "and if" at the beginning of each conditional expression made rules easier to understand.

These early tests also pointed out some more fundamental problems. Users would sometimes expect that there was only a fixed set of names that they could use for properties, as if the properties were predetermined by the system. We surmised that part of the problem was that the system properties, like "name," were listed together with the user properties. Although system properties are distinguished by displaying their names in blue, this distinction was evidently too subtle. Also, it seems that the visual appearance of properties is too heavyweight, and that it implies that the computer is doing something special with them. We are therefore switching to a design that uses Boxer-style boxes (diSessa and Abelson 1989) and that displays system properties in a separate area.

An encouraging result of our studies is that girls seem to enjoy using KidSim just as much as boys. We want to design a system that does not have a gender bias, and we are interested in conducting further studies to better understand which features of an interactive environment are particularly appealing to girls, and which are particularly unappealing.

Gilmore Study

Once the prototype was working, Prof. David Gilmore conducted an informal user study at the Centre for Research in Development, Instruction and Training at the University of Nottingham. His study involved 56 children between the ages of 8 and 14. Their exposure to KidSim varied from one to eight hours, in multiple sessions, with the children working together in groups of two or three. Most of the children claimed some computer experience, although generally not with Apple Macintosh computers. Minimal instruction in KidSim was provided, consisting of approximately ten minutes with an introductory worksheet.

The sessions were quite open-ended. Initially, the students were given some ideas of rules to write, such as "move a creature rightwards along the ground." Most all children found the rule-writing interface easy to use and were able to generate multiple rules for their characters. Most importantly, it was evident that the system provoked their imaginations—children invented goals for themselves and created their own characters and situations. They created a soccer game, PacMan, a maze traversal game, ninja turtles, and an aquarium.

These efforts do not constitute a formal test of KidSim. Nevertheless, the results are so positive that we are encouraged to think that the KidSim approach has promise. We are planning to conduct a structured test in the fifth-grade classrooms from our "Post-It Notes" study. The teachers in these classrooms have developed a curriculum around a particular simulation based on Dewdney (1984).

Design Changes

Our main design goal was to produce a tool that children would be able to use to create their own simulations. Every step in the design involved tradeoffs between making KidSim powerful enough that children would find it expressive and engaging, and making it simple enough that they would not find it frustrating or confusing. Our periodic user testing has helped us to see where our initial design choices erred in one direction or the other.

Simple Inheritance

In the original version of KidSim, it was possible to create arbitrarily deep hierarchies of character types. For instance, one could create clown fish, which are a type of fish, which are a type of animal, which is a type of object. We wanted users to create new rules and properties by adding them to a particular charac-

Figure 16. An "Obstacle" Jar, containing fences and rocks.

When the user clicks on a fence in a rule (Figure 17), a popup menu lists "Fence 27," "Fence," "Object," and "Obstacles." The user can select any one as the desired interpretation of what that object is to represent in the rule. Thus Jars can compensate somewhat for the absence of a deep hierarchy.

ter on the game board, but we were not satisfied with any of our schemes for determining how to propagate new rules and properties up the inheritance hierarchy. Furthermore, the deep hierarchy led to potentially confusing situations, since users could instantiate abstract superclasses. Thus, it was possible to have an object on the game board which was an instance of animal, while other objects were instances of clown fish and sharks.

As a result of these difficulties, we changed to a simple inheritance scheme that admits only a single level of character types. This mechanism is certainly less powerful. For example, to add a "swimming" rule to all clown fish, sharks, and whales, users must put a copy of that rule in each of these three character types.

Independent of the "deep hierarchy" issue, we have been interested in allowing children to create new categories at any time. After creating a rule for jumping over fences, for instance, a user might want to use the same rule for jumping over rocks. We therefore added a new feature to KidSim, called "Jars" (figure 16). The user can create a new jar, name it "Obstacles," and put Fences and Rocks in the jar.

Characters Larger than a Square

Our current implementation assumes that every character fits into a single square on the board. This simplifying assumption makes it much easier to specify rules in terms of the squares neighboring a character.

Although we were quite content with this simple approach, our users were not. They frequently want to create worlds where some characters are much

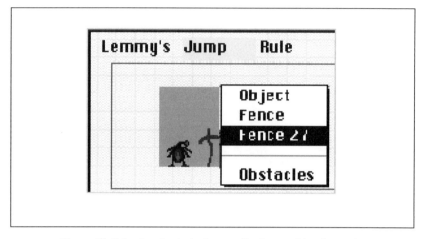

Figure 17. Selecting the desired generality for an object in a rule.

larger than others. This means that our initial design decision resulted in a tool that was not sufficiently expressive. For instance, one user wanted to create a large horse that could carry several riders, and found it very unsatisfying to have to draw the horse in a single square. Therefore, our user studies have convinced us to modify KidSim to allow characters larger than a square, even though this will complicate the rule system.

Related Work

KidSim draws on four traditions in computer programming and human-computer interaction: production systems, graphical rewrite rules, programming by demonstration, and simulations.

Executing the first matching rule in a list of test-action rules comes from production systems. Graphical rewrite rules are used as a programming language in BITPICT (Furnas 1991) and are used to program simulations in Tableau (Kay 1988), ChemTrains (Bell 1993), and AgentSheets (Repenning 1993). Mondrian (Lieberman 1993) uses programming by demonstration to create rules represented by before-after pictures, similar to the storyboard representation of Chimera's macros (Kurlander 1993). The mixed icons and text used to represent program steps was used in Shoptalk (Cohen 1991).

KidSim is a successor to Playground (Fenton 1989). Playground had the same goal of enabling children to create simulations. The most important positive thing that we learned from Playground was that its basic model of allowing children to create their own characters, and to attach rules to characters, was powerful and engaging. The most important negative thing that we learned was that scripting languages are too hard for children, even though Playground characters had a nice structure for storing programs, and the system provided a structure editor for creating syntactically correct statements. We also learned that characters should be allowed to directly manipulate other characters, since Playground did not allow this, and users found it too restrictive.

The system closest to KidSim is AgentSheets (Repenning 1993). AgentSheets is a general-purpose simulation environment, which experienced developers can use to create a variety of domain-specific applications. That is, AgentSheets itself is not intended for end users, but it provides a set of tools that programmers can use to produce a great variety of systems tailored to specific end users. Notably, Repenning produced a domain-specific application for Turing machines that uses graphical rewrite rules, with end users creating Turing machine programs by demonstrating the steps in the program.

LiveWorld (Travers 1994) is similar to KidSim in the style of the simulations that its users can create. Users make objects that move around on a board and interact with nearby objects. However, all programming in LiveWorld is done in Lisp, and therefore it is a much more powerful environment. Also, LiveWorld characters can contain sensors, which are a general and very effective means for specifying regions and objects of interest in a rule. LiveWorld also employs a powerful inheritance scheme.

Pinball Construction Set and SimCity are games that allow users to create interesting simulations, but users are limited to the pre-programmed behavior built into the objects that come with the application. KidSim is more akin to Rocky's Boots, which lets users create simple programs from a small set of primitives.

Summary

KidSim is a tool kit that makes it easy for children and nonprogramming adults to construct and modify simulations by programming their behavior. It takes a new approach to programming by getting rid of the traditional programming language syntax. Drawing on the lessons learned from personal computer user interfaces, KidSim combines two powerful ideas: graphical rewrite rules and programming by demonstration. The result appears to solve the end-user programming problem for some types of simulations.

There are several features that we are planning to add to KidSim. We would like rules to be able to produce sounds and to be able to test for sounds. We plan to introduce a feature to rules for referring to objects that are not spatially close to the character. We want to add buttons and switches so that users can interact with a simulation as it is running, as in video games. And we are adding subroutines so that rules can be grouped together. Subroutines should help to manage the complexity of having large numbers of rules and also provide some additional control over the order in which rules are tested. We would like to conduct further user tests to see whether children are able to use properties effectively and whether they can understand large sets of rules. We would also like to determine whether KidSim is suitable for younger children.

Ultimately we want to extend KidSim to adult programming tasks (AdultSim?). At the moment, we do not know how to do this, and we suspect that the effort required will be nontrivial. However, we do feel that we can characterize the result: all successful end-user programming systems for adults (or kids) will follow the UI principles we have described.

Acknowledgments

We wish express our gratitude to the many people who have helped design and test KidSim: to the two marvelous fifth-grade teachers Betty Jo Allen-Conn in the Los Angeles Open Magnet School and Phyllis Lewcock in the Cupertino Stevens Creek Elementary School, as well as to Julaine Salem, a technical support teacher in the Cupertino Union School District who has assisted both; to all their kids who have told us what they like and do not like, especially Brad Harrah, Liz Wertz, Emily Dean, Shane Varaiya, Joey Steger, Colin Yamaoka, Marcus Contro, Elnas Farnam, Alison Lucero, and Andrew Noto; to Alan Kay's Vivarium project for endowing the Open School with computers and innovative ideas and to Apple's Classroom of Tomorrow (ACOT) project for doing the same with the Stevens Creek School; to Apple Computer for its generous support and continuing interest in education. We would like to thank Alan Kay for many important ideas. His respect for teachers, for the art of teaching, and for the importance of powerful ideas has informed our work. Thanks to David Maulsby, Edwin Bos, Kurt Schmucker, Stephanie Houde, Jeff Bradshaw and Rachel Bellamy for many valuable discussions. We appreciate the following people for advocating important features: Alex Repenning, for sequential execution; Enio Ohmaye, for jars; and Peter Jensen, for simple inheritance. Many thanks to the programmers who have assisted us: Peter Jensen, for the port to Prograph; Rodrigo Madanes, for appearances; Dave Vronay, for the drawing editor; David Maulsby, for jars; Edwin Bos, for subroutines; and Don Tilman and Ramón Felciano. For his strikingly creative animations and graphics, we thank Mark Loughridge. Thanks to the SK8 team. KidSim wouldn't exist without this wonderful environment: Ruben Kleiman (architecture), Adam Chipkin (scripting), Hernan Epelman-Wang (graphics), Brian Roddy (interface), and Alan Peterson (support). For management and support, we thank Dana Schockmel, Kurt Schmucker, Jim Spohrer, Mark Miller, and Rick LeFaivre. For the UK user test, we thank David Gilmore, Karen Pheasey, and Jean and Geoff Underwood. Their study was funded by the UK Economic and Social Research Council and NATO. And finally, a special thank you to Professor Dewdney for the *Planiverse*, the microworld which launched the KidSim effort.

References

Apple Computer, Inc. 1992. *Macintosh Human Interface Guidelines*. Reading, Mass.: Addison-Wesley.

Baecker, R. M., and Buxton, W. A. S. 1987. *Readings in Human-Computer Interaction*. San Francisco, Calif.: Morgan Kaufmann.

Bell, B., and Lewis, C. 1993. CHEMTRAINS: A Language for Creating Behaving Pictures. In Proceedings of the IEEE Workshop on Visual Languages, 188–195. Washington, D.C.: IEEE Computer Society.

Cohen, P. 1991. Integrated Interfaces for Decision Support with Simulation, Technical Note 507, AI Center, SRI International, Menlo Park, California.

Cypher, A. 1993a. EAGER: Programming Repetitive Tasks by Demonstration. In *Watch What I Do: Programming by Demonstration,* ed. A. Cypher, 205–217. Cambridge, Mass.: MIT Press.

Cypher, A., ed. 1993b. *Watch What I Do: Programming by Demonstration*. Cambridge, Mass.: MIT Press.

Davis, R., and King, J. 1975. An Overview of Production Systems, Technical Report, STAN-CS-75-524, Computer Science Department, Stanford University.

Dewdney, A. K. 1984. *The Planiverse, Computer Contact with a Two-Dimensional World*. New York: Poseidon.

diSessa, A. A., and Abelson, H. 1989. BOXER: A Reconstructible Computational Medium. In *Studying the Novice Programmer*, 467–481. Hillsdale, N.J.: Lawrence Erlbaum.

Fenton, J., and Beck, K. 1989. PLAYGROUND: An Object-Oriented Simulation System with Agent Rules for Children of All Ages. In Proceedings of Object-Oriented Programming: Systems, Languages, and Applications '89, 123–137. New York: Association of Computing Machinery.

Furnas, G. 1991. New Graphical Reasoning Models for Understanding Graphical Interfaces. In Proceedings of Computer-Human Interaction '91, 71–78. New York: Association of Computing Machinery.

Halbert, D. 1984. Programming by Example. Ph D. diss., Department of Electrical Engineering and Computer Science, University of California at Berkeley.

Heckel, P. 1982. *The Elements of Friendly Software Design*. San Francisco, Calif.: Sybex.

Kurlander, D. 1993. CHIMERA: Example-Based Graphical Editing. In *Watch What I Do: Programming by Demonstration,* ed. A. Cyper, 271–290. Cambridge, Mass.: MIT Press.

Laurel, B., ed. 1990. *The Art of Human-Computer Interface Design*. Reading, Mass.: Addison-Wesley.

Lieberman, H. 1993. MONDRIAN: A Teachable Graphical Editor. In *Watch What I Do: Programming by Demonstration,* ed A. Cyper, 341–358. Cambridge, Mass.: MIT Press.

Maher, M. L.; Sriram, D.; and Fenves, S. J. 1984. Tools and Techniques for Knowledge-Based Expert Systems for Engineering Design. *Advances in Engineering Software* 6(4): 178–188.

Newell, A., and Simon, H. A. 1972. *Human Problem Solving*. Englewood Cliffs, N.J.: Prentice-Hall.

Repenning, A. 1993. AGENTSHEETS: A Tool for Building Domain-Oriented Dynamic, Visual Environments. Ph.D. diss., Department of Computer Science, University of Colorado at Boulder.

Rychener, M. D. 1976. Production Systems as a Programming Language for Artificial Intelligence. Ph.D. diss., Department of Computer Science, Carnegie-Mellon University.

Scardamalia, M., and Bereiter, C. 1991. Higher Levels of Agency for Children in Knowledge Building: A Challenge for the Design of New Knowledge Media. *Journal of the Learning Sciences* 1(1): 37–68.

Sloman, A. 1971. Interactions between Philosophy and Artificial Intelligence: The Role of Intuition and Non-Logical Reasoning in Intelligence. In Proceedings of the Second International Joint Conference on Artificial Intelligence, 270–278. Menlo Park, Calif.: International Joint Conferences on Artificial Intelligence.

Smith, D. C. 1977. PYGMALION, *A Computer Program to Model and Stimulate Creative Thought*. Basel, Switzerland: Birkhäuser Verlag.

Smith, D. C.; Irby, C.; Kimball, R.; Verplank, W.; and Harslem, E. 1982. Designing the STAR User Interface. *Byte* 7(4): 242–282.

Soloway, E., and Spohrer, J. 1989. *Studying the Novice Programmer*. Hillsdale, N.J.: Lawrence Erlbaum.

Tesler, L.; Enea, H.; and Smith, D. C. 1973. The Lisp70 Pattern-Matching System. In Proceedings of the Third International Joint Conference on Artificial Intelligence, 671–676. Menlo Park, Calif.: International Joint Conferences on Artificial Intelligence.

Travers, M. 1994. Recursive Interfaces for Reactive Objects. In Proceedings of Computer-Human Interaction '94, 379–385. New York: Association of Computing Machinery.

CHAPTER 10

Lifelike Computer Characters:
The Persona Project at Microsoft

Gene Ball, Dan Ling, David Kurlander, John Miller, David Pugh, Tim Skelly, Andy Stankosky, David Thiel, Maarten Van Dantzich, & Trace Wax

The computing industry of the 1990s is in the process of fully adopting the graphical user interface metaphor pioneered by Xerox PARC in the 1970s. This metaphor, first explored by the Smalltalk system on the Alto (Goldberg 1984), was already firmly defined in most significant respects when the Xerox Star was introduced in 1980 (Smith et al. 1982). The concepts of WYSIWYG editing, overlapping screen windows, and the direct manipulation of system objects as icons had all been thoroughly demonstrated. The subsequent decade has seen considerable refinement of the original ideas, particularly regarding usability issues and the idea of visual affordances (Norman 1988), but the essence of the original metaphor is intact. As GUIs become the industry standard, it is appropriate to look ahead to the next major metaphor shift in computing. While there are undoubtedly many further improvements that can (and will) be made to the GUI metaphor, it seems unlikely that computing in 2015 will still be primarily a process of clicking and dragging buttons and icons on a metaphorical desktop (Nielson 1993). Improvements in display technology, miniaturization, wireless communication, and of course processor performance and memory capacity will all contribute to the rapid proliferation of increasingly sophisticated personal computing devices. But it is the evolution of software capability that will trigger a basic change in the user interface metaphor: computers will become assistants rather than just tools.

The coming decade will see increasing efforts to develop software which can perform large tasks autonomously, hiding as many of the details from the user as possible. Rather than invoking a sequence of commands which cause a program to carry out small, well-defined, and predictable operations, the user will specify the overall goals of a task and delegate to the computer responsibility for working out the details. In the specification process, the user will need to describe tasks rather than just select them from predefined alternatives. Like a human assistant, the machine may need to clarify uncertainties in its understanding of the task and may occasionally need to ask the user's advice on how best to proceed. And like a human, it will make suggestions and initiate actions that seem appropriate, given its model of the user's goals. Finally, a successful assistant will sometimes take risks, when it judges that the costs of interrupting the user outweigh the potential costs of proceeding in error.

Requirements for an Assistive Interface

The machinelike metaphor of a direct manipulation interface is not a good match to the communication needs of a computer assistant and its boss. In order to be successful, an assistant-like interface will need to:

- *Support interactive give and take.* Assistants don't respond only when asked a direct question. They ask questions to clarify their understanding of an assignment, describe their plans and anticipated problems, negotiate task descriptions to fit the skills and resources available, report on progress, and submit results as they become available.

- *Recognize the costs of interaction and delay.* It is inappropriate to require the user's confirmation of every decision made while carrying out a task. Current systems usually ask because they have a very weak understanding of the consequences of their actions. An assistive interface must model the significance of its decisions and the potential costs of an error so that it can choose to avoid bothering the user with details that aren't important. Especially as the assistant becomes responsible for ongoing tasks, the cost of interrupting a user who is concentrating on something else (or of waiting when the user isn't available), must be taken into account.

- *Manage interruptions effectively.* When it is necessary to initiate an interaction with the user, the assistant needs to do so carefully, recognizing the likelihood that the user is already occupied to some degree. The system may be able to tell that the user is typing furiously, or talking on the telephone, and should wait until an appropriate pause (depending on the urgency of the interruption). Even when apparently idle, the user might be deep in thought, so a noncritical interruption should be tentative in any case.

- *Acknowledge the social and emotional aspects of interaction.* A human assistant quickly learns that "appropriate behavior" depends on the task, the time of day, and the boss's mood. To become a comfortable working partner, a computer assistant will need to vary its behavior depending on such variables as well. Social user interfaces have tremendous potential to enliven the interface and make the computing experience more enjoyable for the user, but they must be able to quickly recognize cues that non-critical interactions are not welcome.

Conversational Interfaces: The Persona Project

How will we interact with computer assistants? The most natural and convenient way will be by means of a natural spoken dialogue. Since we are convinced that users will be unwilling to speak to the computer in specialized command languages, spoken conversational interaction will only become popular when the assistant can understand a broad range of English paraphrases of the user's intent. However, sufficient progress has now been made on speech recognition and natural language understanding that the prospect of a useful conversational interface has become a realistic goal.

The Persona project at Microsoft Research began in late 1992 to undertake the construction of a lifelike computer assistant, a character within the PC which interacts with the user in a natural spoken dialogue and has an expressive visual presence. The project set out to build on the ongoing research efforts at Microsoft in speech recognition (Huang et al. 1995) and natural language processing (NLP) (Jensen 1993), as well as develop new reactive three-dimensional computer animation techniques (Ball et al. 1994).

The goal was to achieve a level of conversational competence and visual reactivity that allows a user to suspend disbelief and interact with our assistant in a natural fashion.

As a first step, we have constructed a prototype conversational system in which our character (a parrot named Peedy) acts as music assistant, allowing the user to ask about a collection of audio CDs and select songs to be played. Peedy listens to spoken English requests and maintains a rudimentary model of the dialogue state, allowing him to respond (verbally or with actions) in a conversationally appropriate way.

Related Work

The creation of a lifelike computer character requires the integration of a wide variety of technologies and skills. A comprehensive review of all the research relevant to the task is therefore beyond the scope of this chapter. Instead, this section simply attempts to provide references to the work which has most directly influenced our efforts.

The work of Cliff Nass and Byron Reeves at Stanford University (Reeves and Nass 1996) has demonstrated that interaction with computers inevitably evokes human social responses.

Their studies have shown that in many ways people treat computers *as human*, even when the computer interface is not explicitly anthropomorphic. Their work has convinced us that since users will anthropomorphize a computer system in any case, the presence of a lifelike character is perhaps the best way to achieve some measure of control over the social and psychological aspects of the interaction.

The Microsoft (1995) "Bob" product development team has created a collection of home computer applications based entirely on the metaphor of a *Social User Interface*, in which an animated personal guide is the primary interface to the computer. The guide communicates to the user through speech balloons which present a small group of buttons for the operations most likely to be used next. This allows the user to focus on a single source of relevant information without becoming overwhelmed by large numbers of options. The guides also provide tips and suggestions to introduce new capabilities or to point out more efficient ways of completing a task. User studies with Bob have verified that for many people, the social metaphor reduces the anxiety associated with computer use.

Efforts to create lifelike characters are underway in a number of other research organizations, including the Oz project at Carnegie-Mellon University (Bates 1994), Takeuchi's work at Sony Computer Science Laboratory (Takeuchi and Nagao 1993), the Jack project at the University of Pennsylvania (Badler, Phillips, and Webber 1993), the CAIT project at Stanford (Hayes-Roth et al. 1995), and the Autonomous Agents Group at the MIT Media Laboratory (Maes 1994).

In the linguistic processing required of a conversational assistant, we attempt to find a practical balance between knowledge intensive approaches to understanding (e.g. Lockheed's Homer [Vere and Bickmore 1990]) and more pragmatic natural command languages (e.g. CMU's Phoenix [Ward 1991]).

We are convinced that useful conversational interfaces will have to simulate many of the subtle dialogue mechanisms that humans use to communicate effectively. Our (still very preliminary) efforts in that direction are based on the work of Cohen (1992), Clark (1992), and Walker and Whittaker (1990).

Relevant references on the visual presentation of a character include work on physically realistic animation at Georgia Tech (Hodgins 1994) and DEC (Waters 1987), procedural generation of natural motion at NYU (Perlin 1994), and the coordination of simulation and animation at IBM (Lewis, Koved, and Ling 1991). Our work on pre-compiled action plans is most similar to the work of Schoppers (1987). Key issues for the effective audio presentation of lifelike characters include work on emotive speech (Cahn 1989) and rich soundscapes (Gaver, Smith, and O'Shea 1991).

Persona System Overview

For the reasons discussed above, it seems quite likely that conversational assistants will play a major role in our interactions with computers in the next century. Many of the technologies involved, including speech recognition, natural language understanding, animation, and speech synthesis, have been the focus of significant research efforts for many years. In addition to specialized research efforts in those topics, we decided in 1992 to undertake the construction of a complete conversational assistant. That decision was motivated by two complementary goals:

- First, an integrated system could serve as a testing ground for the individual technologies. The requirements of a conversational assistant would stress each technology in specific (and sometimes unexpected) ways, and serve to motivate and guide research for those components. Further, many integration issues will have to be resolved before conversational assistants can become a mainstream capability, and a prototype system can be a productive way to explore methods for combining complex technologies into a coherent architecture.

- Second, the overall experience of interacting with a computer assistant is likely to be profoundly different from using the component technologies individually. The anthropomorphic nature of the assistant ensures that it will generate social and psychological responses in the user which are qualitatively different from those encountered with traditional computer interfaces. In addition, the use of spoken conversation is likely to raise expectations of human competence that must be controlled (i.e. lowered) in order to avoid disappointing the user. We expected that a conversational prototype would be a useful testbed for exploring the dynamics of interaction with a computer character—dynamics that can't be experienced without an integrated system.

A diagram of the prototype system that we built (named Personal Digital Parrot One: i.e., PDP1, or Peedy for short) can be seen in Figure 1. Because of the anthropomorphic nature of the system, the name Peedy naturally transferred to our initial character (a parrot) as well. In the remainder of the chapter, "Peedy" (or "he") will be used to refer to the prototype system and the character interchangeably.

Each time Peedy receives a spoken input, he responds with a combination of visual and audio output. Figure 2 shows a transcript of a brief interaction with Peedy. For purposes of discussion here, the system will be split into three subsystems:

- *Spoken language processing* (consisting of the Whisper, Names, NLP, and Semantic modules in figure 1), which accepts microphone input and translates it into a high level input event description,

- *Dialogue management* (Dialogue in figure 1), which accepts input events and decides how the character will respond,

- *Video and Audio output* (Player/ReActor & Speech Controller), which, in response to dialogue output requests, generates the animated motion, speech, and sound effects necessary to communicate to the user in a convincingly lifelike way.

These subsystems constitute the user interface of the system, which controls a

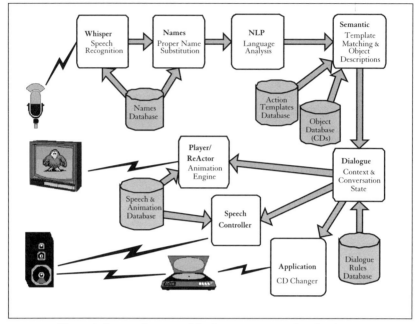

Figure 1. System diagram of the Persona conversational assistant.

simple application that allows the user to select and play music from a collection of audio compact discs (labeled Application in figure 1).

Goals for the Subsystems

In each of these three areas, we began the prototype with a number of long-term goals in mind and then tried to achieve a minimum workable subset on a realistic path toward those goals. In this section, we enumerate those goals and summarize the prototype's status with respect to them. Discussion of future work has been deferred to the end of the chapter.

Language Our eventual goal for the spoken language subsystem is to allow users to express requests in natural conversational English, without any need to learn a specialized command language. The character should be able to understand any likely paraphrase of a request that is within its capabilities.

In the current prototype, we have tried to construct a framework that could be extended to meet that goal, but its current capabilities are quite limited. Spoken commands must currently come from a limited set of about 150 "typical" utterances that might be encountered in the CD audio application. These utterances are recognized as paraphrases of one of 17 canonical requests that Peedy understands.

[Peedy is asleep on his perch.]
User: Good morning, Peedy.
[Peedy rouses]
Peedy: Good morning.
User: Let's do a demo.
[Peedy stands up, smiles]
Peedy: Your wish is my command, what would you like to hear?
User: What have you got by Bonnie Raitt?
[Peedy waves in a stream of notes, and grabs one as they rush by.]
Peedy: I have "The Bonnie Raitt Collection" from 1990.
User: Pick something from that.
Peedy: How about "Angel from Montgomery"?
User: Sounds good.
[Peedy drops note on pile]
Peedy: OK.
User: Play some rock after that.
[Peedy scans the notes again, selects one]
Peedy: How about "Fools in Love"?
User: Who wrote that?
[Peedy cups one wing to his 'ear']
Peedy: Huh?
User: Who wrote that?
[Peedy looks up, scrunches his brow]
Peedy: Joe Jackson
User: Fine.
[Drops note on pile]
Peedy: OK.

Figure 2: Sample dialogue with Peedy.

Dialogue. The dialogue controller is probably the most open-ended component of the system (Figure 2). Since it acts as Peedy's "brain," deciding how to respond to perceptual stimuli, it could eventually become a quite sophisticated model of a computer assistant's memory, goals, plans, and emotions. However, in order to reduce complexity, we decided to limit ourselves to "canned plans"—e.g. predefined sequences of actions that can be authored as part of the creation of a character, then activated in response to input events. This mechanism must be made flexible enough to allow multiple sequences to be active simultaneously (e.g. to let a misunderstanding correction subdialogue occur at any point within a music selection interaction). In addition, to enhance the believability of a character, we feel that its behavior should be affected by memories of earlier interactions within the dialogue (or in previous conversations) and by a simple model of its emotional state.

The dialogue controller in the current system includes sequences for only a few conversational interactions, with no facility for managing subdialogues. We have experimented with some preliminary implementations of episodic memory and an emotional model but haven't fully integrated those with the rest of the system.

Video and Audio Output. For the animation subsystem, our goal is to create a convincing visual and aural representation of a character, which when given fairly abstract requests for action by the dialogue controller, can then carry out those requests with smoothly believable motion and synchronized sound. Because the character's actions must fit into the ongoing dialogue, the ability to instantly produce an appropriate animation is critical. We also wish to use film techniques to enhance the clarity and interest of the visual presentation and to create a rich and convincing acoustic environment. Finally, some variation is needed in the animation sequences so as to avoid obvious repetition and to maintain the illusion of natural motion.

The Player/ReActor runtime animation system has been very successful at producing reactive real-time sequences of high quality animation. In the current system, however, all camera control and movement variability must be hand authored. We also chose to forego the flexibility of a general text-to-speech system because such systems currently lack the naturalness and expressivity that our character requires. Thus in the current system, the authoring effort required to produce new animation sequences (defining character motion, camera control, sound effects, and pre-recorded speech) is much higher than we would like.

Hardware Environment

The language and dialogue subsystems of the Peedy prototype currently run on a 90 MHz Pentium PC under Windows NT, without any specialized signal processing hardware. ReActor (including graphics rendering at 8 to 15 frames per second) runs on a Silicon Graphics Indigo2. The system is coded in G (language transformation rules), C, C++, and Visual Basic. Language processing for each utterance, exclusive of database searches, typically takes well under a second. However, database queries and communication delays between system components increase the typical response latency to several seconds. While much of this delay can be attributed to the prototyping development environment, we expect the reduction of system latency to be a major ongoing challenge.

Implementation

This section describes the capabilities and implementation of each subsystem of the Persona prototype in detail. The prototype is quite shallow in its capabilities, yet it is very effective at producing the illusion of conversational interaction. The implementation specifics therefore serve both to document the shortcuts and tricks that we've used to achieve that illusion and also to demonstrate that the system organization can support continued development toward the goals outlined above.

The final section outlines the next steps that we feel are appropriate for each component and discusses our plans for continued development.

Spoken Language Processing

As described above, a key goal for the spoken language subsystem of the Persona project is to allow users flexibility to express their requests in the syntactic form they find most natural. Therefore, we have chosen to base the interface on a broad-coverage natural language processing system, even though the assistant currently understands requests in only a very limited domain.

It is precisely the flexibility (and familiarity) of spoken language that makes it such an attractive interface: users decide what they wish to say to the assistant and express it in whatever fashion they find most natural. As long as the *meaning* of the statement is within the (limited) range that the assistant understands, then the system should respond appropriately. Attempts to define specialized English subsets as command languages can be frustrating for users who discover that natural (to them, if not the designer) paraphrases of their requests cannot be understood.

The approach taken in Peedy combines aspects of both knowledge-intensive understanding systems and of more pragmatic task-oriented systems. Our system is built on a broad-coverage natural language system which constructs a rich semantic representation of the utterance, which is then mapped directly into a task-based semantic structure. The goal is to provide the flexibility and expressive power of natural language within a limited task domain and to do so with only a moderate amount of domain-specific implementation effort. In this respect, our approach is most similar to pragmatic natural command language systems, but we have chosen to base our efforts on a rich natural language foundation, so that we will be able to expand the system's linguistic capabilities as the language processing technology continues to develop.

The remainder of the spoken language processing section describes the language processing in the current Persona prototype, focusing especially on the interface between the broad-coverage natural language processing system and the Persona semantic module (labeled NLP and Semantic in figure 1).

Whisper Speech Recognition. Spoken input to the Persona assistant is transcribed by Whisper, a real-time, speaker-independent continuous speech recognition system under development at Microsoft Research (Gaver, Smith, and O'Shea 1991). In the current Peedy prototype, all possible user utterances are described to the system by a context free grammar. For example, Figure 3 shows the portion of the grammar which generates the 16 variations of "Play something by Madonna after that" that Peedy recognizes.

```
STATEMENT play something by ARTIST TIMEREF
TIMEREF after that
TIMEREF next
ARTIST madonna
ARTIST joe jackson
ARTIST claude debussy
ARTIST andrew lloyd webber
ARTIST synchro system
ARTIST pearl jam
ARTIST joe cocker
ARTIST bonnie raitt
```

Figure 3: Grammar for one legal Peedy statement.

The user speaks one statement at a time, using a push-to-talk button to indicate the extent of the utterance. Because Whisper is a continuous recognizer, each sentence can be spoken in a naturally fluid way, without noticeable breaks between words. The recognizer uses a voice model based on speech recorded by a large variety of male English speakers (female speakers use a separate voice model), so no specialized training of the system is required for a new speaker (although the limited grammar currently means that speakers must know which sentences can be understood).

Whisper compares its HMM phoneme models to the acoustic signal and finds the legal sentence from the grammar that most closely matches input. If the match is reasonably close, it forwards the corresponding text string (along with a confidence measure) to the next module.

Name Substitution. In the music selection task, user utterances may contain the names of artists, songs, or albums. These proper names (particularly titles) are likely to confuse a parser because they can contain out-of-context English phrases: e.g. "Play *before you accuse me* by Clapton." Unfortunately, current speech recognizers cannot detect the prosodic clues that indicate the inline

Therefore Peedy includes a name substitution step which scans the input text for possible matches to our database of names and titles (rating them according to plausibility) and substitutes placeholder nouns before passing the input to the parser. Alternative interpretations are presented to the parser (first substituting exact matches, then making no substitutions, and finally trying partial matches), stopping when a successful interpretation is found (figure 4). Because "Clapton" is only a partial match to the database entry "Eric Clapton," the proper interpretation is not the first one tried, but the earlier ones fail to produce a sensible interpretation.

This approach quite reliably finds the correct interpretation of understand-

```
#1 play track1 by clapton
   track1 = "before you accuse me"

#2 play before you accuse me by clapton

#3 play track1 by artist1
   track1 = "before you accuse me"
   artist1 = "Eric Clapton"

#4 play before you accuse me by artist1
   artist1 = "Eric Clapton"
```

Figure 4: Possible name substitutions for "Play before you accuse me by Clapton." Alternative #3 is interpreted successfully.

able sentences, but cannot deal with references to names that are not in our database. Currently, such references result in a failure to understand the input.

English Parsing. After names have been substituted, the input string is passed to the MS-NLP English processor, which produces a labeled semantic graph (referred to as the *logical form*) which encodes case frames or thematic roles. For example, the statement "I'd like to hear something composed by Mozart" results in a graph (figure 5) that represents "I (the speaker) would like that I hear something, where Mozart composed that something." Several strict English paraphrases produce identical logical forms, e.g.:

I'd like to hear something that was composed by Mozart.
I would like to hear something that Mozart composed.
I'd like to hear something Mozart composed.

MS-NLP processes each input utterance in three stages:

- *Syntactic Sketch:* syntactic analysis based on augmented phrase structure grammar rules (bottom-up, with alternatives considered in parallel)
- *Reassignment:* resolution of most syntactic ambiguities by using semantic information from on-line dictionary definitions,
- *Logical Form:* construction of a semantic graph which represents predicate-argument relations by assigning sentence elements to "deep" cases, or functional roles, including: Dsub (deep subject), Dobj (deep object), Dind (deep indirect object), Prop (modifying clause), etc.

The resulting graph encodes the semantic structure of the English utterance. Each graph node represents the root form of an input word; arcs are labeled by the appropriate deep cases.

```
like1 (+Modal +Past +Futr)
 Dsub——i1 (+Pers1 +Sing)
 Dobj——hear1
           Dsub——i1
           Dobj——something1 (+Indef +Exis +Pers3 +Sing)
                      Prop——compose1
                                Dsub——mozart1 (+Sing)
                                Dobj——something1
```

Figure 5: Logical Form produced by parse of
"I'd like to hear something composed by Mozart."

Application-Specific Transformations. The logical form is then processed by applying a sequence of graph transformations which use knowledge of both the interaction scenario and the task domain. These application-specific transformations recognize:

- Artifacts that commonly occur in conversational speech
- Language interpretations that are appropriate in the context of a user-assistant conversation
- Task-specific vocabulary
- Colloquial expressions and specialized grammatical constructs common in the task domain
- Descriptive qualifications of objects in the application

They convert them into a normalized domain-specific semantic representation that we call a *task graph* (see figure 6).

The task graph represents the same meaning as the logical form, but in terms of the concepts defined within a specific application. The application designer defines:

- *Abstract verbs*, which correspond to actions that the assistant can do, or knows about (e.g. vbPlay refers to playing a piece of music)
- *Object classes,* which name the categories of conceptual objects in the task domain (e.g. obTrack)
- *Object properties,* which label the possible attributes of each object class (e.g. pArtist, pRole)
- *Property values,* which enumerate sets of legal property values (e.g. vComposer, vRandom)

Object properties are used to label arcs in the task graph; the other application identifiers serve as graph nodes.

```
vbPlay1
  \Dsub——you1 (+Pers2 +Sing +Plur)
  \Dobj——obTrack1 (+Indef +Exis +Pers3 +Sing)
            \Prop——compose1
                       \Dsub——mozart1 (+Sing)
                       \Dobj——obTrack1
           \pSetSize—vOne
           \pSetChoice—vRandom
```

*Figure 6: Task graph produced from figure 5
by application of music assistant transformations.*

These application-specific transformations are carried out by rules written in G, a custom language developed as part of the MS-NLP project. Each rule specifies a structural pattern for a semantic graph: whenever the graph for the current utterance matches the pattern, the rule fires. The body of the rule can then modify the semantic graph appropriately.

Our rules are designed to translate a language-based representation of the user's utterance into an unambiguous application-specific representation. The driving force behind these rules is the need to recognize all legitimate English paraphrases of a request and reduce them to a single canonical structure. The canonical form allows the application to deal with a single well-specified representation of meaning while giving users nearly complete freedom to express that meaning in whatever fashion they find most comfortable.

A single English statement can be paraphrased in a variety of ways: by modifying vocabulary or syntactic structure or (especially in spoken communication) by employing colloquial, abbreviated, or nongrammatical constructions. In addition, spoken communication occurs within a social context that often alters the literal meaning of a statement. In Persona, we try to identify and deal with each category of paraphrase independently, for two reasons. First, many of our graph transformations might be applicable in related task domains, so they are grouped to facilitate possible reuse. Secondly, our transformations are designed to be applied in combination: each rule deals with a single source of variation, and the G processor executes all the rules which match a given utterance. Thus a small collection of individual rules can combine to cover a very wide range of possible paraphrases.

Verbal Artifacts. Verbal expression is often padded with extra phrases which contribute nothing essential to the communication (except perhaps time for the speakers to formulate their thoughts). Rules which remove these artifacts, converting (for example)

"Let's see, I think I'd like to hear some Madonna."

into

"I'd like to hear some Madonna."

are appropriate for applications using spoken input.

User-Assistant Interactions: Persona attempts to simulate an *assistant* helping the user in a particular task domain. This social context evokes a number of specialized language forms which are commonly used in interactions with assistants. For example, polite phrases, such as "please" and "thank you," do not directly affect the meaning of a statement. Other social conventions are critical to a correct understanding of the user's intent; in particular, an expression of desire on the user's behalf should generally be interpreted as a request for action by the assistant. Therefore, Persona includes rules which recognize the semantic graphs for forms such as:

"I'd like to hear some Madonna."
"I want to hear some Madonna."
"It would be nice to hear some Madonna."
and translate them into a graph corresponding to the explicit imperative:
"Let me hear some Madonna."

These transformations would be appropriate for interaction with Persona in any application domain.

Synonym Recognition: A major source of variability in English paraphrases comes from simple vocabulary substitution. For each abstract verb and object class in the application, we use a Persona rule to translate any of a set of synonyms into the corresponding abstract term. These synonyms often include ones which are context dependent; for example in our music selection application, "platter" and "collection" are transformed into *obCD*, "music" and "something" become *obTrack*, and "start" and "spin" translate into *vbPlay*. This approach generates correct interpretations of a wide variety of task-specific utterances, including:

"Spin a platter by Dave Brubeck."
"I'd like to hear a piece from the new Mozart collection."
"Start something by Madonna."

However, it does so at the expense of finding valid interpretations for very unlikely statements, e.g.:

"Spin a music from the rock platter."

In practice, we expect this to cause little difficulty within narrow domains; however, as we generalize to related applications, we expect conflicts to arise. By first translating generic or ambiguous words into more general abstract terms (e.g. "Play something" into *vbPlay obPlayable*) we can postpone interpretation to the necessary point, so that in "Play something by Hitchcock," "something" can be resolved as *obMovie* based on the results of the database search.

Colloquialisms. Another class of application-specific transformations deals with specialized grammatical conventions within the domain. To understand a statement like:

"How about some Madonna."

we treat "how about" as equivalent to "play," and employ a rule which recognizes "play artist" as an abbreviation for "play something by artist." In a similar fashion, an isolated object description can be assumed to be a request for the default action, as in "A little Mozart, please." We expect that each task domain will require a few idiosyncratic rules of this sort, which compensate for the tendency of speakers to omit details which are obvious from the interaction context. In effect, these rules define a model of the default interaction context, which depends only on the task domain. An explicit model of the current dialogue context is used to properly interpret anaphoric references and fragments used to clarify earlier miscommunications (e.g. "The one by Mozart.").

Object Descriptions. The majority of our application-specific transformation rules are designed to interpret descriptions of objects within the task domain. Much of the expressive power of natural language comes from the ability to reference objects by describing them, rather than by identifying them with unambiguous names. Therefore it is critical that Persona be able to properly interpret a wide variety of domain object descriptions.

A Persona application defines a collection of descriptive properties which can be used to qualify references to objects within the domain. For example, a track from a CD can be described by combinations of the following attributes: title, title of containing CD, position on CD, year, musical genre, energy level, vocal/instrumental, year produced, date acquired, music label, length, or the names of its singers, composers, lyricists, musicians, producers, etc. Persona rules evaluate the modifiers of each object in the logical form and transform them into the appropriate property values. Typical examples include:

- Adjectives that imply both a property and its value ("jazz CD" implies pGenre:vJazz);
- Nouns that identify an object and also specify other attributes ("concerto" implies pGenre: vClassical);
- Cases where the interpretation cannot be determined without additional context ("new CD" could refer to either pDateAcquired or pYearProduced, so a generic property pAge is passed to the action routines); and
- Propositional Modifiers ("the CD I bought yesterday" transforms into pDateAcquired: vYesterday).

While the collection of descriptive attributes will vary for each application, we expect that there will be many similarities across related domains, and it will therefore be possible to migrate many rules into new domains.

Action Templates. After all legal transformations have been applied, the resulting task graph is matched against a collection of *action templates* which represent utterances that the application "understands," in other words, knows how to respond to. If the Persona matcher locates a template with the same abstract verb and deep case fillers, then processing continues with the evaluation (e.g. by running a database query) of any *object descriptions* in the task graph. For example, the template for any request that Persona play one or more tracks from a CD:

vbPlay Dsub: you Dobj: obTrack

matches the task graph in figure 6. Then the description of obTrack, consisting of properties such as pArtist, pSetSize, and pSetChoice can be evaluated. In this case, a database query is executed which finds all tracks in the music collection which have Mozart listed as composer. Finally, an event descriptor corresponding to the matched template (including the results of the object evaluations) is transmitted to the dialogue module.

Dialogue Management

Upon receipt of an input event descriptor from the language subsystem, the dialogue manager is responsible for triggering Peedy's reaction: an appropriate set of animations, verbal responses, and application actions, given the current dialogue situation. In the Peedy prototype, that situation is represented in two parts: the current conversational state and a collection of context variables.

Conversational State Machine. The conversational state is represented by a simple finite state machine, which models the sequence of interactions that occur in the conversation. For each conversational state (e.g. Peedy has just suggested a track that the user may wish to hear), the state machine has an action associated with every input event type. The current state machine has just five conversational states and seventeen input events, which results in approximately 100 distinct transitions (in a few cases, there are multiple transitions for a single state/event pair, based on additional context as described below).

Each transition in the state machine can contain commands to trigger animation sequences, generate spoken output, or activate application (CD player) operations. For example, Figure 7 shows the rule that would be activated if Peedy had just said "I have The Bonnie Raitt Collection, would you like to hear something from that?" (stGotCD), and the user responded with "Sure" (evOK). Peedy's response would be to:

- Trigger the *pePickTrack* animation, which causes Peedy to look down at the CD (note) that he's holding as if considering a choice,
- Expand the description of the current CD into a list of the songs it contains (genTracks),
- Select one or two tracks, based on the parameters given in the interaction (doSelect)— in this example, Peedy would pick one track at random, and

State	Event	NewState	Action
stGotCD	evOK	stSuggested	do
pePickTrack	genTracks;	doSelect;	Say <!PDSays(howAbout)>

Figure 7. Example dialogue state transition.

- Verbally offer the selected song, e.g. "How about *Angels from Montgomery?*", with the appropriate beak-sync.

Context and Anaphora. In addition to the conversational state, the Peedy dialogue manager also maintains a collection of context variables, which it uses to record parameters and object descriptions that may affect Peedy's behavior. This mechanism is used to handle simple forms of anaphora and to customize behavior based upon the objects referenced in the user's request.

For example, the question "Who wrote that?" generates the action template:

vbTell Dsub: you Dobj: obArtist(pRole: vComposer, pWork: refObX)

which corresponds to the paraphrase "Tell me the artist who composed that work." *refObX* is interpreted as the last referenced object, and the identifier of that object is retrieved from the corresponding context variable. The specified database query is then performed (i.e.: what Artist composed "Angel From Montgomery") and the result is stored in context variables. Then the input event *evWhoWroteTrack* is sent to the dialogue manager. State transition rules can be predicated upon context expressions; so in figure 8 the appropriate rule will fire, depending on the number of artists that were found by the query, and Peedy will respond with either "Bonnie Raitt" or "I don't know." (More than one artist match isn't currently handled.)

Verbal Responses by Template Expansion. In the examples above, the *Say* action in a dialogue state transition was used to generate Peedy's spoken output. The argument to *Say* is a template expression, which specifies the category of verbal response that is desired. Figure 9 shows the four templates for the category *haveCD* in the current system, which Peedy would use to respond to "Have you got anything by Bonnie Raitt?" The system chooses one of the templates based on the specified probabilities; in this case, the choices are equally likely (the first is chosen 1 in 4 times; otherwise, the second has a 1 in 3 chance, etc.). This allows some variation in Peedy's responses, including an occasional cute or silly remark. The selected template is then expanded, by evaluating queries (*getLastCD* loads all attributes of the last referenced CD into context) and substituting context variables (*Title* and *Year* are values assigned by *getLastCD*).

Episodic Memory. As illustrated in figure 10, when Peedy fails to understand a spoken input, he raises his wing to his ear and says "Huh?" This action is a natural way to concisely inform users that there was a miscommunication and

State	Event	Predicate	NewState	Action
stAttending	evWhoWroteTrack	cnt0=1	stAttending	doSelect; Say <!PDSays(artist)>
stAttending	evWhoWroteTrack	cnt0=0	stAttending	Say <!PDSays(DontKnow)>

Figure 8: Dialogue rules for evWhoWroteTrack.

Category	Prob	Result
haveCD	0.25	i have <!getLastCD><=Title> from <=Year>
haveCD	0.33	ive got <!getLastCD><=Title>
haveCD	0.5	ive got <!getLastCD><=Title>, would you like to hear something from that?
haveCD	1	i have <!getLastCD><=Title> from <=Year>, would you like to hear something from that?

Figure 9: Variations of saying I have a CD.

quite effectively cues them to repeat. However, when repeated speech recognition failures occur for the same input (as they occasionally do), the exact repetition of the "Huh?" sequence is very awkward and unnatural. This is a basic example of Peedy's need to understand the history of the interaction, and to adapt his behavior accordingly.

We have recently experimented with additions to the prototype system which record a detailed log of events that occur during interactions with Peedy and then use that history to adjust his behavior to be more natural. The memory has been used to enable three new types of context dependent behavior:

- Depending on previous (or recent) interactions, Peedy's reaction to a given input can vary systematically. For example, the second time he fails to understand an utterance, he says "Sorry, could you repeat that?" and then becomes progressively more apologetic if failures continue to reoccur.

- The selection of an output utterance can depend on how frequently (or recently) that particular alternative has been used. For example, a humorous line can be restricted to be used no more than once (or once a week) per user. (The interaction memory is retained separately for each user.)

- Dialogue sequences can adjust a simple model of Peedy's emotional state (e.g. happy because of successful completion of a task or sad because of repeated misrecognitions). His emotional state can then affect the choice of utterance or animation in a particular situation.

Video and Audio Output

An important element in the "believability" of an agent is its ability to produce richly expressive visual behavior and to synchronize those visual elements with appropriate speech and sound effects. We found that in order to achieve the

Figure 10: Peedy indicating a misrecognition.

necessary level of realism and expression, most of the output elements must be carefully authored. The three dimensional model of Peedy's body, his movements, facial expressions, vocalizations, and sound effects were all individually and painstakingly designed. But in order to create a believable conversational interaction, it is equally important that Peedy react quickly and flexibly to what the user says. To make that reactivity possible, we divided the animations and sounds up into short fragments (*authored elements*) and developed a run-time controller for Peedy (called Player) which uses our reactive animation library (ReActor) to sequence and synchronize those elements in real-time. This approach also lets us combine the authored elements into a wide variety of longer animations so that long repetitive sequences can be avoided.

ReActor. ReActor represents a visual scene as a named hierarchy decorated with properties. The hierarchy includes all the visible objects and additional entities such as cameras and lights. Properties such as position or orientation of a camera, the material or color of an object, or the posture of an articulated figure can all be animated over time. Camera (and lighting) control provides the ability to support cinematic camera and editing techniques in a real-time computer graphics environment. More abstract properties of an agent such as its "state of excitement" can also be defined and animated.

ReActor explicitly supports temporal specifications in terms of wall clock time and relative time, where relative time is defined in terms of a hierarchy of embedded time lines. These specifications include when and for how long actions take place. This support for time allows ReActor to also synchronize multiple time-based streams such as sound, speech, and animation.

The Scene Hierarchy and Properties. The scene is represented by a *named hierarchy,* which includes all the visible objects and additional entities such as cameras and lights. These are all first class objects which can be manipulated in a uniform way by the animation system.

The hierarchy is decorated with *properties,* which include geometric specifications such as position and orientation. However, as we shall see later, these properties can also be more abstract, where changes are reflected in the visual (or sonic) representation of the object via an application-defined function. Any of these properties can be readily altered, and their changes over time form the basis of all animations.

Properties and Controls. To animate over a specific time interval, a property is bound to a *control.* The control is a function of *wall clock time* which specifies the value of a property. The control may be a standard interpolation function or a more specialized, application-defined function.

Scripts. Scripts specify the bindings of properties to controls during an interval on a local time line. The local time line is translated to wall clock time when the script is invoked. The script is useful for two reasons. First, one can collect related controlled properties into a larger named object which can be invoked as a unit. Second, and more importantly, the script provides a mechanism to describe things in terms of *relative time* rather than wall clock time.

Support for Real-Time. ReActor ensures correct real-time behavior so that events in the underlying model occur at the correct times independent of the rendering process. Relative timings among events are thus always maintained. ReActor estimates the time at which the next frame will be displayed, and properties are updated to values correct for that time. On a slower (or busier) machine, the update rate will be lower, but the appearance of each frame will be correct for the time at which it is displayed.

ReActor also allows us to specify *critical times,* which are times at which frames must be displayed. Critical times are needed because sometimes a certain instant needs to be portrayed to produce a convincing animation; for example, in a hammering sequence, it is important to show the instant when the hammer hits the nail. At lower frame rates, the use of critical times produces much more satisfying animations.

Similarly we can readily synchronize other types of time-based streams, such as sound. As an example, the sound of the hammer hitting the nail can be made to occur at the time specified for the strike.

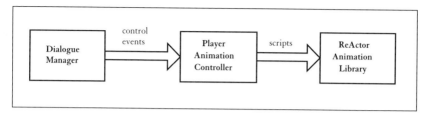

Figure 11: Architecture of Peedy's animation control.

Directors. Complex reactive behavior of objects is implemented via *directors*. Our overall goal is to be able to control and animate, in real-time, characters and objects with complex behaviors which respond to user input. Directors, supported by the lower level abstractions, provide this capability. Directors are triggered by various events, including temporal events, changes to properties, user input, and events generated by other directors. Directors create and/or invoke scripts or directly specify bindings of properties to controls.

In the prototype system, directors are used to give Peedy a variety of subtle ongoing behaviors: he blinks and makes other small movements occasionally, and after a period of inaction will sit down, wave his legs, and eventually fall asleep.

Player. ReActor provides tools for scheduling and synchronizing many fine-grained animations. However, the animation requests that are made by Peedy's Dialogue Manager are at a much higher level. These requests trigger fairly long sequences which correspond to complete steps in Peedy's interaction with the user. An animation controller, called Player, is responsible for converting the high-level requests into the appropriate sequences of fine-grained animations. Since the appropriate sequence of scripts to use can depend upon the current state of the character (e.g. standing or sitting, holding a note or not, etc.), selecting and coordinating the scripts to produce natural behavior can involve complex dependencies. Player supports a convenient plan-based specification of animation actions and compiles this specification into a representation that can be executed efficiently at run time.

Figure 11 illustrates the slice of the Persona architecture that handles animation control. The dialogue manager sends control events to the animation controller. This controller interprets the incoming events according to its current internal state, informs the low-level graphics system (ReActor) what animations to perform, and adjusts its own current internal state accordingly.

For example, consider the path of actions when the user asks Peedy "What do you have by Bonnie Raitt?" This is illustrated in figure 12. First the application interprets the message and sends a peSearch event to the animation controller to have Peedy search for the disc. The animation controller knows that Peedy is in his "deep sleep" state, so it sequentially invokes the wakeup, standup, and search animations. It also changes Peedy's current state (as repre-

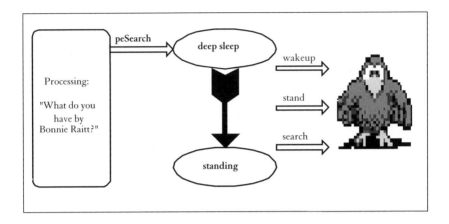

Figure 12: An animation control example.

sented in the animation controller) to standing, so that if another peSearch event is received immediately, Peedy will forego the wakeup and standup animations and immediately perform a search.

One can view the animation controller as a state machine that interprets input events in the context of its current state to produce animation actions and enter a new state. Originally we specified the animation controller procedurally as a state machine, but as new events, actions, and states were added, the controller became unwieldy and very difficult to modify and debug. It became clear that we needed a different manner of specifying the controller's behavior. One of the difficulties of specifying this behavior is that graphical actions make sense in only limited contexts for either semantic reasons (Peedy cannot sleep and search at the same time) or animation considerations (the search script was authored with the expectation that Peedy would be in a standing position).

Player calculates these transitions automatically, freeing the implementer from part of the chore of constructing animated interfaces. To accomplish this, Player uses planning, a technique traditionally used by the AI community to determine the sequence of operators necessary to get from an initial start state to a goal state. In our system, the operators that affect system state are animation scripts, and the programmer declares preconditions and postconditions that explain how each of the scripts depend on and modify state. One of the major problems with planning algorithms is that they are computationally intensive. Animation controllers, however, have to operate in real time. Our solution is to precompile the conveniently specified planning notation into an efficient to execute state machine.

The language for specifying the behavior of the animation controller has five components. Recall that the animation controller accepts high-level animation events and outputs animation scripts. So the language must contain both event and script definitions. The language also contains constructs for defining state variables that represent animation state, autonomous actions called autoscripts, and a state class hierarchy that makes defining preconditions easier. Each of these language constructs will now be described in turn.

State Variables. State variables represent those components of the animation configuration that may need to be considered when determining whether a script can be invoked. State variable definitions take on the form:

(state-variable *name type initial-value <values>*)

All expression in the language are LISP s-expressions (thus the parentheses), and bracketed values represent optional parameters. The first three arguments indicate the name, type, and initial value of the variable. State variables can be of type boolean, integer, float, or string. The last argument is an optional list of possible values for the variable. This can turn potentially infinitely-valued types, such as strings, into types that can take on a limited set of values (enumerative types). Examples of state-variable definitions are:

(state-variable 'holding-note 'boolean false)
(state-variable   'posture 'string 'stand '(fly stand sit))

The first definition creates a variable called holding-note, which is a boolean and has an initial value of false. The second creates a variable called posture, which is a string that is initialized to stand. It can take on only three values (fly, stand, and sit), and this should be expressed to the system because in some cases the system can reason about the value of the variable by knowing what it is not.

There is a special class of state variable, called a time variable. Time variables are set to the last time one of a group of events was processed.

Autoscripts. Autoscripts make it easy to define autonomous actions, which are actions that occur typically continuously when the animation system is in a particular set of states. Examples of this would be having an animated character snore when it is asleep, or swing its legs when it is bored. Autoscripts are procedures that are executed whenever a state variable takes on a particular value. For example, to have the snore procedure called when a variable called alert is set to sleep, we write the following:

(autoscript 'alert 'sleep '(snore))

The third argument is a list, because we may want to associate multiple autonomous actions with a given state variable value. Note that though we typically bind autoscripts to a single value of a state variable, we could have an autoscript run whenever an arbitrary logical expression of state variables is true, by binding the autoscript to multiple variable values, and evaluating whether the expression is true within the autoscript itself before proceeding with the action.

Event Definitions. For every event that might be received by the animation controller, an event definition specifies at a high-level what needs to be accomplished and the desired timing. Event definitions take on the form:

(event name <directives>*)

The term <directives>* represents a diverse set of statements that can appear in any number and combination. The :state directive tells the controller to perform the sequence of operations necessary to achieve a particular state. The single argument to this directive is a logical expression of state variables, permitting conjunction, disjunction, and negation. This high-level specification declares the desired results, not how to attain these results. In contrast, the :op directive instructs the system to perform the operation specified as its only argument. The animation controller may not be in a state allowing the desired operation to be executed. In this case, the controller will initially perform other operations necessary to attain this state, and then execute the specified operation.

For example, the peBadSpeech event is received by Player whenever our animated agent cannot recognize an utterance with sufficient confidence. Its effect is to have Peedy raise his wing to his ear, and say "Huh?" This event definition is as follows:

(event 'evBadSpeech :state 'wing-at-ear :op 'huh)

When an evBadSpeech event comes over the wire, the controller dispatches animations so that the expression wing-at-ear (a single state variable) is true. It then makes sure that the preconditions of the huh operator are satisfied and then executes it. Note that wing-at-ear could have been defined as a precondition for the huh operator, and then the :state directive could have been omitted above. However, we chose to specify the behavior this way because we might want huh to be executed in some cases when wing-at-ear is false.

By default, the directives are achieved sequentially in time. Above, wing-at-ear is made to be true, and immediately afterwards huh is executed. The :label and :time directives allow us to override this behavior and define more flexible sequencing. The :label directive assigns a name to the moment in time represented by the position in the directives sequence at which it appears. The :time directive adjusts the current time in one of these sequences.

```
(event 'evThanks
  :op 'bow
  :label 'a
  :time '(+ (label a) 3)
  :op 'camgoodbye
  :time '(+ (label a) 5)
  :op 'sit)
```

As defined above, when the animation controller receives an evThanks event, Peedy will bow. The label a represents the time immediately after the bow due to its position in the sequence. The first :time directive adjusts the scheduling clock to 3 seconds after the bow completes, and this is the time that camgoodbye operator executes, moving the camera to the "goodbye" position. The second :time directive sets the scheduling clock to 5 seconds after the bow, and then Peedy sits. If Peedy must perform an initial sequence of actions to satisfy the sit precondition, these will begin at this time, and the sit operation will occur later. Note that these two timing directives allow operations to be scheduled in parallel or sequentially.

Four additional directives are used, albeit less frequently. The :if statement allows a block of other directives to be executed only if a logical expression is true. This allows us, for example, to branch and select very different animation goals based on the current state. Occasionally it is easier to specify a set of actions in terms of a state machine rather than as a plan. The :add and :sub directives change the values of state variables and, in conjunction with the :if directive, allow small state machines to be incorporated in the controller code. The :code directive allows arbitrary C++ code to be embedded in the controller program.

Operator Definitions. Scripts are the operators that act on our graphical scene, often changing the scene's state in the process. Operator definitions are of the following form:

```
(op opname       <:script scriptname>
    <:precond precondition>
    <:add postcondition>
    <:sub postcondition>
    <:must-ask boolean>)
```

This creates an operator named opname associated with the script called scriptname. The operator can only execute when the specified precondition is true, and the postcondition is typically specified relative to this precondition using :add or :sub. Since operators typically change only a few aspects of the state, relative specification is usually easiest. The :must-ask directive defaults to false, indicating that the planner is free to use the operator during the planning process. When :must-ask is true, the operator will be used only if explicitly requested in the :op directive of an event definition. An example script definition appears below:

```
(op     'search
    :script 'stream
        :precond '((not holding-note) and ...)
    :add 'holding-note)
```

This defines an operator named search associated with a script called stream. The precondition is a complex logical expression that the state class hierarchy, described in the next section, helps to simplify. The part shown here says that Peedy cannot be holding a note before executing a search. After the search is executed, all of the preconditions will still hold, except holding-note will be true.

Though we have so far referred to operators and scripts interchangeably, there are really several different types of operators in Player. Operators can be static scripts, dynamic scripts (procedures that execute scripts), or arbitrary code. In the latter two cases, the :director or :code directives replace the :script directive.

We can also define macro-operators, which are sequences of operators that together modify the system state. As an example, the hard-wake macro-operator appears below:

```
(macro-op      'hard-wake
    :precond '(alert.snore and ...)
    :add 'alert.awake
    :seq '(:op snort :op exhale :op focus))
```

The above expression defines a macro-operator that can only be executed when, among other things, the value of alert is snore. Here, the '.' ("dot") comparator denotes equality. Afterwards, the value of alert will be awake. The effect of invoking this macro-operator is equivalent to executing the snort, exhale, and focus operators in sequence, making Peedy snort, exhale, then focus at the camera in transitioning from a snoring sleep to wakefulness in our application. The :time and :label directives can also appear in a macro definition to control the relative start times of the operators; however, our system requires that care be taken to avoid scheduling interfering operators concurrently.

State Class Hierarchy. In the last two examples, the preconditions were too complex to fit on a single line, so parts were omitted. Writing preconditions can be a slow, tedious process, especially in the presence of many interdependent state variables. To simplify the task, we allow programmers to create a state class hierarchy to be used in specifying preconditions. For example, the complete precondition for the search operator defined earlier is:

```
((not holding-note) and alert.awake and
posture.stand and (not wing-to-ear) and
(not wearing-phones))
```

Since this precondition is shared by five different operators, we defined a state class (called standing-noteless) that represents the expression and is used as the precondition for these operators. This not only makes the initial specification easier, but also subsequent modifications, since changes can be made in a single place.
Class definitions take the following form.

```
(state-class classname states)
```

State class hierarchies support multiple inheritance. Here, states is a list of state variable expressions or previously defined state classes. A state-class typically inherits from all of these states, and in the case of conflicts, the latter states take precedence. State hierarchies can be arbitrarily deep. The stand-noteless class is not actually defined as the complex expression presented earlier, but as:

```
(state-class      stand-noteless
    '(stand-op (not holding-note)))
```

In other words, the stand-noteless class inherits from another class called stand-op. We have found that the semantics of an application and its animations tend to reveal a natural class hierarchy. For example, for our animated character to respond with an action, he must be awake, and for him to acknowledge the user with an action, he must not have his wing to his ear as if he could not hear, and cannot be wearing headphones. These three requirements maske up the class ack-op (for acknowledgment operation), from which most of our operations inherit, at least indirectly.

Algorithm. Typical planning algorithms take a start state, goal state, and set of operators, compute for a while, then return a sequence of operators that transforms the start into the goal. Since our animated interface must exhibit real-time performance, planning at run-time is not an option. Instead, Player pre-compiles the plan-based specification into a state machine that has much better performance. This places an unusual requirement on the planning algorithm—it must find paths from any state in which the system might be to every specified goal state.

A naive approach might apply a conventional planner to each of these states and goals independently. Fortunately, there is coherence in the problem space that a simple variation of a traditional planning algorithm allows us to exploit. Our planning algorithm, like other goal regression planners, works by beginning with goals and applying operator inverses until finding the desired start state (or in our case, start states). The algorithm is a breadth-first planner and is guaranteed to find the shortest sequence of operators that takes any possible start state to a desired goal.

The next step, after the planning algorithm finishes, is to build the actual state machine. Our system generates C++ code for the state machine, which is compiled and linked together with the Reactor animation library and various support routines. The heart of the state machine has already been calculated by the planner. Recall that plans are (state conditional, action sequence) pairs, which the planner computed for every goal state. These plans can readily be converted to if-then-else blocks, which are encapsulated into a procedure for their corresponding goal. These procedures also return a value indicating whether or not the goal state can be achieved. We refer to these procedures as state-achieving procedures, since they convert the existing state to a desired state.

Next, the system outputs operator-execution procedures for every operator referenced in event definitions. These procedures first call a state-achieving procedure, attempting to establish their precondition. If successful, the operator-execution procedures execute the operator and adjust state variables to reflect the postcondition. When multiple operators share the same precondition, their operator-execution procedures will call the same state-achieving procedures.

Finally, we generate event procedures for every event definition. These procedures, called whenever a new event is received from the application interface, invoke state-achieving procedures for each :state directive and operator-execution procedures for each :op directive in the event definition. The :time directive produces code that manipulates a global variable, used as the start time for operator dispatch. The :label directive generates code to store the current value of this variable in an array, alongside other saved time values.

The planner and ancillary code for producing the state machine are implemented in Lucid Common Lisp and run on a Sun Sparcstation. Our animation controller specification for the Peedy prototype contains 7 state variables (including 1 time variable), 5 auto-scripts, 32 operators, 9 state classes, and 24 event definitions. The system took about 4 seconds to generate a state machine from this controller specification on a Sparcstation 1+, a 15.6 MIPS, 1989-class workstation. It is important to note that in our Peedy application, not all animation is scheduled via planning. We have found that low-level animation actions, such as flying or blinking, are conveniently implemented as small procedural entities or state machines that are invoked by the higher-level animation planner. These state machines can be activated through autoscripts and the :director directive, and they can maintain their own internal state or reference and modify the animation controller's state variables at run-time. As mentioned earlier, state machines can also be embedded into the animation controller using the event definition's :if directive. Our experience suggests that planning-based specification should not entirely replace procedurally based specification. The two techniques can best be used together.

Speech and Sound Effects. In the audio component of Persona, we set out to give Peedy an appropriate voice and to place him in a convincing aural environment. Our goals include the ability to easily add new remarks to the character's speech repertoire and to synchronize the audio properly with his lip (or beak) movement. Because speech and sound effects have such a large effect on the user's perception of the system, we think it's important to concentrate significant effort on attaining aural fidelity and richness—both by situating cinema-quality sound effects properly within a realistic acoustic environment, and by maximizing the naturalness and emotional expressivity of the character's voice.

The character's voice needs to sound natural while having a large vocabulary. Text to Speech (TTS) systems can deliver excellent language coverage, but the quality of even the best TTS products destroys the anthropomorphic illusion of the agent. In the prototype, we chose instead to pre-record speech fragments, which vary from single words ("one," "Madonna") to entire utterances ("Another day, another CD. What do you want to hear?").

To maintain a suspension of disbelief, Peedy's voice must be synchronized with his visual rendering. To get accurate "beak sync", we analyze each speech fragment with the speech recognition system to determine the offset of every phoneme within the recording. This information is then used to automatically create a ReActor script which plays the audio fragment and synchronizes Peedy's beak position to it. (Sound effects are handled similarly, except that they are triggered by commands placed into animation scripts by hand.) When the Dialogue Manager selects a statement for Peedy to say, it is broken up into its predefined fragments, and a sequence of corresponding script activations is sent to ReActor.

This approach means that every phrase that the character uses must be individually recorded, a tedious process which makes additions to Peedy's vocabulary difficult. The current system is also limited to producing one sound effect or vocalization at a time, a restriction which limits the richness possible in the soundscape. In addition, application actions (e.g. control of CD audio) are currently not triggered by the animation system and are therefore difficult to synchronize properly.

Future Directions

As we had hoped, the creation of a lifelike conversational assistant has proven to be a powerful force for discovering and exploring interactions among a wide variety of efforts at Microsoft Research. Many significant research challenges remain before the creation of a competent "assistant" will become feasible. We list here research topics in which we have active efforts that we feel are critical to continued progress toward that goal.

Language

The speech recognizer in the prototype will understand only those sentences which appear in its grammar; however, writing a grammar for all likely utterances (even about a limited domain like music selection) is very difficult. Instead, we would like to switch to an approach which uses a statistical grammar, so that the recognizer searches for matches to the acoustic data where each sequence of words within the match occurs frequently in common speech. Developing a stochastic grammar for conversational speech (including common disfluencies) is therefore an important research objective.

While we feel that our approach to collapsing paraphrases into canonical utterances by means of application-specific transformations is promising, the specification of those transformations is currently too difficult. We are exploring the creation of tools that let application developers define those rules simply by providing examples of the canonical statement and of paraphrases which should be treated equivalently.

Dialogue

We've found that the current dialogue manager based on a simple finite state machine doesn't give us enough flexibility. We're working to reorganize it as a collection of rules which make it easier to handle subdialogues, multiple active goals, and character initiation of interchanges. We'd also like to explore ways in which Bayesian decision theory might be used to control the character's responses to events.

Our experiments with giving Peedy an episodic memory and simple emotional response to his interactions with the user have convinced us that those capabilities can give him an important additional sense of naturalness and sociability. We plan to include and extend them in future versions of the system.

We expect that Peedy's abilities will remain limited to quite narrow task domains for the foreseeable future. However, we think it may be feasible for Peedy to have enough background knowledge to guide a new user into his area of competence through a natural conversation. This process would involve a mixture of knowing about things that new users are likely to say and having strategies for dealing constructively with input that lies completely beyond his range of understanding.

Video and Audio Output

For the creation of more realistic and variable animations, we plan to focus on the use of ReActor directors to control subtle behaviors. For example, a director can be used to create intelligent cameras which track moving objects automatically, or to adjust the parameters of animations and sound effects to reflect Peedy's emotional state.

The addition of inverse kinematics to the ReActor runtime system is another goal. This capability will allow the animator to author natural motions for just a few components of a complex linked figure (e.g. hands and feet) and let the system calculate appropriate motions of the rest of the figure. This has the potential to significantly reduce the effort required to author new animations.

We are also investigating improvements to the quality of speech synthesis systems by using rules based on a deep language analysis of the input text. That analysis might allow us to automatically generate a natural rhythm and pitch contour for our character's speech and free us from the need to prerecord all spoken output.

References

Badler, N.; Phillips, C. B.; and Webber, B. L. 1993. Simulating Humans. Computer Graphics, Animation, and Control. Oxford, U.K.: Oxford University Press.

Ball, J. E.; Ling, D. T.; Pugh, D.; Skelly, T.; Standkosky, A.; and Thiel, D. 1994. Demonstration of REACTOR: A System for Real-Time Reactive Animations. In CHI'94 Conference Companion, 39–40. New York: ACM Press.

Bates, J. 1994. The Role of Emotion in Believable Agents. Communications of the ACM 37(7): 122–125.

Cahn, J. E. 1989. Generating Expression in Synthesized Speech. Master's thesis, Department of Architecture, Massachusetts Institute of Technology.

Clark, H. H. 1992. Arenas of Language Use. Chicago: The University of Chicago Press and The Center for the Study of Language and Information.

Cohen, P. R. 1992. The Role of Natural Language in a Multimodal Interface. In ACM Symposium on User Interface Software and Technology, 143–149. New York: ACM Press.

Gaver, W. W.; Smith, R. B.; and O'Shea, T. 1991. Effective Sounds in Complex Systems: The Arkola Simulation. In Proceedings of CHI'91: Human Factors in Computing Systems, 85–90. New York: ACM Press.

Goldberg, A. 1984. SMALLTALK-80: The Interactive Programming Environment. Reading, Mass.: Addison-Wesley.

Hayes-Roth, B.; Sinkoff, E.; Brownston, L.; Huard, R.; and Lent, B. 1995. Directed Improvisation with Animated Puppets. In CHI'95 Conference Companion, 79–80. New York: ACM Press.

Hodgins, J. K. 1994. Simulation of Human Running. In Proceedings of the IEEE International Conference on Robotics and Automation, 1320–1325. Washington, D.C.: IEEE Press.

Huang, X.; Acero, A.; Alleva, F.; Hwang, M.; Jiang, L.; and Mahajan, M. 1995. Microsoft Highly Intelligent Speech Recognizer—WHISPER. Presented at the International Conference on Acoustic, Speech, and Signal Processing, 9–12 May, Detroit, Michigan.

Jensen, K.; Heidorn, G. E.; and Richardson, S. D., eds. 1993. Natural Language Processing: The PLNLP Approach. Boston, Mass.: Kluwer Academic.

Lewis, J. B.; Koved, L.; and Ling, D. T. 1991. Dialogue Structures for Virtual Worlds. In Proceedings of CHI'91: Human Factors in Computing Systems, 131–136. New York: ACM Press.

Maes, P. 1994. Agents That Reduce Work and Information Overload. Communications of the ACM 37(7): 31–40.

Microsoft. 1995. Microsoft Bob. Redmond, Wash.: Microsoft.

Nielson, J. 1993. Noncommand User Interfaces. Communications of the ACM. 36(4): 83–99.

Norman, D. A. 1988. The Design of Everyday Things. New York: Doubleday.

Perlin, K. 1994. A Remarkably Lifelike Implementation of a Synthetic Computer Character. Presented at Lifelike Computer Characters '94, 4–7 October, Snowbird, Utah.

Reeves, B., and Nass, C. 1996. The Media Equation. Stanford, Calif.: CSLI Publications.

Schoppers, M. J. 1987. Universal Plans for Reactive Robots in Unpredictable Environments. In Proceedings of the Tenth International Joint Conference on Artificial Intelligence, 1039–1046. San Mateo, Calif.: International Joint Conference on Artificial Intelligence.

Smith, C.; Irby, C.; Kimball, R.; Verplank, B.; and Harslem, E. 1982. Designing the STAR User Interface. Byte 7(4): 242–282.

Takeuchi, A., and Nagao, K. 1993. Communicative Facial Displays as a New Conversational Modality. In INTERCHI'93 Conference Proceedings, 187–193. New York: ACM Press.

Vere, S., and Bickmore, T. 1990. A Basic Agent. Computational Intelligence 6(1): 41–60.

Walker, M. A., and Whittaker, S. 1990. An Investigation into Discourse Segmentation. In Proceedings of the Twenty-Eighth Annual Meeting of the ACL, 70–79. Morristown, N.J.: Association for Computational Linguistics.

Ward, W. 1991. Understanding Spontaneous Speech: The PHOENIX System. In Proceedings of 1991 International Conference on Acoustics, Speech, and Signal Processing, 365–367. Washington, D.C.: IEEE Computer Society.

Waters, K. 1987. A Muscle Model for Animating Three-Dimensional Facial Expressions. *Computer Graphics (SIGGRAPH'87)* 21(4): 17–24.

Chapter 11

Software Agents for Cooperative Learning

Guy A. Boy

A crucial issue for the integration of new *information technology* (IT) in the education system is the enhancement of the access to knowledge and culture in order for the education system to improve its role of knowledge transfer and citizen training. It can be used for at least three reasons:

- To develop autonomy and individual learning
- To remove barriers caused by geographical isolation
- To open the education system to the external world and facilitate synergy with local resources

In this chapter, it is assumed that IT is typically supported by CD-ROMs or the Internet. This project fits with the current cognitive science initiative of the French Ministry of Research. A crucial chapter of this initiative is devoted to *cultural technologies*. The main issues that are currently raised are the following: Would the computer-mediated information technology give birth to a new world? What would this world be like? What would be the role of human beings in this world? It often happens that humans are the victims of new information technology because they do not assimilate or integrate it in the right way, and/or at the right time. The use of the new IT leads to the creation of new artifacts enabling the management of knowledge. It seems that implicit behavior characterizing traditional culture is evolving towards explicit behavior with the use of new IT. A major issue is the extension of the human memory to *external memories*. Computer technology enables knowledge management and storage. New concepts such as corporate memory or organizational memory are emerging. The education system is certainly a good example of a generator of corporate knowledge that is reused for the benefit of students.

This chapter introduces a concept of *educational memory* (EM), i.e., corporate memory (CM) for the education system. CM work currently developed at EU-RISCO is multidisciplinary and multidomain, even if it is currently focused on the construction of CM concepts for the aeronautical industry (Attipoe and Boy 1995; Boy 1995; Durstewitz 1994). In many ways, CM problems encountered in the industry domain are very similar to the CM problems encountered in the education domain. CM is also related to the development of information highways. Information highways will enable massive information transfer. But they do not solve the major problem of existence or availability of the right information at the right time in the right place, and in the right understandable format. In this perspective, I propose the use of *software agents* as *intelligent assistant systems* (Boy 1991b) that would facilitate human-computer interaction, as well as human-human interaction through new IT.

The agent-orientation of human-machine interaction is not new. Autopilots have been commonly used since the 1930s. Such agents perform tasks that human pilots usually perform, such as following a flight track, maintaining an altitude, etc. Transferring such tasks to the machine modifies the original task of the human operator. The job of the human operator evolves from a manipulation task (usually involving sensory-motor skills) to a supervisory task (involving cognitive processing and situation awareness skills) (Sheridan 1992). Creating *software agents* involves new cooperation and coordination processes that were not explicitly obvious before. Agents are taken in the sense of Minsky's (1985) terminology.

I would like to convince the reader that software agent technology enables the understanding and learning of various kinds of concepts, since they involve active behavior of the users. They enable users to center their interactions at the content level (semantics), partially removing syntactic difficulties. They also enable users to index (contextualize) content to specific situations that they understand better (pragmatism).

The second section of this chapter presents my view on *computer-supported cooperative learning* (CSCL). The evolution of learning technology shows that we are heading towards the construction of pedagogical tools that enhance current educational materials. A specific case of cooperative learning in physics is given. The third section focuses on the requirements for an educational environment based on the construction and exchange of active documents. Examples of software agents for cooperative learning are provided in the fourth section. An application is developed in the fifth section. The balance of the chapter is devoted to a discussion on and the perspectives of the current research effort.

Computer-Supported Cooperative Learning

Education is fundamentally a cooperative process. But in the new world of technologically mediated instruction, how can this cooperation be supported or amplified? In this section, I argue that educational materials can directly support co-operation through electronic documents that provide context critical to learning.

Cooperation Via Electronic Documents

Using new IT involves the exchange of electronic documents of various *types*. These documents can be *ephemeral*, *draft*, or *edited*. An ephemeral document is a document providing useful information that can be forgotten after it has been used. It is usually called a "message" in the electronic mail language. In addition, sending a few lines using electronic mail has become acceptable, a practice which is not the current way of doing things with a standard letter format. The fact that an electronic mail message can be very precise but informal facilitates communication between people. A draft document is a working document that will be annotated and modified. It is usually exchanged back and forth between people until it becomes satisfactory. An edited document is a crisp, completed and nonmodifiable document.

Documents can be considered as mediating tools that support exchanges of viewpoints and concepts. Several viewpoints can be merged into a concept when a common agreement has been reached. They can be left as they are otherwise. In practice, documents are organized into chunks, such as paragraphs, sections, chapters, and so forth. These chunks include consistent viewpoints or concepts. In any case, each viewpoint should be *contextualized*, i.e., it should be labeled by the name of the author of the viewpoint, his or her main interests, etc. Context is usually related to other entities such as situation, behavior, point of view, relationships among agents, discourse, dialogue, and so forth.

Cooperation via electronic documents is a new activity that will involve new tools. These tools are information-intensive. They are called *software agents*. Traditional writing and reading becomes human-computer interaction. Furthermore, I claim that introducing such artificial assistants into the education system in effect will contribute to changing the relations among the various actors.

Sometimes documents are designed in such a way that they end up being complex because either technology does not allow them to be simpler, or designers do not have enough human factors knowledge and training to design for simplicity. Software agents should reduce the complexity to improve situation awareness, understanding, and performance. For this reason, we should keep software agents as small applications (Rappaport 1995). Software agents assist users to design, produce, manage, access, choose, and interpret documents.

For instance, in the University of Michigan Digital Library, Birmingham et al. (1994) developed a comprehensive agent-based architecture. They focused on the construction of particular agents and protocols: (1) *user-interface agents* including an interviewing agent, (2) *supporting query-processing agents* incorporating linguistic retrieval and providing information integration, (3) *mediators* to better allocate resources, (4) *ontologies and protocols* to federate any collection of independently generated information sources in a common language, and (5) *collection-interface agents* maintaining the link between autonomous data repositories and the rest of the system.

The Evolution of the Learning Technology

The initial learning technology focused on individualized instruction, i.e., standalone tutoring. The current view has evolved to the point where training and education must support inquiry-based learning and collaboration as it is integrated into the doing and using. What does it mean to learn? What is a learning environment? This section describes the evolution of learning technology from conventional computer-based training to cooperative learning.

Computer-based training (CBT) concerns training where students and teachers use computers to improve conventional training. Each instruction method is based on a model (Boy 1993). This model involves knowledge that needs to be learned, the student, and the way knowledge will be conveyed to the student. Thus, there are at least three major issues in CBT: (1) knowledge representation and elicitation, (2) student modeling, and (3) computer-student interface. Domain knowledge representation can be more or less formal according to its degree of complexity. It is important to capture student knowledge in order to improve training (the feedback issue). In addition, student background and personality need to be taken into account. The computer-student interface should include both domain and student knowledge.

Intelligent tutoring systems (ITS) have been studied for almost two decades. They involve CBT and include several humanlike features in their software. An ITS has explicit models of tutoring and domain knowledge. It is more flexible in its system's response. Unfortunately, the current ITS model supports the philosophy of learning as "knowledge transfer." *This model does not work today because we need to be change-tolerant, as the world changes every day.* In the information age, we need to go from facts to process, and from isolation to cooperation (Soloway 1993).

Interactive learning systems should enable the student to manipulate cognitive artifacts (Norman 1992) from several perspectives or viewpoints. Viewpoints can be shallow (interface level) or deep (interaction level). For instance, an airplane artifact can be seen from several viewpoints: a picture or a text explaining how it should be used (user viewpoint), how it is built (engineering viewpoint), or how much it costs (financial viewpoint).

Cooperative learning systems provide students with access to other people's ideas and concepts (SIGCUE 1992). They make it possible to exchange, discuss, negotiate, defend, and synthesize viewpoints. By using cooperative learning systems, we drastically depart from the usual one-directional way of learning. Students are placed in a dynamic environment where they can express their own viewpoints and incrementally adapt initial viewpoints to more informed and mastered concepts. In addition, cooperative learning systems are mediating tools enhancing cooperation between students, teachers, parents, and other people involved in the education system. In this chapter, I define computer-supported cooperative learning as an environment in which knowledge is exchanged via electronic documents.

Learning is an active and constructive social process. An essential aspect of knowledge is that it is contextualized. This fact is the reason why knowledge is so difficult to acquire and represent. It is vivid. The paradox is that when we think that we have formalized it (e.g., written on paper), it is already deactivated! We have to recontextualize it to adapt it to a new situation and make it vivid again. Contextualization can be seen as indexing in the sense of connecting chunks of knowledge. The contextualization process is facilitated when people learn by doing. It follows that learning technology needs to be highly interactive.

A Specific Case of Cooperative Learning in Physics

It is mandatory to perform a careful analysis of the current practice and the available experience in the use of learning technology to provide the teachers with the appropriate tools. The Toulouse Board of Education is currently working on a cooperative distant learning system in physics. The aim of this experimentation is to help pedagogical teams to cooperatively design physics lab exercises according to global educational directives, obtain pedagogical consistency between schools, and train teachers and students to use modern communication tools.

The current project involves 72 physics teachers from 28 schools distributed in 14 sites. Each site has a coordinator. At least three sites work on the same topic. Each site produces a set of pedagogical sheets that include the directives and necessary materials for lab experiments. Site coordinators meet every month to examine and improve the various productions before testing them in the classroom. Each site is equipped with an interactive workstation used for designing the pedagogical sheets cooperatively with two other sites. This cooperative work leads to the construction of a pedagogical sheet database that is accessible to the entire education community.

This experimentation is very well received by the teachers. A conscious effort has been made to keep this experimentation within a reasonable framework at least in the initial stage. The volume and the quality of the productions show the real interest of the various participants. Teachers who do not participate in this experimentation ask for the productions in order to use them in their classroom. Eurisco currently develops a CSCL environment called ACTIDOC using an approach of cooperation via active documents. The next two sections of this chapter present such an environment based on the construction and evaluation of software agents.

Towards an Environment Based on Active Documents

It is common sense to say "it is much better to get someone who knows than a hundred people who search." From this perspective, the concept of knowledge-able agent is essential. Knowledge acquisition is usually handled through books and human-human interactions. On one hand, books require a reader to infer vivid knowledge from the texts. On the other hand, even when knowledgeable people are available at the right time in the right place (this is extremely rare), they are not necessarily able to explain what they know because knowledge elicitation is an extremely difficult process.

Requirements for Active Documents

Software agents for cooperative learning are designed to transform electronic document basic content into active documents. They convey vivid behavior to static documents. This section provides four requirements for active documents.

Documents have been used for ages to transfer information and knowledge from person to person. These documents have various forms such as text or graphics. But a book without a reader is just ink on paper. The active part of a text is the reader. Sometimes, the reader experiences difficulties in understanding what the writer wanted to convey through the text. Instead of mobilizing user cognition on basic interaction problems, the larger part of user's cognitive activity should be focused on learning the content of documents. Thus, an active document includes artifacts that provide the *appropriate illusion* useful and natural for the user to understand its content (first requirement).

Even if we claim that a natural interaction tends to improve information access, the shallow user interface level is not enough to qualify an active document. In particular, intelligent indexing, such as providing good metaphors supported by appropriate search mechanisms, improves human-machine interaction. Indexing is used in the sense of connecting a document with other documents that are likely to enhance understanding. Current hypertext technology (Nielsen 1990) enables the user to navigate in a document space from the consultation of an initial document. Not only does this capacity extend the user's memory, but it is also a suggestive facility that enhances associative learning. Thus, an active document has *appropriate indexing mechanisms* (second requirement).

Document user-friendliness and indexing facilitate exploration. In addition, the agent-orientation provides a framework for automatic adaptivity to users. In the Computer Integrated Documentation (CID) project, an adaptive indexing software agent incrementally updates the context of the information retrieval. The notion of context has been used to tailor documentation to users' information requirements (Boy 1991a). Thus, an active document is *adaptive* to users (third requirement).

Finally, it often requires cognitive efforts to figure out dynamic aspects of complex matters when they are available on a static medium such as paper. Computer programs enable the simulation of dynamic features that paper technology cannot provide. Computer simulations enable better understanding of such dynamic aspects. Thus, an active document enables *dynamic simulations* (fourth requirement).

Integrating Software Agents into Active Documents

As I have already advocated, one way to avoid extra training is to produce documents that can be naturally used by people. Direct manipulation is likely to improve the design and use of (active) documents. A user-centered answer to facilitate the integration of CSCL environments is to satisfy conditions such as consistency of knowledge, internal consistency of the system that insures human reliability, context-sensitivity to the task, expert advice when it is needed, etc.

Current documents are constructed from a variety of knowledge sources. They may have various formats according to the target and the available technology. The form and content of a document are both task-dependent (context of use) and domain-dependent (content). One of the main difficulties in designing active documents is to anticipate a very large number of contexts of use. Context of use is usually related to other entities such as situation, behavior, viewpoint, relationships among agents, discourse, dialogue, etc. Contextualization is extremely difficult using the conventional paper technology. It is easier using computer technology when appropriate software agents are available or easy to construct. The CID project is an example of integration of software agents into active documents.

If active documents are understood by the user without external help, then they are self-explanatory. Complementary documents are commonly used to explain original documents. In active documents, explanation should be formalized and transferred into a software agent that will help the user to better understand. For instance, in the physics lab exercises, diagrams are presented to the students with missing parts that the students need to add in order to complete a consistent electrical circuit. On paper, these diagrams are presented to the student with a text explanation to explain what he or she needs to do. On the computer, the same diagrams are active, so that by clicking on each part of them, hypertextual information (text or graphics) appears and explains what to do.

I make a distinction between a *shallow* and a *deep interface*. A shallow interface includes the necessary devices and displays (handled using metaphors) to enable a user-friendly human-machine interaction. Metaphors are designed to improve the interface transparency. A deep interface consists of internal mechanisms (see the next section). These internal mechanisms help users in the management of the complexity of the tasks and the system itself. This distinction is a departure from the conventional software development cycle where the shallow interface is built on top of an already existing software mechanism. Agent programming happens on top of existing documents; they provide life to these documents. In this sense, they constitute a deeper interface, i.e., they enable mediation between users (readers) and documents (writers).

SRAR, Blocks and Software Agents

Knowledge is not contextual, it is contextualized. In practice, there must be a voluntary act of contextualizing acquired knowledge; i.e., knowledge is incrementally modified to fit with contextual requirements. This act is not trivial. Context is incrementally constructed and added to current knowledge. This raises the context representation issue. What is context? In this chapter, context is a set of conditions on world parameters that are *persistent* in a variation domain. For instance, a flight phase such as "cruise" defines persistent conditions such as "the aircraft is in the air within a prescribed flight level envelope."

The *Situation Recognition and Analytical Reasoning* (SRAR) model was developed to take into account the way operations procedures were used in the control of complex systems (space shuttle, aircraft, industrial process, etc.) The SRAR model has been described extensively in (Boy 1991a), and used in KAoS (see Bradshaw et al. chapter, also in this volume). In SRAR, it is assumed that knowledge is divided into chunks that consist of a situational part (including context) and an analytical part. When a situation is recognized, analytical reasoning is performed. It is very difficult (often impossible) to elicit situational knowledge. Situational knowledge is domain-specific and incrementally acquired by training. It consists of compiled expertise at the skill level in Rasmussen's sense (Rasmussen 1986).

Analytical knowledge is elicited when we ask someone to explain what he/she knows about a domain. The underlying principle of SRAR is that situational knowledge is incrementally constructed from analytical knowledge integrated with situated explanations and observations. This learning process is performed by experimentation (Boy and Rappaport 1987).

I have shown that some analytical knowledge chunks used in a novice's analytical reasoning were compiled into an expert's situational patterns for solving the same problem (Boy and Caminel 1989; Boy 1987). Furthermore, such situation patterns are active interface agents that represent local pragmatism useful in human-machine interaction.

Knowledge blocks were born from the need to model the construction of situational knowledge (Boy 1990; Mathé 1990; Boy and Caminel 1989). They were designed to enable the representation of situated analytical chunks at any representational grain level. A knowledge block consists of a problem statement including a context, triggering preconditions, abnormal conditions and a goal, and a procedure (a solution to the problem statement) to reach the goal. Contextual conditions (context) are distinguished from triggering conditions because they are more persistent in time and/or space. Context (situational patterns) is incrementally acquired and refined (Boy 1991a, 1991b). It is used to label and organize knowledge blocks.

Smith *et al.* already defined an *agent* as a persistent software entity dedicated to a specific purpose (Smith, Cypher, and Spohrer 1994). In this chapter, an agent[1] is a software entity that can be represented by a knowledge block with an interface metaphor (appearance). Even if these kinds of agents can be "generic,", they must be flexible enough to be tailored to each individual. It is recognized that the most flexible way to tailor a software agent is to program it. However, programming must be natural and easy to do. If users need to learn a conventional programming language, most of them will not develop such agents. My software agents research agenda focuses on two directions:

- The construction of *internal mechanisms* based on knowledge blocks that enable users to manipulate natural concepts without knowing what is going on behind the scene (what really happens is machine learning "crunching"); natural concepts manipulated by users are for instance "I like that," "this is not what I need at the moment," "this is related to another concern which is...," etc.

- The construction of *metaphors* that enable users to think and play with "natural" entities such as simulation objects, consistent symbols and signs (specific to the domain), etc.; these metaphors are not necessarily human-like expressions, but rather symbolic, meaningful, and consistent[2] interface entities; they are mainly focused on the adaptation of appropriate media to various kinds of knowledge that need to be transferred for supportability purposes

The ACTIDOC Environment

ACTIDOC (ACTIve DOCuments) is a CSCL environment. It is based on the principle that conventional documents, usually paper-based, can be improved by the addition of appropriate software agents. Currently, ACTIDOC is implemented on top of HyperCard (HC).

An ACTIDOC document is an ordered set of pages (typically HC cards in the current implementation). A page consists of a *content* and *software agents* that make the content vivid (or active). The content of a page is common knowledge that is shared by a community of people, e.g., teachers, students, parents, etc. For instance, it comes from a text book. Software agents are overlaid on top of the edited part of an ACTIDOC page. An ACTIDOC agent is an active knowledge block that is composed of the following:

- A name
- A context that is a list of triplets (author(s); time of creation/modification; reasons for creation/modification)
- A set of triggering conditions (TCs): a TC is usually reduced to a mouse click or a message coming from another agent

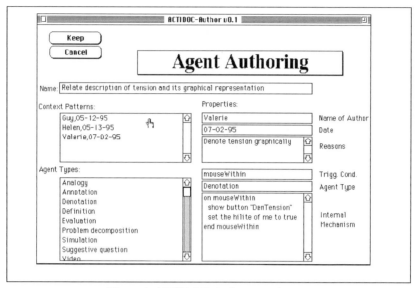

Figure 1. ACTIDOC-Author typical entry.

- A set of internal mechanisms (IMs) typically implemented in HyperTalk, each IM is associated with a TC
- A set of interface metaphors: typically an agent has an initial interface metaphor that can be modified by one of its internal mechanisms

ACTIDOC-Author is a system that enables the creation and modification of ACTI-DOC agents (figure 1).

Examples of Software Agents for Cooperative Learning

A major strength of the French education system is its unity: teachers must follow an official program elaborated by the National Education Ministry. It is also a strong constraint. If it is followed to the letter, it turns out to be a page-turning activity. Such an alternative assumes that the student must absorb the information contained in each page and answer questions before going on to the next page. I believe that the assimilation and accommodation of these linear courses can be improved if appropriate pragmatism is used. In my approach, pragmatism is introduced using software agents that assist both the learner and the teacher in the assimilation and accommodation of the content. In this section, I introduce both a methodology and examples of agents that support this approach.

Schank's Learning Architectures as Classes of Agents for the Design of Active Documents

The main problem in building such software agents is putting the student in an appropriate learning situation that affords exploration, understanding, and remembering. Each active document includes a learning situation that must satisfy the following requirements : timely information, appropriate content, and appropriate presentation and support. Schank and Juna have proposed six learning architectures that I use to assist the design of software agents supporting active documents (Schank and Jona 1991).

Case-based learning software agent. This architecture is based on two ideas. The first idea is that the expert memory includes facts. Doctors and lawyers, for instance, remember cases that were processed in the past and reuse them in analogous situations. Situation recognition is then extremely important. It is essential to recognize analogies with previous cases. The second idea, dear to Roger Schank, is that people are good storytellers. In particular, when students are ready to listen to a story, they are ready to learn from this story. The task of a software agent that would use this architecture would be to motivate students to listen to the story to encourage them to look for more information, to ask questions (exploration), and eventually to criticize the story.

Incidental learning software agent. Sometimes people are not motivated to learn in specific situations. When specific knowledge is essential in everyday life, people remember it by heart, e.g., multiplication tables. They remember essential knowledge in context by recalling some of its attributes. The trick in incidental learning is to provide students with the attributes that are sufficiently motivating for them. An incidental learning software agent enables the presentation of interesting situations about a concept that is not easy to learn because it is not intrinsically motivating.

Problem-solving software agent. Problem solving is usually learned by giving the students rules to apply and situations-problems in which these rules can be useful. I then increase the complexity of a problem, and hope that students will be able to adapt. Each student must perform an exercise before being allowed to go to the next one. An architecture including a set of cascading problems includes a problem space where problems are related to each other by various degrees of complexity. In other words, if you cannot solve problem A, you will not be able to solve problem B, because B is a logical follow-up to A. There are problems that we need to be able to solve before others. A software agent that enables the implementation of this architecture must provide a library of cascading problems, with semantic connections between them. Each problem is decomposed into sub-problems with lower granularity, and thus is easier to solve. This assumes a sufficiently fine analysis of the domain to elicit a hierarchy of sub-problems.

Software agent that enables exploration directed by video databases. The best teachers who taught us were good storytellers. Human beings use their memory to index and retrieve anecdotes at will. Video databases would be very interesting instruments that would serve as storytellers. The main problem is to index them in such a way that the student could easily browse them and retrieve useful information. The corresponding software agent helps the user to index and retrieve video images in the right context.

Software agent that enables learning by doing based on simulations. The simulation technique enables students to learn by exploration. It is becoming easier to implement as computer technology improves. Most microcomputers are equipped with games involving learning by doing and trial-and-error. Such simulation constitutes an environment in which students do not fear making errors. Rapid prototypes of simulation could help in the development of global skills. Heavier simulators are often necessary to learn fine grain concepts and situations. This type of software agent is more complex because it must be integrated into the simulation.

Suggestive-questions software agent. This technique is based on the fact that everyone can be his or her own teacher. We often have a good idea, a problem, or just a question that we would like to discuss. A suggestive-questions software agent is a knowledge-based system that helps in learning from interaction by listening to the student and asking good questions. It must be able to ask students questions about one of their problems or ideas. These questions are often questions that students would not think of, even if they know the topic very well. This mechanism enables students to learn from their own ideas. A software agent that would ask such questions would be useful even if it does not understand the student's ideas.

Evaluation Software Agent (Student Level)

An *evaluation software agent* manages the strengths and weaknesses of the student. This software agent is a knowledge-based system. An expert instructor very rarely discovers many new cases that he has not experienced before. There are observable patterns of student behavior (i.e., individual strengths and weaknesses) that the instructor is able to recognize. Recognition of such patterns leads to prelearned appropriate answers. This representation allows the implementation of production rules that a computer expert system can run. Such a computer evaluation mechanism would allow instructors to focus more on one of their main tasks, which is to answer student needs more appropriately. Thus, students would benefit from this human feedback.

The construction of the evaluation software agent that assists the instructor in the evaluation task should improve the relevance and completeness of the feedback. Students would perceive and correct their flaws faster. Performance would be much improved. The evaluation software agent should enable the analysis of student needs and further improve instructor acts. It should make it possible for the instructor to focus on the students' most important strengths and weaknesses.

The evaluation software agent would allow an instructor to find classes of students according to their strengths and weaknesses. This classification capability would enhance better use of scarce pedagogical resources. The efficiency of training would be improved.

Instructor aid Software Agent

An instructor aid software agent should satisfy the following requirements:

- Reduce instructor workload of tedious, repetitive, and time-consuming tasks such as preparing lectures and correcting exercises; it should be connected to office automation software agents that are extremely relevant here; video hardware should be directly accessible from the computer
- Facilitate understanding and learning from their own experience; the instructors may consult a database including their own teaching strengths and weaknesses; they would improve the courses by considering the students' overall performance; this effect would be the same as transforming training into a self-correction activity; this feedback system would enable instructors to improve the courses incrementally by experimentation
- Offering access to other experiences; today the exchange of experience between instructors is very limited, because of weak exchange support; an instructor aid software agent should improve this support and provide an appropriate framework facilitating human-human interactions

Thus an instructor aid software agent facilitates course management including authoring of courses, storing and retrieving experience, and accessing the experience of other instructors.

General Purpose Networking Software Agent

Concepts that have already been developed would not be applied if the psychological and social reality were not taken into account. A danger would be to implement these software agents in a centralized system. The overall system should be decentralized and interconnected. The last thing an instructor would like is to be spied on by a system. Conversely, if an instructor perceives the benefits of the *cooperation* with other colleagues (including coordinators), he or she would certainly interact with equals within an interconnected system. Electronic mail systems are good examples of such interconnected communication systems.

This issue leads to the definition of a general purpose networking software agent that would enable anyone in a domain-specific network to benefit from the experience of others. A general purpose networking software agent used by a coordinator would provide generalizations of experience for the overall training network. It is a knowledge-sharing tool for the overall training system in the application domain. It enables the management of cases that are incrementally stored when they are discovered by educators or instructors. It enables ac-

Notion of Potential Difference or Tension

We observe a river water current. The altitude difference between two points of the river causes the existence of a water current between these two points.

In the same way, we observe an electrical current in a closed circuit. The potential difference between two points of the circuit causes the existence of an electrical current between these two points.

This analogy is displayed in the following figure:

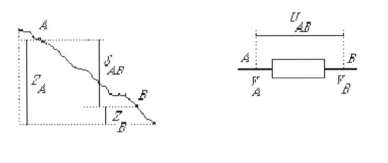

Figure 2. Basic pedagogical document.

cess to evaluation records from any location in the network at any time. It enables instructors to compare various performances. Local practices would be kept, but the definition of a common ontology would improve the understanding of student backgrounds and capabilities.

Developing an Example

In the following example, software agents are added to existing documents to enhance their usability. Software agents provide pragmatism to the existing documents where syntax and semantics are already fixed and will not be modified. This feature corresponds to the French unified school program. Even if this approach fits well with the French education system, I think that the separation of semantics and pragmatism is a general and useful concept for the design of active documents.

An Example in Physics

Let us take an example of a formal course on electrical tension. In this example, I show how a conventional physics exercise can be transformed into an active

Notion of Potential Difference or Tension

We observe a river water current. The altitude difference between two points of the river causes the existence of a water current between these two points.

In the same way, we observe an electrical current in a closed circuit. The potential difference between two points of the circuit causes the existence of an electrical current between these two points.

This analogy is displayed in the following figure:

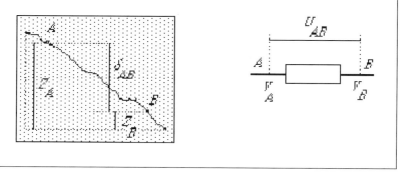

Figure 3. Use of a denotation agent.

document by the addition of appropriate software agents. A conventional page describing the notion of potential difference or tension follows (figure 2).

Teachers may add appropriate agents such as *denotation* agents that show relevant parts of graphics explained in the text. These agents associate text descriptions to corresponding graphical objects, and vice versa. For instance, when the mouse is dragged on the sentence "We observe a river water current," the denotation agent shows the relevant part (figure 3).

In the same way, a *definition* agent can be programmed to establish a correspondence between a text description and a mathematical formula. When the text "altitude difference between two points" is activated by putting the mouse on top of it, a mathematical formula appears in context. The context is defined by the corresponding picture and the denotation of the two points A and B (figure 4).

An *analogy* agent gives the equivalence between various entities such as V_A and Z_A. If the mouse is dragged on top of V_A, the altitude Z_A is highlighted and shows the analogy (figure 5).

These are very simple software agents that enhance the pragmatics of already designed physics courses. In this particular case, agents are basically hypermedia links between objects. Objects can be overlaid on top of graphical or textual parts

Notion of Potential Difference or Tension

We observe a river water current. The *altitude difference between two points* of the river causes the existence of a water current between these two points.

In the same way, we observe an electrical current in a closed circuit. The potential difference between two points of the circuit causes the existence of an electrical current between these two points.

This analogy is displayed in the following figure:

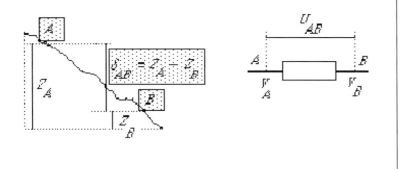

Figure 4. Use of a definition agent.

of a conventional document to create active documents. There is a tool box of agent types that teachers can choose from to program their own agents by analogy. Agent types can be denotation, definition, analogy, suggestive question, problem solving (decomposition of a problem into sub-problems), video management, evaluation, hypermedia link to another active document, etc. Once the teacher has chosen an agent type in the tool box, a procedure helps him or her design the corresponding agent by clicking on appropriate objects or locations on the screen.

When the system is in use, both students and teachers browse active documents related to the lesson of the day at their own speed. Individual backtracking is possible and encouraged. Eventually new agents can be created to enhance understanding of the concept to be learned. Students practice exercises by solving problems presented in an active document exercise. In these documents, problem statements are put in context using agents in the same way as presented above. Suggestive questions guide the students. Hypermedia links to other relevant documents enable the student to remember concepts previously learned. An evaluation agent records student's paths in the various active documents, as well as the answers to the questions posed. By the end of a session active documents are collected and analyzed by the teacher either on-line with the students or off-line.

Notion of Potential Difference or Tension

We observe a river water current. The altitude difference between two points of the river causes the existence of a water current between these two points.

In the same way, we observe an electrical current in a closed circuit. The potential difference between two points of the circuit causes the existence of an electrical current between these two points.

This *analogy* is displayed in the following figure:

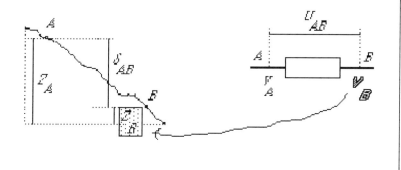

Figure 5. Use of an analogical agent.

An Educational Memory in Use

Typical active documents such as those described in the previous subsection are exchanged between teachers, students, parents, schools, and homes. An educational memory is not a dead body of information but an actively growing accumulation of beliefs that have been put together (related or not) by people involved in the education process. These beliefs may evolve with time according to tests. An active document cannot become a stable and trustable knowledge entity[1] until it has been adequately communicated to and approved by other people. This is a reason to enhance the educational memory interactivity both within the education system itself and with other parties such as industry and the civil organizations. The educational memory can be seen as a large set of interconnected active documents that are logically and historically organized. This logical and historical organization is performed using contextual descriptions of the documents as described previously. It also includes a classification of software agents. This classification is incrementally acquired using a concept clustering process applied to software agents constructed by teachers. The block representation handles the construction and re-construction of such documents' organization (Boy 1991a).

The second requirement described in the Requirements for Active Documents subsection states that active documents should have appropriate indexing mechanisms. In the CID system, an indexing mechanism has already been developed that is suitable for incrementally updating descriptors of documents and attaching context to these descriptors. A descriptor is a partial description of the document that defines a particular semantic direction of search. A document is always partially described. This is why information retrieval is an *abduction* process (Peirce 1931–58). Context is added to the descriptors within a document to reduce the uncertainty characterizing the information retrieval process. Context is usually added either positively or negatively to descriptors after successful or unsuccessful document retrievals. When a document is retrieved, it provides not only content knowledge, but also contextual information such as who designed it, why it was designed the way it is (design rationale), who used it, who did not like it (user feedback), and so forth.

Let us take a scenario of active document search and reuse. First, a physics teacher decides to give a course on the notion of potential difference and tension. She decides to retrieve active documents generated by other people. She makes the assumption that by using the educational memory, she will get interesting active documents that she can reuse and adapt to her course. She tries to describe what she needs by specifying a list of descriptors such as "potential difference" or "tension." After a first information retrieval attempt, she gets more than 100 active documents. She does not have time to examine the whole set. She then decides to add some context to the descriptors by specifying "tenth grade" and "physics course." She then gets 7 documents that she can browse. She sees that some of the documents mention that the evaluation feedback provided by other teachers on 4 of them is not acceptable. She decides not to consider these anymore. To decide which one of the 3 remaining documents she will keep, she reads the annotations provided by other teachers and uses the documents themselves. Once she has used the selected active document, she provides feedback information on her own use of it. She may say that some children could not understand some parts of it. Thus, she has made some modifications that are included and contextualized in the current active document. The document is returned to the educational memory.

In addition, a physics teacher may design a set of software agents that he/she can send to the educational memory for experimentation. Other teachers may use them and give their feedback. I think that this is a way to converge towards a normalization of pragmatics in the teaching of physics. The main problem is for the teachers to carefully annotate the active documents that they create, modify or use. In the current project, the aim is to better understand the human factors involved in the use of such an educational memory, as well as the underlying mechanisms that are required to support it.

Discussion and Perspectives

This chapter presents an approach of cooperative learning that is based on the design and use of software agents. Alain Rappaport (1988) was one of the first researchers to introduce the concept of cognitive primitives for the design of user interfaces and expert systems. In cooperative learning, cognitive primitives (basic software agents) are essential to better respond to students' needs and problems and improve cooperative learning. Teachers should be faced with software agents that they understand directly in order to better generate active documents. Both teachers and students should be able to create new agents easily, as well as modify old ones. To facilitate active document design and publishing, libraries of software agents need to be created and maintained.[4]

In the aeronautical domain, Airbus Training has implemented a procedure used by instructors that enables them to provide experience feedback, i.e., instructors ask for improvements or corrections of flaws in training tools based on the experience they have on these tools. Experience feedback is based on positive or negative experience that is interpreted by training specialists to generate or modify corporate knowledge. A corporate memory of the description of the various pedagogical tools is maintained with this procedure. The main point of such an organization is the optimization of the end product destined for the students.

The education system needs to better understand the notion of a product designed by a team of people for the needs of an evolving society. What do we want our children to learn? For doing what? Design rationale of educational products should be more explicit. In these conditions, teachers will be able to communicate about concrete descriptions of their pedagogical requirements by exchanging, using, and refining software agents.

Standardization is a key factor to enhancing communication between people within a professional community. In the education system, the need for standardization is a trigger for appropriating new technologies, contrary to the aeronautical domain where standardization is a late, but crucial issue. In other words, it is now important to develop an ontology of the education domain that enables teachers and instructors to establish workable communication links, especially with upcoming software agents. Standardization is consistent with the engineering approach. One of the drawbacks of standardization in education is the risk of the reduction of natural concepts.

In this chapter, three main concepts have emerged: active documents, software agents, and organization. Active documents are used as repositories of pedagogical knowledge. Software agents are observers, information processors, and proposers. They can be active entities added to conventional documents transcribed into an electronic form. Some of them observe a user's interactions. They are able to produce actions from the data they have acquired from the user. The action performed by a software agent ranges from the activation of other agents to the execution of (computational) operations. They implicitly or explicitly include user models. Software agents are easy to manipulate and relate to each others. They provide vivid behavior to a user interface. They can be visible (audible), or invisible (inaudible). When they are sensorial, they have a presentation shape (usually called a metaphor) on the screen, or a sound, and a behavior. Otherwise, the user does not know that they exist. In the field of electronic documentation, agent adaptivity has been shown to be extremely useful in information retrieval (Boy 1991a). In this case, software agents are knowledge-based mechanisms that enable the management of active documents.

> Technology is not a panacea for education. But, it can serve the proximal cause for mobilizing folks to actions *(Soloway 1995)*.

As active documents are manipulated, it is anticipated that the education organization will evolve. It will produce a shareable memory that can be capitalized by the corpus of the teaching profession. I claim that humans will experience several changes in their professional lives, because of technology changes as well as job changes. Training is no longer only a matter of an initial learning phase but is becoming a lifetime continuous education process that is based on intelligent assistance (Boy 1991b, 1987) or performance support. Even if initial training (including theoretical courses) enables the acquisition of conceptual frameworks, intelligent assistance based on software agents can be seen as hands-on training with the possibility of zooming into deeper knowledge. Training as intelligent assistance is intrinsically cooperative. This chapter proposes several dimensions that are relevant to this cooperation factor. In particular, it is claimed that *system agent-orientation* is not neutral to the evolution of our information-based world. Since software agents carry various viewpoints, these viewpoints need to be documented. This documentation requires more human-human coordination, participation, and distributed decision making. This project is ongoing, and further results will become available over the next few years.

Summary

This chapter describes an approach to the design of software agents for cooperative learning. This approach is based on a careful analysis of current education practices, e.g., user needs and cultural constraints, bearing in mind the technological possibilities and goals. I claim that information technology (IT) should be designed to preserve a reasonable continuity with current practice, to facilitate knowledge transfer and access, to show a good cost/benefit ratio, where cost includes financial cost as well as additional workload. In the ACTIDOC environment, active documents are generated and managed using current learning documents improved with a pragmatic layer of appropriate software agents. Such agents for cooperative learning are proposed and discussed using typical examples.

Acknowledgments

Many thanks to Jeffrey Bradshaw and Alain Rappaport for many useful and vivid exchanges on the topic. Thanks to Helen Wilson, Rob Jaspers, Martin Hollender and Said Tazi who provided astute comments towards improving the quality of this chapter. Some of the views presented in this section have been developed over the last 13 years by the author in cooperation with others. Some results from other researchers are presented because they have been judged important for this chapter and the comprehension of the whole.

Notes

1. Why is the concept of "agent" useful for capturing intelligence in the interaction between human and machine? Interaction can be divided into two conceptual entities: the interface between agents and the procedures that they use to interact through this interface. Thus, I claim that intelligence is both in the interface and in the procedures. Usually, the more the interface makes the system transparent to the user (i.e., the user understands how to use the system to perform what he or she needs to do), the less he or she needs procedures (i.e., direct interaction is sufficient without any external help). In many cases, however, it is hardly possible to avoid the use of procedures because of the complexity of the tasks and the system itself.

2. According to Donald Norman, "People will be more accepting of intelligent agents if their expectations are consistent with reality. This is achieved by presenting an appropriate conceptual model—a system image—that accurately depicts the capabilities and actions" (Norman 1994).

3. A trustable knowledge entity is guaranteed to work in a given context of validity. This is the case of physics formulas such as Newton's law "f=ma" to measure forces at the surface of the Earth.

4. A major issue is the interoperability of software developed in a specific software environment. Software agents should be platform-independent. Furthermore, the combination of object-oriented techniques (a software agent is a software object) and component-based software has some essential benefits listed by Rappaport (1995): reuse, extendibility, customization, distributability, and standardization. An example of standardization of agent-based software is given in General Magic (1994).

References

Attipoe, A., and Boy, G. A. 1995. Modeling Knowledge and Access in Corporate Distributed Information Systems. Paper presented at the IJCAI '95 Workshop on Artificial Intelligence in Distributed Information Systems, 19 August, Montreal, Quebec, Canada.

Birmingham, W. P.; Drabenstott, K. M.; Frost, C. O.; Warner, A .J.; and Willis, K. 1994. The University of Michigan Library: This Is Not Your Father's Library. Paper presented at Digital Libraries '94, The First Annual Conference on the Theory and Practice of Digital Libraries, 19–21 June, College Station, Texas.

Boy, G. A. 1995. Supportability-Based Design Rationale. Paper presneted at the IFAC Conference on Human-Machine Systems, 27–29 June, Boston, Massachusetts.

Boy, G. A. 1993. Operator and Student Models in Computer-Based Training, EURISCO

Report T-93-005-GB-VI, European Institute of Cognitive Sciences and Engineering, Toulouse, France.

Boy, G. A. 1991a. Computer-Integrated Documentation, NASA Technical Memorandum, No. 103870, National Aeronautics and Space Administration, Moffett field, California.

Boy, G. A. 1991b. *Intelligent Assistant System.* San Diego, Calif.: Academic.

Boy, G. A. 1987. Operator Assistant Systems. *International Journal of Man-Machine Studies* 27:541–554.

Boy, G. A., and Caminel, T. 1989. Situation Pattern Acquisition Improves the Control of Complex Dynamic Systems. Paper presented at the Third European Workshop on Knowledge Acquisition for Knowledge-Based Systems, July, Paris.

Boy, G. A., and Rappaport, A. T. 1987. Operator Assistant System in Space Telemanipulation: Knowledge Acquisition by Experimentation. Paper presented at ROBEX'87, 4–5 June, Pittsburgh, Pennsylvania.

Durstewitz, M. D. 1994. Reuse of Experience for Industrial Applications—A Formal Approach. Paper presented at CSI'94, Cognitive Science in Industry, 28–30 September, Luxembourg.

General Magic. 1994. Telescript Technology: The Foundation of the Electronic Marketplace, White Paper, General Magic, Inc., Mountain View, California.

Minsky, M. 1985. *The Society of Mind.* New York: Simon and Schuster.

Nielsen, J. 1990. *Hypertext and Hypermedia.* San Diego, Calif.: Academic.

Norman, D. 1994. How Might People Interact with Agents. *Communications of the ACM* 37(7): 68–71.

Norman, D. A. 1992. Cognitive Artifacts. In *Designing Interaction: Psychology at the Human-Computer Interface*, ed. J. M. Carroll, 17–38. Cambridge, U.K.: Cambridge University Press.

Papert, S. 1995. Deeper Implications of Computation for Learning: Changing the Representations of Knowledge Used by Introductory Math and Science. Talk presented at the Fourth International Workshop on Human and Machine Cognition, May, Seaside, Florida.

Peirce, C. S. 1931–58. *Collected Papers.* Edited by C. Hartshorne, P. Weiss, and A. Burks. 8 vols. Cambridge, Mass.: Harvard University Press.

Piaget, J. 1977. *The Equilibration of Cognitive Structures.* Chicago: University of Chicago Press.

Rappaport, A. T. 1995. Context, Cognition, and Intelligent Digital Information Infrastructure. Talk presented at the Fourth International Workshop on Human and Machine Cognition, May, Seaside, Florida.

Rappaport, A. T. 1988. Cognitive Primitives. *International Journal of Man-Machine Studies* 29:733–747.

Rasmussen, J. 1986. *Information Processing and Human-Machine Interaction. An Approach to Cognitive Engineering.* System Sciences and Engineering Series, ed. A. P. Sage. New York: North Holland.

Schank, R. 1991. Where's the AI? *AI Magazine* 12(4): 38–49.

Schank, R. C., and Jona, H. Y. 1991. Empowering the Student: New Perspectives on the Design of Teaching Systems. *Journal of the Learning Sciences* 1(1).

Sheridan. T. B. 1992. *Telerobotics, Automation, and Human Supervisory Control.* Cambridge, Mass.: MIT Press.

SIGCUE. 1992. Computer-Supported Collaborative Learning. *Bulletin of the Special Interest Group for Computer Uses in Education (SIGCUE)* 21(3): 1–65.

Smith, D. C.; Cypher, A.; and Spohrer, J. 1994. KIDSIM: Programming Agents without a Programming Language. *Communications of the ACM* 37(7): 55–67.

Soloway, E. 1995. Beware, Techies Bearing Gifts. *Communications of the ACM* 38(1): 17–24.

Soloway, E. 1993. Interactive Learning Environments. Paper presented at INTER-CHI'93 Tutorial Notes, 24–29 April, Amsterdam.

CHAPTER 12

The M System

Doug Riecken

The study of software agents has resulted in a diverse set of views and realizations. One such view has focused on building specialized agents which assist users by performing specific tasks such as creating an itinerary, filtering e-mail, or optimizing human-computer interaction (Etzioni and Weld 1994; Maes 1994; Riecken 1992a). A second area of study aims to integrate the performance of sets of these specialized agents (Genesereth and Ketchpel 1994). For example, several individuals might delegate the task of scheduling a meeting to their respective agents.

The present study concerns a third focus of research: how to integrate different reasoning processes *(societies of agents)* to implement a software assistant capable of performing a broad range of tasks. As a result of this research, I have developed M, a software assistant which attempts to recognize, classify, index, store, retrieve, explain, and present information. M integrates multiple *reasoning agents* whose joint results assist groups of users working in a desktop multimedia conferencing environment.

Multistrategy reasoning and learning has been an active research area (Guha and Lenat 1994; Michalski and Tecuci 1994; Michalski 1993; Pazzani 1990; Gasser and Huhns 1989; Bond and Gasser 1988; Engelmore and Morgan 1988; Huhns 1987; de Kleer 1977). From my studies in this domain, the design and implementation of M's architecture posed many interesting questions:

- How do you coordinate and manage a diverse set of agents?
- How do the agents communicate?
- What knowledge is required by an agent and is it shared with other agents?
- Do the agents know of each other, and if so, what relationships exist?
- Does an agent demonstrate intelligent behavior or does intelligent behavior emerge from the coexistence of the active states of the many diverse agents?

To address these questions, I defined and implemented a design theory for an architecture of integrated agents, influenced by Minsky's *Society of Mind* (SOM) theory (Minsky 1985, 1980). Aspects of spatial, structural, functional, temporal, causal, explanation-based, and case-based reasoning capabilities were integrated in M by means of the following:

- An I/O system
- A semantic network
- A rule-based system
- A scripting system
- A blackboard system
- A history log file system

The theory takes the position that an assistant which can classify and explain actions performed on objects within a dynamic environment can function effectively by simultaneously generating and testing multiple domain theories in relation to a given goal.

In this chapter I will provide a general discussion of an architecture which supports integrated multiple reasoning processes, the *agents*. This architecture has been applied in several different domains:

- A system which learns to compose music (Riecken 1992b)
- Intelligent user interface agents (Riecken 1992a, 1991a, 1991b)
- The M assistant, which classifies and manages objects in an electronic conferencing system

M and the Virtual Meeting Room Application

To test design methods for prototyping such an assistant, I identified several tasks relating to collaborative electronic work environments. M was applied at AT&T Bell Laboratories to perform these tasks within a virtual meeting room (VMR) "world" which supports multimedia desktop conferencing. In a VMR, participants collaborate via pen-based computers and telephone. In this context, the goal of a software assistant is to classify and index the changing states of the VMR shared by the participant(s) and the assistant.

The VMR World

The VMR "world" is composed of domain objects such as electronic documents, electronic ink, images, markers, white boards, copy machines, and staplers on which actions may be performed. Each user is supported by a personalized assistant, which attempts to recognize and define relationships between domain objects, based on the actions performed by the users and the resulting new states of the world. For example, VMR participants may perform actions on a group of electronic documents such as joining them as a set or annotating them collectively. M attempts to identify all domain objects and classify relationships between various subsets based on their physical properties and relevant user actions.

User actions are taken as indicators of semantic associations between subsets of objects. A simple example of an association would be two adjacent documents which a user annotates by drawing a circle around them. Thus, based on (1) spatial reasoning about the proximity of the documents and the circle, (2) structural and functional reasoning about the circle surrounding the two documents, and (3) causal reasoning about the user's action of drawing the circle, M can infer and explain a plausible relationship between the documents. This functionality provides a new kind of framework for users to work together electronically.

Conceptually, a VMR is a virtual place where one or more persons can work together despite their physical separation. In such an "electronic place," individuals physically located in New Jersey and England can "meet" and work, sharing and creating information in a variety of media.

In a VMR, the assistant attempts such tasks as recognizing, classifying, indexing, and explaining the actions performed by users on all the objects within a VMR during a given meeting. VMRs may also be persistent, existing over arbitrarily long periods of time. A VMR is thus like a real meeting room where individuals can exit at the end of a working session, leaving behind necessary documents and other objects, and return later to continue the work at hand.

If collaborative work environments are to be successful, then the expressiveness of the participants must be improved, and distracting computer-related actions must be minimized. Below are two examples of the kinds of VMR tasks where M can help improve the performance of participants.

Organizing the Electronic Workspace

Consider a typical group of designers working in a brainstorming session held within a real physical room. By the end of such a working session, the designers will have created and used many documents, bullet lists, diagrams, notes, post-it notes, and other such items. Based on the properties of a physical room, the participants could organize themselves and the objects in the room using tables, walls, and whiteboards. Documents and other objects could be spatially organized and located for ease of access by the meeting participants. Typically, the designers would be able to view, engage, review, and reformulate various conceptual relationships between the physical materials and information generated as the meeting progressed.

When we port the designers' brainstorming session to a VMR, their view of the work environment is significantly constrained to the physical size of their respective computer screens. What if a software assistant took on the responsibility of organizing the creative output and interactions of all the participants? In essence, the assistant helps users to access and manipulate many different materials created and used during a meeting, independent of where the materials are located within a VMR or when the materials were last used or created.

M can define, generate, and explain an extensive set of relationships and classifications which represent various conceptual information and views of both (1) the set of objects created and used by the participants in a VMR and (2) the actions performed on VMR objects by the participants. Thus, via dialog boxes or direct manipulation techniques, participants can ask their respective assistants to present organized views of the various related materials used during a meeting.

M observes the actions performed by VMR participants and attempts to infer how the current actions applied to VMR objects relate to other VMR objects and previous actions. For example, as participants interact with an electronic document, M can provide them with contextual hyperlinks to related objects such as other documents, drawings, notes, lists, pen annotations, and voice annotations.

One of M's fundamental responsibilities is to assist a user in defining or reformulating relationships between objects in a VMR. M attempts to maintain simultaneous theories of how objects in a VMR might relate. This function enables M to provide participants with multiple views or access to related materials. While M maintains an extensive schema for organizing a VMR, it must adhere to an assistant's prime directive: never take control away from the user, who is ultimately responsible for defining relations and hyperlinks.

Figure 1 displays a computer screen where a participant in a VMR is annotating a document. Present on the computer screen are several other VMR objects and a menu-list provided by M of other VMR objects (currently out of view) which might be related to the annotated document. M can bring these other objects into view and explain why they are believed to be related. Figure 2 is one of M's diagrammatic representations of some of the relationships which exist in figure 1.

Grouping Things

As a direct result of M's classifying functions, a user has access to individual and sets of related VMR objects. This feature is significant since user actions can be performed on groups of VMR objects represented at various levels of abstraction.

M classifies objects as members of sets based on object properties and user actions. For example, all text documents or all annotated bullet lists respectively form sets based on their properties. Similarly, a sequence of actions applied to VMR objects in a given space and time can form a set. Consider a group of objects consisting of a text document, an embedded graphic image, and annotations. When a user performs an action to integrate these objects visually, M uses its spatial, temporal, structural, and functional knowledge to relate them logically as a set.

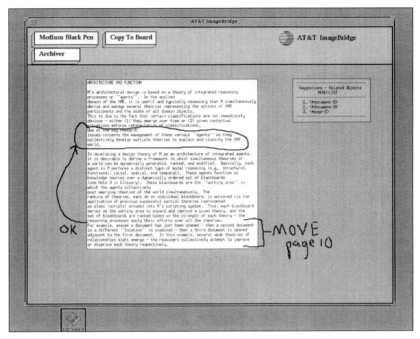

Figure 1: A VMR session where a document is being annotated and an M-provided menu-list is presented to provide access to other related objects.

Classifying objects as members of sets allows users and M to perform such important operations as (1) evaluating sets (e.g., explaining the composition of a set), (2) comparing sets (e.g., explaining how sets differ and intersect), (3) joining sets, (4) copying sets, and (5) moving sets.

By grouping related things, an assistant minimizes actions required by the user. An assistant could automatically perform such tasks as grouping related visual objects in a drawing package so they could be moved. In a VMR, if a participant moves an object in a defined group, the entire group can be moved along with it, while maintaining consistency with all constraints present in the current state of the VMR.

Figure 3 displays a group of related VMR objects composed of two individual documents and some pen annotations. This group is seen along with some other objects not in the group. Figure 4 displays the resulting group after a user moved one of the documents. Figure 5 displays the resulting group after the same document is moved again. In both moves, the task of grouping was performed by M.

While moving groups of visual objects on a computer screen addresses one type of task, it is useful to consider that movement can be visual, physical, virtual, and conceptual. M could apply the function of grouping to such tasks as

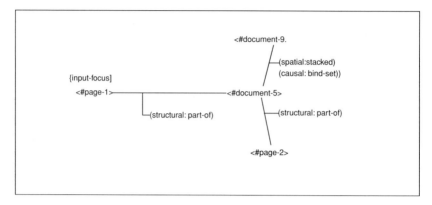

Figure 2: M's diagrammatic representations of some of the relationships between the annotated document and the objects presented in the menu-list shown in figure 1.

transferring information to another person (e.g., transmitting a set of multimedia documents via e-mail), performing queries over sets of information, and copying sets of documents to a specified storage resource.

Enumeration is another kind of grouping task. For example, if M observes a repetitive action being performed by a user over a group of objects, then M could suggest that the user apply the action globally on the group or ask to complete the task on the remaining objects for the user. The ability of M to provide user access to groups can improve the interaction between users and their computers.

Overview of M

In this section I breifly describe the role agents play in M, the different agent types M uses, and how M applies SOM theory. The section concludes with a sketch of M's overall architecture and implementation.

Role of Agents

M's architectural design is based on a theory of integrated reasoning processes called *agents*. In the VMR application, it is necessary that M simultaneously derive and manage several theories representing the actions of VMR participants and the state of all domain objects. This process is necessary because certain classifications are not immediately obvious, because either (1) they emerge over time or (2) they evolve over time. One of the key research issues concerns the management of these various agents as they collectively develop multiple theories to explain and classify the VMR world.

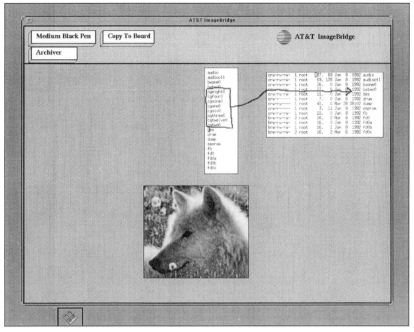

Figure 3: A VMR session where two documents and some pen annotations are grouped.

Agent Types

Within M there are five major reasoning processes, each of which are viewed as individual agents:

- *Spatial:* based on location-related properties;
- *Structural:* based on the relationships between the parts of an object;
- *Functional:* based on how the object is intended to be used;
- *Temporal:* based on time-related properties;
- *Causal:* based on relationships between events and subsequent state changes.

In addition to these five major agent types, the M system also includes many "simpler" processes which function as *supporting agents*. These supporting agents serve to represent knowledge related to qualitative properties of the domain world for a VMR. For example, within the VMR application, supporting agents represent conceptual knowledge about things like color, shape, spatial relationships (e.g., left-of, under), and structural relationships (e.g., part-of, edge-to). These simpler processes function as a collection of *memory machines* within M's semantic network, as explained below.

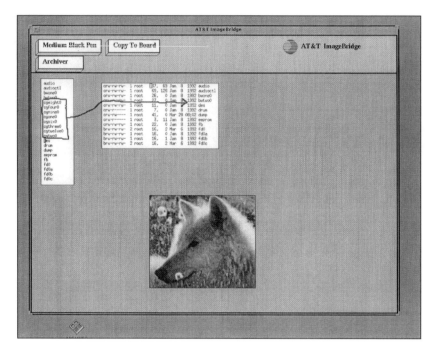

Figure 4: The layout of the grouped objects after a user moved only the document with the annotated circle drawn in it.

M as an Application of SOM Theory

M attempts to model and leverage key aspects of Minsky's SOM theory. As an architecture of integrated agents, M needed to be capable of dynamically generating, ranking, and modifying simultaneous theories of the world. In SOM theory, intelligent behavior is the result of many diverse *memory machines*, functionally distinct *societies of agents,* collaborating to reformulate current beliefs about the world.

M relies on a rich and diverse knowledge of a world—a commonsense knowledge base which represents an extensive set of permissible actions and relationships for all domain objects defined in that world. This knowledge constitutes, in essence, the world's legal grammar. Specific relationships between objects are based on domain qualifiers defining structure, space, time, function, and causal effects. This extensive knowledge enables M to process and represent a situation in a world in several different ways. A VMR world is simple and tractable enough for such an approach to be practical with our current technology and understanding.

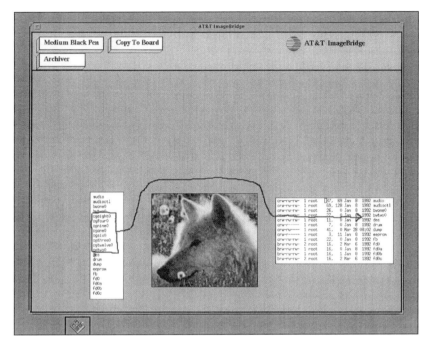

Figure 5: The new layout of the grouped objects after a user moved only the document with the annotated circle drawn in it a second time. Note that M adjusted the position of the annotations because of spatial constraints.

Architecture and Implementation

The M system integrates several traditional AI technologies in order to realize several information processing techniques discussed in SOM theory. These technologies include an *I/O system,* a *semantic network*, a *rule-based system*, a *scripting system*, a *blackboard system*, and a *history log file system.* The following discussion is a short overview to introduce the M system's architecture. A more complete discussion is given in the Architecture and Implementation of M section.

Input of a situation from the VMR world comes into M's semantic network via an I/O system. This system activates given nodes and establishes specific states in the individual state machines representing conceptual qualitative knowledge of VMR domain properties such as color and shape that are encoded into the semantic network. As state is asserted in the various qualifier machines which compose the semantic network, these assertions enable given rules to fire in M's rule-based system; these in turn may generate additional assertions to be applied to the semantic network.

The five reasoning agents monitor the changing states of the semantic network and rule-based system and select scripts from M's script-base that seem relevant to the situation in the VMR world. These scripts are then applied as partial solutions or explanations to generate a theory of the VMR situation. Finally, the highest ranked theories are provided as output to the user.

The blackboard system makes use of the five agents, which constitute knowledge sources that function over a dynamically ordered set of blackboards. These blackboards are the working area where the agents collectively post emerging theories of the world. The ranking of theories, each on an individual blackboard, is achieved via the application of previous successful partial theories represented as partial solutions or explanations encoded into M's scripting system. Thus, each blackboard serves as the working area to expand and improve a given theory, and each member of the set of blackboards is ranked based on the strength of each theory—the reasoning processes apply their efforts over all current theories posted on the ranked blackboards.

For example, assume a document as just been opened. Following this, a second document in a different location is examined, then a third is opened adjacent to the first document. As a result of M's reasoning processes, several weak theories of relationships between the three documents might emerge; the reasoning agents collectively attempt to improve or disprove each theory respectively, with each theory represented on one of the ranked ordered blackboards.

An individual theory for a VMR situation is represented on a single blackboard. Each blackboard serves as an individual "short-term memory" machine of a given situation in a world. Thus, several blackboards representing different views of a situation can actually be applied to change views quickly and reformulate the representation of the situation. This change is accomplished simply by toggling between blackboards to change the focus of attention.

Architecture and Implementation of M

We can explore how M functions and adapts its performance through a general discussion of the components that make up M's system architecture. M consists of the following subsystems (Figure 6):

- An I/O system.
- A spreading activation semantic network, to implement Minsky's K-lines (polynemes);
- A rule-based system;
- A scripting system;
- A blackboard system, to implement Minsky's trans-frames and pronomes;
- A history log file system

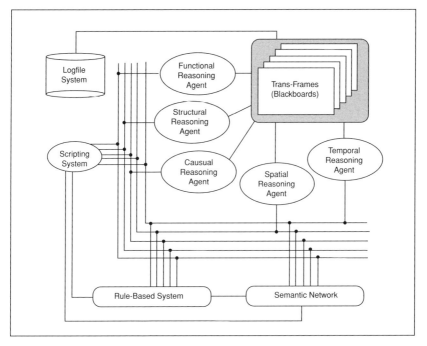

Figure 6: The M software architecture.

The I/O System

When a VMR event occurs, such as an individual annotating a document or moving one piece of "paper" on top of another, M's I/O system is responsible for representing "who did what." This is achieved by: (1) noting which actor, VMR participant or VMR object performed the action, (2) noting the type of action performed (e.g., annotating, moving, cutting), (3) noting the VMR object(s) which were involved in the action.

The input information, represented in an *input record,* entails a set of facts about state changes in the relevant objects. The I/O system is based on the input technique for the OCCAM system (Pazzani 1990), which uses some aspects of Schank's Conceptual Dependency theory (Schank 1975, 1973).

Conceptual Dependency theory is a way of representing knowledge about events expressed as sets of legal actions that can be performed on a given set of objects in some "world." It was developed in order to provide a language-independent representation and a set of conceptual primitives to reason about sentences in natural language.

Each input record identifies an ACT consisting of an action-type-identifier, an actor, an object, and a from-to qualifier. For example, an ACT represents an ACTOR (a VMR participant or object) which performed a specific type of legal

```
ACTOR: (#doug ((class:participant) (host: wolfgang)))
ACTION: (move-object)
OBJECT: (#book23 (class:book))
FROM: (coordinate (100, 100))
TO: (coordinate (150, 200))
```

Figure 7: A typical M input record.

ACTION on a given OBJECT, and a set of properties associated with the object (e.g., spatial position, composition/structure, size) which have changed FROM some existing value TO a new value. Figure 7 displays an input record where the ACTOR <doug> applied a <move> ACTION to the OBJECT <book23>, which moved the object FROM <coordinate(x1, y1)> TO <coordinate(x2, y2)>. When a VMR action is performed, the I/O system asserts the facts in the input record to the semantic net.

The Semantic Network

Semantic networks are a type of knowledge representation consisting of a set of nodes interconnected by various relationships. Within such a network, the level of *activation* of a particular node is intended to correspond with the amount of "attention" that the system should pay to a particular piece of knowledge associated with that node.

The semantic network in M propagates new knowledge about the user's actions, as represented in the input record, through spreading activation over sets of qualifiers (e.g., size, position, color). Each qualifier acts as a state machine, a member of a "society of property agents." For example, a domain object qualifier representing shape is implemented as a state machine, which can represent any one of a set of legal shapes such as square or circle. When an actor or object is identified by the I/O system, the corresponding qualifiers within the semantic network collectively are activated. Qualifiers are set to the legal state corresponding to the states of the properties of the domain objects. As these qualifiers become active in a specific state, they serve as the facts which are used to drive the inferences of the rule-based system.

A important aspect of the M design is the application of Minsky's *K-line* theory (Minsky 1985, 1980). According to the theory, each time a person 'gets an idea,' 'solves a problem,' or has a 'memorable experience,' a K-line is created. This K-line gets connected to those 'mental agencies' that were actively involved in the memorable mental event. When that K-line is later activated, it reactivates some of those same mental agencies, creating a 'partial mental state' that resembles the original. The related concept of a *polyneme* refers to an agent that arouses different activities in different agencies at the same time as a result of learning from experience. Within M, each distinct domain object is uniquely represented as a K-line/polyneme structure which links and activates the correct property states for the "society of property agents" represented in the semantic network. The state of activation of these agents corresponds to a set of facts about the state of the VMR.

The Rule-Based System

Rule-based systems (also called *production systems*) implement a model of processing based on logical constructs called *production rules.* Production rules have two parts: the *antecedent* (often called the left-side or IF portion of the rule) and the *consequent* (often called the right-side or THEN portion of the rule). The antecedent specifies some condition to be satisfied, and the consequent some action to be performed when the antecedent is true. In a rule-based system, the production rules are organized and collected in a structure called a knowledge base. As the conditions of given production rules in the knowledge base are satisfied, the rule is "fired" to produce actions that direct the behavior of the system.

M's rule-based system performs several significant functions. As various facts in the semantic network are asserted to be true, these facts satisfy specific preconditions expressed in the antecedent of given rules. The "firing" of such a rule can lead to two results: First, new facts expressed in a rule's consequent may be propagated in the semantic network, leading to a potential cascading effect where additional facts are inferred. Second, M's reasoning agents apply this new information to create, purge, strengthen, or weaken the various theories being used simultaneously by M to explain the state of the VMR world.

As new facts are asserted, they directly influence the scripting system and the behavior of the reasoning agents. The reasoning agents evaluate and apply the scripts of partial plans provided by the scripting system. In essence, we can view the rule based system as a collection of domain methods to organize facts and bias the selection of partial plans by M's reasoning agents.

The Scripting System

Scripts can be used to represent some consistent sequence of events (Schank and Abelson 1977). They must include a set of *entry conditions* that must be satisfied before the script can be invoked, a set of *resulting properties* which will be true following the script's events, and a set of objects and actions representing the sequence of events themselves.

In the case of M, the scripting system includes of a corpus of partial plans which have demonstrated frequent success in previous classification problems.

For M, a script is a partial ordering of elements in a set—the set corresponds to an interval of time to which a consistent pattern of facts and rules has been successfully applied to predict the state of some objects following a given action.

The scripting system uses coefficients to weight each script's potential to either initiate or improve upon a theory. Each theory is an attempt to classify and explain some set of actions, objects, and relationships within a VMR. The weighted scripts bias the various reasoning agents as they dynamically rank the competing theories as they are formulated on their respective blackboards. This approach minimizes combinatorial growth of the classification theories available to the reasoning agents. The reasoning agents select weighted scripts which formulate or improve only the seven most highly ranked theories.

As an example, let us assume that some VMR participants have just opened an electronic document. After several actions have been performed on this document, the participants "move" to another location in the VMR. During this time, they perform some actions on other objects.[1] Let us now assume that the participants move back to the location of the first document, open a second document near the first document, and perform some actions only on the second document. At this time, a weak theory of relationship between the two documents might be suggested by a partial plan based on spatial and structural properties; for this example, assume the weak theory is suggested because a script is applied which has a low coefficient. Now let us assume that the participants then move to some other objects, perform some actions, but then return to the location of the two adjacent documents. As they repeatedly return to this same location, there probably is no rule or script which significantly strengthens the relationship between the two documents. However, should a participant drag one of the documents toward the other, cut-and-paste between them, or create an annotation that spans them, a corresponding more highly weighted script could be applied to suggest a stronger theory of relationship.

Over time M can dynamically adjust the weights of the scripts so as to adapt its performance to the behavior and needs of an individual user. M makes this adjustment by (1) generating new rules and scripts and (2) adjusting the weights of individual scripts.

The Blackboard System

Blackboard systems are a means of implementing dynamic, opportunistic behavior among cooperating reasoning processes that share intermediate results of their efforts by means of a global data structure (the blackboard). Nii (1989) describes the basic structure of a blackboard system in terms of three components:

- The knowledge sources. The knowledge needed to solve the problem is partitioned into knowledge sources, which are kept separate and independent. [Note: in the case of M, the five reasoning agents constitute the knowledge sources]

- The blackboard data structure. The problem-solving state data (objects from the solution space) are kept in a global data store, the blackboard. Knowledge sources produce changes to the blackboard, which lead incrementally to a solution to the problem. Communication and interaction among the knowledge sources take place solely through the blackboard.

- Control. What knowledge source to apply when and to what part of the blackboard are problems addressed in control.

M's blackboard system provides a shared workspace in which the reasoning agents develop their classification theories about the VMR world. The blackboard system contains a dynamic set of up to seven ranked blackboards, which are created and disposed of as needed. Each blackboard contains an emerging classification theory over some subset of actions and objects. An emerging theory can be thought of as a hypothesis to be proved by M's reasoning agents. As new facts are asserted as true, new rules fire, and new scripts become applicable. M's reasoning agents collaborate by applying these facts, rules, and scripts as axioms to their respective blackboards. The dynamic ranking of the blackboards is determined by the weights assigned to the theory each one contains.

Minsky's (1985) *trans-frames* are data structures which are used to represent actions. An action is thought of as being a trajectory between two situations, one for <before> and the other for <after>. A *pronome* is a type of agent associated with a particular 'role' or aspect of a representation, corresponding, for example, to the actor, trajectory, or cause of some action. In M, an action is represented by the following set of properties: an <actor> which caused the action, some set of <domain object(s)> which the action was applied to, and the <before> and <after> features of those <objects>.

When a reasoning agent posts an axiom to a blackboard, this information can be viewed either as a modality of reasoning (e.g., spatial, temporal) or as an action represented by Conceptual Dependency information. New modal information could, for example, be structural or functional information which describes an object and which is posted into a graph-based schema (e.g., like a semantic network) as described by Winston et al. (1983) and Mitchell, Keller, and Kedar-Cabelli (1986). The conceptual dependency information could include such qualifiers as actor, action, object, goal, origin, and destination. This information describes actions associated with before and after states of the world, represented as trans-frames. Both types of modal and conceptual dependency information are extremely useful.

As an example of modal information, consider a functional reasoning agent which posts specific functional features of an object to a blackboard. This new information can serve to bias a structural or causal reasoning agent to derive any structural or causal features of the object that have strong correspondence with the already-posted functional features. As for the conceptual dependency information, the Minsky trans-frames allow different "things" and theories to be represented on individual blackboards using conceptual dependency schema. The trans-frame approach provides a canonical form which enables M to effectively compare different theories or sub-theories posted over the ranked blackboards.

Both types of information, the graph-based schema and the trans-frame schema, serve an additional significant function. They provide names for each schema element—in essence the names of the particular "fields" for each schema "record." Based on the names of each schema element and the respective semantics, M can generate explanations describing relationships among VMR objects and actions.

After M develops a simultaneous set of classification theories of the state of a VMR, these theories are collapsed into a ranked set of linked data structures. The set of competing theories is eventually stored in a history log file system, at which time the respective blackboards are deleted and new blackboards may be created for the next set of classification tasks.

The History Log File System

As M continues to process new VMR events and generate new classifications, all information in the log file system is retrievable and available to the reasoning agents. The information stored in the log file system is indexed according to the temporal ordering of VMR events, the spatial position of VMR events, and the individual identifiers to index and access each VMR object directly. This indexing allows M to update and reformulate previous theories based on the sequence of VMR actions which continue to occur. Basically the history log file system is a complex representation of an entire VMR world over time.

Knowledge Required

Several types of knowledge are required. In this section, I describe domain object definitions, the general classes of domain objects, and domain object qualifiers.

Domain Object Definitions

M's five reasoning agents share a common body of domain knowledge relating to the VMR. This knowledge consists of individual definitions representing each type of VMR object and the legal actions that may be performed by each object. Each definition entails a set of qualifiers represented as facts in the semantic network and rules in the rule-based system. The facts define the properties of each domain object and relationships between them. The rules define the actions that can be performed on or by each object as well as the actions which serve to focus the problem-solving process.

The use of these definitions simplifies the design of M and minimizes the effort required to modify and maintain it. In addition, these definitions provide a framework that can guide the designer during implementation of a function provided by a given object and can clarify relationships with existing objects.

General Classes of Domain Objects

M's knowledge is partitioned over five general classes, which are all subclasses of the root class *VMR-object.*:

- *Primitive drawable objects:* Knowledge about general properties of VMR objects upon which users may perform such actions as typing text, annotating with pens, and pasting other visual graphics and images. Examples of primitive drawable objects include sheets of paper, whiteboards, bulletin boards, and post-it notes.
- *Composite drawable objects:* Knowledge about such things as a chapter in a notebook composed of sheets of paper and a notebook composed of chapters.
- *Drawing tools:* Knowledge about tools which generate visual results such as pens, erasers, paint brushes, keyboards, cameras, fax machines, and scanners.
- *Primitive editing tools:* Knowledge about tools which perform actions (e.g., cut, join, move, transform) on graphical VMR objects.
- *Composite editing tools:* Knowledge about tools composed of editing tools (e.g., a stapler which performs joins, a "copy machine" which performs cut, copy, and move).

Domain Object Qualifiers

Individual domain objects are represented as instances of the five general classes using a set of qualifiers. Obtaining the best possible set of qualifiers is critical for two reasons. First, these qualifiers enable M to derive plausible classifications over the current state of a VMR. Second, the definition of qualifiers that can be viewed by both M and humans in the same way ensures a consistent view, by both M and the VMR participants, of the various reasoning processes which are applicable to VMR classification tasks.

An important consideration in the selection of qualifiers for M was the identification of contextual properties associated with objects and actions in a VMR, rather than the actual determination of the content of the VMR objects. Some of the most general qualifiers applied to all the domain objects included service and functionality, type identifier, author, group and affiliation, origin, conceptual set, content, composition, appearance and geometry, color, time and date, and space.

Service and Functionality. The service and functionality qualifier specifies the legal actions which a given object can perform. This knowledge is critical, since it enables M to apply functional in addition to structural and causal reasoning.

Type Identifier. A *type identifier* denotes a specific type of VMR object (e.g., piece of paper, whiteboard, picture image, multimedia document). In some cases, this identifier may also include a *tag field* containing several key words or phrases defining a user's purpose for the object.

Author. The *author* qualifier identifies the person responsible for the event generated by an action. It also defines an individual as the author of some VMR object just created.

Group and Affiliation. Typically, an individual is associated with some group of persons and some type of affiliation in an organization. For example, I am a member of the Computer Systems Research Laboratory (the group) and I am an employee of AT&T Bell Laboratories (the affiliation). These qualifiers enable M to infer relationships to actions I perform based on my *group and affiliation* relationships.

Origin. The *origin* qualifier identifies sources of information accessed by participants. Examples include fax, e-mail, netnews, voice mail, and electronic news, journals, newspapers, magazines, and books. Identifying an information source has many useful characteristics. For example, based on <origin> and <functionality> qualifiers, M can classify documents composed from information extracted from a real-time electronic news service as being very recent or new information compared with information extracted from an electronic book.

Conceptual Set. Sometimes VMR participants group objects into *conceptual sets*. These actions are significant in various ways. This qualifier identifies that in a specified context, a given object belongs to a set of objects. For example, a piece of paper might be positioned by a participant near or on top of other pieces of paper to form a set. Other examples of manual set construction by participants include binding pages into documents or documents into a book. As a somewhat different use of this qualifier, consider that several distinct objects might be spatially adjacent to each other during some interval of time in a meeting. M's ability to represent and replay this history of spatial and temporal information is a useful feature for VMR participants who need to recall some earlier context.

Content. In some cases it is possible to represent the *content* of a VMR object. Such representation is achieved via tag fields and the application of standard information retrieval techniques. While M's ability to qualify an object based on content is limited, it still is a useful feature and an important area for future work.

Composition. An object can also be qualified based on its *composition*. For example, a document might be composed of several different media, such as text, audio, graphics, and video. This knowledge supports various structural reasoning processes.

Appearance and Geometry. Another qualifier relates to the visualization of an object, its *appearance and geometry*. These features include the object's size, shape, and presentation as being either 2-dimensional (2D) or 3-dimensional (3D). These qualifiers also support various structural and spatial reasoning processes.

Color. The color and texture qualifier provides M with another useful means to classify actions. For example, sometimes VMR participants listing information on a whiteboard will intentionally select different color electronic markers as they generate the list. M might be led to infer that the author of the list is noting some type of classification over subsets of the list, based on the different colors.

Time and Date. *Time and date* information identifies when an action occurred. Examples include the time and date when an object was first created and when an action was last applied on the object. Based on a given task, M applies such qualifiers to derive various partial orderings of temporal events relating to different objects.

Space. The *space* selected by VMR participants to perform actions is a powerful qualifier. Participants can organize objects over the virtual space of a VMR. Through the aid of multimedia and multimodal technologies, it is possible to simulate the spatial context of the real room; thus, spatial reasoning over a simulated space provides another classification technique.

Summary

I have described a general architecture, implemented in the M system, which integrates multiple reasoning processes. This architecture allows the reasoning agents to collectively formulate and examine multiple classifications of domain objects simultaneously. This approach is useful for classification problems which exhibit time-variant characteristics. In order to minimize combinatorial growth of individual classification trajectories, a set of weighted and ranked partial plans represented in M's scripting system guides the reasoning processes of the agents.

I have described several key architectural aspects of the system. First, M integrates causal, functional, structural, spatial, and temporal reasoning. Second, M's architecture is composed of six components: a semantic net, a rule-based system, a scripting system, a dynamically ranked set of blackboards, a log file, and an I/O system. Third, the M view of agents consists of the five reasoning agents but also includes a hierarchical view of "societies of agents" built throughout all of M's system components (e.g., the simple qualifier property agents of which the semantic network is composed). Our overall perspective is based on Minsky's SOM theory—his trans-frames, implemented as blackboards, are a significant component which allows theories to be represented and compared and provides a short-term memory resource.

So, in conclusion, how should we think about agents? I hope that in time some of the confusion about the meaning of the term will disappear. Within SOM theory, an agent is a simple, specialized "reasoning" process. However many of the "agents" in the research literature resemble something more like what I would call an "assistant." To me, an assistant is an "intelligent machine" (biological or otherwise), composed of many "agencies of agents." To be an assistant one needs to understand many things, whereas the term "agent" implies some kind of specialist. To handle a common sense problem, one would not typically call on an individual agent—instead, one would want an assistant endowed with the talents of many integrated agents.

Acknowledgments

The author is deeply indebted to Marvin Minsky, Ed Pednault, and Stacy Marsella for their helpful interest and comments in this research. I especially wish to thank Sudhir Ahuja, Wayne Armour, John Carson, Alex Kononov, Yann LeCun, David Neal, and David C. Smith for valuable discussions concerning my work.

Note

1. For this example it is not necessary to consider the relationships which might exist between the actions on the first document and those performed on the other objects.

References

Bond, A. H., and Gasser, L., eds. 1988. *Readings in Distributed Artificial Intelligence.* San Francisco, Calif.: Morgan Kaufmann.

de Kleer, J. 1977. Multiple Representations of Knowledge in a Mechanics Problem-Solver. In Proceedings of the Fifth International Joint Conference on Artificial Intelligence, 299–304. Menlo Park, Calif.: International Joint Conferences on Artificial Intelligence.

Engelmore, R., and Morgan, T., eds. 1988. *Blackboard Systems.* Reading, Mass.: Addison-Wesley.

Etzioni, O., and Weld, D. 1994. A Softbot-Based Interface to the Internet. *Communications of the ACM* 37(7): 72–79.

Gasser, L., and Huhns, M. N., eds. 1989. *Distributed Artificial Intelligence, Volume 2.* San Francisco, Calif.: Morgan Kaufmann.

Genesereth, M. R., and Ketchpel, S. P. 1994. Software Agents. *Communications of the ACM* 37(7): 48–53.

Guha, R. V., and Lenat, D. B. 1994. Enabling Agents to Work Together. *Communications of the ACM* 37(7): 126–142.

Huhns, M. N., ed. 1987. *Distributed Artificial Intelligence.* San Francisco, Calif.: Morgan Kaufmann.

Maes, P. 1994. Agents That Reduce Work and Information Overload. *Communications of the ACM* 37(7): 30–40.

Michalski, R., ed. 1993. *Machine Learning* (Special Issue on Multistrategy Learning) 11(2–3).

Michalski R., and Tecuci, G., eds. 1994. *Machine Learning: A Multistrategy Approach, Volume 4.* San Francisco, Calif.: Morgan Kaufmann.

Minsky, M. 1985. *The Society of Mind.* New York: Simon and Schuster.

Minsky, M. 1980. K-Lines: A Theory of Memory. *Cognitive Science* 4:117–133.

Mitchell, T. M.; Keller, R. M.; and Kedar-Cabelli, S. T. 1986. Explanation-Based Generalization: A Unifying View. In *Machine Learning,* ed. R. Michalski. Norwell, Mass.: Kluwer Academics.

Nii, H. P. 1989. Introduction. In *Blackboard Architectures and Applications,* eds. V. Jagannathan, R. Dodhiawala, and L. Baum. San Diego, Calif.: Academic.

Pazzani, M. 1990. *Creating a Memory of Causal Relationships: An Integration of Empirical and Explanation-Based Learning Methods.* Hillsdale, N.J.: Lawrence Erlbaum.

Riecken, D. 1991a. Adaptive Direct Manipulation. In Proceedings of the IEEE International Conference of Systems, Man, and Cybernetics, 1115–1120. Washington, D.C.: IEEE Computer Society.

Riecken, D. 1991b. Auditory Adaptation. In Proceedings of the IEEE International Conference of Systems, Man, and Cybernetics, 1121–1126. Washington, D.C.: IEEE Computer Society.

Riecken, D. 1992a. Human-Machine Interaction and Perception. In *Multimedia Interface Design,* eds. M. Blattner and R. Dannenberg. New York: ACM Press.

Riecken, D. 1992b. WOLFGANG—A System Using Emoting Potentials to Manage Musical Design. In *Understanding Music with AI: Perspectives on Music Cognition,* eds. M. Balaban, K. Ebcioglu, and O. Laske. Menlo Park, Calif.: AAAI Press.

Schank, R. C. 1975. *Conceptual Information Processing.* Amsterdam: North-Holland.

Schank, R. C. 1973. Identification of Conceptualizations Underlying Natural Language. In *Computer Models of Thought and Language,* eds. R. C. Schank and K. M. Colby. San Francisco, Calif.: Freeman.

Schank, R. C., and Abelson R. P. 1977. *Scripts, Plans, Goals, and Understanding.* Hillsdale, N.J.: Lawrence Erlbaum.

Winston, P. H.; Ginford, T. O.; Katz, B.; and Lowry, M. 1983. Learning Physical Descriptions from Functional Definitions, Examples, and Precedents. In Proceedings of the Third National Conference on Artificial Intelligence, 433–439. Menlo Park, Calif.: American Association for Artificial Intelligence.

Agent Communication, Collaboration, & Mobility

CHAPTER 13

An Overview of
Agent-Oriented Programming

Yoav Shoham

I have been working in areas related to software agents for a number of years now, together with many students and other colleagues. Recently, terms such as "(intelligent) (software) agents," "knowbots," and "softbots" have become quite popular. The work taking place under this umbrella is diverse, varying in content, style, and quality sufficiently to render terms such as "software agent" meaningless in general. I have spent a fair amount of time in the past two years trying to understand various agent-related work in industry and academia. However, in this chapter I will not attempt to put any order into this area, nor position our own work at Stanford within it. This is the topic of another paper currently in the works. The discussion here will be confined to reviewing our own work on multi-agent systems in general and agent-oriented programming in particular.

Agent-Oriented Programming: Software with Mental State

In 1989 I coined the term *agent-oriented programming* (AOP) to describe a new programming paradigm, one based on cognitive and societal view of computation. Although new, the proposal was inspired by extensive previous research in Artificial Intelligence (AI), distributed computing, and other neighboring disciplines. This chapter will summarize some of the major ideas from previous research. A more detailed discussion of AOP appears in Shoham (1993).

What Is an Agent?

Most often, when people in AI use the term "agent," they refer to an entity that functions continuously and autonomously in an environment in which other processes take place and other agents exist. This is perhaps the only property that is assumed uniformly by those in AI who use the term. The sense of "autonomy" is not precise, but the term is taken to mean that the agents' activities do not require constant human guidance or intervention. Often certain further assumptions are made about the environment, for example that it is physical and partially unpredictable. In fact, agents are sometimes taken to be robotic agents, in which case other issues such as sensory input, motor control, and time pressure are mentioned.

Finally, agents are often taken to be "high-level." Although this sense is quite vague, many take some version of it to distinguish agents from other software or hardware components. The high level is manifested in symbolic representation and/or some cognitive-like function: agents may be "informable" (Genesereth 1989), may contain symbolic plans in addition to stimulus-response rules (Torrance 1991; Hayes-Roth et al. 1989; Mitchell 1990), and may even possess natural-language capabilities. This sense is *not* assumed uniformly in AI, and in fact a certain counter-ideology deliberately denies the centrality or even existence of high-level representation in agents (Agre and Chapman 1987; Brooks 1986).

Clearly, the notion of agenthood in AI is anything but crisp. I should therefore make it clear what *I* mean by the term "agent," which is precisely this: *An agent is an entity whose state is viewed as consisting of mental components such as beliefs, capabilities, choices, and commitments.* These components are defined in a precise fashion and stand in rough correspondence to their commonsense counterparts. In this view, therefore, agenthood is in the mind of the programmer: What makes any hardware or software component an agent is precisely the fact that one has chosen to analyze and control it in these mental terms.

The question of what an agent is is now replaced by the question of what entities can be viewed as having mental state. The answer is that *anything* can be so described, although it is not always advantageous to do so. This view is not original to me. For example, in Dennett (1987) and other publications, Dennett proposes the "intentional stance," from which systems are ascribed mental qualities such as intentions and free will. The issue, according to Dennett, is not whether a system really is intentional, but whether we can coherently view it as such. Similar sentiments are expressed by McCarthy (1979), who also distinguishes between the legitimacy of ascribing mental qualities to machines and its usefulness:

> To ascribe certain *beliefs, free will, intentions, consciousness, abilities,* or *wants* to a machine or computer program is *legitimate* when such an ascription expresses the same information about the machine that it expresses about a person. It is *useful* when the ascription helps us understand the structure of the machine, its past or future behavior, or how to repair or improve it. It is perhaps never *logically required* even for humans, but expressing reasonably briefly what is actually known about the state of the machine in a particular situation may require mental quali-

ties or qualities isomorphic to them. Theories of belief, knowledge and wanting can be constructed for machines in a simpler setting than for humans, and later applied to humans. Ascription of mental qualities is *most straightforward* for machines of known structure such as thermostats and computer operating systems, but is *most useful* when applied to entities whose structure is very incompletely known.

In Shoham (1989), I illustrate the point through the light-switch example. It is perfectly coherent to treat a light switch as a (very cooperative) agent with the capability of transmitting current at will, who invariably transmits current when it believes that we want it transmitted and not otherwise; flicking the switch is simply our way of communicating our desires. However, while this is a coherent view, it does not buy us anything, since we essentially understand the mechanism sufficiently to have a simpler, mechanistic description of its behavior. In contrast, we do not have equally good knowledge of the operation of complex systems such robots, people, and, arguably, operating systems. In these cases it is often most convenient to employ mental terminology; the application of the concept of "knowledge" to distributed computation, discussed below, is an example of this convenience.[1]

Agent- Versus Object-Oriented Programming

I mentioned previously that the ascription of mental constructs must be coherent and useful. The application of the logic of knowledge in distributed computation, given there as an example, used the mental construct "knowledge" in a particular way: it mapped it onto an existing computational framework (a distributed network of processors) and used it to reason about the system. The use we will make of mental constructs is different: rather than use them for mere analysis, we will employ them to *design* the computational system. The various mental categories will appear in the programming language itself, and the semantics of the programming language will be related to the semantics of the mental constructs. This is similar in spirit to a development within the distributed computation community, where a proposal has been made to include tests for epistemic properties in the protocols themselves (Halpern and Zuck 1987); however, up till now there has been no follow up on the proposal.

I have proposed a computational framework called *agent-oriented programming* (AOP). The name is not accidental, since from the engineering point of view AOP can be viewed as a specialization of the *object-oriented programming* (OOP) paradigm. I mean the latter in the spirit of Hewitt's original Actors formalism (Hewitt 1977), rather than in some of the senses in which it used today.

Intuitively, whereas OOP proposes viewing a computational system as made up of modules that are able to communicate with one another and that have individual ways of handling incoming messages, AOP specializes the framework by fixing the state (now called *mental state*) of the modules (now called *agents*) to consist of precisely defined components called beliefs (including beliefs about

	OOP	AOP
Basic unit	object	agent
Parameters defining state of basic unit	unconstrained	beliefs, commitments, capabilities, choices…
Process of computation	message passing and response methods	message passing and response methods
Types of message	unconstrained	inform, request, offer, promise, decline…
Constraints on methods	none	honesty, consistency…

Figure 1. OOP versus AOP.

the world, about themselves, and about one another), capabilities, choices, and possibly other similar notions. A computation consists of these agents' informing, requesting, offering, accepting, rejecting, competing, and assisting one another. This idea is borrowed directly from the speech act literature (Grice 1989; Searle 1969; Austin 1962).

Speech act theory categorizes speech, distinguishing between informing, requesting, offering and so on; each such type of communicative act involves different presuppositions and has different effects. Speech-act theory has been applied in AI, in natural language research as well as in plan recognition. To my knowledge, AOP and McCarthy's Elephant2000 language are the first attempts to base a programming language in part on speech acts. Figure 1 summarizes the relation between AOP and OOP.[2]

On the Responsible Use of Pseudo-Mental Terminology

The previous discussion referred to mentalistic notions such as belief and commitment. In order to understand the sense in which I intend these, consider the use of logics of knowledge and belief in AI and distributed computation. These logics, which were imported directly from analytic philosophy first to AI and then to other areas of computer science, describe the behavior of machines in terms of notions such as knowledge and belief. In computer science these mentalistic-sounding notions are actually given precise computational meanings and are used not only to prove properties of distributed systems, but to program them as well. A typical rule in such a knowledge-based systems is "if processor A does not *know* that processor B has received its message, then processor A will not send the next message." AOP augments these logics with formal notions of choices, capabilities, commitments, and possibly others. A typical rule in the resulting systems will be "if agent A *believes* that agent B has *chosen* to do something harmful to agent A, then A will *request* that B change its choice." In addition, temporal information is included to anchor belief, choices, and so on in particular points in time.

Here again we may benefit from some ideas in philosophy and linguistics. As in the case of knowledge, there exists work in exact philosophy on logics for choice and ability. Although they have not yet had an effect in AI comparable to that of logics of knowledge and belief, they may in the future.

Intentional terms such as knowledge and belief are used in a curious sense in the formal AI community. On the one hand, the definitions come nowhere close to capturing the full linguistic meanings. On the other hand, the intuitions about these formal notions do indeed derive from the everyday, common sense meaning of the words. What is curious is that, despite the disparity, the everyday intuition has proven a good guide to employing the formal notions in some circumscribed applications. AOP aims to strike a similar balance between computational utility and common sense.

Two Scenarios

Below are two scenarios. The first is fairly complex and serves to illustrate the type of future applications envisioned. The second is a toy example and serves three purposes: it illustrates a number of AOP ideas more crisply; it is implementable in the simple AGENT-0 language described later in the chapter; and it illustrates the fact that agents need not be robotic agents.

Manufacturing Automation. Alfred and Brenda work at a car-manufacturing plant. Alfred handles regular-order cars, and Brenda handles special-order ones. The plant has a welding robot, Calvin. The plant is controlled by a coordinating program, Dashiel. The following scenario develops, involving communication between Alfred, Brenda, Calvin and Dashiel. It contains communication acts such as informing, requesting, committing, permitting, and commanding and requires agents to reason about the beliefs, capabilities, and commitments of other agents.

8:00: Alfred requests that Calvin promise to weld ton bodies for him that day, Calvin agrees to do so.

8:30: Alfred requests that Calvin accept the first body, Calvin agrees, and the first body arrives. Calvin starts welding it and promises Alfred to notify him when it is ready for the next body.

8:45: Brenda requests that Calvin work on a special-order car which is needed urgently. Calvin responds that it cannot right then but that it will when it finishes the current job, at approximately 9:00.

9:05: Calvin completes welding Alfred's first car, ships it out, and offers to weld Brenda's car. Brenda ships it the car, and Calvin starts welding.

9:15: Alfred inquires why Calvin is not yet ready for his (Alfred's) next car. Calvin explains why and also that it (Calvin) expects to be ready by about 10:00.

9:55: Calvin completes welding Brenda's car and ships it out. Brenda requests that it reaccept it and do some painting, but Calvin refuses, explaining that it does not know how to paint. Calvin then offers to weld another car for Alfred and proceeds to weld Alfred's cars for a while.

12:15: Brenda requests that Calvin commit to welding four more special-order cars that day. Calvin replies that it cannot, since that conflicts with its commitment to Alfred, who still has six unwelded cars. Brenda requests Alfred to release Calvin from its commitment to Alfred. Alfred refuses. Brenda requests that Dashiel (remember Dashiel?) order Calvin to accept her important request and revoke its commitment to Alfred. Dashiel orders Calvin to weld two of Brenda's cars, and then as many of Alfred's as time allows.

3:30: Calvin senses it is low on lubricant, and, without interrupting its work, asks Alfred for when the next lubrication is scheduled. Alfred responds that he doesn't know, but that Dashiel should know. Calvin asks Dashiel, who informs it that the next lubrication is scheduled for 4:00. Since that is sufficiently soon, Calvin continues to weld.

Airline Reservation. This example is a minor modification of one due to John McCarthy (1990), who uses it to illustrate his Elephant2000 programming language. The example involves three agents: a passenger P, an airline clerk C, and C's supervisor S. P and S are human, and C is a program (or is it the other way around? Or perhaps all three are programs?). Note that by confirming a reservation, the airline enters into a commitment to issue a boarding pass to the passenger at the appropriate time. Again, the following exchange involves requesting (a query is a request to inform), informing, permitting, and denying, as well as mental components such as knowledge and commitment.

March

P to C: Please inform me what flights you have from San Francisco to New York on April 10.

C to P: Flight 354 departs at 08:30, flight 293 departs at 10:00, flight 441 departs at noon.

P to C: Please book me on 354.

C to P: That is sold out.

P to C: Please book me on 293.

C to P: That is confirmed; your reservation number is 112358.

P to C: Please book me also on 441.

C to P: That conflicts with 293; I am not allowed to double book a passenger.

P to C: Please get permission to do so.

C to S: I request permission for the following double booking.

S to C: Permission denied.

C to P: Sorry, I cannot get approval.

April 18, at the airport

P to C: My name is P; I have a reservation for flight 293.

C to P: Here is your boarding pass.

Overview of the AOP Framework

A complete AOP system will include three primary components:

- A restricted formal language with clear syntax and semantics for describing mental state. The mental state will be defined uniquely by several modalities, such as belief and commitment.
- An interpreted programming language in which to program agents, with primitive commands such as REQUEST and INFORM. The semantics of the programming language will depend in part on the semantics of mental state.
- An "agentifier," converting neutral devices into programmable agents.

In the remainder of this document I will start with a short discussion of mental state. I will then present a general family of agent interpreters, a simple representative of which has already been implemented as AGENT-0. Related work is described in the fifth section. I will end with a summary of recent research results related to AOP.

On the Mental State of Agents

The first step in the enterprise is to define agents; that is, to define the various components of mental state and the interactions between them. There is not a unique "correct" definition, and different applications can be expected to call for specific mental properties.[3] In this section I summarize what could be viewed as a bare-bones theory of mental state, a kernel that will in the future be modified and augmented.

Components of a Language for Mental State

In related past research by others in AI, three modalities were explored: belief, desire, and intention (giving rise to the pun on BDI agent architectures). Other similar notions, such as goals and plans, were also pressed into service. These are clearly important notions; they are also complex ones, however, and not necessarily the most primitive ones.[4]

By way of motivation, here is an informal view of the world which underlies the selection. At any point in time, the future is determined by two factors: the past history, and the current actions of agents. For example, past history alone does not (in this view) determine whether I raise my arm; that is determined by whether in fact I take the appropriate action. The actions of an agent are determined by its *decisions*, or *choices*.[5] In other words, some facts are true for natural reasons, and other facts are true because agents decided to make them so. Decisions are logically constrained, though not determined, by the agent's beliefs; these beliefs refer to the state of the world (in the past, present or future), to the mental state of other agents, and to the capabilities of this and other agents. For example, given that the robot believes that it is incapable of passing through the narrow doorway, it will not decide to go through it. Decisions are also constrained by prior decisions; the robot cannot decide to be in Room 5 in five minutes if it has already decided to be in Room 3 at that time.

In the first instantiation of AOP, a language called AGENT-0 (Torrance 1991), we too started with quite basic building blocks, in fact much more basic than those mentioned so far. We incorporated two modalities in the mental state of agents: *belief* and *obligation* (or *commitment*). We also defined *decision* (or *choice*) as an obligation to oneself. Finally, we included a third category which is not a mental construct *per se: capability*.

By restricting the components of mental state to these modalities we in some informal sense excluded representation of motivation. Indeed, we did not assume that agents are "rational" beyond assuming that their beliefs, obligations and capabilities are internally and mutually consistent. This assumption stands in contrast to the other work mentioned above, which makes further assumptions about agents acting in their own best interests, and so on. Such stronger notions of rationality are obviously important, and I am convinced that in the future we will wish to add them. In fact, in her dissertation, Thomas introduced an AOP language that includes the notions of intending and planning (Thomas 1993).

Properties of the Various Components

I have so far not placed any constraints on the various modalities defined, and therefore have not guaranteed that they in any way resemble their common sense counterparts. We will now place such constraints. Just as there is no objectively "right" collection of mental categories, there is no "right" list of properties for any particular mental category. I have already stated that the correspondence between the formal definition and common sense will always be only approximate and that I would like to strike a balance between common sense and utility. Indeed, I expect different applications of AOP to call for different properties of belief, commitment, and capability. In this section I will briefly and informally define a number of properties I assume about the modalities. Formal definitions of these properties may be found in Shoham (1993).

These properties are quite weak, but they are sufficient to justify the terminology, and necessary for the design of the interpreter. The weakness of the assumptions ensures that the interpreters apply to a wide variety of applications. Still, even these assumptions will be inappropriate for some purposes, in which case a new type of interpreter will be required.

Internal consistency. I assume that both the beliefs and the obligations are internally consistent.

Good faith. I further assume that agents commit only to what they believe themselves capable of, and only if they really mean it.

Introspection. Although in general I do not assume that agents have total introspective capabilities, I *do* assume that they are aware of their obligations. On the other hand, I do not assume that agents are necessarily aware of commitments made to them.

Persistence of mental state. I have only placed restrictions on mental attitudes at a single instant of time. I conclude this section by discussing how mental states change or persist over time. Unlike with the previously discussed properties, precise constraints cannot currently be specified, but only informal guidelines.

Consider, for example, belief. The previously discussed restrictions allow agents which at one time believe nothing at all, shortly afterwards to have a belief about *every* sentence, and then again to become quite agnostic. Common sense suggests that beliefs tend to be more stable than that, and it would indeed be difficult to rely on the behavior of agents with such volatile beliefs. I will now place a strong condition on belief: I will assume that agents have perfect memory of and faith in their beliefs, and only let go of a belief if they learn a contradictory fact. Beliefs therefore persist *by default*. Furthermore, I will assume that the *absence* of belief also persists by default, although in a slightly different sense: if an agent does not believe a fact at a certain time (as opposed to believing the negation of the fact), then the only reason he will come to believe it is if he learns it.

How to formally capture these two kinds of default persistence is another story, which touches on issues that are painfully familiar to researchers in nonmonotonic temporal reasoning and belief revision. In fact, a close look at the logical details of belief (or knowledge) persistence reveals several very subtle phenomena, which have so far not been addressed in the literature.

In addition, obligations should persist—otherwise they wouldn't be obligations. As in the case of belief, however, the persistence is not absolute. Although by default obligations persist, there are conditions under which obligations are revoked.

These conditions presumably include explicit release of the agent by the party to which it is obligated, or alternatively a realization on the part of the agent that it is no longer able to fulfill the obligation. (In their discussion of the persistence of commitment, Cohen and Levesque [1990] actually propose a more elaborate second condition, one that requires common knowledge by the committer and committee of the impossibility; however, further discussion of their position and arguments against it would be too long a detour.)

Since decision is defined in terms of obligation, it inherits the default persistence. Notice, however, an interesting point about the persistence of decision: while an agent cannot unilaterally revoke obligations it has towards others, it can cancel obligations held towards it—including obligations it holds towards itself, namely decisions. An agent is therefore free to modify an existing decision, but unless he explicitly does so the decision will stand.

Finally, capabilities too tend not to fluctuate wildly. In fact, in this document I assume that capabilities are fixed: What an agent can do at one time it can do at any other time. However, I will allow to condition a capability of an action on certain conditions that hold at the time of action.

The Contextual Nature of Modal Statements

I have throughout the discussion talked of "unequivocal" statements regarding beliefs, obligations, and capabilities. Common sense, however, suggests that each of these modalities is context sensitive: I can print the document right now, but only in the context of the network being up; I am obligated to you to finish the work by tomorrow, but if my child has just been rushed to hospital then all bets are off (even though I am still capable of finishing the work). Indeed, McCarthy has argued that all statements, not only modal ones, should be viewed in context. Although I agree in principle and discuss it further in Shoham (1991), in this article I will ignore the issue of context sensitivity.

A Generic Agent Interpreter

In the previous section I discussed the first component of the AOP framework, namely the definition of agents. I now turn to the programming of agents and will outline a generic agent interpreter.

The behavior of agents is governed by programs; each agent is controlled by its own private program. Agent programs themselves are not logical entities, but their control and data structures refer to the mental state of the agent using the logical language.[6]

The Basic Loop

The behavior of agents is, in principle, quite simple. Each agent iterates the following two steps at regular intervals:

1. Read the current messages and update your mental state (including your beliefs and commitments);

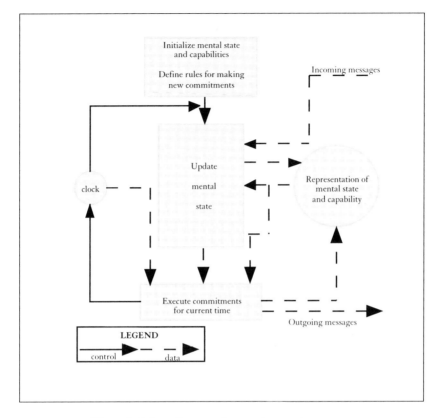

Figure 2. A flow diagram of a generic agent interpreter.

2. Execute the commitments for the current time, possibly resulting in further belief change. Actions to which agents are committed include communicative ones such as informing and requesting.

The process is illustrated in figure 2; the dashed arrows represent flow of data, while the solid arrows show temporal sequencing.

Assumptions about Message Passing

Agent programs will include, among other things, communication commands. In order that those be executable, I will assume that the platform is capable of passing messages to other agents addressable by name, whether those reside in the same machine or in others. The programming language will define the form of these messages, and the interpreter will determine when messages are sent.

Assumption about the Clock

Central to the operation of the interpreter is the existence of a clock; agents are inherently "real time" (to use another overloaded term). The main role of the clock is to initiate iterations of the two-step loop at regular intervals (e.g., every 10 milliseconds, every hour). The length of these intervals is determined by the settable variable "time grain."

I do not discuss the implementation of such a clock, which will vary among platforms, and simply assume that it exists. I also assume a variable "now," whose value is set by the clock to the current time in the format defined in the programming language (e.g., an integer, date:hour:minute).

In previous work, I have made the very strong assumption that a single iteration through the loop lasts less than the time grain; in future versions of the language I will relax this assumption and correspondingly will complicate the details of the loop itself.

Of course, the fact that agents use the same temporal language does not ensure that their clocks are synchronized. If all are agents are running on the same machine; there will be no problem, but otherwise the possibility of clock drift exists. Although synchronization does not impact the design and programming of single agents, it is crucial for ensuring that a society of agents is able to function usefully. Fortunately, there exist synchronization protocols which ensure limited drift among clocks (for an overview, see Schneider [1987]), and we expect to use these in our applications.

AGENT-0: A Simple Language and its Interpreter

Agent interpreters may vary along many dimensions and in general pose many challenging problems. We have implemented a particular programming language called AGENT-0, whose interpreter is an extremely simple instance of the generic agent interpreter. In fact, the simplifications embodied in AGENT-0 are so extreme that it may be tempting to dismiss it as uninteresting. However, it was recognized early on that one would not gain good insight into the strengths and weaknesses of AOP without writing actual programs. It was decided therefore to implement a simple interpreter first, and design more complex languages and interpreters based on this experience. It turned out the design of AGENT-0 itself posed some challenges, and we have been surprised by the diversity of applications that even this simple language admits. Furthermore, AGENT-0 is designed in a way that suggests obvious extensions; a few are being currently pursued and are described in the final section.

The implemented interpreter is documented in Torrance (1991). A second, more complex interpreter was designed and implemented in collaboration with the Hewlett Packard Corporation.

Related Work

So far, I have not discussed related work in any depth. The body of related work is in fact so rich that in this section I will mention only the most closely related work, and briefly at that. I will omit further discussion of past work on logics of knowledge and belief, which the logic of mental state extends, since I already did that in the introduction. For the same reason, I will not discuss object-oriented programming and Hewitt's work. The following is ordered in what I see as decreasing relevance to, and overlap with, AOP. The order (or, for that matter, inclusion in the list) reflects no other ranking, nor is it implied that researchers high up on the list would necessarily endorse any part of AOP.

McCarthy's (1990) work on Elephant2000

This language under development is also based on speech acts, and the airline-reservation scenario I have discussed is due to McCarthy. One issue explored in connection with Elephant2000 is the distinction between illocutionary and perlocutionary specifications, which I have not addressed. In contrast to AOP, Elephant2000 currently contains no explicit representation of state, mental or otherwise. Conditional statements therefore refer to the history of past communication rather than to the current mental state.

Distributed AI

There is related work within Distributed AI community (cf. MCC [1990]). Although AOP is, to my knowledge, unique in its definition of mental state and the resulting programming language, others too have made the connection between object-oriented programming and agenthood (Ferber and Carle 1990; Hewitt 1990).

The Intelligent Communicating Agents Project (1987-1988)

This ambitious project, carried out jointly at Stanford, SRI and Rockwell International (Nilsson, Rosenschein, Cohen, Moore, Appelt, Buckley, and many others) had among its goals the representation of speech acts and connection between the intensional level and the machine level. See discussion of some of the individual work below.

Cohen and Levesque's Work on Belief, Commitment, Intention, and Coordination

These two researchers (Cohen and Levesque 1997, 1990) have also investigated the logical relationships between several modalities such as belief and choice. Although they have not approached the topic from a programming-language perspective as I have, they too have been interested in speech acts and mental state as building blocks for coordination and analysis of behavior. Their work has its roots in earlier work in natural language understanding by Allen, Cohen, and Perrault (Allen 1983; Cohen and Perrault 1979). Despite some similarities, crucial differences exist between the mental categories employed by Cohen and Levesque and ours.

Contract Nets

AOP shares with early work on contract nets (Smith 1980) the computational role of contracts among agents. However, the similarity ends there. Contract nets are based on broadcasting contracts and soliciting bids, as opposed to the intimate communication in AOP. Contract nets had no other notion of mental state, no range of communicative speech acts, nor any aspect of the asynchronous, real-time design inherent in AOP.

Situated Automata

Rosenschein and Kaelbling's situated automata (Kaelbling 1988; Rosenschein and Kaelbling 1986; Rosenschein 1985) is relevant in connection with the process of agentification. We adopt their idea of decoupling the machine language from the programmer's intensional conceptualization of the machine, but differ on the specific details.

Coordination

Several researchers have been concerned with the process of coordination in modern environments. For example, as a part of their more global project, Winograd and Flores have developed a model of communication in a work environment (Winograd and Flores 1986). They point to the fact that every conversation is governed by some rules, which constrain the actions of the participants: a request must be followed by an accept or a decline, a question by an answer, and so on. Their model of communication is that of a finite automaton, with the automaton states corresponding to different states of the conversation. This is a *macro* theory, a theory of societies of agents, in contrast to the *micro* theory of AOP. In related work, Malone and his associates are aiming towards a general theory of coordination, drawing on diverse fields such as computer science and economics (Malone 1991).

Informable Agents

Genesereth's work on informable agents (see Genesereth chapter, also in this volume). Genesereth's interest lies primarily in agents containing declarative knowledge that can be informed of new facts and that can act on partial plans. In this connection, he has investigated also the compilation of declarative plans and information into action commands. Genesereth uses the term "agents" so as to include also low-level finite-automaton-like constructs. AOP's structure of mental state is consistent with Genesereth's declarative regime but is not required by it.

Plan Representation and Recognition

Work on plan representation and recognition by Kautz, Pollack, Konolige, Litman, Allen, and others (e.g., Kautz 1990, Litman and Allen 1990, Pollack 1990, and Bratman 1987) also addresses the interaction between mental state and action, but it is usually concerned with finer-grained analyses, involving the actual representation of plans, reasoning limitations, and more complex mental notions such as goals, desires, and intentions.

Nilsson's Action Nets

ACTNET is a language for computing goal-achieving actions that depends dynamically on sensory and stored data. The ACTNET language is based on the concept of action networks. An action network is a forest of logical gates that select actions in response to sensory and stored data. The connection to AOP, albeit a weak one, is that some of the wires in the network originate from database items marked as "beliefs" and "goals." The maintenance of these databases is not the job of the action net.

Summary of Results and Ongoing Research

Work on mental state is proceeding on different fronts. Here are some pointers to ongoing research:
- In Moses and Shoham (1993) we provide some results on the connection between knowledge and (one kind of) belief.
- Thomas (1993) tackles the notions of capability, plan, and intentions.
- In Lamarre and Shoham (1994) we argue for the three-way distinction between knowledge, certainty, and belief.
- Brafman and Tennenholtz (1992) lay out a framework in which beliefs, preferences, and strategy are maintained in a form of "rational balance."
- Del Val and Shoham (1994) argue that the properties of belief update should be derived methodically from a theory of action and that doing so reveals some limitations of the KM postulates.
- Del Val and Shoham (1994) propose to reduce the notion of belief revision to that of belief update, and thus also to theories of action.
- In Shoham and Cousins (1994) we provide an initial survey of logics of mental state in AI.

In parallel with the logical aspects of action and mental state, we have investigated algorithmic questions:

- We have proposed a specific mechanism for tracking how beliefs change over time, called *temporal belief maps* (Isozaki and Shoham 1992).
- In Brafman, Latombe, and Shoham (1993) and Brafman et al. (1993) we show that, similar to distributed systems, the formal notion of knowledge can be applied to algorithmic robot motion planning. Recently, we proposed knowledge complexity as a useful general complexity measure in robotics, with an application to automating the distribution of robotic algorithms.

We have recently begun contemplating the role of agents in the context of digital libraries, whether or not they are of the AOP variety. We have so far conducted one experiment:

- There is an experiment to deploy adaptive agents that perform automated browsing of the World Wide Web on behalf of the user.

Finally, we are interested in how multiple agents can function usefully in the presence of other agents. In particular, we are interested in mechanisms that minimize conflicts among agents and have been investigating the utility of social laws in computational settings:

- In Shoham and Tennenholtz (1992) we propose a general framework for representing social laws within a theory of action and investigate the computational complexity of automatically synthesizing useful social laws. We also study a special case of traffic laws in a restricted robot environment.
- In Shoham and Tennenholtz (1995) we study ways in which such conventions emerge automatically in a dynamic environment. Early results were reported on in Shoham and Tennenholtz (1992).
- In Kittock (1994), he refines these results to take into account the topology of the agent network and the existence of asymmetric interactions among agents.

Notes

1. Elsewhere, I discuss how the gradual elimination of animistic explanations with the increase in knowledge is correlated very nicely with both developmental and evolutionary phenomena. In the evolution of science, theological notions were replaced over the centuries with mathematical ones. Similarly, in Piaget's stages of child development, there is a clear transition from animistic stages around the ages of 4-6 (when, for example, children claim that clouds move because they follow us around) to the more mature later stages.

2. There is one more dimension to the comparison, which I omitted from the table, and it regards inheritance. Inheritance among objects is today one of the main features of OOP, constituting an attractive abstraction mechanism. I have not discussed it since it is not essential to the idea of OOP, and even less so to the idea of AOP. Nevertheless a parallel can be drawn here, too. In OOP, specialized objects inherit the methods of more general ones. One analogous construct in AOP would be group agents, that is, agents

that are made up of a group of simpler agents. If we define the beliefs of this composite agent as the "common beliefs" of the individual agents and the commitments of the composite agents as their "common commitments," then the mental attitudes of the group are indeed inherited by the individual.

3. In this respect our motivation here deviates from that of philosophers. However, I believe there exist sufficient similarities to make the connection between AI and philosophy mutually beneficial.

4. Cohen and Levesque (1990), for example, propose to reduce the notion of intention to those of goal and persistence. Their pioneering work introduces mental categories that are different from ours. The two frameworks share the essential view of belief and time. They each introduce modalities absent from the other: obligation and capability in our framework, goals and intentions in theirs. However, even two notions that at first appear to be similar—such as our "decision" and their "choice"—turn out to be quite different.

5. The term choice is somewhat ambiguous; I discuss various senses of choice later.

6. However, an early design of agent programs by Akahani was entirely in the style of logic programming; in that framework program statements themselves were indeed logical sentences.

References

Agre, P., and Chapman, D. 1987. PENGI: An Implementation of a Theory of Activity. In Proceedings of the Sixth National Conference on Artificial Intelligence, 268–272. Menlo Park, Calif.: American Association for Artificial Intelligence.

Allen, J. F. 1983. Recognizing Intentions from Natural Language Utterances. In Computational Models of Discourse, eds. M. Brady and R. C. Berwick, 107–166. Cambridge, Mass.: MIT Press.

Austin, J. L. 1962. How to Do Things with Words. Cambridge, Mass.: Harvard University Press.

Brafman, R., and Tennenholtz, M. 1994. Belief Ascription and Mental-Level Modeling. In Proceedings of the Fourth International Conference on Principles of Knowledge Representation and Reasoning (KR'94). San Francisco, Calif.: Morgan Kaufmann.

Brafman, R. I.; Latombe, J.-C.; and Shoham, Y. 1993. Toward Knowledge-Level Analysis of Motion Planning. In Proceedings of the Eleventh National Conference on Artificial Intelligence, 670–675. Menlo Park, Calif.: American Association for Artificial Intelligence.

Brafman, R. I.; Latombe, J.-C.; Moses, Y.; and Shoham, Y. 1993. Knowledge as a Tool in Motion Planning under Uncertainty. In Theoretical Aspects of Reasoning about Knowledge: Proceedings of the Fifth Conference (TARK 1994). San Francisco, Calif.: Morgan Kaufmann.

Bratman, M. E. 1987. Intention, Plans, and Practical Reason. Cambridge, Mass.: Harvard University Press.

Brooks, R. A. 1986. A Robust Layered Control System for a Mobile Robot. IEEE Journal of Robot Automation 2(1): 14–23.

Cohen, P. R., and Levesque, H. J. 1990. Intention Is Choice with Commitment. Artificial Intelligence 42(3): 213–261.

Cohen, P. R., and Levesque, H. J. 1997. Rational Interactions as the Basis for Communication. In *Intentions in Communication*, eds. P. R. Cohen, J. Morgan, and M. E. Pollack. Cambridge, Mass.: MIT Press. Forthcoming.

Cohen, P. R., and Perrault, C. R. 1979. Elements of a Plan-Based Theory of Speech Acts. *Cognitive Science* 3:177–212.

Del Val, A., and Shoham, Y. 1994. Deriving Properties of Belief Update from Theories of Action. *Journal of Logic, Language, and Information* 3(2): 81–119.

Del Val, A., and Shoham, Y. 1996. A Unified View of Belief Revision and Update. *Journal of Logic and Computation* 4(5): 797–810.

Dennett, D. C. 1987. *The Intentional Stance.* Cambridge, Mass.: MIT Press.

Drummond, M. 1989. Situated Control Rules. In *Proceedings of the First International Conference on Knowledge Representation and Reasoning,* eds. R. J. Brachman and H. J. Levesque, 103–113. San Francisco, Calif.: Morgan Kaufmann.

Ferber, J., and Carle, P. 1990. Actors and Agents as Reflective Concurrent Objects: A Mering IV Perspective. In Proceedings of the Tenth International Workshop on Distributed Artificial Intelligence, Technical Report ACT-AI-355-90, MCC, Austin, Texas.

Genesereth, M. R. 1989. A Proposal for Research on Informable Agents, Technical Report, Logic-89-4, Computer Science Department, Stanford University.

Grice, P. 1989. *Studies in the Ways of Words.* Cambridge, Mass.: Harvard University Press.

Halpern, J. Y., and Zuck, L. D. 1987. A Little Knowledge Goes a Long Way: Simple Knowledge-Based Derivations and Correctness Proofs for a Family of Protocols. In Proceedings of the Sixth ACM Symposium on Principles of Distributed Computing, 269–280. New York: Association of Computing Machinery.

Hayes-Roth, B.; Washington, R.; Hewett, R.; Hewett, M.; and Seiver, A. 1989. Intelligent Monitoring and Control. In Proceedings of the Eleventh International Joint Conference on Artificial Intelligence, 243–249. Menlo Park, Calif.: International Joint Conferences on Artificial Intelligence.

Hewitt, C. 1990. Toward Open Information Systems Semantics. In Proceedings of the Tenth International Workshop on Distributed Artificial Intelligence, Technical Report ACT-AI-355-90, MCC, Austin, Texas.

Hewitt, C. 1977. Viewing Control Structures as Patterns of Passing Messages. *Artificial Intelligence* 8:323–364.

Isozaki, H., and Shoham, Y. 1992. A Mechanism for Reasoning about Time and Belief. In Proceedings of the Conference on Fifth-Generation Computer Systems, 694–701. Amsterdam. IOS Press.

Kaelbling, L. P. 1988. Goals as Parallel Program Specifications. In Proceedings of the Seventh National Conference on Artificial Intelligence, 60–65. Menlo Park, Calif.: American Association for Artificial Intelligence.

Kautz, H. A. 1990. A Circumscriptive Theory of Plan Recognition. In *Intentions in Communication,* eds. P. R. Cohen, J. Morgan, and M. E. Pollack, 60–65. Cambridge, Mass.: MIT Press.

Kittock, J. E. 1994. The Impact of Locality and Authority on the Emergence of Conventions. In Proceedings of the Twelfth National Conference on Artificial Intelligence, 420–425. Menlo Park, Calif.: American Association for Artificial Intelligence.

Lamarre, P., and Shoham, Y. 1994. Knowledge, Certainty, Belief, and Conditionalization. In *Proceedings of the Fourth International Conference on Principles of Knowledge Representation and Reasoning (KR'94),* eds. J. Doyle, E. Sandewall, and P. Torasso, 415–424. San Francisco, Calif.: Morgan Kaufmann.

Litman, D. J., and Allen, J. F. 1990. Discourse Processing and Commonsense Plans. In *Intentions in Communication*, eds. P. R. Cohen, J. Morgan, and M. E. Pollack. Cambridge, Mass.: MIT Press.

McCarthy, J. 1979. Ascribing Mental Qualities to Machines, Technical Report Memo, 326, AI Lab, Stanford University.

Malone, T. W. 1991. Toward an Interdisciplinary Theory of Coordination, Technical Report, CCS 120, Sloan School of Management, Massachusetts Institute of Technology.

MCC. 1990. Proceedings of the Tenth International Workshop on Distributed Artificial Intelligence, Technical Report ACT-AI-355-90, MCC, Austin, Texas.

Mitchell, T. M. 1990. Becoming Increasingly Reactive. In Proceedings of the Eighth National Conference on Artificial Intelligence, 1050–1058. Menlo Park, Calif.: American Association for Artificial Intelligence.

Moses, Y., and Shoham, Y. 1993. Belief as Defeasible Knowledge. *Journal of Artificial Intelligence* 64(2): 299–321.

Pollack, M. E. 1997. Plan as Complex Mental Attitudes. In Intentions in Communication, eds. P. R. Cohen, J. Morgan, and M. E. Pollack. Cambridge, Mass.: MIT Press. Forthcoming.

Rosenschein, S. J. 1985. Formal Theories of Knowledge in AI and Robotics, Technical Report 362, SRI International, Menlo Park, California.

Rosenschein, S. J., and Kaelbling, L. P. 1986. The Synthesis of Digital Machines with Provable Epistemic Properties. Paper presented at Conference on Theoretical Aspects of Reasoning about Knowledge, 19–22 March, Monterey, California.

Schneider, F. 1987. Understanding Protocols for Byzantine Clock Synchronization, Technical Report, Computer Science Department, Cornell University.

Searle, J. R. 1969. *Speech Acts: An Essay in the Philosophy of Language.* Cambridge, U.K.: Cambridge University Press.

Shoham, Y. 1993. Agent-Oriented Programming. *Journal of Artificial Intelligence* 60(1): 51–92.

Shoham, Y. 1991. Varieties of Context. In *Artificial Intelligence and Mathematical Theory of Computation*, 393–408. San Diego, Calif.: Academic.

Shoham, Y. 1989. Time for Action. In Proceedings of the Eleventh International Joint Conference on Artificial Intelligence, 954–959. Menlo Park, Calif.: International Joint Conferences on Artificial Intelligence.

Shoham, Y., and Cousins, S. 1994. Logics of Mental Attitudes in AI: A Very Preliminary Survey. In *Advances in Knowledge Representation and Reasoning,* eds. G. Lakemeyer and B. Mebel, 296–309. New York: Springer Verlag.

Shoham, Y., and Tennenholtz, M. 1992. Emergent Conventions in Multi-Agent Systems: Initial Experimental Results and Observations. In *Proceedings of the Conference on Principles of Knowledge Representation and Reasoning,* 225–231. San Francisco, Calif.: Morgan Kaufmann.

Shoham, Y., and Tennenholtz, M. 1995. Computational Social Systems: Offline Design. *Journal of Artificial Intelligence* 73(1–2): 231–252.

Smith, R. G. 1980. The Contract Net Protocol: High-Level Communication and Control in a Distributed Problem Solver. *IEEE Transactions of Computer Science* 29(12): 1104–1113.

Thomas, B. 1993. PLACA, An Agent-Oriented Language. Ph.D. diss., Department of Computer Science, Stanford University.

Torrance, M. 1991. The AGENT0 Programming Manual, Technical Report, Department of Computer Science, Stanford University.

Winograd, T., and Flores, F. 1986. *Understanding Computers and Cognition.* Norwood, N.J.: Ablex.

Chapter 14

KQML as an Agent
Communication Language[1]

Tim Finin, Yannis Labrou, & James Mayfield

t is doubtful that any conversation about agents will result in a consensus on the definition of an agent or of agency. From personal assistants and "smart" interfaces to powerful applications, and from autonomous, intelligent entities to information retrieval systems, anything might qualify as an agent these days. But, despite these different viewpoints, most would agree that the capacity for interaction and interoperation is desirable. The building block for intelligent interaction is knowledge sharing that includes both mutual understanding of knowledge and the communication of that knowledge. The importance of such communication is emphasized by Genesereth, who goes so far as to suggest that an entity is a software agent if and only if it communicates correctly in an agent communication language (Genesereth and Ketchpel 1994). After all, it is hard to picture cyberspace with entities that exist only in isolation; it would go against our perception of a decentralized, interconnected electronic universe.

How might meaningful, constructive, and intelligent interaction among software agents be provided? The same problem for humans requires more than the knowledge of a common language such as English; it also requires a common understanding of the terms used in a given context. A physicist's understanding of velocity is not the same as that of a car enthusiast's,[2] and if the two want to converse about "fast" cars, they have to speak a "common language." Also, humans must resort to a shared etiquette of communication that is a result of societal development and that is partially encoded in the language. Although we are not always conscious of doing so, we follow certain patterns when we ask questions or make requests. Such patterns have common elements across human languages. Likewise, for software agents to interact and interoperate effectively requires three fundamental and distinct components: (i) a common language, (ii) a common understanding of the knowledge exchanged, and (iii) the ability to exchange whatever is included in (i) and (ii). We take effective interaction to be the exchange (communication) of information and knowledge that can be mutually understood. The more applications that can communicate with one another, and the wider the range of knowledge they can exchange, the better.

This perspective on interoperability in today's computing environment has been the foundation of the approach of the Knowledge Sharing Effort (KSE) consortium. We present the approach of the KSE and the solutions suggested for the subproblems identified by the consortium, emphasizing the KSE's communication language and protocol KQML (Knowledge Query and Manipulation Language). In addition to presenting specific solutions, we are interested in demonstrating the conceptual decomposition of the problem of knowledge sharing into smaller more manageable problems and in arguing that there is merit to those concepts independent of the success of individual solutions.

In the remainder of this chapter, we provide a brief coverage of the objectives and approach of the Knowledge Sharing Effort and a summary of the major results of the KSE. In the Communication Languages and their Desired Features section we attempt to define the notion of a communication language and its desired features. In the Knowledge Query and Manipulation Language (KQML) section we present the agent communication language KQML along with our notion of an environment of KQML-speaking agents. In the Evaluation of KQML as an Agent Communication Language section we evaluate KQML as a communication language. The Applications of KQML section provides an overview of applications and environments that have used KQML, and the final section surveys some other agent communication languages and approaches.

The Approach of the Knowledge-Sharing Effort (KSE)

Let us address the issue of software agents and interoperability in more detail. We will refer to software agents as applications for which the ability to communicate with other applications and share knowledge is of primary importance. Figure 1 summarizes the possible components of such an agent; they are grouped into representation components, communication components, and components that are not directly related to shared understanding.

Mutual understanding of what is represented may be divided into two subproblems: (i) translating from one representation language to another (or from one family of representation languages to another); and (ii) sharing the semantic content (and often the pragmatic content) of the represented knowledge among different applications. Translation alone is not sufficient because each knowledge base holds implicit assumptions about the meaning of what is represented. If two applications are to understand each other's knowledge, such assumptions must also be shared. That is, the semantic content of the various tokens must be preserved.

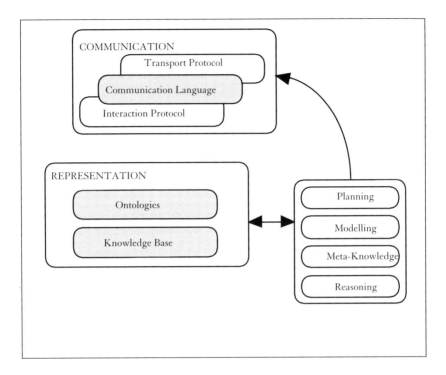

Figure 1. Our abstract model for interoperating software agents identifies three classes of components: representation components, communication components, and components not directly related to shared understanding.

Communication is a threefold problem involving knowledge of (i) interaction protocol; (ii) communication language; and (iii) transport protocol. The interaction protocol refers to the high-level strategy pursued by the software agent that governs its interaction with other agents. Such a protocol can range from negotiation or liaison and game theory protocols to protocols as simple as "every time you do not know something, find someone who knows and ask." The communication language is the medium through which the attitudes regarding the content of the exchange are communicated. It is the communication language that suggests whether the content of the communication is an assertion, a request or some form of query. The transport protocol is the actual transport mechanism used for the communication, such as TCP, SMTP, and HTTP. Practical considerations may favor the use of one of those over others.[3]

Software agents may (or may not) have other components to help the agent carry out its business. The ability to reason about its own actions, to represent meta-knowledge, to plan activities, or to model other agents can enhance the capabilities of an application. Such components are peripheral to the virtual knowledge base, although they are usually built on top of it. Although they may use the virtual knowledge base or the communication language to implement their agendas, the issues associated with them should be viewed as orthogonal to the issues of mutual understanding and communication.

The Knowledge-Sharing Effort (KSE), sponsored by the Advanced Research Projects Agency (ARPA), the Air Force Office of Scientific Research (ASOFR), the Corporation for National Research Initiative (NRI), and the National Science Foundation (NSF), is an initiative to develop technical infrastructure to support knowledge sharing among systems (Neches et al. 1991). The KSE is organized around the following three working groups, each of which addresses a complementary problem identified in current knowledge representation technology: *Interlingua*, *Shared Reusable Knowledge Bases*, and *External Interfaces*.

The *Interlingua Group* is developing a common language for expressing the content of a knowledge-base. This group has published a specification document describing the *Knowledge Interchange Format*, or KIF (Genesereth and Fikes 1992).

KIF can be used to support translation from one content language to another, or as a common content language between two agents which use different native representation languages. Information about KIF and associated tools is available over the Internet.[4] A group within the KSE with a similar scope is the *KRSS Group* (Knowledge Representation System Specification). This group focuses on the definition of common constructs within families of representation languages. The group has produced a common specification for terminological representations in the KL-ONE family.[5]

The *SRKB Group* (Shared Reusable Knowledge Bases) is concerned with facilitating consensus on the content of sharable knowledge bases, with sub-interests in shared knowledge for particular topic areas and in topic-independent development tools and methodologies. It has established a repository for sharable ontologies and tools, which is available over the Internet.[6]

The scope of the *External Interfaces Group* is run time interaction between knowledge-based systems and other modules in a run-time environment. Special attention has been given to two important cases: communication between two knowledge-based systems and communication between a knowledge-based system and a conventional database management system (Pastor, McKay, and Finin 1992). The KQML language is one of the main results to come out of the external interfaces group of the KSE.[7]

These three groups of the KSE roughly address the interoperability issues at the levels identified by the three shaded boxes of figure 1; the results of the research efforts, namely KIF, Ontolingua and KQML, are the specific solutions suggested for them.

The Solutions of the Knowledge-Sharing Effo

KIF is the solution suggested by the KSE for the syntactic aspects of representations for knowledge sharing. The language is intended as a powerful vehicle to express knowledge and meta-knowledge. There were two different motivations behind the development of a language like KIF: (i) creation of a *lingua franca* for the development of intelligent applications, with an emphasis on interoperation (in cooperation with the other components of the "package solution" of the KSE); and (ii) creation of a common interchange format so that with the use of "translators" one could translate from language A to KIF and from KIF to language B instead of translating from A to B.[8] KIF has found its way into applications,[9] but it remains to be proven whether it will fulfill any of its intended roles.

Next we provide a brief coverage of KIF, the ideas behind ontologies and *Ontolingua* (the framework for the development of ontologies) and KQML. This is not intended as a detailed analysis, but rather as an introduction to the main ideas of these research efforts. The remainder of this presentation is primarily concerned with KQML and its function as a communication language for software agents.

Knowledge Interchange Format (KIF)

KIF[10] is a prefix version of first order predicate calculus with extensions to support nonmonotonic reasoning and definitions. The language description includes both a specification for its syntax and one for its semantics. First and foremost, KIF provides for the expression of simple data. For example, the sentences shown below encode three-tuples in a personnel database in which the fields represent employee ID number, department assignment, and salary, respectively:

(salary 015-46-3946 widgets 72000)
(salary 026-40-9152 grommets 36000)
(salary 415-32-4707 fidgets 42000)

More complicated information can be expressed through the use of complex terms. For example, the following sentence states that one chip is larger than another:

(> (* (width chip1) (length chip1)) (* (width chip2) (length chip2)))

KIF includes a variety of logical operators to assist in the encoding of logical information (such as negation, disjunction, rules, quantified formulas, and so forth). The expression shown below is an example of a complex sentence in KIF. It asserts that the number obtained by raising any real-number '?x'[11] to an even power '?n' is positive:

(=> (and (real-number ?x) (even-number ?n)) (> (expt ?x ?n) 0))

KIF provides for the encoding of knowledge about knowledge, using the backquote ("`") and comma (',') operators and related vocabulary. For example, the following sentence asserts that agent Joe is interested in receiving triples in the salary relation.[12]

(interested joe `(salary ,?x ,?y ,?z))

KIF can also be used to describe procedures—in other words to write programs or scripts for agents to follow. Given the prefix syntax of KIF, such programs resemble Lisp or Scheme. The following is an example of a three-step procedure written in KIF. The first step ensures that there is a fresh line on the standard output stream; the second step prints 'Hello!' to the standard output stream; the final step adds a carriage return to the output.

(progn (fresh-line t) (print "Hello!") (fresh-line t))

The semantics of the KIF core (KIF without rules and definitions) is similar to that of first order logic. There is an extension to handle nonstandard operators (like 'and'), and there is a restriction that models satisfy various axiom schemata (to give meaning to the basic vocabulary in the format). Despite these extensions and restrictions, the core language retains the fundamental characteristics of first order logic, including compactness and the semi-decidability of logical entailment.

Ontologies and Ontolingua

The SRKB Working Group is also working on the problem of sharing the content of formally represented knowledge. Sharing content requires more than a formalism (such as KIF) and a communication language (KQML). Although the problem of understanding what must be held in common among communicating agents is a fundamental question of philosophy and science, the SRKB is focusing on the practical problem of building knowledge-based software that can be reused as off-the-shelf technology. The approach is to focus on common ontologies (Neches et al. 1991). Every knowledge-based system relies on some conceptualization of the world (objects, qualities, distinctions, and relationships that matter for performing some task) that is embodied in concepts, distinctions, and so forth in a formal representation scheme. A common ontology refers to an explicit specification of the ontological commitments of a set of programs. Such a specification should be an objective (i.e., interpretable outside of the program) description of the concepts and relationships that the programs use to interact with other programs, knowledge bases, and human users. An agent commits to an ontology if its observable actions are consistent with the definitions in the ontology.

The SRKB Group has worked on the construction of ontologies for various domains. Ontologies are written in KIF, using the definitional vocabulary of Ontolingua.[13] Each ontology defines a set of classes, functions, and object constants for some domain of discourse, and includes an axiomatization to constrain the interpretation. The resulting language (the basic logic of KIF *plus* the vocabulary and theory from the ontologies) allows for the sentences to be inter-preted unambiguously and independent of context, making the relevant detail explicit. These ontologies can then be used by communicating applications. There has been a considerable number of ontologies developed by the group, on a variety of domains that might be of interest to software applications.

Knowledge Query Manipulation Language (KQML)

KQML was conceived as both a message format and a message-handling proto-col to support run-time knowledge sharing among agents. The key features of KQML may be summarized as follows:

- KQML messages are opaque to the content they carry. KQML messages do not merely communicate sentences in some language, but they rather communicate an attitude about the content (assertion, request, query).
- The language's primitives are called performatives. As the term suggests, the concept is related to speech act theory. Performatives define the per-missible actions (operations) that agents may attempt in communicating with each other.
- An environment of KQML speaking agents may be enriched with special agents, called facilitators, that provide such functions as the following: as-sociation of physical addresses with symbolic names; registration of databases and/or services offered and sought by agents; and communica-tion services (e.g., forwarding, brokering). To use a metaphor, facilitators act as efficient secretaries for the agents in their domain.

Intelligent interaction is more than an exchange of messages. As suggested in the first section of this chapter, KQML is an attempt to dissociate these issues from the communication language, which should define a set of standard mes-sage types that are to be interpreted identically by all interacting parties. A *uni-versal* communication language is of interest to a wide range of applications that need to communicate something more than predefined or fixed statements of facts. KQML is the centerpiece of this presentation and is described in more de-tail in the Knowledge Query and Manipulation Language (KQML) section.

Communication Languages and their Desired Features

It is fair to ask whether one can talk about an agent communication language without referring to the properties of agency. Instead of providing a compre-hensive definition of agency, we suggest that agents are commonly taken to be "high-level" (i.e., they use symbolic representation, display cognitive-like func-tion, and/or have a belief and/or a knowledge store) and are commonly viewed as having an intentional level description (i.e., their state is viewed as consisting of mental components such as beliefs, capabilities, choices, commitments etc.).

We take this "description" to be a helpful *abstract* model for *viewing* software agents, even if their actual implementation does not make claims to such ambitious concepts. Agents then reside at the *knowledge level* (Newell 1993, 1982) and are not well served by general languages and protocols developed for distributed computing. Such languages and protocols focus on *processes* rather than on the programs or collection of programs that constitute the agents. As a result, a communication language should be powerful enough to support communication between programs that are viewed as being at this higher level (with an intentional description); otherwise, the agents will have to bear the task of translating between the lower level and the agent's level.

It should also be made clear that a communication language is not a protocol, although both may be concerned with communication and communication-related issues. The distinction between a communication language and a protocol is often fuzzy. A protocol, as used or mentioned in the context of communication languages, may have any of the following three meanings: (i) a transport protocol, like HTTP, SMTP, FTP, etc.; (ii) a high level framework for interaction, such as negotiation, game theory protocols, or planning; or (iii) constraints on the possible valid exchanges of communication primitives.[14] A communication language may use protocols of the first kind as transport mechanisms, may be used by protocols of the second kind as a way to implement them, and usually includes protocols of the third kind as part of its description; but a communication language definitely is not merely a protocol itself.

In this section we suggest requirements for agent communication languages. We divide these requirements into seven categories: form, content, semantics, implementation, networking, environment, and reliability. We believe that an agent communication language will be valuable to the extent that it meets these requirements. At times, these requirements may be in conflict with one another. For example, a language that can be easily read by people might not be as concise as possible. It is the job of the language designer to balance these various needs. In the Evaluation of KQML, as an Agent Communication Language section, we evaluate KQML with respect to these requirements.

Form

A good agent communication language should be declarative, syntactically simple, and readable by people. It should be concise, yet easy to parse and to generate. For a statement of the language to be transmitted to another agent, the statement must pass through the bit stream of the underlying transport mechanism. Thus, the language should be linear or should be easily translated into a linear form. Finally, because a communication language will be integrated into a wide variety of systems, its syntax should be extensible.

Content

A communication language should be layered in a way that i
systems. In particular, a distinction should be made between tl
language, which expresses communicative acts, and the cc
which expresses facts about the domain. Such layering facilita   ...cssful
integration of the language to applications while providing a conceptual framework for the understanding of the language. The language should commit to a
well-defined set of communicative acts (primitives). Although this set could be
extensible, a core of primitives that capture most of our intuitions about what
constitutes a communicative act irrespective of application (database, object-oriented system, knowledge base, etc.) will ensure the usability of the language by
a variety of systems. The choice of the core set of primitives also relates to the
decision of whether to commit to a specific content language. A commitment to
a content language allows for a more restricted set of communicative acts because it is then possible to carry more information at the content language level.
The disadvantage is that all applications must then use the same content language; this is a heavy constraint.

Semantics

Although the semantic description of communication languages and their
primitives is often limited to natural language descriptions, a more formal description is necessary if the communication language is intended for interaction
among a diverse range of applications. Applications designers should have a
shared understanding of the language, its primitives, and the protocols associated with their use, and abide by that shared understanding. The semantics of a
communication language should exhibit those properties expected of the semantics of any other language. It should be grounded in theory, and it should be
unambiguous. It should exhibit canonical form (similarity in meaning should
lead to similarity in representation). Because a communication language is intended for interaction that extends over time amongst spatially dispersed applications, location and time should be carefully addressed by the semantics. Finally, the semantic description should provide a model of communication, which
would be useful for performance modeling, among other things.

Implementation

The implementation should be efficient, both in speed and in bandwidth uti-
lization. It should provide a good fit with existing software technology. The interface should be easy to use; details of the networking layers that lie below the
primitive communicative acts should be hidden from the user. Finally, the language should be amenable to partial implementation, because simple agents
may need to handle only a subset of the primitive communicative acts.

Networking

An agent communication language should fit well with modern networking technology. This ability is particularly important because some of the communication will be *about* concepts involving networked communications. The language should support all of the basic connections—point-to-point, multicast and broadcast. Both synchronous and asynchronous connections should be supported. The language should contain a rich enough set of primitives that it can serve as a substrate upon which higher-level languages and interaction protocols can be built. Moreover, these higher-level protocols should be independent of the transport mechanisms (e.g., TCP/IP, email, http) used.

Environment

The environment in which intelligent agents will be required to work will be highly distributed, heterogeneous, and extremely dynamic. To provide a communication channel to the outside world in such an environment, a communication language must provide tools for coping with heterogeneity and dynamism. It must support interoperability with other languages and protocols. It must support knowledge discovery in large networks. Finally, it must be easily attachable to legacy systems.

Reliability

A communication language must support reliable and secure communication among agents. Provisions for secure and private exchanges between two agents should be supported. There should be a way to guarantee authentication of agents. We should not assume that agents are infallible or perfect—they should be robust to inappropriate or malformed messages. The language should support reasonable mechanisms for identifying and signaling errors and warnings.

Knowledge Query and Manipulation Language (KQML)

To address many of the difficulties of communication among intelligent agents, we must give them a common language. In linguistic terms, this means that they must share a common syntax, semantics, and pragmatics. Getting information processes or software agents to share a common syntax is a major problem. There is no universally accepted language in which to represent information and queries. Languages such as KIF (Genesereth and Fikes 1992), extended SQL, and LOOM (MacGregor and Bates 1987) have their supporters, but there is also a strong position that it is too early to standardize on any representation language (Ginsberg 1991).

As a result, it is currently necessary to say that two agents can communicate with each other if they have a common representation language or use languages that are inter-translatable. Assuming the use of a common or translatable language, it is still necessary for communicating agents to share a framework of knowledge in order to interpret the messages they exchange. This is not really a shared semantics, but rather a shared ontology. There is not likely to be one shared ontology, but many. Shared ontologies are under development in many important application domains such as planning and scheduling, biology and medicine. The pragmatics of communicating software agents involves such issues as knowing with whom to talk and how to find them as well as knowing how to initiate and maintain an exchange. KQML is concerned primarily with this kind of pragmatics and secondarily with semantics. It is a language and a set of protocols that support software agents in identifying, connecting with, and exchanging information with other such agents.

In the next two sections we present the KQML language, its primitives and protocols supported, and the software environment of KQML-speaking applications.

A Description of KQML

The KQML language can be thought of as consisting of three layers: the *content* layer, the *message* layer, and the *communication* layer. The content layer bears the actual content of the message, in the programs own representation language. KQML can carry expressions encoded in any representation language, including languages expressed as ASCII strings and those expressed using a binary notation. Some KQML-speaking agents (e.g., routers, very general brokers) may ignore the content portion of the message, except to determine where it ends.

The communication level encodes a set of message features which describe the lower level communication parameters, such as the identity of the sender and recipient, and a unique identifier associated with the communication.

It is the message layer that is used to encode a message that one application would like to transmit to another. The message layer forms the core of the KQML language and determines the kinds of interactions one can have with a KQML-speaking agent. A primary function of the message layer is to identify the protocol to be used to deliver the message and to supply a speech act or performative which the sender attaches to the content (such as that it is an assertion, a query, a command, or any of a set of known performatives). In addition, since the content may be opaque to a KQML-speaking agent, this layer also includes optional features which describe the content language, the ontology it assumes, and some type of description of the content, such as a descriptor naming a topic within the ontology. These features make it possible for KQML implementations to analyze, route and properly deliver messages even though their content is inaccessible.

The syntax of KQML is based on a balanced parentheses list. The initial element of the list is the performative; the remaining elements are the performative's arguments as keyword/value pairs. Because the language is relatively simple, the actual syntax is not significant and can be changed if necessary in the future. The syntax reveals the roots of the initial implementations, which were done in Common Lisp; it has turned out to be quite flexible.

A KQML message from agent *joe* representing a query about the price of a share of IBM stock might be encoded as:

(*ask-one* :sender joe :content (PRICE IBM ?price) :receiver stock-server :reply-with ibm-stock :language LPROLOG :ontology NYSE-TICKS)

In this message, the KQML performative is *ask-one*, the content is *(price ibm ?price)*, the ontology assumed by the query is identified by the token *nyse-ticks*, the receiver of the message is to be a server identified as *stock-server* and the query is written in a language called *LPROLOG*. The value of the ':content' keyword is the content level, the values of the ':reply-with,' ':sender,' ':receiver' keywords form the communication layer and the performative name, with the ':language' and ':ontology' form the message layer. In due time, 'stock-server' might send to *joe* the following KQML message:

(*tell* :sender stock-server :content (PRICE IBM 14) :receiver joe :in-reply-to ibm-stock :language LPROLOG :ontology NYSE-TICKS)

A query similar to the *ask-all* query could be conveyed using standard Prolog as the content language in a form that requests the set of all answers as:

(*ask-all* :content "price(ibm,(Price, Time))" :receiver stock-server :language standard_prolog :ontology NYSE-TICKS)

The first message asks for a single reply; the second asks for a set as a reply. If we had posed a query which had a large number of replies, would could ask that they each be sent separately, instead of as a single large collection by changing the performative. (To save space, we will no longer repeat fields which are the same as in the above examples.):

(*stream-all* :comment "?VL is a large set of symbols" :content (PRICE ?VL ?price))

The *stream-all* performative asks that a set of answers be turned into a set of replies. To exert control of this set of reply messages, we can wrap another performative around the preceding message:

(*standby* :content (stream-all :content (PRICE ?VL ?price)))

The *standby* performative expects a KQML language content, and it requests that the agent receiving the request take the stream of messages and hold them and release them one at a time; each time the sending agent transmits a message with the *next* performative. The exchange of next/reply messages can continue until the stream is depleted or until the sending agent sends either a *discard* message (i.e., discard all remaining replies) or a *rest* message (i.e., send all of the remaining replies now).

A different set of answers to the same query can be obtained (from a suitable server) with the query:

Category	Name
Basic Query	evaluate, ask-if, ask-about, ask-one, ask-all
Multi-response (query)	stream-about, stream-all, eos
Response	reply, sorry
Generic informational	tell, achieve, cancel, untell, unachieve
Generator	standby, ready, next, rest, discard, generator
Capability-definition	advertise, subscribe, monitor, import, export
Networking	register, unregister, forward, broadcast, route

Table 1. There are about two dozen reserved performative names that fall into seven basic categories.

(*subscribe* :content (stream-all :content (PRICE IBM ?price)))

This performative requests all future changes to the answer to the query. In other words, it is a stream of messages which are generated as the trading price of IBM stock changes.

Though there is a predefined set of reserved performatives, it is neither a minimal required set nor a closed one. A KQML agent may choose to handle only a few (perhaps one or two) performatives. The set is extensible; a community of agents may choose to use additional performatives if they agree on their interpretation and the protocol associated with each. However, an implementation that chooses to implement one of the reserved performatives must implement it in the standard way.

Some of the reserved performatives are shown in table 1. In addition to standard communication performatives such as *ask*, *tell*, *deny*, *delete*, and more protocol-oriented performatives such as *subscribe*, KQML contains performatives related to the nonprotocol aspects of pragmatics, such as *advertise*—which allows an agent to announce what kinds of KQML messages it is willing to handle; and *recruit*—which can be used to find suitable agents for particular types of messages (the uses of these performatives are described in the next section). For example, the server in the above example might have earlier announced:

(*advertise* :ontology NYSE-TICKS :language LPROLOG :content (stream-all :content (PRICE ?x ?y)))

Which is roughly equivalent to announcing that it is a stock ticker and inviting monitor requests concerning stock prices. This *advertise* message is what justifies the subscriber's sending the *stream-all* message.

There are a variety of interprocess information exchange protocols in

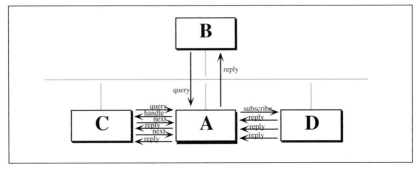

Figure 2. Several basic communication protocols are supported in KQML.

KQML. In the simplest, one agent acts as a client and sends a query to another agent acting as a server and then waits for a reply, as is shown between agents A and B in figure 2. The server's reply might consist of a single answer or a collection or set of answers. In another common case, shown between agents A and C, the server's reply is not the complete answer but a handle which allows the client to ask for the components of the reply, one at a time. A common example of this exchange occurs when a client queries a relational database or a reasoner which produces a sequence of instantiations in response. Although this exchange requires that the server maintain some internal state, the individual transactions are as before—involving a *synchronous* communication between the agents. A somewhat different case occurs when the client subscribes to a server's output and an indefinite number of *asynchronous* replies arrive at irregular intervals, as between agents A and D in figure 2. The client does not know when each reply message will be arriving and may be busy performing some other task when they do.

There are other variations of these protocols. Messages might not be addressed to specific hosts, but broadcast to a number of them. The replies, arriving synchronously or asynchronously have to be collated and, optionally, associated with the query that they are replying to.

Facilitators, Mediators, and the Environment of KQML Agents

One of the design criteria for KQML was to produce a language that could support a wide variety of interesting agent architectures. Our approach to this is to introduce a small number of KQML performatives which are used by agents to describe the meta-data specifying the information requirements and capabilities and then to introduce a special class of agents called *communication facilitators* (Genesereth and Ketchpel 1994). A facilitator is an agent that performs various useful communication services, such as maintaining a registry of service names, forwarding messages to named services, routing messages based on content,

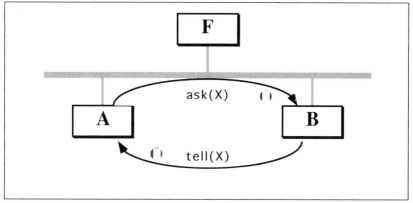

*Figure 3. When A is aware of B and of the appropriateness of querying
B about X, a simple point-to-point protocol can be used.*

providing "matchmaking" between information providers and clients, and providing mediation and translation services.

As an example, consider a case where an agent A would like to know the truth of a sentence X, and agent B may have X in its knowledge-base, and a facilitator agent F is available. If A is aware that it is appropriate to send a query about X to B, then it can use a simple *point-to-point* protocol and send the query directly to B, as in figure 3.

If, however, A is not aware of what agents are available, or which may have X in their knowledge-bases, or how to contact those of whom it is aware, then a variety of approaches can be used. Figure 4 shows an example in which A uses the *subscribe* performative to request that facilitator F monitor for the truth of X. If B subsequently informs F that it believes X to be true, then F can in turn inform A.

Figure 5 shows a slightly different situation. A asks F to find an agent that can process an *ask(X)* performative. B independently informs F that it is willing to accept performatives matching *ask(X)*. Once F has both of these messages, it sends B the query, gets a response, and forwards it to A.

In figure 6, A uses a slightly different performative to inform F of its interest in knowing the truth of X. The recruit performative asks the recipient to find an agent that is willing to receive and process an embedded performative. That agent's response is then to be directly sent to the initiating agent. Although the difference between the examples used in figures 5 and 6 are small for a simple ask query, consider what would happen if the embedded performative was *subscribe(ask-all(X))*.

As a final example, consider the exchange in figure 7 in which A asks F to "recommend" an agent to whom it would be appropriate to send the performa-

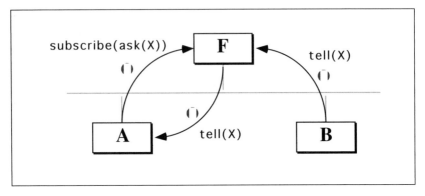

Figure 4. Agent A can ask facilitator agent F to monitor for changes in its knowledge-base. Facilitators are agents that deal in knowledge about the information services and requirements of other agents and offer such services as forwarding, brokering, recruiting, and content-based routing.

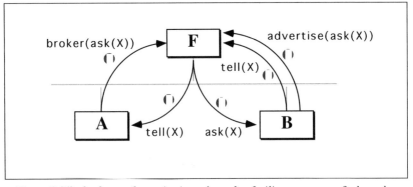

Figure 5. The broker performative is used to ask a facilitator agent to find another agent which can process a given performative and to receive and forward the reply.

tive *ask(X)*. Once F learns that B is willing to accept *ask(X)* performatives, it replies to A with the name of agent B. A is then free to initiate a dialogue with B to answer this and similar queries.

From these examples, we can see that one of the main functions of facilitator agents is to help other agents find appropriate clients and servers. The problem of how agents find facilitators in the first place is not strictly an issue for KQML and has a variety of possible solutions.

Current KQML-based applications have used one of two simple techniques. In the PACT project (Cutkosky et al. 1993), for example, all agents used a central, common facilitator whose location was a parameter initialized when the agents were launched. In the ARPI applications (Burstein 1994), finding and es-

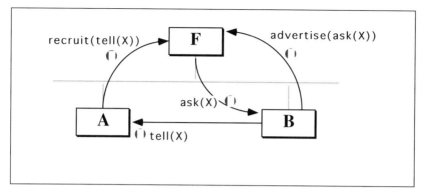

Figure 6. The recruit performative is used to ask a facilitator agent to find an appropriate agent to which an embedded performative can be forwarded. Any reply is returned directly to the original agent.

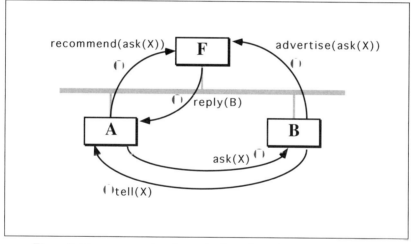

Figure 7. The recommend performative is used to ask a facilitator agent to respond with the "name" of another agent which is appropriate for sending a particular performative.

tablishing contact with a local facilitator is one of the functions of the KQML API. When each agent starts up, its KQML router module announces itself to the local facilitator so that it is registered in the local database. When the application exits, the router sends another KQML message to the facilitator, removing the application from the facilitator's database. By convention, a facilitator agent should be running on a host machine with the symbolic address *facilitator.domain* and listening to the standard KQML port.

Evaluation of KQML as an Agent Communication Language

In this section, we evaluate the KQML language as it stands today, relative to our requirements for agent communication languages, given in the Communication Languages and their Desired Features section.

Form

Performatives, the only primitives of the languages, convey the communicative act and the actions to be taken as a result. Thus the form should be deemed to be declarative. In format, KQML messages are linear streams of characters with a Lisp-like syntax. Although this formatting is irrelevant to the functions of the language, it makes the messages easy to read, to parse, and to convert to other formats.[15] The syntax is simple and allows for the addition of new parameters, if deemed necessary, in future revisions of the language.

Content

The KQML language can be viewed as being divided into three layers: the content layer, the message layer, and the communication layer. KQML messages are oblivious to the content they carry. Although in current implementations of the language there is no support for non-ASCII content, there is nothing in the language that would prevent such support. The language offers a minimum set of performatives that covers a basic repertoire of communicative acts. They constitute the message layer of the language and are to be interpreted as speech acts. Although there is no "right" necessary and sufficient set of communicative acts, KQML designers tried to find the middle ground between the two extremes: (i) providing a small set of primitives thereby requiring overloading at the content level; and (ii) providing an extensive set of acts, where inevitably acts will overlap one another and/or embody fine distinctions. The *communication* layer encodes a set of features to the message which describe the lower level communication parameters, such as the identity of the sender and recipient, and a unique identifier associated with the communication.

Semantics

KQML semantics is still an open issue. For now there are only natural language descriptions of the intended meaning of the performatives and their use (protocols). An approach that emphasizes the speech act flavor of the communication acts is a thread of ongoing research (Labrou and Finin 1994).

Implementation

In two current implementations of KQML interfaces, the Lockheed KQML API and the Loral/UMBC KQML API, each provides a content-independent message router and a facilitator. The application must provide handler functions for the performatives in order for the communication acts to be processed by the application and eventually return the proper response(s). It is not necessary that an application should handle all performatives since not all KQML-speaking applications will be equally powerful. Creating a KQML speaking interface to an existing application is a matter of providing the handler functions. The efficiency of KQML communication has been investigated. Various compression enhancements have been added which cut communication costs by reducing message sizes and also by eliminating a substantial fraction of symbol lookup and string duplication.

Networking

KQML-speaking agents can communicate directly with other agents (addressing them by symbolic name), broadcast their messages, or solicit the services of fellow agents or facilitators for the delivery of a message by using the appropriate performatives (see the Applications of KQML section). KQML allows for both synchronous-asynchronous interactions and blocking-nonblocking message sending on behalf of an application through assignment of the appropriate values for those parameters in a KQML message.

Environment

KQML can use any transport protocol as its transport mechanism (HTTP, SMTP, TCP/IP, etc.). Also, because KQML messages are oblivious to content, there are no restrictions on the content language beyond the provision of functions that handle the performatives for the content language of the application. Interoperability with other communication languages remains to be addressed as such languages appear. The existence of facilitators in the KQML environment can provide the means for knowledge discovery in large networks, especially if facilitators can cooperate with other knowledge discovery applications available in the World Wide Web.

Reliability

The issues of security and authentication have not been addressed properly thus far by the KQML community. No decision has been made on whether they should be handled at the transport protocol level or at the language level. At the language level, new performatives or message parameters can be introduced that allow for encryption of either the content or the whole KQML message. Since KQML speaking agents might be imperfect, there are performatives (such as *error* and *sorry*) that can be used as responses to messages that an application cannot process or comprehend.

Applications of KQML

The KQML language and implementations of the protocol have been used in several prototype and demonstration systems. The applications have ranged from concurrent design and engineering of hardware and software systems, military transportation logistics planning and scheduling, flexible architectures for large-scale heterogeneous information systems, agent-based software integration, and cooperative information access planning and retrieval. KQML has the potential to significantly enhance the capabilities and functionality of large-scale integration and interoperability efforts now underway in communication and information technology such as the national information infrastructure and OMG's CORBA, as well as in application areas in electronic commerce, health information systems, and virtual enterprise integration. The content languages used have included languages intended for knowledge exchange including the Knowledge Interchange Format (KIF) and the Knowledge Representation Specification Language (KRSL) (Lehrer 1994) as well as other more traditional languages such as SQL. Early experimentation with KQML began in 1990. The following is a representative selection of applications and experiments developed using KQML.

The design and engineering of complex computer systems, whether exclusively hardware or software systems or both, today involves multiple design and engineering disciplines. Many such systems are developed in fast cycle or concurrent processes which involve the immediate and continual consideration of end-product constraints, such as marketability, manufacturing and planning. Further, the design, engineering, and manufacturing components are also likely to be distributed across organizational and company boundaries. KQML has proved highly effective in the integration of diverse tools and systems, enabling new tool interactions and supporting a high-level communication infrastructure reducing integration cost as well as flexible communication across multiple networking systems. The use of KQML in these demonstrations has allowed the integrators to focus on what the integration of design and engineering tools can accomplish and appropriately de-emphasized how the tools communicate (Mark et al. 1994; Kuokka et al. 1993; Tenenbaum, Weber, and Gruber 1993; Genesereth 1991).

KQML has been used as the communication language in several technology integration experiments in the ARPA Rome Lab Planning Initiative. One of these experiments supported an integrated planning and scheduling system for military transportation logistics linking a SIPE planning agent (Bienkowski, des-Jardins, and Desimone 1994; Wilkins 1988), with a Common Lisp scheduler, a LOOM knowledge base (MacGregor and Bates 1987), and a Common Lisp case-based reasoning tool. All of the components integrated were preexisting systems ƒwhich were not designed to work in a cooperative distributed environment.

In a second experiment, an information agent was constructed by integrating CoBASE (Chu and Yang 1994), a cooperative front-end; SIMS (Arens et al. 1994; Arens 1992; the Arens and Ambite chapter, also in this volume), an information mediator for planning information access; and LIM (Pastor, McKay, and Finin 1992), an information mediator for translating relational data into knowledge structures. CoBASE processes a query, and, if no responses are found, relaxes the query based upon approximation operators and domain semantics and executes the query again. CoBASE generates a single knowledge-based query for SIMS which uses knowledge of different information sources to select which of several information sources to access, partitions the query, and optimizes access. Each of the resulting queries in this experiment is sent to a LIM knowledge server which answers the query by creating objects from tuples in a relational database. A LIM server front-ends each different database. This experiment was run over the Internet involving three geographically dispersed sites.

Agent-Based Software Integration (Genesereth 1993) is an effort underway at Stanford University, which is applying KQML as an integrating framework for general software systems. Using KQML, a federated architecture incorporating a sophisticated facilitator is developed, which supports an agent-based view of software integration and interoperation (Genesereth and Ketchpel 1994). The facilitator in this architecture is an intelligent agent which processes and reasons about the content of KQML messages, supporting tighter integration of disparate software systems.

Other work done at Stanford involves ACL (Agent Communication Language), an implementation of KQML that differs from "pure" KQML in the commitment it makes to KIF as the content language of the interacting applications. ACL has been used in several large-scale demonstrations of software interoperation, and the results are promising. Full specifications are available, and parts of the language are making their way through various standards organizations. Several start-up companies are proposing to offer commercial products for processing ACL; and a number of established computer system vendors are looking at ACL as a possible language for communication among heterogeneous systems. Genesereth provides more about the specifics of this approach (Genesereth and Ketchpel 1994), whose success is tied to the advantages and features of KIF.

We have also successfully used KQML in other smaller demonstrations integrating distributed clients (in C) with mediators which were retrieving data from distributed databases. Mediators are not just limited distributed database access. In another demonstration, we experimented with a KQML URL for the World Wide Web. The static nature of links within such hypermedia structures lends itself to being extended with virtual and dynamic links to arbitrary information sources as can be supported easily with KQML.

Other Communication Languages

There has not been much work on communication languages from a practitioner's point of view. If we set aside work on network (transport) protocols or protocols in distributed computing as being too inefficient for the purposes of intelligent agents (as opposed to processes) the rest of the relevant research may be divided into *theoretical* and the *applied* approaches. The more theoretical work offers constructs and formalisms which address issues of agency in general and communication in particular, as a dimension of agent behavior, with an emphasis on the intentional description of an agent.[16] The more applied work is aimed at developing agent languages and associated communication protocols focused on tools, interfaces, and supporting applications. To our knowledge, there has not been any work on communication languages that is part of a broader project that commits to specific architectures.

Agent-Oriented Programming

Although Agent-Oriented Programming (AOP) could be classified in the first one of the categories mentioned above, the fact that it comes with a programming language in which one can program agents that communicate and evolve makes it more than a construct of a theoretical interest. In AOP (Shoham 1993) agents are defined as entities whose state is viewed as consisting of mental components such as beliefs, capabilities, choices, and commitments. Although this so called *intentional* description of a software system is nothing new, AOP introduces a formal language with syntax and semantics to describe the mental states and an interpreted programming language, called AGENT-0 that has semantics consistent with those of the mental states and in which a programmer can program an agent. A part of AGENT-0[17] is a communication language that introduces primitives for the interaction of agents. The primitives are speech acts; their semantics are provided in terms of their execution (the communication acts update the belief and the commitment space of an agent) and may be executed conditionally (according to whether certain mental states hold). Since AGENT-0 was intended as a prototype to illustrate the principles of AOP, it is limited in many important ways. For example, facts have to be atomic sentences (i.e., no conjunction, disjunction, or modal operators allowed), and commitments can be made only for primitive actions (i.e., no planning). An attempt to alleviate some of the deficiencies of AGENT-0 was done with PLACA by including operators for action planning and goal achievement, but PLACA is also an experimental language and has not reached production state. AGENT-K[18] is a language in the AOP that essentially extends AGENT-0 to use KQML for communication. This still retains the issue of cooperation of agents written in the AOP paradigm with agents that do not fall in the AOP paradigm. Finally it remains to be proven the extent to which the AOP paradigm provides a powerful enough framework for serious agent programming.

Telescript

General Magic's *Telescript* defines an environment for transactions between software applications over the network, with a focus on applications in the area of electronic commerce. In the Telescript paradigm agents "travel" over the network (carrying both procedures and data) and perform actions on data at the transport location, instead of exchanging the data. Its developers suggest that this approach offers advantages on issues of bandwidth use and security, with respect to the predominant client-server paradigm. Telescript is an interpreted, communication-centric language executed by the Telescript engine that has access to the application environment through an API. A typical communicating application is written partly in Telescript and partly in some other (host) language, with Telescript having control of all communication-related issues, such as transporting the agent, handling conditions, scheduling the agents activities, and gathering and modifying information. Telescript has attracted the interest of commercial vendors for electronic commerce applications. Can Telescript agents interoperate with other (non-Telescript) agents? First of all, Telescript agents do not communicate; they transport themselves on location and execute a predefined script. Even if some form of communication was allowed, it is unknown (i) how communication would be integrated to this new paradigm of transportable, script-executing paradigm of agents (will agents exchange scripts?) and (ii) how Telescript agents can interoperate with agents whose interaction follows the traditional client-server paradigm. Although such questions have not been addressed yet, it seems that Telescript agents will be confined to a Telescript universe.

Conclusions

There is no silver bullet for the problem of knowledge sharing. The difficulties of addressing this issue go beyond the plethora of applications and systems that would be candidates for knowledge sharing. The problem itself is not a single, well-defined problem but rather a wide range of subproblems (and corresponding approaches). From this point of view, we feel that the KSE approach and KQML have merits that go beyond the success of the individual solutions that have been suggested. Above all the KSE promotes an approach to the problem and the fundamental subproblems to be addressed. This approach includes (i) translating between representations, (ii) sharing the semantic (and often pragmatic) content of the knowledge that is represented, and (iii) communicating attitudes about the shared knowledge. Whether the respective solutions for these three problems will be KIF, Ontolingua, and KQML is to be proven in time, but we believe that these are the three levels at which the overall problem should be attacked.

We believe the same argument to be true for KQML. The communication language should be dissociated from interaction and transport protocols, should be oblivious to the content and concerned only with attitudes about the content. The idea of a communication language that offers primitives (the performatives), modeled after speech acts, that have a meaning outside the context of a specific application or representation is not necessarily a new one, but KQML is a first attempt for a communication language based on this concept. The number and the variety of the primitives will always be a matter of debate; KQML developers tried to balance the two extremes of having very few primitives (and thus overloading the content) and offering an extensive set of performatives that would inevitably overlap and would be hard to standardize. The other idea offered by KQML is that of having specialized agents, called *facilitators*, that with the use of the appropriate KQML performatives can help agents find other agents (or be found by other agents) that can perform desired tasks for them.

Acknowledgments

This work has been the result of very fruitful collaborations with a number of colleagues with whom we have worked on KQML and other aspects of the Knowledge Sharing Effort. We wish to specifically thank and acknowledge Don McKay, Robin McEntire, Richard Fritzson, and Chelliah Thirunavukkarasu.

Notes

1. This work was supported in part by the Air Force Office of Scientific Research under contract F49620-92-J-0174, and by the Advanced Research Projects Agency monitored under USAF contracts F30602-93-C-0177 and F30602-93-C-0028 by Rome Laboratory.

2. Unless, of course, the physicist also happens to be interested in cars.

3. For example, for systems that use firewalls or are connected to a network only intermittently, SMTP may be preferred over TCP as a transport mechanism.

4. The URL is http://www.cs.umbc.edu/kse/kif/.

5. This document and other information on the KRSS group is available as http://www.cs.umbc.edu/kse/krss/.

6 The URL is http://www.cs.umbc.edu/kse/srkb/

7. General information about KQML is available from http://www.cs.umbc.edu/kqml/.

8. So for n languages the number of translators needed would be 2n instead of $n*(n-1)$. Of course the advantages of having a common interchange format go beyond such a reduction; but defining the advantages (and disadvantages) of such an approach has been an issue of debate.

9. Primarily in conjunction with ACL, an implementation of KQML, which is standard KQML with a commitment to KIF as the content language.

10. This presentation of KIF is based on a similar presentation (Genesereth and Ketchpel 1994).

11. Symbols beginning with a question mark are taken to be variables.

12. The use of commas signals that the variables should not be taken literally. Without the commas, this sentence would say that agent joe is interested in the sentence (salary ?x ?y ?z) instead of its instances.

13. See http://www-ksl.stanford.edu/knowledge-sharing/ontologies/README.html for more information on ontologies and the various projects with which the SRKB Group has been involved.

14. Very much as in meaningful communications between sane human beings, where a question about the time for example will be followed by a response (hopefully about time) and not by another question about the weather.

15. Simple programs exist to convert KQML messages to predicate-like format.

16. An agent theory is concerned with how an agent's knowledge, actions, and cognitive state relate to one another, guide the agent's "behavior," and affect both the agent and the environment in which the agent finds itself, through time.

17. AGENT-0 is only one of the possible programming languages in the AOP paradigm. In AOP there is no "proper" programming language. Extensions or replacements of AGENT-0 may be introduced, but they will have to be consistent with the intentional description imposed by the paradigm.

18. Look at URL http://www.csd.abdn.ac.uk/~pedwards/publs/agentk.html for more details.

References

Arens, Y. 1992. Planning and Reformulating Queries for Semantically-Modeled Multi-database Systems. In Proceedings of the First International Conference on Information and Knowledge Management. New York: Association of Computing Machinery.

Arens, Y.; Chee, C.; Hsu, C.-N.; In, H.; and Knoblock, C. A. 1994. Query Processing in an Information Mediator. In *Proceedings of the ARPA/Rome Lab 1994 Knowledge-Based Planning and Scheduling Initiative Workshop*. San Francisco, Calif.: Morgan Kaufmann.

Bienkowski, M.; desJardins, M.; and Desimone, R. 1994. SOCAP: System for Operations Crisis Action Planning. In *Proceedings of the ARPA/Rome Lab 1994 Knowledge-Based Planning and Scheduling Initiative Workshop*. San Francisco, Calif.: Morgan Kaufmann.

Burstein, M., ed. 1994. *Proceedings of the ARPA/Rome Lab 1994 Knowledge-Based Planning and Scheduling Initiative Workshop*. San Francisco, Calif.: Morgan Kaufmann.

Chu, W., and Yang, H. 1994. COBASE: A Cooperative Query Answering System for Database Systems. In *Proceedings of the ARPA/Rome Lab 1994 Knowledge-Based Planning and Scheduling Initiative Workshop*. San Francisco, Calif.: Morgan Kaufmann.

Cutkosky, M.; Engelmore, E.; Fikes, R.; Gruber, T.; Genesereth, M.; and Mark, W. 1993. PACT: An Experiment in Integrating Concurrent Engineering Systems. *IEEE Computer* 26(1): 28–38.

Genesereth, M. 1993. An Agent-Based Approach to Software Interoperability, Technical Report, Logic-91-6, Logic Group, Computer Science Department, Stanford University.

Genesereth, M. 1991. DESIGNWORLD. In Proceedings of the IEEE Conference on Robotics and Automation, 2-785–2-788. Washington, D.C.: IEEE Computer Society.

Ginsberg, M. 1991. Knowledge Interchange Format: The KIF of Death. *AI Magazine* 12(3): 57–63.

Genesereth, M., and Fikes, R. 1992. Knowledge Interchange Format, Version 3.0, Reference Manual, Technical Report, Computer Science Department, Stanford University.

Genesereth, M. R., and Ketchpel, S. P. 1994. Software Agents. *Communications of the ACM* 37(7): 48–53, 147.

Kuokka, D.; McGuire, J. G.; Pelavin, R. N.; Weber, J. C.; Tenenbaum, J. M.; Gruber, T.; and Olsen, G. 1993. SHADE: Technology for Knowledge-Based Collaborative Engineering. In *AI and Collaborative Design: Papers from the 1993 AAAI Workshop,* eds. J. S. Gero and M. L. Maher, 245–262. Menlo Park, Calif.: AAAI Press.

Labrou, Y., and Finin, T. 1994. A Semantics Approach for KQML—A General-Purpose Communication Language for Software Agents. In the Third International Conference on Information and Knowledge Management. New York: Association of Computing Machinery.

Lehrer, N. 1994. The Knowledge Representation Specification Language Manual, Technical Report, ISX Corporation, Thousand Oaks, California.

MacGregor, R., and Bates, R. 1987. The LOOM Knowledge Representation Language, Technical Report ISI/RS-87-188, USC/Information Sciences Institute, Marina del Rey, California.

Mark, W., et. al. 1994. COSMOS: A System for Supporting Design Negotiation. *Journal of Concurrent Engineering: Applications and Research* 2(3).

Neches, R.; Fikes, R.; Finin, T.; Gruber, T.; Patil, R.; Senator, T.; and Swartout, W. 1991. Enabling Technology for Knowledge Sharing. *AI Magazine* 12(3): 36–56.

Newell, A. 1993. Reflections on the Knowledge Level. *Artificial Intelligence* 59:31–38.

Newell, A. 1982. The Knowledge Level. *Artificial Intelligence* 18:87–127.

Pastor, J.; McKay, D.; and Finin, T. 1992. View-Concepts: Knowledge-Based Access to Databases. In Proceedings of the First International Conference on Information and Knowledge Management. New York: Association of Computing Machinery.

Shoham, Y. 1993. Agent-Oriented Programming. *Artificial Intelligence* 60:51–92.

Tenenbaum, M.; Weber, J.; and Gruber, T. 1993. Enterprise Integration: Lessons from SHADE and PACT. In *Enterprise Integration Modeling,* ed. C. Petrie. Cambridge, Mass.: MIT Press.

Wilkins, D. 1988. *Practical Planning: Extending the Classical AI Planning Paradigm.* San Francisco, Calif.: Morgan Kaufmann.

Chapter 15

An Agent-Based Framework for Interoperability

Michael R. Genesereth

The software world today is one of great richness and diversity. Many thousands of software products are available to users today, providing a wide variety of information and services in a wide variety of domains. While most of these programs provide their users with adequate value when used in isolation, there is increasing demand for programs that can interoperate to exchange information and services with other programs, thereby solving problems that cannot be solved alone.

Unfortunately, getting programs to work together often necessitates extensive work on the part of users and developers. They must learn the characteristics of completed programs and how to negotiate communication formats and protocols for programs under development. What's more, the resulting systems are usually very rigid: components often cannot be modified or replaced without subsequent rounds of negotiation and programming.

Approaches to Software Interoperation

In order to deal with these problems, the systems community has developed various pieces of technology to transfer the burden of interoperation from the creators and users of programs to the programs themselves (figure 1). This technology includes such things as standard communication languages, subroutine libraries to assist programmers in writing interoperable software, and system services to facilitate interoperation at runtime.

Communication language standards facilitate the creation of interoperable software by decoupling implementation from interface. So long as a program abides by the details of the communication standards, it does not matter how it is implemented. Today, standards exist for a wide variety of domains. For ex-

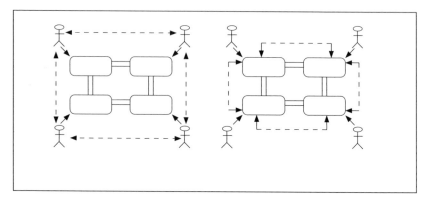

Figure 1. Programmer coordination vs. automatic coordination.

ample, electronic mail programs from different vendors manage to interoperate through the use of mail standards like SMTP. Disparate graphics programs interoperate using standard formats like GIF. Text formatting programs and printers interoperate using languages like Postscript.

There is also a wide range of systems services. Directory assistance programs help by providing a way for programs to discover which programs can handle which requests and which programs are interested in which pieces of information. Automatic brokers (such as the Publish-and-Subscribe capabilities on the Macintosh, DDE, BMS, ToolTalk, OLE, and CORBA) take the directory notion one step further: they not only compute the appropriate programs to receive messages but also forward those messages, handle any problems that arise, and, where appropriate, return the answers to the original senders.

Unfortunately, this kind of technology is too limited to support the ideal of automated coordination suggested in figure 1. To begin with, existing standards are not sufficiently expressive to allow the communication of definitions, theorems, assumptions, and the other types of information that programmers can communicate with each other and that may be needed for one system to communicate effectively with another. Current subroutine libraries provide little support for increased expressiveness. Directory assistance programs and brokers are limited by the lack of expressiveness of the languages used to document resources and their lack of inferential capability.

Furthermore, there can be inconsistencies in the use of syntax or vocabulary. One program may use a word or expression to mean one thing while another program uses the same word or expression to mean something entirely different. At the same time, there can be incompatibilities. Different programs may use different words or expressions to say the same thing.

As a simple example of these inadequacies, consider two computer-assisted design programs, one running on a Macintosh, the other on a Unix workstation.

The goal is to establish communication betv
can exchange information about the posit
board. The problem is that they use differe
positions. In the Macintosh program, each
integer $(65536*column+row)$. In the Unix |
ized by two quantities, a row and a column.

Now, it is a simple matter for two progra
They can either rewrite the programs so th
positions, or they can interject some tran
The question of interest here, however, is
with automatically. It is really a simple matter of having each program document the coordinate system it uses. For example, the Macintosh program could
emit the equation relating its point notation to the alternative row and column
notation. After that, it should be able to continue to export point information,
leaving it to the system software to translate between this notation and that of
the Unix program. Unfortunately, none of the existing approaches to interoperation supports this sort of interaction.

The Knowledge Sharing Effort Approach to Interoperability

Agent-based software engineering attacks these problems by mandating a universal communication language, one in which inconsistencies and arbitrary
variations in notation are eliminated. There are two popular approaches to the
design of such a language: *procedural* and *declarative*.

The *procedural* approach is based on the idea that communication can be best
modeled as the exchange of procedural directives. Scripting languages (such as
TCL, AppleScript, Java, and Telescript) are based on this approach. They are
both simple and powerful. They allow programs to transmit not only individual
commands but entire programs, thus implementing delayed or persistent goals
of various sorts. They may typically be executed directly and efficiently.

Unfortunately, there are disadvantages to purely procedural languages. For
one, devising procedures sometimes requires information about the recipient
that may not be available to the sender. Secondly, procedures are unidirectional.
Much information that agents must share should be usable in both directions; for
example, to compute quantity from quantity at one time and to compute quantity from quantity at another. Most significantly, scripts are difficult to merge.
This is no problem so long as all communication is one-on-one. However, things
become more difficult when an agent receives multiple scripts from multiple
agents that must be run simultaneously and may interfere with each other.
Merging procedural information is much more difficult than merging declarative specifications or mixed mode information (like condition-action rules).

In contrast with this procedural approach, the *declarative* approach to language design is based on the idea that communication can be best modeled as

. declarative statements (definitions, assumptions, and the like). ...ally useful, a declarative language must be sufficiently expressive ..nicate information of widely varying sorts (including procedures). At ..e time, the language must be reasonably compact; it must ensure that .nunication is possible without excessive growth over specialized languages. ..⌐ an exploration of this approach to communication, researchers in the ARPA Knowledge Sharing Effort have defined the components of an agent communication language (ACL) that satisfies these needs.

In the approach to interoperation described here, programs (called *agents*) use ACL to supply machine-processable documentation to system programs (called *facilitators*), which then coordinate their activities. Since agents and facilitators assume the burden of interoperation, application programmers are relieved of this responsibility and can construct their programs without having to learn the details of other programs in the runtime environment.

Facilitators and the agents they manage are typically organized into what is often called a *federated system*. Figure 2 illustrates the structure of such a system in the simple case in which there are just three machines, one with three agents and two with two agents apiece. As suggested by the diagram, agents do not communicate directly with each other. Instead, they communicate only with their local facilitators, and facilitators, in turn, communicate with each other. In effect, the agents form a "federation" in which they surrender their autonomy to the facilitators.

As with most other brokering approaches, messages from servers to facilitators are undirected; i.e., they have content but no addresses. It is the responsibility of the facilitators to route such messages to agents able to handle them. There can be an arbitrary number of facilitators, on one or more machines, and the network of facilitators can be connected arbitrarily.

The federation architecture provides assisted coordination of other agents based on a *specification-sharing* approach to interoperation. Agents can dynamically connect or disconnect from a facilitator. Upon connecting to a facilitator, an agent supplies a specification of its *capabilities* and *needs* in ACL. In addition to this meta-level information, agents also send application-level information and requests to their facilitators and accept application-level information and requests in return. Facilitators used the documentation provided by these agents to transform these application-level messages and route them to the appropriate agents. The agents agree to service the requests sent by the facilitators, and in return, the facilitators manage the requests posted by the agents.

A major difference between the knowledge-sharing approach to software interoperation and previous approaches lies in the sophistication of the processing done by these facilitators. In some cases, facilitators may have to translate the messages from the sender's form into a form acceptable to the recipient. In some cases, they may have to decompose the message into several messages, sent to different agents. In some cases, they may combine multiple messages. In some

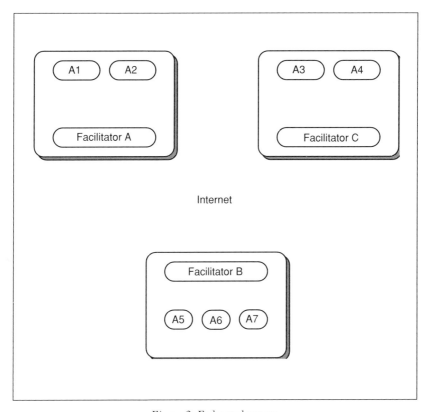

Figure 2. Federated system.

cases, this assistance can be rendered interpretively, with messages going through the facilitators; in other cases, it can be done in one-shot fashion, with the facilitators setting up specialized links between individual agents and then stepping out of the picture.

The knowledge-sharing approach to software interoperation has been devel oped into a practical technology that has been put to use in a variety of applications necessitating interoperation.

In the next section, I introduce the ACL language and describe various approaches to building agents capable of communicating in ACL. In the Software Agents section, I show how ACL can be used by agents in communicating their specifications to other agents. I then describe the implementation of facilitators (Facilitators section) and give a detailed example of the federation architecture (Example section). In the Applications section, I describe three applications of the technology, and conclude in the final section with a discussion of remaining issues and a summary of key points.

Agent Communication Language

The basis for the approach to interoperation described here is a language called ACL (Agent Communication Language). The design of this language follows the recommendations of the various committees involved in the Knowledge Sharing Effort sponsored by ARPA.

ACL can best be thought of as consisting of three parts: an "inner" language called KIF (Knowledge Interchange Format), its vocabulary, and an "outer" language called KQML (Knowledge Query and Manipulation Language). An ACL message is a KQML expression in which the "arguments'" are terms or sentences in KIF formed from words in the ACL vocabulary.

The example below illustrates the use of ACL in an exchange of information between an agent named Joe and an agent named Bill. Joe starts off by sending a message to Bill asking him to store the fact that either p or q is true of every object in the world. He then sends a second message asking Bill to store the fact that p is not true of the object named a. In the third message Joe asks Bill for some object ?x for which (q ?x) is true. Since either p or q is true of every object and p is not true of a, then q must be true of a. In this example, it is assumed that Bill is able to draw such conclusions, with the result that he responds to Joe's request with the answer a.

Joe to Bill:
(request :sender joe :receiver bill
:content (stash '(or (p ?x) (q ?x))))
Joe to Bill:

(request :sender joe :receiver bill
:content (stash '(not (p a))))

Joe to Bill:
(request :sender joe :receiver bill :reply-with msg1
:content (ask-one '?x '(q ?x))))

Bill to Joe:
(respond :sender bill :receiver joe :in-reply-to msg1
:content a)

Knowledge Interchange Format (KIF)

As mentioned above, "arguments" in an ACL message are expressions in a formal language called KIF (Knowledge Interchange Format). KIF is a prefix version of the language of first order predicate calculus, with various extensions to enhance its expressiveness.

The basic vocabulary of the language includes variables (the first column in the examples below), operators (the second column), object constants (the third column), function constants (the fourth column), and relation constants (the fifth column). Individual variables are distinguished by the presence of ? as initial character, and sequence variables are distinguished by the presence of an initial @. There is a fixed set of operators. All others words are constants.

?x not	chip1	sin	prime	
?res	and	theta	cos	left
@lor	123	+	>	

From words, we can build KIF terms to refer to objects in the universe of discourse. In addition to variables and constants, the language includes operators to build complex terms, conditional terms, set descriptors, and quoted expressions (which refer to expressions).

```
(size chip1)
(+ (sin theta) (cos theta))

(if (> theta 0) theta (- theta))
(setofall ?x (above ?x chip1))
(quote (above chip1 chip2))
```

From terms, we can build sentences. These include simple sentences, as well as logical sentences involving Boolean operators like "and," "or" and "=>" (the implication operator).

```
(prime 565762761)
(> (sin theta) (cos phi))

(not (> sin theta) 0))
(or (< 0 (log h)) (< (log h) 1))
(=> (> ?x 0) (positive ?x))
```

Finally, there are rules and definitions. Rules differ from implications (sentences involving the =>) in that they can be used in only one direction. The presence of the operator "consis" in the first part of a rule signals that the rule can applied so long as the enclosed sentence is consistent with the database. Without the "consis," the sentence must be contained in the database in order for the rule to be applied. New object constants, function constants, and relation constants can be defined using the appropriate definitional operators. Such definitions are not essential in order for new constants to be used; however, they provide a convenient grouping for the sentences defining those concepts and allow one to distinguish facts that are true by definition from assertions about the world.

```
(=>> (consis (not (conn ?x ?y))) (not (conn ?x ?y))) (defrelation leq (?x ?y) := (not
(> ?x ?y)))
```

The semantics of the KIF core (KIF without rules and definitions) is similar to that of first order logic. There is an extension to handle nonstandard operators (like "quote," "if," and "setof"), and there is a restriction to models that satisfy various axiom schemata (to give meaning to the basic vocabulary in the format). Despite these extensions and restrictions, the core language retains the fundamental characteristics of first-order logic, including compactness and the semidecidability of logical entailment.

The semantics of rules and definitions is not first order and leads to potential noncompactness and potential nonsemidecidability. However, the extension is upwardly compatible, so that these properties are guaranteed for any databases without rules or definitions.

Vocabulary

In order for programs to communicate about an application area, they must use words that refer to the objects, functions, and relations appropriate to that application area, and they must use these words consistently. One way to promote this consistency is to create an open-ended dictionary of words appropriate to common application areas. Each word in the dictionary would have an English description for use by humans in understanding the meaning of the word, and each word would have KIF annotations for use by facilitators in mediating disagreements of terminology.

Note that, in proposing such a dictionary I am not proposing that there be one standard way of encoding information in each application area. Indeed, the dictionary would probably contain multiple *ontologies* for many areas. For example, we would expect it to contain vocabulary for describing three dimensional geometry in terms of polar coordinates, rectangular coordinates, cylindrical coordinates, and so on. Each program could use whichever ontology is most convenient. The formal definitions of the words associated with any one of these ontologies could then be used by the facilitator in translating messages using one ontology into messages using the other ontology. These issues are discussed in more detail in the section on translation.

Knowledge Query and Manipulation Language (KQML)

While it is possible to design an entire communication framework in which all messages take the form of KIF sentences, this would be inefficient. Because of the contextual independence of KIF's semantics, each message would have to include any implicit information about the sender, the receiver, the time of the message, message history, and so forth. The efficiency of communication can be enhanced by providing a linguistic layer in which context is taken into account. This is the function of KQML.

As used in ACL, each KQML *message* is a list of components enclosed in matching parentheses. The first word in the list indicates the type of communication. The subsequent entries are KIF expressions appropriate to that communication, in effect the "arguments."

Intuitively, each message in KQML is one piece of a dialogue between the sender and the receiver, and KQML provides support for a wide variety of such dialogue types.

The expression shown below is the simplest possible KQML dialog. In this case, there is just one message: a simple notification. The sender is conveying the enclosed sentence to the receiver. In general, there is no expectation on the sender's part about what use the receiver will make of this information.

A to B: (tell (> 3 2))

The following dialogue is a little more interesting. In this case, the first message is a request for the receiver to execute the operation of printing a string to its standard i/o stream. The second message tells the sender that the request has been satisfied.

A to B: (perform (print "Hello!" t))
B to A: (reply done)

In the dialogue shown below, the sender is asking the receiver a question in an ask-if message. The receiver then sends the answer to the original sender in a reply message.

A to B: (ask-if (> (size chip1) (size chip2)))
B to A: (reply true)

In the following case, the sender asks the receiver to send it a notification whenever it receives information about the position of an object. The receiver sends it three such sentences, after which the original sender cancels the service.

A to B: (subscribe (position ?x ?r ?c))
B to A: (tell (position chip1 8 10))
B to A: (tell (position chip2 8 46))
B to A: (tell (position chip3 8 64))
A to B: (unsubscribe (position ?x ?r ?c))

In addition to simple notifications, commands, questions, and subscriptions, KQML also contains support for delayed and conditional operations, requests for bids, offers, promises, and so forth.

Software Agents

In the approach to interoperation described here, application programmers write their programs as software agents. Like other agents, a software agent is obliged to communicate in ACL, but it does so in a particularly stylized way:

1. On start up, it initiates an ACL connection to the local facilitator.

2. It supplies the facilitator with a description of its capabilities.

3. It then enters normal operation: it sends the facilitator requests when it is incapable of fulfilling its own needs, and it acts to the best of its abilities to satisfy the facilitator's requests.

A software agent is a special kind of agent in that it surrenders its autonomy to the facilitator. A general agent is not compelled to satisfy the requests of other agents. It can accept them or decline them, or it can negotiate for payment. A software agent does not have this freedom. After registering with its local facilitator and supplying its specification, the software agent is obliged to satisfy the facilitator's requests whenever it can. Of course, this is a good deal in many cases, since the agent gets the facilitator's services in return.

The following subsection describes how software agents specify their capabilities and needs; and the Agent Implementation Strategies subsection discusses various strategies for building them, from writing new programs to dealing with legacy software.

Specifying Agent Capabilities and Needs

In order to provide services to other agents, an agent must communicate its capabilities to the facilitator in ACL. An agent specifies its capabilities by transmitting "handles" facts to its facilitator. For example, an agent capable of answering questions about the dealer of a vendor may transmit the following specification to its facilitator:

    (handles business-agent '(ask-one ,?variables (dealer ,?dealer ,?vendor)))
    (handles business-agent '(ask-all ,?variables (dealer ,?dealer ,?vendor)))

These facts state that agent business-agent is capable of answering queries about a single dealer for a vendor, or all the dealers for a vendor. The actual capability is a quoted KQML expression, such as '(ask-one ,?variables (dealer ,?dealer ,?vendor)) in the first example. This specification is similar to the object interface specifications in CORBA's IDL.

If some other agent A_1 wants to know the dealers of NEC, it may communicate the following request to the facilitator:

    (ask-all ?x (dealer ?x nec))

The facilitator examines its knowledge base and determines that the business-agent can handle the request. The facilitator sends the request to the business-agent, gets the answer, and passes it to A_1. Agent A_1 is completely unaware of the sequence of steps performed in servicing its request.

Capabilities can be more complicated, as in the following conditional specification:

    (<= (handles business-agent '(ask-all ,?variables (dealer ,?dealer ,?vendor))) (=
    ?vendor 'ibm))

This states that the business-agent can answer only queries about the dealers of ibm. The specifications can have arbitrarily complicated preconditions.

An agent specifies its needs by transmitting "interested" facts to its facilitator. For example, the following states that the agent cs-manager is interested in all facts regarding the release of PC-compatible computers.

    (interested cs-manager '(tell (released ,?manufacturer PC ,?model)))

Similar to "handles" statements, "interested" statements can be conditional:

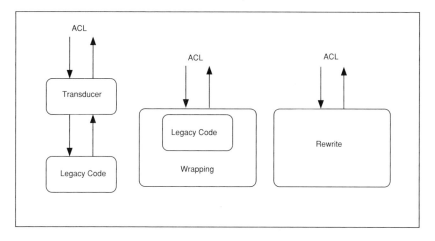

Figure 3. Three approaches to agent implementation.

(< = (interested cs-manager '(tell (released ,?manufacturer PC ,?model))) (member ?manufacturer '(ibm toshiba nec micro-international)))

This states that the cs-manager agent is interested only in the release of PC-compatible computers from IBM, Toshiba, NEC, and Micro-International.
If another agent transmits the following fact to the facilitator:

(tell (released micro-international PC 6500D))

then the facilitator will examine its knowledge base and find that the agent cs-manager is interested in expressions of this form, and it will send the same KQML expression to the cs-manager. We will discuss the specification of agent needs and capabilities from the facilitator's point of view in the Content-Based Routing subsection that follows.

Agent Implementation Strategies

The criterion for agenthood is a behavioral one. A process is a software agent if and only if it acts like one. Any implementation that achieves this behavior is acceptable. Nevertheless, it is natural to ask whether there are any standard strategies for converting legacy programs into software agents. In my work thus far, I have taken different approaches in different cases (figure 3).

One approach is to implement a transducer that mediates between an existing program and the local facilitator. The transducer initiates communication with the local facilitator. It supplies the program's specification to the facilitator. It accepts requests from the facilitator, translates them into the program's native communication language, and passes those messages to the program. It accepts the program's responses, translates them into ACL, and sends the resulting messages to the facilitator.

This approach has the advantage that it requires no knowledge of the program other than its communication behavior. It is therefore especially useful for situations in which the code for the program is unavailable or too delicate to tamper with.

This approach also works for other types of resources, such as files and people. It is a simple matter to write a program to read or modify an existing file with a specialized format and thereby provide access to that file via ACL. Similarly, it is possible to provide a graphical user interface for a person that allows that person to interact with the system in a specialized graphical language, which is then converted into ACL, and vice versa.

A second approach to dealing with legacy software is to implement a wrapper that, in essence, injects code into a program to allow it to communicate in ACL. The wrapper can directly examine the data structures of the program and can modify those data structures. Furthermore, it may be possible to inject calls out of the program into the code so that the program can take advantage of externally available information and services.

This approach has the advantage of greater efficiency than the transduction approach, since there is less serial communication. It also works for cases where there is no interprocess communication ability in the original program.

The third and most drastic approach to dealing with legacy software is to rewrite the original program. The advantage of this approach is that it may be possible to enhance its efficiency or capability beyond what would be possible in either the transduction or wrapping approaches.

The best examples of this approach come from the engineering domain. Many traditional engineering programs are designed to work to completion before communicating with other programs. Recent work in concurrent engineering suggests that there is much advantage to be gained by writing programs that communicate partial results in the course of their activity and that accept partial results and feedback from other programs. By communicating a partial result and getting early feedback, a program can save work on what may turn out to be an unworkable alternative. The expressiveness of ACL allows programs to express partial information. However, many existing programs are unable to take advantage of this expressiveness and the concurrent engineering strategy. In these cases, rewriting the programs is the only alternative.

Facilitators

Facilitators are the system-provided agents that coordinate the activities of the other agents in the federation architecture. Each facilitator keeps the other facilitators in the network informed of which agents are connected to it and what facts have been communicated by them.

Facilitators provide a collection of services, including:

- *White Pages:* finding the identity of agents by name, for example, "What agents are connected?" or "Is agent x connected?"
- *Yellow Pages:* finding the identity of agents capable of performing a task. For example, "What agents are capable of answering the query x?"
- *Direct Communication:* sending a message to a specific agent.
- *Content-based Routing:* the facilitator is given the responsibility of handling a request. It makes use of the specifications and other information provided by the agents to do this, thereby giving the illusion that it is the sole provider of all services.
- *Translation:* agents may use different vocabulary. In order to interoperate, the facilitator may have to translate the vocabulary of one agent into the vocabulary of another.
- *Problem Decomposition:* handling a complex request may require breaking it into sub-problems, getting the answers to the sub-problems, and then combining these answers to obtain the answer to the original request. As in content-based routing, the facilitator makes use of the specifications and application-specific information provided by the agents to accomplish this.
- *Monitoring:* when an agent informs the facilitator of a need, the facilitator monitors its knowledge to determine if the need can be satisfied. For example, an agent may specify the need "I am interested in facts about the position of chips in design x."

The responsibility of the facilitator on each machine is to assist the agents running on that machine to collaborate with each other and, indirectly, with the agents running on other machines. In this section, I describe the communication services a facilitator needs to provide, and I discuss ways in which the facilitator can help agents set up direct communication amongst themselves in order to eliminate the overhead inherent in communicating through the facilitator. I give an overview of the reasoning program in the next subsection, followed by illustrations of how it is used in content-based routing, translation, synthesis, buffering, matchmaking, and connectivity.

Overview of the Implementation

The top-level program of the facilitator is a loop that accepts messages from the agents and facilitators to which it is connected. On receipt of a message, it passes the message to its message handler and goes back to listening for additional messages.

In handling a message, the message handler uses an automated reasoning program on its knowledge base of specification information. Our reasoning program is a variation on the method used in Prolog. There are two primary differences. First of all, it handles KIF syntax rather than Prolog syntax. Secondly, unlike Prolog, it is sound and complete for full first-order predicate calculus: it is based on the model elimination rule of inference, the unification algorithm does an occurcheck, the restriction to Horn clauses is removed, and the search is done in iterative deepening fashion.

A full description of the program is beyond the scope of this paper. However, a simple example should convey sufficient detail for readers to follow the examples in the following subsections.

Consider a database with the sentences shown below. The predicate p holds of three pairs of objects—a and a, a and b, and b and c. The predicate q is also true of three pairs of objects—a and b, b and c, and c and d. The predicate r is defined to be true of two objects if there is an intermediate object such that p is true of the former object and this intermediate object and q is true of the intermediate object and the latter object.

(p a a)
(p a b)
(p b c)

(q a b)
(q b c)
(q c d)

(< = (r ?x ?z)
(p ?x ?y)
(q ?y ?z))

Suppose now, we wanted to know whether r was true of a and c. The trace shown below shows how the reasoning program derives this result.

Call: (r a c)?
Call: (and (p a ?y) (q ?y c))
Call: (p a ?y)
Exit: (p a a)
Call: (q a c)
Fail: (q a c)
Call: (p a ?y)
Exit: (p a b)
Call: (q b c)
Exit: (q b c)
Call: (and (p a b) (q b c))
Exit:(r a c)

The desired conclusion (r a c) unifies with the conclusion of the last sentence in the knowledge base with the variable ?x bound to a and the variable ?z bound to c. The program thus reduces the original question to the subquestion on the second line—in effect the question of whether there is a binding for the variable ?y for which the conjunction is true. In order for this to be true, there must be a binding for ?y for which (p a ?y) is true. The program first finds (p a a) and binds ?y to a. It then tries to prove (q a c). Unfortunately, this fails. So, the program backs up and tries to find another way to satisfy (p a ?y). In so doing, it discovers the fact (p a b) and binds ?y to b. Again it tries to prove (q b c) and in this case succeeds. Since both conjuncts are proved, the conjunction is proved; and, since the conjunction is proved, the original sentence is proved.

This program is both sound and complete. In other words, if the program manages to prove a result, then that result must logically follow from the sentences in the database; and if a conclusion logically follows from the database, the method will prove it.

Unfortunately, as with all sound and complete reasoning methods for the full first-order predicate calculus, the method does not necessarily terminate. If a conclusion does not follow from the database, the method may spend forever trying to prove it. While this situation does not often arise, it is a real danger for a piece of system code.

In order to deal with this difficulty, the facilitator uses a preprocessor to screen sentences before they are added to the facilitator's database. The facilitator adds a sentence if and only if it can prove that doing so will not cause an infinite loop.

Note that the problem of making this determination is itself undecidable; so it is not possible to know in all cases whether a sentence will cause an infinite loop. Our facilitator circumvents this difficulty by taking a conservative approach to proving the "safeness" of a set of sentences: it uses a variety of tests to determine whether an inference will terminate. If a database passes the tests, termination is assured. If not, the database may or may not be safe. Fortunately, the tests are cheap, and they cover a very large fraction of the kinds of sentences that programmers writing communication specifications will need.

One example of a test is the requirement that a database be function-free. If there are no function constants, then the database reduces, in effect, to propositional calculus, for which there is a known decision procedure. The sentence shown below would not pass this test, because of the embedded function f, and it is easy to see how the method described above would enter an infinite loop in using this sentence to prove a simple conclusion like (p a).

(<= (p ?x) (p (f ?x)))

Even if a database contains functions, it is possible to show termination provided that the database contains no recursion. For example, the first sentence below would pass this test, whereas the second would fail, since p is dependent on p

+ (<= (r ?x ?z) (p ?x ?y) (q ?y ?z))
x (<= (p ?x ?z) (p ?x ?y) (p ?y ?z))

Even if the database has recursion and functions, it is possible to show termination provided that every recursive call diminishes the complexity of its arguments. For example, the following database passes this test, because the recursive calls to r all concern a subpart of the original expression.

```
(r 0)
(<= (r (listof ?x ?y)) (r ?x) (r ?y))
```

Of course, other tests are possible. The problem of provable termination has been studied extensively in the database and automated reasoning communities. With additional work, more tests can be employed, thus enlarging the set of sentences the facilitator can handle.

Content-Based Routing

From an application programmer's point of view, communication in a federation architecture is undirected: application programs are free to send messages without specifying destinations for those messages. It is the job of the facilitator to determine appropriate recipients for undirected messages and to forward the messages accordingly. In so doing, the facilitator functions as a broker for the services provided by the servers in its community.

In order to see how this is done, consider how the facilitator handles the message shown below. It is being told via one particular encoding that the object named chip1 is indeed a computer chip.

```
(tell '(member chip1 chips))
```

The facilitator is connected to three agents, named layout, domain-editor, and board-editor. These agents have given the facilitator the specification information shown below.

```
(interested layout '(tell (position ,?x ,?r ,?c)))

(<= (interested domain-editor '(tell (member ,?x ,?y)))
(symbol ?x)
(symbol ?y))

(<= (interested board-editor '(tell (= (,?f ,?x) ,?y)))
(member ?f (setof 'row 'col))
(symbol ?x)
(natural-number ?y))
```

In order to determine which agents are interested in this message, the facilitator forms the query (interested ?a '(tell (member chip1 chips))) and uses its reasoning program to find a binding for variable ?a. In this case, there is just one, the domain-editor. Consequently, the facilitator sends the message to this agent.

```
(tell '(member chip1 chips))
```

Note that in making the determination that the domain-editor agent is interested, the facilitator must not only match the pattern in the first line of its specification but also verify properties of the bindings of the variables, in particular that they are both symbols.

Translation

Agents in a system may interoperate even when they are not created using the same programming language or development framework. Like programming "objects," agents define message-based interfaces that are independent of their respective internal data structures and algorithms. The translation capability of facilitators extends this significantly by making interoperation independent of the agent interface (the KQML expressions the agent can handle). An agent can be replaced with a more capable implementation with a different interface. By providing translation rules to map the old interface to the new, the agent can provide its old functionality in addition to the new and improved one.

There are two parts to the translation process: *vocabulary* and *logical*. The need for *vocabulary translation* arises because of differences between the abstractions inherent in the implementations of different agents. For example, one agent may work with rectangular coordinates, while another works with polar coordinates.

The need for *logical translation* arises because of limits imposed by agents on the logical structure of messages in which they are interested. Some agents are capable of accepting any message in ACL. Other agents are more selective. For example, a Prolog agent might restrict its interest to Horn Clauses; a relational database might restrict its interests to ground atomic formulas.

As an example of translation, consider a situation in which the facilitator receives the message shown below. As before, it is being told via one particular encoding that the position of a particular chip on a printed circuit board is located in the tenth row and sixteenth column.

(tell '(= (pos chip1) (point 10 16)))

The facilitator's agent catalog mentions that an agent named layout is interested in receiving messages of the form (position **), where ** and ** are natural numbers.

(<= (interested kb (tell '(position ?x ?m ?n))
(natural-number ?m)
(natural-number ?n))

Since the incoming sentence does not have the form specified in this interest, content-based routing alone would not cause any message to be sent to layout. However, let us suppose that the facilitator also has information relating pos and position, as in the following sentence:

(<=> (= (pos ?x) (point ?row ?col))
(position ?x ?row ?col))

Using this sentence together with the sentence (= (pos chip1) (point 10 16)), the facilitator is able to deduce the sentence (position chip1 10 16). In other words, it can translate from one form to the other. It then checks whether any agent is interested in this information, finds layout, and sends the message shown below.

(tell '(position chip1 10 16))

An important issue in translation is knowing when to make the effort. When the facilitator receives a message, how does it know that translation will lead to a new message that is of interest to one of its agents without doing the translation? Randomly generating conclusions from the information in the message is impractically expensive. A better alternative is derivation of conclusions after filtering with the results of some connectivity analysis. Given a set of interests and a data base of axioms relating differing vocabularies, it is possible to distinguish lines of reasoning that lead to potentially interesting conclusions from those lines that cannot possibly lead to interesting conclusions. This analysis is efficient and needs to be done just once, before the facilitator receives any messages.

Synthesis

The example of translation in the preceding subsection is particularly simple. One incoming message leads to one outgoing message. In some cases, an incoming message can be handled only by sending multiple messages to multiple agents. In order to handle such messages, the facilitator must be able to synthesize a multi-step communication plan to handle the incoming message.

As an example of this type of message handling, consider the message shown below. As in the last example, the facilitator is being told the position of a particular chip.

(tell '(= (pos chip1) (point 10 16)))

One difference in this example is that the facilitator's agent catalog contains the information shown below, documenting an agent interested in row information and col information but not pos information.

(<= (interested board-editor (tell '(= (,?f ,?x) ,?y)))
(member ?f (setof 'row 'col))
(symbol ?x)
(natural-number ?y))

As before, let us assume that the facilitator's library contains a sentence relating the two vocabularies.

(<=> (= (pos ?x) (point ?row ?col))
(and (= (row ?x) ?row) (= (col ?x) ?col)))

In this case, there are two conclusions from the original sentence. The facilitator discovers these two conclusions and sends them on to the board-editor agent.

(tell '(= (row chip1) 100))
(tell '(= (col chip1) 160))

Note that if the incoming message had been an ask-if message, the facilitator would have been able to reduce this to two questions: one about the row of the chip and another about the column. In this case, it would first send the row question to board-editor; then, on getting an answer, it would send in the col question; and, on getting that answer, would be able to answer the original question.

Buffering

Another important issue in translation is buffering. In some cases, it may not be possible to transform a message into a form that is acceptable to any agent, yet it is possible to merge the information from two or more messages to form an acceptable result.

As an example of how the facilitator handles these cases, consider the incoming message shown below. In this case, the incoming information involves the row of a chip. No col information is provided.

(tell '(= (row chip1) 10))

The facilitator's agent catalog contains information about an agent layout that is interested in pos information.

(interested frame-editor '(tell (= (pos ,?x) ,?y))

The facilitator's library contains information relating row and col to pos, just as before.

(<=> (= (pos ?x) (point ?row ?col))
(and (= (row ?x) ?row) (= (col ?x) ?col)))

Unfortunately, in this case, it is unable to complete its translation since there is no col information. But all is not lost. From looking at its agent catalog and library, the facilitator knows that sentences involving row can lead to sentences involving pos; and it knows that there are agents interested in pos sentences. Also from an examination of its agent catalog, it can conclude that there are no agents that handle requests to store row sentences. Given these two conditions, the facilitator decides to save the incoming fact in its information buffer for potential further use.

(= (row chip1) 10)

Now suppose that, at some point after this, the facilitator receives the missing col information in a message like the following:

(tell '(= (col chip1) 16))

Putting this information together with the preceding fact, it can conclude a pos sentence; and it sends the derived sentence onto the layout agent.

(tell '(= (pos chip1) (point 10 16)))

Note the importance here of knowing when to buffer information and when to discard. If the facilitator were to save every piece of information it receives, it would quickly run out of space. By saving only those pieces of information that are of potential use and that are not being stored elsewhere, the amount of information that must be saved remains manageable.

Matchmaking

As described above, content-based routing, translation, and buffering are all performed by the facilitator. This is necessary for maximum flexibility, thus allowing for agent substitutions, changing interest lists, system reconfiguration, and so forth. However, performing these services at runtime can be needlessly costly from a computational point of view.

As an example of this, consider the case of two agents running on a single machine, one a database program and the other a database editor. Whenever the user of the editor makes a change, the results must be propagated to the database program. The editor must format an appropriate message; the facilitator must route and translate the message; and the database program must unformat the message in order to make the appropriate changes to the database.

Fortunately, under certain circumstances, it is possible to eliminate this overhead by moving portions of the computation to server initialization time. Suppose, in the example, that we know that a database program and editor are the only two agents interested in the information they are exchanging (at least for the time being). In this case, the facilitator can request that the agents implement their communication via remote procedure call, giving each the address of the other and taking itself out of the picture.

Of course, in order to preserve flexibility, it is essential that the facilitator retain the ability to request that the agents terminate or modify such connections in the event that the environment changes in an incompatible way. Although this check carries with it a certain amount of overhead, the advantage of this approach is that it eliminates the overhead associated with the transmission of messages; instead, the overhead is paid only when there are changes in system configuration, agents' interests, and so forth.

Connectivity

Our final facilitator-related topic concerns the issue of connectivity between facilitators and agents and between facilitators and other facilitators.

Since remote communication is more expensive than local communication, there is good reason for having at least one facilitator on each machine. Otherwise, in order for a program to communicate with another program on the *same* machine, it would have to send a message to a *remote* machine!

On the other hand, there is really no reason to have more than one facilitator per machine. Anything that can be handled by two facilitators can be handled by one facilitator. There can be no computational advantage, unless the two facilitators are running on different processors with the same machine.

What about the connection of agents to facilitators? While it is possible to consider a situation in which every agent is connected to every facilitator, this is impractical in settings, like the Internet, where there are likely to be many agents and many facilitators. For this reason, in federation architecture, I as-

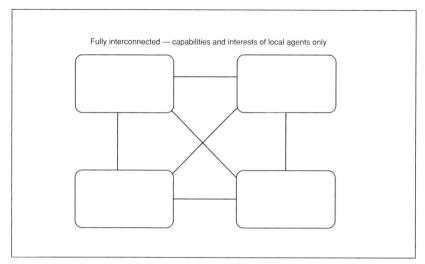

Figure 4. Full interconnection architecture.

sume that every agent is connected to one and only one facilitator.

Finally, there is the issue of inter-facilitator connectivity. Here, there are multiple choices, each with advantages and disadvantages.

The simplest sort of architecture is full interconnection, as suggested by figure 4. In this architecture, every facilitator is connected to every other facilitator. Since these connections are logical connections and not physical wires, this sort of architecture is feasible, though not necessarily desirable.

The disadvantage of this approach is the cost of interconnectivity. On a large network, like the Internet, the number of facilitators could be very large, and under this scheme every one would have to know about every other one.

An alternative that alleviates this difficulty is a spanning tree architecture, as suggested in figure 5. In this approach, facilitators are connected in such a way that there is a path from every facilitator to every other facilitator but there are no loops

This approach is good because it allows connectivity without the cost of numerous connections. It has the disadvantage of being susceptible to failure when one of the nodes goes down, as this can break the network into disconnected components.

Finally, there is the general connectivity architecture. In this architecture, every facilitator is connected at least indirectly with every other facilitator, as in the spanning tree architecture, but there is no restriction that the connectivity be loop free.

Like the spanning tree architecture, a general connectivity architecture can be more economical of connections than a full interconnection architecture. It

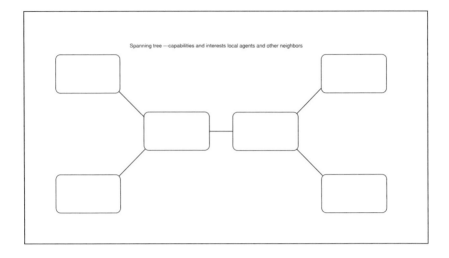

Figure 5. Spanning tree architecture.

has the added advantage that a failure of a node or connection does not necessarily disconnect different segments of the network.

Unfortunately, it has the disadvantage of possible loops. If one facilitator sends a message to a second and the second passes it on to a third and the third passes it on again, it might end up back where it started.

Fortunately, loops of this sort can be caught by adding sender information to each message (as in many mail protocols, for example) and checking for this information when a message is received. It can also be handled by having each facilitator save information about which messages it has sent. Either way the loops can be broken. The programming cost is a little higher, but the efficiency and reliability of the approach recommend it highly.

Another complexity in the spanning tree and general connectivity architectures stems from the need of facilitators to merge the interests of other facilitators in with those of their own agents in complicated ways. In a full connectivity architecture, each facilitator simply aggregates the interests of its local agents and passes those interests on to all other facilitators. Each facilitator uses this information to handle incoming requests. In the other two architectures, the interests passed on to neighbors are more complicated. A facilitator connected to two other facilitators must blend the interests of its first neighbor into the interests of its local agents in the specification it sends to its second neighbor; and it must blend the interests of its second neighbor into the interests of its local agents in the specification it sends to its first neighbor.

Example

This section presents a simple example of the federation architecture. Instead of focusing on the details, I present a broad picture of the types of software inter-operation made possible.

First, a brief overview of the scenario. There is a computer systems manager in a publishing company who wants to upgrade the computers used by the sales staff to portable Pentium-based machines. The computer systems manager informs the facilitator of his interest in Pentium laptops. Sometime later, the computer product agent notifies the facilitator of the availability of a Pentium laptop, and this information is passed on to the computer systems manager by the facilitator. The computer systems manager asks the meeting scheduling agent to set up a joint meeting with the managers of the sales and finance departments to discuss the purchase of the new machines. The meeting scheduling agent gets the available times from the calendar agents for the sales and finance managers to schedule a meeting. We fill in some of the details below.

The computer systems manager sits at his terminal with a graphical user interface (GUI) and tells the facilitator that he is interested in being told of the availability of PC-compatible Pentium laptops. The GUI commands are translated into the following KIF fact, which is transmitted to the facilitator:

```
(<= interested cs-manager '(tell (available ,?manufacturer ,?model-name)))
    (= (denotation ?model-name) ?model) ; the model from its name
    (computer-family ?model PC)
    (laptop ?model))
```

There is a product agent that can answer queries about the computer family a product belongs to (e.g., PC, Apple) and which computers are laptops. It has specified its capabilities by transmitting the following facts to the facilitator:

```
(handles product-agent
    '(ask-one ,?variables (computer-family ,?computer ,?family)))
(handles product-agent '(ask-if (laptop ,?computer)))
```

Whenever a new piece of information is added to the product agent's knowledge base it notifies the facilitator of the fact. A new Micro-International 3600D computer is announced, and information about it is added to the knowledge base of the product agent. The product agent communicates the following KQML message to the facilitator:

```
(tell (available Micro-International 3600D))
```

The facilitator performs inference to see if any agent is interested in this fact. It finds that the cs-manager agent is interested, but only if the computer family of the 3600D is PC, and if the 3600D is a laptop. The facilitator cannot answer these questions locally. However, it forwards the queries to the product-agent, who can answer them. The product-agent responds positively to both queries, and the cs-manager is notified of the previous availability of the 3600D. A message indicating this pops up on the GUI of the computer systems manager.

The computer systems manager uses his GUI to ask the facilitator to schedule a one hour meeting with the managers of the sales and finance groups during the week of December 12th to 16th. The GUI transmits the following KQML message to the facilitator:

(schedule-meeting (listof sales-manager finance-manager)
    (interval 12-12-94 12-16-94)
    60)

There is a scheduling agent that can schedule meetings. It previously transmitted the following fact to the facilitator:

(handles scheduler '(schedule-meeting ,?people ,?interval ,?meeting-duration))

The original meeting request is passed on to the scheduler agent by the facilitator. The scheduler is not able to schedule a meeting directly, since it does not have access to the calendars of the sales and finance managers. Therefore, the scheduling agent passes on the following query to the facilitator:

(ask-one ?x (calendar sales-manager (interval 12-12-94 12-16-94) ?x))

There is a datebook agent for the sales manager that records his calendar. It had previously notified the facilitator of its capability with the following fact:

(handles sales-manager-datebook
    '(ask-one ,?x (calendar sales-manager ,?interval ,?x)))

Similarly, there is a synchronize agent that can answer queries regarding the calendar of the finance manager.

The facilitator passes on the two queries of the scheduler to the sales-manager-datebook agent and the finance-manager-synchronize agent. The calendars returned by these agents are sent to the scheduling agent, who schedules the earliest possible meeting. The first available meeting time is transmitted to the facilitator, who finally forwards the results to the cs-manager.

This example illustrates a collection of points: anonymous interaction of agents through the use of a facilitator, interoperation of a variety of program types, different types of agent implementations incorporating legacy code, and the dual nature of agents as both clients and servers.

Some programs in the example are based on legacy code, such as the product agent which uses an SQL database for recording data about computers, the datebook calendar program, and the synchronize calendar program. Other programs are written from scratch, such as the scheduling agent that computes the intersection of available times for a group of meeting participants.

Different techniques are used to incorporate legacy code. The product agent uses an SQL database for recording facts, and it is "agentified" by providing a transducer to convert ACL into SQL commands and vice versa. The datebook calendar program is agentified by a wrapper: the source code is modified to support ACL communication. The meeting scheduling component of the datebook and synchronize programs was rewritten in the scheduling agent to support a more general notion of time.

Finally, the example also illustrates the dual nature of agents as both providers and consumers of services. For example, the meeting scheduling agent can handle a request to schedule a meeting. However, in order to service this request, the scheduling agent must ask the facilitator for the calendars of the participants.

Applications

In this section, I describe some experiments designed to assess the power and limitations of the knowledge-sharing approach to software interoperation. While knowledge-sharing technology has potential value in many different application areas, I chose to concentrate my experiments on two particular application areas: computer-aided engineering and heterogeneous distributed information access.

Designworld

Designworld is the result of the first integration effort. In its current form, Designworld is an automated prototyping system for small scale electronic circuits built from standard parts (TTL chips and connectors on prototyping boards). The design for a product is entered into the system via a multimedia design workstation; the product is built by a dedicated robotic cell—in effect, a microfactory. If necessary, the product, once built, can be returned to the system for diagnosis and repair.

The Designworld system consists of eighteen processes on six different machines (two Macintoshes and four HP workstations). Each of the eighteen programs is implemented as a distinct agent that communicates with its peers via messages in ACL. Any one of these programs can be replaced by an ACL-equivalent program without changing the functionality of the system as a whole. Any agent can be moved to a different machine (with equivalent capabilities). Any agent can be deleted and the system will continue to run correctly, albeit with reduced functionality.

In the development of the system, there was virtually no communication between programmers, except at the very end; the discussion, when it occurred, was limited to negotiation on message vocabulary; and no reimplementation took place as a result of this negotiation (since the mediation of all disagreements was handled by the system's facilitator). The Designworld system is a good example of software interoperation through knowledge-sharing technology. However, as an experiment in interoperation, it is somewhat suspect since all of the software was developed by a single team.

PACT

Our second application of the technology deals with this experimental weakness. PACT (the Palo Alto Collaborative Testbed) is a multi-institutional testbed for research in the integration of engineering tools. PACT differs from Designworld in its emphasis on the integration of previously developed tools and tools developed by multiple teams without the benefit of institutionally enforced coordination.

The system in its current form incorporates four previously existing systems (i.e., Designworld, NVisage, NextCut, and DME) and includes several commercial products (e.g., Mathematica). Overall, there are thirty processes on eighteen different machines.

We have demonstrated the interoperation of the components of PACT by applying the system to the design of a particular electromechanical device, viz. an electronically controlled robotic manipulator. The various parts of the manipulator are modeled by the different systems participating in PACT. There is a simulation of the manipulator system as a whole based on coordinated piecemeal simulations performed by the participating systems. There is an example of a design change and effective communication of this change among the various systems.

Infomaster

Infomaster is a virtual information system that allows users to access a variety of heterogeneous distributed information sources from multiple perspectives. Infomaster accesses information stored in databases or knowledge bases using ACL, and uses facilitators to decompose, route, and translate requests, and assemble, route and translate responses.

The first information available through Infomaster concerns rental housing in the San Francisco Bay area. Every morning, an agent extracts the latest classified advertisements for rental housing from the World Wide Web sites of several newspapers. These are then separated into individual advertisements, parsed into a structured format, and loaded into a KIF knowledge base. This knowledge base has advertised that it can handle queries for rental housing. Once users have specified their query, they may determine how many rental advertisements satisfy their requirements and further constrain query in an iterative fashion. In the first day of availability for new Stanford students, Infomaster handled 3,000 queries. Support for additional sources and kinds of information are planned.

Issues and Summary

In order to provide adequate power and scalability for agent-based capabilities, current implementations of facilitators take advantage of automated reasoning technology developed by the artificial intelligence and database research communities. Powerful search control techniques are used to enhance normal message-processing performance, and automatic generation of message routing programs and pairwise translators is used for cases requiring greater efficiency.

Even with these enhancements, these implementations consume more time in the worst case than simpler processing techniques, like the pattern matching method used in BMS. This is sometimes acceptable, especially when the alternative is no interoperation at all. However, in time-critical applications such as machine control, the extra cost can be prohibitive.

Scalability is an important concern in the design of the federation architecture. There are three important issues: consistent vocabulary, inference cost, and knowledge base size. Interoperation in the federation architecture relies on the assumption that all agents agree to a shared ontology. However in a large system, multiple overlapping ontologies must be supported. Ideally, specialized ontologies can be built using existing ontologies. The ontologies are related in a directed graph, where each ontology can incorporate some or all of the terms and definitions of its parent ontologies, while overriding those that it must define differently.

The second scalability issue concerns inference cost. As the number of agents increases, the number of facts about agent capabilities, needs, and application-specific facts increases. However, the performance of the system should not degrade because of irrelevant facts. Ontologies help address some of the complexity. All requests are relative to an ontology, and the graph structure of the ontologies partitions the knowledge into smaller relevant sets. In addition, the facilitator controls the inference process by selecting the cheapest agent to handle a request and by avoiding infinite loops. Additionally, it is possible to guarantee desirable performance properties by placing restrictions on the rules a facilitator may accept. For example, if all facts are ground atomics (as in CORBA's IDL specification), then inference is reduced to database lookup, and the cost is logarithmic in the number of facts. If the facts are stratified (i.e., no recursive definitions), then it is possible to compute time bounds on inference. It is important to note that inference is expensive only with complex rules, and it is possible to enforce a policy of accepting only simple rules.

The third scalability issue deals with managing the size of the knowledge base. There are two aspects to this: application-specific facts, and meta-level specifications. Facilitators run continuously, and it is not possible to put a bound on the number of application-specific facts it may be told. The maintainer of each facilitator can enforce a policy for deciding what information to record. For example, a facilitator may follow the policy of recording only ground atomic facts, or it may record only facts in a given ontology. There may be a limit to the number of facts that a facilitator records, and it may discard some facts when a space limit is reached. Similarly, it is not possible to put a bound on the total number of agents in the system. A system can have a network of facilitators, with different agents connected to different facilitators. Each facilitator must be capable of transmitting a request to any agent that can handle it, independent of its location. To minimize the number of capability and interest specification facts, each facilitator summarizes the capabilities and interests of its directly connected agents, and passes on this summary to its neighboring facilitators. The summary reduces the number of facts and may involve generalization. For example, if one directly-connected agent can answer questions about the dealers of Apple computers and another directly-connected agent can answer questions about IBM dealers, then the facilitator may summarize the answers by informing its neighboring facilitators that it can answer questions about the dealers of all personal computers. There is a space-time tradeoff here: fewer less-precise specifications vs. a larger number of more precise specifications. It is acceptable for an agent to handle a request by indicating that it cannot answer it, for example if its specifications are too general.

In my treatment so far, I have assumed that there is sufficient common interest among the agents that they will frequently volunteer to help each other and receive no direct reward for their labor. As the Internet becomes increasingly commercialized, I envision a world where agents act on behalf of their creators to make a profit. Agents will seek payments for services provided and may negotiate with each other to maximize their expected utility, which might be measured in a form of electronic currency. These problems mark the intersection of economics and distributed artificial intelligence (DAI). Several researchers in DAI are using tools developed in economics and game theory to evaluate multi-agent interactions. I am currently examining extensions to the federation architecture to incorporate some of these capabilities.

I have ignored several other key problems in my presentation, such as security, crash recovery, inconsistencies in program specifications, and so forth. Although I have partial solutions to these problems, further work is needed.

There are many applications of knowledge-sharing technology in offline software integration that I have not discussed, such as in software documentation, retrieval of components from software libraries based on this documentation, and software verification.

In this chapter, I have taken a brief look at how knowledge-sharing technology can be used to promote software interoperation. My long-range vision is one in which any system (software or hardware) can interoperate with any other system, without the intervention of human users or their programmers. Although many problems remain to be solved, I believe that the introduction of knowledge-sharing technology will be an important step toward achieving this vision.

Acknowledgments

Many people contributed to the ideas presented in this chapter. The most significant contributions came from participants in the ARPA Knowledge Sharing Initiative, the Designworld Project, the PACT Project, and the ABSE Project, most notably Mark Cutkosky, Richard Fikes, Rich Fritzson, Mark Gisi, Tom Gruber, Jon Gustafson, Pierre Huyn, Marta Kosarchyn, Reed Letsinger, Don MacKay, Ofer Matan, Bill Mark, Greg Olsen, Vishal Sikka, Marty Tenenbaum, and Jay Weber. This chapter is as much theirs as it is mine. Support for the authors' work was provided by Hewlett-Packard under grant number 172S338 and by the Office of Naval Research under contract number N00014-90-J-1533.

Bibliography

Cutkosky, M.; Englemore, R.; Fikes, R.; Gruber, T. R.; Genesereth, M.; Mark, W.; Tenenbaum, J. M.; and Weber, J. 1993. PACT: An Experiment in Integrating Concurrent Engineering Systems. *IEEE Computer* 26(1): 28–37.

Finin, T.; Weber, J.; Wiederhold, G.; Genesereth, M.; Fritzson, R.; McGuire, J.; McKay, D.; Shapiro, S.; Pelavin, R.; and Beck, C. 1992. Specification of the KQML Agent Communication Language (Official Document of the DARPA Knowledge Sharing Initiative's External Interfaces Working Group), Technical Report 92-04, Enterprise Integration Technologies, Inc., Menlo Park, California.

Genesereth, M. R. 1991a. An Agent-Based Approach to Software Interoperation, Logic-91-6, Department of Computer Science, Stanford University.

Genesereth, M. R. 1991b. DESIGNWORLD. In Proceedings of the IEEE Conference on Robotics and Automation, 2-785–2-788. Washington, D.C.: IEEE Computer Society.

Genesereth, M. R., and Fikes, R. 1992. Knowledge Interchange Format Version 3.0 Reference Manual, Logic Group Report, Logic-92-1, Department of Computer Science, Stanford University.

Gruber, T. R. 1993. A Translation Approach to Portable Ontology Specification. *Knowledge Acquisition* 5(2): 199–220.

Gruber, T. R. 1992. ONTOLINGUA: A Mechanism to Support Portable Ontologies, Version 3.0, Stanford Knowledge Systems Laboratory Technical Report, KSL 91-66, Department of Computer Science, Stanford University.

Neches, R.; Fikes, R.; Finin, T.; Gruber, T.; Patil, R.; Senator, T.; and Swartout, W. R. 1991. Enabling Technology for Knowledge Sharing. *AI Magazine* 12(3): 36–56.

CHAPTER 16

Agents for Information Gathering

Craig A. Knoblock & José Luis Ambite

With the growing number of information sources available, the problem of how to combine distributed, heterogeneous information sources becomes more and more critical. The available information sources include traditional databases, flat files, knowledge bases, programs, etc. Traditional approaches to building distributed or federated systems do not scale well to the large, diverse, and growing number of information sources. Recent Internet systems such as World Wide Web browsers allow users to search through large numbers of information sources but provide very limited capabilities for locating, combining, processing, and organizing information.

A promising approach to this problem is to provide access to the large number of information sources by organizing them into a network of *information agents* (Papazoglou, Laufmann, and Sellis 1992). The goal of each agent is to provide information and expertise on a specific topic by drawing on relevant information from other information agents. To build such a network, we need an architecture for a single agent that can be instantiated to provide multiple agents. We will base our design on our previous work on SIMS (Arens, Knoblock, and Shen 1995; Knoblock, Arens, and Hsu 1994; Arens et al. 1993), an information mediator that provides access to heterogeneous data and knowledge bases.

This chapter focuses on the design of an individual (SIMS) agent and discusses the issues that arise in using this design to build a network of information-gathering agents. In the Agent Organization Section, we present an approach to organizing a group of information agents. Then, in the next four sections , we present the design of the individual agents. The Knowledge of an Agent section describes how the knowledge of an agent is represented as a set of interrelated models. The Communication Language and Protocol section describes how the agents exchange queries and data with one another. The Query Processing section describes how information requests are flexibly and efficiently processed. The Learning section describes how an agent learns about the other agents in order to improve its accuracy and performance over time. The final two sections describe closely related work in this area and conclude with a discussion of the current status and the work that remains to be done.

Agent Organization

In order to effectively use the many heterogeneous information sources available in large computer networks, such as the Internet, we need some form of organization. The concept of an agent that provides expertise on a specific topic, by drawing on relevant information from a variety of sources, offers the basic building block. We believe that agents will be developed to serve the information needs of users in particular domains. More complex agents that deal with wider and/or deeper areas of knowledge will appear in an evolutionary fashion, driven by the market forces of applications that can benefit from using them.

Similar to the way current information sources are independently constructed, information agents can be developed and maintained separately. They will draw on other information agents and data repositories to provide a new information source that others can build upon in turn. Each information agent is another information source, but provides an abstraction of the many information sources available. An existing database or program can be turned into a simple information agent by building the appropriate interface code, called a *wrapper*, that will allow it to conform to the conventions of the organization. Note that only one such wrapper would need to be built for any given type of information source (e.g., relational database, object-oriented database, flat file, etc.). The advantage of this approach is that it greatly simplifies the individual agents since they need to handle only one underlying language. This arrangement makes it possible scale the network into many agents with access to many different types of information sources.

Some agents will answer queries addressed to them, but will not actively originate requests for information to others; we will refer to these as data repositories. Usually, these agents will correspond to databases, which are systems specially designed to store a large amount of information but in which the expressive power of their data description languages and their reasoning abilities have been traded off for efficiency. In the rest of the chapter, we will use the term "data repository" when we want to emphasize such behavior; otherwise we will use the terms "information agent" or "information source" (interchangeably).

Figure 1 shows an example network of information agents that will be used throughout the chapter to explain different parts of the system. The application domain of interest is logistics planning. In order to perform its task, this agent needs to obtain information on different topics, such as transportation capabilities, weather conditions and geographic data. The other agents also integrate a number of sources of information that are relevant to their domain of expertise.

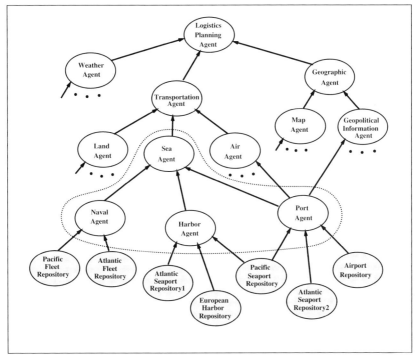

Figure 1. Network of information-gathering agents.

For example, the *Sea_Agent* combines assets data from the *Naval_Agent* (such as ships from different fleets), harbor data from the *Harbor_Agent* and the *Port_Agent* (such as storage space or cranes in harbors, channels, etc., information that has been obtained, in turn, from repositories of different geographical areas). These four agents (circled by the dotted line in the figure) will be examined in greater detail in the following sections.

There are several points to note about this network that relate to the autonomy of the agents. First, each agent may choose to integrate only those parts of the ontologies of its information sources necessary for the task that it is designed for. For example, the *Transportation_Agent* might have a fairly complete integration of the *Sea, Land,* and *Air* agents, while the *Logistics_Planning_Agent* might draw on only some parts of the knowledge of the *Weather* and *Geographic* agents. Second, we may need to build new agents if we cannot find an existing one that contains all the information needed. For example, if the *Geographic_Agent* did not include some particular geopolitical facts required by the *Logistics_Planning_Agent,* the latter could access directly the *Geopolitical_Information_Agent.* However, if much of the information was not represented, an alternative geographic agent would need to be constructed (and linked). Third, the network forms a directed acyclic graph, not a tree, because a particular agent may provide information to several others that focus on different aspects of its expertise (like the *Port_Agent,* that is accessed by the *Geopolitical, Air,* and *Sea* agents). Nevertheless, cycles should be avoided; otherwise a query may loop end-lessly without finding some agent that can actually answer it. In summary, in spite of the complexity introduced by respecting the autonomy of the agents in the organization, the fact that individual agents can be independently built and maintained makes the system flexible enough to scale to large numbers of infor-mation sources and adaptable to the needs of new applications.

In order to build a network of specialized information agents, we need an ar-chitecture for a single agent that can be instantiated to provide multiple agents. In previous work we developed an information server, called SIMS, which pro-vides access to heterogeneous data and knowledge bases (Arens et al. 1993). We use the Loom Interface Manager (LIM) (Pastor, McKay, and Finin 1992) as a wrapper for relational databases. Using SIMS and LIM, we built a small net-work of information-gathering agents that interact over the Internet. Each SIMS agent contains a detailed model of its domain of expertise and models of the information sources that are available to it. Given an information request, an agent selects an appropriate set of information sources, generates a plan to retrieve and process the data, uses knowledge about the information sources to reformulate the plan for efficiency, and executes the plan. An agent can also learn about other agents to improve their overall efficiency and accuracy. The following sections describe the knowledge representation, communication, query processing, and learning capabilities of the individual agents.

The Knowledge of an Agent

Each agent contains a model of its domain of expertise and models of the other agents that can provide relevant information. We will refer to these two types of models as the domain model and information-source models. These models constitute the general knowledge of an agent and are used to determine how to process an information request.

The domain model is an *ontology* that represents the domain of interest of the agent and establishes the terminology for interacting with the agent. The infor-mation-source models describe both the contents of the information sources and their relationship to the domain model. These models do not need to contain a complete description of the other agents, but rather only those portions that are directly relevant. They constitute the resources that are available to an agent to answer information requests when they cannot be handled locally.

Both the domain and information-source models are expressed in the Loom knowledge representation language (MacGregor 1990). Loom is an AI knowl-edge representation system of the KL-ONE family[1] (Brachman and Schmolze

1985). Loom provides a language for representing hierarchies of classes and relations, as well as efficient mechanisms for classifying instances of classes and reasoning about descriptions of object classes.

The Domain Model of an Agent

Each information agent is specialized to a single *application domain* and provides access to the available information sources within that domain. The domain model is intended to be a description of the application domain from the point of view of users or other information agents that may need to obtain information about the application domain.

The domain model of an agent defines its area of expertise and the terminology for communicating with it. That is, it provides an ontology to describe the application domain. This ontology consists of descriptions of the classes of objects in the domain, relationships between these classes (including subsumption), and other domain-specific information. These classes and relationships do not necessarily correspond directly to the objects described in any particular information source. The model provides a semantic description of the domain, which is used extensively for processing queries.

The largest application domain that we have to date is a logistics planning domain, which involves information about the movement of personnel and materiel from one location to another using aircraft, ships, trucks, etc. Currently, we are building another network of agents for a trauma-care domain.

Figure 2 shows a fragment of the domain model of the *Sea_Agent* that belongs to the organization of figure 1. The nodes represent concepts (i.e., classes of objects), the thick arrows represent subsumption (i.e., subclass relationships), and the thin arrows represent concept roles (i.e., relationships between classes). Some concepts that specify the range of roles have been left out of the figure for clarity. Some are simple types, such as strings or numbers (such as *ship-name*), while others are defined concepts (such as *geoloc-code*).

Modeling Other Agents

An agent will have models of several other agents that provide useful information for its domain of expertise. Each information-source model has two main parts. First, there is the description of the contents of the information source. This comprises the concepts of interest available from that information source in terms of the ontology of that information source. The terms in the ontology provide the language that the information source understands (and that will be used to communicate with it, as described in the Communication Language and Protocol and Query Processing sections). Second, the relationship between these information source concepts and the concepts in the domain model needs to be stated. These mappings are used for transforming a domain model query into a set of queries to the appropriate information sources.

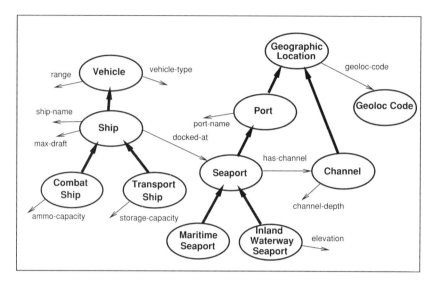

Figure 2. Fragment of the domain model of the Sea_Agent.

Figure 3 illustrates how an information source is modeled in Loom and how it is related to the domain model. All of the concepts and roles in the information-source model are mapped to concepts and roles in the domain model. A mapping link between two concepts or roles (dashed lines in the figure) indicates that they represent the same class of information and, more precisely, that their extensions are equivalent. Thus, if the user (of the *Sea_Agent*) requests *all* seaports, that information can be retrieved from the concept *Harbor* of the *Harbor_Agent*. Note that the domain model may include relationships that involve concepts coming from different agents (like the role *docked-at* of the *Ship* concept) but are not explicitly present in any one information source.

Communication Language and Protocol

We use a *common* language and protocol to communicate among agents (in order to avoid the n^2 translation problem). Strictly speaking, there are two different aspects in agent communication: the content of the communication and the particular communicative act that is intended. This fact is reflected, respectively, in the choice of Loom as the language in which to describe the desired information requested by agents, and the Knowledge Query and Manipulation Language (KQML) (Finin, Fritzson, and McKay 1992; Finin, Labrou, and Mayfield, chapter 14 of this volume) as the protocol to organize the dialogue among agents.

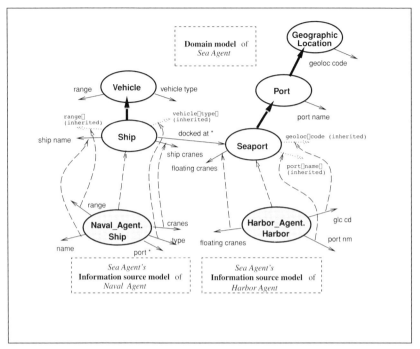

Figure 3. Relating an information-source model to a domain model in the Sea_Agent.

Queries to an information agent are expressed in a subset of the Loom query language. These queries are composed of terms of its domain model, so there is no need for other agents or a user to know or even be aware of the terms used in the underlying information sources. Given a query, an information agent identifies the appropriate information sources and issues queries to those sources to obtain the requisite data for answering the query. To do this, an information agent translates the domain-level query into a set of queries to more specialized information agents using the terms appropriate to each of those agents (by reasoning with the mappings introduced in the Modeling Other Agents subsection).

Figure 4 illustrates a query expressed in the Loom language. This query requests all seaports and the corresponding ships that can be accommodated within each port. The first argument to the *retrieve* expression is the parameter list, which specifies which parameters of the query to return (analogous to the projection operation in the relational algebra). The second argument is a description of the information to be retrieved. This description is expressed as a conjunction of concept and relation expressions, where the concepts describe the classes of information, and the relations describe the constraints on these classes. The first clause of the query is an example of a concept expression and specifies

```
(retrieve (?port_name ?ship_type)
        (:and (seaport ?port)
              (port_name ?port ?port_name)
              (channel_of ?port ?channel)
              (channel_depth ?channel ?depth)
              (ship ?ship)
              (vehicle_type ?ship ?ship_type)
              (max_draft ?ship ?draft)
              (> ?depth ?draft)))
```

Figure 4. Example Loom query.

that the variable *?port* describes a member of the class *Seaport*. The second clause is an example of a relation expression and states that the relation *port_name* holds between the values of *?port* and *?port_name*. More precisely, this query requests all *seaport-name* and *ship-type* pairs where the depth of the port exceeds the draft of the ship.

In addition to sending queries to other agents, the agents also need the capability to send back information in response to their queries. We use an implementation of KQML to handle the interface protocols for transmitting queries, returning the appropriate information, and building the appropriate internal structures. Messages among SIMS agents, and between SIMS agents and the LIM agents, which provide access to relational databases, are all uniformly expressed in KQML. Recall that making an existing database or other application program available to the network of agents requires building a wrapper around the existing system. This wrapper should include the capability of handling the relevant KQML performatives and understand the expressions of the common content language, i.e., the Loom query language. Currently, the operations supported by SIMS are retrieve, update, insert, delete, and notify.

To summarize, the communication among agents proceeds through the following phases. Once the example of figure 1 has been translated into queries in terms of each information source, each subquery (in its Loom query language form) will be enclosed in a KQML message and transmitted to the appropriate information source. Then, the wrapper of the receiver will unpack it, translate the Loom expression into the language originally handled by that agent (for example, SQL in the case of a relational database), collect the results, and send them back as a KQML reply. Recall also that only one such wrapper would need to be built for any given type of information source, a fact which reduces the complexity of the translation among heterogeneous systems from quadratic to linear in the number of different data description languages.

Query Processing

A critical capability of an information agent is the ability to flexibly and efficiently retrieve and process data. The query processing requires developing an ordered set of operations for obtaining the requested set of data. Developing such a set includes selecting the information sources for the data, the operations for processing the data, the sites where the operations will be performed, and the order in which to perform them. Since data can be moved around between different sites and processed at different locations, and the operations can be performed in a variety of orders, the space of possible plans is quite large.

We have developed a flexible planning system to generate and execute query access plans. The planner is based on an implementation of UCPOP (Barrett et al. 1993). We augmented this planner with the capability of producing parallel execution plans (Knoblock 1994), added the capability of interleaving planning and execution (Etzioni, Golden, and Weld 1994; Ambros-Ingerson and Steel 1988), and added support for run-time variables (Etzioni et al. 1992; Ambros-Ingerson and Steel 1988) for gathering information at run time. This work extends previous work on interleaving planning, execution, and sensing with the ability to perform these operations in parallel and applies these ideas to query processing. In the context of query processing, it allows the system to execute operations in parallel, augment and replan queries that fail while executing other queries, gather additional information to aid the query processing, and accept new queries while other queries are being executed.

This section describes how this planner is used to provide flexible access to the available information sources. First, we describe how we cast a query as an information goal. Second, we describe how an agent *dynamically* selects an appropriate set of information sources to solve an information goal. Third, we present our approach to producing a flexible query access plan. Fourth, we describe how the interleaving of the planning and execution can be used to execute actions in parallel, employ sensing operations to gather additional information for planning, handle new information requests as they come in, and replan when actions fail. Finally, we describe how an agent optimizes queries using semantic knowledge about the contents of other information sources.

An Information Goal

A planning problem consists of a goal, an initial state, and a set of operators that can be applied to transform the initial state into the goal. In this subsection, we will describe the goal and initial state, and in the following two subsections we present the operators used in the planning process.

For information gathering, the goal of a problem consists of a description of a set of data as well as the location where that data is to be sent. For example, figure 5 illustrates a goal which specifies that the set of data be sent to the *output*

```
(available output sims
        (retrieve (?port_name ?ship_type)
            (:and (seaport ?port)
                (port_name ?port ?port_name)
                (has_channel ?port ?channel)
                (channel_depth ?channel ?depth)
                (ship ?ship)
                (vehicle_type ?ship ?ship_type)
                (range ?ship ?range)
                (> ?range 10000)
                (max_draft ?ship ?draft)
                (> ?depth ?draft))))
```

Figure 5. Example planner goal.

```
((source-available Naval_Agent isd12.isi.edu)
 (source-available Harbor_Agent isd14.isi.edu)
 (source-available Port_Agent isd14.isi.edu))
```

Figure 6. Example initial state.

device of a SIMS agent. The data to be retrieved is defined by the query expressed in the Loom knowledge representation language, as described in the The Knowledge of an Agent section.

The initial state of a problem defines the information agents that are available as well as which server they are running on. The example shown in figure 6 defines three available agents. Each clause defines the name of the agent and the machine it is running on. For example, the first clause defines the Naval_Agent, which is running on the machine isd12.isi.edu. In addition, there are also the domain and information models, that are static (for the duration of the query processing) and are accessed directly from a Loom knowledge base.

Information Source Selection

An information goal sent to an agent is expressed in terms of the domain model of that agent. Part of the planning for an information goal requires selecting an appropriate set of information sources (other information agents or data repositories). A set of reformulation operators selects the information sources by trans-

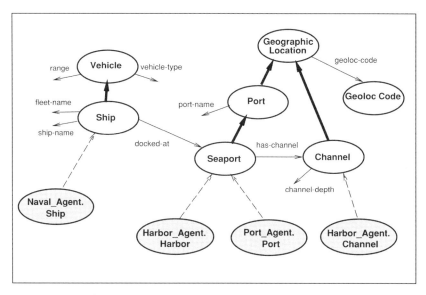

Figure 7. Fragment of the domain and information-source models.

forming the domain-level terms into terms about information that can be retrieved directly from an information source (Arens, Knoblock, and Shen 1995). If a query requests information about ports and there is a single information source that provides such information, then the mapping is straightforward. However, in some cases there may be several information sources that provide access to the same information, and in other cases no single information source can provide the required information and it will need to be drawn from several different sources.

Consider the fragment of the knowledge base shown in figure 7, which covers the knowledge relevant to the example query in figure 5. The concepts *Seaport, Channel,* and *Ship* have links to information source concepts, shown by the shaded circles, which correspond to information that can be retrieved from some information agent. Thus, the *Harbor_Agent* contains information about both seaports and channels, and the *Port_Agent* contains information about seaports.

The system has a number of truth-preserving reformulation operations that can be used for reformulating a domain-level query. The basic operations include the following:

- *Information source selection* maps a domain-level concept directly to an information-source-level concept. In many cases this will simply be a direct mapping from a concept such as *Seaport* to a concept that corresponds to the seaports in some information source. There may be several information sources that contain the same information, in which case the domain-level query can be reformulated in terms of any one of the information source concepts. In general, the choice is made so as to minimize the overall cost of executing the query.

- *Concept generalization* uses knowledge about the relationship between a concept and a superconcept to reformulate a query in terms of the more general concept. In order to preserve the semantics of the original request, one or more additional constraints may need to be added to the query in order to avoid retrieving extraneous data. For example, if a query requires some information about seaports, but the information sources that correspond to the *Seaport* concept do not contain the requested information, then it may be possible to generalize *Seaport* to *Port* and retrieve the information from some information source that contains port information. In order to ensure that no extraneous data is returned, the reformulation will include a join between *Seaport* and *Port*.

- *Concept specialization* replaces a concept with a more specific concept by checking the constraints on the query to see if there is an appropriate specialization of the requested concept that would satisfy it. For example, if a query requests all *Seaports* with an elevation greater than 300 feet, it can be reformulated into a request for all *Inland-Waterway Seaports* using knowledge in the model that only inland-waterway seaports have an elevation above 300 feet.

- *Definition substitution* replaces a relation defined between concepts in the domain model with equivalent terms that are available in the information-source models. For example, *has_channel* is a property of the domain model, but it is not defined in any information source. Instead, it can be replaced by joining over a key, *geoloc-code,* that occurs both in *Seaport* and *Channel.*

For example, consider the query shown in figure 5. There are two concept expressions—one about ships and the other about seaports. In the first step, the system attempts to translate the seaport expression into an information-source-level expression. Unfortunately, none of the information sources contain information that corresponds to *has_channel.* Thus, the system must reformulate *has_channel,* using the substitute definition operator. This enforces the fact that *has_channel* can be materialized by performing a join over the keys for the *Seaport* and *Channel* concepts. The resulting reformulation is shown in figure 8.

Another step in the reformulation process is to select information sources for the information requested in the query. This can be done using the select-information-source operator, which selects among the available information sources. Figure 9 shows a reformulation of a query for information about seaports, which could be provided by either the *Harbor_Agent* or *Port_Agent.* In this case, *Harbor_Agent* is selected because the information on channels is available only in the *Harbor_Agent.*

```
(retrieve (?port_name ?ship_type)
        (:and (seaport port)
                (port_name ?port ?port_name)
                (geoloc_code ?port ?geocode)
                (channel ?channel)
                (geoloc_code ?channel ?geocode)
                (channel_depth ?channel ?depth)
                (ship ?ship)
                (vehicle_type ?ship ?ship_type)
                (range ?ship ?range)
                (> ?range 10000)
                (max_draft ?ship ?draft)
                (> ?depth ?draft)))
```

Figure 8. Result of applying the definition substitution operator to eliminate has_channel.

```
Domain-Level Query:
(retrieve (?port_name ?depth)
        (:and (seaport ?port)
                (port_name ?port ?port_name)
                (geoloc_code ?port ?geocode)
                (channel ?channel)
                (geoloc_code ?channel ?geocode)
                (channel_depth ?channel ?depth)))

Source-Level Query:
(retrieve (?port_name ?depth)
        (:and (harbor_agent.harbor ?port)
                (harbor_agent.port_nm ?port ?port_name)
                (harbor_agent.glc_cd ?port ?glc_cd)
                (harbor_agent.channel ?channel)
                (harbor_agent.glc_cd ?channel ?glc_cd)
                (harbor_agent.ch_depth_ft ?channel ?depth)
```

Figure 9. Result of selecting information sources for channels and ships.

```
(define (operator join)
    :parameters (?join-ops ?data ?data-a ?data-b)
    :precondition (:and (join-partition ?data ?join-ops ?data-a ?data-b)
                        (available local sims ?data-a)
                        (available local sims ?data-b))
    :effect (:and (available local sims ?data)))
```

Figure 10. The join operator.

Generating a Query Access Plan

In addition to selecting the appropriate information sources to solve an information goal, the planner must also determine the appropriate data manipulation and ordering of those operators to generate the requested data. Therefore, besides the operators for source selection, there are five operators for manipulating the data:

- *Move:* Moves a set of data from one information agent to another.
- *Join:* Combines two sets of data using the given join operation.
- *Retrieve:* Specifies the data to be retrieved from a particular information source.
- *Select:* Selects a subset of the data using the given constraints.
- *Compute:* Constructs a new term in the data from some combination of the existing data.

Each of these operations manipulates one or more sets of data, where the data is specified in the same terms that are used for specifying the original query.

Consider the operator shown in figure 10 that defines a join performed locally. This operator is used to achieve the goal of making some information available in the local knowledge base of a SIMS agent. It does so by partitioning the request into two subsets of the requested data, getting that information into the local knowledge base of an agent and then joining that data together to produce the requested set of data. The operator states that (1) if a query can be broken down into two subqueries that can be joined together over some join operator, and (2) the first set of data can be made available locally, and (3) the second set of data can also be made available locally, then the requested information can be made available. The predicate join-partition is defined by a program that produces the possible join partitions of the requested data.

To search the space of query access plans efficiently, the system uses a simple estimation function to calculate the expected cost of the various operations. Using this evaluation function in a branch-and-bound search, the system will produce a plan that has the lowest overall parallel execution cost. In the exam-

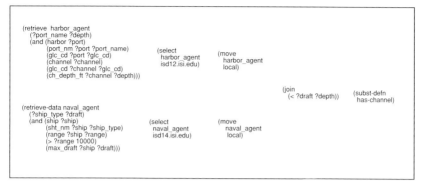

Figure 11. Parallel query access plan.

ple, the planner leaves the join between the *Harbor* and *Channel* to be performed by the *Harbor_Agent* since this will be cheaper than moving the information into the local knowledge base of an agent and joining it together.

The plan generated for the example query in figure 5 is shown in figure 11. This plan includes the source selection operations as well as the data manipulation operations since these operations are interleaved in the planning process. In this example, the system partitions the given query such that the ship information is retrieved in a single query to the *Naval_Agent,* and the seaport and channel information is retrieved in a single query to the *Harbor_Agent.* All of the information is brought into the local knowledge base of the agent originating the query, where the draft of the ships can be compared against the depth of the seaports. Once the final set of data has been generated, it is returned to the agent or application that requested the information.

Interleaving Planning and Execution

The previous two sections described the operators for both selecting an appropriate set of information sources and for manipulating the data retrieved from those information sources. This section describes how this planning is tightly integrated with the execution to provide the ability to flexibly and efficiently process queries (Knoblock 1995). The interleaving of the planning and execution provides a number of important capabilities for the agents:

- An agent can run continuously, accepting queries and planning for them while it is executing other queries.
- If a failure occurs, an agent can replan the failed portion of the plan while it continues to execute queries that are already in progress. After replanning, the system will redirect the failed subquery to a different agent or information repository.
- An agent can issue sensing actions to gather additional information for

query processing. This allows an agent to gather additional information to formulate more efficient queries to other information sources. Information gathering can also help to select among a number of potentially relevant information sources (Knoblock and Levy 1994).

Rather than having a separate execution module, the execution is tightly integrated in the planner. This is done by treating the execution of each individual action as a necessary step in completing a plan. Thus, the goal of the planner becomes producing a complete and executed plan rather than just producing a complete plan. This allows the planner to interleave the planning process with the execution, which makes it possible to handle new goals, replan failed goals, and execute actions to gather additional information.

The execution of an action is viewed as a commitment to the plan in which the action occurs. This means that the planner will consider only the plan from which the action is executed and all valid refinements of that plan. Since execution of an action commits to the corresponding plan, we would like the planner to be selective in choosing to execute an action. Such selectivity is achieved by delaying the execution of any action as long as possible. The idea is that the planner should find the best complete plan within some time limit before any action is executed. Then once execution is begun, it would resolve any failed subplans or new goals before executing the next action.

Execution of an action may take considerable time, so the planner does not execute an action and wait for the results. Instead the system spawns a new process to execute the action, and then that process notifies the planner once it has completed. At any one time there may be a number of actions that are all executing simultaneously.

On each cycle of the planner, the system will check if any executing actions have completed. Once an action has completed, the executing action is removed from the agenda. If it completes successfully, it is left in the plan and marked as completed. Other actions that depend on this action may now be executable if all of their other dependencies have also been executed. If an action fails, the system produces a refinement of the executing plan that eliminates the failed portion of the plan. This replanning can be performed while other actions are still executing.

If a new goal is sent to the planner, the system simply inserts an open condition for that new top-level goal. The additional open condition will be handled before initiating execution of any new operators, so the planner will augment the existing plan to solve this new goal in the context of the existing executing plan.

The planner also supports run-time variables (Etzioni et al. 1992; Ambros-Ingerson and Steel 1988), which allow the planner to perform sensing operations in the course of planning. These variables appear in the effects of operators and essentially serve as place holders for the value returned by the operator when it is actually executed. Run-time variables are useful because the result can be incorporated and used in other parts of the plan.

```
(retrieve (?ship-type ?draft)
        (:and (naval_agent.ship ?ship)
              (naval_agent.sht_nm ?ship ?ship-type)
              (naval_agent.max_draft ?ship ?draft)
              (naval_agent.range ?ship ?range)
              (> ?range 10000)))
```

Figure 12. Example subquery.

Semantic Query Optimization

Before executing any actions in the query plan, the system first performs semantic query optimization to minimize the overall execution cost (Hsu and Knoblock 1993). The semantic query optimizer uses semantic knowledge about the information sources to reformulate the query plan into a cheaper but semantically equivalent query plan. The semantic knowledge is learned by the system as a set of rules (see the Learning Rules for Semantic Query Optimization subsection).

Consider the example shown in figure 12. The input query retrieves ship types whose ranges are greater than 10,000 miles. This query could be expensive to evaluate because there is no index placed on the range attribute. The system must scan all of the instances of Ship and check the values of the range to retrieve the answer.

An example semantic rule is shown in figure 13. This rule states that all ships with range greater than 10,000 miles have a draft greater than 12 feet. Based on these rules, the semantic query optimizer infers a set of additional constraints and merges them with the input query. The final set of constraints left in the reformulated query is selected based on two criteria: reducing the total evaluation cost, and retaining the semantic equivalence. A detailed description of the algorithm may be found in (Hsu and Knoblock 1993). In this example, the input query is reformulated into a new query where the constraint on the attribute *range* is replaced with a constraint on the attribute *max_draft*, which turns out to be cheap to access because of the way the information is indexed. The reformulated query can therefore be evaluated more efficiently. The system can reformulate a query by adding, modifying or removing constraints. The resulting query is shown in figure 14.

We can reformulate each subquery in the query plan with the subquery optimization algorithm and improve their efficiency. However, the most expensive aspect of queries to multiple information sources is often processing and transmitting intermediate data. In the example query plan in figure 11, the constraint on the final subqueries involves the variables *?draft* and *?depth* that are bound in the preceding subqueries. If we can reformulate these preceding sub-

```
(:if (:and (naval_agent.ship ?ship)
        (naval_agent.range ?ship ?range)
        (naval_agent.fuel_cap ?ship ?fuel_cap)
        (> ?range 10000))
 (:then (> ?draft 12)))
```

Figure 13. An example semantic rule.

```
(retrieve (?sht-type ?draft)
    (:and (naval_agent.ship ?ship)
        (naval_agent.sht_nm ?ship ?ship-type)
        (naval_agent.max_draft ?ship ?draft)
        (> ?draft 12)))
```

Figure 14. Reformulated query.

queries so that they retrieve only the data instances possibly satisfying the constraint *(< ?draft ?depth)* in the final subquery, the intermediate data will be reduced. This reformulation requires the query plan optimization algorithm to be able to propagate the constraints along the data flow paths in the query plan. We developed a query plan optimization algorithm which achieves this by using the semantic rules to derive possible constraints and propagating these constraints around the query plan.

Consider an example of reformulating the query plan shown in figure 11. The system is given the fact *41 ≤ ?depth ≤ 60.* The subquery optimization algorithm can infer from the constraint *(< ?draft ?depth)* a new constraint *(< ?draft 60)* and then propagate this constraint to constrain the maximum draft. The algorithm will insert the new constraint on *?draft* in that subquery.

The resulting query plan is more efficient and returns the same answer as the original one. The amount of intermediate data is reduced because of the new constraint on the attribute *?draft.* The entire algorithm for query plan optimization is polynomial. Our experiments show that the overhead of this algorithm is very small compared to the overall query processing cost. On a set of 26 example queries, the query optimization yielded significant performance improvements with an overall reduction in execution time of 59.84% (Hsu and Knoblock 1995).

Learning

An intelligent agent for information gathering should be able to improve both its accuracy and performance over time. To achieve these goals, the information agents currently support three forms of learning. First, they have the capability to cache frequently retrieved or difficult to retrieve information. Second, for those cases where caching is not appropriate, an agent can learn about the contents of the information sources in order to minimize the costs of retrieval. Finally, an information agent can analyze the contents of its information sources in order to refine its domain model to better reflect the currently available information. All these forms of learning can improve the efficiency of the system, and the last one can also improve its accuracy.

Caching Retrieved Data

Data that is required frequently or is very expensive to retrieve can be cached in the local agent and then retrieved more efficiently (Arens and Knoblock 1994). An elegant feature of using Loom to model the domain is that cached information can easily be represented and stored in Loom. The data is currently brought into the local agent for processing, so caching is simply a matter of retaining the data and recording what data has been retrieved.

To cache retrieved data into the local agent requires formulating a description of the data so it can be used to answer future queries. This description can be extracted from the initial query, which is already expressed in the form of a domain-level description of the desired data. The description defines a new subconcept, and it is placed in the appropriate place in the concept hierarchy. The data then become instances of this concept and can be accessed by retrieving all the instances of it.

Once the system has defined a new class and stored the data under this class, the cached information becomes a new information source concept for the agent. The reformulation operations, which map a domain query into a set of information source queries, will automatically consider this new information source. Since the system takes the retrieval costs into account in selecting the information sources, it will naturally gravitate towards using cached information where appropriate. In those cases where the cached data does not capture all of the required information, it may still be cheaper to retrieve everything from the remote site. However, in those cases where the cached information can be used to avoid an external query, the use of the stored information can provide significant efficiency gains.

The use of caching raises a number of important questions, such as which information should be cached and how the cached information is kept up to date. We are exploring caching schemes where, rather than caching the answer to a specific query, general classes of frequently used information are stored. This is especially useful in the Internet environment where a single query can be very expensive and the same set of data is often used to answer multiple queries. To avoid problems of information becoming out of date, we have focused on caching relatively static information.

Learning Rules for Semantic Query Optimization

The goal of an information agent is to provide efficient access to a set of information sources. Since accessing and processing information can be very costly, the system strives for the best performance that can be provided with the resources available. This means that when it is not processing queries, it gathers information to aid in future retrieval requests (Hsu and Knoblock 1995, 1994).

The learning is triggered when an agent detects an expensive query. In this way, the agent will incrementally gather a set of rules to reformulate expensive queries. The learning subsystem uses induction on the contents of the information sources to construct a less expensive specification of the original query. This new query is then compared with the original to generate a set of rules that describe the relationships between the two equivalent queries. The learned rules are integrated into the agent's domain model and then used for semantic query optimization. These learned rules form an abstract model of the information provided by other agents or data repositories.

Reconciling Agent Models

So far we have assumed that the domain and information-source models of an agent are perfectly aligned. That is, the mappings among concepts in these models perfectly correspond to the actual information. In a network of autonomous agents, this assumption will not hold in general. First, the designer of the models might not have had a complete understanding of the semantics of the information provided by each agent. Second, even if at design time the models were accurate, the autonomy of the agents will cause some concepts to drift from their original meaning. The dynamic nature of the information implies that we need to provide mechanisms to detect inconsistency and/or incompleteness in the agent's knowledge. In this section we describe an approach to automatically reconcile agent models, which will improve both the accuracy of the represented knowledge and the efficiency of the information gathering. It consists of three phases. First, an agent checks for misalignments between the domain and source models. Second, it modifies the domain model to represent the new classes of information detected. Third, if possible, it learns from the actual data a description that declaratively describes these new concepts.

We will illustrate the main ideas of this approach through an example from the domain of the *Sea_Agent* (figure 7). Assume that initially both *Harbor_Agent.Harbor* and *Port_Agent.Port* contain the same information about major commercial seaports, which for the purposes of the application is in agreement with the intended semantics of the concept *Seaport.* However, the *Port_Agent* evolves to contain information about recreational, small fishing harbors, etc. The *Harbor_Agent* and *Port_Agent* are no longer equivalent providers of Seaport information.

First, analyzing their actual extensions, our agent will notice that *Harbor_Agent.Harbor* is now a subset of *Port_Agent.Port.* Second, the domain model is automatically modified as shown in figure 15. A new concept commercial-seaport is added to the domain model as a subconcept of the original *Seaport.Harbor_Agent.Harbor* will map now into *Commercial-Seaport.* Third, we apply machine learning algorithms (currently ID3 [Quinlan 1986]) in order to obtain a concise description of this new concept. For example, it might construct a description that distinguishes commercial seaports from generic seaports by the number of cranes available. With this refined model, a query like "retrieve all the seaports that have more than 15 cranes and channels more than 70 feet deep," which describes information only satisfied by commercial seaports, could be appropriately directed to the *Harbor_Agent,* saving both in communication (less data transmitted) and processing costs (less data considered in any subsequent join), because the concept *Harbor* has a smaller number of instances. Moreover, a query about a small-craft harbor will not be incorrectly directed to the *Harbor_Agent,* but to the *Port_Agent,* which is the only one that can provide such information.

A more detailed explanation of these techniques can be found in Ambite and Knoblock (1994), including other cases in which the extensions are overlapping or disjoint, or deal with more than two information source concepts.

The benefits of the reconciliation are twofold. First, increased accuracy of the knowledge represented in the system—these new concepts provide a more precise picture of the current information available to an agent system. This mechanism adapts automatically to the evolution of the information sources, whose contents may semantically drift from the original domain model mappings. Also, human designers may revise these concepts to both refine the domain model and detect errors. Second, increased efficiency of query processing. A SIMS agent will use those concepts that yield a cheaper query plan. These new concepts provide better options for retrieving the desired data.

Related Work

A great deal of work has been done on building agents for various kinds of tasks. This work is quite diverse and has focused on a variety of issues. First, there has been work on multi-agent planning and distributed problem solving, (see Bond and Gasser [1988]). The body of this work deals with the issues of coordination, synchronization, and control of multiple autonomous agents. Second, a large body of work has focused on defining models of the beliefs, intentions, capabili-

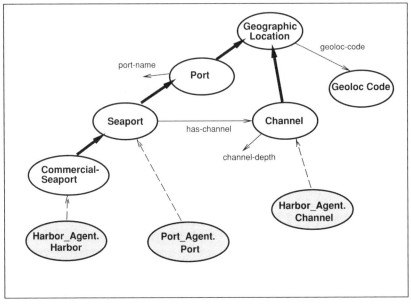

Figure 15. Reconciled model.

ties, and needs of an agent. Shoham (1993) provides a nice example of this work and a brief overview of the related work on this topic. Third, there is more closely related work on developing agents for information gathering.

The problem of information gathering is also quite broad, and the related work has focused on various issues. Kahn and Cerf (1988) proposed an architecture for a set of information-management agents, called Knowbots. The various agents are hard-coded to perform particular tasks. Etzioni et al. (Etzioni, Golden, and Weld 1994; Etzioni et al. 1992) have built agents for the Unix domain that can perform a variety of Unix tasks. This work has focused extensively on reasoning and planning with incomplete information, which arises in many of these tasks. In contrast to this work, the focus of our work is on flexible and efficient retrieval of information from heterogeneous information sources. Since these systems have in-memory databases, they assume that the cost of a database retrieval is small or negligible. One of the critical problems in dealing with large databases is how to issue the appropriate queries to efficiently access the desired information. We are focusing on the problems of how to organize, manipulate, and learn about large quantities of data.

Research in databases has also focused on building integrated or federated systems that combine information sources (Landers and Rosenberg 1982; Sheth and Larson 1990). The approach taken in these systems is to first define a global schema, which integrates the information available in the different information sources. However, this approach is unlikely to scale to the large number of evolving information sources (e.g., the Internet) since building an integrated schema is labor intensive and difficult to maintain, modify, and extend.

The Carnot project (Collet, Huhns, and Shen 1991) also integrates heterogeneous databases using a knowledge representation system. Carnot uses a knowledge base to build a set of articulation axioms that describe how to map between SQL queries and domain concepts. After the axioms are built, the domain model is no longer used or needed. In contrast, the domain model of one of our agents is an integral part of the system and allows an agent to both combine information stored in the knowledge base and to reformulate queries.

Levy el al. (Levy, Sagiv, and Srivastava 1994) are also working on building agents for information gathering. The focus of their work has been on developing a framework for selecting a minimal set of sites to answer a query. In contrast, SIMS integrates the site selection process in the query planning process in order to provide greater flexibility. This integration allows SIMS to generate a query plan and a corresponding set of sources that will produce the requested information most efficiently.

Discussion

This chapter described the SIMS architecture for intelligent information agents. This particular architecture has a number of important features: (1) modularity in terms of representing an information agent and information sources, (2) extensibility in terms of adding new information agents and information sources, (3) flexibility in terms of selecting the most appropriate information sources to answer a query, (4) efficiency in terms of minimizing the overall execution time for a given query, and (5) adaptability in terms of being able to track semantic discrepancies among models of different agents. We will discuss each of these features in turn.

First, the uniform query language and separate models provide a *modular* architecture for multiple information agents. An information agent for one domain can serve as an information source to other information agents. This can be done seamlessly since the interface to every information source is exactly the same — it takes a query in a uniform language (i.e., Loom) as input and returns the data requested by the query. The domain model provides a uniform language for queries about information in any of the sources to which an agent has access. The contents of each agent is represented as a separate information source and is mapped to the domain model of an agent. Each information agent can export some or all of its domain model, which can be incorporated into another information agent's model. This exported model forms the shared terminology between agents.

Second, the separate domain and information-source models and the dynamic information source selection make the overall architecture easily *extensible*.

Adding a new information source simply requires building a model of the information source that describes the contents of the information source as well as how it relates to the domain model. It does not require integrating the new information-source model with the other information-source models since the mapping between domain and information-source models is not fixed. Similarly, changes to the contents of information sources require only changing the model of the specific information source. Since the selection of the information sources is performed dynamically, when an information request is received, the agent will select the most appropriate information source that is currently available.

Third, the separate domain and information-source models and the dynamic information source selection also make the agents very *flexible*. The agents can choose the appropriate information sources based on what they contain, how quickly they can answer a given query, and what resources are currently available. If a particular information source or network goes down or if the data is available elsewhere, the system will retrieve the data from sources that are currently available. An agent can take into consideration the rest of the processing of a query, so that the system can take advantage of those cases where retrieving the data from one source is much cheaper than retrieving it from another source because the remote system can do more of the processing. This flexibility also makes it possible to cache and reuse information without extra work or overhead.

Fourth, building parallel query access plans, using semantic knowledge to optimize the plans, caching retrieved data, and learning about information sources provide *efficient* access to large numbers of information sources. The planner generates plans that minimize the overall execution time by maximizing the parallelism in the plan to take advantage of the fact that separate information sources can be accessed in parallel. The semantic query optimization provides a global optimization step that minimizes the amount of intermediate data that must be processed. The ability to cache retrieved data allows an agent to store frequently used or expensive-to-retrieve information in order to provide the requested information more efficiently. And the ability to learn about the contents of the information sources allows the agent to exploit time when it would not otherwise be used to improve its performance on future queries.

Fifth, the ability to compare and reconcile models of different agents make the agents *adaptable* to changes in the information sources. Using the detailed semantic models of the information sources, an agent can track changes in the information sources and update its own models appropriately. This information is critical for both the accuracy and the efficiency of the query processing.

To date, we have built information agents that plan and learn in the logistics planning domain. These agents contain a detailed model of this domain and extract information from a set of relational databases. The agents generate query access plans to the appropriate information sources, execute the queries in parallel, and learn about the information sources. Future work will focus on extending the planning and learning capabilities of these agents.

Acknowledgments

We gratefully acknowledge the contributions of the other members of the SIMS project, Yigal Arens, Chin Chee, Chunnan Hsu, Wei-Min Shen, and Sheila Tejada for their work on the various components of SIMS. We also thank Don Mckay, Jon Pastor, and Robin McEntire at Unisys for setting up the LIM agents and providing us with an implementation of KQML.

The research reported here was supported in part by Rome Laboratory of the Air Force Systems Command and the Advanced Research Projects Agency under contract no. F30602-91-C-0081, and in part by the National Science Foundation under grant number IRI-9313993. J.L. Ambite is supported by a Fulbright/Spanish Ministry of Education and Science Scholarship. The views and conclusions contained in this report are those of the authors and should not be interpreted as representing the official opinion or policy of RL, ARPA, NSF, the U.S. Government, the Fulbright program, the Government of Spain, or any person or agency connected with them.

Note

1. These type of languages are also known as description logics, terminological logics, or concept languages.

References

Ambite, J. L., and Knoblock, C. A. 1994. Reconciling Agent Models. In Proceedings of the Workshop on Intelligent Information Agents. Gaithersburg, Md.: National Institute of Standards and Technology.

Ambros-Ingerson, J., and Steel, S. 1988. Integrating Planning, Execution, and Monitoring. In Proceedings of the Seventh National Conference on Artificial Intelligence, 83–88. Menlo Park, Calif.: American Association for Artificial Intelligence.

Arens, Y., and Knoblock, C. A. 1994. Intelligent Caching: Selecting, Representing, and Reusing Data in an Information Server. In Proceedings of the Third International Conference on Information and Knowledge Management (CIKM'94), 433–438. Gaithersburg, Md.: National Institute of Standards and Technology.

Arens, Y.; Knoblock, C. A.; and Shen, W. M. 1996. Query Reformulation for Dynamic Information Integration. Journal of Intelligent Information Systems (Special Issue on Intelligent Information Integration) 6(2–3): 99–130.

Arens, Y.; Chee, C. Y.; Hsu, C.-N.; and Knoblock, C. A. 1993. Retrieving and Integrating Data from Multiple Information Sources. International Journal on Intelligent and Cooperative Information Systems 2(2): 127–158.

Barrett, A.; Golden, K.; Penberthy, S.; and Weld, D. 1993. UCPOP User's Manual, Version 2.0, Technical Report, 93-09-06, Department of Computer Science and Engineering, University of Washington.

Bond, A. H., and Gasser, L. 1988. Readings in Distributed Artificial Intelligence. San Francisco, Calif.: Morgan Kaufmann.

Brachman, R. J., and Schmolze, J. G. 1985. An Overview of the KL-ONE Knowledge

Representation System. *Cognitive Science* 9(2): 171–216.

Collet, C.; Huhns, M. N.; and Shen, W.-M. 1991. Resource Integration Using a Large Knowledge Base in CARNOT. *IEEE Computer* 24(12): 55–62.

Etzioni, O.; Golden, K.; and Weld, D. 1994. Tractable Closed-World Reasoning with Updates. In *Proceedings of the Fourth International Conference on Principles of Knowledge Representation and Reasoning,* eds. J. Doyle, E. Sandewall, and P. Torasso, 178–189. San Francisco, Calif.: Morgan Kaufmann.

Etzioni, O.; Hanks, S.; Weld, D.; Draper, D.; Lesh, N.; and Williamson, M. 1992. An Approach to Planning with Incomplete Information. In *Proceedings of the Third International Conference on Principles of Knowledge Representation and Reasoning,* eds. B. Nebel, C. Rich, and W. Swartout, 115–125. San Francisco, Calif.: Morgan Kaufmann.

Finin, T.; Fritzson, R.; McKay, D.; and McEntire, R. 1994. Agent Communication Language. In Proceedings of the Third International Conference on Information and Knowledge Management (CIKM'94), 456–463. New York: Association of Computing Machinery.

Hsu, C.-N., and Knoblock, C. A. 1995. Using Inductive Learning to Generate Rules for Semantic Query Optimization. In *Advances in Knowledge Discovery and Data Mining,* eds. Gregory Piatetsky-Shapiro and Usama Fayyad, 201–218. Menlo Park, Calif.: AAAI Press.

Hsu, C.-N., and Knoblock, C. A. 1994. Rule Induction for Semantic Query Optimization. In *Proceedings of the Eleventh International Conference on Machine Learning (ICML'94),* 10–13 July, New Brunswick, New Jersey. San Francisco: Morgan Kaufmann.

Hsu, C.-N., and Knoblock, C. A. 1993. Reformulating Query Plans for Multidatabase Systems. In Proceedings of the Second International Conference on Information and Knowledge Management, 423–432. New York: Association of Computing Machinery.

Kahn, R. E., and Cerf, V. G. 1988. An Open Architecture for a Digital Library System and a Plan for Its Development, Technical Report, Corporation for National Research Initiatives, Reston, Virginia.

Knoblock, C. A. 1995. Planning, Executing, Sensing, and Replanning for Information Gathering. In Proceedings of the Fourteenth International Joint Conference on Artificial Intelligence (IJCAI'95), 1686–1693. Menlo Park, Calif.: International Joint Conferences on Artificial Intelligence.

Knoblock, C. A. 1994. Generating Parallel Execution Plans with a Partial-Order Planner. In *Proceedings of the Second International Conference on Artificial Intelligence Planning Systems,* 13–15 June, Chicago, Illinois, 98-103. Menlo Park, Calif.: AAAI Press.

Knoblock, C. A., and Levy, A. 1994. Efficient Query Processing for Information-Gathering Agents. In Proceedings of the Workshop on Intelligent Information Agents. Gaithersburg, Md.: National Institute of Standards and Technology.

Knoblock, C. A.; Arens, Y.; and Hsu, C.-N. 1994. Cooperating Agents for Information Retrieval. In *Proceedings of the Second International Conference on Cooperative Information Systems,* 17–20 May, Toronto, Canada. Toronto: University of Toronto Press.

Landers, T., and Rosenberg, R. L. 1982. An Overview of Multibase. In *Distributed Data Bases,* ed. H. J. Schneider, 153–184. New York: North-Holland.

Levy, A. Y.; Sagiv, Y.; and Srivastava, D. 1994. Towards Efficient Information- Gathering Agents. In *Software Agents: Papers from the AAAI 1994 Spring Symposium,* 64–70. Technical Report SS-94-03. Menlo Park, Calif.: AAAI Press.

MacGregor, R. 1990. The Evolving Technology of Classification-Based Knowledge Representation Systems. In *Principles of Semantic Networks: Explorations in the Representation of Knowledge,* ed. J. Sowa, 385–400. San Mateo, Calif.: Morgan Kaufmann.

Papazoglou, M. P.; Laufmann, S. C.; and Sellis, T. K. 1992. An Organizational Framework for Cooperating Intelligent Information Systems. *International Journal of Intelligent and Cooperative Information Systems* 1(1): 169–202.

Pastor, J. A.; McKay, D. P.; and Finin, T. W. 1992. View-Concepts: Knowledge-Based Access to Databases. Paper presented at the First International Conference on Information and Knowledge Management, 8–11 November, Baltimore, Maryland.

Quinlan, J. R. 1986. Induction of Decision Trees. *Machine Learning* 1(1): 81–106.

Sheth, A. P., and Larson, J. A. 1990. Federated Database Systems for Managing Distributed, Heterogeneous, and Autonomous Databases. *ACM Computing Surveys* 22(3): 183–236.

Shoham, Y. 1993. Agent-Oriented Programming. *Artificial Intelligence* 60(1): 51–92.

CHAPTER 17

KAoS: Toward An Industrial-Strength Open Agent Architecture

Jeffrey M. Bradshaw, Stewart Dutfield, Pete Benoit, & John D. Woolley

The complexity of modern engineered systems motivates the require-ment for timely access to technical and operational documentation (Boy 1991, 1992). Documents are both the most valuable and the most expensive knowledge resource in engineering organizations (Carter 1992). Product and product-related documents may be intended for use by thousands of people over a life cycle of many years (Nelson and Schuler 1995; Malcolm, Poltrock, and Schuler 1991). Designers, engineers, operators, maintenance technicians, suppliers, and subcontractors often require access to the same doc-uments, but for different purposes and with different perspectives and termi-nology. Because documentation specialists cannot anticipate all the circum stances and questions that may arise, they try to organize and index text, graphic, and multimedia in a context-free manner. People, however, resist reading manuals that describe system features in a task-neutral way (Rettig 1991) Instead they use information retrieval strategies that are context-*depen-dent* (Mathé and Chen 1994; Boy and Mathé 1993; Boy 1991). For example, they remember that information about the diameter of a particular rivet was (or was not) relevant to the selection of a tool for repairing the fuselage. They organize their work by posting frequently-referred-to pages of a maintenance manual in prominent places in their work area, thus exploiting situational knowledge not available to the manual's original authors.

Agents for Technical Information Management and Delivery

The rapidly growing amount and complexity of information available has com-pounded the problems of technical information delivery. Until relatively recently, computing resources were so scarce and the bandwidth of human-computer interaction so low that every effort was made to increase access to online information (Nelson 1980). Now the amount of data that can be manipulated is so overwhelming and the barriers to access so much more permeable that we need to be seriously concerned about how to actively, selectively keep only the most relevant information at the forefront of user interaction.

The Promise of Software Agents

Software agents have been proposed as one way to help people better cope with the increasing volume and complexity of information and computing resources. Researchers are hopeful that this approach will help restore the lost dimension of individual perspective to the content-rich, context-poor world of the next decade. As Paul Saffo ((1994) expresses it:

> It is not content but context that will matter most a decade or so from now. The scarce resource will not be stuff, but point of view…. The future belongs to neither the conduit nor content players, but those who control the filtering, searching, and sense-making tools we will rely on to navigate through the expanses of cyberspace… Without a doubt, the agent arena will become a technological battleground, as algorithms rather than content duel for market dominance.

What will such agents do? At the user interface, they will work in conjunction with component integration frameworks to select the right data, assemble the needed components, and presentand format the information in the most appropriate way for a specific user and situation. Behind the scenes, additional agents will take advantage of distributed object management, database, document management, workflow, messaging, transaction, searching, indexing, and networking capabilities to discover, link, and securely access the appropriate data and services. Documents assembled through the use of such agents are termed "virtual" because they may never have existed as such until the moment they were dynamically composed and presented through the current "information lens." They are termed "adaptive" because the tools, content, and user interface learn to tailor themselves over time to the requirements of particular users and situations (Browne, Totterdell, and Norman 1990).

A variety of agent theories, architectures, languages, and implementations have been proposed.[1] Simple script-based agents have proven themselves useful in repetitive administrative tasks; more complex procedural agents have been applied to applications such as systems or network management (Reinhardt 1994; Richman 1995). Additional agent work has focused on areas such as Internet resource discovery and information integration (Brown et al. 1995; Etzioni and Weld 1995, 1994; Knoblock and Ambite 1997; Woelk, Huhns, and Tomlinson 1995; Bowman et al. 1994; Virdhagriswaran 1994; and Wiederhold 1992), intelligent coordination of distributed problem-solvers (Genesereth 1997; Kuokka and Harada 1995; Tambe et al. 1995; Hanks, Pollack, and Cohen 1993;

Gassero 1991; and Hewitt and Inman 1991; Finin, Labrou, and Mayfield 1997; O'Hare and Jennings 1996), and active user assistance (Ball et al. 1997; Boy 1997; Maes 1997; Malone, Grant, and Lai 1997; Riecken 1997; and Cypher 1993). Yet other agent implementations are beginning to appear that will enable mobile agents to perform business transactions in a safe and secure manner (Wayner 1995; White 1997). In contrast, the use of agents for context-dependent assembly of virtual documents from distributed information is a relatively new research area. The initial impetus has come from the explosion of distributed information on the public Internet (Bowman et al. 1994) and is now being recognized as a requirement for business organizations needing more flexible and dynamic access to private sources of heterogeneous, distributed information.

Lack of Semantics and Extensibility of Communication Languages

While several approaches to agent technology are showing significant promise, many critical issues remain unsolved. For one thing, agents created within one agent framework can seldom communicate with agents created within another.

KQML has been proposed as a standard communication language for distributed agent applications (Finin 1997, Labrou and Mayfield 1997; Genesereth 1997). The core concept is that agents communicate via "performatives," by analogy with human performative sentences and speech acts (e.g., "I hereby request you to send me file ABC.TEX"). Unfortunately, KQML developers have not yet reached full consensus on many issues. Agent designers are free to add new types of performatives to the language. However, there exist a number of confusions in the set of performatives supplied by KQML and no constraints are provided to agent designers on what can be a performative (Cohen and Levesque 1997). These problems are compounded as agent communication language designers are increasingly concerned with policies for full agent conversations, rather than simple one-way exchange at individual performatives (Labrou 1996).

Without a clearly-defined semantics of individual performatives as they are employed within particular types of agent-to-agent dialogue, developers cannot be sure that the communication acts their agents are using will have the same meaning to the other agents with whom they are communicating. Such a semantics is needed to determine the appropriateness of adding new performatives to a particular agent communication language, and to define their relationship to preexisting ones.

Lack of Infrastructure, Scalability, and Security

In addition to the current limitations of agent communication languages, the potential for large-scale, cross-functional deployment of general purpose agents in industrial and government settings has been hampered by insufficient progress on infrastructural, architectural, security, and scalability issues. Considerable research has been done on these issues by the distributed computing community, and in some cases commercial products exist that could address many of them, yet up till now relatively little effort has been made to incorporate these technologies into agent development frameworks.

The current lack of standards and supporting infrastructure has prevented the thing most users of agents in real-world applications most need: *agent interoperability* (Gardner 1996; Virdhagriswaran, Osisek, and O'Connor 1995). A key characteristic of agents is their ability to serve as universal mediators, tying together loosely-coupled, heterogeneous components—the last thing anyone wants is an agent architecture that can accommodate only a single native language and a limited set of proprietary services to which it alone can provide access.

To address some of these problems, we are developing KAoS (Knowledgeable Agent-oriented System), an open distributed architecture for software agents. Although the framework is still far from complete, our experience with KAoS to date leads us to believe that an approach of this type can become a powerful and flexible basis either for implementing or integrating diverse types of agent-oriented systems. The following section provides the background of KAoS. We then present the aims and major components of the KAoS architecture: agent structure, dynamics, and properties; the relationship between agents and objects; and the elements of agent-to-agent communication. Following this, we briefly summarize our experience in building KAoS applications and discuss issues and future directions.

KAoS Background

KAoS grows out of work beginning in 1988 on a general purpose interapplication communication mechanism for the Macintosh called MANIAC (Manager for InterApplication Communication) (Bradshaw et al. 1991, 1988). Plans for coordination among MANIAC-enabled applications were modeled and executed by means of an integrated planner we developed using ParcPlace Smalltalk. A later version, NetMANIAC, extended messaging capabilities to other platforms through the use of TCP/IP.

In 1992, we began a collaboration with the Seattle University (SU) Software Engineering program to develop the first version of KAoS (Tockey et al. 1995; George et al. 1994). We replaced the integrated planner with a fully object-oriented agent framework, borrowing ideas from Shoham's (1997) AGENT-0 work. The following year, a new group of students replaced the MANIAC capability with HP Distributed Smalltalk's version of OMG's Common Object Request Broker Architecture (CORBA) (Siegel 1996).[2]

Providing Infrastructure, Scalability, and Security through a Foundation of Distributed Object Technology

To the extent KAoS can take advantage of architectures such as CORBA, we can concentrate our research efforts on the unique aspects of agent interaction rather than on low-level distributed computing implementation issues. CORBA provides a means of freeing objects and agents from the confines of a particular address space, machine, programming language, or operating system (Siegel 1996). The Interface Definition Language (IDL) allows developers to specify object interfaces in a language-neutral fashion. Object Request Brokers (ORBs) allow transparent access to these components and services without regard to their location. The CORBA 2.0 specification extends the architecture to deal with the problem of interoperability between ORBs from different vendors. A set of system services is bundled with every ORB, and an architecture for "common facilities" of direct use to application objects is being defined. Among these common facilities will be a compound document facility based on an enhanced version of the CI Labs OpenDoc specification (Orfali, Harkey, and Edwards 1995).[3]

Our collaborations with SU have produced increasingly sophisticated versions of KAoS that are designed to take advantage of the capabilities of commercial distributed object products as a foundation for agent functionality. To date, we have investigated the use of two object request broker (ORB) products: IBM's System Object Model (SOM) (Campagnoni 1994), and Iona's Orbix. We have also explored agent interaction with Microsoft Component Object Model (COM) underlying ActiveX/OLE (Brockschmidt 1994), and are developing a Java version of KAoS.

We are encouraged by the increased cooperation among research teams and product development groups working on agent technology. For example, we are closely following the progress of the *Mobile Agent Facility*, currently being defined by the common facilities task force of the Object Management Group (OMG) (Chang and Lange 1996; Lange 1996; Virdhagriswaran, Osisek, and O'Connor 1995). We have also been active participants in the *Hippocrene* project of the Aviation Industry Computer-Based Training Committee (AICC) (Bradshaw, Madigan, et al. 1993; Bradshaw, Richards, et al. 1993) and are working with members of the KQML subgroup of the knowledge-sharing initiative to better understand and resolve interoperability issues. As research progresses, we will continue to advocate industry-wide agent interoperability standards that are neutral with respect to particular hardware platforms, operating systems, transport protocols, and programming languages. Promising standards will replace aspects of or be incorporated into KAoS as appropriate in the future.

Providing an Extensible Language Semantics Through an Agent Communication Meta-architecture

It is challenging to define an architecture that is general enough to be implemented in many different ways and applied to diverse problems, yet specific enough to guarantee support for the requirement of agent interoperability. A prime example of this difficulty is the CORBA specification, which required successive refinement over a period of years until sufficient experience and consensus to assure that cross-vendor interoperability could be achieved.

The KAoS architecture dictates neither a single transport-level protocol, nor the form in which content should be expressed, and allows agents to be configured with whatever set of communication primitives is desired. For this reason, it may be properly regarded as an open agent communication *meta*-architecture.[4]

While not incompatible with languages such as KQML, KAoS provides a more flexible and robust foundation for industrial-strength agents. We have optimized the architecture for extensibility so that new suites of protocols and capabilities can be straightforwardly accommodated as needed. Our goal is not to lead the invention of new languages and methods of agent interaction but rather to anticipate and easily adapt to new research, standards, and domain-specific enhancements as they emerge in the future.[5] If desired, for example, the set of KQML "performatives" or the communication primitives of some future specialized agent language could easily be implemented within KAoS.

Implementation Context

Figure 1 illustrates the primary long-range application context in which KAoS is being defined. Though we have optimized our implementation to address Boeing's current needs, we intended the general architecture to support rapid evolution. We are currently preparing versions of the basic KAoS implementation that will be placed in the public domain where they can be evaluated and improved upon.

KAoS Architecture

The KAoS architecture currently aims to provide the following:

- A form of agent-oriented programming, based on a foundation of distributed object technology
- Structured conversations between agents, which may preserve their state over time
- An approach for extending the language of inter-agent communication in a principled manner, taking into account the repertoire of illocutionary acts ("verbs") available to agents, the set of conversation policies available to agents, the content of messages, and a means for agents to locate and access desired services
- A framework supporting interoperability with other agent implementations as well as with non-agent programs
- An environment in which to design agents to engage in specialized suites of interactions

KAoS Agents. Basic characteristics of KAoS agents are described in the Basic Characteristics of Agents subsection that follows. A consistent structure pro-

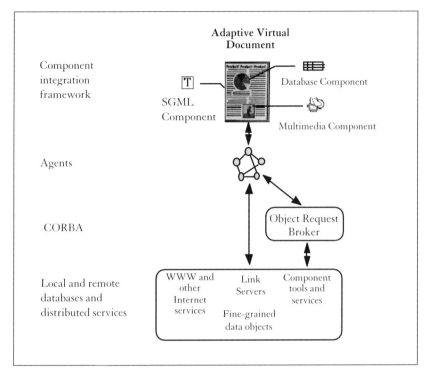

Figure 1. The context in which the KAoS agent architecture is being defined.

vides mechanisms allowing the management of knowledge, desires, intentions, and capabilities. Agent dynamics are managed through a cycle that includes the equivalent of agent birth, life, cryogenic state, and death.

The Agents and Objects subsection describes the relationship between agents and objects. Each agent has a *generic agent instance,* which implements as a minimum the basic infrastructure for agent communication. Specific extensions and capabilities can be added to the basic structure and protocols through standard object-oriented mechanisms. *Mediation agents* provide an interface between a KAoS agent environment and external nonagent entities, resources, or agent frameworks. *Proxy agents* extend the scope of the agent-to-agent protocol beyond a particular agent domain. The *Domain Manager* carries off policies set by a human administrator, such as keeping track of agents that enter and exit the domain. The *Matchmaker* can access information about the location of the generic agent instance for any agent that has advertised its services.

Agent Communication. *Messages* are exchanged between agents in the context of *conversations* (see the Agent-to-Agent Communication subsection). *Verbs* name the type of illocutionary act (e.g., *request, promise*) represented by a message. Unlike most agent communication architectures, KAoS explicitly takes into account not only the individual message, but also the various sequences of messages in which it may occur. Shared knowledge about message sequencing conventions *(conversation policies)* enables agents to coordinate frequently recurring interactions of a routine nature simply and predictably. *Suites* provide convenient groupings of conversation policies that support a set of related services (e.g., the *Matchmaker suite*). A starter set of suites is provided in the architecture but can be extended or replaced as required.

Scope of the Current Work. The current version of the architecture aims only to specify those generic capabilities which are basic to agent lifecycle management and communication. We are investigating extensions to the architecture to deal with additional issues, including:

- End-user authoring
- Mobile agents
- Semantics of agent communication for emergent conversation behavior
- Joint intention
- Planning
- Complex negotiation
- Vague goal specification
- Learning and adaptive behavior
- Anthropomorphic or other visual presentation
- Message translation

Some of these potential enhancements and technical issues are discussed in the Issues and Future Directions section.

Basic Characteristics of Agents

Agent-oriented programming (Shoham 1997) is a term that has been proposed for the set of activities necessary to create software agents. In the context of KAoS, an agent can be thought of as an extension of the object-oriented programming approach, where the objects are typically somewhat autonomous and flexibly goal-directed, respond appropriately to some basic set of speech acts (e.g., request, offer, promise), and ideally act in a way that is consistent with certain desirable conventions of human interaction such as honesty and non-capriciousness.[6] From this perspective, an agent is essentially "an object with an attitude."

But it is important to note that an agent's "attitude" is not really an *attribute* but rather an *attribution* on the part of some person (Van de Velde 1995). That is what makes coming up with a once-and-for-all definition of an agent so difficult: one person's "intelligent agent" is another person's "smart object"; and today's "smart object" is just a few years away from being seen tomorrow as just another "dumb program." The key distinction is in our point of view. For agent

proponents, the claim is that just as so[...]
pressed and understood in an object-orie[...]
ral one (Kaehler and Patterson 1986), so [...]
ers and users to think in terms of inten[...]
(Dennett 1987).[7] Singh (1994) lists sever[...]
the appeal of viewing agents as intention[...]

> "They (i) are natural to us, as desig[...]
> cinct descriptions of, and help und[...]
> of complex systems; (iii) make ava[...]
> terns of action that are independen[...]
> tion of the agent in the system; a[...]
> themselves in reasoning about each other."

Agent Structure. The KAoS architecture and generic agent class provide a consistent structure for agents; this includes mechanisms for storing, updating, querying, and "inheriting" knowledge (facts and beliefs), desires, intentions, and capabilities.[8] These structures are shown in the box on the right of figure 2. *Knowledge* is defined as a collection of *facts* and *beliefs*. Facts are simply beliefs about the agent and the environment in which the agent has complete confidence.[9] Facts or beliefs may be held privately or potentially made public (e.g., using a blackboard). *Desires* represent the goals and preferences that motivate the agent. *Intentions* represent the commitment of the agent to being in a state where it believes it is about to actually perform some set of intended actions (Cohen and Levesque 1990). All agents are required to appropriately handle external requests to provide information about their structure. An appropriate response might be sometimes simply, "I am unable to give you the information you request."

While the KAoS architecture provides the "hooks" for implementing sophisticated agents based on these structures and related mechanisms, it does not require that agents use these hooks in an "intelligent" fashion. The minimal requirement is that agents be able to carry out successful conversations related to services they are requesting or ones which they have advertised—the determination of the mechanisms by which this is accomplished is left to the agent designer.

Capabilities are the services or functions that an agent can provide as defined in specific extensions to the generic agent implementation. Our goal is to allow as much flexibility as possible in how agent capabilities are defined. For example, on the Windows platform, generic agents are currently packaged as OLE automation servers or OLE/ActiveX controls, and on the Macintosh platform generic agent functionality is exposed through Apple Events. The Java implementation of KAoS currently relies on sockets. Because KAoS relies on popular messaging schemes for communication between extensions and the generic agent, agent capabilities can be defined or extended straightforwardly using any

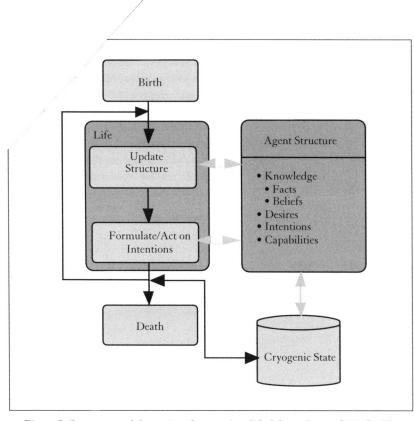

Figure 2. Structure and dynamics of agents (modified from George [1994]). The black arrows represent state transitions, and the gray arrows data flows.

combination of standard programming languages, general-purpose scripting languages (e.g., AppleScript, Visual Basic, Tcl, Perl, JavaScript) and declarative logic-based programming languages (e.g., KIF, Prolog). We see this kind of extensibility as being a positive step toward the eventual (more ambitious) goal of powerful visual and user authoring environments wherein complete agents can be defined (Cypher 1993; Repenning 1993; Spohrer, Vronay, and Kleiman 1991; Smith, Cypher, and Spohrer 1997; Malone, Grant, and Lei 1997).

Agent Dynamics. Figure 2 shows how each agent goes through the equivalent of birth, life, and death. At birth, agents instantiated and initialized with some amount of innate structure. During their lives, agents go through a continuous cycle of reading, processing, and sending messages. Agents may acquire additional knowledge, desires, and capabilities as they interact with other agents and with their environment. As messages come in, agents update their structure, formulate their intentions, and send new messages in order to act on them.

In specific applications, agent death may be required to free resources or simply deal with agents that are no longer useful. Agent death poses special problems. Depending on the application, it may be necessary to include domain-specific procedures for dealing with it. These may include notification of other agents, transfer of any pending commitments, or transfer of knowledge.

KAoS agents that are declared as persistent must be able to go into a form of "suspended animation" (called *cryogenic state*). Each persistent agent is responsible for saving the aspects of its structure required allow it to be reactivated when required. The process of saving and restoring structure may also be simple or complex, depending on the situation.[10]

Agents and Objects

The KAoS architecture defines a basic structure and default core speech-act-based agent-to-agent protocol that is normally shared among all agents. To this basic capability, specific extensions and capabilities can be added as needed through inheritance or aggregation. Communication between agents takes place through the use of *messages*. A message consists of a packet of information, usually sent asynchronously, whose type is represented by a *verb* corresponding to some kind of illocutionary act (e.g., *request, inform*).[11] Messages are exchanged by agents in the context of *conversations*. Each message is part of an extensible protocol—consisting of both message names and conversation policies—common to the agents participating in the conversation. Table 1 enumerates distinctions between communication in classical object-oriented programming and in the agent-oriented architecture.

Like KQML, we make a distinction between communication, content, and contextual portions of agent messages (Finin, Labrou, and Mayfield 1997). The communication portion encodes information enabling proper message routing, such as the identity of the sender and recipient. The content portion contains the actual gist of the message (e.g., the specific request or information being communicated) and may be expressed in any notation or form desired, including binary executables. The contextual portion describes the type of message being sent (e.g., request, inform) and tells how it relates to the larger scope of the particular conversation taking place. Optionally, the message context may also contain other descriptive information, such as the language used to express the content and (if the content is declarative) references to particular ontologies associated with it. The combination of all these features allows agents to analyze, route, and deliver messages properly without necessarily requiring interpretation of content until they reach their final destination.[12]

Table 2 identifies the characteristics of an operation and compares these to the characteristics of a message. By "operation," we mean the invocation of a procedure or a method.

Though operations may take place in isolation, messages occur only in the context of a conversation. The meaning of a given operation may vary between in-

	Objects	Agents
Basic unit	instance	agent
State-defining parameters	unconstrained	knowledge, desires, intentions, capabilities,...
Process of computation	operations	messages
Message types	defined in classes	defined in suites
Message sequences	implicit	defined in conversations
Social conventions	none	honesty, consistency,...

*Table 1. Objects versus agents
(modified from Shoham 1997).*

Operation	Message
Operation name	Verb
Signature	Conversation Parameters
Return Value	(none)

Table 2. Message characteristics.

stances of different classes, but a message always has a meaning defined by its place in a particular conversation (see the Agent-to-Agent Communication subsection). For example, a *decline* message in the context of an *Offer* conversation means something different from the same message in the context of a *Request*.

The parameters of a message contain any necessary meta-information about message processing (e.g., maximum response delay, whether acknowledgment is required) and the message content (e.g., content language).

Composition of Agents. Figure 3 shows two agents communicating within a particular agent domain. Each agent contains an instance of the generic agent class (or of a specialization of that class) which is called the *generic agent instance*.[13] The generic agent class implements as a minimum the basic infrastructure for agent communication. It understands conversation policies (see the Conversations Policies subsubsection), and how to initiate and end specific conversations based on a particular policy. The generic agent also monitors the current state of the conversations in which the agent is participating, and is able to judge whether new con-

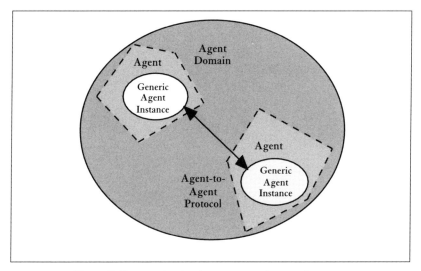

Figure 3. Communication between generic agent instances.

versational moves being proposed at a particular time are permissible.

The agent *domain* denotes the extent of inter-agent messaging; that is, no agent can communicate directly with any other agent across the bounds of an agent domain. For example, in a CORBA environment the bounds of the agent domain would typically be the bounds of a set of communicating ORBs.[14]

Specific capabilities of particular agents may be defined by any combination of *inheritance* (i.e., by creating specialized subclasses of the generic agent class) or *aggregation* (by incorporating an extension implemented as a set of separate objects).[15] Figure 4 shows an agent implemented as an aggregation of an agent extension with an instance of the generic agent class. Some extensions may be very active, others may function passively as data repositories.

Defining specialized agents by inheritance generally has the advantage of more efficient performance and tighter integration with the generic agent implementation. Defining them by aggregation has the advantage of allowing the implementation of agent capabilities to be determined dynamically at run-time. For example, a particular agent designed to monitor resource consumption on a set of machines may encounter a situation that requires human intervention. If the agent contains a "hot pluggable" extension, the automated agent capability can be unplugged from the generic agent instance on-the-fly and a human be put in its place without interrupting the ongoing agent conversations, and without the other agents even being aware that it is a person rather than a program that is now directly controlling agent behavior.

Examples of agent extensions might include:

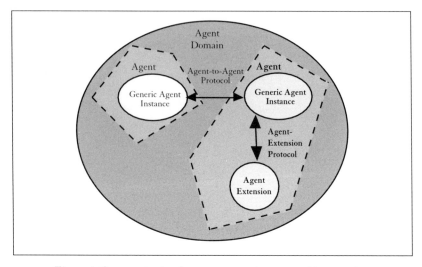

Figure 4. Communication between a generic agent and its extension.

- Unique programs implementing specific agent capabilities
- Encapsulations of internal resources over which the agent has exclusive control, such as knowledge and commitments
- Representations of external resources over which the agent has exclusive control, such as a mailbox

If an object is not exclusively owned by a particular agent, then any part of any agent may interact with it directly. Examples might include:

- Encapsulations of internal resources over which the agent does not have exclusive control. For example, instances of an "agent conversation object" data structure might, in a particular KAoS implementation, be shared between the agents participating in flat conversation
- External resources over which the agent does not have exclusive control, such as a display or an ODBMS.

Agent Environments: Bridging Domains through Proxy Agents. An agent *environment* comprises the set of all agent domains that fall within the range of the agent-to-agent protocol and is thus potentially unbounded. The agent-to-agent protocol extends beyond a particular domain through the use of *proxy agents* (figure 5). Proxy agents are useful in cases where two agent domains share agent-to-agent protocols but cannot communicate because they are implemented within different distributed object environments.[16] For example, communication between different implementations of KAoS (e.g., Java, ActiveX, CORBA) might require proxy agents. Separate agent domains, whether similar or not, may use proxy agents that communicate through

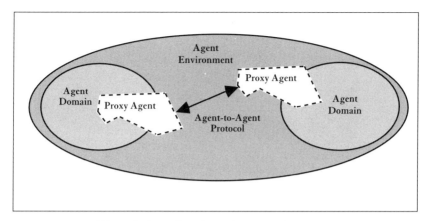

Figure 5. Agent domains and agent environments.

sockets or through some other mechanism.[17] Any extension of the range of the agent-to-agent protocol beyond the bounds of an agent domain by definition uses a proxy.

To extend the range of the agent-to-agent protocol beyond the agent domain requires that:

- Agents in both domains understand the agent-to-agent protocol
- One or more agents in each domain are capable of transmitting and receiving the agent-to-agent protocol over some form of connection between the two domains, and in so doing act as gateways to their counterparts in the remote domain.

Mediation Agents. A *mediation agent* is any agent that communicates with external (i.e., nonowned) entities or resources. Hence, a proxy agent is a special case of a mediation agent. A mediation agent provides in essence a gateway or wrapper for external non-agent entities, allowing them to access resources via the agent domain, and in turn allowing other agents to make use of them through normal agent-to-agent protocols. A single mediation agent may manipulate many external resources, and several mediation agents may share a single external resource. Figure 6 illustrates some of the kinds of resources that mediation agents might manipulate.

In a typical KAoS application, most or all agents perform some form of mediation. Since external resources such as a database can be shared among agents, the system designer need not design a single agent as a dedicated resource manager (otherwise that resource manager could become a bottleneck for an otherwise distributed system). For such cases it is preferable that several agents be allowed—where appropriate—to access a given resource through an external resource management facility (for example, a database API).

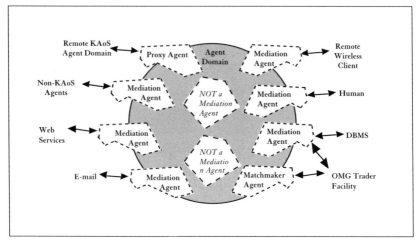

Figure 6. Mediation agents.

Domain Managers and Matchmakers. For an agent domain to become active, two agents must be started. One is the *Matchmaker*, by which agents access information about services within a domain (analogous to the yellow pages in a telephone book). The other is the *Domain Manager*, which controls the entry and exit of agents within a domain, and maintains a set of properties on behalf of the domain administrator.

For an agent to become part of a domain, it first registers itself with the Domain Manager, whose location must be known or accessible to the agent at initialization time. The Domain Manager ultimately lets an agent join a domain, or prevents it from joining based on policies set by the administrator who is responsible for set up of the domain. The Domain Manager relies on a separate naming service (white pages) to associate agent names with implementation specific object references.

In our implementations to date, Matchmakers have been defined as special cases of mediation agents which use external repositories such as system registries or databases to store data about services. The Matchmaker's major function is to help client agents find information about the location of the generic agent instance for any agent within the domain that has advertised its services, and to forward that request to Matchmakers in other domains where appropriate.[18] In a CORBA environment, an OMG *trader facility* could be used in support of the Matchmaker function.

The Domain Manager provides the address of the Matchmaker to agents within its domain. An agent *advertises* a service to the Matchmaker if it is prepared to respond to messages from other agents wishing to use that service. An advertise message may specify whether there are any restrictions on which agents may have access to and visibility of the advertised service. For example, certain services may be made available only to client agents within the advertising agent's own domain. An agent desiring to use a service may ask a Matchmaker to *recommend* available agents that have previously advertised that service. A recommend query may involve simple or sophisticated pattern-matching against an arbitrary collection of potential service provider properties.

The Matchmaker does not currently track agents that consume services but do not provide them. Neither does it directly provide a general repository for shared agent knowledge—if required, this could be implemented by a separate mechanism such as a blackboard. Specific message types used for communication with the Matchmaker are discussed in the Matchmaker Suite subsection.

Agent-to-Agent Communication

Conversations. Unlike most agent communication architectures,[19] KAoS explicitly takes into account not only the individual message in isolation, but also the various sequences in which a particular message may occur. We believe that social interaction among agents is more appropriately modeled when *conversations* rather than isolated illocutionary acts are taken as the primary unit of agent interaction. As Winograd and Flores (1986) observe:

> The issue here is one of finding the appropriate domain of recurrence. Linguistic behavior can be described in several distinct domains. The relevant regularities are not in individual speech acts (embodied in sentences) or in some kind of explicit agreement about meanings. They appear in the domain of conversation, in which successive speech acts are related to one another. (p. 64]

We define a conversation to be a sequence of messages between two agents, taking place over a period of time that may be arbitrarily long, yet is bounded by certain termination conditions for any given occurrence. Conversations may give rise to other conversations as appropriate.

Messages occur only within the context of conversations. Each message is part of an extensible protocol common to the agents participating in the conversation. The content portion of a message encapsulates any semantic or procedural elements independent of the conversation policy itself.

Conversation Policies. A major issue for designers of agent-oriented systems is how to implement policies governing conversational and other social behavior among agents. Walker and Wooldridge (1995) have termed the two major approaches: *off-line design,* in which social laws are hard-wired in advance into agents, and *emergence,* where conventions develop from within a group of agents.

For performance reasons, and because the deeper logic of conversations has yet to be satisfactorily articulated by researchers, the current KAoS architecture provides only for an off-line approach. Just as the KQML agent protocol embodies a separate linguistic messaging layer allowing agents to circumvent the inefficiencies that otherwise would be imposed by the contextual independence of KIF's semantics (Genesereth 1997), KAoS provides an explicit set of mechanisms encoding message-sequencing conventions[20] that, in most situations, frees agents from the burden of elaborate inference that otherwise might be required to determine which next message types are appropriate.[21] Shared knowledge about message sequencing rules enables agents to coordinate frequently recurring interactions of a routine nature simply and predictably.

Conversation policies[22] prescriptively encode regularities that characterize communication sequences between users of a language. A conversation policy explicitly defines what sequences of which messages are permissible between a given set of participating agents.

In current versions of KAoS, state transition diagrams are used to represent each conversation policy.[23] Every transition leads to exactly one state. All transitions lead to a state labeled with a unique identifier such as a number. The scope of the identifier is confined to the conversation policy—that is, no similarity can be inferred between states of the same number in different conversation policies. Exactly one transition (the first transition) in each conversation policy does not originate in a state. Each transition represents a message and is labeled with the originator and recipient, and each but the first transition is labeled with the message name. All states have transitions entering them. Any state with no transition leaving it is a final state; reaching a final state ends the conversation. Some conversation policies implement silence as a valid transition between states; for example, *Inform* may terminate with an acknowledge message or with silence, depending on what option is selected by the initiator of the conversation (see below). Where silence is appropriate, the conversation terminates immediately after the initial transition.

Facilities for implementing conversation policies and carrying out conversations are built into the generic agent capability. A starter set of conversation policies (the *Core suite*) is also provided, but can be replaced or extended as needed. The conversation policies of the default Core suite currently consist of *Inform, Offer, Request, Conversation for Action (CFA),* and *Query* .[24]

Inform. The simplest case of a conversation is Agent A sending a single message to Agent B with the "no response required" option enabled (figure 7). In such a case, Agent B terminates its side of the conversation "silently" and the conversation policy reduces to the kind of atomic message sending encountered in most agent communication languages. A slightly more complex example would be when Agent A requires Agent B to acknowledge receipt of the information. This it does by including a "response required" parameter within the initial message.

Offer. Whereas the effect of an *inform* message is immediate, an *offer* is future-oriented. Hence an offer is something that can be *declined*, while it is impossible to decline to be informed once one already has processed the content of an inform message (figure 8). As an example, a monitoring agent could initiate an *Offer* con-

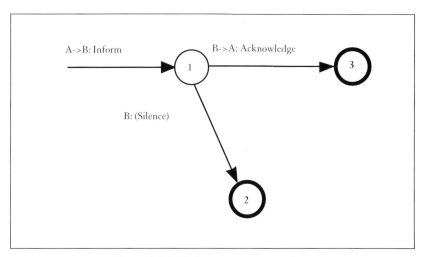

A->B: Inform   B->A: Acknowledge

1   3

B: (Silence)

2

Figure 7. The Inform conversation policy.

versation with another agent that it perceived could benefit from its assistance.

Request. The conversation policy for a *Request* is shown in figure 9. This kind of conversation policy (as opposed to the *Conversation for Action* policy below) is best suited to an agent that known to reliably fulfill its commitments, or for which the consequences of its failure to do so are slight. In the simplest case, Agent B can simply perform the request of Agent A, with an optional acknowledgment. The request may also be declined or countered by Agent B. Agent A can in turn counter again, accept the request, or withdraw it at any time. Once the request has been carried out by B, it optionally sends the *report satisfied* message to A with results returned in the content portion.

We note here that there is a tradeoff between economy of verb types and "naturalness" of expression within a given conversation policy. For example, one could argue that *acknowledge* (in the *Offer* policy) and *report satisfied* (in the *Request* policy) should be replaced by simple *inform* messages. On the other hand, it is clear that the use of the more specific verbs makes it easier to infer the function of the messages in the context of their respective conversation policies.

This tradeoff between economy and naturalness of expression is an issue which cries out for additional study. Based on our informal analysis, we believe that the semantics of the most common types of more specific verbs can be straightforwardly derived from the formal definitions of a small number of basic speech acts.

Conversation For Action. We regard Winograd and Flores' (1986) *Conversation For Action* (CFA) as a more complex variant of Request (figure 10). We include a slightly modified version of their Conversation For Action in our core set of conversation policies, since it seems well-suited to many of the requests

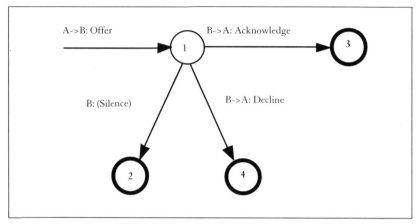

Figure 8. The Offer conversation policy.

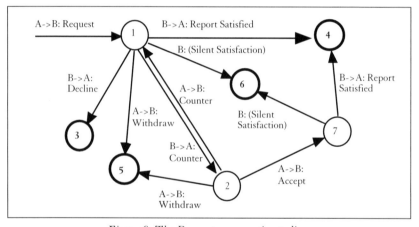

Figure 9. The Request conversation policy.

both that agents make of each other and that humans make of agent systems.[25]

In contrast to the Request conversation policy, Conversation for Action provides a more complex mechanism to handle commitments that persist over time and may not be reliably fulfilled. Additional conversations may well be generated, as the agent negotiates with others to fulfill its commitments. The important feature to note in the state-transition diagram is that communication about commitments is handled explicitly: a definite *promise* must be communicated if B accepts A's initial request, and if B does not intend to fulfill its commitment, it must send a *renege* message to A. A in turn must declare explicitly that it either will *accept* or *decline* the report from B that the request has been satisfied.

Asynchronies in conversations. The implementation of a conversation policy

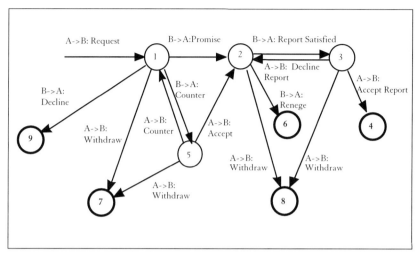

Figure 10. The Conversation For Action (CFA) conversation policy.

must account for asynchronies in conversations (Bowers and Churcher 1988).[26] The major asynchrony of concern is between the time of transmission of a particular message and the time of response.

To handle asynchronies, a conversation policy must be designed to prevent a conversation entering a state from which it cannot process an incoming message. An asynchrony will manifest itself as an attempt to effect an invalid transition on a conversation, and should occur only when more than one participant in a conversation can instigate a valid transition from a state. For example, in figure 10, transitions from state 2 allow messages from either A or B. Each transition from such a state will conform to one of the following rules:

- The transition leads directly to a final state, in which the conversation will no longer exist to process another incoming message. For example, *B:A renege* in figure 10 leaves the conversation in state 6, from which an *A:B withdraw* is irrelevant.

- The transition leads to a non-final state from which any message from another participant valid in the originating state is still valid—for example, because *A:B withdraw* is valid from both states 1 and 2 in figure 10, it will have the desired effect even if *B:A promise* moves the state from 1 to 2.

Conversation policy implementation requirements. The agent initiating a conversation specifies the opening verb and a conversation policy for a conversation, and the responding agent must indicate in return that it is capable of processing both the opening verb and the conversation policy. In implementing a conversation policy, all agents which participate in a conversation will—by definition—correctly generate and interpret all subsequent messages in the conversation.

The capability to implement a conversation policy entails:

- Recognizing incoming messages correctly
- Generating appropriate outgoing messages
- Making the correct state transitions

Verbs. *Verbs* name the type of illocutionary act represented by a message. All verbs fall into one or both of the following categories:

- the name of the initial message in a conversation
- A named state transition in one or more conversation policies

That is, some verbs appear only inside existing conversations; some only initiate conversations, and some may occur in either context.

The agent's capacity to understand any verb which may occur during a conversation is implicit in its capacity to process the conversation policy for that conversation. The capability of understanding a verb which initiates a conversation (an *initial verb*) entails:

- Understanding the initial verb
- Implementing the conversation policy that the verb uses

Suites. A *suite* provides a convenient grouping of conversation policies that support a set of related services.[27] The default *Core suite* of initial verbs and conversation policies is normally available to all agents. In addition to the Core suite, specialized agents such as the Matchmaker would be expected to process at least one additional set of conversations (i.e., the *Matchmaker suite*).

Table 3 represents a conceptual model of the relationship between the basic elements of the Core suite, omitting the *Query* conversation policy which is introduced in the Query subsection that follows. Information about the relationship between a verb and a conversation policy is shown within the cells: an *I* (initial) shows that the verb may act as an initial verb and specify the conversation policy for a new conversation; an *S* (subsequent) shows that the verb may be used during the course of an existing conversation. An *S* in parentheses indicates that the use of the verb within a given conversation policy is optional in some contexts (e.g., acknowledgment of inform messages is not always required)

Rôles. In a typical conversation, the agent requesting a service will select the suite to be used for the conversation. The agent providing the service must have already advertised the service and the set of suites which it requires. Having done so, the two agents may then participate in a conversation, using an appropriate conversation policy in the selected suite.

Since a service-providing agent cannot make its services known to the Matchmaker without first advertising their existence, and since a service-requesting agent cannot access the required services for the first time without having the Matchmaker recommend an appropriate agent, every agent must have access to the Matchmaker suite (described in the Matchmaker Suite subsection that follows). However, there is an important difference between non-

Core Suite	Inform	Offer	Request	CFA
inform	I			
acknowledge	(S)	(S)		
offer		I		
decline		(S)	S	S
request			I	I
counter			S	S
accept			S	S
withdraw			S	S
promise				S
report satisfied			(S)	S
accept report				S
decline report				S
declare satisfied				S
renege				S

Table 3. The basic elements of the Core suite, omitting Query.

Matchmaker and Matchmaker agents in how they will participate in such conversations: the former will only need to know how to *initiate* advertising and recommending conversations in the rôle of a service requester, while the latter must how to *process* them as a service provider.

Rôles serve to partition the available messages, such that a given agent need not implement verbs and conversation policies in ways that it will never use. For example, most KAoS agents will be capable of playing advertiser or requester rôles in conversations with the Matchmaker, but only the Matchmaker agent itself will need to implement capabilities and roles relevant to the processing of *advertise* and *recommend* messages generated by others.

Rôles and suites. A suite maintains the permissible combinations of initial verb, conversation policy, and rôle. It must specify at least two rôles (e.g., one for the initiator of the conversation and one for the respondent). Where appropriate, agents may be permitted to play more than one possible rôle for a given conversation policy. For example, a Matchmaker may act as a service provider during the course of processing a *recommend* conversation for a requesting agent. However, in order to carry out the request, it may subsequently act in the rôle of a service requester by initiating a *recommend* conversation with another

Matchmaker in order to have its assistance in locating service providers consistent with the original *recommend* request.

From table 3, we see that the *Core suite* provides the following combinations of initial verb, conversation policy, and rôle for agents which initiate conversations:

- *Inform, Inform,* informer
- *Offer, Offer,* offerer
- *Request, Request,* requester
- *Request, CFA,* requester

The initial verb of a conversation determines the rôle for the agent originating the conversation. For example, any agent generating an *inform* or *request* verb necessarily acts as an informer or requester, and the agent receiving either of these messages will automatically adopt the rôle or rôles needed to process these incoming messages.

Requirements for conversation initiators and respondents. To allow communication with other agents, each agent must be designed to support one or more conversations. Being a conversation initiator or respondent requires an agent to do the following for one or more combinations of suite, conversation policy, initial verb, and rôle:

- Implement the conversation policies
- Implement the capabilities necessary to process messages appropriate to its rôles in the conversations
- If an initiator, generate the initial verb.

Requirements for agents providing a suite of services. Providing a suite of services entails that an agent must be capable of adopting an appropriate rôle for each conversation in that suite. In other words, an agent must do the following:

- Implement all the suite's conversation policies
- Implement the capabilities necessary to process messages appropriate to its rôles as a service provider within instances of those conversation policies.

Example of Adding a New Conversation Policy: Query. Though the starter set of conversation policies defined in KAoS may be adequate for many common sorts of agent interaction, there will often be a need to add new ones. We will illustrate how this is done by adding a *Query* conversation policy to complete the partial Core suite shown in table 3. The *query* verb can initiate either a *CFA* conversation policy whose state transitions are identical except for the initial verb,[28] or a new *Query* conversation policy (figure 11). The major difference between the *Query* and *Request* conversation policies is that the *B:A report satisfied* message is not optional, and it must by definition contain some result (i.e., a response to the query) as part of its content.

Consistent with the state transition diagram, table 4 shows that the *query* conversation protocol is identical to the *request* conversation protocol except that the use of the *report satisfied* verb is required rather than optional. The shaded cells

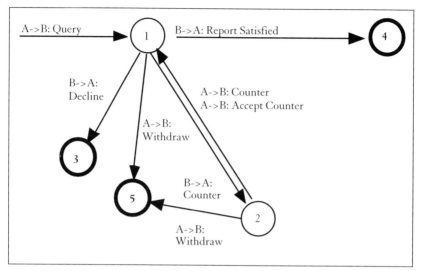

Figure 11. The Query conversation policy.

show what has been newly added: one conversation policy, one verb, and the participation information.

Example of Conversation Policy Reuse: The Matchmaker Suite. One challenge addressed by the KAoS architecture is how to enable developers and consumers of agent services to add a new suite with minimal effort. For example, if a request for a new service could be made by reusing an existing conversation policy combined with a new initial verb, developers could often be spared the trouble of creating a whole new conversation policy and making it available to each potential requester. In the simplest case, any agent desiring access to the service which had already implemented the conversation policy being reused would simply have to extend its data about supported suites with a new initial verb. In many cases, not only the conversation policy but also many of the agent-specific handlers that process the messages of the conversation policy (e.g., countering) could be reused.

As an example, the *Matchmaker suite* is shown as the shaded area of table 5. The suite is implemented by combining existing conversation policies with three new initial verbs: *retire, advertise,* and *recommend.* The *advertise* message is sent to the Matchmaker by any agent wishing to offer services. It uses the *Offer* conversation policy with a more specific verb.[29] The *retire* message is used by an agent to withdraw its services. It uses the *Inform* conversation policy. The *recommend* message is used to request the Matchmaker's help in finding an agent to perform some service. *Recommend* uses the *Query* conversation policy.[30]

The Matchmaker suite thus provides the following combinations of initial verb, conversation policy, and rôle for agents which originate conversations:

Core Suite	Inform	Offer	Request	CFA	Query
inform	I				
acknowledge	(S)	(S)			
offer		I			
decline		(S)	S	S	S
request			I	I	
counter			S	S	S
accept			S	S	S
withdraw			S	S	S
promise				S	
report satisfied			(S)	S	S
accept report				S	
decline report				S	
declare satisfied				S	
renege				S	
query				I	I

Table 4. Completing the Core suite by adding the Query conversation policy.

- *Advertise, Offer*, advertiser
- *Retire, Inform*, retiree
- *Recommend, Query*, requester

Emulating Common KQML Agent Interactions. Using the Core and Match-maker suites as described, one could straightforwardly emulate common types of KQML interactions described by Finin, Labrou, and Mayfield (1997):

- The simple KQML *ask/tell* sequence is identical to the simplest case of the KAoS *Query* where an *A:B query* message would be followed by a *B:A report satisfied* message.
- The KQML *subscribe* example could be implemented as a *Request* that resulted in a series of *inform* messages sent from state 1 whenever the variable of interest changed. The conversation would continue until B decided to send a *decline* message to end the original request for the subscription service. Alternatively, a new *subscribe* verb and/or conversation policy could be added.
- The KQML *recruit* example could be implemented as three separate conversations: the first as an *advertise* conversation between the Matchmaker and

Core	Inform	Offer	Request	CFA	Query
inform	I				
acknowledge	(S)	(S)			
offer		I			
decline		(S)	S	S	S
request			I	I	
counter			S	S	S
accept			S	S	S
withdraw			S	S	S
promise				S	
report satisfied			(S)	S	S
accept report				S	
decline report				S	
declare satisfied				S	
renege				S	
query				I	I
Matchmaker					
advertise		I			
retire	I				
recommend					I

Table 5. The Core and Matchmaker suites.

Agent B, the second as a *recommend* conversation between the Matchmaker and Agent A, and the third, once Agent B was located, as a *query* from A to B. Alternatively, a new, more complex conversation policy for *recruit* or *recommend* could be defined.

- The KQML *broker* conversation would be handled in a similar fashion to *recommend,* except that a new verb would need to be added to the Matchmaker to handle the indirection of the reply.

- The KQML *recommend* example is equivalent to the KAoS Matchmaker's *recommend* conversation.

Applications

In this section we describe some of the applications of KAoS to date.

Initial Prototypes and Agent Utilities

Early versions of KAoS were used to build demonstrations of agent-oriented programming and simulations of various agent activities. The first prototype implemented a multi-agent version of a battleship game, defining specializations of the generic agent class for one or many cooperating ship captains on each team, a game board Matchmaker, an Excel spreadsheet mediation agent, and a referee (Tockey et al. 1995; Atler et al. 1994).

A maintenance performance support prototype demonstrated how mediation agents could help coordinate the interaction between airline maintenance mechanics and their supervisors and adapt the presentation of task-related information through a dynamic OpenDoc component interface (Bos et al. 1995). Generic agent capability was specialized to create a supervisor agent, a job administration agent, a user administration agent, and a client mediation agent that handled interaction between OpenDoc "clients" and a KAoS agent domain.

A scheduling environment prototype showed how KAoS could be used to implement assistants to aid in the process of scheduling meetings and meeting rooms (Barker et al. 1995). A simulation of interaction with the agent system through electronic mail and agent learning of user preferences was also created. The scheduling environment consisted of a set of scheduling agents, a scenario agent, a mail mediation agent handling interaction between a MAPI mail application and the agent domain, and an OLE journaling mediation agent that communicated with Microsoft Excel.

Our experience indicated that a set of utilities to aid the construction, debugging, and maintenance of agents would be invaluable for future applications. We created an agent construction kit prototype based on Microsoft Foundation Classes for the Windows platform, and a visual interface construction kit prototype using HyperCard on the Macintosh. We created a Conversation Monitor to allow particular sets of agent conversations to be logged, passively monitored, or intercepted. A Service Viewer provides a view on the services currently registered with a Matchmaker, and an Agent Structure Viewer allows one to inspect the persistent state of a particular agent. Finally, we have explored the use of NASA's CLIPS development environment to represent and operate on Matchmaker knowledge.

Gaudi Intelligent Performance Support Architecture

The Boeing Company is exploring the use of portable airplane maintenance aids (PMA) and online Web-based tools (Boeing OnLine Data—BOLD) to provide training and support to customers (Guay 1995; Bradshaw et al. 1993) A new version of KAoS is being incorporated into one such prototype of an intelligent performance support system (Bradshaw, et al. 1997). The system, named *Gaudi,*[31] is being designed around the actual processes, activities, and resources of the work environment. It is intended to directly and actively support necessary tasks, adapting information to the requirements of the user and situation. A similar architecture is being developed to support large-scale collaberation between medical staff at the Fred Hutchinson Cancer Research Center and primary-care physicians worldwide (Bradshaw et al. 1997).

Seven requirements guide *Gaudi's* evolution in the long-term:

1. *Think tasks, not documents.* The current transition in desktop computing is from an application-centric to a document-centric paradigm. Distributed component integration technologies (e.g., WWW, OpenDoc, ActiveX, Java) are fueling this trend. However, as component integration technologies increase in power and flexibility, user interfaces will move beyond a document-centric approach to a task-centric one. Large undifferentiated data sets will be restructured into small well-described elements, and complex monolithic applications will be transformed into a dynamic collection of simple parts, driving a requirement for new intelligent technology to put these pieces back together in a way that appropriately fits the context.

2. *Pave where the path is.* This phrase comes from the old story of the college planner who built a new campus with no paths built in at all (Brand 1994, p. 187). After the first winter, she photographed where people made paths in the snow between the buildings, and paved accordingly in the spring. The lesson is that some elements of the design of the system need to be postponed, and learned instead through actual experience with the user. As part of a collaboration with NASA Ames, we are working to incorporate an adaptive engine into *Gaudi.* The adaptive component is described in more detail in the Learning and Adaptivity subsection that follows.

3. *Make all parts replaceable.* The idea is that future users of such a system would be able to easily add to or replace the software applications Boeing provides with applications of their own choosing in conjunction with their own or Boeing-provided data. A migration path from legacy monolithic applications to distributed component-based software must also be provided

4 *Link to anything (without requiring markup).* SGML and HTML-based software typically provides for hyperlinking based on embedded markup of textual data. However embedded markup becomes problematic (Malcolm, Poltrock, and Schuler 1991): where context-sensitive linking is needed, since appropriate links may vary according to the user, task, or situation; where linking needs to be added after the fact to data provided in a read-only format such as CD-ROM, or where the unpredictable nature of the content requires dynamic query-based links rather than static pre-determined ones.

Additionally, new techniques need to be developed to allow linking to complex data elements such as individual frames in a video stream or pieces of 3D geometry. Linking to a variety of live dynamic datafeeds is of particular importance We have implemented an agent-assisted external linking facility that implements dynamic links without requiring markup.

5. *Run it everywhere*. This requirement underlines the necessity of developing a cross-platform approach (i.e., Mac, Windows, UNIX). It also requires that progress in wearable and mobile computing platforms and networking approaches (such as developments in wireless communication) be taken into account.

6. *Pull data from anywhere*. Rather than delivering a closed-box containing a static set of Boeing data, users must be able to dynamically access and integrate data that may reside on a networked server. This data may include anything from a private airline spares database, to a Boeing-managed media server for digital video, to other sources of information residing anywhere on the public Internet.

7. *Let your agents handle the details*. The fragmentation of data into smaller-grain-sized objects and the decomposition of large applications into sets of pluggable components could prove a nightmare for users if there is no support to help them put all the pieces together again. KAoS agents will enable intelligent interoperability between heterogeneous system components, and will help filter and present the right information at the right time in the most appropriate fashion to users who would otherwise be overwhelmed by a flood of irrelevant data.

Issues and Future Directions

Work in progress on mobile agents, formalizing semantics and modeling dialogue as a joint activity, and learning and adaptivity are described in this section.

Mobile Agents

We are working on the issue of agent mobility on two fronts: 1) allowing mobile users of small computing devices to interact with a KAoS agent domain residing on a remote machine, 2) integrating the KAoS architecture with mobile agent approaches that permit the physical migration and secure, managed execution of agent programs on "guest" hosts not belonging to the sender of the agent.

With regard to the first issue, we have completed a prototype of a mediation agent serving a mobile client of the *Gaudi* application by a wireless connection. In the prototype, agents involved in a currently running session can be transferred from one client to another at the request of a user. Though the current session context is preserved in the transfer, the agents are responsible for adapting to the characteristics of the client platform as required. For example, a user can transfer a session running on a desktop with a high-resolution display to a laptop with a low-resolution display. The user interface will adapt to the new hardware configuration, and hyperlinks not appropriate for the new client (e.g., high-resolution multimedia) will be filtered out automatically. A serial connection is maintained only as needed between the mobile client and the machine on which KAoS is running. To preserve power and bandwidth, the connection is an intermittent rather than an exclusive, continuous one.

With regard to the second issue, we are developing a Java implementation of KAoS and are enhancing the KAoS OLE/ActiveX implementation to take advantage of DCOM. Agents will be able to transport themselves in two ways: 1) by transferring an entire agent from one domain to another (*teleportation*), or 2) by transferring only the agent's extension (e.g., as an applet) to a different host (*telesthesia*). In this second scenario, the mobile portion of the agent could execute on remote hosts while remaining in communication with its generic agent in the home domain. Agent communication with other programs may be facilitated by the ability of agents to plug into an open protocol bus hosted as part of client or server Web application services (e.g., LiveConnect on Netscape). We will incorporate industry standards for agent transfer protocols as they emerge (e.g., the *dispatch, retract,* and *fetch* verbs defined in Lange [1996]).[32]

Formalizing Semantics and Modeling Dialogue as a Joint Activity

To date, we have attempted no formal description of the semantics of KAoS agent communication. Ongoing progress in such formalizations is summarized by Cohen and Levesque (1997) and Labrou (Labrou 1996; Labrou and Finin 1994). We anticipate continued collaboration with these and other researchers as this work moves forward.

A more general issue concerns the manner in which such a set of social laws (e.g., conversation policies, collaboration strategies, policies governing reconsideration of conventions) comes to exist within an agent society (Durfee, Gmytrasiewicz, and Rosenschein 1994; Wooldridge and Jennings 1994; Jennings 1993; and Shoham and Tennenholtz 1992). We have noted in the discussion of conversations the distinction between the approaches of *off-line design* and *emergence* of agent social behavior. While the off-line design of social laws generally makes for simpler design and more predictable agent behavior, we see value in allowing for emergent behavior where the situation demands (e.g., complex negotiations [Zlotkin and Rosenschein 1994], teamwork [Cohen and Levesque 1991]).

For example, Cohen (1994) discusses the limitations of "state models" of conversations, such as those we have proposed as part of the current KAoS architecture. While many of the problems he describes (nonliteral language, multifunctional utterances, etc.) are more important for human-human or human-agent communication than for agent-agent interaction using a very restricted language, he makes a good case that, over the long term, "state model" ("dialogue grammar") approaches need to function in concert with more powerful plan-based approaches that require agents to infer one another's intentions at runtime. Cohen summarizes the rationale for plan-based dialogue theories as follows:

> Plan-based models are founded on the observation that utterances are not simply

strings of words, but rather are the observable performance of speech acts… Plan-based theories of communicative action and dialogue assume that the speaker's speech acts are part of a plan, and the listener's job is to uncover and respond appropriately to the underlying plan, rather than just to the utterance. (p. 187).

As an argument he cites Grice's (1975) well-known example of a pedestrian with an empty gas can who asks "Where is the nearest gas station?" The answer "it's two blocks down the road" may be truthful, and a perfectly conformant response given the conversation policy in force, "but would be useless if the speaker knew that the gas station were closed. Rather, what a cooperative dialogue participant is *supposed* to do is provide an answer that addresses the speaker's goals, plans, here, one that directs him to the nearest *open* gas station." (Cohen 1994, p. 187)

Cohen and Levesque (1991) develop the concept of a "joint intention" that applies to a set of agents involved in cooperative dialogue.[33] According to theory, team behavior is more than coordinated individual behavior: it involves the mutual adoption of beliefs, intentions, and goals. For example, when an agent agrees to respond to the query for the nearest gas station, a helpful answer should be seen in terms of its having adopted some subset of the requester's goal structure, agreeing not only to fulfill the manifest request but also to do whatever is reasonable to help satisfy the questioner and meet his objectives. This may include, for example, finding and removing obstacles to the success of the plan, or even recommending a different plan if it is known that the current one will fail.

The KAoS architecture assumes that agents identify each other by the services they advertise; such an environment need not treat random encounters between unrelated agents as a primary concern. Accordingly, the concept of "joint intention" is dealt with only implicitly by considering at design time the services and the rules within conversation policies associated with those services.

Increasing the flexibility and power of agents will require elaboration of joint action theory. Smith and Cohen (1996) have begun the development of a semantics of agent communication that would allow the rigorous analysis of conversation policies such as those described in this chapter (see also Cohen and Levesque 1997). Among other things, they have demonstrated that the behavior of the state transition model of the Winograd and Flores CFA policy is consistent with an emergent behavior of agents operating according to the principles in their model of interagent communication. We expect to accommodate an emergent model of agent communication in a future version of KAoS.[34]

Learning and Adaptivity

It is very difficult to write successful general-purpose agents. That is why some of the most successful applications of adaptive agents (Maes 1997) and programming-by-demonstration environments (Cypher 1993) have been for applications such as mail and calendar managers, where the learning algorithms could operate within a strong task-model that defined context.

Unlike more routine applications, the complexity and dynamic nature of many aerospace problems make it very difficult to anticipate situations or contexts that agents will be encountering. Thus not only the situation patterns, but also much of the task model and contextual knowledge must be acquired online and incrementally as agents perform tasks in the real world.

We intend to provide a framework for the acquisition of situational knowledge by reimplementing and refining the Situation Recognition and Analytical Reasoning (SRAR) model (Bradshaw 1994; Boy and Mathé 1993; Boy 1991; Mathé 1990). The SRAR model was originally developed in 1986 as part of a project to aid astronauts in diagnosing faults in the orbital refueling system of NASA's space shuttle. It has subsequently been applied at NASA Ames to develop a suite of computer-integrated documentation (CID) (Boy 1992; Chen and Mathé 1992) and telerobotics (Mathé and Kedar 1992) applications. Working in collaboration with the originators of this approach, we have begun to integrate and extend selected CID contextual learning mechanisms into the KAoS architecture to assess their value in performance support applications (Mathé and Chen 1994).

The SRAR model provides a formal framework for integrating situational (problem statement situational patterns) and analytical (problem-solving resources) knowledge (figure 12). In the beginning, agents are "inexperienced" and must rely on broad analytic knowledge (e.g., nominal models of tasks and procedures that may be incomplete and incorrect). These analytic models may be acquired through automated knowledge acquisition (Bradshaw et al. 1993) or process- and task-modeling tools (Bradshaw et al. 1992). Learning mechanisms rely on the reinforcement of successful actions, the discovery of failure conditions, and the generation of recovery actions to improve performance. Elements of the analytical knowledge are transferred into situation patterns that embody refinements of how procedures are carried out in real fact by particular people in particular contexts. Over time, situational patterns multiply and become more complex, while analytical knowledge becomes more structured. The result over time is a set of agents that have learned by experience how to adapt to particular people and situation patterns.

Conclusions

The KAoS architecture will succeed to the extent that it allows agents to carry out useful work while remaining simple to implement. Although it is still far from complete, our experience with the current KAoS architecture has shown it to be a powerful and flexible basis for diverse types of agent-oriented systems. The strength of the architecture derives from several sources:

- It is built on a foundation of distributed object technology and is optimized to work with component integration architectures such as Open-

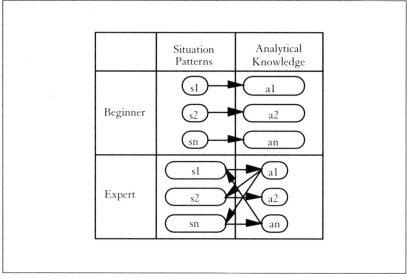

Figure 12. The SRAR model.

Doc, ActiveX, and Java and with distributed object services such as those provided by CORBA, DCOM, and the Internet

- It supports structured conversations that preserve and make use of the context of agent communication at a higher level than single messages; allow differential handling of messages depending on the particular conversation policy and the place in the conversation where the message occurs; and permit built-in generic handlers for common negotiation processes such as countering

- It allows the language of inter-agent communication to be extended in a principled manner, permitting verbs and conversation policies to be straightforwardly reused, adapted, or specialized for new situations

- It groups related sets of conversation policies into suites supporting a coherent set services

- It provides facilities for service names (yellow pages), which are advertised to the Matchmaker by agents offering services

- It provides facilities for agent names (white pages), which allow a Domain Manager to uniquely identify an agent as long as it persists

- It is appropriate for a wide variety of domains and implementation approaches and is platform- and language-neutral

- It allows simple agents to be straightforwardly implemented, while providing the requisite hooks to develop more complex ones

- It supports both procedural and declarative semantics

- It is designed to interoperate with ot[...]
  and protocols (e.g., KQML) either by ex[...]
  to-agent protocol or by defining special[...]

We are optimistic about the prospects for a[...]
tensible object frameworks and look forward[...]
erable agent implementations that will surely r[...]

Acknowledgme[...]

We appreciate all those whose contributions h[...]
cially Jack Woolley (advisor), Steve Tockey (adv[...]
93 Seattle University KAoS team (Nick Georg[...]per, Monica Rosman
LaFever, Katrina Morrison, Dan Rosenthal, Steve Tockey), the 1993-94
AgONy! team (David Atler, Mike Bingle, Tim Cooke, John Morgan, Dan Van
Duine, Michael Zonczyk), the 1994-95 KAoS-CORBA (Dwight Barker, Pete
Benoit, Jim Tomlinson, Sheryl Landon) and TAINT (Mary Bos, Robert Boyer,
Stewart Dutfield, E. J. Jones) teams, and the 1995-96 KAoS OpenDoc (Khalighi
Dariush, Harold Edwards, Dennis O'Brien, James "Bat" Masterson, Feliks
Shostak, Norm Thorsen) and KAoS OLE (David Chesnut, Phil Cooper, Mike
Faulkner, Dan Klawitter, Phuoc Huu Nguyen, Jaimie Roeder) teams. Thanks
also to Ian Angus, Larry Baum, Isabelle Bichindaritzz, John Boose, Guy Boy,
Kathleen Bradshaw, Alberto Cañas, Bob Carpenter, Dick Chapman, Jim Chen,
Phil Cohen, Dave Cooper, Stan Covington, Rob Cranfill, Al Erisman, Megan
Eskey, Ken Ford, Peter Friedland, Brian Gaines, Ralph Giffin, Kirk Godtfred-
sen, Roger Guay, Pat Henderson, Pete Holm, Earl Hunt, Renia Jeffers, Dick
Jones, Randy Kelley, Oscar and Sharon Kipersztok, Cathy Kitto, Vicki Lane,
Henry Lum, David Madigan, Jack Martz, Cindy Mason, John McClees, Bill
McDonald, Mark Miller, Nathalie Mathé, Peter Morton, Ken Neves, Janet
Nims, Sue Pickett, Luis Poblete, Steve Poltrock, Judy Powell, Josh Rabinowitz,
Alain Rappaport, Tyde Richards, Tom Robinson, Kurt Schmucker, John
Schultemaker, Doug Schuler, Dick Shanafelt, Kish Sharma, Mildred Shaw,
Dave Shema, David C. Smith, Jim Spohrer, Keith Sullivan, Amy Sun, Steve
Tanimoto, Rob Thompson, Jim Tomlinson, Sankar Virdhagriswaran, Helen
Wilson, and Debra Zarley. The work described in this chapter was supported in
part by grant R01HS09407 from the Agency for Health Care Policy and Re-
search and by a collaborative research agreement with NASA-Ames.

We expect to make a version of KAoS publically available in late 1997. For
information on the availability of KAoS, contact Jeff Bradshaw at jeffrey.m.
bradshaw@boeing.com, (206) 865-6086.

Notes

1. For surveys illustrating the variety of software agents research, see, for example, Bradshaw (1997), Wooldridge and Jennings (1995), and Nwana (1996).

world's largest software development consortium with a membership [of] ware vendors, developers and end users. Established in 1989, its goal is to [provide a] common architecture framework for distributed object-oriented applications [through] widely available interface specifications.

[Wi]thin the OMG, work is underway to provide standards for interoperability between [M]icrosoft's Distributed Component Object Model (DCOM) and CORBA. Many ORB vendors already provide their own versions of this capability. Various approaches to providing object system interoperability are discussed by Foody (1995).

4. In the spirit of Hewitt's "open systems" (Hewitt 1991; Hewitt and Inman 1991), we do not believe that it is practical or desirable that future systems rely on a specific common agent architecture. What is important is that societies of different kinds of agents, regardless of internal structure, be able to coordinate their activities (Haddadi and Sundermeyer 1996), and that specialized agent architectures and languages optimized for particular domains can proliferate while still being able to interoperate with more general ones.

5. If a particular third-party agent implementation does not conveniently lend itself to direct implementation or emulation in KAoS, one or more mediation agents can be defined to act as a gateway between the disparate agent worlds (see the Mediation Agents subsubsection).

6. It is still too early to tell if agent-oriented programming will require fundamentally different models of software development (Raccoon 1995) and user-interface design (Gentner and Nielsen 1995; Erickson 1997).

7. Russell and Norvig (1995, p. 821) discuss the fact that while the concept of an intentional stance might help us avoid the paradoxes and clashes of intuition, the fact that it is rooted in a relativistic folk psychology can create other sorts of problems. Resnick and Martin (Resnick and Martin 1990; Martin 1988) describe examples of how, in real life, people quite easily and naturally shift between the different kinds of descriptions of designed artifacts. See Erickson (1997) for an additional useful perspective on the advantages and disadvantages of encouraging users to think in terms of agents.

8. See Haddadi and Sundermeyer (1996) for a survey of belief-desire-intention (BDI) agent architectures. Note that the idea of "inheriting" knowledge is somewhat different than that of inheriting methods, or attributes.

9. Alternatively, we have considered whether facts should be defined as beliefs that are global (i.e., all agents pointed to the same set of facts). This definition would prevent the problem of two agents having contradicting "facts" (which is otherwise possible in our architecture). However this approach would impose the daunting requirement that all agents in a potentially unbounded and dynamic agent environment have continuous access to the current global set of facts.

10. There are many issues related to agent persistence that currently remain unsolved. For example, there are problems associated with deactivating an agent while it is involved in an ongoing conversation. If the agent is saved then restored to an environment that has significantly changed, much of its previous knowledge, desires, and intentions may no longer apply.

11. The basic message unit in KAoS is the message tag: {tag = value; }, which can be expanded by recursively replacing the value with another message tag or series of message tags. Our approach is similar in spirit to that of Sims, who has argued the benefits of "semantic data" in OMG forums and in various publications (e.g., Sims 1994, pp. 138–144).

12. The KAoS architecture neither requires interpretation of content by Matchmaker and proxy agents nor disallows it when it is possible and desirable to do so. By way of

comparison, Finin's description of KQML (Finin, Labrou, and Mayfield 1997) states that every implementation "ignores the content portion of the message," whereas Genesereth's (1997) ACL (Agent Communication Language) description of KQML currently makes the commitment to KIF (Knowledge Interchange Format) as the content language, so that the content is always available for interpretation.

13 An agent that comprises more than one agent is called a composite agent. It would necessarily contain more than one instance of the generic agent.

14 Strictly speaking, the bounds of the set of communicating ORBs would constitute the maximum bounds of a particular agent domain; the actual bounds of a particular agent domain could be much smaller according to what was most convenient for agent developers. The domain constitutes the logical unit of administration for some set of agents, so in principle several agent domains with different policies or application scope could co-exist on a single ORB.

15. In object-oriented programming literature, aggregation means one of two things: 1. An alternative to inheritance, used by COM, in which a class picks and chooses attributes and methods—or groups thereof—from other classes (Brockschmidt 1994). The new class has a subset of the union of the attributes and methods from the other classes, together with any attributes and methods which the new class introduces; 2. The sense used here—namely, the composition of an entity (such as an agent) from several object instances.

16. As Finin et al. (1995) observe, proxies can be used to provide a number of services: firewall gateways, protocol gateways, message processing, filtering and annotating, and agent composition.

17. The ability to carry on socket-based communication is currently required of all proxy agents, who optimally may implement additional protocols as well.

18. The Matchmaker performs a similar rôle to a KQML "agent server" facilitator which uses the advertise and recommend performatives (Finin, Labrou, and Mayfield 1997). See Kuokka and Harada (1995) for a discussion of KQML and matchmaking, and Decker, Williamson, and Sycara (1996) for a comparison of matchmaking and brokering approaches. Future versions of KAoS may include brokering capability.

19. Notable exceptions are Barbuceanu and Fox's (1995) COOL, Kuwbara's (1995) AgenTalk, and the GOAL cooperation service framework (Cunningham 1995). Labrou (1996) and Labrou and Finin (1994) have suggested a scheme by which a future version of KQML could implement conversation policies.

20. For an excellent discussion on the role of convention in language use, see Deuchar (1990).

21. Nothing in the architecture precludes a more sophisticated approach, based on an emergent model of agent communication and notions such as joint intention and planning (see the Formalizing Semantics and Modeling Dialogue as a Joint Activity subsection).

22. A concept similar to our conversation policies is that of dialogue grammars (Cohen 1994). We discuss limitations of dialogue grammar models for agent communication in the Formalizing Semantics and Modeling Dialogue as a Joint Activity subsection.

23. An object-oriented design for a finite state machine is described by Ackroyd (1995).

24. The Query conversation policy is described in the Query subsubsection.

25. We are not, however, claiming that the conversation for action model is necessarily well suited for human-to-human conversation (Cohen 1994; DeMichelis and Grasso 1994; Suchman 1993; Cohen and Levesque 1991; Robinson 1991; Bowers and Churcher 1988).

26. See von Martial (1992) for a discussion of asynchronous conversation design techniques abased on finite state models.

27. There is an analog to Apple Event Suites, which group high-level interprocess events supporting a functional area (Apple 1993). Requirements for suite conformance in KAoS, however, are somewhat more stringent than in Apple Event Suites.

28. Replacement of the initial verb of a conversation policy in a specialized suite is permissible when the new initial verb is a strict specialization of the generic illocutionary act in the original conversation policy. For example, *query* is a more specialized *request,* and *decline* is a more specific kind of *inform.*

29. The reason that an advertisement uses the Offer conversation policy rather than the one for Inform is to give the Matchmaker an opportunity to refuse the services of the agent, if it deems it necessary for some reason (e.g., the credentials of the advertising agent are not acceptable). On the other hand, the Inform conversation policy is used for retire, since the agent providing the service should be able to control when its services are no longer available (i.e., the Matchmaker should not be able to refuse the agent's announcement that it is withdrawing its services).

30. The Domain Manager suite and the Proxy suite also reuse conversation policies from the Core suite.

31. The system is named for the Spanish artist and architect, Antonio Gaudi (1852-1926), who is most widely known for his work on the Sagrada Familia temple in Barcelona (Tarrago 1992). This monumental unfinished structure, on which construction still continues after more than a hundred years, symbolizes our desire to investigate architectures capable of outliving its designers and of providing a suitable foundation for unanticipated additions of significant new features. We believe that complex, long-living structures are something that need to be started by designers, but continually "finished" by users (Brand 1994).

32. Standardization of agent transfer protocols is an increasing topic of concern. See for example, discussions by White (Gardner 1996; White 1996), Chang, and Lange (Lange 1996; Chang and Lange 1996).

33. A related concept is Clark's (1992, p. 258) notion of joint conversational or perceptual experiences. The idea is that two people "cannot talk successfully to each other without appealing to their common ground," i.e., "the sum of their mutual knowledge, mutual beliefs, and mutual suppositions" (Clark 1992, p. 3).

34. An implementation of the joint action model would require that KAoS allow for conversations between more than two agents. We have not yet implemented such a capability.

References

Ackroyd, M. 1995. Object-Oriented Design of a Finite-State Machine. *Journal of Object-Oriented Programming* June: 50–59.

Apple. 1993. *Inside Macintosh: Interapplication Communication.*, Reading, Mass.: Addison-Wesley.

Atler, D.; Bingle, M.; Cooke, T.; Morgan, J.; Duine, D. V.; and Zonczyk, M. 1994. *AGONY! Battleship Documentation*, Department of Software Engineering, Seattle University.

Ball, G.; Ling, D.; Kurlander, D.; Miller, J.; Pugh, D.; Skelly, T.; Stankosky, A.; Thiel, D.; Dantzich, M. V; and Wax, T. 1996. Lifelike Computer Characters: The Persona Project at Microsoft Research. In *Software Agents,* ed J. M. Bradshaw. Menlo Park, Calif.: AAAI Press.

Barbuceanu, M., and Fox, M. S. 1995. COOL: A Language for Describing Coordination in Multi-Agent Systems. In Proceedings of the First International Conference on Multi-Agent Systems, ed. V. Lessor, 17–24. Menlo Park, Calif.: American Association for Artificial Intelligence.

Barker, D.; Benoit, P.; Tomlinson, J.; and Landon, S. 1995. kaos corba Design Document, Department of Software Engineering, Seattle University.

Bos, M.; Boyer, R.; Dutfield, S.; and Jones, E. J. 1995. TAINT OPEN JOB Design Document, Department of Software Engineering, Seattle University.

Bowers, J., and Churcher, J. 1988. Local and Global Structuring of Computer-Mediated Representation: Developing Linguistic Perspectives on CSCW in COSMOS. In Proceedings of the Conference on Computer-Supported Cooperative Work. New York: Association of Computing Machinery.

Bowman, C. M.; Danzig, P. B.; Manber, U.; and Schwartz, M. F. 1994. Scalable Internet Resource Discovery: Research Problems and Approaches. Communications of the ACM 37(8): 98–107, 114.

Boy, G. 1992. Computer-Integrated Documentation. In Sociomedia: Multimedia, Hypermedia, and the Social Construction of Knowledge, ed. E. Barrett, 507–531. Cambridge, Mass.: MIT Press.

Boy, G. A. 1997. Software Agents for Cooperative Learning. In Software Agents, ed J. M. Bradshaw. Menlo Park, Calif.: AAAI Press.

Boy, G. A. 1991a. Indexing Hypertext Documents in Context. In Proceedings of the Third ACM Conference on Hypertext, 1–11. New York: Association of Computing Machinery.

Boy, G. A. 1991b. Intelligent Assistant Systems. San Diego, Calif.: Academic.

Boy, G. A., and Mathé, N. 1993. Operator Assistant Systems: An Experimental Approach Using a Telerobotics Application. In Knowledge Acquisition as Modeling, eds. K. M. Ford and J. M. Bradshaw, 271–286. New York: Wiley.

Bradshaw, J. M.; Robinson, T.; and Jeffers, R. 1995. GAUDI: An Unfinished Architecture for Performance Support. Paper presented at the Fifth International Conference on Human-Machine Interaction and Artificial Intelligence in Aerospace (HMI-AI-AS '95), Toulouse, France.

Bradshaw, J. M. 1997. An Introduction to Software Agents. In Software Agents, ed J. M. Bradshaw. Menlo Park, Calif.: AAAI Press

Bradshaw, J. M. 1994. Adaptivity in KAOS, A Knowledgeable Agent-Oriented System. Paper presented at the International Conference on Information Processing and Management of Uncertainty in Knowledge-Based Systems (IPMU), Paris, France.

Bradshaw, J. M.; Boose, J. H.; Covington, S. P.; and Russo, P. J. 1988. How to Do with Grids What People Say You Can't. Proceedings of the Third Knowledge Acquisition for Knowledge-Based Systems Workshop, 4.1–4.20. Banff, Alberta, Canada: SRDG Publications.

Bradshaw, J. M.; Carpenter, R.; Cranfill, R.; Jeffers, R.; Poblete, L.; Robinson, T.; and Sun, A. 1997. The Many Roles of Agent Technology in Knowledge Management: Examples from Applications in Aerospace and Medicine. Presented at the AAAI Spring Symposium on Knowledge Management, Stanford University, Stanford, California, March.

Bradshaw, J. M.; Ford, K. M.; Adams-Webber, J. R.; and Boose, J. H. 1993. Beyond the Repertory Grid: New Approaches to Constructivist Knowledge-Acquisition Tool Development. In Knowledge Acquisition as Modeling, eds. K. M. Ford and J. M. Bradshaw, 287–333. New York: Wiley.

Bradshaw, J. M.; Holm, P.; Kipersztok, O.; and Nguyen, T. 1992. *EQUALITY:* An Application of *AXOTL II* to Process Management. In *Current Developments in Knowledge Acquisition: EKAW-92, eds.* T. Wetter, K.-D. Althoff, J. H. Boose, B. R. Gaines, M. Linster, and F. Schmalhofer, 425–444. Berlin: Springer-Verlag.

Bradshaw, J. M.; Holm, P.; Kipersztok, O.; Nguyen, T.; Russo P. J.; and Boose, J. H. 1991. Intelligent Interoperability in DDUCKS. Paper presented at the AAAI-91 Workshop on Cooperation among Heterogeneous Intelligent Systems, Anaheim, California.

Bradshaw, J. M.; Richards, T.; Fairweather, P.; Buchanan, C.; Guay, R.; Madigan, D.; and Boy, G. A. 1993. New Directions for Computer-Based Training and Performance Support in Aerospace. Paper presented at the Fourth International Conference on Human-Machine Interaction and Artificial Intelligence in Aerospace, 28–30 September, Toulouse, France.

Brand, S. 1994. *How Buildings Learn: What Happens after They're Built..* New York: Viking Penguin.

Brockschmidt, K. 1994. *Inside OLE 2*. Redmond, Wash.: Microsoft.

Brown, C.; Gasser, L.; O'Leary, D. E.; and Sangster, A. 1995. AI on the WWW: Supply-and-Demand Agents. *IEEE Expert*, 10(4): 50–55.

Browne, D.; Totterdell, P.; and Norman, M., eds. 1990. *Adaptive User Interfaces*. San Diego, Calif.: Academic.

Campagnoni, F. R. 1994. IBM's System Object Model. *Dr. Dobb's* 24–28.

Carter, J. 1992. Managing Knowledge: The New Systems Agenda. *IEEE Expert*, 3–4.

Chang, D. T., and Lange, D. B. 1996. Mobile Agents: A New Paradigm for Distributed Object Computing on the WWW. In Proceedings of the OOPSLA 96 Workshop "Toward the Integration of WWW and Distributed Object Technology."

Chen, J. R., and Mathé, N. 1995. Learning Subjective Relevance to Facilitate Information Access. Submitted to CIKM-95.

Clark, H. H. 1992. *Arenas of Language Use*. Chicago, Ill.: University of Chicago Press.

Cohen, P. R. 1994. Models of Dialogue. In Cognitive Processing for Vision and Voice: Proceedings of the Fourth NEC Research Symposium, ed. T. Ishiguro, 181–203. Philadelphia: Society for Industrial and Applied Mathematics.

Cohen, P. R.; and Levesque, H. 1997. Communicative Actions for Artificial Agents. In *Software Agents,* ed J. M. Bradshaw. Menlo Park, Calif.: AAAI Press

Cohen, P. R., and Levesque, H. J. 1991. *Teamwork*, Technote 504, SRI International, Menlo Park, California.

Cohen, P. R., and Levesque, H. J. 1990. Intention Is Choice with Commitment. *Artificial Intelligence* 42(3).

Cunningham, J. 1995. GOAL Cooperation Service Framework. In Proceedings of the First International Conference on Multi-Agent Systems, ed. V. Lessor, addendum. Menlo Park, California: American Association for Artificial Intelligence.

Cypher, A., ed. 1993. *Watch What I Do: Programming by Demonstration*. Cambridge, Mass.: MIT Press.

Decker, K.; Williamson, M.; and Sycara, K. 1996. Matchmaking and Brokering. In *Proceedings of the Second International Conference on Multiagent Systems (ICMAS-96)* Menlo Park, Calif.: AAAI Press.

DeMichelis, G., and Grasso, M. A. 1994. Situating Conversations within the Language-

Action Perspective: The MILAN Conversation Model. In Proceedings of the Conference on Computer-Supported Cooperative Work, eds. R. Furuta and C. Neuwirth, 89–100. New York: Association of Computing Machinery.

Dennett, D. C. (1987). *The Intentional Stance.*, Cambridge, MA: MIT Press.

Deuchar, M. 1990. Are the Signs of Language Arbitrary? In*Images and Understanding,* eds. H. Barlow, C. Blakemore, and M. Weston-Smith. Cambridge, U.K.: Cambridge University Press.

Durfee, E. H.; Gmytrasiewicz, P.; and Rosenschein, J. S. 1994. The Utility of Embedded Communications: Toward the Emergence of Protocols. In Proceedings of the Thirteenth International Distributed Artificial Intelligence Workshop, eds. M. Klein and K. Sharma, 85–93, Boeing Information and Support Services, SEattle, Washington.

Englemore, R., ed. 1988. *Blackboard Systems.* Reading, Mass.: Addison-Wesley.

Etzioni, O., and Weld, D. S. 1995. Intelligent Agents on the Internet: Fact, Fiction, and Forecast. *IEEE Expert* 10(4): 44–49.

Etzioni, O., and Weld, D. 1994. A Softbot-Based Interface to the Internet. *Communications of the ACM* 37(7): 72–76.

Finin, T., Labrou, Y., & Mayfield, J. 1997. KQML as an agent communication language. In *Software Agents,* ed J. M. Bradshaw. Menlo Park, Calif.: AAAI Press.

Finin, T.; Potluri, A.; Thirunavukkarasu, C.; McKay, D.; and McEntire, R. 1995. On Agent Domains, Agent Names, and Proxy Agents. Paper presented at the CIKM Workshop on Intelligent Information Agents, Baltimore, Maryland.

Foody, M. 1995. Providing Object System Interoperability with Middleware. *Cross-Platform Strategies: Supplement to SIGS Publications* 11–21.

Gardner, E. 1996. Standards Hold Key to Unleashing Agents. *Web Week* 5.

Gasser, L. 1991. Social Conceptions of Knowledge and Action: DAI Foundations and Open Systems Semantics. *Artificial Intelligence* 47:107–138.

Genesereth, M. R. 1997. An Agent-based Framework for Interoperability. In *Software Agents,* ed. J. M. Bradshaw. Menlo Park, Calif.: AAAI Press.

Gentner, D., and Nielsen, J. 1995). The Anti-Mac: Violating the MACINTOSH Human-Interface Guidelines. In Proceedings of CHI-95, 183–184. New York: Association of Computing Machinery.

George, N.; Imper, R.; Dwor, M. R.; Morrison, K.; Rosenthal, D.; Tockey, S.; Woolley, J.; Bradshaw, J. M.; Boy, G.; and Holm, P. D. 1994. KAOS: A Knowledgeable–Agent-Oriented System. Paper presented at the AAAI Spring Symposium on Software Agents, 21–23 March, Stanford, California.

Grice, H. P. 1975. Logic and Conversation. In *Syntax and Semantics: Speech Acts,* ed. H. P. Grice. San Diego, Calif.: Academic.

Guay, R. L. 1995. Notebook Simulations as Electronic Performance Support Tools for Airline Maintenance. Paper presented at the Royal Aeronautical Society Flight Simulation Group Simulation in Aircraft Maintenance Training Conference, DATE, London, United Kingdom.

Haddadi, A., and Sundermeyer, K. 1996. Belief-Desire-Intention Agent Architectures. In *Foundations of Distributed Artificial Intelligence,* eds. G. M. P. O'Hare and N. R. Jennings, 169–185. New York: Wiley.

Hanks, S.; Pollack, M. E.; and Cohen, P. R. 1993. Benchmarks, Test Beds, Controlled Experimentation, and the Design of Agent Architectures. *AI Magazine* 14(4): 17–42.

Hewitt, C. 1991. Open Information Systems Semantics for Distributed Artificial Intelligence. *Artificial Intelligence* 47:79–106.

Hewitt, C., and Inman, J. 1991. DAI Betwixt and Between: From "Intelligent Agents" to Open Systems Science. *IEEE Transactions on Systems, Man, and Cybernetics* 21(6): 1409–1419.

Jennings, N. R. 1993. Commitments and Conventions: The Foundation of Coordination in Multi-Agent Systems. *Knowledge Engineering Review* 8(3): 223–250.

Kaehler, T., and Patterson, D. 1986. A Small Taste of Smalltalk. *BYTE* 145–159.

Knoblock, C. A., & Ambite, J.-L. 1996. Agents for Information Gathering. In *Software Agents,* ed. J. M. Bradshaw. Menlo Park, Calif.: AAAI Press.

Kuokka, D., and Harada, L. 1995. On Using KQML for Matchmaking. In Proceedings of the First International Conference on Multi-Agent Systems (ICMAS-95), ed. V. Lesser, 239–245. Menlo Park, Calif.: American Association for Artificial Intelligence.

Kuwabara, K. 1995. AGENTALK: Coordination Protocol Description for Multiagent Systems. In Proceedings of the First International Conference on Multi-Agent Systems, ed. V. Lesser, addendum. Menlo Park, Calif.: American Association for Artificial Intelligence.

Labrou, Y. 1996. Semantics for an Agent Communication Language. Ph.D. diss., University of Maryland at Baltimore County.

Labrou, Y., and Finin, T. 1994. A Semantics Approach for KQML—A General-Purpose Communication Language for Software Agents. In Proceedings of the Third International Conference on Information and Knowledge Management, eds. N. R. Adam, B. K. Bhargava, and Y. Yesha, 447–455. New York: Association of Computing Machinery.

Lange, D. B. 1996. Agent Transfer Protocol ATP/0.1 Draft 4, IBM Research Laboratory, Tokyo.

Maes, P. 1997. Agents that Reduce Work and Information Overload. In *Software Agents,* ed. J. M. Bradshaw. Menlo Park, Calif.: AAAI Press.

Malcolm, K. C.; Poltrock, S. E.; and Schuler, D. 1991. Industrial-Strength Hypermedia: Requirements for a Large Engineering Enterprise. In Proceedings of the Third ACM Conference on Hypertext, PP–PP. New York: Association of Computing Machinery.

Malone, T. W.; Grant, K. R.; and Lai, K.-Y. 1996. Agents for Information Sharing and Coordination: A History and Some Reflections, In *Software Agents,* ed. J. M. Bradshaw. Menlo Park, Calif.: AAAI Press.

Martin, F. 1988. Children, Cybernetics, and Programmable Turtles. Master's thesis, Media Laboratory, Massachusetts Institute of Technology.

Mathé, N. 1990. A Space Remote Control Application: Cognitive Modeling and Blackboard-Based Implementation. Paper presented at the Conference on Human-Machine Interaction in Aeronautics and Space, Toulouse-Blagnac, France.

Mathé, N., and Chen, J. 1994. A User-Centered Approach to Adaptive Hypertext Based on an Information Relevance Model. Paper presented at the Fourth International Conference on User Modeling (UM '94), Hyannis, Massachusetts.

Mathé, N., and Kedar, S. T. 1992. Increasingly Automated Procedure Acquisition in Dynamic Systems. Paper presented at the Seventh Banff Knowledge Acquisition for Knowledge-Based Systems Workshop, Banff, Canada.

Nelson, P. R., and Schuler, D. 1995. Managing Engineering Information with Hypermedia, Boeing Commercial Airplane Group, Seattle Washington.

Nelson, T. 1980a. Interactive Systems and the Design of Virtuality, Part 1. *Creative Computing* 56–62.

Nelson, T. 1980b. Interactive Systems and the Design of Virtuality, Part 2. *Creative Computing* 95–106.

Nwana, H. S. 1996. Software Agents: An Overview. *Knowledge Engineering Review* Forthcoming.

O'Hare, G. M. P.; and Jennings, N. R. ed. 1996. *Foundations of Distributed Artificial Intelligence*. New York: John Wiley and Sons.

Orfali, R.; Harkey, D.; and Edwards, J. 1995. Client-Server Components: CORBA meets OPENDOC. *Object Magazine* 55–59.

Raccoon, L. B. S. 1995. The CHAOS Model and the CHAOS Life Cycle. *ACM SIGSOFT Software Engineering Notes* 20(1): 55–66.

Reinhardt, A. 1994. The Network with Smarts. *BYTE* 10: 50–64.

Repenning, A. 1993. AGENT SHEETS: A Tool for Building Domain-Oriented Dynamic, Visual Environments. Ph.D. diss., University of Colorado.

Resnick, M., and Martin, F. 1990. Children and Artificial Life, E&L Memo, 10, Media Laboratory, Massachusetts Institute of Technology.

Rettig, M. 1991. Nobody Reads Documentation. *Communications of the ACM* 34(7): 19–24.

Richman, D. 1995. Let Your Agent Handle It. *InformationWeek* 44–56.

Riecken, D. 1997. The M System. In *Software Agents,* ed. J. M. Bradshaw. Menlo Park, Calif.: AAAI Press.

Robinson, M. 1991. Computer-Supported Cooperative Work: Case and Concepts. In *Groupware 1991: The Potential of Team and Organisational Computing,* eds. P. R. Hendriks, 59–75, Utrecht, The Netherlands: SERC.

Russell, S., and Norvig, P. 1995. *Artificial Intelligence: A Modern Approach*, New York: Prentice-Hall.

Saffo, P. 1994. It's the Context, Stupid. *Wired* 3:74–75.

Shoham, Y. 1997. An Overview of Agent-oriented Programming. In *Software Agents,* ed J. M. Bradshaw. Menlo Park, Calif.: AAAI Press.

Shoham, Y. 1991. Agent Oriented Programming. *Artificial Intelligence*, 60(1): 51–92.

Shoham, Y., and Tennenholtz, M. 1992. On the Synthesis of Useful Social Laws for Artificial Agent Societies. In Proceedings of the Tenth National Conference on Artificial Intelligence, 276–281. Menlo Park, Calif.: American Association for Artificial Intelligence.

Siegel, J. 1996. *CORBA: Fundamentals and Programming.* New York: John Wiley.

Sims, O. 1994. *Business Objects: Delivering Cooperative Objects for Client-Server.* New York: McGraw-Hill.

Singh, M. P. 1994. *Multiagent Systems: A Theoretical Framework for Intentions, Know-How, and Communication.* Berlin: Springer-Verlag.

Smith, I. A., and Cohen, P. R. 1996. Toward a Semantics for an Agent Communications Language based on Speech-Acts. In *Proceedings of the Thirteenth National Conference on Artificial Intelligence,* 24-31. Menlo Park, Calif.: AAAI Press.

Spohrer, J. C.; Vronay, D.; and Kleiman, R. 1991. Authoring Intelligent Multimedia Applications: Finding Familiar Representations for Expressing Knowledge. Paper presented at the 1991 IEEE International Conference on Systems, Man, and Cybernetics, Charlottesville, Virginia.

Suchman, L. 1993. Do Categories Have Politics? The Language-Action Perspective Reconsidered. In *Proceedings of the Third European Conference on Computer-Supported Cooperative Work,* 1–14. Dordrecht, The Netherlands: Kluwer Academic.

Tambe, M.; Johnson, W. L.; Jones, R. M.; Koss, F.; Laird, J. E.; Rosenbloom, P. S.; and Schwamb, K. 1995. Intelligent Agents for Interactive Simulation Environments. *AI Magazine* 16(1): 15–39.

Tarrago, S. 1992. *Gaudi.* Barcelona: Editorial Escudo de Oro, S.A.

Tockey, S.; Rosenthal, D.; Rosman LaFever, M.; Jasper, R.; George, N.; Woolley, J. D.; Bradshaw, J. M.; and Holm, P. D. 1995. Implementation of the KAOS Generic Agent-to-Agent Protocol. *Northwest AI Forum (NAIF) Journal.*

Van de Velde, W. 1995. Cognitive Architectures—From Knowledge Level to Structural Coupling. In *The Biology and Technology of Intelligent Autonomous Agents,* ed. L. Steels, 197–221. Berlin: Springer-Verlag.

Virdhagriswaran, S. 1994. Heterogeneous Information Systems Integration: An Agent-Messaging–Based Approach. Presented at the CIKM-94 Workshop on Intelligent Agents, Gaithersburg, Maryland.

Virdhagriswaran, S.; Osisek, D.; and O'Connor, P. 1995. Standardizing Agent Technology. *ACM Standards View.* Forthcoming.

von Martial, F. 1992. *Coordinating Plans of Autonomous Agents.* Heidelberg, Germany: Springer-Verlag.

Walker, A., and Wooldridge, M. 1995. Understanding the Emergence of Conventions in Multi-Agent Systems. In Proceedings of the First International Conference on Multi-Agent Systems, ed. V. Lessor, 384–389. Menlo Park, Calif.: American Association for Artificial Intelligence.

Wayner, P. 1995. Free Agents. *BYTE* 105–114.

White, J. 1996. A Common Agent Platform, General Magic, Inc. Sunnyvale, Calif.

Wiederhold, G. 1992. Mediators in the Architecture of Future Information Systems. *IEEE Computer* 38–49.

Winograd, T., and Flores, F. 1986. *Understanding Computers and Cognition.* Norwood, N.J.: Ablex.

Woelk, D.; Huhns, M.; and Tomlinson, C. 1995. Uncovering the Next Generation of Active Objects. *Object* 4:33–40.

Wooldridge, M. J., and Jennings, N. R. 1995. Agent Theories, Architectures, and Languages: A Survey. In *Intelligent Agents: ECAI-94 Workshop on Agent Theories, Architectures, and Languages*, eds. M. J. Wooldridge and N. R. Jennings, 1–39. Berlin: Springer-Verlag.

Wooldridge, M. J., and Jennings, N. R. 1994. Formalizing the Cooperative Problem-Solving Process. In Proceedings of the Thirteenth International Distributed Artificial Intelligence Workshop, eds. M. Klein and K. Sharma, 403–417. Seattle, Wash.: Boeing Information and Support Services.

Zlotkin, G., and Rosenschein, J. 1994. *Rules of Encounter: Designing Conventions for Automated Negotiation among Computers.*, Cambridge, Mass.: MIT Press.

CHAPTER 18

Communicative Actions for Artificial Agents

Philip R. Cohen & Hector J. Levesque

A language for interagent communication should allow agents to enlist the support of others to achieve goals; to commit to the performance of actions for another agent; to monitor their execution; to report progress, success, and failure; to refuse task allocations; to acknowledge receipt of messages, etc. Crucially, a collection of agents needed to accomplish a task will frequently include humans who have delegated tasks to the agents, and/or humans who will be performing some of the work. As such, it is essential that the functions being offered by the communication language be common across the language of intelligent agents and the language that people will use to communicate with them.

It so happens that there is such a language, the language of "speech acts" (Austin 1962, Searle 1969), or more precisely, "illocutionary acts." Such actions include requesting, promising, offering, acknowledging, proposing, accepting, etc. Philosophers of language noted that human utterances are the observable byproduct of such actions, and moreover, that utterances may realize more than one such action simultaneously (such as being both an assertion and a request). AI researchers have modeled such actions as operators in planning systems (Allen and Perrault 1980, Appelt 1985, Bruce 1975, Cohen and Perrault 1979) and have developed logical frameworks for providing their semantics (Cohen and Levesque 1990b, Perrault 1990, Sadek 1991).

Recently, a number of researchers have proposed artificial languages based on speech act theory as the foundation for interagent communication (ARPA 1993, Labrou 1994, McCarthy 1989, Shoham 1993, Sidner 1994). The most elaborate and developed of these is KQML (ARPA 1993). In this language, agents communicate by passing so-called "performatives" to each other. KQML is offered to the agent community as an *extensible* language with an open-ended set of performatives, whose meaning is independent of the propositional content language (e.g., Prolog, first-order logic, SQL, etc.) However, the authors of KQML have yet to provide a precise semantics for this language, as is customary with programming languages.[1] Without one, agent designers cannot be certain that the interpretation they are giving to a "performative" is in fact the same as the one some other designer intended it to have. Moreover, the lack of a semantics for communication acts leads to a number of confusions in the set of reserved "performatives" supplied. Lastly, designers are left unconstrained and unguided in any attempt to extend the set of communication actions.

This chapter claims that substantive confusions exist in the KQML specification that undermine its semantical basis. As an example of how semantics can be given to communicative actions, we propose adequacy criteria for a semantical treatment and illustrate how our semantics of speech acts obeys them. Finally, we discuss the impact these analyses may have on various design decisions made in KQML.

Background: Performatives

In natural languages, a performative utterance is one that succeeds simply because the speaker *says* or *asserts* she or he is doing so. Usually, in English, such utterances arise in a first-person, present tense declarative utterance, often accompanied by "hereby," as in "I hereby request you to get off my foot." However, this is not always the case, and performatives can occur in the third person ("We request you to attend the marriage of our son,") in the passive ("Passengers are requested to refrain from smoking"), and even brokered via third parties (as when a translator might say "The King requests you to remove your shoes.") The important commonality among these uses is that the action is performed by saying so. Essentially, the speaker is *asserting* that *this* utterance is a request, order, or whatever.

When does saying so make it so? There are a number of cases to be considered, but we discuss only one here (for a more complete discussion, see Cohen and Levesque [1990c]). Performative uses of illocutionary verbs succeed because, on our analysis, such verbs are defined as *attempts*. That is, the semantics of the illocutionary act is that the speaker is attempting to communicate his or her mental state. By asserting that she or he is doing so, the act succeeds in doing so because the speaker is taken to be an expert on his or her own mental state. In most cases, then, the listener will immediately assume the speaker is in the requisite mental state, and the act succeeds. (See Cohen and Lesveque 1990a for proofs of the relevant theorems.) Importantly, it should be noticed that many verbs, namely, perlocutionary verbs, *cannot* be used performatively. For example, in English, "I hereby convince you that your birthday is March 3" cannot be a performative utterance because one cannot be guaranteed that the listener will be convinced.

A second constraint to be observed is that some verbs are *self-defeating* when used performatively. For example, "I hereby lie to you that I took out the garbage" cannot be a successful lie. Our semantics shows logically why this cannot be so, and thus provides a model for the kinds of constraints that can apply on the formation of new performatives.

The problem of performatives for natural language speech act theories, then, is how a declarative utterance, which looks like an assertion, can in fact (also) be something else, namely the act it names. That is, what is uttered appears to be something with a truth value. But most illocutionary acts, for example, requests, do not have a truth value. Rather, what has a truth value is the proposition that *this* utterance constitutes the named action.

KQML

Briefly, KQML is a communication language that has been designed to facilitate high-level cooperation and interoperation among artificial agents (Finin etal 1994a, Genesereth and Ketchpel 1994, Labrou and Finin 1994). Agents may range from simple programs and databases to more sophisticated knowledge-based systems. The language is proposed as a general-purpose standard for interagent communication (Labrou 1994), and is being used in a number of projects in the USA. KQML offers an extensible set of so-called "performatives" that specify what kinds of communications agents can have with one another. Examples include *achieve, advertise, ask-if, ask-all, broker, deny, error, stream-all, tell,* and *unachieve.* For example, the following is the description of the "performative" *deny,* taken from KQML 1993:

```
deny
       :content <performative>
       :language KQML
       :ontology <word>
       :in-reply-to <expression>
       :sender <word>
       :receiver <word>
```

Performatives of this type indicate that the meaning of the embedded <performative> is *not* true of the sender. A *deny* of a *deny* cancels out.

Communicative actions such as these are considered performatives in the sense that "the message is intended to perform some action in virtue of being sent" (ARPA 1993, p. 4).

Coupled with KQML is a set of policies that dictate constraints on legal sequences of communication acts, which are enforced through some combination of constraints on KQML developers, agent developers, and specific modules (e.g., the conversation module, Labrou and Finin 1994). These policies induce a set of interagent conversation patterns using the communication actions.

Critique of KQML as an Agent Communication Language

We have identified three general difficulties with the draft KQML specification (ARPA 1993): ambiguity and vagueness, misidentified performatives, and missing performatives.

Ambiguity and Vagueness

The meaning of the reserved or standard performatives is rather unclear. Performatives are given English glosses, which often are vague or ambiguous. For example, given that the definition of *deny* says that the embedded performative is not true of the speaker, if an agent *denys* a *tell*, does that mean the agent did not *tell* earlier, or does not believe what is being said now? A close reading of this definition reveals another confusion lurking — it says that what agents deny is a performative, and it is no longer true of the speaker. This implies that performatives do in fact have truth values, and are not actions after all. If so, then the semantic type of a performative is most likely a proposition. We therefore return to the problem of natural language performative utterances, namely how the uttering of an expression with a truth value constitutes the performance of an action. Actually, we do not believe this interpretation is intended by the authors of KQML. Rather, the definition of *deny,* as well as those of many other "performatives," are simply miscast. However, given that other performatives are defined in terms of *deny,* such as *unregister* and *untell,* it is no small error.[2]

Misidentified Performatives

KQML labels as performatives actions that should be the argument of a directive speech act, e.g., requesting. For example, *achieve* is glossed in English as a request to get the addressed agent to make something true. But, the formalism omits the request. Accordingly, it is an error to include acts such as *achieve, broker, stream-all* as performatives because an agent cannot execute another agents' actions or satisfy another agent's goals, merely by saying so (i.e., sending a message). In fact, the relevant performative should be a directive act (e.g., a request).

In summary, there are really only two types of speech acts discussed in the draft specification for KQML, the directive and assertive. Semantics of these actions has been given in great detail elsewhere (Cohen and Levesque 1990c, Sadek 1991) and will be briefly discussed below.

Missing Performatives

Although KQML offers an extensible language, a most important class of communication actions seems to be missing entirely—the commissives, which commit an agent to a course of action. The prototypical example of a commissive is promising; other examples include accepting a proposal, and agreeing to perform a requested action. Without these actions, it is hard to see how any multiagent system could work robustly. Whenever an agent is busy and cannot immediately execute a requested action, the requesting agent would be blocked, as it has no reason to believe that it can proceed, and that an answer will be forthcoming. The requesting agent cannot even receive a confirmation that its requested action has been accepted by a given agent, as there are no acceptances in the language.[3]

Some researchers have suggested that the language does not need commissive performatives. Rather, it is argued that a *tell* that the sender *will* do an action *A* should suffice. We believe there are numerous problems with this suggestion. First, the logical form of this *tell* is essentially that of a prediction —the sender is asserting what *will* be true in the future. When a prediction fails, it is open to the agent merely to say "well, I was wrong," and to revise its beliefs. This is simply too weak. Someone who proposes marriage and hears the performative "I assert that I will marry you (eventually)" in response is unlikely to rent a wedding hall.[4] A commitment, however, would be cause for celebration. The agent is supposed to *make* commitments true, to screen out incompatible options, to track its success, etc. (Bratman 1987, Cohen and Levesque 1990a).

The second option is to approximate a commitment with an agent's telling what *it* will do. The only way this can succeed is if we insist that agents do not come to this conclusion in any way other than by having a commitment/intention. Otherwise, the agent may fall victim to the "Little Nell" problem (Cohen and Levesque 1990a, McDermott 1982), in which the agent never forms the intention to act because it already believes the action will happen. But, if the conclusion that the agent eventually acts arises because the agent is committed, why not have the agent just say so?

The third difficulty with trying to avoid commitment by issuing a *tell* of what the sender will do, is that acknowledging this special case would violate the KQML design decision of having the performatives be independent of the content language. Here, one would have to stipulate special rules for contents of the apppropriate form (i.e., a future operator applied to the agent's actions).

It appears to us that KQML is underspecified, and in need of a semantical treatment to clarify what in fact agents and agent designers are supposed to mean by performing communicative actions. This lack of a semantics has not gone unnoticed, as Labrou and Finin (1994) have attempted an initial semantics using a simple pre/post-condition analysis of speech acts, loosely based on Searle and Vanderveken's multidimensional semantics (1985). We have discussed elsewhere (Cohen and Levesque 1990b) problems with this type of semantics, specifically that much of what is stipulated can be derived. As an example, of the kind of semantics we believe is called for, we review our analysis of speech acts, which is appropriate to both human and artificial agents. Although we provide semantics in terms of mental states, the agents themselves need not reason using these attitudes, but need only behave according to the principles they entail.

We begin by giving an abbreviated description of our analysis of rational action upon which we erect a theory of speech acts. The theory is cast in a modal logic of belief, goal, action, and time. Further details of this logic can be found in Cohen and Levesque (1990a). Then, we show how the speech acts of requesting and informing compose, using as an example, the asking of a yes-no question.

Abbreviated Theory of Rational Action

In this section, we describe our analysis of rational action upon which our theiry of speech acts is built .

Syntax

The language we use has the usual connectives of a first-order language with equality, as well as operators for the propositional attitudes and for talking about sequences of events: $(BEL\ x\ p)$ and $(GOAL\ x\ p)$ say that p follows from x's beliefs or goals (a.k.a choices) respectively; $(BMB\ x\ y\ p)$ says that x believes that p is a mutual belief with y; $(AGT\ x\ e)$ says that x is the only agent for the sequence of events e; $e_1 \le e_2$ says that e_1 is an initial subsequence of e_2; and finally, $(HAPPENS\ a)$ and $(DONE\ a)$ say that a sequence of events describable by an action expression a will happen next or has just happened, respectively.

An action expression here is built from variables ranging over sequences of events using the constructs of dynamic logic: $a;b$ is action composition; $a|b$ is nondeterministic choice; $a\|b$ is concurrent occurrence of a and b; $p?$ is a test action; and finally, a^* is repetition. The usual programming constructs such as *IF/THEN* actions and *WHILE* loops, can easily be formed from these. Because test actions occur frequently in our analysis, yet create considerable confusion, read $p?;a$ as "action a occurring when p holds," and for $a;p?$, read "action a occurs after which p holds." We use e as a variable ranging over sequences of events, and a and b for action expressions.

We adopt the following abbreviations:

$(DONE\ x\ a) \stackrel{\text{def}}{=} (DONE\ a) \wedge (AGT\ x\ a)$.

$(HAPPENS\ x\ a) \stackrel{\text{def}}{=} (HAPPENS\ a) \wedge (AGT\ x\ a)$.

$(AFTER\ a\ p) \stackrel{\text{def}}{=} (HAPPENS\ a;p?)$

$\Diamond p \stackrel{\text{def}}{=} \exists e\ (HAPPENS\ e;p?)$.

$(LATER\ p) \stackrel{\text{def}}{=} \neg p \wedge \Diamond p$.

$\Box p \stackrel{\text{def}}{=} \neg \Diamond \neg p$.

$(PRIOR\ p\ q) \stackrel{\text{def}}{=} \forall c\ (HAPPENS\ c;q?) \supset \exists a\ (a \le c) \wedge$
$(HAPPENS\ a;p?)$.

The proposition p will become true no later than q.

$(KNOW\ x\ p) \stackrel{\text{def}}{=} p \wedge (BEL\ x\ p)$.

Individual Commitments and Intentions

To capture one grade of commitment that an agent might have toward his goals, we define a persistent goal, *P-GOAL*, to be one that the agent will not give up until he thinks certain conditions are satisfied. Specifically, we have

Definition 1—Internal Commitment:

(P-GOAL x p q) $\stackrel{\text{def}}{=}$

(1) (BEL x ¬ p) $\wedge$

(2) (GOAL x (LATER p)) $\wedge$

(3) [KNOW x (PRIOR [(BEL x p)$\vee$(BEL x $\square$¬ p)$\vee$(BEL x ¬ q)]

¬ [GOAL x (LATER p)])].

That is, the agent *x* believes *p* is currently false, chooses that it be true later, and knows that before abandoning that choice, he must either believe it is true, believe it never will be true, or believe *q*, an escape clause (used to model subgoals, reasons, etc.) is false.

Intention is a kind of persistent goal in which an agent commits to having done an action, in a particular mental state.[5]

Definition 2—Intention:

(INTEND$_1$ x a q) $\stackrel{\text{def}}{=}$

(P-GOAL x [DONE x (BEL x (HAPPENS a))?;a] q).

Intending to do an action *a* or achieve a proposition *p* is a special kind of commitment (i.e., persistent goal) to having done the action *a* or having achieved *p*. However, it is not a simple commitment to having done *a* or *e;p?* for that would allow the agent to be committed to doing something accidentally or unknowingly. Instead, we require that the agent be committed to arriving at a state in which he believes he is about to do the intended action next.

This completes a brief discussion of the foundational theory of intention and commitment. Next, we proceed to define the communicative actions.

Illocutionary Acts as Attempts

Searle (1969) points out that an essential condition for a request is that the speaker be attempting to get the addressee to perform the requested action. We take this observation one step further and define all illocutionary acts as attempts, hence defined in terms of the speaker's mental states. Attempts involve both types of goal states, GOAL (merely chosen) and INTEND (chosen with commitment):

Definition 3—{ATTEMPT x e Ψ Φ } $\stackrel{\text{def}}{=}$

[(GOAL x (LATER Ψ)) $\wedge$

(INTEND$_1$ x e;Φ? (GOAL x (LATER Ψ)))]? ; e

That is, an attempt to achieve Ψ via Φ is a complex action expression in which x is the agent of event e, and just prior to e, the agent chooses that Ψ should eventually become true and intends that e should produce Φ relative to that choice. So, Ψ represents some ultimate goal that may or may not be achieved by the attempt, while Φ represents what it takes to make an honest effort.[6]

Adequacy Criteria for a Semantics for Communicative Actions

In Cohen and Perrault (1979) we provided a strong adequacy criterion for theories of human speech acts, namely compositionality. Speech acts that take actions as arguments, such as requests, should be able to take other speech acts as arguments. Moreover the appropriateness and success conditions of the composite communicative act should be based on those of the elementary ones. Thus, yes-no and wh-questions should be correctly handled as composite speech acts, with the proper semantics derived from both request and inform (Cohen and Perrault 1979, Perrault and Allen 1980, Sadek1991). Similarly, a request should properly embed a request to an intermediating agent (Cohen and Perrault 1979), and provide reasonable conditions on the knowledge of the intermediating agent about the ultimate recipient. Appropriateness conditions that arise include whether or not the intermediating agent has to believe the recipient can in fact do the requested action. Intuitively, if the original request is simply forwarded to a named recipient, the answer should be "no." However, if the middle agent (i.e., facilitator) is supposed to *recruit* an agent to satisfy a request directed at no one in particular, then the answer should be "yes."

Below we provide a semantics for illocutionary acts that provides such compositionality. For space considerations, we consider only the case of a yes/no question. We first define speech acts that are appropriate to both human and software agents, and then we discuss where the two kinds of communicative actions may diverge.

Definitions of Request and Inform

Illocutionary acts (IAs) are modeled as complex action expressions in the dynamic logic. Essentially, an IA is an event performed in the "right" circumstances, namely when the agent is attempting to achieve a certain type of effect —to communicate its mental state.

To characterize a request or, for that matter, any illocutionary action, we must decide on the appropriate formulas to substitute for Φ and Ψ in the definition of an attempt. We constrain illocutionary acts to be those in which the speaker is committed to *understanding,* that is, to achieving a state of *BMB* that he is in a certain mental state. Moreover, we will for now adopt the strong assumption that agents that are part of the network are in fact sincere, although the semantics provided does not depend on sincerity. Our definition of sincerity from Cohen and Levesque (1990a) is:

Definition 4 —Sincerity:

(SINCERE x y p) $\stackrel{\text{def}}{=}$
   $\forall$e (GOAL x (HAPPENS x e; (BEL y p)?)) $\supset$
    (GOAL x (HAPPENS x (KNOW y p))?)

In other words, agent x is sincere to y about p if whenever x wants y to come to believe p, x wants y to come to know p.

Below is a definition of a speaker's requesting an addressee to achieve α, where α is an action expression containing a free variable e'. The idea is that requesting α is requesting the action to be performed for some value of the free variable. For example, a request to perform the action *{ClosedWindow?;e';OpenWindow?}* is a request to open the window. Complete definitions and an extensive justification of the various conditions can be found in Cohen and Levesque (1990a).

Definition 5—{REQUEST spkr addr e α} $\stackrel{\text{def}}{=}$

{ATTEMPT spkr e $\exists$e' (DONE addr α)
  [BMB addr spkr
    (GOAL spkr $\exists$e'
      [$\Diamond$(DONE addr α) $\wedge$
      (INTEND$_1$ addr α
        (GOAL spkr
          [$\Diamond$[DONE addr α) $\wedge$
          (HELPFUL addr spkr)])])]) }

That is, event e is a request if it is an attempt at that time to get the addressee to do α, while being committed to making public that the speaker wants first, that α be done, and second, that the addressed party should intend to achieve it relative to the speaker's wanting it and relative to the addressee's being helpfully disposed towards the speaker.[7] This means that the addressee is allowed to "get off the hook" if the speaker changes its mind about desiring the action α done.

The illocutionary act of informing can be defined as an attempt get the addressee to know that some proposition is true:

Definition 6— { INFORM spkr addr e p } $\stackrel{\text{def}}{=}$

{ATTEMPT spkr addr e
  (KNOW addr p)
  [BMB addr spkr
    (P-GOAL spkr
      (KNOW addr (KNOW spkr p)))] }

So an inform is defined as an attempt in which to make an "honest effort," the speaker is committed to making public that he is committed to the addressee's knowing that he knows p. That is, just like a request, the speaker is committed to the addressee's knowing what mental state he is in. Although he is committed to getting the addressee to believe something about his *goals,* what he hopes to achieve is for the addressee to come to know p.

At this point in our analysis of human speech acts, utterance events were characterized as producing a *BMB* that the speaker is in the mental state characterized by the mood indicators in the utterance (e.g, imperative or indicative). However, the general framework for artificial agents differs somewhat from our analysis of the human case. Our notion of an attempt included a commitment to making an "honest effort," which requires an agent to overcome obstacles to successful delivery and understanding of the message. Let us assume that the KQML framework, with its routers and matching of content languages between the sending and receiving agents, functions as specified. We therefore make the further assumption that the second condition in the attempt, the one the agent is committed to, in fact becomes true after the act.[8]

Semantics for a Yes-No Question

Using these speech acts, it is now easy to characterize a yes-no question. We simply use the following action expression (suggested in Sadek 1991):

{REQUEST spkr addr e
{INFORM addr spkr e′ p} | {INFORM addr spkr e′ ¬p}}

That is, using the nondeterministic choice operator (a disjunction for actions), we have a request for the addressee to either inform the speaker that p or inform the speaker that ¬p.[9] Notice that we have not needed to postulate a new species of inform, namely *informif* as done in Allen and Perrault (1980), Cohen and Perrault (1979), or *ask-if* in KQML.

Now, among the various felicity conditions for use of this composite action, we need to identify the sincerity condition. We show that in x's asking the question to y whether or not $p,$ the asking agent, is in the following mental state:

(GOAL x ◇[(Know x p) ⋁ (Know x ¬p)])

Theorem 1. Questions:

(Done x {REQUEST x y e
{INFORM y x e′ p} | {INFORM y x e′ ¬p} }) ⊃
(GOAL x ◇[(KNOW x p) ⋁ (KNOW x ¬p)]).

Proof Sketch. Given what was discussed above, we assume that the network has in fact functioned as designed, and that the requesting event has been observed, understood, and its reception acknowledged by the receiver. Thus, we assume that

(BMB y x
(GOAL x
∃e′[◇(DONE y α) ⋀
(INTEND₁ y α
(GOAL x [◇(DONE y α) ⋀
(HELPFUL y x)])))])
where α is {INFORM y x e′ p} | {INFORM y x e′ ¬p}

That is, the receiver y thinks it is mutually believed that the sender x wants y to inform x that p or inform x that $\neg p$, and to intend to do so relative to x's desires and y's helpfulness.

Let us consider only the first conjunct of the *BMB,* namely that the speaker wants α to be done. What follows applies to each case separately, embedded within the (GOAL x $\diamond$ ...). Specifically, we consider next the performance of α, after which the following holds:

[BMB x y (P-GOAL y [KNOW x (KNOW y p)])] $\bigvee$
(BMB x y (P-GOAL y [KNOW x (KNOW y ¬p)]))

Because knowledge entails truth,

$\models$ [KNOW x (KNOW y p)] $\supset$[KNOW x p]

therefore, we have

[BMB x y (P-GOAL y [KNOW x p] $\bigwedge$ [KNOW y p])] ,

and analogously for informing that p is false.

Now, not only was the "honest effort" condition true, but by the definition of attempting, it was also intended. Therefore, the above condition was intended after e'. In other words, we have, roughly,

(INTEND$_1$ y e';
  ([BMB x y (P-GOAL y (KNOW x p))] $\bigvee$
  [BMB x y (P-GOAL y (KNOW x ¬ p))])?...)

Assuming agent y is sincere, we conclude that

(INTEND$_1$ y e';
    ([KNOW x (P-GOAL y (KNOW x p))] $\bigvee$
    [KNOW x (P-GOAL y (KNOW x ¬p))])) ,

because a sincere y would not intend for x to believe something falsely. Furthermore, our analysis of the relationship between *(P-GOAL y q)* and $\diamond q$ (described in Theorem 4.5 in Cohen and Levesque (1991a, p. 239) indicates that this conclusion can be drawn provided that y remains competent about q (i.e., whenever y comes to believe q, it is correct), and y does not drop its goal to achieve q believing it never will be true. Thus, if we assume y does not come to the conclusion that *(KNOW x p)* lightly, and does not come to the conclusion that x will never know that p, x will eventually come to know that p. Hence, we derive that

(KNOW x $\diamond$[(KNOW x p) $\bigvee$(KNOW x ¬p)]),
which entails $\diamond$[(KNOW x p) $\bigvee$ (KNOW x ¬ p)].[10]

Given that these conclusions were drawn within the operator *(GOAL x$\diamond$...)*, we reach the conclusion that the requestor in fact wants to know whether or not p. □

Summary

We have shown how one can determine the sincerity condition of a composite communicative action by combining the definitions of the composed acts.[11]

Similar kinds of analyses can be performed for other composed performatives, of which KQML offers many. For example, the so-called *achieve* performative should be analyzed as a *request* to achieve *p*, or in our framework, a request to do an *e* such that ¬*p?;e; p ?*. To model the contract net protocol (Smith and Davis 1988c), a *bid* action first needs to be defined, after which one can analyze *request for bid*.

As a last example, a proper semantics should distinguish among various kinds of requests, such as requests to *request*, and *broker, recruit*, and *forward* (in KQML). A third-party request involves one agent's requesting another to then request a third agent to perform an action (Cohen and Perrault 1979). Because of the semantics we have given, the middle agent will need to have various beliefs and goals about the ultimate recipient. In KQML, a *request* to *forward* differs from a *request* to *recruit* in that the first requires the requestor to know what agent should receive the forwarded action. The second requires the recipient to find an agent to perform the requested action, at the same time requesting that agent to perform the action. Thus, *forward* would seem to be more specific than *recruit*. But, in the KQML draft specification, *recruit* is described as an instance of *forward,* differing only in the originating agent's specifying the ultimate agent. It would seem, then, that a semantics should provide a common definition, differing only in the scope of a quantifier into a modal operator (if that is how one represents "knowing who"). However, the *request* to *recruit* also shares with the *request* to *request* the effect that the ultimate recipient is asked to perform some action. Thus, perhaps *recruit* should be a species of *request*. Finally, to complicate matters further, *forward* seems not to be a species of *request* in that an agent can *forward* a message without the agent's having any beliefs or goals regarding the receiver's subsequent actions. Thus, there are arguments that *recruit* is a species of *forward,* and vice-versa, and is also a species of *request,* but *forward* is not a species of *request*. To clarify these definitions, one needs to define *forward* and *recruit* formally and perform the compositions with *request*. Moreover, only with a formal semantics can one define precisely what is meant by "being a species of."

The point of providing a semantics for a composed action is only to illustrate how a semantics such as ours may be helpful in analyzing communicative acts. There is no recommendation here being made that agent designers should use this semantics, or any semantical treatment, for analyzing their systems. Rather, the KQML community needs to know that the language *has* a semantics, and that a strong foundation is present upon which to build.

Impact on KQML Design Decisions

Two major decisions have influenced the design of KQML, namely extensibility and content independence. Given that we have questioned the nature of the basic KQML elements (i.e., performatives), what impact will this critique have on those decisions?

Extensibility

By allowing the set of performatives to be extended, KQML requires developers to carry the burden of ensuring that agents know how to behave with these new communication actions. Unfortunately, developers are given no guidance on how to formulate new performatives. Merely providing a new label does not ensure that the act does anything new. Moreover, without a true semantics, it is difficult to rule out incoherent and/or self-defeating definitions.

As the language currently stands, the directive force of most performatives is implicit in the semantics. Therefore, developers need to implement correctly that implicit directive force for each new action of this class. Moreover, those new speech acts need to enter into old and new agent conversation patterns correctly. For example, the designer needs to understand how it is that requests are acknowledged, committed to, discharged, etc. Rather than have to reimplement separate interaction patterns for each of the new actions, the relevant conversation patterns should only be defined once, and then all species of that class should inherit the basic structure.

Content Independence

In the interest of modularity, KQML handles the communicative actions independently of the content language. This decision can be maintained so long as the content language does not allow any attitude operators (so far, attitude operators are allowed). If $BEL, GOAL, INTEND,$ etc. are allowed in the content language, then agents can easily send self-defeating speech acts to one another, causing undefined behavior. For example, an agent x could $TELL$ a message expressing Moore's paradox, namely, $(p \land \neg(BEL\ x\ p))$. To generalize, an agent could say both that it requests an act, and that it does not want the act done, etc. Thus, agents could deny the sincerity conditions or preparatory conditions (Searle 1969) of the relevant speech act. Without a semantics, this situation may not be detectable by an agent designer. It is unlikely, however, that the agent architecture could detect such semantic anomalies automatically.

A disadvantage of content independence is that it prevents the content from being checked for compatibility with the speech act type. For example, directives employ future actions, and actions that are promised should be only those to be performed by the promising agent.

Comparison with Other Agent Communication Languages

A number of other agent communication languages have been proposed, including AOP (Shoham 1993, Thomas 1993) and Telescript (White 1997).

Agent Oriented Programming (AOP)

AOP shares with the approach proposed here a concern for agents' commitments as a crucial part of any agent communication language and framework. Although our definitions and semantics of the foundational concepts of choice and intention are different, their importance to both efforts is similar. We differ in that the approache presented here attempts to provide a logical semantics of communicative acts per se, whereas AOP essentially provides rules for responding to or issuing a message with a speech act label (i.e., *request, inform,* or *query-whether*). This operational semantics leaves it open to the agent developer what the communicative acts in fact mean, and how they affect the agents' mental states. We advocate there being an agreement or specification about what the communication acts are supposed to mean, as it may be important for technical, as well as legal reasons, to show that agents behaved according to the specifications.

There are technical differences, of course, in the details of communicative action. For example, because there is no nondeterministic choice operator that can form disjunctive actions in AOP, a yes/no question is defined as three requests to inform about whether the queried proposition is true, false, or unknown. In our model, there is only one request, but for a disjunctive act. The "I don't know" response is handled at a higher level, and need not be specified as part of the semantics of a question.

Telescript

Telescript seems not to be an agent communication language, per se, but rather a scripting language. Agents do not communicate in the sense of sending messages to one another. Rather, they transport themselves to various "places," at which they "meet" other agents. It is claimed, then, that agents "interact using object-oriented programming techniques." This raises the questions of what the agents' methods are, and how one agent knows what another's are. Let us assume that all agents are specializations of a given class, and share a common set of methods. Then, one might expect that an agent would communicate by executing another agent's public methods rather than execute any communicative acts per se. For example, one agent may execute another's "sell a ticket" method, which would start the process of ticket sales. This type of interaction makes sense when a homogeneous network is involved, in which agents share methods and have knowledge of each other's methods. For example, the ticket buyer does not share a "sell a ticket" method with the seller; rather it must somehow be designed to expect such a method when it reaches the ticket seller. In the heterogeneous world of the Internet, it is unclear how such agent-programming would take place. Moreover, and especially in a business context, we are concerned about the nature of communicative actions in an environment in which some agents are insincere, deceptive, or merely antagonistic. Our semantics is designed to insulate an agent's mental states from being operated upon directly by other agents. On receiving a message, an agent is supposed to have a "model" of what the other agent *wants* it to do/believe, etc. By representing the effects of communicative actions in this way, the receiving agent then has the option to reason about the sincerity of the sender, while still protecting its innermost states. A developer of Telescript agents may in fact be able to afford such protection to its agents, but as specified publicly so far (in White 1997), no guidance is given on how to do this.

Agent Architectures May Include People

We began this chapter by observing that an agent architecture needs to interact with people. End users will give the architecture tasks to be performed, and in the course of execution the agents may need to make requests of other people. For example, in the open agent architecture (Cohen et al. 1994), the *notify* agent may need to have a telephone phone conversation with the person who answers the telephone in order to pass a message to the intended recipient. Thus, to specify a *hybrid* agent architecture, including people and software agents, the semantics will need to make reference to "states" that the human may be in, such as being committed to bringing the intended recipient to the telephone. The agents will need to expect certain behavior of human agents who may take part, perhaps accidentally, in their activities, and they themselves will need to engage in behavior that is at least sufficiently familiar that people can readily adapt to their limitations. Rather than have two sets of semantics, it would be parsimonious to develop one model and language that can scale from simple software agents to even an overly simplistic approximation of people.

Our speech act theory has the virtue that essentially the same analysis can be given for human and software agents' communication acts, though obviously, the mental states and surface linguistic forms inherent in human communication are far richer. Still, one may argue that very limited user interfaces could be generated based on a much simpler agent model —for example, the Magic Cap[TM] interface employs Telescript as its core, which does not have the richness advocated here. Again, this may work for the case of simple devices, with simple functionality, in a homogenous agent environment. But, we are dubious for more complex and heterogenous environments, especially those that might involve telephone interactions. We are not advocating that natural language interaction be the only way users interact with their agents (in fact, we build multimodal interfaces [see Cohen 1990b, Cohen et al. 1994, Oviatt et al. 1994]). But, agent architectures will certainly need to be developed that can support telephone-based interaction.

Future Work: Interagent Dialogues

The communicative action definitions given here are in need of modification and repair, as they are too one-sided. They express the sender's mental states, but are not sufficient to initiate team behavior (Cohen and Levesque 1991). The reason is that neither sender nor receiver ends up with the right kinds of commitments that together can establish a joint intention. In Cohen (1993) and Smith and Cohen (1996), we redefine the communicative actions of request, refuse, etc., showing how joint intentions are established, monitored, and discharged. Moreover, we demonstrate how joint intention theory can predict the structure of finite-state models of interagent dialogue, which have been claimed to provide an adequate model of interagent dialogue (Bradshaw 1997).

Conclusion

KQML has shown its versatility in supporting agent architectures as a viable computational paradigm. However, the language is still in need of a more precise definition and semantics before agent designers can be confident that their contributions rest on solid foundations. In particular, commercial uses of agent architectures will at some point emerge, and it will be important for legal as well as technical reasons to be able to show that agents correctly performed according to their specifications and those of the language. We believe a semantics something like the one illustrated here will be necessary as part of this effort.

Acknowledgements

This research was supported in part by the Information Technology Promotion Agency, Japan, as part of the Industrial Science and Technology Frontier Program "New Models for Software Architecture" sponsored by NEDO (New Energy and Industrial Technology Development Organization) and also in part by grant N00014-95-1-1164 from the Office of Naval Research.

Notes

1. A first attempt has been made (Labrou and Finin 1994), but much work remains.

2. Labrou and Finin (1994) propose a different definition of *deny,* in which the sender essentially states that it does not believe a proposition. According to this semantics, the language of KQML has changed dramatically to include embedded propositions instead of embedded performatives.

3. We are aware that numerous researchers are attempting to add new performatives, many in the commmissive class. Our point is that the basic language should provide gthe generic commisive speech act, which other agent designers should specialize for their needs.

4. The addition of "eventually" here is logically unnecessary but serves to draw the distinction more clearly.

5. In Cohen and Levesque 1990a , we define two types of intention, those to do actions and those to achieve states of affairs.

6. In a more adequate analysis, there should be a stronger relationship, say contingent causality, between Φ and Ψ.

7. A *command* speech act would be identical to a request except that instead of involving helpfulness, the intent would be relative to some sort of authority relationship between the speaker and the addressee. "Helpfulness" is defined in Cohen and Levesque (1990a).

8. Note that we could derive conditions under which it comes true, as in Cohen and Levesque (1990a).

9. The case of "I don't know" would handled by the need to discharge the standing joint intention (Cohen and Levesque 1991) that underlies the agent architecture, namely that agents jointly intend to interact.

10. Now that we have moved back to the level that analyzes what x has chosen, we note that the assumptions that gate the conclusion of $\Diamond p$ from the persistent goal are actually chosen conditions. That is, the x is choosing that y be competent about x's knowing p and chooses that y does not drop its goals too soon.

11. Compare with the stipulations of Labrou and Finin (1994).

References

Allen, J. F., and Perrault, C. R. 1980. Analyzing Intention in Dialogues. *Artificial Intelligence,* 15(3): 143–178.

Appelt, D. 1985. *Planning English Sentences.* New York: Cambridge University Press.

ARPA 1993. ARPA Knowledge Sharing Initiative External Interfaces Working Group 1993. Specification of the KQML Agent-Communication Language. Working Paper, ARPA.

Austin, J. L. 1962. *How to Do Things with Words.* London: Oxford University Press.

Bradshaw, J. M.; Dutfield, S.; Benoit, P.; andWooley. J. D. 1997. KAoS: Toward an Industrial-Strength Open Agent Architecture. In *Software Agents* ed. J. Bradshaw. Menlo Park, Calif.: AAAI Press / The MIT Press.

Bratman, M. 1987. *Intentions, Plans, and Practical Reason.* Cambridge, Mass.: Harvard University Press.

Bruce, B. C. 1975. Belief Systems and Language Understanding. Technical Report 2973, Bolt Beranek and Newman Inc., Cambridge, Masschusetts.

Cohen, P. R. 1992. The Role of Natural Language in a Multimodal Interface. In *Proceedings of UIST'92,* 143-149. New York: ACM Press.

Cohen, P. R. 1993. Models of Dialogue. In Cognitive Processing for Vision and Voice: Proceedings of the Fourth NEC Research Symposium, ed. M. Nagao *SIAM.*

Cohen, P. R.; Cheyer, A.; Wang, M. Q.; and Baeg, S. C. 1994. An Open Agent Architecture. Presented at the AAAI Spring Symposium on Software Agents, 23-24 March, Stanford, California.

Cohen, P. R. and Levesque, H. J. 1990a. Intention Is Choice with Commitment. *Artificial Intelligence,* 42(3).

Cohen, P. R. and Levesque, H. J. 1990b. Performatives in a Rationally Based Speech Act Theory. In *Proceedings of the Twenty-Eighth Annual Meeting, Association for Computational Linguistics,* Pittsburgh, Pennsylvania. San Francisco: Morgan Kaufmann.

Cohen, P. R. and Levesque, H. J. 1990c. Rational Interaction as the Basis for Communication. In *Intentions in Communication,* ed. P. R. Cohen, J. Morgan, and M. E. Pollack. Cambridge, Mass.: The MIT Press.

Cohen, P. R.; and Levesque, H. J. 1991. Teamwork. *Noûs* 25(4): 487–512.

Cohen, P. R.; and Perrault, C. R. 1979. Elements of a Plan-Based Theory of Speech Acts. *Cognitive Science,* 3(3):177–212.

Finin, T.; Fritzson, R.; McKay, D.; and McEntire, R. 1994. KQML as an Agent Communication Language. In Proceedings of the Third International Conference on Information and Knowledge Management (CIKM'94), New York, November. New York: ACM Press.

Genesereth, M.; and Ketchpel, S. 1994. Software Agents. *Communications of the ACM,* 37(7):100–105.

Labrou Y., and Finin, T. 1994. A Semantics Approach for KQML—A General Purpose Communication Language for Software Agents. Paper presented at the Third International Conference on Information and Knowledge Management (CIKM'94), Washington, D.C.

McCarthy, J. 1989. Elephant: A Programming Language Based on Speech Acts. Department of Computer Science, Stanford University.

McDermott, D. 1982. A Temporal Logic for Reasoning about Processes and Plans. *Cognitive Science,* 6(2):101–155, April-June.

Oviatt, S. L.; Cohen, P. R.; and Wang, M. Q. 1994. Toward Interface Design for Human Language Technology: Modality and Structure as Determinants of Linguistic Complexity. *Speech Communication* 15(3-4).

Perrault, C. R. 1990. An Application of Default Logic to Speech Act Theory. In *Intentions in Communication,* ed. P. R. Cohen, J. Morgan, and M. E. Pollack. Cambridge, Mass.: The MIT Press.

Perrault, C. R., and Allen, J. F.1980. A Plan-based Analysis of Indirect Speech Acts. *American Journal of Computational Linguistics,* 6(3):167–182.

Sadek, D. 1991. Dialogue Acts Are Rational Plans. Paper presented at the ESCA/ETRW Workshop on the Structure of Multimodal Dialogue (VENACO II), Maratea, Italy, September.

Searle, J. R. 1969. *Speech Acts: An Essay in the Philosophy of Language.* New York: Cambridge University Press.

Searle, J. R.; and Vanderveken, D. 1985. *Foundations of Illocutionary Logic.* New York: Cambridge University Press

Shoham Y. 1993. Agent-Oriented Programming. *Artificial Intelligence* 60(1) 51–92.

Sidner, C. 1994. An Artifical Discourse Language for Collaborative Negotiation. In *Proceedings of the National Conference on Artificial Intelligence,* 814–819. Menlo Park, Calif.: AAAI Press.

Smith, I. and Cohen, P. R. 1996. Toward a Semantics for an Agent Communication Language Based on Speech Acts. In *Proceedings of the Thirteenth National Conference on Artificial Intelligence.* Menlo Park, Calif.: AAAI Press / The MIT Press.

Smith, R. G.; and Davis, R. 1988. The Contract Net Protocol: High-level Communication and Control in a Distributed Problem Solver. In *Readings in Distributed Artificial Intelligence,* ed. A. H. Bond and L. Gasser, 357–366. San Francisco: Morgan Kaufmann.

Thomas, B. 1993. PLACA, an Agent Oriented Language. PhD diss., Department of Computer Science, Stanford University, Stanford, California,.

White, J. E. 1997. Mobile Agents. In *Software Agents* ed. J. Bradshaw. Menlo Park, Calif.: AAAI / TheMIT Press.

CHAPTER 19

Mobile Agents

James E. White

The economics of computing, the growth of public information networks, the convergence of computers and communication, and advances in graphical user interfaces enable powerful new electronics products to be placed in the hands of consumers. Personal intelligent communicators provide one example. Intelligent televisions, providing access to vast amounts of scheduled program material and video on demand, will offer another.

In principle, such products could put people in closer touch with one another (e.g., by means of electronic postcards), simplify their relationships (e.g., by helping them make and keep appointments), provide them with useful information (e.g., television schedules, traffic conditions, restaurant menus, and stock market results), and help them carry out financial transactions (e.g., purchase theater tickets, order flowers, and buy and sell stock).

New devices alone are insufficient to deliver to the consumer services like those above. Also needed is a new breed of computer software I call the *communicating application*. Unlike the standalone applications of today's personal computer (e.g., word processing programs), communicating applications will adeptly use the public networks to which they give access to find and interact with people and information on the consumer's behalf.

Communicating applications will have qualities of timeliness and effectiveness that today's uncommunicative applications do not. One such application might maintain my stock portfolio, buying and selling stock under conditions that I establish for it in advance. Another might arrange that every Friday evening a romantic comedy of its choosing is ready for viewing on my television and that my favorite pizza is delivered to my door.

Today's networks pose a barrier to the development of communicating applications. The barrier stems from the need for such applications to physically distribute themselves, that is, to run not only on the computers dedicated to individual users, but also on the computers that users share, the servers. For example, a communicating application that is to provide a forum for buying and selling used cars necessarily has two parts. A user interface component in a user's personal communicator gathers information from an individual buyer or seller. A database component in a public server records the information and uses it to bring buyers and sellers together.

The barrier posed by a public network is insurmountable. A user of an enterprise network might well be allowed to install any application she wishes on her own desktop computer. She might even persuade her network administrator to install a new application on the departmental servers. However, a user of a commercial on-line service would find that no amount of persuasion would succeed in making her software a part of that service.

The success of the personal computer is due in large part to third-party software developers. On the platform provided by hardware and operating system manufacturers, developers built standalone applications that made personal computers indispensable tools for people in all walks of life. One might expect that the success of the information superhighway will depend on developers in a similar way. Unless public networks are platforms on which third-party developers can build communicating applications, the networks will respond much too slowly to new and varied requirements and so will languish. Unfortunately, today's networks are not platforms.

This chapter explores the concept of a public network designed as a platform for application developers. It introduces a new communication paradigm, the *mobile agent*, which provides the organizing principle for such a network, and a new communication software technology, *Telescript technology*, which implements the concept in a commercial setting. The chapter also presents and explores the vision of an electronic marketplace that allows automated access by agents, as well as conventional, interactive access by people.

The remainder of the chapter is divided into four parts. The "Enabling Mobile Agents" section introduces and motivates the concept of a mobile agent, explains how Telescript technology implements the concept, and describes an electronic marketplace based upon the technology. The "Programming Mobile Agents" section explains by example how a communicating application works. The example serves as an introduction to the Telescript language in which mobile agents are programmed. The "Using Mobile Agents" section explores the variety of applications that mobile agents make possible. These are scenes from the electronic marketplace of the future. In the final section, I briefly summarize related work.

Enabling Mobile Agents

This section introduces and motivates the concept of a mobile agent, explains how Telescript technology implements the concept, and describes an electronic marketplace based upon the technology.

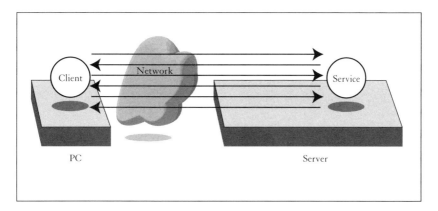

Figure 1. Remote procedure calling.

The Mobile Agent Paradigm

The concept of a mobile agent sprang from a critical examination of how computers have communicated since the late 1970s. This section sketches the results of that examination and so presents the case for mobile agents.

Current Approach. The central organizing principle of today's computer communication networks is *remote procedure calling (RPC)* (figure 1). Conceived in the 1970s, the RPC paradigm views computer-to-computer communication as enabling one computer to call procedures in another. Each message that the network transports either requests or acknowledges a procedure's performance. A request includes data which are the procedure's arguments. The response includes data which are its results. The procedure itself is internal to the computer that performs it.

Two computers whose communication follows the RPC paradigm agree in advance upon the effects of each remotely accessible procedure and the types of its arguments and results. Their agreements constitute a *protocol*.

A user computer with work for a server to accomplish orchestrates the work with a series of remote procedure calls. Each call involves a request sent from user to server and a response sent from server to user. To delete from a file server, for example, all files at least two months old, a user computer might have to make one call to get the names and ages of the user's files and another for *each* file to be deleted. The analysis that decides which files are old enough to delete is done in the user computer. If it decides to delete n files, the user computer must send or receive a total of $2(n + 1)$ messages.

The salient characteristic of remote procedure calling is that each interaction between the user computer and the server entails two acts of communication, one to ask the server to perform a procedure, another to acknowledge that the server did so. Thus *ongoing interaction requires ongoing communication*.

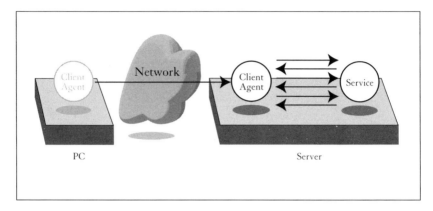

Figure 2. Remote programming.

New Approach. An alternative to remote procedure calling is *remote programming (RP)* (figure 2). The RP paradigm views computer-to-computer communication as enabling one computer not only to call procedures in another, but also to supply the procedures to be performed. Each message that the network transports comprises a procedure which the receiving computer is to perform and data which are its arguments. In an important refinement, the procedure is one whose performance the sending computer began (or continued) but the receiving computer is to continue; the data are the procedure's current state.

Two computers whose communication follows the RP paradigm agree in advance upon the instructions that are allowed in a procedure and the types of data that are allowed in its state. Their agreements constitute a *language*. The language includes instructions that let the procedure make decisions, examine and modify its state, and, importantly, call procedures provided by the receiving computer. Note that such procedure calls are local rather than remote. We call the procedure and its state a *mobile agent* to emphasize that they represent the sending computer even while in the receiving computer.

A user computer with work for a server to accomplish[1] sends to the server an agent whose procedure there makes the required requests of the server (e.g., "delete") based upon its state (e.g., "two months"). Deleting the old files of the previous example—no matter how many—requires just the message that transports the agent between computers. The agent, not the user computer, orchestrates the work, deciding "on-site" which files should be deleted.

The salient characteristic of remote programming is that a user computer and a server can interact without using the network once the network has transported an agent between them. Thus *ongoing interaction does not require ongoing communication*. The implications of this are far-reaching.

Tactical Advantage. Remote programming has an important advantage over remote procedure calling. The advantage can be seen from two different perspectives. One perspective is quantitative and tactical, the other qualitative and strategic.

The tactical advantage of remote programming is *performance*. When a user computer has work for a server to do, rather than shout commands across a network, it sends an agent to the server and thereby directs the work locally, rather than remotely. The network is called upon to carry fewer messages. The more work to be done, the more messages remote programming avoids.

The performance advantage of remote programming depends in part upon the network: the lower its throughput or availability, or the higher its latency or cost, the greater the advantage. The public telephone network presents a greater opportunity for the new paradigm than does an Ethernet. Today's wireless networks present greater opportunities still. Remote programming is particularly well suited to personal communicators, whose networks are presently slower and more expensive than those of personal computers in an enterprise; and to personal computers in the home, whose one telephone line is largely dedicated to the placement and receipt of voice telephone calls.

A home computer is an example of a user computer that is connected to a network occasionally rather than permanently. Remote programming allows a user with such a computer to delegate a task—or a long sequence of tasks—to an agent. The computer must be connected to the network only long enough to send the agent on its way and, later, to welcome it home. The computer need not be connected while the agent carries out its assignment. Thus remote programming lets occasionally connected computers do things that remote procedure calling would make impractical.

Strategic Advantage. The strategic advantage of remote programming is *customization*. Agents let manufacturers of user software extend the functionality offered by manufacturers of server software. Returning once again to the filing example, if the file server provides one procedure for listing a user's files and another for deleting a file by name, a user can effectively add to that repertoire a procedure that deletes all files of a specified age. The new procedure, which takes the form of an agent, customizes the server for that particular user.

The remote programming paradigm changes not only the division of labor among software manufacturers but also the ease of installing the software they produce. Unlike the standalone applications that popularized the personal computer, the communicating applications that will popularize the personal communicator have components that must reside in servers. The server components of an RPC-based application must be statically installed by the user. The server components of an RP-based application, on the other hand, are dynamically installed by the application itself. Each is an agent.

The advantage of remote programming is significant in an enterprise net-

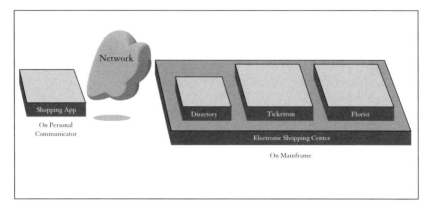

Figure 3. Places.

work but profound in a public network whose servers are owned and operated by public service providers (e.g., America Online™). Introducing a new RPC-based application requires a business decision on the part of the service provider. For an RP-based application, all that's required is a buying decision on the part of an individual user. Remote programming thus makes a public network, like a personal computer, a *platform*.

Mobile Agent Concepts

The first commercial implementation of the mobile agent concept is General Magic's *Telescript technology*™ which, by means of mobile agents, enables automated as well as interactive access to a network of computers. The commercial focus of Telescript technology is the *electronic marketplace*, a public network that will let providers and consumers of goods and services find one another and transact business electronically. Although the electronic marketplace doesn't exist today, its beginnings can be seen in the Internet.

Telescript technology implements the following principal concepts: places, agents, travel, meetings, connections, authorities, and permits. An overview of these concepts indicates how the remote programming paradigm provides the basis for a complete and cohesive remote programming technology.

Places. Telescript technology models a network of computers—however large—as a collection of places. A *place* offers a service to the mobile agents that enter it (figure 3).

In the electronic marketplace, a mainframe computer might function as a shopping center. A very small shopping center (illustrated) might house a ticket place where agents can purchase tickets to theater and sporting events, a flower place where agents can order flowers, and a directory place where agents can learn about any place in the shopping center. The network might encompass

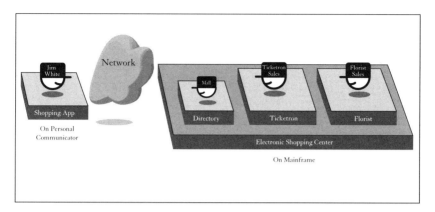

Figure 4. Agents.

many independently operated shopping centers, as well as many individually operated shops, many of the latter on personal computers.

While servers provide some places, user computers provide others. A home place on a user's personal communicator, for example, might serve as the point of departure and return for agents that the user sends to server places.

Agents. Telescript technology models a communicating application as a collection of agents. Each *agent* occupies a particular place. However, an agent can move from one place to another, thus occupying different places at different times. Agents are independent in that their procedures are performed concurrently (figure 4).

In the electronic marketplace, the typical place is permanently occupied by one distinguished agent. This stationary agent represents the place and provides its service. The ticketing agent, for example, provides information about events and sells tickets to them, the flower agent provides information about floral arrangements and arranges for their delivery, and the directory agent provides information about other places, including how to reach them.

Travel. Telescript technology lets an agent *travel* from one place to another—however distant. Travel is the hallmark of a remote programming system (figure 5).

Travel lets an agent obtain a service offered remotely and then return to its starting place. A user's agent, for example, might travel from home to a ticketing place to obtain orchestra seats for *Phantom of the Opera*. Later the agent might travel home to describe to its user the tickets it obtained.

Moving software programs between computers by means of a network has been commonplace for 20 years or more. Using a local area network to download a program from the file server where it's stored to a personal computer where it must run is a familiar example. But moving programs *while* they run,

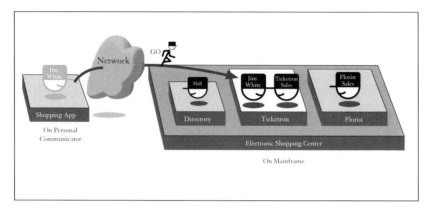

Figure 5. Travel.

rather than *before*, is unusual. A conventional program, written for example in C or C++, cannot be moved under these conditions because neither its procedure nor its state is portable. An agent can move from place to place throughout the performance of its procedure because the procedure is written in a language designed to permit this. The *Telescript language* in which agents are programmed lets a computer package an agent—its procedure and its state—so that it can be transported to another computer. The agent itself decides when such transportation is required.

To travel from one place to another an agent executes an instruction unique to the Telescript language, the *go* instruction. The instruction requires a *ticket*, data that specifies the agent's destination and the other terms of the trip (e.g., the means by which it must be made and the time by which it must be completed). If the trip cannot be made (e.g., because the means of travel cannot be provided or the trip takes too long) the *go* instruction fails; the agent handles the exception as it sees fit. However, if the trip succeeds, the agent finds that its next instruction is executed at its destination. Thus in effect the Telescript language reduces networking to a single instruction.

In the electronic marketplace, the *go* instruction lets the agents of buyers and sellers co-locate themselves so they can interact efficiently.

Meetings. Telescript technology lets two agents in the same place meet. A *meeting* lets agents in the same computer call one another's procedures (figure 6).

Meetings are what motivate agents to travel. An agent might travel to a place in a server to meet the stationary agent that provides the service the place offers. The agent in pursuit of theater tickets, for example, travels to and then meets with the ticket agent. Alternatively, two agents might travel to the same place to meet each other. Such meetings might be the norm in a place intended as a venue for buying and selling used cars.

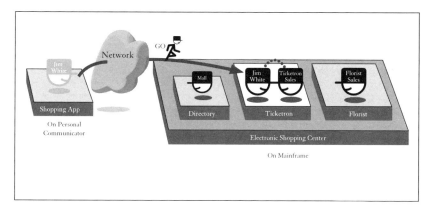

Figure 6. Meetings.

To meet a co-located agent, an agent executes the Telescript language's *meet* instruction. The instruction requires a *petition*, data that specifies the agent to be met and the other terms of the meeting (e.g., the time by which it must begin). If the meeting cannot be arranged (e.g., because the agent to be met declines the meeting or arrives too late) the *meet* instruction fails; the agent handles the exception as it sees fit. However, if the meeting occurs, the two agents are placed in programmatic contact with one another.

In the electronic marketplace, the *meet* instruction lets the co-located agents of buyers and sellers exchange information and carry out transactions.

Connections. Telescript technology lets two agents in different places make a connection between them. A *connection* lets agents in different computers communicate (figure 7).

Connections are often made for the benefit of human users of interactive applications. The agent that travels in search of theater tickets, for example, might send to an agent at home a diagram of the theater showing the seats available. The agent at home might present the floor plan to the user and send to the agent on the road the locations of the seats the user selects.

To make a connection to a distant agent, an agent executes the Telescript language's *connect* instruction. The instruction requires a *target* and other data that specify the distant agent, the place where that agent resides, and the other terms of the connection (e.g., the time by which it must be made and the quality of service it must provide). If the connection cannot be made (e.g., because the distant agent declines the connection or is not found in time or because the quality of service cannot be provided) the *connect* instruction fails; the agent handles the exception as it sees fit. However, if the connection is made, the two agents are granted access to their respective ends of it.

In the electronic marketplace, the *connect* instruction lets the agents of buyers

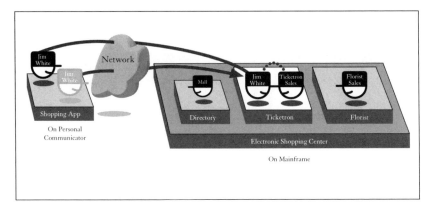

Figure 7. Connections.

and sellers exchange information at a distance. Sometimes, as in the theater lay-out phase of the ticking example, the two agents that make and use the connection are parts of the same communicating application. In such a situation, the protocol that governs the agents' use of the connection is of concern only to that one application's designer. It need not be standardized.

If agents are one of the newest communication paradigms, connections are one of the oldest. Telescript technology integrates the two.

Authorities. Telescript technology lets one agent or place discern the authority of another. The *authority* of an agent or place in the electronic world is the individual or organization in the physical world that it represents. An agent or place can discern but neither withhold nor falsify its authority. Anonymity is precluded (figure 8).

Authority is important in any computer network. To control access to its files, a file server must know the authority of any procedure that instructs it to list or delete files. The need is the same whether the procedure is stationary or mobile. Telescript technology verifies the authority of an agent whenever it travels from one region of the network to another. A *region* is a collection of places provided by computers that are all operated by the same authority. Unless the source region can prove the agent's authority to the satisfaction of the destination region, the agent is denied entry to the latter. In some situations, highly reliable, cryptographic forms of proof may be demanded.

To determine an agent's or place's authority, an agent or place executes the Telescript language's *name* instruction. The instruction is applied to an agent or place within reach for one of the reasons listed below. The result of the instruction is a *telename*, data that denotes the entity's identity as well as its authority. *Identities* distinguish agents or places of the same authority.

Authorities lets agents and places interact with one another on the strength of

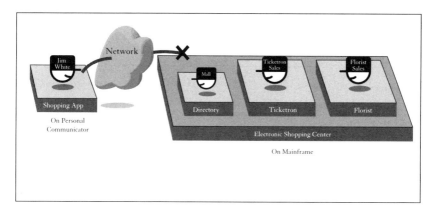

Figure 8. Authorities.

their ties to the physical world. A place can discern the authority of any agent that attempts to enter it and can arrange to admit only agents of certain authorities. An agent can discern the authority of any place it visits and can arrange to visit only places of certain authorities. An agent can discern the authority of any agent with which it meets or to which it connects and can arrange to meet with or connect to only agents of certain authorities.

In the electronic marketplace, the *name* instruction lets programmatic transactions between agents and places stand for financial transactions between their authorities. A server agent's authority can bill a user agent's authority for services rendered. In addition, the server agent can provide personalized service to the user agent on the basis of its authority or can deny it service altogether. More fundamentally, the lack of anonymity helps prevent viruses by denying agents that important characteristic of viruses.

Permits. Telescript technology lets authorities limit what agents and places can do by assigning permits to them. A *permit* is data that grants capabilities. An agent or place can discern its capabilities but cannot increase them (figure 9).

Permits grant capabilities of two kinds. A permit can grant the right to execute a certain instruction. For example, an agent's permit can give it the right to create other agents.[2] An agent or place that tries to exceed one of these qualitative limits is simply prevented from doing so. A permit can also grant the right to use a certain resource in a certain amount. For example, an agent's permit can give it a maximum lifetime in seconds, a maximum size in bytes, or a maximum amount of computation, its *allowance*. An agent or place that tries to exceed one of these quantitative limits is destroyed.[3]

To determine an agent's or place's permit, an agent or place executes the Telescript language's *permit* instruction. The instruction is applied to an agent

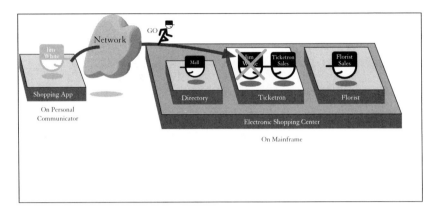

Figure 9. Permits.

or place within reach for one of the reasons listed in "Authorities."

Permits protect authorities by limiting the effects of errant and malicious agents and places. Such an agent threatens not only its own authority but also those of the place and region it occupies. For this reason the technology lets each of these three authorities assign an agent a permit. The agent can exercise a particular capability only to the extent that all three of its permits grant that capability. Thus an agent's effective permit is renegotiated whenever the agent travels. To enter another place or region, the agent must agree to its restrictions. When the agent exits that place or region, its restrictions are lifted, but those of another place or region are imposed.

In the electronic marketplace, the *permit* instruction and the capabilities it documents help guard against the unbridled consumption of resources by ill-programmed or illintentioned agents. Such protection is important because agents typically operate unattended in servers rather than in user computers where their misdeeds might be more readily apparent to the human user.

Putting Things Together. An agent's travel is not restricted to a single round-trip. The power of mobile agents is fully apparent only when one considers an agent that travels to several places in succession. Using the basic services of the places it visits, such an agent can provide a higher-level, composite service (figure 10).

In my example, traveling to the ticket place might be only the first of the agent's responsibilities. The second might be to travel to the flower place and there arrange for a dozen roses to be delivered to the user's companion on the day of the theater event. Note that the agent's interaction with the ticket agent can influence its interaction with the flower agent. Thus, for example, if instructed to get tickets for any evening for which tickets are available, the agent can order flowers for delivery on the day for which it obtains tickets (figure 10).

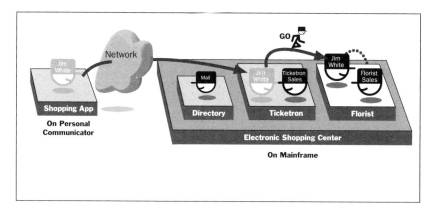

Figure 10. Composite service.

This simple example has far-reaching implications. The agent fashions from the concepts of tickets and flowers the concept of special occasions. In the example as presented, the agent does this for the benefit of an individual user. In a variation of the example, however, the agent takes up residence in a server and offers its special occasion service to other agents. Thus agents can extend the functionality of the network. Thus the network is a platform.

Mobile Agent Technlogy

New communication paradigms beget new communication technologies. A technology for mobile agents is software. That software can ride atop a wide variety of computer and communication hardware, present and future.

Telescript technology implements the concepts of the previous section and others related to them. It has three major components: the language in which agents and places (or their "facades") are programmed; an engine, or interpreter, for that language, and communication protocols that let engines in different computers exchange agents in fulfillment of the *go* instruction.

Language. The Telescript programming language lets developers of communicating applications define the algorithms agents follow and the information agents carry as they travel the network[4]. It supplements systems programming languages such as C (or C++). Entire applications can be written in the Telescript language, but the typical application is written partly in C. The C parts include the stationary software in user computers that lets agents interact with users and the stationary software in servers that lets places interact, for example, with databases. The agents and the "surfaces" of places to which they are exposed are written in the Telescript language (figure 11).

The Telescript language has a number of qualities that facilitate the development of communicating applications:

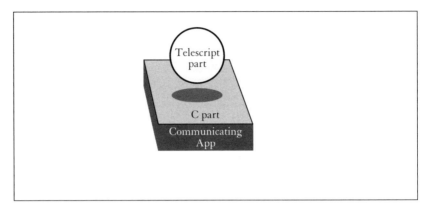

Figure 11. Telescript language.

- *Complete*. Any algorithm can be expressed in the language. An agent can be programmed to make decisions; to handle exceptional conditions; and to gather, organize, analyze, create, and modify information.
- *Object-Oriented*. The programmer defines classes of information, one class inheriting the features of others. Classes of a general nature (e.g., Agent) are predefined by the language. Classes of a specialized nature (e.g., Shopping Agent) are defined by communicating application developers.
- *Dynamic*. An agent can carry an information object from a place in one computer to a place in another. Even if the object's class is unknown at the destination, the object continues to function: its class goes with it.
- *Persistent*. Wherever it goes, an agent and the information it carries, even the program counter marking its next instruction, are safely stored in non-volatile memory. Thus the agent persists despite computer failures.
- *Portable and Safe*. A computer executes an agent's instructions through a Telescript engine, not directly. An agent can execute in any computer in which an engine is installed, yet it cannot directly access its processor, memory, file system, or peripheral devices. This restriction helps prevent viruses.
- *Communication-Centric*. Certain instructions in the language, several of which have been discussed, let an agent carry out complex networking tasks: transportation, navigation, authentication, access control, and so forth.

A Telescript program takes different forms at different times. Developers deal with a high-level, compiled language not unlike C++. Engines deal with a lower-level, interpreted language. A compiler translates between the two.

Engine. The Telescript engine is a software program that implements the Tele-

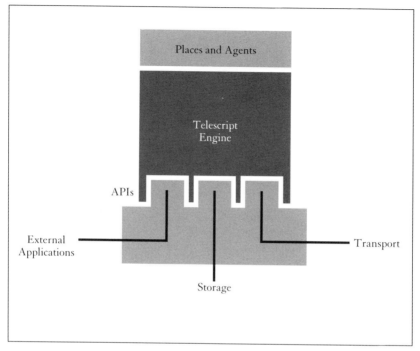

Figure 12. Telescript engine.

script language by maintaining and executing places within its purview, as well as the agents occupying those places. An engine in a user computer might house only a few places and agents. The engine in a server might house thousands (figure 12).

At least conceptually the engine draws upon the resources of its host computer through three application program interfaces (APIs). A storage API lets the engine access the nonvolatile memory it requires to preserve places and agents in case of a computer failure. A transport API lets the engine access the communication media it requires to transport agents to and from other engines. An external applications API lets the parts of an application written in the Telescript language interact with those written in C.

Protocols. The Telescript protocol suite enables two engines to communicate. Engines communicate in order to transport agents between them in response to the *go* instruction. The protocol suite can operate over a wide variety of transport networks including those based upon the TCP/IP protocols of the Internet, the X.25 interface of the telephone companies, or even electronic mail (figure 13).

The Telescript protocols operate at two levels. The lower level governs the transport of agents, the higher level their encoding (and decoding). Loosely speaking, the higher level protocol occupies the presentation and application

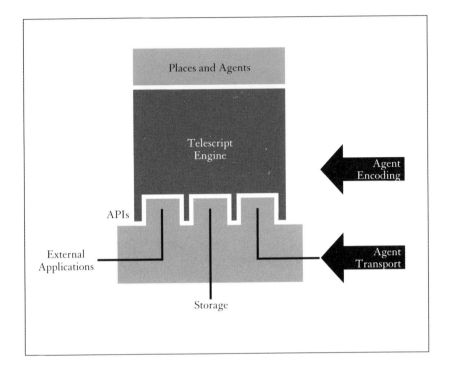

Figure 13. The Telescript protocol suite.

layers of the seven layer Open Systems Interconnection (OSI) model.[5]

The Telescript *encoding rules* specify how an engine encodes an agent—its procedure and its state—as binary data and sometimes omits portions of it as a performance optimization. Although free to maintain agents in different formats for execution, engines must employ a standard format for transport.

The Telescript *platform interconnect protocol* specifies how two engines first authenticate one another (e.g., using public key cryptography) and then transfer an agent's encoding from one to the other. The protocol is a thin veneer of functionality over that of the underlying transport network.

Programming Mobile Agents

This section explains by example how a communicating application works. The example serves as an introduction to the Telescript language in which mobile agents are programmed.

Telescript Object Model

In this section I explain how a communicating application works. I do this by implementing, in the Telescript language, both an agent and a place. First I explain the low level concepts and terminology that underlie the example. In particular, I sketch the Telescript *object model* which governs how either an agent or a place is constructed from its component parts.

Object Structure. The Telescript language, like SmallTalk™, the first object-oriented language, treats every piece of information—however small—as an object. An *object* has both an external interface and an internal implementation.

An object's *interface* consists of attributes and operations. An *attribute*, an object itself, is one of an object's externally visible characteristics. An object can *get* or *set* its own attributes and the *public*, but not the *private*, attributes of other objects. An *operation* is a task that an object *performs*. An object can *request* its own operations and the *public*, but not the *private*, operations of other objects. An operation can accept objects as *arguments* and can *return* a single object as its *result*. An operation can *throw* an exception rather than return. The *exception*, an object, can be *caught* at a higher level of the agent's or place's procedure to which control is thereby transferred.

An object's *implementation* consists of properties and methods. A *property*, an object itself, is one of an object's internal characteristics. Collectively, an object's properties constitute its dynamic state. An object can directly get or set its own properties, but not those of other objects. A *method* is a procedure that performs an operation or that gets or sets an attribute. A method can have *variables*, objects that constitute the dynamic state of the method.

Object Classification. The Telescript language, like many object-oriented programming languages, focuses on classes. A *class* is a "slice" of an object's interface combined with a related slice of its implementation. An object is an *instance* of a class.

The Telescript programmer defines his or her communicating application as a collection of classes. To support such *user defined* classes the language provides *many predefined* classes a variety of which are used by every application. The example application presented in this section consists of several user-defined classes which use various predefined classes[6].

Classes form a hierarchy[7] whose root is Object, a predefined class. Classes other than the Object class inherit the interface and implementation slices of their superclasses. The *superclasses*[8] of a class are the root and the classes that stand between the class and the root. A class is a *subclass* of each of its superclasses. An object is a *member* of its class and each of its superclasses.

A class can both define an operation (or attribute) and provide a method for it. A subclass can provide an overriding method unless the class *seals* the operation. The overriding method can invoke the overridden method by *escalating* the operation using the language's "^" construct. The overriding

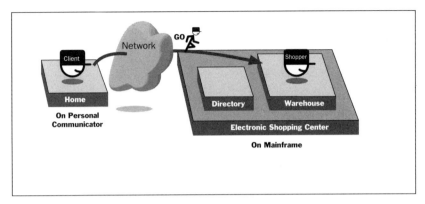

Figure 14. Programming a place.

method selects and supplies arguments to the overridden method.

One operation, which the Object class defines, is subject to a special escalation rule. The *initialize* operation is requested of each new object. Each method for the operation initializes the properties of the object defined by the class that provides the method. Each method for this operation must escalate it so that all methods are invoked and all properties are initialized.

Object Manipulation. The Telescript language requires a method to have *references* to the objects it would manipulate. References serve the purpose of pointers in languages like C, but avoid the "dangling pointer" problem shared by such languages. References can be replicated, so there can be several references to an object.

A method receives references to the objects it creates, the arguments of the operation it implements, and the results of the operations it requests. It can also obtain references to the properties of the object it manipulates.

With a reference to an object in hand, a method can get one of the object's attributes or request one of the object's operations. It accomplishes these simple tasks with two frequently used language constructs, for example.

file.length

file.add("isEmployed", true)

The example application makes use of the predefined Dictionary class. A dictionary holds pairs of objects, its *keys* and *values*. Assuming *file* denotes a dictionary, the first program fragment above obtains the number of key-value pairs in that dictionary while the second adds a new pair to it. If these were fragments of a method provided by the Dictionary class itself, *file* would be replaced by "*", which denotes the object being manipulated.

References are of two kinds, *protected* and *unprotected*. A method cannot modify an object to which it has only a protected reference. The engine intervenes by throwing a member of the predefined Reference Protected class.

Programming a Place

The agent and place of the example enable this scene from the electronic marketplace. A shopping agent, acting for a client, travels to a warehouse place, checks the price of a product of interest to its client, waits if necessary for the price to fall to a client-specified level, and returns when either the price reaches that level or a client-specified period of time has elapsed. Beyond the scope of the example are the construction of the warehouse place and the client's construction and eventual debriefing of the shopping agent (figure 14).

The warehouse place and its artifacts are implemented by three user-defined classes, each of which is presented and discussed below.

The Catalog Entry Class. The user-defined Catalog Entry class implements each entry of the warehouse's catalog, which lists the products the warehouse place offers for sale. Implicitly below, this class is a subclass of the predefined Object class.

A catalog entry has two public attributes and two public operations. The *product* attribute is the name of the product the catalog entry describes, the *price* attribute its price. The two operations are discussed below.

```
CatalogEntry: class =
(
    public
        product: String;
        price: Integer; // cents
        see initialize
        see adjustPrice
    property
        lock: Resource;
);
```

The special *initialize* operation initializes the properties of a new catalog entry. There are three. The *product* and *price* properties, implicitly set to the operation's arguments, serve as the *product* and *price* attributes. The *lock* property, set by the method to a new resource, is discussed below.

```
initialize: op (
    product: String;
    price: Integer /* cents */ ) =
{
    ^();
    lock = Resource()
};
```

A catalog entry uses a resource to serialize price modifications made using its *adjustPrice* operation. A Telescript *resource* enables what some languages call critical conditional regions. Here the resource is used to prevent the warehouse place and an agent of the same authority, for example, from changing a product's price simultaneously and, as a consequence, incorrectly.

The public *adjustPrice* operation adjusts the product's price by the percentage supplied as the operation's argument. A positive percentage represents a price increase, a negative percentage a price decrease.

```
adjustPrice: op (percentage: Integer)
throws ReferenceProtected =
{
    use lock
    {
        price = price + (price*percentage).quotient(100)
    }
};
```

A catalog entry, as mentioned before, uses a resource to serialize price modifications. Here the language's *use* construct excludes one agent (or place) from the block of instructions in braces, so long as another is executing them.

The operation may throw an exception. If the catalog entry is accessed using a protected reference, the Engine throws a member of the predefined Reference Protected class. If the shopping agent, for example, rather than the warehouse place, tried to change the price, this would be the consequence.

The Warehouse Class. The user-defined Warehouse class implements the warehouse place itself. This class is a subclass of the predefined Place and Event Process classes.

A warehouse has three public operations, which are discussed below.

```
Warehouse: class (Place, EventProcess) =
(
    public
        see initialize
        see live
        see getCatalog
    property
        catalog: Dictionary[String, CatalogEntry],
);
```

The special *initialize* operation initializes the one property of a new warehouse place. The *catalog* property, implicitly set to the operation's argument, is the warehouse place's catalog. Each key of this dictionary is assumed to equal the *product* attribute of the associated catalog entry.

```
initialize: op (
    catalog: owned Dictionary[String, CatalogEntry]) =
{
    ^()
};
```

A region can prevent a place from being constructed in that region the same way it prevents an agent from traveling there (see "Permits"). Thus a region can either prevent or allow warehouse places and can control their number.

The special *live* operation operates the warehouse place on an ongoing basis. The operation is special because the engine itself requests it of each new place. The operation gives the place autonomy. The place *sponsors* the operation, that is, performs it under its authority and subject to its permit. The operation never finishes; if it did, the engine would terminate the place.

```
live: sponsored op (cause: Exception|Nil) =
{
    loop {
        // await the first day of the month
        time: = Time();
        calendarTime: = time.asCalendarTime();
        calendarTime.month = calendarTime.month + 1;
        calendarTime.day = 1;
        *.wait(calendarTime.asTime().interval(time));

        // reduce all prices by 5%
        for product: String in catalog
        {
            try { catalog[product].adjustPrice(-5) }
            catch KeyInvalid { }
        };

        // make known the price reductions
        *.signalEvent(PriceReduction(), 'occupants)
    }
};
```

On the first of each month, unbeknownst to its customers, the warehouse place reduces by 5% the price of each product in its catalog. It signals this event to any agents present at the time. A Telescript *event* is an object with which one agent or place reports an incident or condition to another.

The public *getCatalog* operation gets the warehouse's catalog, that is, returns a reference to it. If the agent requesting the operation has the authority of the warehouse place itself, the reference is an unprotected reference. If the shopping agent, however, requests the operation, the reference is protected.

```
getCatalog: op () Dictionary[String, CatalogEntry] =
{
    if sponsor.name.authority == *.name.authority {catalog}
    else {catalog.protect()@}
};
```

One agent or place, as mentioned before, can discern the authority of another. Using the language's *sponsor* construct, the warehouse place obtains a reference to the agent under whose authority the catalog is requested. The place decides whether to return to the agent a protected or unprotected reference to the catalog by comparing their *name* attributes.

The Price Reduction Class. The user-defined Price Reduction class implements each event that the warehouse place might signal to notify its occupants of a reduction in a product's price. This class is a subclass of the predefined Event class.

PriceReduction: class (Event) = ();

Programming an Agent

Once it opens its doors, the warehouse needs customers. Shopping agents are implemented by the two user-defined classes presented and discussed below.

The Shopper Class. The user-defined Shopper class implements any number of shopping agents. This class is a subclass of the predefined Agent and Event Process classes.

A shopping agent has four public operations and two private ones, all of which are discussed individually below.

```
Shopper: class (Agent, EventProcess) =
(
    public
        see initialize
        see live
        see meeting
        see getReport
    private
        see goShopping
        see goHome
    property
        clientName: Telename; // assigned
        desiredProduct: String;
        desiredPrice, actualPrice: Integer; // cents
        exception: Exception|Nil;
);
```

The special *initialize* operation initializes the five properties of a new shopping agent. The *clientName* property, set by the operation's method to the telename of the agent creating the shopping agent, identifies its client. The *desired-Product* and *desiredPrice* properties, implicitly set to the operation's arguments, are the name of the desired product and its desired price. The *actualPrice* property is not set initially. If the shopping agent finds the desired product at an acceptable price, it will set this property to that price. The *exception* property is set by the method to a nil. If it fails in its mission the agent will set this property to the exception it encountered.

```
initialize: op (
    desiredProduct: owned String;
    desiredPrice: Integer) =
{
    ^();
    clientName = sponsor.name.copy()
};
```

A region can prevent an agent from being constructed in that region the same way it prevents one from traveling there (see "Permits"). Thus a region can either prevent or allow shopping agents and can control their number.

The special *live* operation operates the shopping agent on an ongoing basis. The engine requests the operation of each new agent. The new agent, like a new place, sponsors the operation and gains autonomy by virtue of it. When the agent finishes performing the operation, the engine terminates it.

```
live: sponsored op (cause: Exception|Nil) =
{
    // take note of home
    homeName: = here.name;
    homeAddress: = here.address;

    // arrange to get home
    permit: = Permit(
        (if *.permit.age == nil {nil}
         else {(*.permit.age *90).quotient(100)}),
        (if *.permit.charges == nil {nil}
         else {(*.permit.charges*90).quotient(100)})
    );

    // go shopping
    restrict permit
    {
        try { *.goShopping(Warehouse.name) }
        catch e: Exception { exception = e }
    }
    catch e: PermitViolated { exception = e };

    // go home
    try { *.goHome(homeName, homeAddress) }
    catch Exception { }
};
```

The shopping agent goes to the warehouse and later returns. The private *goShopping* and *goHome* operations make the two legs of the trip after the present operation records as variables the telename and teleaddress of the starting place. A *teleaddress* is data that denotes a place's network location.

Using the language's *restrict* construct the shopping agent limits itself to 90%

of its allotted time and computation. It holds the remaining 10% in reserve so it can get back even if the trip takes more time or energy than it had anticipated. The agent catches and records exceptions, including the one that would indicate that it had exceeded its self-imposed permit.

The private *goShopping* operation is requested by the shopping agent itself. The operation takes the agent to the warehouse place, checks the price of the requested product, waits if necessary for the price to fall to the requested level, and returns either when that level is reached or after the specified time interval. If the actual price is acceptable to its client, the agent records it.

```
goShopping: op (warehouse: ClassName)
throws ProductUnavailable =
{
    // go to the warehouse
    *.go(Ticket(nil, nil, warehouse));

    // show an interest in prices
    *.enableEvents(PriceReduction(*.name));
    *.signalEvent(PriceReduction(), 'responder);
    *.enableEvents(PriceReduction(here.name));

    // wait for the desired price
    actualPrice = desiredPrice+1;
    while actualPrice > desiredPrice
    {
        *.getEvent(nil, PriceReduction());
        try
        {
            actualPrice =
                here@Warehouse.getCatalog()[desiredProduct].price
        }
        catch KeyInvalid { throw ProductUnavailable() }
    }
};
```

The shopping agent travels to the warehouse place using the *go* operation. Upon arrival there the agent expresses interest in the price reduction event which it knows the place will signal. Each time it sees a price reduction, the agent checks the product's price to see whether it was reduced and was reduced sufficiently. The agent contrives one such event to prompt an initial price check. If a price reduction is insufficient, the agent waits for another.

The agent provides the *go* operation with a ticket specifying the warehouse place's class but neither its telename nor its teleaddress. In an electronic marketplace of even moderate size, this limited information would not suffice. The agent would have to travel to a directory place to get the place's name, address, or both.

The operation may throw an exception. If the warehouse doesn't carry the product, a member of the user-defined Product Unavailable class is thrown.

The private *goHome* operation is requested by the shopping agent itself. The operation returns the agent to its starting place and initiates a meeting with its client. Before initiating the meeting, the agent asks to be signaled when it ends. After initiating the meeting, the agent just waits for it to end. During the meeting, the client is expected to request the *getReport* operation.

```
goHome: op (homeName: Telename; homeAddress: Teleaddress) =
{
    // drop excess baggage
    *.disableEvents();
    *.clearEvents();

    // go home
    *.go(Ticket(homeName, homeAddress));

    // meet the client
    *.enableEvents(PartEvent(clientName));
    here@MeetingPlace.meet(Petition(clientName));

    // wait for the client to end the meeting
    *.getEvent(nil, PartEvent(clientName))
};
```

The shopping agent leaves the warehouse place using the *go* operation. Before leaving it retracts its interest in price reductions and, to lighten its load, discards any notices of price reductions it received but did not examine.

The agent provides the *go* operation with a ticket giving the telename and teleaddress of the agent's starting place, information it recorded previously.

The special *meeting* operation guards the agent's report by declining all requests to meet with the shopping agent. The agent itself initiates the one meeting in which it will participate. The operation is special because the engine itself requests it whenever a meeting is requested of an agent.

```
meeting, sponsored op (
    agent: protected Telename; // assigned
    _class: protected ClassName;
    petition: protected Petition) Object|Nil
throws MeetingDenied =
{
    throw MeetingDenied();
    nil
};
```

The operation may throw an exception. Indeed the shopping agent always throws a member of the predefined Meeting Denied class.

The public *getReport* operation returns the actual price of the desired product. The actual price is less than or equal to the desired price.

getReport: op () Integer // *cents*
throws Exception, FeatureUnavailable =
{
   if sponsor.name != clientName
    { throw FeatureUnavailable() };
   if exception != nil
    { throw exception };
   actualPrice
};

The operation may throw an exception. If the agent requesting the operation is not the shopping agent's client, the operation's method throws a member of the predefined Feature Unavailable class. If the shopping agent failed in its mission, the method throws a member of the predefined Exception class.

The Product Unavailable Class. The user-defined Product Unavailable class implements each exception with which the shopping agent might notify its client that the warehouse doesn't carry the product. This class is a subclass of the predefined Exception class.

ProductUnavailable: class (Exception) = ();

Using Mobile Agents

Having explained in the previous section how communicating applications work, I speculate in this final section about the myriad of applications that third-party developers could call into being. Each of three subsections adopts a theme, develops one variation on that theme, and sketches four others. These are the promised scenes from the electronic marketplace of the future.

Monitoring Changing Conditions

The User Experience. Two weeks from now, Chris must make a two-day business trip to Boston. He makes his airline reservations using his personal communicator. He's ready to go. Chris's schedule in Boston proves hectic. On the second day, he's running late. Two hours before his return flight is scheduled to leave, Chris's personal communicator informs him that the flight has been delayed an hour. That extra hour lets Chris avoid cutting short his last appointment.

The hour Chris saved was important to him. He could have called the airline to see whether his flight was on time, but he was extremely busy. Chris was startled—pleasantly so—when notice of his flight's delay hit the screen of his personal communicator. When he used his communicator to arrange his trip two weeks ago, Chris had no idea that this was part of the service.

How Agents Provide the Experience. Chris can thank one mobile agent for

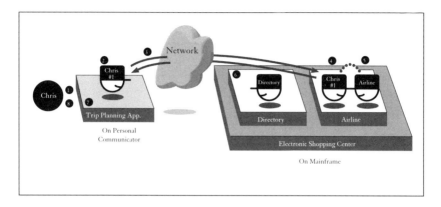

Figure 15. Monitoring changing conditions.

booking his round-trip flight to Boston and another for monitoring his return flight and notifying him of its delay. The first of these two tasks was accomplished in the following steps (figure 15):

1. Chris gives to the trip planning application he bought for his personal communicator the dates of his trip, his means of payment (e.g., the number and expiration date on his Visa card), his choice of airline, etc. If he's used the application before, it has much of this information already.

2. The application creates an agent of Chris's authority and gives Chris's flight information to it. The part of the application written in C creates and interacts with the part written in the Telescript language, the agent, through the Telescript engine in Chris's personal communicator.

3. The agent travels from Chris's communicator to the airline place in the electronic marketplace. It does this using the *go* instruction and a ticket that designates the airline place by its authority and class.

4. The agent meets with the airline agent that resides in and provides the service of the airline place. It does this using the *meet* instruction and a petition that designates the airline agent by its authority and class.

5. The agent gives Chris's flight information to the airline agent, which compares the authority of Chris's agent to the name on Chris's Visa card and then books his flight, returning a confirmation number and itinerary.

6. The agent returns to its place in Chris's communicator. It does this using the *go* instruction and a ticket that designates that place by its telename and teleaddress which the agent noted before leaving there.

7. The agent gives the confirmation number and itinerary to the trip planning application. Its work complete, the agent terminates.

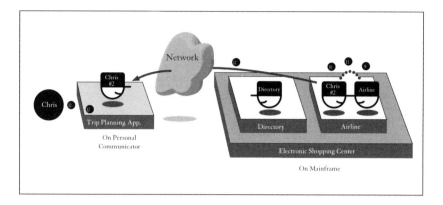

Figure 16. Additional steps.

8. The application conveys to Chris the confirmation number and itinerary, perhaps making an entry in his electronic calendar as well.

The remaining task of monitoring Chris's return flight and informing him if it's delayed is carried out in the following additional steps (figure 16):

9. Before leaving the airline place (in step 6), Chris's agent creates a second agent of Chris's authority and gives Chris's itinerary to it.

10. This second agent puts itself to sleep until the day of Chris's trip. The airline place may charge Chris a fee for the agent's room and board.

11. On the day of Chris's flight, the agent arises and checks the flight once an hour throughout the day. On each occasion it meets with the airline agent using the *meet* instruction and a petition that designates it by its authority and class. On one occasion it notes a delay in Chris's flight.

12. The agent returns to Chris's personal communicator (as in step 6), notifies the trip planning application of the delay in Chris's return flight and then terminates (as in step 7), and the application gives Chris the information that allows him to complete his meeting (as in step 8).

Variations on the Theme. This first scenario demonstrates how mobile agents can monitor changing conditions in the electronic marketplace. There are many variations:

• Chris learns by chance that the Grateful Dead are in town next month. He tries to get tickets but learns that the concert sold out in 12 hours. Thereafter Chris's agent monitors Ticketron every morning at 9 am. The next time a Grateful Dead concert in his area is listed, the agent snaps up two tickets. If Chris can't go himself, he'll sell the tickets to a friend.

• Chris buys a television from The Good Guys. Chris's agent monitors the local consumer electronics market for 30 days after the purchase. If it finds the same set for sale at a lower price, the agent notifies Chris so that he can exercise the low price guarantee of the store he patronized.

- Chris invests in several publicly traded companies. Chris's agent monitors his portfolio, sending him biweekly reports and word of any sudden stock price change. The agent also monitors the wire services, sending Chris news stories about the companies whose stock he owns.

- Mortgage rates continue to fall. Chris refinances his house at a more favorable rate. Thereafter Chris's agent monitors the local mortgage market and notifies him if rates drop 1% below his new rate. With banks foregoing closing costs, such a drop is Chris's signal to refinance again.

Doing Time-Consuming Legwork

The User Experience. John's in the market for a camera. He's read the equipment reviews in the photography magazines and in *Consumer Reports* and has visited his local camera store. He's buying a Canon EOS A2. The only remaining question is: from whom? John asks his personal communicator. In 15 minutes, he has the names, addresses, and phone numbers of the three shops in his area with the lowest prices. A camera store in San Jose, 15 miles away, offers the A2 at $70 below the price his local camera shop is asking.

The $70 that John saved, needless to say, was significant to him. John could have consulted the three telephone directories covering his vicinity, made a list of the 25 camera retailers within, say, 20 miles of his office, and called each to obtain its price for the EOS A2, but who has the time? John now considers his personal communicator to be an indispensable shopping tool.

How Agents Provide the Experience. John can thank a mobile agent for finding the camera store in San Jose, a task that was accomplished in the following steps (figure 17):

1. John gives to the shopping application he bought for his personal communicator the make and model of the camera he's selected. He also identifies the geographical area for which he wishes pricing information.

2. The application creates an agent of John's authority and gives John's shopping instructions to it. The C part of the application creates and interacts with the agent through the engine in John's communicator.

3. The agent travels from John's communicator to the directory place in the electronic marketplace. It uses the *go* instruction and a ticket that designates the directory place by its authority and class.

4. The agent meets with the directory agent that resides in and provides the service of the directory place. It uses the *meet* instruction and a petition that designates the directory agent by its authority and class.

5. The agent obtains from the directory agent the directory entries for all camera retailers about which the place has information. John's agent nar-

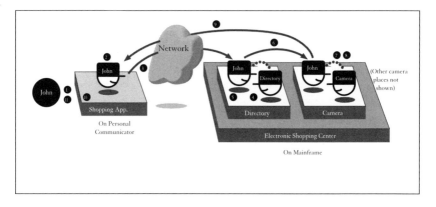

Figure 17. Doing time-consuming legwork.

rows the list to the retailers in the geographical area it is to explore.

6. The agent visits the electronic storefront of each retailer in turn. Each storefront is another place in the electronic marketplace. For each trip the agent uses the *go* instruction with a ticket that gives the telename and teleaddress that the agent found in the storefront's directory entry.

7. The agent meets with the camera agent it finds in each camera place it visits. It uses the *meet* instruction and a petition that designates the camera agent by its authority and class.

8. The agent gives to the camera agent the camera's make and model and is quoted a price. The agent retains information about this particular shop only if it proves a candidate for the agent's top-three list.

9. The agent eventually returns to its place in John's communicator. It does so using the *go* instruction and a ticket that designates that place by its telename and teleaddress, which the agent noted before leaving there.

10. The agent makes its report to the shopping application. Its work complete, the agent terminates.

11. The application presents the report to John, perhaps making an entry in his electronic diary as a permanent record.

Variations on the Theme. This second scenario demonstrates how mobile agents can find and analyze information in the electronic marketplace. There are many variations:

• John hasn't talked to his college friend, Doug, in 20 years. He remembers that Doug was a computer science major. John's agent searches the trade journals and conference proceedings—even very specialized ones—in the hope that Doug has written or spoken publicly. The agent finds that Doug has published several papers, one just two years ago. The agent returns with Doug's address in LA where he has lived for 5 years.

- It's Friday. John has been in Chicago all week on business. Expecting to go home today, John is asked to attend a Monday morning meeting in New York. He faces an unplanned weekend in midtown Manhattan. John's agent learns that Charles Aznavour—John has every recording he ever made—is performing at Radio City Music Hall on Saturday night. With John's approval, the agent purchases him a ticket for the concert.

- John is in the market for a used car. He's had great experience with Toyotas. John's agent checks the classified sections of all 15 Bay Area newspapers and produces for John a tabular report that includes all used Toyotas on the market. The report lists the cars by model, year, and mileage, allowing John to make comparisons between them easily.

- John yearns for a week in Hawaii. His agent voices his yearning in the electronic marketplace, giving details John has provided: a few days on Kauai, a few more on Maui, beach-front accommodations, peace and quiet. The agent returns with a dozen packages from American Airlines, Hilton Hotels, Aloha Condominiums, Ambassador Tours, and so forth. Unlike the junk mail John receives by post, many of these offers are designed specifically for him. The marketplace is competing for his business.

Using Services in Combination

The User Experience. Mary and Paul have been seeing each other for years. Both lead busy lives. They don't have enough time together. But Mary's seen to it that they're more likely than not to spend Friday evenings together. Using her personal communicator, she's arranged that a romantic comedy is selected and ready for viewing on her television each Friday at 7 pm, that pizza for two is delivered to her door at the same time, and that she and Paul are reminded earlier in the day of their evening together and of the movie to be screened

Paul and Mary recognize the need to live well-rounded lives but their demanding jobs make it difficult. Their personal communicators help them achieve their personal as well as their professional objectives. And it's fun.

How Agents Provide the Experience. Mary relies upon a mobile agent to orchestrate her Friday evenings. Born months ago, the agent waits in a quiet corner of the electronic marketplace for most of each week; each Friday at noon it takes the following steps (figure 18):

1. Mary's agent keeps a record of the films it selected on past occasions in order to avoid selecting one of those films again.

2. The agent travels from its place of repose to one of the many video places in the electronic marketplace. It uses the *go* instruction and a ticket that designates the video place by its authority and class.

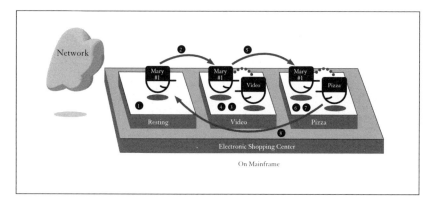

Figure 18. Using services in combination.

3. The agent meets with the video agent that resides in and provides the service of the video place. It uses the *meet* instruction and a petition that designates the video agent by its authority and class.

4. The agent asks the video agent for the catalog listing for each romantic comedy in its inventory. The agent selects a film at random from among the more recent comedies, but avoids the films it's selected before, whose catalog numbers it carries with it. The agent orders the selected film from the video agent, charges it to Mary's Visa card, and instructs the video agent to transmit the film to her home at 7 pm. The video agent compares the authority of Mary's agent to the name on the Visa card.

5. The agent goes next to Domino's pizza place. It uses the *go* instruction and a ticket that designates the pizza place by its authority and class.

6. The agent meets with the pizza agent that resides in and provides the service of the pizza place. It uses the *meet* instruction and a petition that designates the pizza agent by its authority and class.

7. The agent orders one medium-sized Pepperoni pizza for home delivery at 6:45 p.m. The agent charges the pizza, as it did the video, to Mary's Visa card. The pizza agent, like the video agent before it, compares the authority of Mary's agent to the name on the agent's Visa card.

8. Mary's agent returns to its designated resting place in the electronic marketplace. It uses the *go* instruction and a ticket that designates that place by its telename and teleaddress, which it noted previously.

What remains is for the agent to notify Mary and Paul of their evening appointment. This is accomplished in the following additional steps (figure 19):

9. The agent creates two new agents of Mary's authority and gives each the catalog listing of the selected film and the names of Mary and Paul, respec-

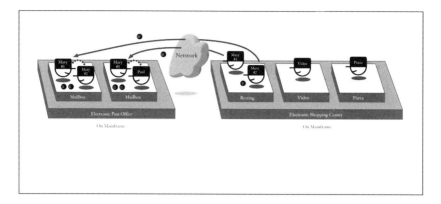

Figure 19. Additional steps.

tively. Its work complete, the original agent awaits another Friday.

10. One of the two new agents goes to Mary's mailbox place while the other goes to Paul's. To do this they use the *go* instruction and tickets that designate the mailbox places by their class and authorities.

11. The agents meet with the mailbox agents that reside in and provide the services of the mailbox places. They use the *meet* instruction and petitions designating the mailbox agents by their class and authorities.

12. The agents deliver to the mailbox agents electronic messages that include the film's catalog listing and that remind Mary and Paul of their appointment with each another. The two agents terminate. The mailbox agents convey the reminders to Mary and Paul themselves.

Variations on the Theme. This third scenario demonstrates how mobile agents can combine existing services to create new, more specialized services. There are many variations:

- Mary plans to take Paul to see *Phantom of the Opera* next weekend. Her agent tries to book orchestra seats for either Saturday or Sunday, gets them for Sunday, reserves a table at a highly regarded Indian restaurant within walking distance of the theater, and orders a dozen roses for delivery to Paul's apartment that Sunday morning.

- Mary's travel plans change unexpectedly. Rather than return home this evening as planned, she's off to Denver. Mary's agent alters her airline reservation, books her a nonsmoking room at a Marriott Courtyard within 15 minutes of her meeting, reserves her a compact car, and provides her driving instructions to the hotel and the meeting. The agent also supplies Mary with a list of Indian restaurants in the vicinity.

- Mary receives and pays her bills electronically. Her agent receives each bill as it arrives, verifies that Mary has authorized its payment, checks that it is in the expected range, and issues instructions to the bank if so. Mary's agent prepares for her a consolidated monthly report and, at tax time, sends to her accountant a report of her tax deductible expenses.

- Mary takes a daily newspaper, but it isn't her idea of news. At 7 a.m. each day Mary's agent delivers to her a personalized newspaper. It includes synopses of the major national and international news stories, of course, but it also reports the local news from her hometown in Virginia; the major events of yesterday in her field, physics; the market activity of the stocks in her portfolio; and Doonesbury, which always gives her a chuckle.

Related Work

Computer scientists have long explored how programming languages tailored for the purpose could ease the development of communicating applications. An overview of their work is found in Bal, Steiner, and Tanenbaum (1989).

The RP paradigm was conceived and first implemented in the mid-1970s (White 1976), was formalized and in other ways advanced in the mid-1980s (Birrell and Nelson 1984), and is today the basis for client-server computing.

The RP paradigm in its most basic form involves transporting procedures before they begin executing, not after (i.e., before they develop state). A persuasive argument for the basic paradigm is made in Gifford and Stamos (1990). The basic paradigm has been implemented in many settings. In the Internet the most recent effort is Java (Gosling and McGilton 1995).

The RP paradigm in the form described in this chapter involves transporting executing procedures. The case for this more advanced form is made in Chess, Harrison, and Kershenbaum (1994). An early noncommercial implementation is Emerald (Black et al. 1988). In the Internet the most recent undertaking is Obliq (Bharat and Cardelli 1995).

The RP paradigm arose not only in the field of programming languages but also in that of electronic mail, where procedures can be transported as the contents of messages. One of the earliest efforts is described in Vittal (1981). In the Internet the most recent work is Safe-Tcl (Ousterhout 1995).

If mobile agents actually become an important element of the electronic marketplace, standards for mobile agents will arise and technologies for mobile agents will one day be taken for granted. Attention will shift to higher-level matters, for example, agent strategies for effective negotiation. A foretaste of the work to come is found in Rosenschein and Zlotkin (1994).

Acknowledgments

A talented team of software engineers at General Magic led by Steve Schramm conceived Telescript technology and implemented it for servers. A second team at AT&T led by Alex Gillon used the technology to create a commercial service, AT&T's PersonaLink™. A third team at General Magic led by Darin Adler implemented the technology for user computers, initially Sony's MagicLink™ and Motorola's Envoy™ personal communicators. In July 1995Nippon Telegraph and Telephone, AT&T, and Sony announced a joint venture to deploy a second mobile agent-based service in Japan.

General Magic licenses its technologies to members of a global alliance of computer, communication, and consumer electronics companies which include Apple, AT&T, Cable and Wireless, France Telecom, Fujitsu, Matsushita, Mitsubishi, Motorola, NorTel, NTT, Oki, Philips, Sanyo, Sony, and Toshiba.

Notes

1. The opportunity for remote programming (like that for remote procedure calling) is bi-directional. The example depicts a user's agent visiting a server, but a server's agent can visit a user's computer as well. In an electronic marketplace, if the user's agent is a shopper, the server's agent is a door-to-door salesperson.

2. An agent can grant any agents it creates only capabilities it has itself. Furthermore, it must share its allowance with them.

3. An agent can impose temporary permits upon itself. The agent is notified, rather than destroyed, if it violates them. An agent can use this feature of the Telescript language to recover from its own misprogramming.

4. Despite its name, the Telescript language is not a scripting language. Its purpose is not to allow human users to create macros, or scripts, that direct applications written in "real" programming languages like C. Rather, it lets developers implement major components of communicating applications.

5. The Telescript protocols are not OSI protocols. The OSI model is mentioned here merely to provide a frame of reference for readers acquainted with OSI.

6. The example uses the predefined Agent, Class, Class Name, Dictionary, Event Process, Exception, Integer, Meeting Place, Nil, Object, Part Event, Permit, Petition, Place, Resource, String, Teleaddress, Telename, Ticket, and Time classes and various subclasses of Exception (e.g., Key Invalid).

7. The language permits a limited form of multiple inheritance by allowing other classes which extend the hierarchy to a directed graph.

8. The language permits a class to have implementation superclasses that differ from its interface superclasses. Such classes are rare in practice.

References

Bal, H. E.; Steiner, J. G.; and Tanenbaum, A. S. 1989. Programming Languages for Distributed Computing Systems. *ACM Computing Surveys* 21(3).

Bharat, K. A., and Cardelli, L. 1995. Migratory Applications, DEC Systems Research

Center, Merrimack, New Hampshire.

Birrell, A. D., and Nelson, B. J. 1984. Implementing Remote Procedure Calls. *ACM Transactions on Computer Systems* 2(1): 39–59.

Black, A.; Hutchinson, N.; Jul, E.; and Levy, H. 1988. Fine-Grained Mobility in the EMERALD System. *ACM Transactions on Computer Systems* 6(1): 109–133.

Chess, D. M.; Harrison, C. G.; and Kershenbaum, A. 1994. Mobile Agents: Are They a Good Idea? *IBM Research Report* RC 19887, IBM, Gaithersburg, Maryland.

Gifford, D. K., and Stamos, J. W. 1990. Remote Evaluation. *ACM Transactions on Programming Languages and Systems* 12(4): 537–565.

Gosling, J., and McGilton, H. 1995. The JAVA Language Environment: A White Paper, Sun Microsystems, Mountain View, California.

Ousterhout, J. K. 1995. Scripts and Agents: The New Software High Ground. Talk presented at the Winter 1995 Usenix Conference, 16–20 January, New Orleans, Louisiana.

Rosenschein, J. S., and Zlotkin, G. 1994. *Rules of Encounter*. Cambridge, Mass.: MIT Press.

Vittal, J. 1981. Active Message Processing: Messages as Messengers. *Computer Message Systems*. New York: North-Holland.

White, J. E. 1976. A High-Level Framework for Network-Based Resource Sharing. *AFIPS Conference Proceedings*, 561–570. New York: FOCUS.

Index

Composed in Granjon,
a typeface recreated by Adobe Systems Inc.
from a 1928 design created by
George Jones for the Linotype Company.
This design mimics the designs and characteristics
of the typefaces created by French printer, publisher,
and type designer Robert Granjon (d. 1579).
Granjon, a craftsman from
Lyonnaise France,
was one of the first independent
type designers from whom
printers could buy type.

Printed and Bound by
Braun-Brumfield, Inc., Printers,
in Ann Arbor Michigan.